Lancaster

Also by Leo McKinstry

Fit to Govern?

Turning the Tide

Boycs: The True Story

Jack and Bobby: A Story of Brothers in Conflict

Rosebery: Statesman in Turmoil

Sir Alf: A Major Reappraisal of the Life and Times of
England's Greatest Football Manager

Spitfire: Portrait of a Legend

Lancaster

The Second World War's Greatest Bomber

LEO McKINSTRY

JOHN MURRAY

First published in Great Britain in 2009 by John Murray (Publishers)
An Hachette UK Company

3

© Leo McKinstry 2009

The right of Leo McKinstry to be identified as the Author of the Work
has been asserted by him in accordance with the
Copyright, Designs and Patents Act 1988.

A CIP catalogue record for this title is
available from the British Library

Hardback ISBN 978-0-7195-2353-3
Trade paperback ISBN 978-1-84854-338-6

Typeset in Monotype Bembo by Ellipsis Books Limited, Glasgow

Printed and bound by Clays Ltd, St Ives plc

John Murray policy is to use papers that are natural, renewable and
recyclable products and made from wood grown in sustainable forests.
The logging and manufacturing processes are expected to conform to the
environmental regulations of the country of origin.

John Murray (Publishers)
338 Euston Road
London NW1 3BH

www.johnmurray.co.uk

To my darling wife Elizabeth
who understands everything

Contents

Illustrations

33. Dresden, in ruins, after the most infamous RAF attack of the war
34. A Lancaster delivering food supplies during Operation Manna
35. A Lancaster Mark III refuelling a Gloster Meteor
36. The Avro Shackleton
37. A post-war maritime reconnaissance Lancaster

Picture Acknowledgements: Corbis: 2 bottom, 11 bottom, 14 top right, 15 bottom. Mary Evans Picture Library: 7 top left. Getty Images: 3 bottom, 5 top right, 6 top left and right, 7 top right, 8 top, 12 top. Imperial War Museum London: 3 top left (CH18684) and right (TR198), 5 bottom (CH15362), 6 bottom (CH8795), 8 bottom (TR1386), 9 top (CL1405), 10 top (C3371) and bottom (CL650), 11 top left (CH13626), 12 bottom left (FLM2365), 13 top (CH18005), 14 top left (C4776). By kind permission of the Trustees of the Royal Air Force Museum: 1, 4, 5 top left, 7 bottom, 9 bottom, 11 top right, 12 bottom right, 13 bottom, 14 bottom, 15 top, 16. Rex Features: 2 top.

Introduction

'Goddam, it's a flying bomb bay'

❧

I SWITCHED OFF MY tape recorder and started to gather up my papers. Just as I rose from my seat, William Walker, the twinkle-eyed air force veteran whom I had been interviewing for a book about the Spitfire, said: 'It was a wonderful plane and I hope you do it justice. But that's not the book that really needs to be written about the RAF.'

'Oh?'

'Ever heard of Roy Chadwick?' asked Flight Lieutenant Walker.

'The man who designed the Lancaster bomber?'

'That's right,' he replied, a broad smile on his face. Now in his nineties, the former Spitfire pilot still retained that lively spirit of independence he had once displayed in the Battle of Britain. 'Yes, that's the story that should be told: Roy Chadwick and the Lancaster. It was his plane that won the war, you know.'

'Not the Spitfire?'

'Well, the Spitfire saved us in 1940, of course, but it was the Lancaster that brought us victory. Yet Chadwick never got the credit.'

We chatted for a few more moments. Then I had to leave for my next interview. I turned to shake William Walker's hand as I reached the door.

'Thank you for coming,' he said, his smile wider than ever. 'And don't forget Roy Chadwick and the Lancaster. That should be your next book.'

I did not forget. Even as I became engrossed in my Spitfire project, Flight Lieutenant Walker's parting words echoed in the back of my mind. So it was perhaps inevitable that once the Spitfire biography was published in the late autumn of 2007, I should turn to the Lancaster. Apart from the accuracy of William Walker's observation that fuller justice should be done to the genius of Roy Chadwick, there were several other reasons to see a Lancaster book as the natural successor to one on the Spitfire. After all, both aircraft are regarded as the twin icons of the RAF's triumph in the Second World War, their names synonymous with courage and glory in the air. At displays given by the Battle of Britain Memorial Flight throughout the country, they are the two planes whose outlines are instantly recognized by the public. Both were powered by the Rolls-Royce Merlin engine, whose distinctive throb exuded reliability and strength. Both inspired deep respect in the enemy. 'Give me a squadron of Spitfires,' the German fighter commander Major Adolf Galland famously told Hermann Göring in September 1940, when asked what he needed to win the Battle of Britain.[1] Similarly, Generalleutnant Josef 'Beppo' Schmid, the commander of the Luftwaffe in the west, confessed in a military interrogation in October 1945 that the performance of the Lancaster in terms of range and loading capacity was 'remarkable', while 'the success in target finding at night and in bad weather had increased in an astonishing measure by the autumn of 1944', the moment when the Lancasters were at their peak of operations.[2] One of the Luftwaffe's top fighter pilots, Wolfgang Flack, was even more certain that the influence of the Lancaster was decisive. 'It didn't only make the fighting more difficult, it was the beginning of the end of the war as far as I was concerned. The Lancaster had a longer range, it could fly for a longer period of time, it could carry more bombs and it had good protection. That's why our losses became so high, and that's when we began to feel the superiority of the RAF.'[3]

For all its size, the Lancaster's surprising manoeuvrability was sometimes compared to that of a Spitfire. 'We handled them just like the fighter boys handled their Spitfires. We were that confident,' wrote Group Captain John Searby, who led the raid on the German rocket station at Peenemünde on the Baltic coast in 1943.[4] In the same vein, Michael Maltin, a Lancaster pilot with 550 Squadron, later recalled of battles over Germany: 'You used to treat the Lanc a bit like a Spitfire. You couldn't break that aircraft. You could pull it about and do steep turns and all that. And the more you made the crew sick the happier they were. I was lucky to have flown the best. The Lancaster was magnificent.'[5] The Spitfire's aesthetics and the responsiveness of its controls captivated pilots. The Lancaster inspired a similar reaction in its crews. Leonard Miller, a Bomber Command engineer, even admitted that when he first saw the Lancaster, he 'drooled. It was *the* machine, four engines and it was terrific in handling with all the weight it could carry. It was beautiful to fly. As much as the Spits are admired, so is the Lancaster. It was a perfect design. The power that surged through the machine was terrific. It was wonderful.'[6] Spitfire pilots often commented on their sense of unity with their aircraft, almost as though the plane was part of them. Even with its four engines, the Lancaster could provoke the same feelings. Jack Currie, who was a stretcher-bearer in the London Blitz before he gained his wings, later wrote this passage about returning home after one of his early operations: 'After six hours at the controls, my contact with the aircraft was instinctive and relaxed. We rolled into a turn together, held the turn steadily, without adjustment, with no anxious glances at the dials or searches for the dim horizon. I could scan the sky or talk to the crew, while my sense told me that the turn was accurate. How satisfying it was to fly the Lancaster.'[7] Just as the Spitfire's role in the Battle of Britain was guided by Fighter Command's idiosyncratic chief Hugh Dowding, who treated the rest of the military establishment with suspicion, even hostility, so the Lancaster's part in the European offensive was largely decided by the ferociously individualistic head of Bomber Command, Sir Arthur Harris. As single-minded as Dowding, Harris was fixed on pursuing his own strategy with his force of Lancasters, much to the exasperation of other commanders who found their alternative plans derided.

Yet in other respects the Spitfire and the Lancaster could hardly have been more different. The first was a rapier, the second a mighty broadsword. The little fighter was essentially an instrument of defence whose most famous action took place over her homeland. The heavy bomber was a pulverizing weapon of attack, flying night after night over enemy territory. The Spitfire's role was to provide protection, helped only by the bullets from its Browning guns, whereas the Lancaster's sole purpose was destruction, using its ability to carry up to ten tons of explosives. The Spitfire's legendary heroics took place against a backdrop of blue skies, but Lancaster sorties were usually shrouded in darkness. In aerial duelling with German fighters, the Spitfire could almost seem like a throwback to the medieval age of chivalry, whereas the Lancaster embodied the destructive power of modern total war. For the Spitfire, the target usually meant a German plane. For the Lancaster, the target was a point on the ground, often lit up by the raging inferno of a firestorm. Unlike Spitfire pilots, Lancaster crews were never seen as 'the glamour boys'. Their planes breathed menace and aggression, not the excitement of a Spitfire. Indeed, the RAF was only too aware of the greater public appeal of the fighter plane. In May 1942 the head of RAF training Guy Garrod told Harris how he stressed to new recruits 'that they must not allow themselves to be misled by the glamour of the Fighter Boy, which is emphasized in films, and that they must realize that it is the Bomber Boy who is going to win the air war'.[8]

The imagery of both planes is entirely different. The Spitfire is redolent of golden summer days in Kent or Sussex, of eager scrambles across

3

grass airfields, of thrilling speed and sporadic gunfire. The Lancaster, in contrast, conjures up pictures of bleak Lincolnshire bases in the depths of winter, with icy winds sweeping across concrete runways, or streams of black aircraft, weaving their anxious way through the German night, then suddenly plunging into the turmoil of bright searchlights and exploding flak shells. The Spitfire is remembered with near universal affection, but the Lancaster has been enveloped in controversy ever since 1945 because of its central role in the strategic bombing of Germany. The Spitfire was the hero of Biggin Hill and Malta. The name of the Lancaster is associated with the horrors of Hamburg in 1943 and Dresden in 1945. No one has ever accused Spitfire airmen of complicity in war crimes, but Bomber Command was facing that charge even before the conflict had finished.

The Lancaster's tale is fascinating precisely because it has so many shades, from the awesome bravery of the young crews to the terror they inflicted with their cargoes of death, from the remarkable advances in technology that the plane encapsulated to the political rows that gripped the British Government over the use of this almost revolutionary aircraft. It was undoubtedly the greatest bomber of the Second World War in terms of destructive influence. As Harris wrote in his memoirs: 'The Lancaster far surpassed all the other types of heavy bomber. Not only could it take heavier bomb loads, not only was it easier to handle, and not only were there fewer accidents with this than with other types; throughout the war the casualty rate of Lancasters was consistently below that of other types.'[9] That was a verdict with which most bomber crews would have agreed. As navigator Bill Burke put it: 'The first time I went on board a Lanc, I realized what a wonderful plane it was. It's impossible to over-emphasize the importance of Lanc bombers. It totally transformed the damage which could be done by bombing operations.'[10] Even the massive American B-29, which won its place in history by dropping the two atomic bombs on Japan in 1945, could not carry as big a payload as the Lancaster. Bob Woolf, a wireless operator with the Royal Australian Air Force, recalled how impressed the Americans were by the Lancaster when his plane was forced by bad weather to make a landing at a US base near Newark in Nottinghamshire. 'When we opened the bomb doors, one Yank looked up in awe and shouted, "Goddam, it's a flying bomb bay."'[11]

The phenomenal capacity of the Lancaster put it right at the centre of the debate that raged within the government and the military commands about the direction of the air war from 1941. Dividing lines opened up over the nature of strategic bombing, its morality, purpose and effectiveness. Some, especially those in the army and navy, questioned the vast resources devoted to the heavy-bomber campaign, which came to dominate Britain's war economy. Such critics wanted to see more of the RAF's effort devoted to tactical support for the other two services in campaigns beyond the German cities. In May 1942, just as the production of Lancasters accelerated, the government minister Leo Amery, a sceptic of strategic bombing, recorded in his diary, 'the whole conduct of the war has been prejudiced by the Air Ministry's obsession with bombing, i.e. long-distance bombardment, divorced from actual attack and all the consequences of that obsession in the failure to provide enough at all the places where they have been most urgently wanted from Crete to Singapore and Burma.'[12] Even where there was acceptance of the wider concept of strategic bombing – which can be defined as the use of the RAF to destroy the ability of the German war machine to function – conflict could still erupt over its application. Some planners called for precision attacks, exploiting the growing technical capabilities of the Lancaster and the experience of its crews, while Harris always favoured area bombing to bring about the widest possible destruction across Germany. One of the justifications he frequently voiced for the heavy-bomber offensive was his desire to avoid a repeat of the wholesale slaughter on the western front in the First World War. By obliterating Germany from above, he argued, there would be no need for huge Allied armies to try to fight their way into the Reich. 'The outcome of this war will only be decided in our favour by the realization that the coming of the heavy long-range bomber has completely altered the whole conception and the whole face of warfare,' wrote Harris in July 1942:

> If the ancient and ivory-headed warriors are permitted to have their way, another one to six million of the flower of the youth of this under-populated country and of America will be unnecessarily massacred in proving for the second time that these Ancient Soldiers and Mariners were wrong. It is but cold comfort to realize in the circumstances that not only is the Bomber the only thing that can win the War for us, but that it is going to win the War for us eventually in spite of all the procrastinations and futile diversions which the old battle-horses are determining to stage in the interim.[13]

The tragic paradox of Harris's approach is that his own men in Bomber Command suffered an even greater level of bloodshed than was experienced by the British Expeditionary Force in 1914, with more than half of the 125,000 men who served losing their lives in action.

The story of this unique aircraft features all the most heroic and harrowing elements of wartime: the vivid memories of the crews who flew the planes over the Reich, knowing that their chances of surviving a tour of operations were minimal; the appalling experiences of German civilians under bombardment, watching as buildings crumbled and tarmac roads turned to combustible treacle in the savage heat created by incendiaries; the magnificent daring of exploits like the Dambusters raid in 1943 or the sinking of the German battleship *Tirpitz* off the Norwegian coast in 1944; the emotional contradictions of life in Bomber Command, one moment facing death over Berlin, the next indulging in drunken high jinks in the mess; the radical leaps in aerial technology, from the invention of primitive computers for bombsights to the development of complex radar images on cathode-ray tubes; and the sense of making history as the Axis tyranny was defeated through milestones like D-Day and the fall of Italy. There is also the rich cast of personalities, led by Harris, whose vituperative correspondence is one of the literary treasure chests of the war. The saga also embraces a wide range of other figures such as Guy Gibson, the courageous but emotionally flawed Lancaster pilot; Sydney Bufton, the Air Ministry official and former pilot who waged a long battle against Harris over policy; Barnes Wallis, the shy, ascetic designer of the bouncing bomb; and, of course, Roy Chadwick, the dapper, punctilious architect of the Lancaster, who created not only the finest bomber of the war but also presided over one of the most admired companies within the aircraft industry.

When I embarked on this history of the Lancaster, I feared that I might have nothing new to say since there is already a wealth of literature on the subject. Yet as I began to conduct my research, I soon realized that I need not have worried. Within the archives there were many wells of new information waiting to be tapped. As well as providing new accounts of the Lancaster's role in the Second World War, a number of these sources highlighted the political dimension that has often been ignored in other works. At the Imperial War Museum in London I worked my way through a sound library of more than 135 interviews with Lancaster airmen, ground crews and other people involved with the aircraft, including one fascinating discussion with Norman Boorer, who worked alongside Barnes Wallis and shed new light on the origins of the Dambusters. Apart from these tapes, the Imperial War Museum also has a fine collection of over 40 written memoirs about the Lancaster. Other archives were equally useful. The Bufton papers at Cambridge University revealed the intensity of the quarrels between the Air Ministry and Harris over bombing strategy. More insights into the views of the air staff, Winston Churchill and Bomber Command were provided by the Portal papers at Christ Church College, Oxford, while the Beaverbrook collection in the House of Lords contained intriguing material on the painful birth of the Lancaster. The papers of Sir Arthur Harris at the RAF Museum in Hendon, north London, show not only his devotion to the Lancaster at the expense of any other bomber, but also his utter disdain for anyone who dared to question his approach. There are the voluminous bundles of official files at the National Archives in Kew, south London, which deal with everything from Lancaster production to the development of new guns. I was also provided with interesting material in direct interviews, particularly with staff who had built the Lancaster at the Avro plants around Manchester.

A new picture of the Lancaster offensive emerged from this research. The bombing campaign was more bloody, Harris more obdurate, the origins of the plane more difficult, the political disputes more bitter and the production more troubled than previous studies have indicated. Arthur Harris can now be seen as a man of epic tunnel vision, who refused to allow anything to distract from his goal of hammering Germany's urban population. His ruthless focus was reflected in a letter he sent to his most senior officers soon after taking charge of Bomber Command in early 1942. Concerned about the effects of Nazi propaganda which highlighted the deaths of civilians in recent raids, he told his group commanders: 'You will have realized that the Boche is weeping crocodile tears over the destruction of Lübeck and Rostock. Naturally enough, there are always a number of dyed-in-the-wool pacifists, disappointed spinsters and interested parties in the services who are ready vehicles for his propaganda.' Harris doubted that this mood had extended to Bomber Command, but he asked his commanders to check that there were no signs of disaffection within their groups. 'All war is brutal. It is going to be a damned sight more brutal still. The fact remains that if there are any weaker brethren who cannot stomach it, the sooner we dispose of them, the better.'[14]

It has sometimes been claimed that the Lancaster crews did not wholly share the brutal simplicity of their commander-in-chief's outlook, but, as the archives and interviews demonstrate, the picture is a more complex one. Some airmen had their doubts about the efficiency and morality of area bombing, feeling that some of the raids could barely be justified on military grounds, as evidenced by the recollection of Michael Maltin of 550 Squadron about a raid on the historic town of Freiburg in northern

Germany. 'They sent a huge force loaded with nothing but incendiaries. The aiming point was the cathedral and the time was Sunday at six o'clock. You could not have got out of that town in a fast car. We did not have a single loss. There was no flak. I am not proud of that one.'[15] Most crews, however, felt that they were doing a tough job on behalf of their country, hitting back at Germany in the only way that was feasible. They did not tend to think much about the fate of civilians at all, and when they did, they believed that the Germans were receiving their just reward for inflicting the Blitz on Britain. This was the view shared by most of the British public, prompting the widespread affection for the 'Bomber Boys'. As Henry Hooper, a pilot with 115 Squadron, said: 'The vast majority of people thought it was a great thing to hit back at the Germans. The press did. The public did. I regarded it as a military necessity. I did what the guys up top wanted. We did as we were told. It did not bother me in the slightest. I just thought about killing Germans. It did not occur to me that they were civilians as well.'[16] To David Ware, a pilot with 635 Pathfinder Squadron, 'There was only one good German as far as I was concerned and that was a dead one. I had absolutely no compunction whatsoever.'[17] The prevailing attitude was well captured by Squadron Leader Larry Curtis, a wireless operator and subsequent signals leader of 617 Squadron, the unit that carried out the Dambusters raid. Curtis joined the RAF immediately after he left school in 1940. 'It was the only way we thought we could hit back at them. Let's face it, our own people were being killed in the same way. When there is a factory producing munitions or planes and there are civilians living around it, I'm afraid that is one of the tragedies of war. You didn't like doing it but you knew it had to be done. As the war went on, I felt we were winning and the main concern was to get it over with as soon as possible. If I had it all to do again, I'd do it again.'[18] But there were others who claimed to relish the carnage because of their implacable hatred of the Nazi regime. For them, the collective guilt of the German people meant that they should be shown no mercy. That is the spirit shining through the wartime diary of John Byrne, a stock clerk from Blackpool who joined the RAF in 1942 and began flying as a Lancaster wireless operator in late 1944. On his very first trip, to Düsseldorf on 2 November 1944, he recorded: 'Now the bombing run. I was almost shouting aloud, cursing the Hun to do his damnest. The filthy Hun. How proud I was at that moment. Let the bastards die like the rats they are.' A few weeks later, flying on another raid, he wrote that at 19,500 feet over the target, 'I called Jerry so much shit. I sincerely hoped our bombs would smash his wicked filthy skull clean open. My heart is cold now.'[19] Byrne was killed two months later on the operation against Dresden.

Archive material reveals a number of other intriguing themes. One is the continual tension between the Air Ministry and Bomber Command over Lancaster operations. This can be seen in Harris's initial reluctance to use his force in the preparations for D-Day in 1944 and in his luke-warm approach to the Air Staff's demand to target oil installations in the winter of 1944–5, something Harris perceived as a distraction from hitting cities. Another ferocious argument arose in 1942 over the Air Ministry's proposal to establish a separate target-finding force, subsequently known as Pathfinders, to improve the accuracy of the heavy bombers. Harris strongly objected to the scheme, claiming it would undermine morale, but such opposition was seen within the Ministry as indicative of Bomber Command's negativity. 'The overwhelming mood in Bomber Command is frustration. There is a burning desire to do more. The crews feel they can do more than they are doing. They grope blindly in an effort to discover where failure lies,' wrote the Air Ministry's Deputy Director of Bombing Operations Sydney Bufton in September 1942. 'Bomber Command is a well organised machine but it needs the breath of life. Until we put the right people in the right places we will never extract the utmost from our crews.'[20]

For all their differences, the Air Ministry could be just as ruthless as Harris about the mass killing of German civilians, even at the height of the row over oil targets in 1944–5. The bombing of Dresden in February 1945, by far the most controversial episode in Bomber Command's history, was more the work of the Air Staff and the politicians than Harris. Again, unpublished papers reveal new angles on this lethal affair, particularly the determination of the Air Ministry to terrorize civilians across east Germany. One candid letter written just a few weeks before the assault on Dresden by Wing Commander Arthur Morley, a senior figure in the Directorate of Bomber Operations, argued: 'That this operation is an attack on enemy morale needs no apology. This basic principle of true morale bombing is that to provoke a state of terror, the attacks when launched must be of such density that there is created in the mind of the individual the conviction that if he is in the area attacked, then his chances of escaping death or serious injury are extremely remote.'[21] The longest-running theme of all, again rarely analysed in previous studies, was Harris's enormous admiration for the Lancaster and his utter disdain for the other two types of heavy bomber, the Short Stirling and the Handley Page Halifax. From the moment he took charge of Bomber

Command in February 1942, he lobbied the Ministry to switch production at the aircraft factories from the Stirling and Halifax to the Lancaster. In his fight for the Lancaster, Harris developed an intemperate loathing for Frederick Handley Page, the eponymous head of the Halifax manufacturing company, as he explained in late 1942 to the Secretary of State for Air, Sir Archibald Sinclair. 'Nothing will be done until Handley Page and his gang are also kicked out, lock, stock and barrel . . . We cannot do this by polite negotiation with these crooks and incompetents. In Russia it would have long ago been arranged with a gun and to that extent I am a fervid communist.'[22]

At the heart of the Lancaster saga lies the testimony of the air and ground crews who experienced the war at first hand. Interviews, diary extracts and memoirs help to explain what it was really like to fly the Lancaster, from the start of the operational briefing when the target was revealed, through the preparations for take-off, the climb into the night sky, the passage through the German flak, the heart-stopping moments of the bombing run, the brief sense of relief once the bombs were released and finally the long anxious journey home. 'On the run to the target, you could feel the Lancaster lifting up and down from the blast of the anti-aircraft guns. Searchlights absolutely filled the sky over all the Ruhr. It was like daylight inside the aircraft, with everything visible,' said gunner J. W. Henderson of 50 Squadron, describing a mission to the industrial city of Duisburg in 1943.

> The target was covered in smoke and fire-tracks. Our bomb aimer, once he had seen the barrage of flak that the Germans were sending up, cried out to the pilot, 'How the hell do you go through this?' But undaunted, the skipper flew on. It was nerve-wracking, having to fly straight and level to bomb the target precisely. You could hear the guns above the throb of your engines. You imagined that if you got home your aircraft would be filled with holes.[23]

Recollections like these bring to life the atmosphere inside the plane at 20,000 feet, the gunners almost freezing in their rear and mid-upper turrets as they endlessly searched for German fighters, the bomb aimer preparing his sight for the run, the navigator trying all the time to ascertain the windspeed and the plane's position, the engineer constantly checking fuel gauges and the pilot coping with the responsibility of guiding the plane through pitch blackness, with the constant risk of collision or exploding shells always on his mind. The smell of cordite, the sense of raw fear, the blinding impact of searchlights and the sweeping arc of tracer bullets are all described in vivid first-hand accounts, as are the horror of crashes on take-off or the alarm of trying to land a badly damaged plane.

One characteristic recollection comes from John Sanders, a pilot with 617 Squadron. Interviewed about a raid on Augsburg in southern Germany on the night of 25–6 February 1944, Sanders provided a graphic illustration of both the heroism of a typical Lancaster crew and the toughness of the plane, his words made all the more powerful by his low-key style:

> We climbed up from the airfield like we always did and as we were heading for the coast of France, the sky was still light behind us. Where the sun was setting, there was a golden tinge to the sky. Obviously a German fighter, coming up from the coast, must have seen us silhouetted against the sky. From down to my left, he fired a short burst of cannon fire. He must have been a pretty good pilot to be able to do that, coming from the opposite direction and hitting us with about six or seven cannon shells. One of them exploded right on the side of the cockpit at my eye level. There was a fairly thick bar across the windscreen on that side, but the shell blew a hole in the Perspex.

Despite being temporarily blinded by the exploding shell, Sanders was able to put the plane into a dive to escape the fighter. As he began to pull out, he realized that some vision had returned to his left eye:

> So if I turned my head sideways, I could see the instrument panel. I managed to straighten up. The next thing I did was to feel my face. There was nothing wrong. I told the flight engineer to check everything in the plane. He found that various cannon shells had hit the aircraft and done some superficial damage. But there was no leak of petrol so we decided to press on.

The Lancaster continued on its way to Augsburg:

> Just as we were approaching the target and getting ready to line up, there was an almighty blast behind me. A fighter's cannon had hit us in the tail and flung the aircraft nose down. We went screaming into a dive and, when I looked round, all I could see was a wall of fire. The back of the aircraft was just yellow with flames. I managed to pull the aircraft out of the dive with great difficulty, feet braced against the rudder pedals and pulling like mad.

While Sanders wrestled with the plane, some crew members tackled the fire, putting it out with their extinguishers. Another went to the aid of the rear gunner, who had collapsed in his turret because his oxygen supply had been severed. Amidst all the mayhem, the navigator had retained his calm, working out the best course for home. Because of the noise of the four Rolls-Royce Merlin engines, it was always impossible to speak normally within a Lancaster, so the crews had to rely on an intercom. But in this case, the intercom had broken down when the cannon shells ripped through the wiring. So the navigator wrote out the course on a note which he passed to Sanders. By now, despite having lightened the Lancaster through jettisoning its bomb load at the bottom of the dive, Sanders was 'finding the plane most difficult to handle. I could not keep it level. If I loosened the pressure on the wheel, it just slammed against the instrument panel. I had to hold it back but I could feel something grating all the time. I sensed that something was going to break.' From his cockpit Sanders could not have known that the cannon shells had torn all the fabric off the port elevator, leaving it little more than a wire skeleton. But he found that by wrapping his arms around the wheel and bracing his feet against the rudder pedals he could just keep the nose up. He now had a journey home of more than four hours in this position. 'Every so often I would get the flight engineer to reach across my shoulder and take over the wheel while I had a rest because it was getting very tiring.' In the journey back to base, Sanders was also supported by the exceptional skills of the navigator, a Glaswegian solicitor before the war, who had to plot by dead reckoning and the stars, since his equipment had been hit in the attack. Just as creative was the wireless operator, who managed to fix up a primitive intercom using battery cables from lifejackets, which he plugged into his Marconi wireless. 'All of a sudden I could hear somebody speak to me. So the navigator and I were able to talk. It was much simpler to fly and pass instructions after that.'

When the Lancaster reached the English coast, Sanders used the makeshift intercom to warn the crew that landing would be extremely difficult, given the damage. He therefore gave them the option to bail out. After discussing the problem, however, they decided to put their faith in him. The journey continued until the Lancaster came within a short distance of its base at Fiskerton in Lincolnshire:

> As the plane got lower, it got heavier and heavier on the wheel because the air was denser. It was really hard work. There was a solid sheet of cloud at 2,000 feet. The navigator put me in position, saying, 'Right, you're lined up to start the descent.' As I came out of the cloud, there was the runway in front of me, absolutely perfect. I told the wireless operator, who had the Very pistol, to keep loading reds and firing them to let them know that we were coming in without radio. There were other aircraft landing so control had to know that we were a plane without lights or any way of talking. I got the aircraft lined up and the runway was coming up nicely. Then I realized, to my absolute horror, that I was not going to make it.

As hard as I pulled back on the stick, I could not get the nose up any further. By my own judgement, I could see that we were going to be short of the runway by about half a mile. I thought to myself, 'Good grief, after all this, it isn't going to work.' Then I suddenly remembered that in a Lancaster, the first ten degrees of flap increase the lift. So I tried it. I popped down ten degrees of flap, and the nose came up just enough. I put the wheels on the end of the concrete, but once the tyres bit on the runway, there was no way I could get the stick back and bring the tail down. The poor old Lanc kicked up at an alarming angle, but eventually it crashed onto the tail wheel. And we were down safely. I taxied into dispersal, and all the crew bundled out of the aeroplane. I got into the crew bus, and it was the first and last time in my life that I was kissed by another man. The mid upper gunner threw his arms around me and said, 'You made it.'[24]

There are other memorable individual stories, such as that of Jack West, a navigator with 115 Squadron. On a raid to Homberg, southern Germany, in July 1944, his Lancaster came under both flak and fighter attack, riddling the plane with bullets, destroying most of the instruments, stopping two of the engines, starting a fire in the cockpit and injuring most of the crew. As the blaze intensified, the skipper gave the order to bail out. Blood pouring from his wounds, West made his way towards the escape hatch at the front of the Lancaster. There he was greeted by the strange sight of the bomb aimer 'crouched over the hole in the floor where the escape hatch should have been. When he saw me, he screamed at me to stay back and not come any closer. I ignored this remark and proceeded forward, but then I stopped when I saw he had drawn the six-inch knife that we all carried as part of our escape equipment.' With his face creased in anger, the bomb aimer explained that in his panic he had accidentally dropped his own parachute out the hatch. He then warned West that 'if he couldn't escape no one else would'. West had no option but to retreat and inform the pilot of the bomb aimer's lethal threat. By this time, the engineer had managed to put out the fire, enduring severe burns in the process. In the circumstances the pilot decided that, though the plane was losing height, he would try to keep flying as long as he could. Eventually he reached the English coast, with the Lancaster 'almost touching the water of the North Sea'. As the plane struggled towards the RAF base at Woodbridge in Suffolk, the two remaining engines stuttered, while the undercarriage would not lock down because of the lack of hydraulic fluid. But the heroic skipper came in straight, then 'made a crash landing only for the undercarriage to collapse and the bomb bay doors swing open'. Once the aircraft had come to a halt after falling over to the port side, the injured crew were pulled outside and taken to hospital, West spending ten days having shrapnel removed from his body. When he returned to base he learnt that the Lancaster had sustained 450 bullet holes and over 100 shrapnel holes from the German fighters and anti-aircraft guns. It was a tribute to the resilience of the aircraft that it had reached England. Almost as remarkable as the plane's survival was the attitude of the crew towards the treacherous, knife-wielding bomb aimer. Instead of reporting him, which would almost certainly have resulted in a court martial, they decided to keep quiet about the incident, though 'we indicated that we would rather not fly with him'.[25] Jack West carried on right to the end of the war, winning the Distinguished Flying Medal and enduring further dramas.

The adventures of the airmen contained an immense variety of experiences, some gripping, some horrifying, some bizarre. They feature tales of bailouts over Germany, shattering collisions, bomb-release failures, empty fuel tanks, jammed guns and dangerous landings. In one case, a pilot managed to bring his damaged plane down on a narrow Normandy beachhead soon after D-Day. In another, a crewman fell out of his burning Lancaster at 19,000 feet without a parachute, but landed in a thick snowdrift in a pine forest and survived. Unsurprisingly, the Germans initially did not believe his story when they captured him, concluding that he must be a spy. In the airmen's recollections, there are also rich descriptions of weather conditions during Lancaster raids, like the phenomenon of St Elmo's fire where a thunderstorm could generate an electrical field, turning the four propellers, technically known as airscrews, into circles of blue fire, covering the plane in violent flashes and sending long jets of flame from the guns. But sometimes the surroundings in the sky could be uplifting, as Jack Currie wrote of one climb through the clouds on a daylight raid:

> Suddenly the cockpit of the Lancaster breasts the cloud tops and there is the sky, vast and clear and brilliantly blue. The wisps of cloud that rush past you are so white that you can't believe that you've ever seen true whiteness before. High above, there are some scattered streaks of cirrus, underlining the splendour of the sun, and as for those six hundred bombers, you can see less than a dozen, at different heights and tiny in the distance. If there were time to spare for fun, it would be good to hold this height for a while and run along the cloud crests, like surf-riding on a sea of cotton wool.[26]

Epic courage was needed by all airmen to keep the offensive going. One navigator was sick at the start of every single trip he made, vomiting discreetly into a bag by his desk. Naked fear could be hidden from others with shows of bravado or nonchalance, but not from oneself. Frank Waddington, a member of No. 7 Pathfinder Squadron, confessed:

> I cannot tell you how frightened I was. I used to imagine being shot down, being in a plane that was blazing and we were all fighting to get out. I used to drink like a fish in the hope that I would get to sleep but it did not help. I really just wanted to go home to Mummy. I suppose many of us felt like that but it was a thing you never, ever talked about. I never remember saying to anyone, 'God I'm bloody scared of this.' Or anyone saying it to me. You just carried on with this mock humour, cracking jokes.[27]

But sometimes it was impossible to disguise the terror. One pilot, during a raid on Düsseldorf, became so frightened by the barrage of flak that he simply left the wheel and tried to bail out, only to be pulled back by his crew. As in the case of Jack West's knife-wielding bomb aimer, the crew decided to keep the incident quiet. Others who displayed panic had to face more severe consequences. The lucky ones ended up at an RAF rehabilitation centre at Matlock in Derbyshire. The less fortunate or openly cowardly would be charged with the offence of 'Lack of Moral Fibre', leading to expulsion from their squadron to a harsh RAF correction facility.

Through all their tribulations the crews' greatest asset was the Lancaster, whose dependability was a constant source of comfort amid the chaos of war. Due to its rugged design and Merlin engines, it could absorb huge amounts of punishment. It was unusual for a Lancaster to return from a mission over Germany without holes in its wings and fuselage, yet it rarely surrendered the fight. David Scholes, the Australian pilot, was flying back from Nuremburg in October 1944 when his Lancaster was badly hit by flak, damaging the hydraulics and ripping through the fuselage and the bomb doors. As he recorded in his diary the next day, 'I cannot maintain a good speed with the bomb doors open and we become a straggler. We begin to ice up and I cannot climb. Chunks crash through the Perspex off the airscrews.' But the Lancaster still staggered home and landed. 'I now find that the tail wheel is missing but I don't give a damn because we're down and alive. The old crate is full of holes, petrol is pouring out of her and the fuselage is broken near the mid upper turret, where there is a huge hole.'[28] Faith in the Lancaster was enhanced by its unparalleled ability to keep going after engine failure, another tribute to its superb design. Bob Knights of the Dambusters squadron said: 'The Lancaster handled very well on three engines. It would even fly on two engines. Even with no engines, it would still glide, though it would go down of course. It was a beautiful flying machine.'[29] Noble Frankland, the navigator who later became a renowned historian, had the singular experience of flying on a mission to France in a fully loaded Lancaster when both starboard engines failed before the plane had even crossed the English Channel. Still carrying its huge bomb load, the Lancaster turned round and headed back towards East Anglia. The pilot then made an emergency descent towards RAF Skellingthorpe in Lincolnshire. 'With all the power on one side, the pilot could not entirely straighten his landing line and we came down in something of a sideways skid. The tyres then smoked and melted but the undercarriage held and we came to a rest in a virtually intact aircraft. We heard later that no one had landed a Lancaster before with a full bomb load on board, on two engines on the same side.'[30] A pilot with 44 Squadron once lost an engine on his way to the target, a second when his plane was hit by flak and a third when it seized up within sight of the base. Yet still he was able to land smoothly. 'I thought we were about to run out of engines,' he joked as he left the plane.[31]

It was this resilience, allied to its power and beauty, that inspired such devotion towards the Lancaster from airmen, ground crews and the public. Rarely in history has a weapon of mass destruction been so cherished. As with the Spitfire, RAF personnel talked frankly about the depth of their attachment to the plane. The bomb aimer Campbell Muirhead, whose diary usually reveals a whiff of cynicism about life in Bomber Command, adopted a very different tone when a new Lancaster, named V for Victor, arrived for his crew on 25 June 1944. 'She's beautiful and I've already fallen in love with her. As for her performance: exquisite. Those Rolls-Royce Merlins don't roar; they sing. No country in the world has an engine in the same class as the Merlin.'[32] Just as passionate was Harry Yates, a pilot with 75 Squadron who first flew in a Lancaster during his training at Feltwell, East Anglia, in July 1944. 'I soon discovered that everything that has been said and written about the Avro Lancaster was true. Some products of the hand of man have that uncanny capacity to pull at the heart-strings and the Lancaster was one such. Everything about it was just right. Its muscular, swept lines were beautiful to look at. It flew with effortless grace and had a precise weighted feel. It made the pilot's job easy. You could throw it all over the skies if you had the inclination and the physical strength.'[33] This same feeling ran through the ground crews that operated on the Lancasters and the members of the Women's Auxiliary Air Force (WAAF) who worked at Bomber Command's bases. In his unpublished memoir Stephen Rew, a fitter based at Waddington, Lincolnshire, recalled one twilit summer evening as his aircrew waited at the dispersal site, moments before the men boarded their plane for take-off. 'For a few minutes they sit smoking and watching the lean, menacing but beautiful shape of their aircraft, silhouetted against the reddening sky. She seems to be in a fighting crouch, sitting well down on her undercarriage beneath the weight of fuel and bombs and somehow eager, as if she wants to get at the enemy.'[34]

The success of the Lancaster highlights a wonderful irony at the centre of its story. For the fact is that the Air Ministry did not initially intend to build the plane at all. Instead, the top officials and Air Staff wanted the drive for heavy four-engined bombers to be concentrated on the Halifax and Stirling, while Avro developed a two-engined bomber called the Manchester. When the Manchester turned out to be a disaster, thanks to its hopelessly unreliable engines, the Ministry wanted to see Avro turned over for the manufacture of the Handley Page Halifax. That this plan was not enacted was only because of the persistence of Roy Chadwick and his managing director at Avro, Roy Dobson, who both had long believed that the Manchester could be transformed into a better aircraft if it were given the proper engines. In the face of ministerial hostility, even obstruction, Chadwick and Dobson pursued their goal until they won over the establishment with the brilliance of the Lancaster's design. In this sense, it is no exaggeration to describe the Lancaster as a semi-private venture. It was built to no specification except Chadwick's own. Avro was given no instructions for its development. Indeed, there was not even an official contract for the Lancaster until the prototype had undertaken its test flights. Full credit to the role of Chadwick and Dobson can now be paid, not least through material in an Air Ministry file about the history of the Lancaster, which contains a lengthy interview with Chadwick shortly before his tragic early death in 1947.

The historian Noble Frankland wrote in one of his books about the bomber offensive: 'Aircraft are strange birds and the distinctions between them which render the differences between brilliant success, useful value and outright failure are often hard to see and more often impossible to predict. So too the effect of modification and redevelopment sometimes produces the most unpredictable and the most surprising results.'[35] This was certainly true of the change from the Manchester to the Lancaster, where the addition of two engines turned a dangerous mediocrity into a world-beater. But it was the genius of Chadwick that made this possible. Once more, there is a parallel with the Spitfire, designed by Reginald Mitchell. His first design for an all-metal monoplane fighter was rightly described as 'a dog's breakfast'.[36] But from this unpromising start emerged the finest fighter plane that Britain ever possessed. The development of the Lancaster under Chadwick's guidance followed the same lines, from initial failure, through official doubts and on to ultimate triumph. But in the final analysis that triumph could have been all the greater. For the darkest, most regrettable theme of all running through the latter half of the Lancaster story is that neither the magnificence of the plane nor the abilities of its crews were exploited to the full by the RAF. In its myopic focus on area bombing, Harris's Bomber Command did a disservice to Chadwick's wonderful design, using it all too often as an aerial bulldozer when it had continually proved that it was capable of so much more, whether it be in the Dambusters raid or the precision attacks on France in the lead-up to D–Day. Harris certainly recognized the greatness of the Lancaster, but only in the context of fulfilling his own narrow theory of mass devastation. Under a less dogmatic commander, the Lancaster and its men might have been employed to far greater effect against Germany after 1943. In my book on the Spitfire, I came to the conclusion that Sir Hugh Dowding had failed to use the aircraft to its fullest potential in the Battle of Britain because, trapped in the iron certainties of his own system, he was not flexible enough to adapt to the changing nature of the conflict. Sadly for the Lancaster and its men, a similar charge of inflexibility could be levelled against Harris. The Lancaster undoubtedly helped to win the war, but if only there had been greater imagination at the top of Bomber Command, it could have done so more quickly.

I

'Make it simple'

— ❧ —

'I THINK IT IS well for the man in the street to realize that there is no power on earth that can protect him from being bombed, whatever people may tell him. The bomber will always get through,' said the Conservative leader Stanley Baldwin during a Parliamentary debate on the air threat in 1932.[1] His remark soon became famous because it perfectly encapsulated the mood of fatalism and craven resignation that gripped the National Government of the 1930s under the successive leaderships of Ramsay Macdonald (1931–5), Baldwin (1935–7) and Neville Chamberlain (1937–40). Much of the impulse for the policy of appeasement stemmed from the belief that there was no military defence against the bomber, so the only way to maintain peace was through a process of negotiated concessions to Europe's dictators.

Yet along with Chamberlain's notorious promise to have brought 'peace in our time' after the Munich agreement of 1938, Baldwin's claim that 'the bomber will always get through' proved to be one of the worst predictions of the decade. The early years of the Second World War showed that Baldwin's fears about the invincibility of the bomber were grossly exaggerated. Far from being instruments of all-consuming destructive power, bomber forces turned out to be both vulnerable and ineffectual. In a direct contradiction of Baldwin's prophecy, the Luftwaffe's bombers were badly mauled by Fighter Command during the Battle of Britain in the summer and autumn of 1940, proving easy prey for the Spitfires and Hurricanes. Even in the nocturnal Blitz that followed the Battle of Britain, the damage to cities was much less than had been feared before the war. In April 1941 the Luftwaffe retreated, having been unable to break Britain.

When it came to the RAF, the idea that 'the bomber will always get through' was hopelessly misplaced. Throughout the 1930s the Air Staff had regarded heavy bombing of the enemy as the central purpose of the RAF, the very reason for its existence as an independent force. 'Our belief in the bomber was instinctive, a matter of faith,' wrote Sir John Slessor, one of the RAF's key strategists.[2] But it was a faith without foundation.

Bomber Command lacked a clear strategy and adequate equipment. The head of Bomber Command at the start of the war, Sir Edgar Ludlow-Hewitt, had warned that his force was 'practically useless',[3] containing just 17 squadrons capable of night bombing. The ineffectiveness of Bomber Command was exposed almost from the moment that war began. The first RAF bombing raid, on 4 September 1939 against the naval ports of Wilhelmshaven and Brunsbuttel, proved a fiasco. Twenty-nine Wellingtons and Blenheims, both regarded as advanced types of bombers, set off, but ten of them completely failed to find their target, one dropping its bombs on the Danish town of Esbjerg 110 miles away. Of the remainder, seven were shot down by German fighters, while even those that managed to attack German shipping did little more than cause a few dents and chipped paintwork. This was to set the tone for Bomber Command during the next couple of years, where minimal damage in Germany was achieved at an appalling cost. From September 1939 until January 1941, when the Lancaster first took to the air, Bomber Command flew 19,961 sorties, losing 517 aircraft or 14.8 per cent of those dispatched, a completely unsustainable rate of attrition. In the first three years of the war, the chances of any bomber crewman surviving a full tour were less than one in three.[4]

Bomber Command could initially put some of the blame for its failures on Chamberlain's government, which was so terrified of German reprisals that it allowed a paralysing sense of caution to dictate its bombing strategy. When one minister suggested an urban attack, the Air Secretary Kingsley Wood reacted with outrage, warning that German private property could be put at risk. The inhibiting restrictions were later recalled by Derek French of 50 Squadron. 'We were not allowed to fly over German territory or attack any land targets. The idea was to avoid German civilian casualties and a possible escalation of the war.'[5] Apart from occasional attacks on ports and canals, the main use of the bombers was to drop propaganda leaflets on German cities, which, as Sir Arthur Harris ruefully commented, achieved nothing except to increase the supply of toilet paper within the Reich. But even when Winston Churchill replaced Chamberlain as Prime Minister in May 1940 and unshackled Bomber Command, the RAF was still too weak to hit Germany effectively.

The bomber's lack of success in the early part of the Second World War contradicted the popular belief that aerial bombardment would immediately create an apocalypse. This had been a powerful theme during the interwar years, as writers and military experts grabbed the public imagination with their gruesome warnings about terror from the air. With the invention of the bomber, the dangers of annihilation seemed to have moved from science fiction into reality. Typical of the eagerness to stoke up public fears was a passage by the military historian Basil Liddell Hart in his 1925 book *Paris, or The Future of War*: 'Imagine for a moment London, Manchester, Birmingham and half a dozen other great cities simultaneously attacked, the business localities and Fleet Street wrecked, Whitehall a heap of ruins, the slum districts maddened into the impulse to break loose and maraud, the railways cut, factories destroyed.'[6] In similar fashion Colonel James Fitzmaurice, the former head of Irish Free State Air Corps, put forward this prophetic vision in 1931:

> A hideous shower of death and destruction falls screeching and screaming through space and atmosphere to the helpless, thickly populated earth below. The shock of the hit is appalling. Great buildings totter and tumble in dust like a mean and frail set of ninepins. The survivors, now merely demoralized masses of demented humanity, scatter caution to the winds. They are seized by a demoniacal frenzy of terror. They tear off their gas masks, soon absorb the poisonous fumes and expire in horrible agony, cursing the fate that did not destroy them hurriedly and without warning in the first awful explosions.[7]

It was not just in literature that predictions of anarchy and wholesale massacre could be found. The mood extended to officialdom. In 1937 the Committee of Imperial Defence warned that Germany had the capability to mount an air assault lasting sixty days and killing 600,000 people in the process. A year later the Ministry of Health upped the stakes by estimating that 2.8 million hospital beds might be needed to deal with the casualties from bombing.

Feeding these anxieties were the memories of an event that had taken place towards the end of the First World War. In the summer of 1917 the Germans had launched a series of bombing raids on Kent and London, carried out by giant Gotha biplanes. In one attack on Folkestone, 95 people were killed. In a later attack on London, 162 people died. Though these numbers were tiny compared to the death toll on the western front, the Gotha raids sparked a public outcry and widespread alarm. More than 300,000 Londoners took to shelters every night in the second half of 1917, even though the Gotha menace had faded away by then as a result of British fighter action. Apart from the legacy of fear, the other far-reaching consequence of the Gotha raids was that the government was forced to set up a committee, under the South African statesman (later Prime Minister) Jan Christiaan Smuts, to recommend improvements in

Britain's air defences. As a result of Smuts's report, the Royal Air Force was established as an independent force in April 1918, through a merger of the Royal Flying Corps and the Royal Naval Air Service.

The circumstances of the RAF's birth had a profound influence on its development. Indeed Smuts had written in his report: 'The day may not be far off when aerial operations with their devastation of enemy lands and destruction of industrial and populous centres on a vast scale may become the principal operations of war, to which older forms of military operations may become secondary and subordinate.'[8] Seeing the disruption caused by a few German biplanes, the RAF was committed from the start to the concept of strategic bombing. Its first leader, Air Chief Marshal Sir Hugh Trenchard, was a passionate advocate of air power as an offensive weapon rather than as a provider of tactical support for the army or navy. Filled with domineering self-confidence about his opinions, much like Sir Arthur Harris later, he believed that the bomber had changed the whole concept of war, since a nation could be driven into submission by heavy aerial attack alone. In the 'Trenchard Doctrine', which became the prevailing orthodoxy of the Air Staff between the wars, the impact of bombing on the psychology of the enemy's population was even more important than physical damage. Without any evidence, Trenchard claimed that 'the moral effect of bombing stands to the material effect in proportion of twenty to one'.[9] He was equally certain about the uselessness of fighter planes. 'The aeroplane is not a defence against the aeroplane,' he once said.[10]

The ideology of offensive bombing was buttressed by the writings of the Italian military theorist, Brigadier-General Giulio Douhet, whose 1921 book *The Command of the Air* argued that the outcome of future wars would be decided by aerial attacks. The freedom of bombers to fly over enemy territory, maintained Douhet, inaugurated a new era of total war, where massed armies on the battlefront would be an irrelevance and the distinction between combatants and civilians would dissolve. 'The battlefield will be limited only by the boundaries of the nation at war,' he wrote, 'and all of their citizens will become combatants, since all of them will be exposed to the aerial offensives of the enemy.'[11] At the same time as Douhet was propounding his gospel of ruthlessness, across the Atlantic Billy Mitchell, a senior American air officer who had flown in action over France, was also arguing that it would be vital in future wars to concentrate attacks on industrial centres, thereby destroying the enemy's economy. His truculent intolerance towards any US military figures who disagreed with him led to his departure from the army in 1926, though his views continued to have an influence in Britain. In an echo of Douhet and Mitchell, the leading author and former Air Commodore Lionel Carlton wrote in 1937 that 'air power is bombing capacity and nothing else. An assessment of the air strength of a country should be based exclusively on the weight-carrying capacity, the speed, range and on the number of its bomber squadrons.'[12] Trenchard, who had retired as Chief of the Air Staff in 1930, would have shared that sentiment.

Trenchard's successors were also enthusiasts for strategic bombing, but they hardly had the means to conduct it at the start of the Second World War. Their hope of demolishing German industry remained a fantasy. In the whole of Bomber Command in January 1940 there were only 280 aircraft, none of which represented a genuine threat to Germany. The latest type, the Vickers Wellington, was a durable and versatile plane but it lacked speed, height and bomb-loading capacity, while the Armstrong Whitworth Whitley, which first flew in 1936, was known as the 'flying coffin' because of its vulnerability. Another of the supposedly modern monoplanes, the Handley Page Hampden, could only fly at 155 mph and carry a load of just 4,000 pounds, less than a third of the Lancaster's average payload. Furthermore, these planes had no proper navigational aids, radios or bombsights, so their bombing was woefully inaccurate. Dead reckoning, guesswork, moonlight and blind hope were the methods that often had to be used. In one telling incident from May 1940, a Whitley crew bombed an RAF airbase in Cambridgeshire, thinking they were hitting a German airfield in Holland. Rupert 'Tiny' Cooling, a Wellington pilot with 9 Squadron, recalled the extraordinary lack of any focused strategy on bombing missions during the fall of France in May 1940. 'It was a peculiar time in the war because nobody was sure about what to do. We'd got this force, we'd better use it, but how? We were showing the flag more than anything, roaming the countryside. They told us if we saw anything worth bombing, bomb it. I was second pilot as bomb aimer, staring down at the patterns of hedges and bridges and if we saw a likely looking crossroads or railway line, we'd drop a 250-pound bomb on it. It was like shooting pigeons with a blindfold on.'[13] So wayward was the RAF's bombing that the Germans could not work out what strategy Britain was actually pursuing. When a raid was mounted against Berlin in August 1940, in response to a Luftwaffe attack on London, the results were pitiful. In fact the Nazi propaganda chief Josef Goebbels, seeking to whip up hysteria against Britain, was cynically disappointed in the poor results of the raids. With characteristic manipulation, he therefore created his own phoney bomb explosions just to give the illusion of

British 'atrocities'. As he recorded in his diary, 'Attack on Government quarter . . . Nothing serious, but I organise for the matter to be given a little help through fake incendiary bombs. Wardarg [one of his aides] has this photographed immediately. A splendid propaganda device.'[14]

The inadequacy of Bomber Command caused Churchill to rail at the Chief of the Air Staff, Sir Charles Portal. 'Our need is to increase the bomb dropping tonnage upon Germany. This is at present lamentably small and it constitutes a serious reproach to the organisation of the RAF,' wrote the Prime Minister in November 1940. Two months later Churchill was even more vehement in his charges. 'I am deeply concerned at the stagnant condition of our bomber force. The fighters are going well ahead, but the Bomber Force is not making the progress hoped for.'[15] In his reply to the second missive, Portal said that 'the present state of affairs is the price we are paying for the rapid development of Fighter and Coastal Commands'.[16] There was some justice in this explanation from Portal, a cool-headed officer who had taken up his appointment as Chief of the Air Staff in November 1940. Throughout the second half of the 1930s, in response to aggressive German rearmament, a debate had raged within government as to which part of the RAF should receive increased state funds. In line with their Trenchardian instincts, the Air Staff wanted priority given to the bomber force. The government, under the guidance of Chamberlain, inclined towards fighters. This was as much on the grounds of parsimony as strategy. At a Cabinet meeting in November 1938 where ministers agreed the primacy of the fighter, Chamberlain noted that a bomber cost as much as four fighters. But whatever the reasoning, the Cabinet had made the right decision, for the increase in Fighter Command's strength ensured victory in the Battle of Britain two years later.

But Bomber Command's difficulties in 1940 were not just about funding and aircraft numbers. By far the biggest problem was the lack of a high-quality heavy bomber. The absence of one rendered all the talk about strategic bombing and the Trenchard doctrine meaningless. The Air Ministry were only too aware of this. In the early 1930s the RAF's heavy bombers, or so-called 'heavies', had consisted of obsolescent aircraft like the Handley Page Heyford, a strange-looking, part-fabric biplane with a bulbous fixed undercarriage, an open cockpit and a fuselage attached to the upper wing. But advancing technology, particularly the arrival of all-metal monoplanes, had given the Ministry the opportunity to push for radically different bomber types. As well as the new line in medium bombers, which led to the Wellington, the Hampden and the Whitley, the Ministry began to discuss the development of a new generation of far larger and faster heavy bombers, partly influenced by the experience of the US Army Air Corps which in 1934 had drawn up a proposal for a four-engine heavy bomber. The prototype of Boeing B-17, later to win fame as the Flying Fortress, had first flown in July 1935, causing an immediate impression. In October 1935 Captain R. N. Liptrot of the Air Ministry's Directorate of Technical Development had produced an estimate of the performance of a British heavy bomber with four Rolls-Royce Merlin engines. His opinion was that such a plane could achieve a maximum speed of 275 mph and a cruising speed of 230 mph, a huge improvement on bombers currently in service. But Liptrot's director, Air Commodore R. H. Verney, was less enthusiastic, explaining that he 'was very chary of supporting projects for very large aeroplanes'.[17] His alternative scheme, which displayed ingenuity if ultimately not practicality, was to design a plane that could be catapulted so it could take off with a heavy bomb load. Such an aircraft, claimed Verney, would be 'just as powerful, capable of quite as much range, greater speed, and it would be smaller and cheaper to produce'.[18] It was this innovative proposal that would lead, after much agony, dispute, change and even tragedy, to the creation of the Lancaster.

In the months that followed, there were intense discussions within the Air Ministry about plans for the new bomber. As the debate continued into the spring of 1936, two competing theories developed. One stressed the importance of a large bomb load, sacrificing performance for capacity. The alternative, favoured by Verney, saw high performance as vital, with speed, versatility and range as the key ingredients. The conflict between these two positions proved impossible to resolve. The result was that instead of producing one single proposal for its ideal bomber, the Air Ministry came up with two different specifications, one for a heavy and one for a medium aircraft. The first, named B12/36, was issued in July 1936. Focusing on bombing capacity, it called for a four-engined plane with a crew of six, a bomb load of at least 14,000 pounds and a minimum cruising speed at full weight of 180 mph. Interestingly, even in this proposed heavy bomber, the idea of catapult-assisted take-off was retained because of the short length of prewar airstrips. So it was decreed that the structure of the prototype must be able to withstand the pressure 'from a catapult which imposed an acceleration of two-and-a-half "g" at the end of a launch',[19] though this requirement was soon to be dropped as longer runways began to be installed across Bomber Command's airfields. Another defect was the strength of the armament, something that was continually to plague RAF bombers, including the Lancaster. B12/36 stipulated that the plane should carry two .303 Browning guns in the front turret, two in the centre of the fuselage and four in the rear. The Chief of the Air Staff, Sir Edward Ellington, had asked whether consideration could be given to replacing the Browning guns with more powerful 20-mm cannon, but his request was airily dismissed by Group Captain Robert Oxland, the Deputy Director of Operational Requirements, who said that 20-mm cannon were neither practical nor necessary. Oxland's decision, which was to be applied to all RAF aircraft developed in the mid-1930s, turned out to be dangerously short-sighted, weakening the defensive firepower of Bomber Command throughout the war. As late as July 1944, Harris could be found writing to the Air Staff: 'Nothing will convince me that there has been nothing but the most gross lethargy, lack of drive and negligence over the whole business of Bomber rearmament with the result that we are now in this deplorable situation. It passes beyond belief that Bomber Command is still equipped with pop guns and turrets.'[20]

Other aspects of B12/36 were to be just as damaging to the bomber's effectiveness. The structure of the bomb bay was too restrictive, since it was to be divided into sections, none of which could accommodate any individual bomb larger than 2,000 pounds. With a lack of foresight, the Air Staff in 1936 had not imagined that the weight of bombs would dramatically increase in the coming years. Indeed, during the discussions of the Operational Requirements Committee on B12/36, the experts agreed that the 2,000-pounders would be needed only for attacking ships, while 500-pounders would be used against land targets. Even more serious was the limited wingspan imposed on the bomber. It was to be no wider than 100 feet in order to keep down its weight and improve handling on the ground, particularly on distant airfields of the British empire. Again, the planners showed a serious lack of imagination, for the narrow span would drastically restrict the height that the bomber could achieve.

Two firms were chosen to produce prototypes for the B12/36 specification. One was Vickers Supermarine of Southampton, which had just built the acclaimed Spitfire prototype. Tragically, the Spitfire's designer Reginald Mitchell died from cancer in June 1937, just when he had begun on the detailed design of the new four-engine bomber. The company carried on with the work, though the two Supermarine bomber prototypes were destroyed by a German air raid on Southampton in September 1940 and the project was abandoned. By this time, the other

B12/36 design had already gone into production. This was the S29, built by the Belfast aircraft firm of Short Brothers, which had produced the celebrated Sunderland flying boat. After the prototype's maiden flight in May 1939, the S29 was named the Stirling, following the Air Ministry's new practice of calling its bombers after major British towns. In some respects the Stirling was remarkably advanced for its time, having a bigger payload and more power than even the American and Soviet bomber types then under construction. But its inherent design flaws, dictated in part by the specification, meant that it never lived up to the early hopes of the Air Ministry. With its low ceiling, it proved to be disastrously vulnerable over Germany, while its weak undercarriage led to a catalogue of fatal accidents. 'I was not alone in disliking the Stirling,' recalled the navigator Bob Guthrie. 'It was a dodgy sort of aircraft. You couldn't get much over 15,000 feet in them.'[21]

One of the paradoxes of the Lancaster saga is that the only British bomber designed from the start with four engines should turn out to be a failure, whereas the most successful heavy bomber of the war should have begun as a twin-engined medium bomber. But it is precisely in the Lancaster's origins as a lighter, faster aircraft that the key to its success can be found. For as it evolved, the design was able to marry the early advantages of clean lines and strength to the raw power of the Merlin engine. The demand for a twin-engined medium bomber had arisen at the same time as B12/36, driven by Verney's belief that performance and versatility should be of paramount importance. Again, there were lengthy arguments within the Air Staff over the proposed aircraft, which would undertake a wide variety of bombing roles and would, like the original B12/36, seek to use catapult technology. An outline specification, called P13/36, was drawn up in June 1936 and circulated to officials and bomber commanders for their advice. 'The Air Staff require a twin-engined medium bomber for world-wide use,' read the draft. 'It should be an aircraft that can exploit the alternatives between long-range and very heavy bomb loads which is made possible by catapult launching in a heavily loaded condition. The aircraft must be suitable for operations by day and night at home and abroad. It appears that there is a possibility of combining the Medium Bomber, the General Reconnaissance, the General Purpose and the Torpedo Bomber classes in one basic design.'[22] The draft further suggested a speed of 250 mph at 15,000 feet, a crew of four airmen, a front and rear gun turret, each with 1,000 rounds of ammunition, sound-proofing of the pilot's cabin, modern equipment such as oxygen, a radio-telephone, camera, dinghy, and cockpit heating, and a maximum bomb load of 8,000 pounds, this to be made up of sixteen 500-pounders, or four 2,000-pounders, or two torpedoes. There was also to be provision to act as an army transport, carrying 12 fully equipped troops. Given that manoeuvrability was to be one of the Lancaster's great virtues, it is ironic that the draft specification stated: 'A high degree of manoeuvrability is not essential but the aircraft must be sufficiently manoeuvrable at high speeds for dive bombing.'[23] As with the catapult mechanism, the torpedo requirements were later to prove unnecessary. Yet both were to be crucial for the Lancaster's potency. For the accommodation of two naval weapons, each 18 foot 3 inches long, meant the creation of a single massive bomb bay extending for two-thirds of the fuselage, so different to the Stirling's divided structure, while the need to handle the stress of catapult-assisted take-offs made the airframe immensely strong.

With the drumbeat of impending war now echoing in the background, following Germany's remilitarization of the Rhineland in March 1936, there was a new urgency about internal debates on the RAF's needs, as shown by some of the comments on the P13/36 draft specification. In one thoughtful letter Air Commodore Owen Boyd, Commander of No. 1 Bomber Group, expressed his concern that the medium bomber was being designed for too many different roles. 'I would emphasize that I consider it of the utmost importance that the aircraft should be designed for the primary purpose as a medium bomber to be used in European warfare,' wrote Boyd. 'I do not think that any compromise should be accepted which would detract from its efficiency in this, its primary role.' Boyd, all too aware of the looming conflict, was also worried about performance. 'In my opinion, the speeds laid down in the specification will be too slow in four years' time.'[24] Sir John Steel, the Commander-in-Chief of the Air Defence of Great Britain, which was shortly to be reorganized into Fighter and Bomber Commands, shared Boyd's fears, warning at an Air Ministry meeting that 'the desire for a combination of types will result in an aeroplane which will have nothing like the performance it ought to have as a medium bomber'.[25] One intriguing intervention at this meeting came from the Air Staff's Deputy Director of Plans, a post then held by none other than Arthur Harris. In his first remark on the embryonic plane with which his career would be indelibly linked, Harris argued that improving the range and speed of RAF bombers was vital. 'Unless our aeroplanes had ranges at least equal to that of the foreign aircraft, there was a danger of us being attacked by aircraft from points outside the range of our own aircraft; we should have to submit to attack without being able to retaliate.' On the question of top speed, he pointed out that 'the draft requirements represented our minimum requirements and were likely to be improved upon'. He thought that 'if other countries could give better performance so could we'. And the aggressive spirit of Harris was always near the surface. 'It was necessary that our aeroplanes should have the maximum offensive power in a European war,' he told his colleagues.[26]

In the light of the future development of the Lancaster and the Halifax, the most interesting aspect of the debate over specification P13/36 was whether the bomber should be given an additional two engines. In his letter to group commanders and officials with which he enclosed the draft specification, Group Captain Robert Oxland of the Operational Requirements Directorate asked: 'In the interests of reliability in the air, are four engines considered to be preferable to two, in spite of the increased maintenance difficulties?'[27] The general feeling in 1936 was against the idea. 'In view of the fact that the specification lays down that the aircraft is a twin-engined one and is able to remain in the air with one engine cut out, I do not consider that four engines are necessary from the point of view of reliability,' wrote Air Commodore Boyd. Technical director R. H. Verney, always concerned about making the plane too cumbersome, asserted that 'a higher performance would be obtained with a twin-engined type than with a four engine one', while Arthur Harris showed that fallibility of judgement which would later haunt Bomber Command: 'If it were possible to get home on one engine, there was no need to have four.'[28]

When the consultation was completed, the finalized specification P13/36 was issued to the aircraft firms on 24 August 1936. The document retained the essential features of the draft, including the maximum bomb load of 8,000 pounds, along with the torpedo and troop-carrying capabilities, though the required cruising speed at 15,000 feet was raised to 275 mph and the size of crew was increased to six. Perhaps the most significant element of the final version was the requirement that two Rolls-Royce Vulture engines be used as the power-plants in the bomber. Still in the process of development, the 24-cylinder Vulture was regarded by the Air Ministry as the ideal engine because its unusual construction seemed to promise high power output without excessive weight. In essence, each Vulture consisted of two Rolls-Royce 12-cylinder, liquid-cooled Peregrine engines joined one on top of the other to form an X-type. Theoretically, this should have produced double the power of an orthodox engine in the same amount of space on the wing. But in practice the grafting together of the two crankcases was to prove a recipe for failure, prompting endless difficulties with the coolant system, the bearings and the connecting rods. Moreover, because of the pressures on the Merlin programme caused by RAF expansion, particularly the demand for engines for Spitfires and Hurricanes, Rolls-Royce did not have the time or resources to devote to sorting out the problems once the Vulture prototype had first been run in September 1937. As the aviation historian Francis Mason put it: 'The idea was fundamentally sound, but was not afforded sufficient development priority early on.'[29] For all the anguish that the Vulture was to cause, there was a silver lining to the cloud it created over the bomber programme: without the setbacks it brought, the Lancaster might never have been born.

Eight companies expressed an interest in the P13/36 and were invited by the Air Ministry to submit tender proposals. One of them was A.V. Roe, a world-famous aircraft manufacturer which had been formed in 1910 by Alliott Verdon Roe, universally known as 'AV', and his brother Humphrey. The son of a Manchester doctor, A.V. Roe had a varied career as a surveyor, locomotive apprentice, marine engineer and sailor before he developed a fixation with flight, first sparked while watching seabirds during his long hours of duty on voyages to South Africa. So deep was this enthusiasm that he gave up his job in the merchant navy, and travelled to the USA to work on a pioneering gyroplane. But the project literally never got off the ground and in 1906 Roe returned to England. Headstrong, inventive but somewhat wayward, he now embarked on his own adventures in flight. In this age of technological flux, he was full of bold ideas. He claimed to be the first Englishman to have achieved manned flight, having travelled 75 feet in his fragile Antoinette-powered biplane at the Brooklands racetrack in Surrey on 8 June 1908, but there were no witnesses to the event and, much to his bitterness, the milestone was not officially recognized by the Royal Aero Club. Indeed, despite his eagerness, all too many of Roe's early efforts remained airborne only for a few moments, with the result that in aviation circles he became known as 'Roe the Hopper'.[30] Part of the problem was that he was constantly short of money to finance his experiments. But that changed in January 1910 when his brother Humphrey, an astute businessman, agreed to enter into partnership with him. Humphrey Roe worked for the Manchester webbing manufacturer Everard's, and it was in this company's basement at Brownsfield Mill that the brothers' new company, Avro, began to enjoy real commercial success, both with aircraft and parts production. Through a typically shrewd move by Humphrey, the company sold a wire-strainer, known as the Avro barrelless turnbuckle, which could change the tension on the bracing wires of early biplane wings. Having become standard equipment, it sold in huge quantities during the First World War, with Avro making a £40,000-a-year profit on this item alone.

Initially Avro's planes, which included the Type F, the world's first aircraft with a completely enclosed cabin, were manufactured only in small numbers, but the 504 biplane represented a breakthrough. First flown in 1913, it became the standard trainer in the navy and army air forces during the war because of its incredible safety and ease of handling. 'Make it simple' was one of A. V. Roe's dictums, and the 504 lived up to that principle. Almost 8,500 were built over twenty years, the last one coming off the production line in 1933. But the growing reputation of the company was not enough for Roe's restless spirit, particularly as his independence was diluted by an increasingly powerful Avro board. His last stage of disillusion came in May 1928 when Avro was sold to the engineering group Armstrong-Siddeley. Five months later he left the firm to take a controlling interest in S. E. Saunders, the boat manufacturer on the Isle of Wight, where he enjoyed only limited success before his death in 1958.

Roe's exit from Avro did not stop the company from prospering in the 1930s. Among its rewarding types of plane were an excellent trainer, the Tutor, and a multi-purpose military aircraft, the twin-engined Anson. Such was the reliable Anson's appeal that over 11,000 were made between 1935 and 1952, making its production run the largest in history for any British multi-engined plane apart from the Wellington. The continuing success of Avro during this period was largely down to the unique partnership between two men: Roy Chadwick, the Chief Designer, and Roy Dobson, the General Manager. They had much in common. Both were much the same age, had joined Avro just before the First World War, and were forceful, dynamic characters with a creative flair and a deep understanding of aircraft engineering. Roy Dobson, born into a Yorkshire farming family in 1891, began his career as an apprentice engineer in Manchester before moving to Avro as a draughtsman in 1914. The decision to hire him was actually taken by Roy Chadwick, who later said of him: 'His great point is that he is able to put the pep into people in the most amazing way.'[31] His natural gifts for organization led to his ascent up the management hierarchy to take overall charge of the company in 1934. Vigorous, quick-thinking and self-confident, his driving energy meant that he could be extremely demanding of staff. His fellow aeronautical engineer and industrialist Sir Arnold Hall wrote of him: 'He was warm-hearted and enthusiastic, if sometimes a little hard on others in his outbursts of anger when things went wrong, but always immediately contrite if he had been too hard. He was a colourful man with a tremendous capacity for hard work and overcoming problems.'[32]

Roy Chadwick was a quieter, less explosive figure, though he still had a commanding presence within Avro. A Lancastrian, born in Farnworth near Bolton in 1893, he was the son of a mechanical engineer who worked in Manchester for the British Westinghouse Company, a subsidiary of the US electrical and manufacturing giant. A bright, imaginative boy, Chadwick was captivated by his first sight of an aircraft when a hot-air balloon sailed over Trafford Park. From that moment, aviation was to be the dominant theme of his life. During his youth he adored flying kites and making models of aeroplanes, some of them constructed using material from his mother's old silk blouses. His sister May recalled that his early skill at aeronautical modelling attracted much local interest: 'Our friends would keep asking when Roy was going to fly a model and we would pester him continually until finally the great evening would arrive in quite a big turnout of children and fathers. I think Roy used to try and fox us to avoid this audience in case the model, to his discomfiture, took a sweeping nose-dive into the ground or shot vertically into the air – but I only remember the times when the plane sailed through the skies until the elastic motor gave out and we were rapturously enchanted.'[33]

Roy Chadwick's first post was an apprenticeship at British Westinghouse, secured through the influence of his father. He also attended night school at the Manchester Institute of Technology. But his interest in aviation had become more powerful than ever, deepened by an exhibition in 1910 held by the Manchester Aero Club, which featured one of A. V. Roe's triplanes. Soon Chadwick became frustrated with his job, and decided to leave after he was suspended for fighting with another apprentice.

'Oh Mother, I just do not want to go back to Westinghouse,' he said when he arrived home.

'Well, what do you want?'

'I want to work with Mr Roe and help build his aeroplanes.'[34]

Instead of urging him to stick with his job, his mother encouraged him to seek an interview with A. V. Roe. He immediately did so. After meeting the eighteen-year-old, Roe was impressed with his enthusiasm and offered Chadwick a job as his personal assistant. Starting in 1911 in the drawing office, Chadwick soon demonstrated his talent, quickly absorbing Roe's ethos: 'Lightness for climb; cleanness for speed; unit construction for manufacturing ease.'[35] By the outbreak of the First World War,

Chadwick had acquired an air of technical authority within Avro, and Roe trusted him enough to let him work on the drawings for the 504 biplane. He also enjoyed a substantial pay rise which took his salary to £250 a year, a substantial sum for a young man aged only just twenty-one. His self-assurance, good looks and dapper appearance meant that he was not short of female company. Blondes were said to be his preference.

By the end of the war, it was clear that Chadwick had a unique apti-tude for aircraft design. Working closely with Roy Dobson, he was now responsible for the details of all the company's major projects. 'Much of his genius lay in an uncanny understanding of the need for perfect control,' wrote Dobson.[36] Avro's growing order-book had entailed a major expan-sion, and the company had opened a second base at Hamble on the south coast in Hampshire. In 1917 the entire Chadwick family moved there, including his father, who by now was also working for Avro. But it was at Hamble that a near-tragedy took place that almost finished Chadwick's life. Absorbed in every aspect of flying, he qualified as a pilot in 1920. Just weeks after gaining his licence, he went up in one of his new designs, the 534 biplane, known as the Avro Baby. On a squally day over Hamble village, his aircraft suddenly lost height, stalled and crashed to the ground. Chadwick had to be cut free from the wreckage and taken to the South Hampshire hospital, where he was found to have broken his pelvis, one arm, one leg and a kneecap. His recovery was long and painful, involving extensive operations, though it was enlivened by some banter with his friend and Avro colleague Harold Rogerson. One typical exchange at his hospital bed went as follows:

'So how did they tackle the arm?' asked Rogerson.

'Ulna and radius repaired with rivets and silverplate, just like joining a longeron,' replied Chadwick.

'And the femur?'

'Fastened with three inch screws.'

'So when do you get your certificate of airworthiness?'[37]

Once he was out of hospital, Chadwick decided it was time to settle down. A few months after the accident, he married his fiancée Mary Gomersall, the daughter of the head cashier at the English Sewing Cotton Company. Devoted to her husband throughout his life, she provided him with loving homes in which to bring up their two daughters, at first in Southampton and then, from 1928, in Cheshire, where the Chadwick family moved after the reorganization of Avro. In his domestic content-ment, Chadwick was the epitome of affluent respectability: always smartly dressed, keen on classical and choral music, owner of a large American

Buick and an Armstrong-Siddeley saloon, a regular worshipper at his local Anglican church, a good husband and kind father to his two daughters. His eldest daughter Margaret later left this image of Chadwick at a Sunday service, showing the mix of affection and reverence he inspired: 'He would be the first into the pew, with me beside him, and he would kneel in prayer, forehead cradled in his right hand. I used to look up at him when he stood, tall and slender in his black overcoat, singing the different phrases of the Psalms, just as he did when he was a young man.'[38]

But, as with most driven men, family life had to come second to his work. Full of ambitious ideas, he put in exceptionally long hours, and he expected his staff to do so as well. His rigorous approach and intolerance of any slackness meant that he was regarded with a mixture of fear and awe at Avro's headquarters. One draughtsman, Geoff Bentley, recalls, 'I can see him now, walking through the office, very smartly dressed, his moustache neatly trimmed. He was a brilliant man and had this air of cleverness about him. But he was also a hard man. We were all a little scared of him.'[39] Chadwick, known as 'Chaddie' behind his back but addressed as 'sir' to his face, was a strict disciplinarian who banned smoking on his premises. His habit every morning was to conduct a tour of the office, stopping at each desk to check on progress and interrogate the draughtsmen. Harald Penrose, the distinguished aviator who produced a fine biography of Chadwick, wrote of these visitations to the Drawing Office: 'If the drawing was not to his liking or needed correction, he would take a thick soft pencil and draw what was required on top of the original. Though that meant starting all over again because it could not be erased, the draughtsman took it like a soldier on parade. The completed drawing was therefore Chadwick's expression of what was required.'[40] Throughout the week he would make other, more random descents on the draughtsmen, so they devised a signalling system to warn of his approach. Every desk had a metal anglepoise lamp, and when Chadwick's footsteps could be heard the man nearest the door would hit his lampshade with a ruler. The pinging signal would then be picked up by the others. Another former Avro employee, Dick Marsh, has these memories of the Chadwick regime: 'He was like a God to me. Almost everyone was frightened to death of him. If he was coming into the office, word went round like a shot. He could be bad-tempered. If he was not satisfied with a drawing, he sometimes would put his finger underneath it and just tear it in half.'[41]

Chadwick knew that he would need all his diligence, vision and efficiency to fulfil specification P13/36, for this was by far the most technologically advanced proposal that Avro had undertaken. Metal construction, retractable undercarriage, hydraulic controls and fully feathering airscrews were the central features of the project, far beyond the world of wires and fabric that had created the 504 trainer. But Chadwick was undaunted by the scale of the task. By February 1937 he had completed the design tender, which was now submitted to the Air Ministry. On paper, the proposal was impressive. It envisaged a mid-wing aeroplane with a span of 72 feet, a length of 69 feet, and twin fins and rudders in the tailplanes. Named the Type 679, the aircraft's relative compactness and high wing loading, together with a smooth finish produced by flush riveting, enabled Avro to predict that it would achieve a maximum speed of 341 mph and a cruising speed of 294 mph at 15,000 feet. Just as striking was Avro's promise to be able to build the 679 proto-type within just twelve months, a highly optimistic schedule given that the company had no experience in bomber production. So taken were the Air Staff with the Type 679 that after a design conference on 18 March 1937, it was agreed to order the Avro prototype, though sceptical officials said that the twelve-month timetable to delivery was 'obviously impossible'.[42] A separate order was also placed for a P13/36 prototype from the Handley Page company, whose record in British aviation was as illustrious as Avro's. Indeed, Britain's first-ever heavy night bomber, the HP O/100, had been designed by Frederick Handley Page and made its maiden flight in 1915. With a wingspan of 100 feet, this biplane monster had established the firm's name as a manufacturer of large aircraft.

Having won the P13/36 competition, Chadwick and Dobson threw themselves into the development of the Type 679 prototype. The programme appeared to be moving ahead so successfully that in July 1937, after Chadwick had presented a wooden mock-up of the design, the Air Ministry gave Avro a contract for 200 of the machines. 'The Avro design showed such marked promise that direct production "off the drawing board" was envisaged from the first,' noted the Air Ministry historians.[43] None other than the Chancellor of the Exchequer, Sir John Simon, gave formal approval to the contract, demonstrating the importance of the P13/36 to the government's plans for RAF expansion. All too predictably, however, the optimism soon proved unfounded. As the Ministry had feared, the timetable for the Type 679, now named the Manchester, was hopelessly unrealistic. The contract for 200 Manchesters, though it may have been healthy for Avro's bank balance, also meant that the firm had to devote a great deal of attention to installing the necessary jigs and tools. More worryingly, many of the design features proved unfeasible.

The weight was too low, the wingspan too narrow. In addition, the Ministry regularly demanded modifications, such as dropping the catapult requirement and changing the equipment layout. Chadwick himself said that 'the various changes made by the Air Ministry resulted in the equivalent of completely re-stressing the aeroplane six times'.[44] In one of the strength tests, some of the staff were surprised to see Chadwick jumping up and down on a sample of the fuselage floor. 'We have special gauges to test this specimen, sir,' said one of Avro's experts. 'Never mind,' intervened Harold Rogerson, 'Let him have his fun. He needs the exercise.' Chadwick, who had heard the two whispering, responded with a grin, 'Always the simplest way. Not only does it save expense but it can give you a feel for the problem.'[45]

But not everything could be sorted out in such an instinctive manner. By far the biggest problem was the Rolls-Royce Vulture engine, which was beset with teething troubles. The author Len Deighton once wrote: 'A wonderful engine could make a second-rate plane into a winner, but a superb airframe powered by a poor engine could never be a success.'[46] No aircraft ever validated that truth more powerfully than the Manchester. From the start both Chadwick and Handley Page had doubts about the wisdom of installing Vultures in the P13/36, and the latter openly expressed these concerns to the Air Ministry. As a result, he was given permission to redesign his proposed aircraft, changing in 1937 from a twin-engined bomber into a four-engined one, powered by four Merlins. Eventually this would become the Halifax, and the resulting aircraft turned out to be much closer to the fulfilment of specification B12/36 than P13/36. According to an unpublished interview he gave to Air Ministry officials in January 1944, Chadwick had watched the changeover at Handley Page in 1937 and privately 'wished that he had similar engines'.[47] But the full extent of the Vulture's inadequacy was then not yet apparent. Moreover, the Air Ministry would not have contemplated such a step, partly because it still felt it needed a large twin-engined bomber and partly because there was already such a high demand for Merlins. So Avro had no alternative but to persevere with the Vulture.

The Manchester prototype, serial number L7246, was built in sections at Avro's factory in Newton Heath, Manchester, and then in April 1939 assembled at the firm's experimental station at Ringway airport. By then the weight of the plane had risen dramatically, not least because the pair of Vulture engines had ended up more than a ton heavier than originally planned and the wingspan had been stretched to just over 80 feet. During the ground tests, yet more problems were encountered with the Vultures and the hydraulics, an ominous sign of things to come. Moreover, Manchester was at its dampest during the early weeks of summer, making the grass airfield soggy. Finally, in late July, the weather improved. It is almost universally claimed that the first flight of the Manchester took place on Tuesday, 25 July 1939. In fact, as the diary of Avro's test pilot Sam Brown shows, it happened a day earlier, on Monday 24. His entry for that day reveals a hint of the historic significance of the event, as he flew the revolutionary new bomber with his Avro co-pilot Bill Thorn. 'Weather very indifferent in the morning. Cleared up in the afternoon and I decided to fly the Manchester. Went to Ringway after tea and then the wind changed and weather deteriorated. Took the air with Bill at 6.30 p.m. and everything went off fairly well. All the lads very pleased and we had a few drinks in the restaurant. Got home at 9 p.m.'[48] On landing, Brown was said to have given Chadwick the thumbs-up sign. But both this gesture and his positive description could not disguise the reality that the Manchester was still deeply unsatisfactory. In fact during that maiden flight, which only lasted twenty minutes, the hydraulic pump shaft had broken, while Brown found that the rudders did not provide enough control and the engines ran hot. Subsequent trial flights in mid-1939 revealed further inadequacies. As well as the predictable troubles with the Vultures, the Manchester badly lacked lateral stability, yawed to port on landing, and required a long take-off run, even when lightly loaded. Chadwick himself was dismayed at the poor performance of the plane, whose top speed of 265 mph was far below the 341 mph he had forecast. It was not until 23 October that Brown and Thorn had a trouble-free flight, though only a few weeks later both Vultures failed in the air completely and, using every ounce of their skill, they had to glide the plane down to land in a park. Astonishingly, the airframe and under-carriage were undamaged.

This set the tone for the Manchester programme, which lurched from one crisis to another. In December 1939 the plane was sent to the RAF's Aeroplane and Armament Experimental Establishment at Boscombe Down in Wiltshire, where it was praised for its overall design, particularly the layout of the cockpit, but heavily criticized for its performance. Such concern can have only been reinforced by the catalogue of contin-uing engine failures. On 12 December, soon after take-off, the aircraft had to make a forced landing in a cabbage field. On 23 December it began to lose height from 3,000 feet and crashed in a field near Boscombe Down, the Vulture failure so comprehensive that two connecting rods protruded from the crankcase. Yet the exigencies of war meant that neither the Air Ministry nor Avro could abandon the Manchester. The demand for aircraft was too great, the project already too far advanced. At the beginning of 1940 the only way forward seemed to lie in the hope that improvements could be achieved by Avro and Rolls-Royce. It is a measure of the Air Ministry's desperation that, despite the roll-call of Manchester breakdowns, the government kept increasing the size of its order, adding another 450 to the Avro contract in January 1940 and a further 250 from other aircraft manufacturers. By the spring of 1940, the Ministry had placed orders for no fewer than 1,200.

The fevered quest for solutions continued. Outer wings were redesigned. Aileron hinges were refashioned. New elevators were fitted. Larger tail surfaces were installed. A central fin was placed on the rear of the fuselage. New oil coolers were placed in the engines. In May 1940 Avro completed a second prototype, L7247, which incorporated most of these changes. The performance of this Manchester, which was meant to be the final model for the production run, showed a modest improvement on the original prototype. Yet the directional stability, take-off and climb remained unsatisfactory, while there had also been a disturbing rise of almost 4,500 pounds in the plane's equipped weight. When L7247 was sent to Boscombe Down for official trials in June 1940, new problems emerged with the installation of the Frazer-Nash rear gun turret. 'It was jerky in rotation, causing a nose down pitching movement, and produced violent buffeting when on the beam at the limiting diving speed,' reported the Aircraft and Armament Experimental Establishment (A&AEE).[49] Just as worrying was the elevator balance, which, according to A&AEE, 'has such grave disadvantages that only a limited number of aircraft could be accepted with it.'[50] So yet more alterations had to be made, with the Chief of the Air Staff Sir Charles Portal piling on the pressure. 'The Manchester in its present form is completely useless for operations. I am sure that you will do everything possible to get the necessary modifications incorporated as soon as possible,' he told the Operational Requirements Directorate of the Air Staff.[51] Amidst all this anxious tinkering and testing, Avro was still pressing ahead with the production of the Manchester for delivery to the RAF, promising that the first eight planes would be ready by the end of October.

But Roy Chadwick knew by mid-1940 that the Manchester would not prove to be a successful plane, no matter how many changes were made. Indeed, the continual process of trying to compensate for the Vulture's inadequacy by structural modifications could end up undermining the original strengths of the Manchester's airframe. He recognized that a radical alternative was needed. Long before the Manchester proto-type had even flown, he had been considering one. In the autumn of 1938, following Handley Page's decision to switch to a Merlin-powered four-engined bomber in fulfilment of specification P13/36, Chadwick had instructed his design staff to look at the possibility of converting the Type 679 to a four-engined bomber, using either Rolls-Royce Merlins or Bristol Hercules radials. But at that early stage the project was largely immaterial, since the Manchester looked so promising and the Vulture had performed well in tunnel tests.

The idea was given new momentum in March 1939, when the govern-ment issued specification B1/39, which called for a four-engined, heavily armed bomber, weighing less than 50,000 pounds and capable of achiev-ing 280 mph with a 9,000-pound bomb load. The aim of B1/39 was to create the next generation of RAF bombers after the Stirling and Halifax. Avro was one of the companies that tendered for B1/39, using a proposal based on the earlier scheme, now called Type 683, for a four-engined version of the Manchester. The bid failed, though this was of little im-portance since B1/39 soon fell into abeyance, its requirements too technologically advanced for the late 1930s. In any case, throughout this period Avro remained preoccupied with the Manchester. According to the historian Francis Mason, Chadwick had only six draughtsmen in his experimental department working on the Type 683 for most of 1939.[52]

But three developments drastically changed the position early in 1940. The first was the deepening crisis over the Manchester and the Vulture. Official opinion of the plane was neatly summed up by Sir Kingsley Wood, the Secretary of State for Air under Chamberlain, who told colleagues: 'The controls are somewhat heavy and the stability is bad. The aircraft is overweight and the engines are not giving full power.'[53] The second was the creation by Rolls-Royce of a new type of Merlin, the XX, which was particularly suitable for multi-engined aircraft and could produce 1,200 horsepower at 20,000 feet. The third was growing concern that the two heavy bombers, the Halifax and the Stirling, would not live up to expectations, since both aircraft had been beset with prob-lems and the Halifax was badly behind schedule. In Handley Page's difficulty lay Avro's opportunity. Against the backdrop of Britain's national battle for salvation under the attacks of the Luftwaffe, the scene was now set for a struggle within the Air Ministry over the future direction of the bomber programme.

The existence of Type 683 was still known to few outside the company, apart from some government officials. One of those who was enthusiastic about it was William Farren, appointed Deputy Director of Research and Development in May 1940 when the new Prime Minister, Winston Churchill, created the Ministry of Aircraft Production (MAP), another indicator that the air war was at the heart of Britain's fight for survival. Farren had encouraged Avro to tender for specification B1/39 and now urged Chadwick and Dobson to devote greater effort to the four-engined bomber. He stressed, however, that he could not promise any contract in the immediate future. Another early supporter was Norbert Rowe, MAP's Director of Technical Development, who accompanied Farren on a visit to Avro in late June 1940 and was impressed by Chadwick's plan, as he later recalled:

> He went through his proposals for stretching the wing span in a manner entailing minimum redesign of major components and details, retaining the basic aerodynamic wing profile. On this increased span he would install four Rolls-Royce Merlin engines – again involving no drastic structural or aerodynamic modifications. He showed us on the drawing board how he would plan the work and answered our many questions in a satisfactory way. We accepted this as the best way out of the Manchester impasse. Indeed, Roy Chadwick showed himself to be a most resourceful and courageous designer, ultimately snatching success from failure in the most ingenious way.[54]

As a result of the intervention by Farren and Rowe, Avro expanded the Type 683 team to 30 draughtsmen, now based in Avro's huge new factory at Chadderton in Cheshire, a plant built with government subsidy as part of the air expansion plan. In the design now taking shape, the wingspan was lengthened to 100 feet to accommodate the extra pair of engines, and the tailplane was also enlarged, though most of the Manchester's fuselage was to be retained. The Avro draughtsman in charge of the Type 683 project was a bouncy Londoner called Stuart Davies, known throughout Avro as 'Cocky Davies', not because of any bumptiousness but because of his habit of addressing everyone as 'Old Cock'. From MAP's viewpoint, by far the greatest appeal of the proposed new bomber was that its use of the basic Manchester airframe minimized production difficulties. As a result, there would be no lengthy development programme, nor any need to acquire new jigs and tools. In fact, Davies estimated that 70 per cent of the components would be common to both the Manchester and the Type 683.

The second tier of officials at the Ministry of Aircraft Production might have been won over by the Type 683, but the real task now was to convince the top men: Air Chief Marshal Sir Wilfrid Freeman, the urbane

Chief Executive of MAP, and his deputy Arthur Tedder, the brilliant RAF officer whose capacity for original thinking on tactical air support would later help to win the campaigns in North Africa, Italy and Normandy. On 28 June 1940[55] Tedder and Freeman went up to Chadderton to discuss the Manchester programme and the Vulture, but their talks with the management were soon theatrically diverted, as Tedder recounted in his memoirs:

> The second prototype was running, and we both went up in the back seats for a couple of circuits (and afterwards were called fools for our pains!). We went in from the tarmac to the office of Roy Dobson to talk over matters. It was clear that nobody liked the machine very much and we gathered that Rolls were not at all happy about the Vulture. On the desk in Dobson's office there was a nice model of the Manchester. Before we got any farther on the subject, Dobson asked Freeman a direct question: 'I am told you have plenty of Merlins coming in. Is this right?' To which Freeman answered 'Yes'. 'Then what about this?' said Dobson, taking one of the wing tips off and adding an extra wing and an extra engine on one side and then repeating the process on the other side. 'How's that?' he asked. 'That' was the Lancaster – an afterthought that became one of the most successful and effective bombers of the war.[56]

Rather unfairly, Roy Chadwick did not merit a mention in Tedder's account, but he was certainly present at this meeting and later recalled his exchange with Freeman. 'I told him the Vulture was a flop. Sir Wilfrid was very perturbed and said, "That puts you in the cart." We then put before him the proposal that we could produce a four-engined type by merely making new outer wings and altering the sections of the spars. The existing jigs and tools would be kept. Sir Wilfrid undertook to put the proposals before the Minister and I promised that the firm could do a prototype in six months on condition that we were given a carte blanche.'[57]

Impressed by Avro's initiative, Freeman gave his encouragement to the Type 683, without yet providing formal Whitehall backing. As the early design work proceeded, Avro and MAP continued to liaise closely. In mid-July 1940, for instance, Rowe wrote to Dobson: 'I think we shall have to watch the weight of the Manchester with four Merlin XX's very carefully during its development. In particular, I think it is essential to make the very closest estimates we can of the increase in weight over the Manchester as we know it now, since this increase would clearly govern the amount of redesign which is necessary from the standpoint of strength and stiffness.'[58] But the greatest obstacle now facing the Type

683 project lay at the political summit of the MAP's hierarchy. In one of his more unorthodox appointments, Winston Churchill had put the volatile, eccentric, Canadian-born press tycoon Lord Beaverbrook in charge of aircraft production, believing that his lordship's dynamism would have the same galvanizing effect on aeroplane output as it had achieved on the circulation of the *Daily Express*. While the move might have given a short-term boost to fighter production, it represented a threat to long-term bomber development.

'Give me more planes. I don't care whose heart is broken,' was one of Beaverbrook's battlecries.[59] The only planes he wanted were present types, preferably Spitfires and Hurricanes. Under his mercurial influence, the War Cabinet agreed to concentrate the state's resources on aircraft already in production, while bomber contracts were dramatically scaled back. In particular, the order for 1,200 Manchesters was cut to just 200, while the Cabinet further decided that future bomber production could be rationalized by focusing on the Halifax and the Stirling once the Manchester was completed. Freeman later complained bitterly that 'on Lord Beaverbrook's arrival, planning ceased', and that manufacturers were 'bullied instead of being helped in every possible way to achieve their plans'.[60] The hiatus over Type 683 bore out that truth. In a letter that was the political equivalent of a blockbuster bomb, the Ministry of Aircraft Production wrote to Dobson on 29 July instructing him that once the initial order for 200 Manchesters was finished, the Avro plants would have to be turned over for the manufacture of the Halifax, even though the plane had not even gone into service yet and had already displayed serious flaws in its tailplane and hydraulics. Dobson and Chadwick were outraged. The peremptory command not only contradicted the positive reception they had been given for Type 683 but also ignored the extensive work that had already gone into the Manchester. Moreover, it was insulting to be asked to build an unproven aircraft designed by their closest rival in the aircraft industry. Chadwick, always conscious of his status, found the idea of working as a subcontractor for Handley Page intolerable.

Within twenty-four hours of the receipt of this letter, Dobson and Chadwick had written to the Ministry for Aircraft Production asking for a meeting to present their case for continuing with the Type 683. In reply, they were invited to come to MAP's London offices on 4 August. Among those representing MAP at this conference were Captain R. N. Liptrot, the original instigator of P13/36 specification, William Farren and Patrick Hennessy, an aggressive industrialist who had been seconded from the

Ford Motor Company to work for Beaverbrook. Chadwick later said that Hennessy was 'like a cold fish' and did all he could to obstruct Avro.[61] Liptrot and Farren, however, were more enthusiastic. They were persuaded by Avro's argument that, given the progress made on the Type 683, it would be far more efficient to switch to Avro's own four-engined bomber than change to an entirely different aircraft.

Even though the future of the project still remained in the balance, Avro had managed to avoid its abandonment. In a spirit of renewed optimism, drawings were provided, models produced, statistics analysed. 'Design work is now proceeding on highest priority at Messrs A V Roe's to convert the Manchester to a four-engined aeroplane, using Merlin XX engines. The wing span is to be increased to 100 feet but I know of no other basic changes,' wrote Norbert Rowe of MAP just three days after the conference, asking the Royal Aircraft Establishment at Farnborough to liaise with Avro over the project 'with special reference to its longitudinal and asymmetrical stability'.[62] Having conducted a detailed examination of the design, Captain Liptrot produced MAP's first report on the Four Merlin XX Manchester on 22 August. Throughout his document, Liptrot emphasized the efficiencies that could be achieved with its production. The proposal, he wrote, 'is considered to be entirely practicable. The existing Manchester remains intact up to the wing centre section, the only changes being in the outer wings which are stretched to 100 feet and in increases of material gauges as necessary to cope with the higher take-off weight. The existing wing jigs could easily be modified and the change-over in production would be relatively simple.' On top of these manufacturing advantages, he further predicted that the Type 683 would give just as good a performance as the Halifax. 'It compares quite favourably with the Halifax since it has better take-off and for roughly the same cruising speed carries only 800 pounds less bombs for the same range.'[63] Rowe, long a backer of Avro, also gave his approval. In a minute of 25 August 1940 he stressed the production gains from the switch-over, feeling that they might appeal to Beaverbrook's obsession with numbers. 'The broad conclusion is that the aeroplane should be a satisfactory development from the Manchester I, and that it should be put into production in order to utilise the tools and organisation in being for the production of Manchester I. This is the best way of obtaining the greatest number of aeroplanes in a given time, since it is the only way of using the complete Manchester production organisation which will otherwise have to be turned over to a different aeroplane when production of the Vulture engines ceases.'[64]

Throughout this process Freeman had continued to lend his support. Now the favourable analysis of the Type 683 had been produced, he decided it was time to ask Beaverbrook to approve the scheme. With typical impulsiveness, the minister immediately gave his approval for Avro to proceed with a prototype. He told Avro the news in a brusque phone call to Chadwick: 'But if you don't finish it in six months, you can pay for it yourselves,' he barked down the line in his Canadian accent.[65]

After all the tribulations of recent months, the Type 683 had finally received ministerial sanction. 'For action. Contract to cover one prototype,' wrote Norbert Rowe in an internal MAP instruction on 10 September 1940. The Lancaster was about to be born. As the Air Ministry's historical file on the Lancaster commented, the appearance of the plane 'was a tribute to the perseverance and resourcefulness of its designers, who forced it on an unwilling Ministry of Aircraft Production.'[66]

2

'Oh boy, oh boy, what an aeroplane!'

———◆———

UNLIKE THE RENOWNED RAF leaders of World War Two, such as Harris, Dowding or Tedder, Wilfrid Freeman never became a household name, nor did he command any great forces in action. Yet he played as big a part in the ultimate victory of 1945 as any other air chief. For it was his uncanny judgement that ensured the RAF was equipped to survive the battle against the Luftwaffe, then go on to crush Germany in its homeland. Highly intelligent and drily humorous, his natural authority reinforced by his silver locks and sophisticated manner, Freeman had been the driving force behind the Spitfire's role at the centre of the fighter expansion programme in the late 1930s. He had seen the potential of the Mosquito far earlier than anyone else at the top of the Air Ministry where its wooden construction was derided, so much so that it was initially known as 'Freeman's Folly'. He had pushed for the Merlin to be built by Packard in America as well as Rolls-Royce in Britain, enabling the demand for this unique engine to be met at pivotal moments in the war. And it was his decisiveness in August 1940, when the whole bomber programme was in turmoil, that ensured the Lancaster would be built. 'Beyond doubt, he was the most inspiring man I ever served,' said Major G. P. Bulman, the head of aero engine research at the Air Ministry.[1]

Roy Chadwick, usually the undemonstrative northerner, was equally effusive about the part that Freeman had played in the development of the Lancaster. In his unpublished interview in January 1944 Chadwick said that, in official support for the plane, 'pride of place must go to Sir Wilfrid Freeman, who backed me up and persuaded Lord Beaverbrook to sanction the Lancaster project'.[2] Chadwick was even more fulsome towards Freeman personally. In a letter of 16 August 1941, almost exactly a year after Freeman's crucial expression of support for the Type 683 project, Chadwick wrote in terms of unqualified generosity:

> When we discussed the possibilities of getting the machine into production quickly, I promised you that the First Prototype would fly in six months. This was done with a few days to spare. I am confident that the

Lancaster will prove to be the outstanding bomber of the war and it is, I feel, largely due to you that it has come into existence.[3]

The progress from Beaverbrook's decision in August 1940 towards the full prototype had indeed been swift, a tribute to the Avro design team headed by Roy Chadwick and Stuart Davies. In fact Davies was so confident that he told Dobson he would have the first prototype flying by the end of 1940, more than two months ahead of the timetable that Avro had promised MAP. During the autumn a number of technical issues had arisen because of the increased weight of Type 683, which was 57,000 pounds on take-off compared to 45,000 pounds on the Manchester. The spars in the wing structure were strengthened and 250-gallon fuel tanks installed between the engine nacelles. The undercarriage was largely redesigned, with the adoption of the same wheel size as used on the Halifax. A new tailplane with a 33-foot span was developed, which Chadwick assured the experts at the Royal Aircraft Establishment would mean 'that the machine is stable about all its axes'.[4] One of Avro's engineers, Sandy Jack, left this description of the work carried out in the autumn on the prototype, his words again highlighting Avro's belief that the manufacturing process should be as straightforward as possible:

> Increased wing span was an obvious necessity and could readily be obtained simply and at little tooling cost or delay in production. One simply 'stretched' the original wing. All existing wing ribs were retained, pitched however some three inches further apart. The spars were stretched to suit by extruding longer booms, which could be machined on the existing Avro-designed milling machines, the base of which could easily be adapted to suit.[5]

Aside from these technical questions, another vital point to resolve was the name of the aircraft. Initially, Avro called the Type 683 'The Manchester III', the title Manchester II having been used in a putative earlier design for the twin-engined bomber using either Napier Sabre or Bristol Centaurus engines rather than Vultures, though the project had never advanced far because Chadwick 'had dropped everything to get on with the Manchester III'.[6] But the Ministry of Aircraft Production decided that, since the Type 683 was a different concept from the Manchester, a new designation was needed. On 29 October 1940 the Air Ministry and the firm agreed to continue with the place-name theme for bombers by calling it 'The Lancaster', a sturdy traditional English title reflecting the plane's county of birth.[7]

Yet even after Beaverbrook's approval there were still some government figures who remained deeply sceptical about the Lancaster, believing, in the words of an Air Ministry note, that 'the firm's optimistic promises were unfounded'.[8] According to Sandy Jack, when work was well underway on the prototype, news suddenly reached the company that 'no Merlins could be spared from fighter production'.[9] Roy Chadwick's recollection was even more specific, pointing the finger at Patrick Hennessy, the former Ford executive now at MAP. He later said that when Hennessy 'was told by Sir Wilfrid Freeman that I wanted the materials to complete the prototype, he did not offer to help but merely said, "He can dig for it." I replied that I knew where to dig, but I never got an allocation of material.'[10] When Chadwick said that he 'knew where to dig', he meant the Rolls-Royce company. Fortunately, Roy Dobson was close to Rolls-Royce's general manager, the far-sighted, waspish Sir Ernest Hives, who had pioneered the Merlin engine. Hives had been as anguished as Avro about the failure of the Vulture, and with his instinctive grasp of aeronautical engineering he sensed that the Lancaster could be a success. To prevent any delay in the prototype, Hives discreetly used informal channels to supply Avro with four Merlins, though they were not the XX model which would ultimately be fitted to the first production Lancaster. Chadwick's memory, however, is in conflict with MAP and Air Ministry records which show that, from August, Hennessy appears to have been increasingly favourable towards the Lancaster, despite his occasional scepticism about Chadwick's claims for the aircraft's potential performance, something that may account for the designer's hostility.

By November 1940 the Lancaster project, for so long the subject of such fractious internal controversy, was fast becoming a physical reality. It should be stressed that the chorus of official approval was not because of any prophetic belief in the Lancaster's excellence and superiority to the Halifax, merely that the plane was regarded as the best way of utilizing Avro's productive capacity. 'The alterations from the Manchester to the Lancaster amount to quite a big job,' wrote William Farren to Hennessy, 'but they are very much less than changing over from the Manchester to the Halifax. I cannot say exactly what the bomb and range capacity of the aeroplane will be at its top weight but it may be taken that there will not be much difference between the overall capabilities of the Manchester, modified in this way, and the Halifax. I think the two types will be equally acceptable to the Air Staff. I therefore think that you will be safe in planning for the production of whichever is convenient.'[11] Ease of production was also emphasized by the Royal

Aircraft Establishment, whose research officers visited Chadderton on 22 November. Their report explained that the 'Lancaster is designed to use as many parts of the Manchester without alteration. Where alterations are necessary the aim has been to utilize the existing jigs. For example, the outer wing has been assembled on the same jigs set at a greater distance apart, to suit the new span of 100 feet.' They also noted, with a tone of satisfaction, that 'the fuselage of the Lancaster is identical with the Manchester'.[12] But there was never the slightest belief that the Lancaster might actually be superior to the Halifax. The best that could be hoped for was that its performance might come close to Handley Page's machine, but even this was doubtful to some. 'We may expect to find that the final result is not quite so good as the Halifax,' wrote Norbert Rowe, Deputy Director of Research, the sort of ill-fated prediction with which the history of aviation is littered.[13]

Equipped with the Merlins from Ernest Hives, the Lancaster prototype, serial number BT308, was almost ready by early December, a rare instance of a plane's development running ahead of schedule. Stuart Davies's pledge that he would have the aircraft in the air before the end of the month seemed to be on course. On 6 December the prototype was dismantled at Chadderton ready for the journey to Avro's experimental hangar at Ringway airport in Manchester. But then there were two delays. The first was prompted by a Luftwaffe air raid which caused some damage to Avro production and diverted manpower for a few days. 'I think they were looking for me,' joked Chadwick with his family after he heard the news of the German attack, 'Dobbie says that I'm on the Nazi blacklist of people who will be dealt with by the SS when they conquer England!'[14] The second was the discovery of a fault with the hydraulic system of the Manchester, which had been under production since August in fulfilment of the original order for 200. As a result, Chadwick ordered a change of pipes and couplings on the Lancaster prototype, which largely used the same hydraulic system as the Manchester. The plane was eventually taken to Ringway on 28 December and the final engine runs were started. Then fog and drizzle enveloped Ringway, leading to another hold-up.

Finally, on 9 January 1941, the skies cleared. The moment for the maiden flight of the Lancaster had arrived. As with the Manchester prototype's first trip, the Avro test pilot Sam Brown was at the controls, with Bill Thorn at his side. Chadwick's daughter Margaret, who had been encouraged by her father to take an interest in aviation, left this description of the event:

We drove down to the Avro hangars where my father parked. A few hundred yards away stood the huge new Avro, its four engines already ticking over. Sam Brown and Bill Thorn, distinctive in white overalls, could be seen sitting side by side in the cockpit high above the ground. We strolled across to a crowd intently watching the proceedings and were greeted by Roy Dobson with whom my father talked for a while as we stood together at the left-hand side of the group. Presently the engines began to roar and as the plane moved forward my father turned and walked away with me for quite a distance. Though he seemed calm and expressionless, I'm sure he was very tense. Then the plane began to run and soared upward, climbing into the blue between occasional large white clouds, and sailed away into the distance. Presently it returned and circled the aerodrome; then with an impressive din flew low in front of us, climbed up again and made smoothly banked turns to the left and right before magnificently rumbling in and landing. We all began to move across the field to where it rested. As we approached, the fuselage door opened and Capt. Brown, his white overalls brilliant in the sun, appeared in the doorway. There was an eager cry of, 'How did it go, Sam?' and, smilingly, he said, 'It was marvellous – easy to handle and light on the controls.' Then he descended the steps and everyone was talking to him. When we were in the car going home, I turned to my father and said, 'Well, Daddy, you must be very pleased that this new aeroplane is such a success'. He replied, 'Yes I am, but in this business one cannot rest on one's laurels. There is always another and another aeroplane.'[15]

Chadwick's unemotional reply could not disguise the reality that the Avro team sensed it might have a winner. 'Oh boy, oh boy, what an aeroplane! What a piece of work,' is said to have been the reaction of Roy Dobson at the sight of the prototype.[16]

Nine further flights were made by Brown and Thorn over the following fortnight, during which the initially favourable impression was reinforced. The prototype was then sent to the Aircraft and Armament Experimental Establishment at Boscombe Down for further tests, where its qualities were instantly recognized. The first report from A&AEE commended the plane's general handling, particularly the landing which 'is straightforward and easy'. The directional stability, for so long a problem in the Manchester, also appeared to have improved. 'No sign of bad instability was noticed over the range of conditions covered by the flight,' while the layout in the cockpit was also praised. 'Temperature, coolant and oil gauges are neatly grouped on the engineer's panel and conform to the disposition of the engines.' The main criticisms lay in the force required to open the throttles, the heavy swing to port on take-off and the 'excessively high' noise level, since no attempt had been made to sound-proof the cabin. But in conclusion A&AEE believed 'that the Lancaster possesses very good flying qualities and promises to give a good perform-ance'.[17] What was even more striking in later tests was the excellent speed attained by the prototype, 310 mph on one occasion, and the ability to fly even with two engines feathered. 'The handling qualities with one or two engines stopped are excellent. Turns can be made with or against the running engines at speeds above 140mph'.[18] That encouraging verdict was reinforced by the experience of Air Vice Marshal Norman Bottomley, the commander of 5 Bomber Group, who went up in the Lancaster in February and was 'tremendously impressed with its performance'. He told his chief Richard Pierse, AOC of Bomber Command, that its four Merlins were 'beautifully smooth and I am sure that our crews will be most enthusiastic about the aircraft when it reaches them'.[19] That was exactly the way the first RAF pilots felt. One of them was Thomas Murray of 207 Squadron, who had previous experience of the Manchester: 'I did some prototype flying on the Lanc. It was a delightful aeroplane with-out any vices at all. It flew beautifully and it was terrifically fast because the prototype had no turrets or bomb loads. You could fly it with the inside engines cut out. It really was a great tonic after the Manchester.'[20]

The progress was also followed at a political level. The Air Council, chaired by Churchill's Secretary of State for Air Sir Archibald Sinclair, was told in January that the Lancaster made 'a satisfactory first flight', and then, two months later, that the prototype had reached 310 mph. 'The general handling was excellent,' Sinclair was informed.[21] Sinclair, the leader of the Liberal Party, is often portrayed as an eloquent but weak politician, living in the shadow of Churchill under whom he served in the Royal Scots Fusiliers in the First World War. But contrary to this image, Sinclair showed some decisiveness in driving forward the Lancaster in his role at the head of the Air Ministry, the body responsible for RAF policy. Even before the BT308 had completed its tests at Boscombe Down, his Ministry had decided to place an initial order for 450 Lancasters. In response, Avro promised that the first production aircraft could be delivered by August 1941, with the delivery eventually reach-ing 80 aircraft per month.

Sinclair also demonstrated his early enthusiasm for the Lancaster during a brief spat with Beaverbrook in February. The dispute arose over that perennial issue which had threatened the construction of the prototype: the supply of Merlin engines. Concerned about the demands on Rolls-Royce, Beaverbrook suddenly came up with the suggestion that some of the Lancaster production run be fitted with Bristol Hercules radial engines, enabling enough quantities of Merlins to be retained for the Bristol Beaufighter, a twin-engined fighter. Sinclair had little time for Beaverbrook's idea, not least on logistical grounds. 'We would like to avoid having two types of Lancaster in the RAF,' wrote Sinclair, 'and if the reason for your proposal is that Lancaster production requires more engines, would it not be better to reduce the total number of Merlin-engined Beaufighters so that these engines could be used for the Lancaster in the autumn? The Beaufighters thus deprived of Merlin engines could use the Hercules instead of these latter going into the Lancasters as you propose.'[22] Surprised by Sinclair's dismissive attitude, Beaverbrook made a direct challenge. 'Your proposal is that we should build both Beaufighter and Lancaster airframes for a limited number of Merlin engines. I regret to say that it cannot be done. We cannot spare the airframe capacity. In the circumstances do you wish us to abandon 50 Beaufighters in favour of Lancaster production?'[23] Sinclair's reply showed the importance he now attached to the Lancaster, even though the prototype had flown only weeks earlier. 'If you cannot spare the airframe capacity to build us both Beaufighter and Lancaster airframes, then our choice is for the Lancaster. Heavy bomber production is so important that I am prepared to sacrifice the Beaufighters in order to get the additional 25 Lancasters this year.'[24] The issue of producing a Hercules-powered Lancaster would arise again later in the year, causing more grief in the air establishment.

It is typical of both the irregularity of the Lancaster's early development and the official wrangling over aircraft numbers that the Air Ministry's contract for 450 Lancasters was not formally issued to Avro until June, by which time production was already well advanced. Another indicator of the unorthodox nature of the Lancaster's development was the fact that no Air Ministry specification for the plane was issued until the first planes were almost completed. Roy Chadwick produced his own specification, to act as a guide for the draughtsmen, manufacturers and subcontractors, but the official document did not appear until late August. No matter how unorthodox the procedures, once official approval had been given, Avro moved quickly into action, helped by 'the basically simple and easy to produce design, plus the fact that tooling was little affected by the redesign', to quote the Avro engineer Sandy Jack.[25] A second prototype, DG595, was constructed to be as close to the final production aircraft as possible, featuring a number of changes to the first design and an increased all-up weight of 60,000 pounds. The central fin on the tail was now permanently removed and larger fuel tanks were installed, taking the capacity to 2,160 gallons. In addition, a new Frazer-Nash 50A dorsal turret was fitted, as well as a small ventral turret which could be lowered in flight from the centre of the fuselage and operated remotely.

One technical issue that particularly concerned Avro at this stage was the proposed electrical system for the Lancaster provided by GEC, as Roy Dobson explained in a letter to the Ministry of Aircraft Production:

> I am very worried about this electrical strip wiring business which they are trying to force upon us on the Lancaster. I started on this job with quite an open mind and full of enthusiasm for the strip system but one snag after another has been unearthed and now I am certain we are on a bad egg. Fundamentally the thing is not as sound as the plug and socket type of joint. From a production point of view the new type of plug and socket entirely moulded with no machining whatsoever is by far the quickest, cheapest, lightest and most efficient job.

Dobson warned Trevor Westbrook, a dynamic, sometimes intemperate official who had previously worked for Vickers, that if MAP persisted with putting the strip system into the Lancaster, 'I shall have to say something officially about it because I know that the Lancaster will be let down and so will the crew using it.'[26] In reply, Westbrook tried to assure Dobson that the system would be fine once it was running. Westbrook explained that he had initially experienced the same anxieties when the strip system was installed in the Wellington, but it had 'never given any trouble at all', whereas other types of wiring tended to short and required more work. The vital priority, he argued, was 'to rush ahead with this Lancaster machine and get it out into the Service and have all the troubles ironed out right away. I feel sure that once it is through, it will be a fit-and-forget system, unless there is something fundamentally wrong with it, which was not so with the original scheme . . . I do entreat you to get the first Lancaster out at the very earliest possible date.'[27]

After its marked lack of enthusiasm towards the Lancaster in 1940, it was a bit rich of MAP to demand greater urgency from Avro. Besides, no two men could have shown more drive than Dobson and Chadwick, with most of their waking hours consumed by their Avro responsibilities. 'Dobson was always determined to have things done his way – and at once. He suffered neither fools nor delays in any circumstances,' wrote Sandy Jack.[28] Of Chadwick, Avro employee Charles Goldberg said: 'He was a perfectionist. He was the most diligent man I ever met.'[29]

Chadwick's quest for perfection led to another of his incendiary clashes with the Ministry of Aircraft Production. Just when the prototype was nearing completion, he was asked to attend a MAP conference in London to look at the latest bomber designs emerging from America. Infuriated enough by the loss of his time, he was then incensed to be told by a MAP official that these US types were what modern aircraft should look like. 'Chadwick returned in a most belligerent mood, snorting, "If that's what these —— think are super bombers, I'll show them",' recalled Sandy Jack:

> He promptly brought 20 draughtsmen and their drawing boards out to the hangar and set about modifying the Manchester III to his own satis-faction – regardless of whether or not it agreed with the final design conference decisions. The bomb doors were shorn of the safety locks along their mating edges, along with the hydraulic operating jacks, pipes and valves; the rest bed went out; equipment was rearranged internally to improve access and ease of movement by the crew between stations.[30]

Refined by Chadwick, DG595 was flown to Boscombe Down, where it again revealed its superb quality by reaching 360 mph in a dive with-out any adverse effect, an astonishing speed for a heavy bomber.

One of the great virtues of Avro was that manufacturing consider-ations were an integral part of an aircraft's design rather than an afterthought. A. V. Roe's guiding principle to 'make it simple' remained as powerful as ever during the war. Reflecting that belief, the Design Office at Chadderton was called 'Production Department Number One', while Avro also developed a highly efficient pre-production system for organizing labour, equipment and material supplies. Chadwick, who said he always preferred to call himself 'a practical engineer', insisted that a design was no good 'if it's too expensive or takes too long to produce'.[31] Built of aluminium alloy, the Lancaster itself was the embodiment of the Chadwick ethos, in that the aircraft's structure was divided into self-contained units for ease of manufacturing, assembly and maintenance. Avro was also assisted by a well-organized network of other engineering companies and subcontractors, all guided by Dobson's strong leadership into maximizing production levels. A 'Lancaster Group' of firms was set up in the later summer of 1941, compromising Avro itself and four other major firms: Metropolitan-Vickers, Armstrong Whitworth, Vickers and Austin Motors. Each of this quartet, known as the 'daughter firms', was provided with detailed drawings for jigs and tools. To speed up com-munications, they were linked to Chadderton by teleprinter, another sign of Avro's embrace of innovation. In addition, by September 1941 there were 37 manufacturers contracted to supply Lancaster parts to Avro and its daughter firms, ranging from the London and North Eastern Railway in York, which made mainplane trailing edges, to Tates of Stockport, which produced tailplanes.

Over the long term this complex web greatly expanded production of the Lancaster, though the logistical effort of establishing it in 1941 was an enormous burden on Avro. To give one example, a total of 13,000 drawings had to be produced for the tools. 'Supplies of these drawings are being forwarded to the daughter firms as fast as they can be printed, and it may be possible to supply six or seven hundred drawings to each firm per week,' explained Dobson at the first meeting of the Lancaster Group on 9 September.[32] But privately Dobson feared that the task of setting up the daughter-firm structure was distracting Avro from the initial production drive, telling MAP that 'we are getting absolutely overloaded. Could you give a push to the matter of additional store space here and some office accommodation because our pre-production Department is becoming absolutely blocked up with work for these various companies and I think we shall have to ask each of the companies to give us some staff resident here in order to look after their work?[33] It was partly because of all this work that Avro fell marginally behind its schedule of starting Lancaster deliveries in August 1941. Even so, it was a remarkable feat of engineering and efficiency to be able to complete the first plane only two months late. On 31 October 1941 the first production Lancaster, given the serial number R7257 and designated the Mark I, made its maiden flight from Woodford in Manchester, the main Avro base for final assembly and flight testing. The bomber proved just as good as the two prototypes. To commemorate the event, Avro sent MAP a leather-bound copy of a brochure it had produced on the Lancaster, trumpeting the features of the plane, including the large bomb bay with its streamlined, hydraulically-operated doors. 'The arrangement of the bomb bay enables all the standard sizes of bomb to be accommodated, including the very latest large bombs.' This was among the brochure's list of other qualities, including the 'roomy cabin', the 'very effective defence', the 'high speed of the aircraft', the undercarriage of 'very simple design for so large an aeroplane', and the system of engine controls which 'is remarkably free from friction and enables the rather heavy loads to be easily overcome by the pilot'. Overall, said the brochure, 'the Lancaster is remarkably controllable for its size, which enables it to take effective evasive action when attacked and also during bombing operations'.[34]

None of this could be said of the Manchester, which had slid into a twilight world since production had started to be switched to the Lancaster. Despite continual attempts at modifications, its performance both in tests and in operations confirmed that exactly the right decision had been taken to replace it. The plane first went into operational service with 207 Squadron on 24 February, in a raid against a German cruiser docked in the French port of Brest. No losses were suffered, but neither was any damage done by the Manchester's feeble load of 500-pounders. More ominously, one Manchester had to crash-land on its return due to a hydraulics failure. The following weeks saw further ineffectual raids punctuated by spells of inactivity when all the Manchesters had to be grounded because of more troubles with the Vulture engines. The number of aborted sorties and the death toll continued to mount during the summer of 1941, earning the plane a dismal name among aircrews. 'The reputation of the Manchester was such that a member of a Manchester squadron was to be pitied rather than admired,' wrote air gunner Bob Goss.[35] Perhaps the worst feature of the plane was that it could rarely stay in the air on one engine, a striking contrast to the Lancaster's phenomenal durability. Chan Chandler, a rear gunner who had experience of both planes, wrote that the Manchester 'flew like a brick' on one engine. 'The difference between the Manchester and the Lancaster was unbelievable.'[36]

In retrospect, it may seem strange that the government kept producing Manchesters and sending them to squadrons, long after their inadequacy had become clear. In fulfilment of the original contract for 200, the final Manchester did not come off the line until November 1941. Moreover, sorties continued to be flown well into 1942, the last of them an attack on the Focke-Wulf factory at Bremen in northern Germany on 24 June. But there were two motivations behind this determination to stick with the Manchester until the contract was finished. The first was the continuing strain of Micawberism in the Air Staff that somehow the technical problems could be overcome, reflected in the words of Portal to Beaverbrook during one of the periodic crises: 'I feel that whatever the trouble may be, it cannot be beyond the ingenuity of your experts to put it right.'[37] The second was the residue of the philosophy that had undermined the RAF in the 1930s, in which air strength was measured in sheer numbers, regardless of the quality of the planes. This was the creed that had allowed the disastrous Fairey Battle, a woeful, single-engined light bomber, to remain in production into 1940, even though it had been obsolescent when it first entered service in 1937. In the case of the Manchester, the Air Staff felt it better to give squadrons something rather than nothing, particularly as the Lancaster had only started production and the Halifax and Stirling had not fulfilled expectations.

The failure of the Manchester was symbolic of the mood of permanent crisis that engulfed Bomber Command in 1941. Strategic bombing was meant to be Britain's primary offensive weapon, and the inability of the RAF to strike back at Germany caused profound disillusionment within the government and the military. When Britain stood alone against the Nazi regime, beset with threats not just at home but throughout North Africa, the Mediterranean, the Pacific and the Atlantic, many strategists questioned the growing resources devoted to such an ineffectual instrument of war. Such scepticism was not confined to the army and navy, but extended to other RAF commands, especially Coastal Command which was struggling with the U-boat menace. Bomber Command's defence, which had some justification, was that, far from being excessively rewarded, it had actually been starved of the equipment to do its job. If the government really wanted to deal a blow to the Reich, argued the Air Staff, then Bomber Command needed a substantial heavy-bomber force filled with the latest types.

The primacy of the bomber appeared to have an advocate in Winston Churchill, the great warrior statesman who had served in the cavalry during Queen Victoria's reign. With his visionary gift for seeing the wide strategic picture, the Prime Minister had told Beaverbrook in July 1940, on the eve of the Battle of Britain:

> We have no continental army which can defeat German military power. The blockade is broken and Hitler has Asia and probably Africa to draw from. Should he be repulsed here or not try invasion, he will probably recoil eastwards and we have nothing to stop him. But there is one thing that will bring him back and bring him down, and that is an absolutely devastating, exterminating attack by very heavy bombers from this country upon the Nazi homeland. We must be able to overwhelm him by this means. Without it I do not see a way through.[38]

Unlike his predecessor in Downing Street, Churchill was never squeamish about attacking Germany's infrastructure, even if such bombing involved a heavy civilian toll. Yet Churchill was also a realist rather than an ideologue. He may have been ruthless in his attitude towards Germany because he knew it was the only way, in 1941, to counterattack, but he was not a subscriber to the Trenchard doctrine. He attached little credibility to the claim that aerial bombardment could shatter the will of the enemy population. This pragmatism meant that there was a streak of ambivalence in Churchill's opinion of the bomber offensive. He would support it on the grounds of the tangible results, not because of mere dogma.

But there were no such hesitations among the Air Staff, where the Trenchard doctrine still held sway. Far from causing doubts, the setbacks from 1939 to 1941 were an argument for much more weight to be put behind strategic bombing. Similarly, the German Blitz over urban Britain was seen as a vindication rather than a rejection of bombing theories, even though it had patently failed to crack either industry or people. What the Air Staff contemplated was a vast increase in aircraft numbers, not a change in approach.

This outlook was embraced right at the top of the air force, for the Chief of the Air Staff Sir Charles Portal was a keen Trenchardian. To Portal, strategic bombing was the *raison d'être* of the RAF. A self-contained, hard, aloof man, though not without charm to those he regarded as his equals, Portal was widely admired for his natural air of command. 'The accepted star of the Air Force' was Churchill's description, while Arthur Harris said he always exuded 'a calm confidence' when dealing with a multiplicity of directives.[39] Born in 1893 to a wealthy Berkshire land-owning family and educated at Winchester and Oxford, Portal had fought heroically with the Royal Flying Corps and the RAF in the First World War, winning the Military Cross at the Battle of the Somme and carrying out more than 900 sorties by the time the Armistice was declared. His career during the interwar years had been one of almost unbroken advancement, with one promotion following inexorably on the other. He had been a senior instructor at the RAF Cadet College in Cranwell, a commander of British forces in Aden, and, before he became CAS in November 1940, the head of Bomber Command, in which role he had impressed Churchill with his energy both in bombing German invasion barges on the French coast and in daring to mount retaliatory attacks on Germany. Tall, angular, with a lined face, a widow's peak of black hair and a large beaked nose, Portal was an imposing, charismatic figure. Chips Channon, the American-born Tory MP and bisexual social butterfly, described him as 'a man of granite and ruthlessness'.[40] Rigidly self-disciplined, he worked fifteen hours a day as Chief of the Air Staff, slept only four hours a night and had no time for small talk. Portal's relationship with his nominal superior, the Air Minister Sir Archibald Sinclair, was hardly one of equals. In practice, Sinclair acted largely as a political mouthpiece for the CAS, even on the most ferociously controversial subjects.

As head of the RAF, Portal decided that his overriding priority must be the rapid expansion of Bomber Command. Backed up by Sinclair, he campaigned vigorously for an increase in numbers to create a front-line force of 4,000 bombers by 1943, a dramatic leap from the meagre force of just 450 aircraft that existed in mid-1941, comprising two squadrons of Stirlings, two of Halifaxes and two of Manchesters, with Wellingtons, Whitleys, Hampdens and even a few Battles making up the rest. From the spring of 1941, Sinclair joined in the push at a political level, telling Churchill that 'air predominance can only be won by the Bomber Force. Lack of fighters or aircraft to co-operate with the army or navy might lose us the war. Only bombers can bring us victory. Our task over the next two years or less must be to reverse the ratio and raise the intensity of our bomber offensive against Germany to an intolerable pitch.' Sinclair argued that this could be done only by the proposed force of 4,000, whose build-up would require a phenomenal rise in bomber output to 1,000 aeroplanes a month.

In particular, he said, more industrial support would be needed from America, which was already supplying Britain with fighters, light bombers and aero-engines, but should now be persuaded to manufacture 'heavies' as well. Again demonstrating his early faith in the Lancaster, he informed Churchill: 'The production of Merlin engines in America should be doubled and might suffice for the suggested heavy bomber programme, provided we select aircraft such as the Halifax and the Lancaster.'[41] With so many pressures on other fronts, Churchill was reluctant to give his immediate endorsement to so epic a scheme. But his hesitation exasperated Sinclair, who wrote on 1 May: 'I have not heard whether you agree to a front line strength of 4000 heavy bombers by April 1943.' So determined was Sinclair to implement this plan that he even drafted a telegram to President Franklin D. Roosevelt, which he asked Churchill to sign. The draft explained to the President that the British aircraft industry had insufficient capacity to meet the RAF's future need for heavy bombers: 'Believing as we do that air predominance is the key to victory and will be achieved only with the assistance of a greatly increased flow of the heaviest class of bomber from the USA, we feel that inevitable difficulties must be faced and can be overcome. I therefore ask you, Mr President, to lend us your help in this great project on the results of which so much depends.'[42] Churchill remained unmoved and declined to send any telegram to Roosevelt on the subject. He wanted the Air Staff's demand to be discussed in greater detail, since 'such a vast programme carries with it dominating consequences in almost every sphere of manpower and production'.[43]

A subsequent meeting of ministers failed to provide complete endorsement to the expansion scheme but did authorize bomber output to be raised by 200 planes a month. This limited step was not enough for

Sinclair, who confessed in June to Portal that 'the programme is encountering heavy weather. Ministers are reluctant to commit themselves to so big a concentration of effort upon one means of winning the war.'[44] In reality, however, the aircraft industry was in no position to raise dramatically the output of 'heavies' in mid-1941 because of limited production capacity and the need to train a growing workforce.

The political unwillingness to give full backing to the plan for 4,000 bombers stemmed not just from resources but also from the perception that Bomber Command was ineffective. The results achieved so far had been pitiful. Sinclair might argue that 'we can destroy the war industries of Germany and break the will to fight of the German people', but he could provide not a shred of evidence to back up this claim.[45] Bomber Command's attacks remained limited in weight and inaccurate in direction. The idea that the RAF could hit German targets with precision belonged only to propaganda newsreels. In part, this chronic inaccuracy was the result of bombers having to conduct their operations at night, since daylight raids in the first months of the war had led to unsustainable casualties. As Arthur Harris, then commander of 5 Group, said to Arthur Tedder in late 1940 in typically bullish terms, 'I think everybody is agreed that the metier of the heavy bomber is night bombing and that any idea of using them by daylight is now a "busted flush", even amongst those who were not seized of this childishly obvious fact before the war started.'[46] The problem with night bombing was that the crews had neither the training nor the navigational aids to carry it out properly. The Reich, enveloped in the blackout and protected by flak guns, was no place for guesswork.

The inaccuracy of Bomber Command's aeroplanes was compounded by other problems in this period. One was the absence of any single, clear-sighted objective for bombing. A stream of directives was issued by the Air Staff with ever-changing lists of priorities. One month oil installations would be declared as the prime target, only to be replaced the following month by transport links. Then a new instruction would be issued demanding attacks on U-boat pens on the north German coast. All this fed a climate of despair and confusion in the bomber squadrons. Moreover, the head of Bomber Command in 1941, Air Vice Marshal Sir Richard Pierse, was not a figure to inspire confidence in either his commanders or his crews. An officer in the Royal Naval Air Service during the First World War, he had enjoyed a lengthy series of senior postings before he took charge of Bomber Command as Portal's successor in October 1940. Competent rather than imaginative, he frequently veered between hand-wringing pessimism and dangerous overconfidence. Don Bennett, later one of the greatest Lancaster pilots of the war, said of him: 'During my period as a squadron commander I had seen little to admire. He refused to believe the evidence of the failure of the bomber effort in those days and appeared to lack initiative and drive.'[47]

Pierse had always been a believer in precision bombing rather than wider attacks. But the combination of inaccuracy, poor equipment, night raids and pressure for results meant that Bomber Command was unable to stick to this approach. As early as the autumn of 1940, Portal had privately begun to lose faith in the ability of the RAF to carry out precision assaults, and the failure of raids on oil, railways and ports only reinforced his doubts. From the beginning of 1941, Bomber Command was increasingly urged to embrace the concept of area bombing, trying to hit urban expanses rather than specific targets. Within the Air Staff, there was no pretence that this approach was aimed at Germany's military infrastructure. Instead, in the fulfilment of General Douhet's unsparing theories on air power, the attempt at mass devastation became the core of the bombing strategy. At the start of the war, Sir John Slessor, then the RAF's Director of Plans, had pronounced, with an air of moral certitude, that 'indiscriminate attacks on civilian populations as such will never form part of our policy'.[48] The cold realities of failure ensured the abandonment of such high-minded principles.

After another series of unavailing raids on oil targets in February 1941, Portal told Pierse to concentrate 'on the general dislocation of industry by mass attacks on industrial centres'.[49] Portal's outlook was soon mirrored by his deputy, Sir Norman Bottomley, who called on Bomber Command to aim at 'the destruction of the morale of the population of certain vital industrial centres', a statement of undiluted Trenchardism.[50] The mounting consensus in favour of area bombing culminated in a directive from Portal to Bomber Command on 9 July 1941, which stated that the main effort of the force should work 'towards dislocating the German transportation system and to destroying the morale of the civil population as a whole and the industrial system in particular'.[51] A further instruction, drawn up by Freeman and added to this directive, spelled out what the new policy really meant. 'Priority of selection should be given to those targets in Germany which lie in congested areas where the greatest morale effect is likely to be achieved.'[52]

Given the inaccuracy of the bombers, the policy of area attacks made a strategic virtue of operational necessity. But for all its severity, the move ran with the grain of the press and public mood in Britain. Since the

Blitz, newspapers had been clamouring for the RAF to exact revenge on the German population. Any belief in restraint had been obliterated in the Luftwaffe's raids on British cities, especially the destruction of central Coventry on the night of 14 November 1940 when 60,000 buildings were brought down and 568 civilians killed. In a thunderous editorial of 12 September during the Luftwaffe campaign, the *Daily Mirror* declared: 'Bomb for bomb and the same all round! That is the only policy. And the only policy on which our dauntless suffering people insist. If the Air Minister doesn't agree with them then he must clear out. The air war is no time for lecturers, and gloved persons wishing to live up to a high standard of ancient chivalry. The invention of the bombing plane abolished chivalry forever. It is now "retaliate or go under". We are not dedicated to passive or polite martyrdom. We must hit back.'[53] A year later the anger among large sections of the public was just as intense, reflected in one letter to the *Daily Telegraph*: 'There must be thousands in this country who feel with me that until the people of Germany themselves are made to feel and suffer what they are willing to make others suffer, it will be a very long time before we can shatter the prestige which the Nazi regime continues to enjoy.'[54]

But the greatest impetus towards a wholesale adoption of area bombing came not from public opinion but from an internal government report which exposed the waywardness of the RAF's bombing. Churchill's chief scientific adviser Lord Cherwell, a brilliant but austere German-born physicist once described as holding 'an almost pathological hatred of Nazi Germany and an almost medieval desire for revenge',[55] had long been concerned about the inaccuracy of Bomber Command's aeroplanes, an unease that was deepened by studying reports on the failed attacks against oil targets. Determined to find the truth beyond the wishful thinking of Pierse and the Air Staff, he commissioned his own comprehensive analysis of the intelligence on RAF raids against Germany. This was carried out by D. M. Butt, a civil servant in the War Cabinet secretariat, who examined 630 reconnaissance photographs together with operational papers. Butt's study amounted to a powerful indictment of Bomber Command. It showed that only two-thirds of crews ever claimed to have reached their target, and even then, only a third of them came within five miles of hitting the aiming point. The figure fell to a miserable one-tenth in the well-defended Ruhr valley, and to one-fifteenth when squadrons were operating on moonless nights.

The findings, circulated in August 1941, came as a shock to Bomber Command. Even the most modest claims about the potency of its force had been clinically demolished. At first the twin reactions of the Air Staff were either to dismiss the report as an irrelevance or to dispute its conclusions, claiming that Butt had not taken account of the poor weather during his period of analysis. 'In the good weather of 1940, the results would have been very different and led to quite another conclusion,' noted Portal in his response to the report.[56] But Portal was a canny political operator. Behind his cold veneer there lurked a protective streak of cunning. While Pierse flailed about, alternating between outraged denial and a self-incriminating search for easier targets beyond the Ruhr valley, Portal saw how to turn the Butt report to his advantage. Far from being a source of embarrassment, it could be used to justify both area bombing and a huge expansion in Bomber Command.

The Butt report, it was true, had exposed the persistent failure of the bombers to hit precise targets. Yet if the definition of a target were widened to encompass a much broader area, then Bomber Command would not appear nearly so ineffective. A whole town would always be much easier to bomb than a single factory or dockyard. By changing the criteria for accuracy, success was bound to follow. This flexible and cynical attitude fitted in precisely with the wider enthusiasm for area bombing that now prevailed in the Air Staff. Such thinking is revealed in an astonishingly frank private paper from the Directorate of Bombing Operations at the Air Ministry, written just a week after the Butt report. Never mentioned in any previous history, this document is a graphic indicator of how far the Air Staff had departed from the high-minded inhibitions of September 1939. After the war Portal tried to deny that the RAF's aim was ever to kill civilians. It was, he claimed in one lecture, 'a curious and widespread fallacy that our bombing of the German cities was really intended to kill and frighten Germans and that we camouflaged this intention by the pretence that we would destroy industry. Any such idea is completely and utterly false. The loss of life, which amounted to some 600,000 killed, was purely incidental.'[57] This retrospective defence is comprehensively refuted by the Directorate's paper, dated 25 August 1941. The paper opened by stating that, because of the RAF's inaccuracy: 'It is a waste of effort to continue to attack any specific objective by night.' Instead the bombers should go for cities. 'The attack on a city or an area within a city offers the attacking aircraft a target of considerable size and is possible to identify under clear moon conditions. Moreover, at all times it is easier to find and attack than a specific industrial target. The focus of attack therefore becomes the people in their homes and in factories, also the services such as electricity, gas and water upon which the industrial and domestic life of the area depend.' Warming to this theme, the Directorate then found support for such theories in the German bombing of Coventry. To most Britons this attack had been an outrage. To the Air Staff it was an inspiration. The assault on Coventry was 'one of the most successful raids carried out by the German Air Force on this country', with a ton of high explosive and incendiaries for every 800 citizens. 'If Bomber Command could carry out a raid on the Coventry scale every month, the result would be a complete state of panic in the industrialised west of Germany.' The Germans had invented the word 'Coventrate' to describe lethal concentrated bombing on a city, but the Air Ministry felt that the RAF should now adopt the practice. 'Coventry is the best measuring stick of lasting material and moral [i.e. morale] damage that has occurred in this country. It is suggested that this scale of attack can be used as a basis for estimating the tonnage required to carry out a heavy and concentrated attack on any city or town in Germany, such as to cause considerable loss of life and limb, widespread destruction and damage to the houses of workers.'[58]

But a wider, more lethal target strategy would achieve nothing without resources. Another solution to the inaccuracy of bombing highlighted in the Butt report, argued Portal, was a huge increase in the size of the bomber force, so that a greater number of planes would hit their objectives. According to this logic, sheer quantity of aircraft could overcome the obstacles presented by the navigational problems of night-flying. The demand for a 4,000-strong bomber force by July 1943 was therefore put forward with renewed vigour. Finally, after all the previous months of hesitations, Churchill gave his backing for the programme, not least because, with the military situation as dire as ever in Africa and the Pacific, there was still no realistic alternative to the bomber offensive as a means of attacking Germany. Writing to the War Cabinet on 7 September, Churchill explained that he had asked the Ministry of Aircraft Production 'to draw up a plan for this new programme. I regard this subject as a major factor in the war at the present.' The scheme, he added, would mean a total production of 22,000 planes over the next two years, of which 5,500 could be acquired from America. But the remaining 16,500 bombers could only be manufactured 'by a great concentration of effort and by making inroads on our other requirements. Materials and machine tools should not present an insuperable difficulty and there will be enough pilots to fly the aircraft. The crux of the matter will be the provision of sufficient skilled labour to set up the machines and train great numbers of fresh men and women.'[59] For all the political heat they had generated, these figures were wholly unrealistic for an aircraft industry that had barely started building 'heavies'. The huge new demands were epitomized by the statistic that a Lancaster took 105,000 man hours to build, compared to 25,000 for a Spitfire. With his usual acumen Sir Wilfrid Freeman sensed that, contrary to the intentions of the Air Staff, the aircraft industry would try to concentrate on medium bombers precisely because they were easier and cheaper to build compared to the Lancasters and Halifaxes. 'In our view,' he wrote to the Chief Executive of MAP, Sir Charles Craven, 'it is imperative that we should aim to produce the greatest possible number of heavies within the new quota laid down by the Prime Minister. We are still ahead of the Germans in the quality of our aircraft and it is quality which tells in wartime.'[60] Craven inclined to agree, but warned that such an approach would actually lead to an immediate drop in bomber production as factories would have to take time to gear up for the manufacture of the Lancaster. 'I appreciate that the Wellington to the Lancaster is a tramp to a battleship,' replied Craven, 'but if I should stop the production of Wellingtons at Chester and Blackpool and turn over to Lancasters, you will receive no Lancasters (from those factories) by the Prime Minister's target date.'[61]

Now he had his promise of planes, even if not necessarily the numbers of 'heavies' he had been seeking, Portal wanted to secure Churchill's backing for the more stringent policy of area bombing. But Churchill's agreement to the expansion programme did not imply that he entirely accepted Portal's views. In fact, his doubts about this strategy were to provoke an intense exchange between the Prime Minister and his Air Chief, the outcome of which would help fix the direction of the bomber offensive for the remainder of the war. On 25 September Portal set out the case for concentrated area bombing, using a report from the Directorate of Bombing Operations which had calculated that such a force, numbering 250 squadrons and dropping 18,750 tons of bombs per month, could achieve the destruction of Germany's 43 largest cities and towns.[62] 'It is in bombing, on a scale undreamt of in the last war, that we find the new weapon on which we must principally depend for the destruction of German economic life and morale . . . It must be realized that attack on morale is not a matter of pure killing, although the fear of death is unquestionably an important factor. It is rather the general dislocation of industrial and social life arising from damage to industrial plant and dwelling houses, shops, utility and transportation services, from the resultant absenteeism and in fact from interference with all that goes to make up the general activity of a community.' Portal then produced a rather spurious statistical basis for his claims. 'One ton of bombs per 800 of the population would reduce the general activity of all of them to a point beyond all hope of recovery in six months.' The paper then admitted, in line with Butt's findings, that only 25 per cent of sorties might be effective, based on an average bomb lift of three tons, though the new bomber types could raise the tonnage. 'If our hopes of getting more heavy bombers of the Lancaster/Stirling class mature, the average bomb lift of three tons per aircraft may be unduly conservative.' Portal concluded: 'The estimate of the force required to achieve our aim is therefore tentative. We certainly cannot do with less bombers. We may well need more.'[63] Churchill was still to be convinced, having drawn the opposite conclusion from the Butt report:

> It is very disputable whether bombing by itself will be a decisive factor in the present war. On the contrary, all that we have learnt since the war began shows that its effects, both physical and moral, are greatly exaggerated. There is no doubt that the British people have been stimulated and strengthened by the attack made upon them so far. Secondly, it seems very likely that the ground defences and night fighters will overtake the Air attack. Thirdly, in calculating the number of bombers necessary to achieve hypothetical and indefinite tasks, it should be noted that only a quarter of our bombers hit the targets. Consequently, an increase in the accuracy of bombing to 100 per cent would in fact raise our bombing force to four times its strength. The most we can say is that it will be a heavy and I trust increasing annoyance.[64]

The debate between the Prime Minister and his Air Chief had reached a crucial stage. In effect, Churchill had challenged the whole theoretical basis of the strategic bomber offensive. If Portal had wavered, the entire history of air war could have been different. The RAF would have been compelled to take a new direction, with tactical support, fighter attacks and precision bombing as its priorities. In such circumstances the Lancaster would never have attained its position as the key offensive aircraft of the RAF. That honour would have gone to the twin-engined, multi-purpose, plywood-built Mosquito, capable of carrying a 4,000-pound bomb load to Berlin and flying faster than a Spitfire. Indeed some have argued that if the RAF had given primacy to the Mosquito, then it would have become a more flexible, effective force, deadlier to the enemy and safer for its crews. This was the view held by Professor John Ellis, who worked at the Royal Aircraft Establishment at Farnborough during the war. 'The Mosquito was the ideal bomber, whereas the Lancaster was big and slow. The Mosquito concept was by far the better scheme for bombing. Get in there fast and get out fast, because exposure time is all important.'[65] The aviation historian Jon Lake was even more vehement about the error made by the Air Staff in focusing on the Lancaster rather than the Mosquito:

> The unarmed, high-speed 'Wooden Wonder' could be seen as represent-
> ing the future, while the much-lauded Lancaster was an aircraft which
> represented the end of an era – slow, with heavy defensive armament and
> a heavy bombload. To have expected the Air Staff to have discarded its
> Trenchardian attachment to the doctrine of strategic bombing for morale
> effect when the war broke out is probably unrealistic. It is, however, equally
> incomprehensible that even in the light of operational experience little
> attempt was made to shift the emphasis of the bombing campaign . . . It
> was always the case that the smaller, faster more survivable bombers were
> more likely to hit their targets than the four-engined 'heavies' and that
> their relatively tiny bombloads were thereby more effective.[66]

Such thinking was anathema to Portal in late 1941. He believed in mass bombing, and he was determined to secure the Prime Minister's agreement. In a further memorandum of 2 October, he told Churchill that 'since the fall of France it has been a fundamental principle of our strategy that victory over Germany could not be hoped for until German morale and German material strength had been subjected to a bombing offensive of the greatest intensity'. This policy, he wrote, had been agreed not just by the military chiefs of staff but by Churchill himself. Displaying some boldness towards the Prime Minister, Portal then warned that if the government was not willing to support the heavy bomber offensive, then the entire approach towards waging the war would have to be rethought. 'If the most we can hope to achieve with our bomber forces is growing power and annoyance, then, as I see it, the strategic concept to which we have been working must dissolve and we must find a new plan.' He finished on a note of unapologetic candour about the true purpose of area bombing, explaining that already in 1941 'we have caused the death or injury of 93,000 civilians. This result was achieved with a small fraction of the bomb load we hope to employ in 1943.'[67]

Portal had tried to present Churchill with a stark choice: back the bomber offensive to the hilt or abandon it. This might have been under-standable for an Air Chief who had been reared on the Trenchard doctrine and did not have to take the wider political and military considerations into account. But with Germany all dominant in continental Europe and now marching on Moscow, Churchill could hardly be so dogmatic. His response to Portal was a magnificent, at times prophetic, assessment of

Britain's position in the war, using the sharp edge of realism to puncture the inflated theorizing of the bomber zealots:

We all hope that the Air offensive against Germany will realize the expectations of the Air Staff. Everything is being done to create the Bombing Force desired on the largest possible scale and there is no intention of changing this policy. I deprecate, however, placing unbounded confidence in this means of attack and still more expressing that confidence in terms of arithmetic. It is the most potent method of impairing the enemy's morale at the present time. If the United States enters the war, it would have to be supplemented in 1943 by simultaneous attacks by armoured forces in many of the conquered countries which were ripe for revolt. Only in this way could a decision certainly be achieved. Even if all the towns of Germany were rendered largely uninhabitable, it does not follow that military control would be weakened or even that war industry could not be carried on. The Air Staff would make a great mistake to put their claim too high. Before the war we were greatly misled by the pictures they painted of the destruction that would be wrought by air raids. This is illustrated by the fact that 750,000 beds were actually provided for air raid casualties, never more than 6000 being required.

Churchill then turned to the fashionable assumption that bombardment could break the will of the Germans to fight:

It may well be that German morale will crack and that our bombing will play a very important part in bringing the result about. But all things are always on the move simultaneously and it is quite possible that the Nazi war-making power in 1943 will be so widely spread throughout Europe as to be to a large extent independent of the actual buildings in the homeland. A very different picture would be presented if the enemy's Air Force was so far reduced as to enable accurate daylight bombing of factories to take place. This however cannot be done outside the radius of fighter protection, according to what I am at present told. One has to do the best one can, but he is an unwise man who thinks there is any certain method of winning this war, or indeed any other war between equals in strength. The only plan is to persevere.[68]

Portal refused to be swayed by the Prime Minister's scepticism, professing his satisfaction that the Prime Minister had accepted 'the primary importance of our bomber operations and of building up the bomber force on the largest possible scale'.[69]

But the task of creating that large new force was not straightforward. The process of introducing the newer, heavier bomber types actually slowed down output for a time, because of both their sheer size and the need for tooling and training. In the whole of 1941 total deliveries of 'heavies' were just 498, comprising 165 Manchesters, 162 Halifaxes, 153 Stirlings and 18 Lancasters. Not known for his phlegmatic outlook, Sir Richard Pierse lapsed into despondency at what he called 'the ebbing tide of production'.[70] When Sir Archibald Sinclair tried to raise his spirits by reference to Churchill's support for the expansion plan, Pierse was having none of it. 'I am more depressed than I can say at the failure of the Ministry of Aircraft Production to provide us with what we require, even to maintain the small bomber force that we have, let alone give us the wherewithal for expansion. Moreover, whilst I know that the Prime Minister has given his personal instruction that the rate of progress of the Bomber Force expansion is to be accelerated, if not doubled, yet I can see little or no move to turn this into a fact.'[71]

Recognizing the industrial problems of expansion, the government had tried to enlist the help of the USA and Canada in the manufacture of the Lancaster. The body entrusted with the task of securing such help was the British Air Commission, which conducted lengthy negotiations with the American and Canadian governments through the summer and autumn of 1941. But the talks with the US were fruitless. Ostensibly this was because the Americans wanted to reserve their industrial capacity for their own bomber types. 'I have looked into the business of the possibilities of building the Lancaster here and I find they are very slim,' wrote Harry Hopkins, Roosevelt's key adviser, to Freeman at the end of September. 'We are simply straining every possible effort on our own four-engine bombers and if we try new models all of our production people think it will slow the whole process up.'[72] Freeman expressed his regret to Portal. 'This is a pity. I don't think we shall get the Lancaster built in America now for HH was my last hope,' to which Portal responded with a terse four-word note: 'They are too proud.'[73] But it is possible that the White House was not telling the whole truth. Apart from industrial pressures, the Roosevelt administration may not have had much faith in the Lancaster at this time. In the National Archives there is an intriguing note from the British Air Commission to MAP, dated 17 September, which states: 'The American Air Attache to Canada, Colonel John Gullet, has just returned from England and does not speak well of the Lancaster. He says that it is not in the same class as the Halifax.'[74] For all its fallibility, Colonel Gullet's judgement could have had an indirect influence in US Government circles, though Washington tried to reassure London that his opinion carried little weight. Thankfully, despite the colonel, the Canadians proved more receptive towards the overtures from the British

Air Commission. With the support of Canada's Dominion Government, a contract to build 250 Lancasters was given to the National Steel and Car Corporation of Montreal, with deliveries due to start in 1943. To advise the company, a technician from Avro was sent across the Atlantic.

But none of this was of any immediate help to Bomber Command and its despairing commander Sir Richard Pierse, whose vacillations had provoked a profound loss of faith in his leadership. In a desperate attempt to reassert his authority, he ordered a daring series of raids on the night of 7 November against targets ranging from Berlin and the Ruhr to Boulogne in France. In appalling weather over northern Europe, his plan backfired disastrously. Almost 10 per cent of the aircraft he sent were lost, while in the attack on Berlin the figure rose to 12.4 per cent. A crisis summit was called by Churchill to discuss the fiasco, as a result of which it was agreed that Bomber Command should be restricted to closer targets until it built up its resources. Effectively, the bomber offensive was suspended for the winter months. In January 1942 Pierse was relieved of his command and sent out to serve the RAF in India. He did nothing for his reputation by eloping two years later with the wife of General Claude Auchinleck, finishing his career in disgrace.

In the same month as Pierse departed from Bomber Command, the *Daily Sketch* carried this editorial: 'The British public has for some time been asking what has become of our bombers. Why have they not been making the increasingly severe attacks on Germany which were expected and which were promised?'[75] It was not a question that would be asked again, once Arthur Harris and the Lancaster were operating in tandem. The bomber war was about to start in earnest.

3

'The importance of killing and terrifying the Boche'

⌐⌐

IT WAS TO become the most iconic image of the Blitz: the dome of St Paul's cathedral breaking through the clouds of smoke and soaring flames that had engulfed the surrounding area, a symbol of Britain's defiance against the Nazi assault. On a night in late December 1940, the German bombers had brought fire and death to London but Sir Christopher Wren's masterpiece had survived, almost as if protected by a moral shield. Arthur Harris, Deputy Chief of the Air Staff during the Blitz, was working at the Air Ministry in Whitehall when the Luftwaffe struck. He went up to the roof of the building and was mesmerized by what he saw and heard. 'St Paul's standing in the midst of an ocean of fire – an incredible sight. One could hear the German bombers arriving in a stream and the swish of incendiaries falling into the fire below.'[1] Harris was so amazed that he summoned his chief, Sir Charles Portal, to join him on the roof to witness the scene. Gazing in appalled fascination, Harris was inspired to utter part of that avenging verse from the Old Testament: 'They have sown the wind, and they shall reap the whirlwind.'[2]

The term 'Reaping the Whirlwind' captured the public's imagination when Harris used it in one of his first public broadcasts in 1942: 'The Nazis entered this war under the rather childish illusion that they were going to bomb everybody and nobody was going to bomb them. At Rotterdam, London, Warsaw and half a hundred other places they put that rather naive theory into operation. They sowed the wind and now they are going to reap the whirlwind.'[3] The phrase, so redolent of Biblical redemption, impinged on Britain's consciousness because it was a perfect distillation of the bomber strategy, where the German nation was going to be made to pay for the suffering it had caused across Europe.

In the Lancaster the RAF believed it had the agent to create the whirlwind, though at the end of 1941 it would be some time before there were sufficient numbers of the type to fulfil this role. The first Lancaster had come off the production line in October, and in the months that followed the supply of planes was still only a trickle. At this stage in the war Bomber Command was divided into five groups, based largely on geography and types. No. 1 Group in Yorkshire operated medium and heavy bombers, while No. 2 Group, with its headquarters in Cambridgeshire, was equipped with light bombers and had played a heroic, if barren, role in the Battle of France. No. 3 Group flew Wellingtons and Stirlings out of East Anglian airfields, and No. 4 Group in Yorkshire was gradually switching to Halifaxes. But the bomber group that saw itself as the elite force was No. 5 Group in Lincolnshire, whose airfields like Waddington, Scampton, Woodhall Spa and Coningsby would become synonymous with the bomber offensive in Germany. If No. 11 Group in Fighter Command, covering the southeast of England, had been at the heart of the Battle of Britain, then No. 5 Group in Bomber Command would play a similar essential part in the heavy assaults on Germany. Reflecting the Group's status, its commanders had usually been the most highly regarded operational leaders in the service, such as Sir John Slessor, later Chief of the Air Staff, and Harris himself during the opening year of the war. So it was no surprise that in July 1941, when the Lancaster had proved its quality, the Air Staff decided that the plane should first be sent into service with No. 5 Group. The aircraft was considered so advanced, the testing so limited and the production schedule so rapid that, at the suggestion of Avro, a flying and maintenance crew from No. 5 headquarters in Grantham had to be sent to Boscombe Down 'to assist in the programme, put the Lancasters through their paces and comment on them from an operational point of view'.[4] At the same time the original Lancaster prototype, BT308, was sent to the RAF base at Waddington near Lincoln so some crews could become familiar with the new type. When BT308 began its approach for landing at Waddington, most of the ground staff just dismissed it as one of the Manchesters from 207 Squadron until they saw its four engines. Their surprise was an indicator of how little publicity was given to the Lancaster project outside MAP, the Air Ministry and Avro.

On 24 December 1941, almost exactly a year since the prototype had made its maiden flight, the first three production Lancasters were delivered to 44 (Rhodesia) Squadron in No. 5 Group based at Waddington. The squadron was given its title to commemorate the support shown by the white-ruled African state for the war effort, reflected in the fact that a quarter of all No. 44's personnel came from southern Rhodesia. Since September, word had spread through the squadron about the arrival of the new bombers, which were to replace 44 Squadron's ageing Hampdens.

Pip Beck, a radio-telephone operator with No. 5 Group, later described in her memoirs the dramatic moment on Christmas Eve. 'It was with intense interest that everyone in Flying Control watched their approach and landing. As the first of the three taxied round the perimeter to the Watch Office, I stared in astonishment at this formidable and beautiful aircraft, cockpit as high as the balcony on which I stood and great spread of wings with four enormous engines. Its lines were sleek and graceful, yet there was an awesome feeling of power about it. It looked so right after the clumsiness of the Manchester.' As she explained, there was a short period of adjustment to the new planes, particularly because the number of crew members had expanded from four in the Hampden to seven in the Lancaster. Instruction was also required in the new Frazer-Nash power-operated turrets. The planes' arrival, she wrote, 'meant a new programme of training for the air and ground crews and no operations until the crews had done their share of circuits, bumps and cross-countries and had thoroughly familiarised themselves with the Lancasters. There were one or two minor accidents at this time; changing from a twin-engined aircraft to a heavier one with four engines must have presented some difficulties – but the crews took to them rapidly. I heard nothing but praise for the Lancs.'[5]

Having familiarized themselves with the Lancaster, some members of 44 Squadron were then sent in January to provide guidance to airmen in 97 Squadron, which was the next unit to receive the bomber. The squadron, based at Coningsby in Lincolnsire, had seen its morale badly undermined by the failure of the Manchester throughout 1941. It was therefore with some relief that No. 97 crews began to train on the new bomber. The Lancaster may have been a vast improvement on its predecessor, but it was inevitable that there were a few teething problems during the first months of service. After intensive examination of the early production models, experts from A&AEE at Boscombe Down drew up a wide-ranging list of some 44 defects. These included weak brake connections in the legs of the undercarriage, unsuitable placement of the intercom and oxygen plugs, occasional loss of coolant in one of the engines, too narrow a width on the exhaust stub nuts, defective RPM indicators and leaks from the hydraulic system. After a conference at MAP on 26 January 1941, it was agreed that most of these could be remedied by more rigorous maintenance or minor adjustments in the design.

But there was one defect that caused far greater concern, leading to the grounding of the Lancaster fleet and even the involvement of Winston Churchill. In mid-December, A&AEE reported that on one Lancaster 'some rivets had been pulling out of the wing panel of the outer engines' and that the skin on the wing at this point was also wrinkling.[6] Far from being a singular occurrence, the problem arose in other aircraft once the Lancaster had begun full operations in the early spring. The Lancasters of 44 Squadron had first gone into action on the night of 3–4 March 1942, carrying out mine-laying duties off the north German coast. In the parlance of the RAF, these were known as 'gardening' operations and the mines were called 'vegetables'. The mission passed off without any losses and a week later, on the night of 10–11 March, two Lancasters from 44 Squadron had joined a force of 126 other bombers in attacking Essen in the Ruhr valley, the first sortie conducted by the Lancaster over German soil. It was after 97 Squadron's first operation that the fears about the seriousness of the wing defect grew within Bomber Command.

On 20 March six Lancasters had been dispatched from their new base at Woodhall Spa in Lincolnshire to drop mines in the waters near the Friesian Islands. But soon after take-off in heavy, low cloud, the pilot of one of them, Ernest 'Rod' Rodley, realized to his horror that instead of climbing over the English coast, he was barely above the skyline of Boston in Lincolnshire. As he later recalled, 'I eased her up as gently as possible, not wanting to stall into the town and we roared across the rooftops.' He had begun climbing when suddenly his engineer yelled that one wing tip was missing and the other damaged. 'I looked out and on the starboard side there was just a bright jagged aluminium line where the tip used to be. On the port side, a six-foot high green and sand tip of camouflage paint stood at right angles to the wing.' Rodley knew that, with the weather appalling and the plane damaged, there was no chance of continuing the trip or returning to his base. 'I certainly couldn't fling this Lanc about just trying to make a bad weather circuit. Just then we crossed the coast and I saw a beautiful flat expanse of sand, ample for my purpose, so I decided to put her down.' The spot Rodley had chosen was a beach by the Wash. By the time he had brought the Lancaster to a stop, the rest of the crew had already jumped out. The group of seven then trudged through the mist and stopped at the first pub they found. When they later reached their base, Rodley found that his superior officers were doubtful about his tale of wing tips tearing off so easily. They intimated that he had 'deliberately flown low and knocked my wing tips off on the roofs'.[7] Less sceptical was Roy Chadwick, who drove over to Woodhall Spa to interview the pilot. Rodley later recalled their meeting:

> He said to me, 'I'm from Avros and I would like you to tell me about the wing tip trouble. You will realize that it is terribly important to get the

Lancaster right without delay, so I want you to tell me in complete confidence the whole story and I can assure you that nothing will get back to the Air Force. I don't care what you were up to when the wing tips failed – but I must know.' His demeanour was so straightforward and man-to-man that if I had been looping the Lancaster, I would have confessed. So I repeated my story and was impressed by the way he accepted that my speed was moderate when the tips went.[8]

The initial scepticism towards Rodley evaporated when the wing tips were salvaged, one from Boston and the other from the wreck, and they both showed a structural failure. This caused as much concern in Bomber Command as it did in Avro. Immediately No. 5 Group instructed that all its Lancasters should be grounded while inspections to the wing surfaces were carried out. The inspections revealed a weakness in the tip attachments, so a programme was drawn up to replace them with stronger parts. Such work was not particularly laborious, but it gave Churchill the opportunity to seek more help from Roosevelt with the heavy-bomber strategy. Now that the USA was in the war, following the Japanese attack on Pearl Harbour on 7 December 1941, Churchill was desperate for the American air force to come to England in substantial numbers. 'Our bombing force has not expanded as we hoped,' he wrote on 29 March. 'We have had a heavy disappointment in a structural defect with the wing tips of the Lancasters which required laying up the squadrons of our latest and best for several months.' The first US heavy bombers were due to arrive in July. Churchill now begged Roosevelt to expedite their arrival. 'Never was so much good work to be done and so few to do it. We must not let our summer air attacks fall into a second-rate affair.'[9]

With his gift for melodramatic grandiloquence, Churchill had exaggerated both the influence of the first Lancaster squadrons and the extent of the suspension of operations. 'You will wish to know,' the Directorate of Technical Development told Freeman on the very day that Churchill wrote to Roosevelt, 'that the wing tip trouble on the Lancaster is open to quick remedy which is now being applied. If all goes well according to the present plans, Bomber Command's Lancasters should be modified in three weeks' time and all Lancasters on the production line will be modified for issue.'[10] In fact, while the refitting programme was underway, the Lancasters were allowed to return to flying, on condition that there were daily inspections of their wings. Mine laying resumed and it was on 24–25 March, just four days after the Boston crash, that a Lancaster squadron experienced its first casualties, when a plane from 44 Squadron went missing on a trip off Lorient in Brittany. But the wing problem had not been permanently resolved. That reality became all too tragically clear on 18 April, when a Lancaster with the refashioned wing tip was conducting intensive flying tests for the A&AEE. The establishment's official report described what happened. 'The aircraft was seen to come through the cloud base at about 4000 feet in a slight dive. It then rolled, port wing down through about 180°, came back level right way up again and dived straight into the ground with engines full on. It struck at about 60° and blew up. The explosion was severe enough to break windows 300 yards away and scatter wreckage over several fields.'[11] Despite the devastation, enough of the wing structure survived to reveal that the blame lay with the system of attaching the wing skin panel to the front spar.

Chadwick was summoned to a meeting in London with the Air Ministry's Directorate of Technical Development to discuss the problem. This should not be seen as any kind of crisis for the Lancaster. Compared to the Halifax, Stirling and Manchester, the introduction of the Lancaster had been astonishingly smooth. Indeed, the Air Ministry stressed that even after the accident at Boscombe Down: 'We are reasonably safe in allowing Bomber Command to continue flying the Lancaster, provided they maintain daily inspections.'[12] Furthermore, at the meeting itself, it was confirmed that 'the fully modified wing tip now being supplied retrospectively has a satisfactory reserve of strength', while indirect praise for the Lancaster's aerodynamics could also be found in the possibility, voiced by the Directorate of Technical Development, 'as to whether the high manoeuvrability of the Lancaster was such as to impose unduly large loads on the structure, so that it might be advisable to make the controls heavier'. It was pointed out that the controls actually got heavier with speed so 'no modification was required'.[13] On the key issue of wing construction, Chadwick agreed that he should add extra screws where the panelling was attached to the front spar, strengthen the panelling around the engines and also use traditional rivets rather the 'pop' rivets that Avro had initially favoured because they eased the production process.

It was a tribute to the simplicity, reliability and quality of the Lancaster's design that this was the worst of the Mark I's early problems. As the Air Ministry admitted, there were far fewer teething troubles than was usual with a new aircraft 'because of the extensive experience gained on the Manchester'.[14] During the coming years, there would be changes to the armament, the installation of different engines, the introduction of new equipment and changes in bomb load, resulting in a number of other marks, but the basic structure of the Lancaster remained the same for the rest of its service in the RAF. The inherent excellence of the plane was quickly recognized in government circles once it had entered the squadrons. In his diary early in 1942, the Minister for Economic Warfare and Labour MP Hugh Dalton recorded a conversation with Sir Archibald Sinclair. Having set out the case for an intensification of the bomber offensive, Sinclair then declared: 'There has been great disappointment both over the weather and over the delay in big output of heavy bombers. These last have had severe teething troubles but these are now over and the Air Staff are very pleased with the results. The Lancasters, the latest, are the best of all. Soon, aided by the latest developments, we should see some really formidable results.'[15]

The 'latest developments' were in the field of navigation, where the absence of effective aids and target-finding devices had been one of the causes of the disastrous bombing inaccuracy revealed in the D. M. Butt report. In the opening years of the war, bombers had to rely on primitive manual techniques like dead reckoning, which was essentially a simple method of following a set course to the target, taking account of the effect of predicted winds from the start of the journey. The big problems were not only that forecasts were notoriously unreliable but also that wind directions and speeds often changed dramatically during a sortie, so planes could be blown miles off course. Searching for landmarks on the ground or using astral fixes from the stars could be just as useless in heavy weather over blacked-out territory. In desperation, crews frequently resorted to bombing on Estimated Time of Arrival, or ETA, based on the calculation of how long it would take to reach the target flying at a certain speed from their base. Robin Murray, a Wellington pilot, gave this graphic description of how inaccurate bombing according to ETA could be. 'You couldn't see anything, you didn't know where you were in relation to the place you were supposed to bomb, but that was the estimated time of arrival, so that's the time you bombed.'[16]

It was the Lancaster's good fortune to arrive in service just at the moment when a sophisticated new navigational device had reached the squadrons, thereby greatly enhancing the bomber's capability. This aid was called Gee, short for Ground Electronics Engineering, and it had been in development since the summer of 1940 by the Telecommunications Radio Establishment, under the guidance of the pioneering scientist Robert Dippy. After successful trials in the autumn of 1941, it was first used in Bomber Command's operational aircraft from March 1942. Inspired by radar technology, the system used three transmitters spread out in an arc over 200 miles along the south coast of England, each of them transmitting a wave of precisely timed electronic pulses. These were then picked up by a Gee set, called the TR1335, on board the aircraft at the navigator's table. The TR1335 equipment was basically a cathode-ray receiver, on whose screen the measured time differences between the pulses appeared as blips. Interpreting the blips and then plotting this information on a grid set out in special Gee charts, a well-trained navigator could provide a reasonably accurate 'fix', or assessment of the aircraft's position, at any given moment as long as the Gee transmitters were within range. This distance limitation, though, was one of the drawbacks of the system. Because the pulses travelled in a straight line, Gee was restricted by the curvature of the earth to a maximum range of 400 miles, though even after 200 miles it became increasingly less effective. In addition, the Germans eventually found that it could be jammed by their own transmitters. Nevertheless, it was a significant breakthrough for Bomber Command, bringing the Ruhr valley and the northern German ports within the scope of accurate operations. 'It was a wonderful instrument, very easy to use. You could find your position very accurately,' said Alec Flett, a navigator with 460 and 625 Squadrons.[17]

The navigator was part of a crew of seven in the Lancaster, the other roles being the pilot, engineer, wireless operator, bomb aimer, mid-upper gunner and rear gunner. Most of the configuration was dictated by the obvious requirements of flying, bombing and defensive fire, but there was one aspect that had provoked a lengthy debate within the government. This was the proposal that the Lancaster, unlike the previous generation of bombers, should not have a co-pilot, with the place taken instead by the engineer. There were several reasons for this. One was that, at a stroke, it would halve the number of pilots who would have to be trained, so crews could become operational more quickly. Another was that the greater complexity of the Lancaster's engines, fuel systems and hydraulics would require a specialist. Moreover, according to one Air Ministry technical paper arguing for the change, past experience had shown that 'the presence of a second pilot is more of an embarrassment to the first pilot than an assistance. He feels the responsibility of allowing the second pilot to undertake a proportion of the flying which he himself can carry out more efficiently.'[18] The installation of an automatic pilot, it was argued, would deal with concerns about the captain suffering fatigue on long trips into the Reich. The claim that a second pilot would be needed in an emergency was also dismissed by the Air Ministry's training directorate. 'The number of cases in which a second pilot has flown his aircraft back to the base owing to the death or casualty of the first pilot are extremely few. It would be offset many times by the accidents involved during the training of second pilots.'[19] The discussion dragged on for several weeks, something that annoyed Avro. At the Air Ministry's insistence and much to its own 'very strong opposition', Avro had been asked to design a dual-control arrangement for future Lancasters. Having just come up with a satisfactory scheme, the company was then exasperated to learn that it might not be required if there were to be no co-pilot.[20]

The debate over crew organization was the first that involved Sir Arthur Harris, who had taken over as Commander-in-Chief of Bomber Command on 22 February 1942. A stubborn dislike of almost any suggestion from the Air Ministry was to be one of Harris's trademarks throughout the war, and it was on display in his first week in office. 'I do not agree with the one pilot policy as a matter of preference. On the contrary, I consider that for many reasons it is undesirable,' he wrote, those reasons including the need to support the captain and risks in an emergency.[21] But Harris reluctantly accepted the policy, if only on the grounds of a need to reduce the strain on training resources. He insisted, however, that every Lancaster had to have an automatic pilot and that 'one member of the aircrew must receive sufficient training to enable him to bring the aircraft back over this country in the event of the pilot being killed or seriously injured'.[22] After more discussions and trials, it was finally agreed in June that this job should be given to the engineer.

Harris's arrival had been the equivalent of an electric shock to the system. Since the departure of the discredited Sir Richard Pierse on 8 January 1942, Bomber Command had been under the interim leadership of Jack Baldwin, a former head of No. 3 Group, who later followed Pierse to India. But Harris had been the only possible choice to take over on a permanent basis, since no one else at the top of the RAF had his range of experience, including spells as commander of No. 5 Group and Deputy Chief of the Air Staff. With Bomber Command at its lowest ebb following the disasters of the previous year, Arthur Harris was exactly the man needed to galvanize the organization. Large, slightly portly, with a bristling ginger moustache and sandy hair, he exuded fighting spirit from the moment he entered Bomber Command's headquarters at High Wycombe is Buckinghamshire. His passionate belief in strategic bombing was reflected in one of his first public statements as the new chief: 'A lot of people are in the habit of iterating the silly phrase, "bombing can never win a war". Well, we shall see. It hasn't been tried yet.'[23] Ferociously combative, often bad-tempered and aggressively intolerant of any opinion but his own, he had a gift for creating rows and making enemies. His fierce independence and disdain for officialdom made him resentful of any attempts by the Air Ministry to interfere with his work.

At Bomber Command Headquarters, his dominating personality inspired a mix of admiration, loyalty and fear among those who worked for him. His Senior Air Staff Officer, Robert Saundby, effectively his deputy, showed such unquestioning devotion that he refused all offers to take up an operational command of his own. Others were less enamoured. Wing Commander Thomas Murray, who served for a time at High Wycombe between his Lancaster tours, said, 'He relished this power business and as a person I did not admire him. Of course he believed that he would win the war entirely with bombing. He was an arrogant chap and was pretty difficult to work with.'[24] The strength of Harris's volcanic character was sensed by the men in the front-line squadrons, even though the demands on his time meant he rarely left High Wycombe. Indeed, the sense of distance only seemed to add to his stature. The Lancaster pilot Jack Currie wrote this memorable passage about the influence of Harris:

> He was in fact distanced from us by such far echelons of rank and stations, that he was a figure more of imagination than reality. Uninhibited by any bounds of truth, we were able to ascribe to him any characteristic that our spirits needed. It pleased us to think of him as utterly callous, indifferent to our suffering and unconcerned about our fate. There was a paradoxical comfort in serving such a dread commander: no grievance, no complaint, no criticism could possibly affect him. You might as well complain to Jupiter that the rain was wet.[25]

Harris's acerbic, sometimes morbid, sense of humour added to his image of ruthlessness, which he was only too keen to cultivate. On one notorious occasion, he was being driven at high speed in his black Bentley towards London when his car was stopped by the police. 'You could have killed someone,' said the aggrieved constable through Harris's window. 'Young man, I kill thousands of people every night,' was the laconic reply.[26]

But it is one of the many myths of the war that he was known by his men as 'Butcher' Harris, supposedly a reference to his barbarity not so much towards the Germans as towards his own crews. In fact, he was called 'Butch' throughout the RAF, just a classic English nickname without any connotations of mass slaughter. Rex Oldland, a Lancaster engineer with 75 Squadron, was adamant on this point. 'A lot of writers would have you believe we called him "Butcher". That is quite untrue. He was known as Butch. The term then just meant strong, vigorous, resolute.'[27]

In his own circle, however, Harris preferred to be called Bert, or 'Bud' by his wife Therese, and privately he hated the nickname 'Butch'. For all his grim toughness in running the war, Harris could be a generous host at his official residence of Springfield near the Bomber Command head-quarters at High Wycombe, which he shared with his wife and their young daughter. In fact, he often complained to the Air Ministry about the paltry allowance he was given for entertaining guests in his home, a task that he saw as vital in promoting awareness of the bombing offen-sive. It was his standard practice, after lunch or dinner, to show his official guests his large blue books which provided a detailed photographic commentary on the devastation of Germany. The scientist Solly Zuckerman, who was a key adviser to the Air Staff on the technical aspects of bombing, left this account of his first meeting with Harris:

> I was much taken by his quiet sense of power and determination. No two of the many air marshals whom I already knew were alike but he seemed more remote, more self-contained than any I had met before. He changed into a mulberry-coloured velvet smoking jacket and disappeared into the kitchen to prepare Eggs Benedict with his own hands, so revealing to me that the culinary arts were one of the joys of his life. At the end of the meal he also surprised me by the ceremonial way he prepared what I took to be snuff.[28]

The combination of self-containment and determination, referred to by Zuckerman, was the result of Harris's unconventional background. Adversity forged his self-reliance, isolation his suspicion of established authority. The youngest of six children, he was born in 1892 in Cheltenham. His father, who suffered from profound deafness, was a civil engineer, employed by the government of Madras in India, but there was no hint of imperial grandeur about Harris's upbringing. All but abandoned by his parents when they returned to India, he spent most of his lonely child-hood in a succession of West Country boarding schools or lodging with families who took pity on his plight. By the time he left school, Harris regarded his father almost as a stranger, so understandably he ignored a paternal request to sign up for the British army. Instead he travelled to southern Africa, where he worked in a succession of manual jobs, includ-ing farm labourer, rancher and livestock supplier to local miners.

During the First World War, he initially signed up with the First Rhodesian Regiment, fighting against the German forces in East Africa. But in 1915, bored with endless marching, he travelled to England to join the Royal Flying Corps, becoming a highly resourceful and cour-ageous pilot with an obvious talent for leadership. His experiences flying over the western front, however, gave him an abiding repugnance of trench warfare. After the Armistice, Harris stayed in the newly formed Royal Air Force, serving first in India and then in Iraq. It was in the Middle East that he again displayed his originality when he turned the transport carrier Vickers Vernon into a makeshift bomber by installing a bomb rack under its fuselage and creating a hole in the nose for the aimer. Further steps up the RAF hierarchy followed in the 1930s, including one stint in Palestine and another in Yorkshire as commander of No. 4 Group, before he took over No. 5 Group on the outbreak of war. His performance in this post inspired the head of Bomber Command, Sir Edgar Ludlow-Hewitt, to write to Portal about Harris's character. 'He has an exceptionally alert, creative and enterprising mind balanced by long, practical experience. His particular talents lie mainly along practical lines, but his ideas are inspired by an unusually well-developed imagination.'[29]

Harris's willingness to challenge convention also applied to his surprisingly exuberant private life. During the First World War, he had married Barbara Money, the daughter of an Indian Army officer, but the relationship floundered after Harris embarked on a series of affairs while serving in the Middle East, with the result that the couple were divorced in 1935 on the grounds of Harris's misconduct. In her old age Barbara Money said that she might have been able to put up with his infidelities, but 'not the very rude way' he spoke to her.[30] Soon after the divorce Harris remarried, this time to Therese Hearne, another Indian Army officer's daughter. Despite her strict Catholic upbringing and the age difference between them, it was a successful union, partly because Therese – whom Harris always called Jill – felt devoted to him. 'He was so kind and patient,' she once said, not words that would be echoed by anyone in the Air Ministry.[31]

When Harris arrived at Bomber Command, his front line had a mere 44 medium and heavy bomber squadrons, a force of only about 469 night bombers, of which just 54 were Lancasters. But because of his supreme self-confidence and his clear objectives, he was undaunted by the task that lay before him. The army liaison officer at High Wycombe, Charles Carrington, described his immediate impact. 'As a horse knows by instinct whether his rider holds the reins by a firm hand, so Bomber Command knew it had a master. The whole machine tautened up, seemed to move into a higher gear.'[32] Apart from the introduction of the Lancaster and Gee equipment, Harris had one other great advantage over his predecessor Sir Richard Pierse: the Air Staff was now firmly committed to the policy of area bombing against Germany. Just a week before Harris's arrival, Sir Archibald Sinclair had told Portal that 'the bomber offensive should be resumed' and 'sustained at the maximum intensity of which Bomber Command is capable'.[33] This instruction was given formal effect by a new Air Staff directive which authorized Harris to employ his effort 'without restriction'. The primary object of the renewed campaign 'should now be focused on the morale of the enemy civilian population and, in particular, of industrial workers'.[34] Just to clarify that civilians were the target, Sir Charles Portal wrote a note to his deputy Norman Bottomley stressing that 'the aiming points are to be the built-up areas, not, for instance, the dockyards or aircraft factories. This must be made quite clear if it is not already understood.'[35] The Chief of the Air Staff and his new head of Bomber Command were now in unison.

Harris's position was made even stronger by mounting support from Downing Street, desperate for some military success after the humiliating fall of Singapore to the Japanese on 15 February 1942. In March Churchill's chief scientific adviser Lord Cherwell produced an influential paper which appeared to set out a clear scientific case for area bombing. Using an analysis of the effects of the German Blitz on Birmingham and Hull, Cherwell claimed that 'one ton of bombs dropped on a built-up area demolishes 20–40 dwellings and turns 100–200 people out of house and home'. He then extrapolated these figures for Germany in the context of forthcoming bomber production. 'In 1938 over 22 million Germans lived in 58 towns of over 100,000 inhabitants, which, with modern equipment, should be easy to find and hit. Our forecast output of heavy bombers (including Wellingtons) between now and the middle of 1943 is about 10,000. If even half the total load of 10,000 bombers were dropped on the built up areas of these 58 German towns, the great majority of their inhabitants would be turned out of house and home.'[36] The term 'dehousing' – or sometimes 'unhousing' – would soon become a familiar euphemism within the Air Staff and the government, though most understood that the bombers were aiming just as much for their inhabitants as their buildings.

The lethal reality behind such neutral language could be found in the growing use of incendiaries as the key element of the RAF's bomb load. In the first years of the war, incendiaries made up only 5 per cent of loads, the vast majority of which comprised 1,000-, 500- or 250-pound general-purpose bombs. These were prone to failure and ineffectual in their results, not least because their steel shells meant that they contained almost as much metal as explosive. By the time the Lancaster came into service, a new generation of high-capacity blast bombs had been introduced, the most powerful of them the 4,000 pound 'Cookie'. This was a large, green-painted cylinder, looking like an oil drum, which contained amatol, minol and tritonal. Given its shape, it lacked any aerodynamic qualities but, with its thin shell, it had a far greater charge-to-weight ratio than the general-purpose bomb, so it could create a shock wave that would demolish a large building on impact. Medium-capacity blast bombs had also been developed, ranging from 500 pounds to 4,000 pounds, aimed at exploiting the greater lift capacity of the new 'heavies'. But in the context of area bombing, the Air Staff was not interested in the mere demolition of buildings. Something far more physically devastating was needed to shatter the morale of the enemy, and the answer lay in incendiaries. As Sir Norman Bottomley candidly wrote in an Air Staff paper: 'The ultimate aim of the attack on a town area is to break the morale of the population which occupied it. To ensure this we must achieve two things. First we must make the town physically uninhabitable and secondly we must make the people conscious of constant physical danger.' The best way to achieve those twin objectives, he wrote, was through 'saturation by incendiaries'.[37]

Since 1940 government researchers had been working on weapons that could spread raging fire through a city or town. By far the best they had come up with was the four-pound incendiary charge, a stick 22 inches long, hexagonal in shape and made of magnesium alloy, which melted into a flaming mass once ignited by the bomb's firing mechanism. These deadly four-pounders were delivered from the heavy bombers in containers which opened at around 600 feet over the target, allowing the charges to separate and then descend at high speed over a wide area. Other types of incendiaries were used, including the 30-pound liquid bomb, which could spread a viscous benzole-rubber solution over half an acre, and the 30-pound flame-jet bomb with its gallon and a half of gasoline and methane gas igniter. But for all their pyrotechnics, neither proved as harmful as the four-pounder, of which the RAF dropped more than 80 million during the war, 650,000 of them on Dresden alone.[38] It is another rich irony of the Lancaster saga that its most important bomb should also turn out to be its lightest.

The crucial question facing the Air Staff in early 1942 was what proportion of the heavy bombers' loads should be made up of incendiaries to achieve the maximum amount of destruction. For it was not enough just to start fires on the ground. Those fires needed to be fed by air, which in turn required the roofs, doors and windows of buildings to be blown out in order to create violent draughts across the target area. A balance therefore had to be struck between incendiaries and high explosive (HE). What is fascinating is how far the Air Staff used the lessons of the Blitz to resolve the equation. In March the Directorate of Bombing Operations at the Air Ministry sent a letter to all 12 regional commanders of the National Fire Service in England, asking them which type of bombs had caused the worst conflagrations during the German raids of 1940–1. In all but one case, the chiefs said that incendiaries were responsible for at least 80 per cent of the fires during the Blitz, with some putting the figure as high as 95 per cent.

In the light of this information, the Bombing Operations Directorate wanted incendiaries to have the overwhelming preponderance in the loads dropped on German cities. As Syd Bufton put it: 'The destruction of a city by fire can only be achieved by creating a large-scale conflagration or series of conflagrations within the built-up area of the city.' Stressing that the goal was to hit the population rather than industry, Bufton wrote of 'the paramount importance of bombers aiming at and concentrating their loads in the densest and most vulnerable areas of the city'. But Harris, though a passionate advocate of mass urban assaults, was reluctant to subscribe wholeheartedly to the Ministry's view on incendiaries, partly because of his dislike of being told how to run his operations, and partly because he believed that high explosives had a vital role to play in destruction.

The divergence in outlook was to become apparent after the first two major raids on German towns by Bomber Command under Harris's leadership. Determined to reveal the potential of his force after all the dismal results of the previous two years, Harris decided to mount an area attack that would simultaneously cause a shudder in Germany, raise the morale of his men and demonstrate to the government his willingness to be ruthless in enacting the policy of area bombing. He chose as his first target the ancient port of Lübeck, a historic town full of winding medieval streets. It was singled out for attack not because it had any military importance but for precisely the opposite reason: it had none and therefore had few defences. On the night of 28–9 March 1942, 234 Stirling and Wellington bombers attacked Lübeck, dropping 144 tons of bombs and killing 320 people. By setting the town ablaze, Harris had the impact he wanted. Josef Goebbels, the Nazi propaganda chief, wrote in his diary: 'I have been shown a newsreel of the destruction. It is horrible. We can't get away from the fact that the English air raids have increased in scope and importance. If they continue for weeks on these lines, they might conceivably have a demoralising effect on the population.'[39]

The Air Staff, though gratified at the offensive spirit shown by Harris, feared that he had not recognized the key role of incendiaries and was still placing too much emphasis on high explosives and blast bombs. It was this oversight, they argued, that led to the comparative failure of a heavy attack a few weeks later on the northern port of Rostock, where nothing like the number of incendiaries were dropped as fell on Lübeck. 'The moral seems to be,' wrote Freeman to Harris, 'that unless the incendiary attack is on a large scale and concentrated in time and space, it will not achieve any decisive degree of destruction.' Too much HE, he said, would 'detract' from the chances of 'starting a really satisfactory conflagration'.[40] In his reply, Harris argued that the effect of high explosives was underrated, while incendiaries had caused devastation in Lübeck only because of the unique fabric of its medieval architecture. 'We mustn't expect any more Lübecks because there ain't no such places. We blotted the only one there was. Lübeck was easy money.' He went on: 'I am always being pressed to concentrate entirely on incendiaries but I do not agree with this policy. The moral effect of HE is vast. People can escape from fires and the casualties on a solely fire-raising raid would be as nothing.' After explaining that his ideal proportions in an average bomb load were two-thirds incendiary to one-third high explosive, he then gave his own brutal summation of the aim of area bombing. 'What we want to do in addition to the horrors of the fire is to bring the masonry crashing down on top of the Boche, to kill Boche and to terrify Boche.'[41]

The Air Staff, while agreeing with Harris that the ideal heavy bomber load was generally two-thirds incendiary and one-third HE, felt that he had still not sufficiently embraced the concept of mass fire attacks on the larger cities. 'We continue to urge that, to obtain the devastation from incendiary attack,' wrote Bufton to Freeman, 'it must be carried out on a full scale, employing in the region of 200,000 incendiary bombs plus a relatively small tonnage of HE spread out over the whole operation purely to keep heads down and strike fear into the firefighters.' Bufton further argued that, contrary to Harris's claims, there were 'a great many German towns and cities which are even more vulnerable to incendiary attack than Lübeck'. Cologne, in northwest Germany, was the city specifically mentioned by Bufton as a place where a vast concentration of four-pound incendiaries could achieve 'outstanding results'.[42] This was backed up by the Air Intelligence branch of the Ministry, which asserted that 'we may now hope to unhouse great quantities of the population living in the inner residential zones by fire. There seems no reason why, if we can achieve the proper concentration of incendiary bombs, we should not do proportionately as much damage to Cologne as we did to Lübeck', especially because the inner residential area of Cologne 'has a density of population four times as high as that of the inner town of Lübeck'.[43] The Air Ministry was now just as ruthless as Harris about mass carnage.

The differences between the Air Ministry and Harris were nothing compared to far wider objections in other parts of the government and military towards the entire heavy-bombing strategy. To critics of the RAF, the bomber offensive was misguided, the resources devoted to it misplaced. In particular, at the height of the Battle of the Atlantic and Field Marshal Erwin Rommel's advance in North Africa, the other services were alarmed at the priority given to the Lancaster and Halifax programmes. Sir James Grigg, the Secretary of State for War, pointed out that the heavy-bomber production workforce equalled the British army's manpower and claimed that the RAF would soon consume almost half of Britain's war production.[44] The Cabinet minister Leo Amery thought that, in their determination to avoid the quagmire of the western front, Portal and Harris were actually repeating the First World War's mistaken strategy of trying to grind down the enemy. 'It is in essence the same policy of "killing Germans" and damning "side-shows" which did not directly kill Germans for which Gallipoli and all its incalculable possibilities were sacrificed in the last war,' he told Churchill.[45] Amery believed the RAF had 'exaggerated beyond all measure the idea of independent air action and underestimated the importance of air action as part of land and sea action'.[46]

To undermine the objectors and justify the growing investment in the heavy-bomber programme, Harris knew his Command needed to do something spectacular that would capture the imagination of the British public. Up until the middle of April 1942, the Lancasters had played only a sporadic part in the newly intensified bomber offensive. None of them took part in the attack on Lübeck in March and just seven participated in a raid on Hamburg on 8–9 April. But then a daring operation by 44 and 97 Squadrons won the crews of the RAF's newest bomber an instant reputation for heroism, and dramatically revealed the plane's capability. On 16 April the two squadrons, which had both been undertaking long-distance trials in the Lancaster, were informed that they would be carrying out a sortie the next day. No details were given but the imposition of tight security on their bases, including the disconnection of telephones and confinement to camp, showed that a significant attack was planned.

The next morning at 11 a.m., the crews gathered for their briefings, each held separately at their own stations. To their astonishment, they were told that their mission would be a daylight attack on the southern German town of Augsburg, where the MAN factory (Maschinenfabrik Augsburg Nurnberg AG) turned out diesel engines for U-boats. Rod Rodley of 97 Squadron recalled that moment the target was revealed: 'there was a roar of laughter instead of a gasp of horror. No one believed that the air force would be so stupid as to send 12 of its newest four-engined bombers all that distance inside Germany in daylight.'[47] This would be a trip to tax the courage of the men and the strength of the Lancaster, fifteen hundred miles across enemy territory. The plan was for six Lancasters from each squadron to head for the south coast, fly low across France towards the Swiss border, seeking to avoid German radar, and then turn at Lake Constance towards Augsburg. The raid was to be led by John Nettleton of 44 Squadron, a tall, reticent South African who had trained in the merchant navy before joining the RAF in 1938. Filled with the Lancaster's maximum amount of fuel, 2,154 gallons, each plane was to carry four 1,000-pound general-purpose bombs.

The first Lancasters took off from their bases at 3 p.m., the theory being that the dwindling hours of daylight would offer them just enough visibility to see their target, but then protective darkness would envelop them on the long journey back to England. As planned, the two squadrons reached the Sussex headland of Sesley Bill, and then, with incredible verve, the pilots flew at little more than 60 feet over the English Channel. To provide more cover, several squadrons of Boston medium bombers had been sent over northern French targets to divert the German fighters away from the raid. But the attempt to deceive the Luftwaffe backfired badly. A band of Me 109s were indeed lured into the air, but then the Lancasters of 44 Squadron flew directly into their path over France. As the RAF bombers skimmed over villages and fields, the German aircraft descended on them with cannon blazing. Within half an hour of savage, one-sided combat, four of the squadron's Lancasters had been shot down before the Messerschmitts, concerned about fuel and lack of radar cover over central France, returned to their bases. Despite losing a third of his aircraft, Nettleton pressed on with the raid, demonstrating the kind of unwavering spirit for which Bomber Command would become renowned. The remaining eight Lancasters continued to fly as low as they could, sometimes no more than 25 feet, following the contours of the landscape. As Nettleton said in a subsequent BBC interview: 'You can imagine what that must have been like, 30 tons or so of aircraft, its four engines roaring, driving along at several miles a minute. Horses and cattle in the field scattered in front of us. We saw two German officers out riding. Their horses bolted and they were still out of control when we last saw them.'[48] Rod Rodley of 97 Squadron had equally vivid memories of the sights at low level: 'Occasionally you would see some Frenchmen take a second look and wave their berets or their shovels. A bunch of German soldiers doing PT in their singlets broke hurriedly from their shelters as we roared over. The next opposition was a German officer on one of the steamers on Lake Constance firing a revolver at us. I could see him quite clearly, using his Luger to defend the ladies against 48 Browning guns.'[49]

Still flying at full throttle below 300 feet, the Lancasters sped across southern Germany until they approached Augsburg. Coming over the brow of a hill, they saw the big sheds of the MAN works amid the chimneys and rooftops. But the Germans were ready for them. As the Lancasters roared on towards the factory, the anti-aircraft guns burst into life, sending an intense barrage into the twilit sky. 'I dropped the bombs against the side wall,' recalled Rodley. 'We flashed across the target and down the other side to about 50 feet, because flak was quite heavy. As we went away I could see light flak shells overtaking us, green balls flowing away on our right and hitting the ground ahead of us.'[50] Though the factory was hit and set ablaze, three more of the Lancasters were shot down. The remaining five, with Nettleton still at their head, turned westward, returned across France in the darkness and landed back at the bases at one o'clock in the morning.

The raid on Augsburg had achieved its objective at great human cost, confirming to the RAF the risks of daylight bombing. Pip Beck, the Waddington radio-telephone operator, recorded: 'It was not until the next morning that I learned the terrible toll the raid had exacted. There was no way to express the horror that I, like everyone else on the station, felt. The whole camp seemed shocked and silent.'[51] Moreover, for all the direct hits that the MAN factory had taken, the target had only limited economic significance. In fact Lord Selborne, the Minister of Economic Warfare, complained directly to Churchill about Bomber Command's lack of consultation over the raid, claiming that the attack would only delay submarine production by 'two or three months'. What was disturbing, wrote Selborne, was that 'such a target should have been given priority over all the targets which have been so often recommended by this Ministry and which I believe are accepted by the Air Staff as being of the greatest priority . . . Unless our bombing of economic objectives is planned with the greatest care and the plan strictly adhered to, even the highest skill and courage in directing and carrying out operations will not achieve any commensurate success.'[52] Churchill, who professed to find Selborne's charge 'very disquieting',[53] passed the complaint to Harris. This was exactly the sort of political interference that the Bomber Command chief always despised. He told Churchill that the Ministry of Economic Warfare's ideas often took no account of operational realities, while its priorities 'can seldom, in the nature of things, be the over-riding factor amongst so many that are so often opposed'. Bomber Command's aim with raids like that on Augsburg, he explained, was 'to force the Boche to spread his air and anti-aircraft defences all over the continent'.[54]

Yet, for all the losses and political controversies, the Augsburg Mission was undoubtedly a propaganda triumph for the RAF. It was a glorious narrative of courage in adversity, with the brave Lancaster pilots taking the air war to the heart of the Reich's industrial machine. As so often during these years, Churchill captured the national mood when he called Augsburg 'an outstanding achievement of the RAF'.[55] In recognition of their inspiring tenacity, all the survivors of the raid were decorated, Nettleton with the Victoria Cross and the other survivors with the DSO, DFC or DFM. But perhaps the greatest consequence of Augsburg was that it made the public aware of the Lancaster for the first time. Before the raid, its name had barely been mentioned, as all attention was focused on the Stirling, Halifax and Manchester. Yet now it seemed the most formidable addition to the bomber fleet. It was Nettleton himself who, in his BBC interview, emphasized the importance of the plane:

> We Lancaster crews believe that in the Lancaster we have got the answer for heavy bombing. We have tremendous confidence in everything about the Lancasters and in the workers who are turning them out in such numbers. We know that we are only sent to attack the most worthwhile targets. We believe that the way to win the war is to have our own spring offensive before Hitler has his and in places not of his choice but of ours.[56]

Emboldened by the response to the Augsburg raid, Bomber Command now started planning a far more sensational raid, one that in its breath-taking scale could not fail to shock the enemy and impress at home. The conception of this vast effort would show Harris at his best: decisive, bold, a master of organization and planning, willing to shoulder enormous responsibilities and take audacious risks. At the heart of his plan lay a recognition of the psychological importance of numerical symbolism. He decided that, at the end of May, Bomber Command would mount a raid by over 1,000 planes against a northwestern German city, the attack to be code-named, appropriately, Operation Millennium. At first glance the whole idea seemed absurd. After all, his Command still had fewer than 500 planes in front-line service. Moreover, with so many aircraft flying in the night sky towards one target, there initially appeared to be severe dangers of mass collisions or of bombs hitting other RAF planes. But such fears were soon overcome by a rigorous analysis conducted by the Operational Research Section of Bomber Command, which came up with the theory of the 'bomber stream', a new approach that was to be crucial to operations over the Reich. The bomber stream combined a large concentration of force, always one of Harris's central beliefs, with a high degree of safety by requiring the heavy bombers to cross a given point at the rate of about ten per minute. In practice, this meant that each group of ten planes could be spaced quite thinly in a box about three miles long, and five miles wide. Dr Basil Dickins, head of the Operational Research Section, later described how the conclusions were reached:

> There was a tremendous argument as to whether we should concentrate and accept the resultant risks. The interesting point here is that when a crew failed to return from an operation, that was just too bad, but if the crew returned with a hole in the wing caused by an incendiary bomb from above or if there was a jolly near miss, they would tell everyone about their close shave. This highlighted the collision risk. We had to reduce it all to mathematics and work out the actual chance of a collision. And it became quite obvious to us at ORS that while a collision was half a per cent risk, the chance of being shot down by Flak or fighters was three or four per cent. So we could allow the collision risk to mount quite a bit, provided that in doing so we would bring down the losses from other causes.[57]

The biggest problem facing Harris was how to build his force up to the figure of 1,000, given his limited numbers. The only solution was to call on all his reserves, then hope that the other services and RAF commands could also assist. Churchill lent Harris his support in this initiative, his sense of theatre attracted by the boldness of the plan. But others proved less co-operative. Neither the army nor the navy were willing to supply any aircraft, while Coastal Command also withdrew its backing. Harris refused to give up, and by the last week of May he had managed to cobble together some 1,046 planes, including a large number from training units to be flown by instructors. Through sheer determination, he had ensured that Operation Millennium would take place. His first instinct had been to choose Hamburg as the target, but at the last moment he switched to Cologne because the city seemed to promise both better weather and stronger reception for Gee.

On a moonlit night, on 30 May 1942, the huge aerial armada took off from bases across Lincolnshire and East Anglia, heading for the old centre of Cologne. Seventy-three Lancasters were sent as part of the force, their biggest raid so far. The rear gunner 'Chan' Chandler later joked how crowded the skies were. 'When we got to the coast we could see masses of aircraft and more arriving every minute. This was the bomber stream, and then some! Over the target there were so many aircraft that we could have done with traffic lights.'[58] Thanks to good planning and weak German defences, 90 per cent of the planes reached their target, dropping 1,455 tons of bombs on Cologne. In line with Harris's policy, two thirds of them were incendiaries, which started no fewer than 2,500 fires. What struck Hugh 'Pip' Parrott, a Lancaster wireless operator with 207 Squadron, was the tremendous distance from which the blaze could be seen:

> Before we crossed the English coast, the skipper said to the navigator, 'I think I can see a red glow in the sky. It is a long, long way away.' The navigator replied, 'That's Cologne. You don't need me any more. Just head for it.' We actually could see Cologne burning from England. Looking out, it was just a small red glow on the horizon. When we got there, the whole place was a sea of fire and we dropped our bombs into the middle of it. It was a piece of cake really. There was little real opposition.

Interestingly, Parrott faced up to the moral question of area bombing, the subject that was to cause such controversy in years to come:

> This was the only time I did not feel happy about dropping bombs on Germany because when we got there, the city was already burning, like a red hot fire. It gave no real satisfaction to drop another 15,000 incendiaries into that lot. That is the only time I felt we were going over the top. But I never had any compunction about bombing Germany. We were there to win the war. Whether our bombs hit a factory or the town hall, it made no difference to me. We had been bombed by Germany and we were doing the same thing back, only far more effectively.[59]

In terms of destruction, the raid certainly was effective. In Cologne 6,500 acres were obliterated, with the bombing estimated to have destroyed 13,000 houses, 250 factories, 9 hospitals, 4 hotels, 6 department stores and 16 schools. About 200,000 people were evacuated from the city. However, given the extent of the damage, the death toll was surprisingly low, just 486. This was partly because most northern German cities had a good network of public shelters, something that would increasingly frustrate

Harris as the offensive intensified over the next three years. But Göring, the head of the Luftwaffe who had once boasted that no enemy plane would fly over Germany, was appalled and at first refused to believe what had happened. 'Impossible. That many bombs cannot be dropped in a single night,' he said to the Gauleiter of Cologne, 'I tell you as Reichsmarschall that the figures cited are simply too high. How can you dare to report such fantasies to the Fuhrer?'[60] Having faced up to the reality, the Nazi-controlled press portrayed the event as an inhuman atrocity, led by 'British gangs of murderers who are waging war against the defenceless'.[61] German outrage only reinforced what a success the raid had been for Bomber Command. In wreaking such havoc, 43 bombers might have been lost, but at 3.8 per cent that was lower than the average loss rate up until then.

More importantly, the destruction of Cologne had an enormous impact both on the British public and internationally. 'Thanks Bomber Command, you're doing a grand job,' proclaimed a Gaumont newsreel.[62] The *Daily Mail*'s front page was dominated by the story of the attack, rejoicing in the 'loads unleashed from our gigantic Lancasters, Halifaxes, Stirlings and Manchesters. Last night Cologne, third city in Hitler's Reich, still smoked and smouldered from the greatest single bombardment that has ever been launched – from the land, sea or air.' An editorial in the paper declared that 'Cologne was just the beginning. Nothing will stop the development of this attack now. We are committed to the long-term policy of strategic bombardment.'[63] Having pulled off his phenomenal gamble, Harris was showered with congratulations. Telegrams came in from the Russian and US army air forces, while Churchill told Harris that the raid was a 'remarkable feat of organisation . . . This proof of the growing power of the British Bomber Force is also a herald of what Germany will receive, city by city, from now on.'[64] Harris himself, who was knighted less than a fortnight after the raid, felt his entire approach had been vindicated. 'My own opinion is that we should never have had a real bomber offensive if it had not been for the 1,000 bomber attack on Cologne, an irrefutable demonstration of the power of what was to all intents and purposes an untried weapon.'[65]

The rise in morale was at its keenest within Bomber Command, so used to setbacks before now. The arrival of the Lancaster and Harris signalled a new age, exemplified by the mighty strike against Cologne. The mood was captured in the diary of Paddy Rowling, an Australian who was undergoing his final training as a Lancaster navigator with 50 Squadron at the time of the raid. Though he did not fly with the bomber stream, he described the atmosphere at his base of Skellingthorpe in Lincolnshire, his account made all the more vivid by the use of contemporary RAF slang:

> 31st May: Today will be remembered for many long years, more especially by the residents of Cologne. We lost two out of eighteen kites the first night, but no-one I knew. That 1150 kites definitely reached the target is pukka gen [he slightly overestimated the size of the raid] and the fact that they were all over the area and bombed inside an hour and a half, one every six seconds, speaks for the organisation itself, undreamed of a year ago. It is the most gigantic bombardment from the air in history. Smoke from thousands of fires was visible from the Dutch coast 140 miles away. The boys are thrilled about it.[66]

4

'A piddling mission for the mighty Lanc'

⌁

THE EARLY RAIDS on Germany had confirmed the Lancaster's outstanding qualities. The hopes inspired by the first flights of the
prototype in February 1941 had been fulfilled in the most demanding
forms of action, whether it be low flying or strategic city bombing.
Powerful yet elegant, exuding power from its four Merlin XX engines
and menace from its vast bomb bay, the Lancaster immediately inspired
confidence in those involved with her. That feeling was reflected in an
interview given to the BBC soon after the Rostock raid by Flying Officer
John 'Dim' Wooldridge of 207 Squadron, a colourful pilot who later
became a successful playwright, author and composer:

> It is not very often in the career of a bomber pilot that he finds himself
> seated at the controls of a completely new type of aircraft as he sets off
> on a raid. Such an event stands out as a milestone in his life. And such
> was my experience the other night. Midnight found us at 10,000 feet over
> the North Sea heading eastwards. Our aircraft was one of the new
> Lancasters, our target was Rostock. The four engines beat away comfort-
> ably on either side. Beneath us in the belly of the aircraft was slung the
> heaviest load of high explosives I have ever carried on a raid. The airspeed
> indicator showed that we were going to complete this raid as quickly as
> a much shorter raid in an older type of bomber.

The aiming point in Rostock was the Heinkel factory and Wooldridge
described how, in the darkness, he could see the fire of the town glowing from almost 100 miles away. 'It was an amazing sight. There hardly
seemed to be any part of the town that was not burning.' Then he
approached the factory amid heavy smoke from the fires and anti-aircraft
guns.

> We dropped down to 5,000 feet and skimmed across the factory. Lurid
> coloured shells seemed to be whizzing past in every direction. A building
> went past underneath, blazing violently. Then the nose of the Lancaster
> reared upwards as the heavy bomb load was released. Even from 5,000 feet
> there was a clearly audible 'whoomph' as our heaviest bomb burst. As we

turned to look, we saw debris flying high into the air. 'Look out, pilot,' shouted the navigator, as another stream of tracer shells shot up past the wing tips and we turned away to have a look at the target. All over the place, blocks of buildings were burning furiously, throwing up columns of smoke three thousand feet into the sky. We lost height to about 1,000 feet and then flew across the southern part of the town, giving several good bursts of machine-gun fire. Sticks of bombs and incendiaries were crashing down everywhere and we certainly took our hats off to those anti-aircraft gunners. They continued firing even when their guns seemed to be completely surrounded by burning buildings. The last we saw of Rostock was from many miles away. We turned round and took a last look at the bright red glow on the horizon, then turned back towards England, very well satisfied with our first raid in our Lancaster.[1]

The account, somewhat sanitized for BBC listeners, still conveyed the intensity of combat experienced by the new Lancaster crews.

The Lancaster's early success won over the press as well as Bomber Command and the pilots. The plane's immediate reputation for excellence moved *Flight* magazine to produce these words of praise in July 1942: 'Aerodynamically, it is to be found that the Lancaster is fastest, by a considerable margin, of our heavy, four-engined bombers. The qualities of the aircraft are not to be measured in sheer performance alone; controllability, freedom from vices and the ability to fly with one or two engines out of action are at least as important. In that respect, the Lancaster has already proved its worth.' Turning to the construction of the plane, *Flight* then said: 'It is natural to ask what has made the Lancaster probably the finest four-engined bomber in the world. The answer cannot be given in a few words. The low structure weight is due partly to the constructional methods adopted and to a very careful portioning everywhere of the structure members to the loads they have to carry. Yet this has been achieved without undue complication. In fact, the Lancaster structure is a relatively simple one from a manufacturing point of view.'[2] The magazine was particularly impressed with the core of the Lancaster, its strong 'backbone' formed by the centre-section wing spars joined to the roof of the long bomb bay. So taken was the journal with the Lancaster that in one of its editions in August, it made this bold prophecy: 'Avro Lancaster four-motor heavy bombers are likely to go down in history as one of the greatest war-winning elements of this world war.'[3]

Even the Royal family were struck by the Lancaster. At the end of March, George VI and Queen Elizabeth visited the Avro factory at Yeadon in Yorkshire, which had been opened to relieve the pressure on the firm's works around Manchester. In honour of the visit, two of the Lancasters off the production line were christened 'George' and 'Elizabeth'. After the King had been shown around the Lancaster cockpit by Roy Chadwick, the Queen asked: 'Tell me, Mr Chadwick, how do you manage to design such huge and complex machines such as these?' To which, according to his biographer, Chadwick is said to have replied: 'Well, Mam, you don't have to be crazy but it helps.'[4]

Precisely because it was so effective and easy to produce, the Lancaster was in great demand from the moment it entered service, forming a key element of the Ministry of Aircraft Production's expansion programme which, in theory at least, was meant to produce 12,000 bombers by July 1943. The usual worries about the supply of the Merlins meant that the government felt compelled to consider an alternative power plant for the plane, a move which would ensure that production could be maintained. In early 1941, when the first Lancaster was undergoing its trials, MAP had requested that Avro develop a prototype with the Bristol Hercules VI sleeve-valved, air-cooled radial engine. Though it was recognized that the radial Hercules would generate more drag than the in-line Merlin, MAP felt that this could be compensated by the greater power of the Bristol engine. The first test flights of the prototype Hercules VI Lancaster took place in November 1942, and were promising enough for MAP to order 300 of the type, now called the Lancaster II. In operational practice, however, the performance of the Lancaster II, which first came off the production line in September 1942, proved to be significantly worse than the Mark I, especially because its higher fuel consumption reduced its operational range.

The Lancaster II did not progress beyond the initial contract, with its final output of 300 just a fraction of the 3,444 Mark I Lancasters eventually built. This was because the worst fears over the stock of Merlins never materialized. On the contrary, the supply was dramatically increased just at the moment the Mark II was being produced. In September 1940, Sir Wilfrid Freeman, with his usual perceptiveness, had entered into an agreement with the Packard company of America to build the Merlin, known locally as the V-1650. When the USA had first entered the war, however, the British Government had been worried that the Americans might be reluctant to continue building Rolls-Royce engines, hence the pressure for the Lancaster Hercules II contract. But just the opposite was true. Responding to growing demands from the USAAF for Merlins to equip its own aircraft, Packard massively increased its rate of production, demonstrating again the wisdom of President Roosevelt's famous description of his country as 'the arsenal of democracy'.[5] The Lancaster was one of the many British planes to benefit from this stream of Packard Merlins from across the Atlantic. The first trial installation took place in a converted Mark I in August 1942, and having completed its trials successfully, the new version immediately went into production. It was designated the Mark III, although, apart from the power plant, it was exactly the same plane as the Mark I and gave an almost identical performance. In all 3,020 Mark IIIs were built.[6]

But though the Hercules Lancaster was largely an irrelevance in the overall production of the plane, it was part of a crucial debate about the merits of the RAF's heavy bombers, one that would last right up to the end of 1944 and would show Harris at his most committed, stubborn and intemperate. Ignored in previous histories despite the involvement of Churchill and the War Cabinet, this controversy had its origins in the conflict between Harris's belief that all heavy-bomber production should be concentrated on the Lancaster, and the alternative view of much of the air establishment that such an approach would temporarily lead to such a drastic reduction in numbers that the bombing strategy would have to be curtailed. Harris's outlook, which grew more passionate as the war progressed, was motivated by several factors. One was his recognition of the inherent superiority of the Lancaster over all other types. Another was his respect for Dobson and Chadwick, whose company he rated much more highly than those of Handley Page or the Short Brothers. A third was the poor early performance of the Halifax, which left Harris with a permanent suspicion of the plane even when it had been substantially improved.

Harris could not understand why, if there were a shortage of Merlins, the Rolls-Royce engines should not be reserved for the Lancaster Marks I and III rather than developing the separate Mark II with its inferior engine and worse performance. In his view, if any planes should be changed, it should be the Halifax and the Stirling. His opinion was reinforced by the experiences of his airmen, so many of whom testified to the Lancaster's better operational performances in terms of climb, manoeuvrability and speed. In July 1942 a report by the Operational Research Section of Bomber Command about No. 4 Group, which flew Halifaxes, concluded that pilots had 'a casualty rate well above the average. This must be aircraft related as the Lancaster does not suffer the same problem.'[7] That view was shared by most in Bomber Command as the differences between the two four-engine planes became more apparent. An indication of how much the Lancasters were generally preferred to Halifaxes came from Don Charlwood, an Australian who served as a navigator in 103 Squadron. His unit had suffered terrible losses flying Halifaxes, then one day his commander gathered all the men together to bring 'unbelievably good news. "You will be glad to hear that we are to convert shortly to Lancasters." His voice was drowned by an outburst of cheering and shouting.' On the day that the Halifaxes departed, the squadron gathered to say a sarcastic farewell, shouting 'Goodbye Halibag!', as the Handley Page aircraft was known in Bomber Command. The next day the Lancasters arrived at 103 Squadron's base of Elsham Wolds in Lincolnshire. 'In the morning the first of them circled Elsham. We watched them sweep down to our runway, clean-lined and lady-like, a contrast with the more robust, masculine lines of the Halifaxes. We saw them like relief coming to a hard-pressed army. They were inconquerable; the days of heavy losses were over. Soon there was a Lancaster at each dispersal point and no sign of the Halifaxes.'[8]

The process of transfer could also work in the opposite direction, from Lancaster to Halifax, as Jim McIntosh, a Canadian pilot in 403 Squadron discovered when his squadron made such a switch. For McIntosh, the Lancaster had been 'the perfect flying machine. All the controls were within easy reach and designed for use. It was something else. It didn't fly; it soared! Most important, it gave us confidence. The rounded swept lines, like those of a beautiful woman, gave it "class". No other four-engined kite, RAF or USAAF, could compare.' At first the crews did not want to believe the rumours of the change to Halifaxes, which they had viewed as little more than 'bait for the German defences'. But then the 'Halibag' arrived at their base of East Moor in Lincolnshire. After the Lancasters, wrote McIntosh, the new plane was 'a depressing looking beast, square and squat; no lines at all. A feeling of doom now hung over East Moor.'[9]

Harris was always far more concerned about the welfare of his men than the callous caricature of post-war propaganda, as reflected in this richly eloquent passage from a letter he sent to Churchill in July 1942, referring to 'the two o'clock in the morning courage of lonely men, their actions hidden by darkness from their fellows, determined to press home their attacks through fantastically violent barrages into the searchlight cones, wherein gunfire concentrates immediately on any aircraft illuminated. Their behaviour cannot be watched, it can seldom be adjudged by an individual.'[10] A leader of such empathy found intolerable the idea that Bomber Command should not be equipped with the best possible aircraft for its task. The result was that he was determined to see the Halifax replaced by the Lancaster. If Cologne showed Harris at his most creatively efficient, then his bid to ditch the Halifax showed him at his most tenaciously unyielding.

He began the campaign in August 1942 with a memorandum to Portal complaining that the performance of the Halifax was 'little better than the Wellington. The Lancaster, on the other hand, at the same all-up weight as the Halifax (59,000 lbs) can carry 3000 lbs more bombs or fly 550 miles further. In addition, it is faster and is more manoeuvrable by nature of its better aerodynamic design and greater speed range.' Harris had little faith that promised modifications would bring any real improvements in the Halifax, telling Freeman: 'We will never make a silk purse out of this sow's ear. I am convinced that within a year at most the Halifax will not be operationally fit for European operations. It therefore behoves us to do everything possible drastically to reduce the projected Halifax production by every expedient and to increase the production of the Lancaster.'[11]

Thanks to the prompting of Harris the Ministry of Aircraft Production, without much enthusiasm, began to investigate the feasibility of switching over Halifax production to the Lancaster. The analysis focused on one company, English Electric, which, along with several other firms, had been subcontracted to build the Halifax. Yet as Harris had feared, the priority for heavy-bomber quantity over quality still prevailed. On 11 September 1942 the Minister for Aircraft Production Colonel John 'Jay' Llewellin (soon to be succeeded by the more dynamic Stafford Cripps) wrote to Sinclair dismissing Harris's demand. 'If we gave the order to change over now, English Electric would produce the first Lancaster about November 1943 and would not reach peak production until December 1944. Between about August 1943 and December 1944 you would lose some 220 heavy bombers. This would probably be the firm which would give the best result. In my view, the changeover is not the remedy. The remedy is to modify the Halifax so as to bring its performance more like the Lancaster's. We have already taken steps to this end.'[12]

Never one to follow conventional thinking or the easy approach, Sir Wilfrid Freeman was more sympathetic to the views of Harris than those of the Air Ministry and MAP. He suggested to Sinclair that over the next twelve months English Electric could erect additional capacity with jigs and tools to build the Lancaster at its Preston factory. 'In this way the time lag should be cut down and the Halifax can go at almost peak rate until the Lancaster is in reasonable production. The shops that are now producing the Halifax would eventually turn on to the Lancaster and we should get the combined output of both.'[13] In another memorandum Freeman urged the government to 'recognise the fact that whatever we do to the Halifax it will no more than put it on level terms with the Lancaster as it is today, having done that there is nothing else to come. The Lancaster, however, is a good vintage and will continue to improve for a year or two.'[14] Sir Archibald Sinclair refused to move. He supported MAP's line by pleading pressure on industrial capacity and trumpeting the improvements in the Halifax:

> Men in the Halifax squadrons were telling me that they thought the Halifax had definite advantages in some respects over the Lancaster or Stirling and they would prefer it to the Lancaster or Stirling if 30 or 40 mph speed could be restored to it. In view of the setback to the heavy bomber programme and of the scarcity of manpower, would not the wiser course at this stage be to concentrate on modifying the Halifax and to hold in abeyance the question of switching over Halifax production to Lancasters?[15]

Such sweeping claims about the Halifax infuriated Harris, who wrote to Freeman in October: 'I am convinced, as usual, that Handley Page is covering up behind a mass of verbiage and a lot of pettifogging minor modifications, by which he hopes to postpone either the full realization of the hopelessness of the Halifax or the necessity to switch as far as possible to something better. Unless drastic action is taken we are in for a major disaster where our bomber offensive is concerned before the year is out.'[16]

By now other senior politicians had become involved in the row, which even reached the level of the Cabinet. The intensifying debate over the Halifax versus the Lancaster was complicated by other considerations about the future of bomber production, including the disastrous failure of the Stirling on night operations over Germany and the need to replace the ageing Wellington. To some, like Churchill and his scientific adviser Lord Cherwell, the obvious way forward was to consolidate heavy-bomber development and production around the Lancaster rather than to seek a radical new design. 'In the Lancaster, we had a proved success, the performance of which might well be improved,' Churchill told the War Cabinet. 'There was always a great risk in going to a new type which would certainly have teething troubles and might even prove a failure.'[17] Similarly, Cherwell believed that the excellence of the Lancaster meant that it should predominate. He had calculated that the number of pounds of bombs dropped per factory man-hour from the Lancaster was 3.6, whereas for the Stirling it was just 1.2 and the Halifax only .95.[18] 'Having in mind the fact that the Lancaster could carry three times the weight per man-hour of construction as compared with other types and as it was proving superior in all other respects, he thought the decision should be to standardise on this type as much as possible and then concentrate the best designers in the industry on the design of a new type based on the Lancaster.'[19]

But this outlook was shared neither by MAP, which constantly highlighted the logistical difficulties and potential losses from switching production, nor by the influential Assistant Chief of the Air Staff and technical chief Ralph Sorley, who strongly believed in the concept of a new four-engine bomber. Throughout the months of political wrangling, Sorley kept urging the government to press ahead with a new design from Vickers, built to specification B3/42 and developed by Barnes Wallis, soon to win fame as the mastermind behind the Dambusters. The long-term future of the RAF heavy bomber lay with Wallis's B3/42, claimed Sorley, not the Lancaster. 'The Lancaster has reached its peak in weight and by the time that any change is made at Vickers it would be in decline. Were it to be substituted for the B3/42 at Vickers we should be virtually introducing an obsolescent type and abandoning the prospect of a new type of heavy bomber with a long period of development before it.'[20] In another memorandum to Sinclair, Sorley said that 'by putting a brand new type into production we start with an aeroplane that has a new lease of life in front of it, whereas the Lancaster is on "its last legs" so far as development is concerned',[21] a remarkably ill-judged statement given that the basic airframe of the Lancaster was still to be in RAF service in the early 1990s.

Like Churchill and Cherwell, Harris believed that heavy-bomber production had to be standardized on the Lancaster, though there was precious little sign of that happening. But the political arguments had thwarted his desire to see the Halifax phased out immediately, so he came up with a radical suggestion. If the aircraft had to be improved rather than dumped, it should be fitted with the wings of the Lancaster. 'It may be that if such an alteration were possible we should get virtually another Lancaster without having to go anything like as far in a general change-over.'[22]

Predictably, the Ministry of Aircraft Production rejected this imaginative idea. With a mix of weariness and complacency, Air Marshal John Linnell of MAP explained to Harris: 'There would be little to gain in using the Lancaster wing as both the Lancaster and the Halifax have their wings based upon the same aerofoil section. The Halifax is, in fact, slightly thicker at the root, but this only accounts for a loss of 1% in top and cruising speed over the Lancaster. The Lancaster span is about 3 feet wider than the Halifax and while this gives an increase in range of the order of 3% it will not affect the speed. I am sure that this whole problem can best be resolved by a determined cleaning up of the aircraft.'[23] Harris refused to give up immediately on his proposal. 'I still hanker towards the Lancaster type wing in preference to the Halifax wing. As an amateur, I believe that the thicker wing root of the Halifax has much to do with the disturbed airflow and induced drag as compared with the Lancaster,' he told Linnell on 4 November. He felt even more strongly about the extra three feet of the Lancaster's wingspan. 'You will recall our troubles with the Manchester which led to a considerably increased span, sub-sequently incorporated in the Lancaster. Therefore I would not lightly dismiss the extra effect to be secured by increasing the span of the Halifax to that of the Lancaster and still more by adopting the same wing tip shape as the Lancaster, during the same process of modification.'[24]

Harris's anger, never far from the surface, deepened as the Lancaster II, with its Bristol Hercules engines, prepared to go into operational service. The irrationality of the position, whereby the Halifax had the first choice of the better engine, struck him as outrageous. 'The Lancaster II has a marked falling off in performance which is not acceptable now and will be still less acceptable in 1943,' he told Portal. 'It has over 200 miles less range in theory and in practice we are already finding that it has some seven hours endurance compared with the ten hours of the Lancaster I. It is slightly slower. Its maximum speed is obtained at 15,500 feet (a lethal height) as compared with the 19,500 of the Lancaster I. The Hercules engine is notoriously unreliable, though this may be got over. The *raison d'être* of the Lancaster II is that insufficient Merlin engines are available to put Merlins in the total production of Lancaster fuselages. But Merlin engines are being used in large quantities in the deplorable Halifax. Therefore in order to overproduce one deplorable type we are virtually wrecking a large proportion of the output of a first-class type, the Lancaster I.'[25]

By the end of 1942, the air authorities had inched their way to a form of compromise settlement, though one that had only limited appeal to Harris. It was agreed to postpone any decision on Vickers and the Wellington replacement until the spring of 1943, while work would continue on the B3/42 design. The Halifax would continue to be produced by Handley Page, which would not only introduce further improvements in the type but would also start developing a new version, the Halifax III with Bristol Hercules engines. Apart from the hope that the modifications and a different engine would finally bear fruit, a further justification for advancing the Halifax programme could be found in the pledge to wind down the manufacture of the Stirling, made by Short Brothers in Belfast and Austin's at Longbridge in Birmingham. According to MAP, insufficient supplies of the large special tools required in the construction of the Lancaster meant that two changeovers could not be made simultaneously. Therefore the Short Stirling was chosen to be phased out, both because its plane was seen as a worse long-term prospect than the Halifax, and because the company's management, under the ageing, frequently inebriated Oswald Short, was notoriously weak. Throughout 1941 and 1942 the company had dismally failed to reach production targets.

Far from being assuaged by the promise of a move towards greater production of Lancasters, Harris was incensed at this further demonstration of reluctance to meet Bomber Command's immediate needs. So he fired off to Sinclair one of the most gloriously truculent letters that he produced throughout the whole war:

> I understand that the Stirling is to go in favour of the Lancaster as fast as the changeover can be achieved. But it will not be fast – or achieved at all with goodwill and good intent – as long as His Majesty's Government balk at the issue of taking the Stirling management away from the incompetent drunk who at present holds our fate in his hands. The Stirling Group has now virtually collapsed. They make no worthwhile contribution to our war effort in return for their overheads.

Harris then turned his molten ire on the Halifax:

> Handley Page is always weeping crocodile tears in my house and office, smarming his unconvincing assurances all over me and leaving me with nothing but a feeling of mounting uncertainty that nothing whatever ponderable is being done to make his deplorable product worth for war or fit to meet those jeopardies which confront our gallant crews. Nothing will be done until Handley Page and his gang are also kicked out, lock, stock and barrel. Unless we can get these two vital factors of the heavy bomber programme put right, and with miraculous despatch, we are sunk. We cannot do this by polite negotiation with these crooks and incompetents. In Russia it would have long ago been arranged with a gun and to that extent I am a fervid communist.[26]

Sinclair, ever the diplomat, tried to soothe Harris with the promise that preparations for the change from Stirlings to Lancasters would soon be underway. As it turned out, the Lancaster was never built at Short Brothers during the war because of deepening problems with the firm, which led to its nationalization in 1943. However, the switchover from the Stirling to the Lancaster was enacted at Austin's of Birmingham, with the first planes coming off the Longbridge production line in March 1944.

What drove Harris throughout this episode was the mounting evidence of the Lancaster's effectiveness in operations. Others were dealing in theories about future development. He was grounded in realities about current performance. Throughout 1942, as production of the plane speeded up and the Hampden, Whitley and Manchester were phased out, increasing numbers of squadrons in No. 5 Group were equipped with the bomber. By mid-October 1942 there were nine Lancaster squadrons in Bomber Command, with a theoretical front-line establishment of 162 aircraft. The total number of operational aircraft had risen to 206 by the end of the year, almost 32 per cent of the heavy-bomber strength of the Command. More planes were in reserves, undergoing testing or installation of equipment, awaiting repair or being used in training. During 1942 Avro built a total of 516 Lancasters, and its first two daughter firms, Metropolitan-Vickers of Manchester and Armstrong Whitworth of Coventry, another 172. These impressive figures were another indicator of the simplicity of Chadwick's design. The introduction of the Lancaster, Harris told Portal in late October, had brought a dramatic increase in the potency of Bomber Command. 'The potential bomb lift has gone up by 470 tons since August and we are now showing a steady increase in aircraft. The Lancaster has undoubtedly saved the situation and if I could double the number of squadrons so equipped, I venture to think the bomb lift line would begin to spell victory.'[27] In a report produced in January 1943, Harris noted that the number of heavy-bomber squadrons had more than doubled under his command:

> The increasing power of the bomber force, however, is due not merely to the substitution of heavy for medium bombers. On the material side it arises largely from the immense superiority of the Lancaster over all other types, heavy and medium alike. A few figures will show the extent of the gap. For every Lancaster lost on operations, 68.5 tons of bombs are dropped. Corresponding figures for other types are 30.1 tons for the Halifax and 21.6 tons for the Wellington. Again, for every 100 tons of bombs dropped by the Lancaster, nine aircrew personnel are killed or missing. For other types the figures are Halifax 19, Wellington 23. Finally, the advantage which the Lancaster enjoys in height and range enables it to attack with success targets which other types cannot tackle except on suicide terms.[28]

Like all vigorous commanders Harris always had a clear goal – the devastation of Germany – and he regarded all else as a distraction. Soon after Operation Millennium against Cologne in May 1942, he mounted two further 1,000-bomber raids on western German cities, one on Essen in the central Ruhr valley on the night of 1–2 June and the other on the port of Bremen on the night of 25–6 June, the second being an operation in which 96 Lancasters took part. These two raids turned out to be much less successful than that on Cologne, mainly because poor weather hampered the accuracy of the bomber streams. There were no more 1,000 operations for the rest of the year. Harris believed that he had made his point about the importance of mass concentration, but he continued to mount substantial attacks against the Reich. Hamburg, for instance, suffered five raids by over 150 aircraft in 1942, and Düsseldorf was attacked three times, Harris claiming that '300 acres in the centre of the town were utterly destroyed'.[29] Coal towns in the southern Saar valley came under heavy assault in July and September, and in the biggest Lancaster raid of the year 119 of them hit Munich in the south on 21–2 December. The previous night, 20–1 December, 111 Lancasters had attacked the central city of Duisburg on the Rhine, Europe's largest inland harbour, which lay in the heart of the Ruhr valley, ironically nick-named 'Happy Valley' by bomber crews because of the strength of its defences.

The threat posed by those German defences was well described by the New Zealander pilot Roy Calvert of 50 Squadron in his account of a raid on Hamburg in early November. The outward trip to the target had been difficult because thick, heavy cloud had hampered navigation and led to icing of the wings. Having been flying by dead reckoning, he approached what he presumed was the target. Just as the Lancaster completed its bombing run, a searchlight burst through the cloud, then the anti-aircraft guns opened up. 'There was a crack off our port wing tip and we were sprayed with shrapnel – it sounded like gravel thrown on to a tin roof. In the cockpit a top forward panel of Perspex and the starboard blister [lookout window] were shattered and our intercom went dead. Then another shell burst on our port side, closer this time. The poor old Lancaster shuddered violently and we were sprayed with shrap-nel once again.' In the second blast of flak, the wireless operator was killed and Calvert's arm and face were peppered with splinters and fragments of Perspex. The Lancaster was now badly damaged, with its radio and navigation aids unserviceable, its ailerons smashed and a howl-ing wind rushing through holes in the cockpit. But it is a reflection of the plane's resilience that it managed to keep flying once Calvert had brought it down to 1,000 feet. On reaching the English coast, he had to make an emergency landing at Bradwell in Essex. Fog obscured the runway lights and Calvert came in too steeply. 'I opened the throttles, pulled back on the stick, then cut the throttles. The wheels hit and collapsed and we skidded along on our belly, gradually turning to the right until we slid onto the grass and stopped. I switched everything off.' After a brief stay in an Essex hospital, Calvert went back to the airfield to inspect his battered aircraft. 'She was a sad sight, splattered all over with shrapnel. The elevator and rudder control rods were three quarters shot through in three places, but she hadn't let us down for twenty-four ops over France, Germany and Italy, surely reason enough for my love of the Lancaster.'[30]

Bombing Germany accounted for 75 per cent of the Command's operations in 1942, but the wider requirements of war meant that the Lancasters also had to carry out other duties, including attacks on northern Italy and occupied France, as well as mine-laying and maritime convoy patrols in the Battle of the Atlantic. At the time Harris frequently complained about the diversion of his resources, in one typical letter moaning to Portal that 'practically the whole of No. 44 Lancaster squadron is on indefinite loan to Coastal Command',[31] though the chief urged him to take a broader view of the war, pointing out that unless there were a greater air effort over the sea, 'there will be no petrol for the bombers'.[32] The detachment of Lancasters from 44 Squadron for Coastal Command was based in Northern Ireland in July 1942, where they flew long, ten-hour patrols over the sea. The unit enjoyed only one definite success, when Flight Lieutenant T. P. Barlow, on his very first convoy sortie, saw a surfaced U-boat and sank it with a 250-pound anti-submarine bomb and six depth charges. But there were no other clear victories, a fact that for Harris underlined how the Lancasters were wasted on these patrols. When 44 Squadron returned to Waddington, Lincolnshire, its place in Coastal Command was taken by 61 Squadron, operating from St Eval in Cornwall. Again results were disappointing and there were several losses from ship-borne anti-aircraft fire.

By far the most daring maritime raid took place at the end of August, when 12 Lancasters from 106 Squadron took off from Coningsby, Lincolnshire, to attack the German battleship *Gneisenau* and the aircraft carrier *Graf Zeppelin*, which was under construction in the Polish port of Gdynia. In addition to their usual maritime load of armour-piercing and medium-capacity weapons, four of the Lancasters were carrying the experimental 'Capital Ship Bomb', a bulbous 5,600-pounder once described as looking 'like an elongated turnip'.[33] Because of its strange shape, the Capital Ship Bomb had poor ballistics, so the ideal height from which it should have been dropped was only 1,000 feet, almost suicidally dangerous in an attack on a well-protected battleship or dockyard. The airmen of 106 Squadron, led by Wing Commander Guy Gibson, practised for almost two months to develop accuracy from a safer height. On a night of the full moon, 27 August, Gibson's Lancasters roared down the runway at Coningsby, their all-up weight of 67,000 pounds far above the authorized maximum of 60,000 for the plane. Yet the squadron had little difficulty in climbing over the North Sea and embarking on the five-hour journey to the Polish coast. On arriving at the target, the plan was to make accurate bombing runs from 6,000 feet. 'It should have been easy,' wrote Gibson later. 'The docks in brilliant light should been clear cut squares in the bomb-sight. Everything seemed to point in our favour.'[34] But as they approached Gdynia, they found the port shrouded in haze, reducing visibility to less than a mile. Despite braving savage flak while they made 12 runs, none of the Lancasters was able to hit either ship. When Gibson's Capital Ship Bomb landed 400 yards away from the *Gneisenau*, one of his crew laconically commented: 'That's killed a few fish for the bastards.'[35] After an hour of frustration and near-misses, the squadron had to return to England. 'That's the worst of one big bomb; you go a long way to do your best; then you miss; then you have a five-hours bind on the way home. It is an infuriating business,' said Gibson. His next special mission with a big bomb would not prove so fruitless.

Harris always regarded maritime work as ineffectual compared to the bombing of Germany. 'Whilst it takes apparently some 7000 flying hours to destroy one submarine at sea, that was approximately the amount of flying necessary to destroy one-third of Cologne, the third largest city in Germany in one night, a town of vast industrial import,' he wrote in August 1942.[36] Yet he also boasted that his command had done more to paralyse the German fleet through mine-laying than the Royal Navy, and he frequently trumpeted the job his bombers did in restricting the movements of Germany's premier battleship, *Tirpitz*, with mines and threats of attacks. Mine-laying was not always as life-threatening as flying over the Reich, with its bristling network of anti-aircraft guns and fighters. Indeed, Jack Currie said that his first mine-laying operation 'seemed like a piddling mission for the mighty Lanc'.[37] But German fighters and flak from the shore still represented a major threat, while the risk was also heightened by the need for the Lancasters to fly low and find their target visually. A typical mine-laying operation off the German or Danish coast would involve five bombers, each of them carrying six magnetic mines, which were ten feet long and weighed 1,500 pounds, of which the explosive charge made up 740 pounds. Take-off would usually be in the late afternoon. After flying over the sea the Lancasters would then descend to below 2,000 feet to drop their mines on the chosen target. The risks were highlighted by John A. Johns of 153 Squadron. 'If you were shot down into the sea the chances of survival or of launching a dinghy into the northern seas, where survival times were unlikely to exceed ten minutes, did not bear thinking about.'[38] In his memoir of service in Bomber Command, Harry Yates wrote that:

> mine-laying held not the slightest appeal for me. It had a vernacular all of its own. It was called gardening. Mines were called vegetables. As usual in the RAF, banal language disguised an extreme danger. Hours of low-flying in filthy weather, mostly on your own, was the norm. If you could get a fix on the enemy coast, the next thing was to release the mines at low level. But the German captains were assiduous in taking refuge in inhospitable places, beneath mountainous coastlines or behind a packet of flak ships. No amount of cloud cover hid an incoming bomber from the latter's radar or their Bofors. If the skies were clear it was worse. There was the added menace of fighters.[39]

Norman Ashton, a flight engineer with 103 Squadron, experienced the menace of both flak and fighters on his very first Lancaster sortie, when his crew was instructed to drop mines off the mouth of the Gironde on the French west coast near the Bay of Biscay. His Lancaster flew at 16,000 feet towards the target, then dropped down to below 2,000 feet to commence the run across the mouth of the river. As the Lancaster levelled, the guns on the Atlantic coast opened up. 'The whole aircraft seemed to be wrapped in the flashes, like an ungainly Guy Fawkes perched awkwardly on a flickering bonfire. It was fantastic. I could hear, feel and smell the filthy stuff belting against the aircraft but nothing untoward happened.' Once the Lancaster had dropped the mines, Ashton opened the engines to climbing power and the pilot pulled the aircraft into the clouds. But just then a Luftwaffe Ju 88 fighter whistled past the wing tip. Over the intercom Ashton snapped a warning to the mid-upper gunner, who opened up with his Brownings. The response was enough to allow the Lancaster to escape deeper into the clouds and set course for home.[40]

To some, the combination of the icy sea and flak was even more intimidating than the experience of raids on Germany. Flight Sergeant Edwin Jury, a mid-upper gunner with 419 Squadron, said of one mine-laying trip: 'It was the only time on ops I prayed to the Good Lord to get me out. As we flew in to drop the mines at about 800 feet five or six flak ships opened up and I could see these tennis balls of flak whizzing sideways across the water to us. We were so low they had to depress their guns and all this stuff was going over us. I knew if we got hit we'd go straight in without a chance. We didn't fire back. We were always told not to unless you had to. There was no future in pointing yourself out to a flak ship.'[41]

A further diversion from the offensive against Germany in 1942 was the bombing of the other Axis power, Benito Mussolini's Italy. Harris regarded this too as a distraction. Indeed, there was not a single Lancaster raid on Italy until October. But by the autumn, the American-British military had drawn up their plans for Operation Torch, which, combined with General Bernard Montgomery's westward advance across the Tunisian desert, was aimed at finally driving the Axis powers out of North Africa and giving the Allies control of the Mediterranean sea routes. For Torch to succeed, the British Chiefs of Staff considered it essential for Bomber Command to attack northern Italian cities so that Mussolini would have to retain his fighters at home rather than sending them to North Africa. Because Italy's defences were poor and her morale weak, this bombing campaign was more a test of stamina than raw nerve. As Guy Gibson wrote:

> It is a well-known fact that bombing accuracy and effect increase indirectly with the weakness of flak and morale. Italian flak, though bolstered by certain Nazi regiments, was still bad. We would often bomb at very low level, picking out targets at will, and nothing could be worse for the people below than to see those great Lancasters flying around, making a tremendous noise and dropping their cookies out one after another, on exactly the right spot.[42]

Given the importance of Torch, Harris was compelled on several occasions to send almost his full force of Lancasters against Italian targets. On the night of 22–3 October, 112 of them raided Genoa, and another 88 went to Milan the following night. The first half of November saw four major attacks on Genoa alone, and Turin endured three raids of more than 100 Lancasters between 28 November and 9 December. It was a further reflection of Bomber Command's disdain for the Italian defences that the mission on Milan took place in daylight, something that had become unthinkable on urban Germany by late 1942. The comparative ease of these sorties was captured in an account from Harry Irons, a rear gunner with 9 Squadron, of that raid on Milan by the 88 Lancasters, each of them carrying six 1,000-pounders:

They were so surprised in Milan that they didn't even sound the air raid sirens. We did see some fighters, Italian Air Force, but they stood off and didn't interfere. We were there in the middle of the afternoon and people were in the streets. Some of the Lancs went down with machine guns after they'd bombed. We didn't but some of them did, and there was no opposition . . . I think that raid really shook the Italians. Ninety Lancs hitting a fairly compact town, coming all the way from England and wrecking the industry in broad daylight. Well, I think they lost a lot of their appetite for war.[43]

A less relaxed picture can be found in the diary of the American Lancaster pilot Robert Raymond, who had recently completed his Lancaster training and admitted that the Italian defences could sometimes be inadvertently daunting. Of a sortie to Genoa on 7 November, he wrote: 'I and the rest of the crew, feeling like goldfish exposed to the light of day, winced and ducked mentally every time a nearby shell rocked us. I had one hand on the throttles and suddenly realized that I had instinctively pulled them full open. I pulled them back, grasped the wheel with both hands again and concentrated on maintaining the correct height and airspeed. It's hard to control your natural reactions in such a situation when you're new to the game.'[44]

The autumn campaign in Italy and Operation Torch led to the inevitable rows that Harris always managed to provoke. One arose when the Air Ministry instructed him to send a squadron of Lancasters to North Africa in support of Torch. With his usual determination to cling on to his best planes, he decided to send 20 Halifaxes instead, which led to complaints from the Royal Navy about their inadequate bomb load, another sign of how the Lancaster's reputation had spread right across the armed services. 'I am really not prepared to have the Admiralty telling me which squadron I shall send,' Harris told Portal on 25 October:

You will no doubt wish to impress upon the Chief of the Naval Staff that, quite apart from what the Lancasters are doing at the moment as a contribution to the general war, they are all heavily involved in the anti-Tirpitz mining plan. They are the only aircraft which can compete with the bombing and mining of Gdynia, the place for which the Tirpitz is most likely to make. Therefore if they insist on their pound of flesh with regard to the Lancaster as opposed to the Halifax squadron, they are merely cutting their own throats if the Tirpitz moves. But they always want to eat their cake and have it.[45]

Harris got his way. The Lancasters remained in England.

The other spat was caused by Harris's ruthlessness. To him, anything belonging to the enemy was a legitimate target, including its people and historic architecture. His tough self-reliance, forged in the veld, contained a philistine streak. In this case, his disregard for the masterpieces of Italian civilization caused some consternation, not only to colleagues but also to one Lancaster airman, who was outraged that Milan's magnificent Gothic cathedral had been chosen as the aiming point for a raid on the city. Having informed Harris that this unnamed officer had 'risked court martial' in telling an MP about the instruction, Portal warned: 'The RAF is being accused of vandalism. I know it can be said that the actual aiming mark itself is unlikely to be hit but I cannot think that anyone would regard this as an adequate defence and I hope that you will ensure that historic buildings are not chosen as aiming points in the future.'[46] Over the next two and a half years Harris would completely ignore this request.

As demonstrated in the Italian campaign, Harris was willing to consider the occasional daylight raid outside Germany if the benefits outweighed the potential losses. France was the setting for one such spectacular daylight assault, when on 17 October 1942 88 Lancasters attacked the giant Schneider armament works in Le Creusot, in the Bourgogne region near the Swiss border. With typical RAF humour the assault was code-named Operation Robinson, as in Crusoe, a play on the pronunciation of the French town. The Augsburg raid earlier in the year had been a propaganda triumph but an operational failure. Operation Robinson proved far more successful. Having crossed the Channel in close formation, the Lancasters then raced at low height over northern France. As twilight began to set in, the Lancasters then reached Le Creusot and flew over the 287-acre Schneider works at 4,000 feet, dropping 200 tons of high explosive and incendiary bombs within the space of just seven minutes. Among the ordnance were 1,000-pounders fused to blow up ninety minutes after they had fallen, just at the moment when the firefighters were trying to tackle the blazes started by the incendiaries. Little resistance was encountered as the Lancasters pulverized the armament works. 'The only gun that fired,' wrote Paddy Rowling in his diary, 'put in a couple of bursts as we ran up, which burst a couple of hundred yards in front of us at about the same height, but that was immediately silenced by the effect of the bombing, whether by fright or concussion, I don't know.'[47] According to RAF intelligence, the damage was so severe that the factory was still being repaired eight months later.

Harris always believed that daylight raids by Lancasters should be used only in the most special circumstances. But the Air Staff, particularly Sir Wilfrid Freeman, itched for a more expansive use of such bombing. For

Freeman, the lesson of the crippling air losses at Augsburg was not to abandon daylight operations over Germany but try to find a way of giving better protection to the Lancasters, both through fighter cover and stronger armour on the planes themselves. Except on brief trips over northern France, fighter cover within the RAF was never to be feasible during the mid-war years because of the short range of the Spitfire. Perversely, the RAF did not try to develop a long-range escort with the performance of an interceptor fighter because Portal believed that such an aircraft was a technical impossibility, though the American Mustang would prove him wrong. 'Increased range can only be provided at the expense of perform-ance and manoeuvrability,' he told Churchill in 1942.[48] But the alternative of providing more armour plating on the Lancaster was vigorously pursued by Freeman and Ralph Sorley. The only armour on the original produc-tion Lancaster was a thick plate at the back of the pilot's seat, and some plating at the rear of each engine nacelle.

As early as July 1941, the Air Staff called for an investigation into the possibility of fitting extra detachable armour in the Lancaster specifically for daylight operations. Installed around the tail turret, engines, flying controls and fuel tanks, such armour was expected to weigh about 2,000 pounds so, when in use, the bomb load would have to be reduced by a commensurate amount. At an Air Staff meeting, Sorley explained that the Lancaster had been chosen for the investigation because it 'was the most suitable of the heavy bombers for daylight operations owing to its super-ior speed and manoeuvrability'. If the outcome of the inquiry were positive, he added, he hoped that the specially armoured Lancasters could be used on daylight operations from the spring of 1942.[49] Trials were not actually completed until April 1942, but they appeared to show that the armour would offer 'a fair degree of protection' and would also force the top German fighter, the Me 109, to 'come into close range to gain de-cisive results', in which circumstances 'the chances of being shot down by the bomber's defensive armament would be greatly increased'.[50] Following this positive verdict, Freeman then sent 12 of these specially armoured Lancasters to No. 5 Group, telling Harris he wanted them allo-cated to a squadron that would be freed from night bombing and told to 'devote its whole attention to a technical and tactical study of daylight raiding'. Indeed, Freeman was so impressed with these Lancasters that he had ordered another 100 of them. 'I know you do not like the specially armoured Lancasters but I want you to give them a really thorough trial. The lessons we hope to learn from them about daylight attack may be of enormous value and affect the whole range of tactical doctrine.'[51]

Harris more than disliked Freeman's initiative. He was outraged, believing that it wasted a valuable Lancaster squadron, put his men's lives at risk and made a mockery of the entire thrust of the night bomber offensive against Germany. If Freeman wanted to carry out such experiments, argued Harris, he should confine them to a single Lancaster at the RAF's bomb-testing range on the Suffolk coast, not use aircrews as guinea pigs:

> The object of putting the special aircraft onto day bombing is apparently to attempt assessment of their vulnerability as compared with the ordinary Lancaster, by exposing them to the attacks of enemy fighters and recording the result. A disproportionate price would be paid for this information in the loss of extremely valuable aircraft and crews and in avoidable depression of morale. This price might be very high indeed, since if the formation were intercepted by an overwhelming number of fighters, there is no doubt that very few, whether armoured or unarmoured, would survive.[52]

Harris may have had some justification for this, but his reluctance to co-operate, combined with his customary denigration of others' motives, drew a livid reply from Freeman:

> I thought that over a period of one and a half years I had got accustomed to your truculent style, loose expression and flamboyant hyperbole, but I am not used to being told – for such is the implication of your letter – that I am deliberately proposing to risk human lives in order to test out an idea of my own, which in your opinion is wrong. When it was first decided to add additional armour to the Lancaster, it was considered that a return to daylight raiding would be necessary and that every effort should be made to reduce casualties to the minimum. It was recognised that a reduction in bomb load would be necessary. But why not, if the weight of bombs reaching the target is greater than it otherwise would have been? It is possible, for example, that our casualties on the Augsburg raid might have been 50 per cent less if the additional armour had been carried by our aircraft. Instructions have been given for the armour to be made as far as possible detachable and I should now be glad if you would carry out the orders given to you.[53]

In a handwritten postscript on a copy of this letter he sent to Sydney Bufton, Freeman added: 'The only way to deal with Bert is to treat him rough.'[54]

Though he demanded total loyalty from his Bomber Command officers, Harris adopted a more flexible attitude toward the orders of his own superiors. Thick-skinned and unabashed, he simply refused to obey Freeman. 'I hope it is clear to you that I have good reason for astonishment, if not despair, over the Lancaster position and repeated depredations of already over-mortgaged stock. I therefore ask you to review again the Lancaster situation as a whole with a view to permitting only such demands upon them as are possible of achievement until they become available in greater quantity. If this armoured Lancaster proposal is to stand I must ask for an official directive to which I can register my official protest.'[55] After further months of stalemate, the Air Staff abandoned the scheme. In October the detachable sets of armour were put permanently into storage, Freeman wistfully claiming that 'it may be possible to introduce them at some time into future production'.[56] But they never were.

Harris was so obstinate on this issue because he never wavered in his iron conviction that the night bombing of Germany by his 'heavies' was the only way to win the war. Mass aerial bombardment, he had told Churchill in June, pointed to 'the certain, the obvious, the quickest and easiest way to overwhelming victory. The over-strained, far-stretched and militarily compromised condition of Germany plays right into our hands – if we employ our power properly.'[57] In the first half of 1942, there had been mutterings in political circles that because of the weakness of the air offensive, Bomber Command should be broken up and its aircraft divided between Coastal Command and Army Co-operation. But Harris turned the argument on its head, declaring that Coastal Command's contribution to the war effort was so negligible that it should be taken over by Bomber Command. 'Why nibble at the fringes of the enemy's submarine and sea power when we can obliterate with comparative ease the very sources of that power?' he wrote in a paper for the Cabinet in August 1942.[58] As for Army Co-operation, he told Portal, 'they have been sitting on their fannies doing nothing for the last two and a half years'.[59]

Unlike Lord Trenchard, Harris believed that the key purpose of concentrated urban bombing was the destruction of Germany's infrastructure rather than the breaking of civilian morale; as he pointed out, the question of public morale hardly mattered in a totalitarian dictatorship. But in his belief that 'all war is brutal',[60] he had no qualms about treating the enemy's population as part of that infrastructure. Such an outlook could extend even to the non-German population in the occupied territories. He once explained to Bottomley that French factories were best attacked at night 'when all good Frenchmen should be in bed and those who are still working for the enemy doubly deserve all they get'.[61] By late 1942, after his earlier hesitations, Harris had become fully converted to the lethal destructive power of incendiaries over high explosive, and was infuriated if his operational commanders did not follow his exact instructions on the make-up of bomb loads. 'There has been a vast amount of irrefutable evidence that the major portion of raid damage is done by four pound and 30 pound incendiary bombs,' he told his group commanders in September, complaining that some of them had shown a 'flagrant disregard' for his orders by including too much high explosive. 'The blast bombs are carried solely for the purpose of creating alarm and despondency, while the incendiaries are relied upon to do the actual devastation.'[62]

The duo ultimately responsible for the formulation of policy, Portal and Sinclair, shared Harris's faith in area bombing and regularly put pressure on the War Cabinet to step up the offensive through an expansion of the bomber force. The Chief of the Imperial General Staff Sir Alan Brooke recorded in his diary how he had 'a hammer and tongs argument with Portal on the policy for the conduct of the war. He wants to devote all efforts to an intensive air bombardment of Germany on the basis that a decisive result can be obtained in this war. I am only prepared to look on the bombing of Germany as one of the many ways by which we shall bring Germany to her knees.'[63] Churchill too remained deeply equivocal, torn between his instinctive martial exuberance in going on the attack and his grave doubts about the efficacy of area bombing. He agreed that the 'offensive over Germany or Italy must be regarded as our prime effort in the air. It is of the utmost importance that this should not fall away during these winter months, when the strain of the Russian front will be heavy on the German people.'[64] But when Sinclair told him that '4000 to 6000 bombers operating from this country' could 'pulverise German war industry' and that therefore Churchill should 'now declare unequivocally for the heavy bomber as the main instrument of victory', the Prime Minister replied that he was 'not at all convinced' by Sinclair's arguments. Similarly, after Harris sent a long paper to Churchill telling him that 'the one way in which Germany will be defeated is by air attack' and claiming that saturation raids by massed heavy bombers could win the war 'before next summer', Churchill replied: 'You must be careful not to spoil a good case by overstating it. I am doing all I can to expand Bomber Command and I set a value on your action against Germany. I do not however think that Air bombing will bring the war to an end by itself and still less that anything that could be done with our existing resources could produce decisive results in the next twelve months.'[65]

There were many within the Air Ministry and even Bomber Command itself who shared the scepticism of Churchill and Sir Alan Brooke. A pertinent summary of this position was set out by Dr L. A. C. Cunningham, the Air Ministry's Principal Scientific Officer, who asked in November: 'Even if we completely destroyed all production in the nightly accessible parts of Germany, would this have a decisive effect on the war? It must not be forgotten that Russia is still an effective combatant although she has lost a third of her territory. And the cumulative night bombing threat has been drummed into the Germans now for a long time. They are bound to have taken precautions to meet it. I don't believe that night bombing can of itself be decisive.'[66] Some of these doubters thought that Harris's whole approach, based on sheer weight of numbers, was ill-conceived because the bomber force, even after the introduction of Gee, remained woefully inaccurate.

Such critics believed that better results would be achieved by an improvement in delivery rather than just a remorseless expansion of the bomber fleet. Their proposed solution to the problem of inaccuracy was the creation of an elite force, made up of the best pilots in planes using the latest navigational equipment, which could guide the main bomber stream to its target by illuminating the aiming point with pyrotechnic markers. Such an idea was hardly novel. Portal himself had unsuccessfully experimented with flares to light up targets in the summer of 1940, and during the Blitz the Luftwaffe had established a unit of target-finding raid leaders, the *Kampfgruppe 100*, which used Heinkel 111s equipped with special radio equipment. The *Kampfgruppe 100* had led the infamous raid on Coventry in November 1940, but its effectiveness rapidly diminished when the British discovered how to jam its radios. In 1941 Sir John Slessor, as head of No. 5 Group, had suggested to his chief Sir Richard Pierse the use of 'some special aircraft to go in at dusk and put a packet of incendiaries onto the target' with the object of 'lighting up the target so that the following crews can see it'.[67] The continuing dismal results of Bomber Command through the winter of 1941–2 gave renewed impetus to the concept of a target-finding force. Churchill's adviser Lord Cherwell, always seeking forms of military innovation, turned his fertile if erratic mind to the subject, telling Portal: 'If we could rely on 10–20 machines really getting to the right place, it would surely be possible for others to find the conflagration. I wonder what you think of the idea of trying the experiment of giving one of our Bomber Groups the special task of finding the target.' In response, Portal said that he welcomed the idea, especially the suggestion that the elite force be concentrated in one group.[68]

But the real driving force behind the quest for a target-finding force was Syd Bufton, Deputy Director of Bombing Operations in the Air Ministry. Bufton was no desk-bound official of the type despised by operational commanders. The son of a Welsh tobacconist and local politician, he had gained wide experience in flying, engineering and leadership in a variety of air force roles at home and across the Empire, having joined the RAF in 1927 after a short period as an apprentice at Vickers. He could be both practical and analytical. At the start of the war he was in the RAF headquarters in France but then took command of 10 Bomber Squadron, in which post he undertook 19 operations and won the DFC, a far better record than Harris's contemptuous dismissal of him as 'a junior staff officer whose only qualification was that he had dropped a few leaflets on Europe at the beginning of the war'.[69] It was at 10 Squadron that Bufton also first developed his idea for a bombing pioneer force, for one of his methods, as raid leader, had been to drop coloured flares on the target and then fire a flare from his Very pistol to attract other crews. Once at the Bombing Operations Directorate, which advised the Air Ministry on bombing policy, he had the influence to put his theory into practice.

On 17 March 1942 he sent Harris a lengthy paper setting out the case for an elite target-finding force, to be made up of six squadrons drawn from existing units. His central argument was that the target finders had to be based in one united group, for only in this way would they co-ordinate ideas, share new techniques for marking and develop a mutual sense of responsibility for their vital work. If the target finders were dispersed among the squadrons, however, they 'cannot make headway'. He admitted that the creation of an elite group would mean that 40 high-quality crews would have to be withdrawn from the rest of Bomber Command, which could potentially lead to a temporary reduction in morale. On the other hand, he argued, the greatest cause of declining morale in the Command was the inability of squadrons to hit their targets, so the establishment of a target-finding force could actually raise spirits. Besides, continued Bufton, the necessity for improving performance and thereby reducing the political pressures on Bomber Command had to override all other considerations. 'Our failure to produce results to date is plain to all and it is felt that the formation of a target finding force is an essential and necessary step that must be taken without delay. Unfortunately the little that has been achieved in really hurting Germany is not only apparent to an increasing number of members of the RAF but is also appreciated by the Navy and Army to the extent that unless something is done quickly the arguments for splitting the bomber force between the Senior Services will gain such weight as to prove irresistible.'[70]

It was all too predictable that Bufton's scheme should provoke the captious opposition of Harris, whose hackles were always raised by any hint of interference by the Air Ministry. In a reply that mixed complacency with stubbornness and self-delusion, Harris told Bufton that a single target-finding force would be a setback for Bomber Command since it would shatter morale and weaken his squadrons. 'I am not prepared to accept all the very serious disadvantages of a Corps d'Elite in order to secure possibly some improvement on methods which are already proving reasonably satisfactory.' Amongst his commanders, he said, 'the unanimous opinion was against such a force'. He then concluded with his own faintly crackpot proposal that every month the photographic results of each squadron should be analysed for their bombing accuracy, and then the winning squadron would be designated the group's target-finding force for the following month.[71] The Bombing Operations Directorate were disconcerted by Harris's stance, finding it absurd that he could claim Bomber Command's results were 'reasonably satisfactory' when all the evidence pointed in the opposite direction. As Bufton told Harris, a study of 122 photographs of 8 raids on Essen between March and April 1942 showed that 90 per cent of the aircrafts' bombs fell between 5 and 100 miles from their target. Incredibly, just two aircraft actually hit the target. 'I think you will agree that such dispersal shows that our present methods fail entirely to achieve the aim in highly defended areas.'[72]

Bufton was even more angered by Harris's assertion that Bomber Command was united behind his opposition. He knew that in making such a claim Harris was being either ignorant or dishonest. During the spring Bufton had been directly in contact with many of the Command's front-line officers, and they proved far more receptive to the target-finding force than Harris admitted. Such a policy had 'obviously been needed since the first six months of hostilities', said Group Captain H. Graham of 7 Squadron, adding that 'objections to the formation of a target-finding force cannot be seriously entertained by anyone other than an academic degenerate'. In 'full support' of the force, Wing Commander Trevor Freeman of 115 Squadron reported that he had 'discussed the idea with many senior captains who all entirely agree'. It is interesting that some officers felt that Bufton's scheme was necessary because it could make up for the 'lack of determination' shown by too many average bomber crews. This view was expressed with particular vehemence by Group Captain Charles Whitworth, the commander of RAF Scampton near Lincoln:

> There is no doubt about it – flak and searchlights frighten our people beyond measure and many crews go completely to pieces. I am of the opinion – and I happen to know what I am talking about – that in one average squadron today you will find only one out of five crews who are

good enough and sufficiently courageous to mix it with flak and search-lights in the Ruhr and bomb the target. The remainder just fling their bombs away in the area and are just fringe merchants. The courageous crew will in a very short time be destroyed for the simple reason that he is the only one who is going into the target each time and has everything the ground can give concentrated on him.

Whitworth maintained that the proposed new force would 'serve as a tremendous impetus throughout Bomber Command and it is high time we did have a Corps d'Elite. The lack of discipline and lack of pride in themselves of air crews is, I regret to say, pretty well general.'[73]

During a series of acrimonious meetings at the Air Ministry and Bomber Command at High Wycombe, Harris is reported to have said: 'A target finding force will only be established over my dead body.'[74] His resistance stemmed partly from his prickly, blinkered character which treated Bomber Command as his own personal fiefdom. 'I don't ask opinions, I give orders,' he once said.[75] But his clash with Bufton, whom he described as 'the target-finding fanatic',[76] also reflected a fundamental difference of principle over the conduct of the air war. Bufton's passionate advocacy of target-finding was motivated by his belief that the heavy bomber was best used as a precision weapon. That was why he was more concerned with the performance rather than the size of the bomber force. 'If only we selected the right people to lead our squadrons, we could do more with 100 aircraft than with 1000. The trouble is that the high ups think in terms of 2000 or 4000 bombers,' he once wrote.[77] All this was anathema to Harris, since pinpoint accuracy had little relevance for area bombing where widespread devastation was all that mattered. Freeman Dyson, a leading scientist who worked in Operational Research at Bomber Command, witnessed this telling incident at High Wycombe, which illustrated Harris's insouciance about accuracy:

> I happened to be in his office when a WAAF sergeant came in with a bomb plot of a recent attack on Frankfurt. As usual, the impact points deduced from flash photographs were plotted on a map of the city with a three-mile circle drawn around the aiming point. The plot was supposed to go to the commander-in-chief together with our analysis of the raid. Our chief looked glumly at it for a few seconds and then gave it back to the sergeant. 'Awfully few bombs inside the circle,' he said. 'You'd better change that to a five-mile circle before it goes in.'[78]

To others, area bombing might be an ugly, temporary necessity until technical advances allowed more sophisticated attacks. But to Harris, area bombing was the only proper function of his bomber force.

For all his tenacity Harris was fighting a losing battle. By the early summer Bufton had attracted the powerful support of Portal and Freeman, who both found his arguments irrefutable. Harris's last-ditch proposal to establish raid leaders in every squadron was quickly refuted as missing the whole point of the unified elite force. Given the strength of his opponents and the fact that he had only been in his post a few months, Harris had no alternative but to surrender. In June 1942 it was finally agreed to set up the new force, though as a sop to Harris its name was changed from target finders to pathfinders. Initially the Pathfinding Force (PFF) was to have four squadrons, one from each main bomber type. The Lancaster squadron transferred to the PFF was No. 83 and the three other units were made up of Wellingtons, Stirlings and Halifaxes, the combined organization soon taking the title of No. 8 Group. Another minor triumph for Harris was the selection of the PFF Commander. Bufton had pressed for the charismatic fighter leader Basil Embry, who had recently taken part in the Desert War, but Harris succeeded with his choice: the tough Australian Don Bennett, once described by Harris to Churchill as 'one of the most efficient and the finest youngsters I have ever come across in the service'.[79]

Aged just thirty-two, Bennett was almost two decades younger than most of the other group leaders but he had proved himself one of the most skilful and dauntless pilots in the RAF, with an unrivalled mastery of the arts of flying and navigation. Born on a cattle station in Queensland, he had joined the Royal Australian Air Force in 1930 and transferred to Britain in 1932, where he had spells in Fighter Command and on flying boats, the latter a role in which he served briefly under Harris. After working with Imperial Airways as a pilot in the years immediately before the war, he rejoined the RAF, becoming a squadron leader on Whitley and Halifax bombers. His determination and courage were demonstrated during a raid against the *Tirpitz* in Norway. When his plane was shot down, he managed to bail out, reach neutral Sweden by foot and then gain repatriation to Britain, going back in great secrecy as an item of diplomatic baggage. Admired for his brilliant airmanship and phenomenal knowledge of aeronautics, he was also feared for his brusque personality. Jack Goodman, who flew with the Pathfinder Force, left this memory of him. 'He was an airman extraordinary. He was a great one for showing people how to do things. It did not matter what you thought you could do, he could do it better in the air. He was everlastingly demonstrating this to people. If you thought you could get a target error of 100 yards, Bennett would show that he could get an error of 50 yards.'[80]

The Lancasters of 83 Squadron arrived at the PFF base of Wynton in Huntingdonshire on 15 August 1942 and, barely before their engines had cooled, they were ordered into action, though at the last minute the operation was cancelled. The first full operation of the PFF took place on 18–19 August, with a raid on Flensburg, north of Kiel. But for all Bennett's energy, results of the Pathfinder-led raids were disappointing in the following months. Casualties were high over Germany, accuracy was barely improved. In December, Harris reported to his commanders that a mere 24 per cent of aircraft attacking German and Italian targets were shown to have bombed within three miles of the aiming point. But Bufton and the Bombing Operations Directorate believed that such figures did not weaken the case for the Pathfinder Force but instead highlighted Bomber Command's reluctance to implement the scheme properly. It is often said by the defenders of Harris that one of his virtues was his willingness to act on orders once they were firmly given, but that is just another piece of historical myth-making, as demonstrated by the controversy over the armoured Lancasters. In fact, Bennett himself complained 'he never really gave the Pathfinding force a fair chance relative to the other special units'.[81] Here again, the Bufton papers confirm that Bomber Command remained lukewarm about Pathfinders after the force had been established. Bufton was especially aggrieved by the negative attitude of Harris's Senior Air Staff Officer, Robert Saundby, whom he regarded as a disastrous influence on the Command. 'It is now more than six weeks since the Commander-in-Chief agreed to form a Target Finding Force,' wrote Bufton in early August. 'The lack of enthusiasm and sense of urgency in high quarters permeates the whole command and will inevitably result in the complete failure of the Target Finding Force at its inception.'[82] But soon Harris would be presiding over a dramatic change in Bomber Command's performance and image.

5

'The target for tonight'

$\sim\sim$

SIR ARTHUR HARRIS may have been hopeless at diplomacy and politics, but he was a master of organization. The heavy-bomber sorties
over the Reich, which became the predominant theme of his command
from mid-1942, were feats of immense logistical planning. The selection
of targets, the size of the force, the content of the bomb load, the types
of Pathfinder ground markers and the choice of route, all had to be
decided for every operation, informed not only by weather and military
intelligence, but also policy directives from the Air Staff. For all the faults
of his combustible personality, Harris bore this responsibility with fortitude, resolution and his own brand of scornful humour. He worked
sixteen hours a day for most of the war, never took a holiday, and remained
at his post even when suffering from a duodenal ulcer, an ailment not
helped by his chain-smoking and fondness for rich food. Between 1942
and 1945 he took just two weekends off on leave. 'He never really had
a moment of relaxation,' recalled his wife Therese, Lady Harris. 'He had
a low-ringing phone by his bed so as not to wake me and because of
his instruction to Group Commanders and Operations Staff at Command
Headquarters, they would call him to give him the results of raids and
the extent of casualties. He always wanted to know about the losses –
and he took them to heart so personally.'[1] Lady Harris added that her
husband's devoted SASO and later Deputy C-in-C of Bomber Command,
Robert Saundby, who shared their official residence of Springfield at
High Wycombe, was a great help throughout the war. Known as 'Sandy',
he was a rotund, moustachioed, genial aide with a wide range of inter-
ests, including fishing and model railways, but his spaniel-like devotion
to Harris meant that he was too much in awe of his chief ever to challenge him or give candid advice, precisely what Harris needed when he
was at his most stubborn.

Harris's daily routine began after breakfast, when he was driven to
Bomber Command Headquarters from Springfield by his chauffeur
Maddocks in his two-seater Bentley, which was marked with a lighted

sign 'Priority'. Though it was only a short distance, Harris loathed the idea of walking, a legacy of his endless marches in southern Africa during the First World War.

Harris generally arrived at 8.30 a.m. and was met by his secretary, WAAF officer Peggy Wherry, who brought him the most urgent signals and folders with target information. He was then driven to Bomber Command's Operations Room, an underground bunker concealed beneath a grassy mound. 'The Hole', as it was called, was a large oblong chamber with a rubber floor which had a single point of entry permanently manned by an armed guard. Across all the walls were displayed large quarter-inch maps of Europe, orders of battle, lists of targets, charts with the current month's phases of the moon and blackboards with details of the previous night's raids. At 9 a.m. precisely, Harris presided over the morning conference which would decide that night's target. Attended by most of the top officers in Bomber Command's HQ, it was a solemn event, hence its nickname of 'Morning Prayers' or 'High Mass'. The sense of reverence was increased by the strength of Harris's charisma, as John Searby, a Pathfinder commander recalled:

> A small desk placed in the centre of the Ops Room awaited the arrival of Sir Arthur who was punctual to the minute . . . It was a small drama enacted every morning with unfailing regularity; we heard his quick step as he descended the stairs and braced ourselves for the encounter. There was always a mild air of nervousness; his personality was powerful and there was a hushed silence as he entered the Ops Room. He removed his hat, reached into his left-hand breast pocket and took out his packet of American cigarettes, lit up and asked the first question, which seldom varied: 'Did the Hun do anything last night?'[2]

A report on the raids was given by the Senior Intelligence Officer, who then handed Harris a list of the priority targets. There followed a weather forecast from Bomber Command's Chief Meteorological Officer, Dr Magnus Spence, always a crucial part of the proceedings for the weather could dictate the nature of operations. After interrogating Spence, Harris chose the targets for the coming evening, setting out the number of aircraft, the bomb loads and the timing of the sorties. He allowed no discussion about these decisions. Officers knew they were expected to give factual information, not enter a debate. After only a few minutes 'Morning Prayers' were over. 'He rose and left the room, without another word or smile, and we all relaxed,' recalled Colonel Charles Carrington.[3]

Once Harris had chosen the targets, the detailed planning of the operations was left to Saundby and his colleagues, whose tasks included working out routes, fuel loads, timings, markers and Pathfinder procedures. Because of his love of fishing, Saundby gave every German city a piscine code name; so, for instance, Berlin was 'Whitebait', Hamburg 'Dace' and Nuremburg 'Grayling'. Having finalized the details, Bomber Command HQ would then send the instructions by teleprinter to the relevant Bomber Group headquarters. 'Teleprinting was the most secretive means of communication there was,' said Rita Symons who worked at High Wycombe under Harris and typed many of the signals in code.[4] In turn, the Group would relay the details to the squadrons due to take part in the operation. This was done through the Group broadcast, usually held at ten o'clock, when the commanders and specialist officers of the participating squadrons were summoned to their own station's Operations Room. All the individual Operations Rooms were linked up to the Group HQ by a secure telephone line, down which all the relevant information about the forthcoming raid was fed. After the Group broadcast, the stations swung into action, embarking on all the complex arrangements for preparing the airmen and their bombers.

A Lancaster station generally comprised two squadrons, each of them led by a Wing Commander. The squadrons themselves were made up of two or three flights, each of them normally equipped with eight to ten heavy bombers under the control of a squadron leader. Within the flight, every individual Lancaster was given its own title, such as *G-George*, *S-Sugar* or *Q-Queenie*, names that were easily identifiable over the radiotelephone when preparing to take off or come in to land. Planes were often adorned on one side of the fuselage with painted mascots and symbols indicating the number of missions. But the aircrews themselves were just one part of the huge system established by Bomber Command to sustain the offensive. A typical Lancaster airfield at the peak of the war contained about 2,500 personnel, with the airmen only making up one tenth of that number. The rest included armourers, mechanics, clerks, drivers, caterers, RAF Service Police (SPs) and WAAFs. To maintain this organization, the airfields grew to become like rural towns with their own food stores, canteens, offices and accommodation. Some of the larger bases even had their own cinemas, hospitals, dance halls and sports facilities. Their buildings were often so widely spread out that it was only possible to get around them by bicycle. There was nothing luxurious, however, about life on most of the bomber airfields, which had sprung up rapidly during the early part of the war and whose predominant architectural vernacular was the squat, primitive Nissen hut. For those who served in Bomber Command, their prevailing memories were often of icy winds blasting across the Fens, of dark nights shivering around a stove, of iron beds with rough blankets, and of dirty washrooms and tepid showers. There were some much better quarters, like the wood-panelled splendour of Petwood House near Woodhall Spa in Lincolnshire, which was used by 617 Squadron, but these were the exception.

Posted to the base of Wigsley in Nottinghamshire for heavy-bomber training, Flight Sergeant George Hull wrote to a friend, 'Wigsley, ugh! Pigsley would be more appropriate yet I doubt whether any pig would care to be associated with it. The camp is dispersed beyond reason. If I never had a bike I doubt I could cope with the endless route marches that would otherwise be necessary. Messing is terrible, both for food and room to eat it. Normally we queue for half an hour before we can even sit, waiting for it. Washing facilities are confined to a few dozen filthy bowls and two sets of showers an inch deep in mud and water.'[5] For crews on duty, the food was of a higher standard, the post-operation meal of bacon and eggs being the highlight, but otherwise it was dismal, featuring such dishes as fishpaste. Frank Broome, a Lancaster rear gunner with 626 Squadron based at Wickenby, recalled that he and his mates took any chance they could to visit cafes and teashops in nearby Lincoln, because 'we never seemed to be anything but starving'. Broome also wrote that he only took a shower once a fortnight because the experience was so unpleasant. 'It meant stripping in a cold, concrete-floored, brick-built shower monstrosity. Quite often, the floor immediately outside the communal shower cubicle would be flooded to a depth of 25 mm, especially if used in the last couple of days.'[6]

For everyone except the night-flying crews, the day on the airfield generally began before seven o'clock. Cliff Allen, a Yorkshireman who served as an engine fitter in 467 Lancaster Squadron, gave this description of the scene in his Nissen hut on a typically cold February morning in 1943 at RAF Bottesford on the Lincolnshire–Leicestershire border. 'The combustion stove in the centre of the hut still showed a red dying glow. The air pollution rate was appalling and ready to be cut with a knife; any mice in there could be pronounced dead.' Then one of the early risers burst in with a pot of tea, and the rush of bracing air forced the other men from their beds. Allen and his mates had yet to be issued with bicycles, so they had to walk over a mile to their ablutions. 'The temperature was well below zero and in spite of Balaclavas, scarves and mittens, we arrived at the wash house well and truly frozen. The water supply was inevitably cold but help came from the cookhouse in the shape of several buckets of hot water.'[7] Each man carried his own 'goonbag', a haversack in which he kept his washing and shaving kit, mug, knife, fork and spoon. The men then went for their breakfast, which was enlivened by the Tannoy blaring out the familiar march 'Into Battle'. After washing up their mugs and cutlery, it was onto the buses to be taken out to the dispersal areas where the Lancasters were parked.

The first job for the fitters every morning was to carry out the Daily Inspections, or DIs, of each Merlin engine, the Rolls-Royce masterpiece that powered the RAF throughout the war. The Merlin XX, used on the Lancaster Mark I, was a 12-cylinder, 60-degree, upright Vee, liquid-cooled engine. Supercharged by compressed air to give an improved performance at higher altitudes, each Merlin weighed 1,450 pounds and had a capacity of 27 litres, much lighter and smaller than the Bristol Hercules used on the limited run of Lancaster Mark IIs, which weighed 1,930 pounds and had a capacity of 38.5 litres. The heavy bulk of the Hercules was one reason why it gave the Lancaster II a much lower ceiling than the Mark I. The fuel for the Merlin XX was 100 octane, while the coolant was 30 per cent ethylene glycol and 70 per cent water, making this type less combustible and more durable than engines that ran purely on glycol. Each Merlin provided a drive to the propeller unit, which was generally fitted with a three-bladed De Havilland airscrew, as well as individual drives to other services, such as hydraulic pumps that powered the gun turrets, the undercarriage and the flaps, and the vacuum pumps for the instruments. With 1,300 horsepower, the Merlin was the epitome of strength and reliability, giving the Lancaster Mark I a range of 3,000 miles with a minimum bomb load and a service ceiling of 23,500 feet. 'By God those Rolls-Royce Merlins were bloody magnificent machines,' said Nick Williamson, a New Zealander with 75 Squadron.[8] One indicator of the power of the Lancaster's Merlins came from an incident experienced by a production worker, Mrs M. Wright, at the Avro factory in Yeadon, West Yorkshire. 'I was going by a Lancaster on the tarmac near the flight sheds. I didn't realize there was someone inside doing tests. As I came round the corner, the engines were run up and, as I couldn't dodge out of the way quickly enough, the blast knocked me off my feet and blew me some distance.'[9]

During a mission to Berlin, each Merlin would make one and a quarter million revolutions, an arduous burden on any engine no matter how well built. As Cliff Allen explained, the fitters performing the DIs were looking for damage or faults arising from the strain of such trips:

> The removal of the side cowlings revealed our first objective – the exhaust stubs and the protective shroud. The twelve stubs on each engine took a

terrific pounding from the burning of waste gases and a long trip, some-times ten hours, created havoc during flight. The six stubs on each side of the Merlin were given a 'musical' check by striking each with a screw-driver. Undamaged exhaust stubs gave off the same tone, whilst a lower pitch revealed a cracked stub. This was slight damage, but a common occurrence was to find stubs completely burnt off – even the metal shrouds having disintegrated.

During the DIs, all pipes, connections and plugs were studied for leaks and tightened if necessary; the main oil filter was cleaned; and coolant and oil levels were also checked. 'Give us the tools and we'll finish the job,' was one of Churchill's most famous epigrams of the war, uttered in 1941 when he was appealing to the United States for industrial help with the war effort.[10] But Allen felt that aspiration had never been fulfilled within Bomber Command. 'Frustrations were plenty and the one never eliminated was the gnawing fact that we were working on a first class aero engine with third class tools.' Open-ended spanners, for example, were 'too soft and soon useless'.[11]

Another Lancaster fitter was Stephen Rew, who had fallen in love with aeroplanes in his youth but had been crestfallen when he was rejected for RAF recruitment as a fighter pilot. But his engineering skills enabled him to join the service as a fitter and after his training he was sent to 44 Squadron based at Waddington, Lincolnshire. In an unpublished memoir he described the thrill of his first sight of the Lancaster once he had been allotted to a ground crew:

> Seldom in my life have I felt so proud or excited as when walking across the grass towards the big aircraft, on which the dark red letters KM-J, outlined in yellow, showed up in the dull black of her fuselage sides. Beneath the side of the cockpit canopy, glinting in the sun, were painted 26 little yellow bombs in rows of ten, each indicating an attack on Germany, interspersed here and there with an ice-cream cone, indicating an attack on Italy. From the engine exhausts, wide greyish streaks ran back across the wings, giving her a look of wisdom and experience, while her big gaping bomb doors seemed to lend a certain deadliness to her eager shape. From that moment she was to me the only aircraft in the only flight in the only squadron in Bomber Command.

He admitted that the DIs required 'a lot of physical fitness', for they involved hauling a heavy trestle platform from one engine to another. The fatigue was compounded when serious problems occurred. At Waddington, any technical difficulties arising from a raid were logged in an overnight report, known as the 'snag-book'. On one occasion, Rew saw in the snag-book that his Lancaster had a bad oil leak on the port inner engine and a case of overheating in the starboard outer engine. The former involved replacing the vacuum pump, an arduous task because of its almost inaccessible location. Solving the latter problem was even more complex. First, he discovered a hairline crack in the top of the header tank. When he changed the tank and pressure-tested the new one, he was 'puzzled by a faint, continuous ringing noise, like a tuning fork, which went up in tone as the pressure rose'. After a while he found that 'a very fine jet of coolant was shooting out of the radiator'. There was no alternative but to change the radiator, 'a horrible job', which he only just managed to complete in time before the aircrew arrived in advance of take-off.[12]

In Rew's squadron, there were three fitters assigned to each Lancaster, plus a rigger who was in charge of the plane's flying controls and hydraulic and pneumatic systems. Also attached to every flight was a group of specialists, the 'gash' trades such as radio mechanics, photographic technicians, instrument bashers and electricians, who moved from one Lancaster to another checking all was in order and repairing any faults. In addition, an NCO would go round the dispersals during the DIs, ensuring that the work was proceeding satisfactorily before giving a report to the squadron's Wing Commander on the number of aircraft that would be available for operations. Once the DIs were completed, the Lancaster aircrews were driven out to dispersal to conduct test runs on their aircraft's engines and equipment, the first confirmation that there would be operations that evening. In order to save the plane's own batteries, each engine was individually started using a lead from an accumulator carried on a trolley. Moving from starboard to port, the fitters plugged in the trolley acc lead, pressed the starting button, and, with a reluctant cough, the engine kicked into life and then settled down to a steady rumble. Once all four engines were running, the flight engineer tested each one to maximum rpm, beginning with the starboard outer, as described in Stephen Rew's vivid account:

> The shining disc of the starboard outer propeller shimmers and the engine note grows to a roar, drowning the rumble of the others. More and more full-throated it becomes, falls and rises again as he checks the operation of the propeller, steadies for a moment at rated boost, and swells to a fierce bellow as he checks the take-off power. The kite quivers against the restraints of the brakes and the chocks, and the roar begins to diminish as he eases the throttle back, steadies as the magnetos are checked, when the sensitive ear can detect the normal slight drop in rpm as each magneto is switched

off in turn. Then the noise becomes a discontented rumble again, and the process is repeated on the inboard engine. One by one they are run up and they all sound quite healthy.[13]

Occasionally, if a Lancaster had been on the ground for a few days or had developed a serious fault, a full air test would be held, as explained by Flight Engineer Norman Ashton, who flew with *W-William* in 103 Squadron:

> *William* had not flown for a couple of days and we had to do an air test before lunch. Each member of the crew checked his own equipment for serviceability and all snags were carefully noted. We climbed, dived, banked and weaved; tested fuel tanks and pumps, radio, navigational and bombing equipment; feathered and unfeathered propeller blades; swung turrets and guns; checked oxygen and intercom systems; checked pressures, temperatures, voltages, light switches and instruments – in fact every effort was made to sort out anything which might give trouble on the night's trip. On our return, I reported all snags to the sergeant and the tradesmen concerned, so that everything could be fixed in good time.[14]

At Rew's base of Waddington, checking and repairs continued up to noon, when the ground crews washed their hands in petrol, took off their overalls and cycled to the cookhouse for lunch, then retired for a smoke and more tea in the NAAFI canteen. The early afternoon saw an increase in the intensity of the activity at dispersal, as the Lancasters were loaded with bombs and fuel. The first task in the process of 'bombing-up' was to load the trolleys at the station's bomb dump, which was situated as far as possible from the main camp and was protected by blast walls. The bombs were placed on flat-topped Eagle carriers pulled by a heavyweight David Brown tractor, often driven by a WAAF. Though by 1945 the Lancaster was able to carry a phenomenal 22,400-pound bomb, the type of load for normal operations varied greatly. On a maximum incendiary raid, that favoured by the Air Staff in the early years, there would be 14 Small Bomb Carriers (SBCs), each filled with 236 four-pound incendiaries and looking rather like a box of tightly packed fireworks. Alternatively, an industrial demolition raid might feature 14 1,000-pound medium-capacity bombs, while an area-bombing mission that mixed fire with demolition would have the 4,000-pound cylindrical 'Cookie', 3 tail-armed High Explosive (HE) bombs and 6 SBCs. The tractors then hauled the laden trolleys to each aircraft's dispersal.

Frank Hawkins, an armourer with 9 Squadron, recounted the next stage: 'All bombs would come from the dump with safety devices intact and would be left on trolleys at each aircraft's dispersal, there to be pushed under the bomb bay and positioned correctly for winching up. The drivers certainly acquired a fair amount of skill to be able to back the bomb trolley accurately into position, but the manhandling was left to the armourers who were invariably helped by the rest of the aircraft's crew.'[15] A winch was used to lift the bombs into the Lancaster's voluminous bay, where they were secured into bomb racks, but even with this mechanical assistance it was, as Stephen Rew wrote, 'really hard work for the armourers. They had to carry the winches, weighing more than a hundredweight, through the cramped space of the fuselage, let the cable down through the appropriate hole in the floor, hook it onto the bomb or incendiary can, wind the winch-handles until their arms were nearly dropping off and then engage the bomb-release catch. They would have to repeat this at each of the fourteen bomb stations.'[16] The demanding nature of this task was recalled by Les Bartlett, a bomb aimer in 50 Squadron, in his diary for 3 November 1943. 'What a day I've had. "Ops" tonight – but not for our crew so I went and helped the armourers with "bombing-up" the kites. Gee! – I've never worked so hard in my life. It's no piece of cake winding the winches with a 4000 pound bomb on the end of the cables. It took us an hour to do each kite and the ground crew of the last kite were already running up the engines before we had finished.'[17] Like the fitters, the armourers did not always find that their tools were adequate for the job. Lancaster pilot Mick Maguire once turned up at dispersal to find an armourer attacking the bomb doors with an axe. The armourer explained that it was the quickest way to ensure the doors shut tightly. 'This was the essence of everything. We never had time. It led to magnificent achievement becoming routine, because the job had to be done whether we had the time or not.'[18] During just over three years of wartime operations, Lancaster armourers loaded 51 million incendiaries and 608,612 tons of high explosives. The total tonnage of high explosive dropped by Lancasters would have been enough to fill a goods train 345 miles long.

Throughout the afternoon other assignments would be completed, such as the cleaning of the Browning guns and the loading of their ammunition. Nearly all Lancasters carried eight .303 guns, two in the front turret, each with a capacity for 1,000 rounds, two in the mid-upper turret, again with a capacity of 1,000 rounds, and four in the rear, able to carry 2,500 rounds each, the greater potency reflecting the fact that most fighter attacks came from astern. The total of 14,000 rounds were stored on belts in ammunition tanks, one each by the front and mid-upper turrets, with the quartet of tail guns fed from long channels that ran down the sides of the fuselage to tanks in the centre of the plane. Jim McGilveray, a rear gunner with 115 Squadron, was impressed with this arrangement for the rear turret. 'When you fired the gun, a little motor went round and pulled the ammo down the rails, a good idea which meant there were no tanks or ammo in the turret.'[19] On the early production Lancaster there were also two guns, each with a capacity of 500 rounds, in the ventral turret underneath the fuselage, but the turret was phased out from 1942 because it was regarded as an extravagance that weighed down the plane. The most influential figure behind its removal was Sir John Slessor, in his capacity as Commander of No. 5 Group. He told Harris in February 1942: 'An enormous amount of material and skilled-labour time is being devoted to the installation of a soup-plate under-turret with a periscope sight that will add something like 500 pounds to the weight and take something like 10 mph off the speed of the Lancaster and I believe will probably never be used – and certainly not at night. I cannot believe that this is an economical use of our resources.' Harris agreed that the ventral turret was an irrelevance for night operations.[20] In the long run, however, its removal was to prove one of the most misguided decisions taken about the Lancaster, making the plane disastrously vulnerable to German night fighters once the Luftwaffe changed its tactics in 1943.

The storage of the ammunition belts, maintenance of the guns and testing on the ranges was generally the responsibility of the armoury section, though in some squadrons the gunners liked to look after their own Brownings. In fact, Mick Maguire, a former fighter pilot who had transferred to 9 Squadron, was disturbed at this proprietorial attitude and took tough action: 'This tradition had to go. Look in a rear turret and you might find that each gun had a different girl's name painted on it. Watch a gunner cleaning his guns and you could see him using engine oil which, if you want your gun to freeze at high altitude, was the very best thing to use.'[21]

Supplying the fuel and oil was another major task. It has been estimated that during the war Lancaster sorties consumed no fewer than 228 million gallons of fuel.[22] The Lancaster had six self-sealing fuel tanks mounted in its wings. The No. 1 tanks, situated between the fuselage and the inner engines, could each hold 580 gallons; the No. 2 tanks between the engines 383 gallons; and the No. 3 tanks in the outer wings 114 gallons. This gave a maximum fuel load of 1,077 gallons for each wing, or 2,154 in total. For aircrews still awaiting news of their target for the night ahead, the size of load could be an indicator of the length of journey they faced. With a Lancaster consuming petrol at the rate of 200 gallons an hour, the maximum meant a ten-hour round trip deep into Germany, perhaps to the 'Big City' (Berlin), whereas a much lighter load implied a mission to northern France. Filling up the plane could be 'quite an ordeal', according to fitter Cliff Allen. 'To refuel efficiently and quickly required three men: one to check fuel contents on the flight engineer's panel, the other two to operate nozzles on the port and starboard fuel tanks.'[23] The fuel arrived at each dispersal point in a big six-wheeled AEC Matador bowser, capable of holding 2,500 gallons. The fitters climbed onto the wings to place the heavy nozzles in the tanks, then the hoses poured in the green, pungent 100-octane fuel at a rate of 40 gallons per minute.

After refuelling was completed, along came the oil bowser, a 500-gallon tanker pulled by a tractor. At the rear of each Merlin nacelle was the engine's oil tank, with a capacity for 100 gallons, and the fitters checked that each tank was filled to the correct level. For Rew, oiling-up was the worst job of the day, 'for the hose and nozzle were always smothered in oil and were heavy and awkward to handle. When each tank had been filled, one would turn off the tap on the nozzle but no matter how long it was left to drain, one could always be quite certain that it would drip all over the place.'[24] Throughout the bombing-up, rearming and refuelling, there would be a host of other preparations to be carried out, like ensuring that the Perspex canopies were spotless and that the retractable undercarriage's huge Dunlop tyres, 64 inches in diameter and 19 inches in width, were at the correct pressure. Ian Curtis, a ground crewman (or 'erk' in RAF vernacular) at Ludford Magna in Lincolnshire, painted this picture of the scene on his base while he laboured in the armoury section. 'Time drifted past with the multitude of small jobs which always seemed to accumulate. Outside, the usual noises of an aerodrome echoed around. A metallic clang, pumping noises, the shrill of an electrical drill, voices, the muted rumble of a distant running Merlin, the ripping fast rattle of the .303 Brownings from the butts; the rising and falling note of a tractor in the field beyond the armoury.'[25]

The technical work may have been physically demanding for the ground crews, but the real psychological pressure was faced by the aircrews as the clock ticked towards the moment for take-off. Even for the bravest men, the countdown towards the start of a mission was a time of mounting apprehension. 'I feel deep, dark and depressed and distrustful,' wrote wireless operator Charles Williams, of his foreboding at an imminent mission.[26] The atmosphere of nervous anxiety, never absent from a Lancaster base, was dramatically tightened in the late morning, when the battle order for the night's operation was posted on the noticeboards outside the flight offices and messes, setting out the details of missions and naming the crews who would be participating. At the bottom of the order, there would be a note about the timing of the briefing for aircrews, usually in the late afternoon, but not yet any mention of the target. Bob Woolf, a gunner with 9 Squadron, described the mood when the order was posted. 'All those listed for the trip felt the tension, and this would continue right up through the briefing, the preparation for the flight and the pre-flight meal. Sometimes the reaction would be instant. Sometimes some fellows would need to go to the toilet in great haste. Others would try a forced kind of levity, cracking jokes and laughing too easily. Others would become quiet and withdrawn. Nobody wanted to reveal the fear they felt inside but it was deep in our souls.'[27]

After lunch the aircrews might try to get some sleep in their Nissen huts or write letters to family and loved ones. Or they might have to go through more service tests on their aircraft and liaise with the ground crews. All the while, the pressure was intensifying, symbolized by a more overt presence of the RAF Special Police to impose security around the station and prevent any gossip leaking to the public. On some bases, chains were even put around telephone kiosks to stop outside calls being made. The suspense reached a new pitch as the hour of the briefing approached. Flight commanders and specialist gunnery, wireless, bombing and navigation leaders had been called into earlier pre-briefings so they could familiarize themselves with the detailed plans for the operation. Then the moment arrived for the full squadron assembly, when more than 120 men piled into the briefing room, usually another utilitarian Nissen hut. The air of theatrical anticipation was reinforced by more Special Police on the door and the thick cigarette smoke that quickly filled the room. On a dais at the front of the hall was a stand with a large map of Europe, covered up with a curtain. Few West End shows could have created in their audience such aching expectancy. Like a troupe of actors, the senior officers then marched onto the stage. The Commanding Officer grabbed hold of the corner of the curtain and, with the words 'Gentlemen, the target for tonight is . . .', he pulled it away to reveal the destination, its route marked on the map by a half-inch thick red ribbon. The revelation of the target provoked a noisy response from the crews, its negativity calibrated by the difficulty of the mission. 'There was always a big groan if we were told we were going to Berlin. And there would be a clap if we were going to France,' said George Bilton, an engineer with 434 Squadron.[28] Tail gunner Chan Chandler wrote of the hierarchy of reactions to targets: 'Which is the worst? The flak searchlights of the Ruhr? The long, long drag across enemy territory to Berlin and back? The long hours across the unforgiving sea to the ports of Norway? Each had its own particular brand of terror; each caused that sudden knotting of the stomach to the point of vomit as that red ribbon revealed your fate for the night.'[29]

After the Commanding Officer had revealed the target, he then handed over to the Senior Intelligence Officer, who outlined the importance of the target and gave more details of the operation, the potential flak and searchlights, and the type of markers to be used by the Pathfinders on the target. Bill Jones, the Intelligence Officer from 1942 at Elsham Wolds, Lincolnshire, wrote of how important it was to engage with the crews:

> Although I had my briefing notes in my hand, I always made sure I could do the briefing without having to read from them. If you had to read your notes, you couldn't look at the crews and, in any case, it gave the impression that you were simply reading from a prepared speech. As I take the platform with my three feet long black pointer in my hand, I give a quick look round. It happens at every briefing – how many of them will return to be interrogated in the early hours of the morning, I wonder? It was always a tremendous responsibility to stand up there in front of those aircrews and to give them the best information possible.[30]

Further briefings then followed from the specialists. The Navigation leader provided more information about the route, especially the turning points and the diversions aimed at deceiving the German defences. The Bombing leader set out the payloads, the timing of the attack and target indicators. Then the Meteorological Officer forecast the weather and windspeeds, while details of the radio frequencies came from the Signals Officer. Finally, the head of Flying Control set out the procedures to be used on take-off and landing. Not all of this was treated with the reverence that the commanders expected. 'Sir, can I be excused, only I'm meeting my girlfriend tonight at eight o'clock' was one common joke uttered from the back of the room.[31]

All the briefings completed, the men began to troop out of the room. They were often met at the door by the Medical Officer handing out Benzedrine tablets to anyone who felt they needed them for the long night ahead. Known as 'wakey-wakey' pills, their effect was described by Pathfinder gunner Ron Smith: 'They would keep your eyes open firmly when your body was exhausted, mind ever alert but sometimes distant, unbelieving.'[32] Others found that the pumping adrenalin from a flight over enemy territory was enough to keep them awake. But according to Clayton Moore, an air gunner with 9 Squadron, Benzedrine tablets were always in great demand not merely for heightening mental sharpness but also 'because it was popularly believed that they were an effective aphrodisiac. Resulting from this, the pills were jealously hoarded for the next leave period'.[33] Then it was on to the pre-operational meal, usually consisting of bacon and eggs. With wartime rationing in full force, these were both cherished items denied to other personnel. But because of increasing nerves, such meals were not always appreciated. 'A man about to be hanged can, I understand, choose almost anything for his last meal,' wrote the Lancaster pilot R. E. Wannop in a private memoir. 'I always imagined him having a whale of a time, stuffing down all sorts of delicacies. I've changed my mind. I never enjoyed an operational meal before a trip, just couldn't stomach it.'[34] Others, like flight engineer Maurice Flower, saw how too generous a diet could cause mayhem in the air. 'They started giving us chips on pre-flight meals but at 22,000 feet they don't work too well on the stomach! The smell used to be a bit obnoxious in the aeroplane so we asked them, "Please, no more chips on pre-op meals."'[35]

It was not unknown for airmen to overindulge in other ways. Jack Currie, a pilot with 12 Squadron, was always astonished at the behaviour of another pilot in his squadron, who was fighting 'two wars at the same time. One was our common fight against the Axis powers and the other, more personal, was his perpetual struggle against the demon drink.' His habit led to a consumption of at least four tankards of ale at lunchtime, followed by a sustained outburst of involuntary flatulence. The alcohol-fuelled explosions would be repeated as his Lancaster embarked on its sortie. 'As the air became thinner with height, so his intolerable gases expanded. His cabin crew were accustomed to use emergency oxygen from ground level in their determination to retain consciousness.'[36] Bomb aimer Dennis Steiner's pilot got so paralytic one lunchtime before a night operation that the rest of the crew filled him with black coffee, plunged him into a cold bath and then put him to bed for the afternoon. Anytime he tried to get up, they sat on him until he went back to sleep. Later at the briefing, he kept nodding off. Steiner briefly contemplated reporting him as unfit to fly, which would have meant a court martial, but decided against it, hoping that the pilot would have sobered up by take-off. Amazingly, said Steiner, 'by the time we got out to dispersal, he was almost normal and went aboard to inhale lungfuls of oxygen, a good cure for a hangover. All went well, much to my relief.'[37]

Even without such dramas, the tension kept rising. For many airmen, the period between the end of the briefing and the embarkation of their Lancaster was the most draining, as dark thoughts began to fill the passing minutes. Some played chess, others fitfully read the newspapers. In Les Bartlett's 50 Squadron there was a fixed ritual of listening to a record of the Andrews Sisters singing 'The Shrine of Saint Cecilia': 'If you were the superstitious type it was a must, if not then you still listened to it because it was considered extremely unlucky not to have done so.'[38] Guy Gibson, in his posthumously published memoir, described his own feelings. 'It's a horrible business. Your stomach feels as though it wants to hit your backbone. You can't stand still. You laugh at small jokes, loudly, stupidly. You smoke far too many cigarettes, usually only halfway through, then throw them away. Sometimes you feel sick and want to go to the lavatory. The smallest incidents annoy you and you flare up at the slightest provocation. All this because you are frightened, scared stiff.'[39]

About ninety minutes before take-off, the airmen went along to their crew room to change into their flying gear, which varied according to their role in the aircraft. One of the few flaws in the Lancaster was that its heating was poorly distributed around the fuselage. So the wireless operator, seated near the warm-air outlet, would sometimes become excessively hot, but the men in the extremities – the two gunners and the bomb aimer – received no benefit from the heating system, so they had to rely entirely on clothing for warmth. For the rear gunner conditions could be savagely cold because, on many Lancasters, a Perspex panel was removed to give him a clear view of any approaching fighter, though this also exposed him to the elements. To any gunner sitting in his glacial turret, it was absurd of Air Staff officials to claim that, since his back was to the Lancaster's slipstream, he should have felt little effect from the panel's removal.

There was no absolute standard dress in Bomber Command, but among the most popular items were the famous brown leather, sheepskin-lined Irvin flying jacket (designed by the American aviator Leslie Irvin, who also invented the parachute ripcord system) and a pair of silk long johns. According to the Lancaster navigator Donald Feesey, most of the crew members apart from the gunners wore 'padded half-length inner suits and a canvas outer suit plus silk and woollen gloves. Navigators worked in just the silk ones. Flying boots were fleece-lined. Helmets were lined with oxygen masks which plugged into points in the aircraft and with intercom microphones and earpieces which also plugged into separate points.'[40] Many of the later types of flying boot were designed with the worst hazards of the trip in mind, as bomb aimer Les Bartlett recorded in his diary: 'There was a knife in a small inside pocket of the boot. If you were shot down you could use it to cut off the lamb's wool sides of your flying boots leaving you with a pair of ordinary looking boots.'[41]

As well as a parachute harness, the aircrews also donned their inflatable lifejackets, known as 'Mae Wests' after the well-endowed Hollywood star. Some airmen made their own additions to their equipment. Thomas Murray, a pilot with 207 Squadron, always kept a loaded revolver in one of his boots, not for potential use on the enemy but on himself. 'My great fear was burning to death. You saw it a lot over Germany and as captain you could never leave the aircraft because you would not know if your crew was all out. So the gun was the greatest friend I had. I knew that I would not have to face that last bit. That did my morale a lot of good.'[42] Though aircrews were issued with a regulation steel helmet when they first joined the RAF, they never had any need for them in the aircraft. But Campbell Muirhead learnt through a discussion with some colleagues that the helmets were not totally useless, as he noted in his diary: 'Discovered one interesting item, which is that many bomb aimers, when on the run-in, lie on top of their steel helmet in such a way as to protect their testicles. Must say I hadn't thought of that. Somewhat uncomfortable, I would have thought (but maybe not as uncomfortable as having your wedding tackle shot off!). Anyway, I'll take my chance of ending my tour speaking in a high falsetto voice.'[43]

For the rear gunners, with their unique exposure to the freezing night skies, the process of changing clothes was even more demanding. Many of them alternated between two sets of flying clothing, depending on the weather forecast, as Joe Williams of 625 Squadron noted:

If the Met officer said -30 degrees, I would wear my Sidcot [named after its inventor, the Australian aviation pioneer Sidney Cotton] outer suit with my electrically heated Sidcot inner. I had five pairs of gloves. The first pair were white silk, followed by yellow chamois leather gloves, then brown woollen knitted gloves, then some black electrically heated ones which plugged into the sleeves of the Sidcot suit and finally a pair of brown leather gauntlets. We also wore long silk lined underwear, fisherman's socks in addition to your normal socks, a fisherman's jersey and a woollen balaclava under your flying helmet. We also had a heater in the microphone of the flying helmet to stop the spittle or breath freezing up the mike. Then on top you wore the famous Mae West flotation jacket. If the Met Officer said it would be -40, then we had a massive garment called a Taylor flotation suit. It was yellow with in-built flotation pads. There were zips running in different directions. You needed help to get into it. You looked a bit like the Michelin man and mobility was not very great.[44]

The gunners, whom Lancaster pilot R. E. Wannop described as looking like 'Robot men from some fantastic novel',[45] had to be careful not to sweat too much, for perspiration was liable to freeze at night and cause severe frostbite to the hands.

While the men were in the crew room, they were handed out their rations for the flight, which generally consisted of some boiled sweets, a bar of chocolate, a thermos flask of coffee, and perhaps a sandwich and a tin of orange juice. The men were also given their escape kits for use if they came down in occupied territory. These sealed emergency packages contained a local map, a supply of local currency, some forged identity documents, a compass, chewing gum, some pieces of chocolate and concentrated food capsules. A grimmer task was a reminder of the tenuous nature of the airmen's mortality. They were each given envelopes in which to place all their personal effects and letters, which would be sent to their next of kin in the event that they failed to return. In addition they had to hand over their keys, so that if they died the duty officers would not have to break open their lockers to collect their belongings.

Given the extreme dangers they were facing, it is hardly surprising that many of the airmen carried charms. Rabbits' feet, scarves, medallions, lapel pins, playing cards, coins and photographs were all part of this arsenal of superstition. Norman Ashton's crew in *W-William* always brought on board a little woollen doll of an airman to protect them. 'Joe was a tiny fellow with a man-sized job, as fine a mascot as ever graced a Lancaster,' wrote Ashton.[46] One crew decorated the outside of their Lancaster cockpit on every flight with two pairs of women's knickers stolen from the back of a pub.[47] Some charms were counterproductive. Ronald Olsen, a pilot with 617 Squadron, recalled how one of the instruments on his Lancaster went haywire during a trip to Nuremburg, causing a disastrous loss of direction. It turned out that the navigator had a girlfriend who had given him a large horseshoe as a charm. He had put it in his bag, from where, during some freakish weather activity, it appeared to exert a magnetic pull on the main compass.[48]

The deepening fear before a sortie could induce a frenzied atmosphere in the crew room, as Harry Yates recalled. On the night of an operation to Lille 'the crew room was a scene of total chaos. Parachute harnesses, flying gear, navigation bags, rations of chocolate, chewing gum and flasks of coffee, everything was scattered wildly over the tables and on the floor. Aircrew were darting about the room like men possessed, picking up one thing and putting down another, talking at fever pitch; "Where the hell are my goggles? . . . Who moved my bag? . . For God's sake, stop mixing up your gear with mine!" . . . and so on. If the heroes of the German Night Fighter Wing had seen this they would have laughed all the way to their cockpits.'[49]

Once the men were equipped, they moved along to the parachute section, usually a tall building where the chutes were hung out to dry and then repacked for another trip. Here a team of WAAFs handed out the gear, often engaging in some gallows banter. 'If it doesn't work, bring it back and I'll change it for another' was one standard line. After this the crews were picked up in buses or lorries and driven around the station's perimeter fence to their Lancasters, waiting in the darkness which had now descended on the airfield. It could be a journey of over two miles, giving more time to consider the night ahead. But at least the start was now drawing close. Contemplation would soon be replaced by action. As the vehicles approached, the ground crews were making the final preparations, as Stephen Rew described: 'Oilskin wheelcovers removed and put where they can easily be found in the dark. The already spotless Perspex canopy is given a final polish and the green canvas cover removed from the pitot head. The crew buses come into view around the perimeter track. There is a shout of "Crew Up". Seven young men are deposited at each dispersal. They are greeted by the ground crew who give them a hand with all their paraphernalia: parachutes, harnesses, flying helmets, bags containing maps and charts, thermos flasks and bags of barley sugar.'[50] There was desultory chat for a while, the tension ever more palpable in the air. A couple of anxiously smoked cigarettes might glow in the darkness, a feeble joke cause a ripple of laughter.

A poignant account of these moments can be found in the diary of Jock Colville, Winston Churchill's private secretary who volunteered for fighter service in 1941. One evening while on a sortie he suffered engine failure in his fighter and had to make an emergency landing at an airfield near Cambridge. After his own experience in Fighter Command, he was shocked by the sight of the Lancaster airmen preparing for a massive assault on Berlin. 'I stood outside a hangar and watched one three-ton lorry after another debouch a hundred or more young men, who walked silently and unsmiling to their allotted aircraft. Accustomed as I had already become to the gaiety and laughter of fighter pilots, I was distressed by the tense bearing and drawn faces of the bomber crews . . . Of courage they had plenty, but there was nothing but lip-biting gloom registered on those faces.'[51] A picture of the eerie scene just before a winter night take-off was painted in the private memoir of Lancaster pilot R. E. Wannop:

My thoughts were both disturbing and unpleasant. It was rather uncanny on that drome. Everywhere was white with frost, except the aircraft, which had been brushed clean. The field was silent. A faint trickle of smoke rose from the drain pipes which served as chimneys indicating that, from somewhere, firewood and smoke had been scrounged. I have never been on the eve of a battle and heard the ominous silence but I can imagine it. The field was my battleground. Soon there would be a roar, not of cannons or machine guns but the deafening, ear-splitting thunder of 14 aircraft – 56 mighty engines. We waited. The dull splutter of an obstinate engine made me glance at my watch. Gosh! 10.30 – only 15 minutes to take off. The squadron leader was already starting up. Better get cracking.[52]

It was almost with a sense of relief that the moment had arrived. As the aircrews prepared to climb into their Lancasters, most of them went through one final ritual on the ground: urinating on the tail wheel, both to empty the bladder and bring luck. Hugh Parrott of 207 Squadron said that the habit was so common in his squadron that an official order was sent out forbidding it: '"The practice of urinating on the tail wheel will cease forthwith." We didn't pay much attention to that.'[53] Campbell Muirhead's rather cynical crew even elevated this habit into a competition, seeing which one could pee the furthest, 'a hysterical sight, I think, to a WAAF who passed on her bike in the middle of the proceedings and giggling like mad. Well, it isn't every day a girl sees seven penises, all at the same time, especially seven ejecting competitive parabolas.'[54]

Despite its impressive outward appearance, the Lancaster's interior had restricted space and was not easy to enter, especially for seven men in their full kit. 'From an operational point of view, the Lancaster was superb. But it was designed as a bomber and they thought of the crew afterwards because accommodation was decidedly cramped,' said Ian Anderson, a Pathfinder navigator.[55] The crew boarded the Lancaster by climbing a short ladder and going through a door at the rear of the fuselage on the starboard side. What was immediately striking was the distinctive odour, 'a familiar mixture of oil and petrol and all the rest of it – the "Lancaster smell" we called it,' said John Sanders, a pilot in 617 Squadron.[56] Once inside, the seven men had to go to their respective stations, which involved more physical struggle. For all of them it was something of an obstacle course. In his memoirs Chan Chandler outlined the problems for the rear gunner:

> To get to your turret you had to climb over the tail spar which passed through the fuselage in front of the turret. Your chute was stowed on one side in this 'tunnel' as there was no room for it in the turret. Having got in you had to close and latch two sliding doors behind your back. This was very difficult to do with your flying kit on and if you did not get

them fully closed and latched you not only had a howling draught after take-off but stood a fair chance of falling out, so I always got the wireless operator to latch them for me. If you had to bail out you had to line your turret up, open the doors and get half out of your turret to get your parachute, clip it on, get back into the turret, swing it 90 degrees then fall out backwards.[57]

Once inside the rear turret, the gunner could hardly move, as Bob Pierson recalled: 'My head was just about touching the top of the turret and my shoulders were nearly at the edge. In front there was only enough room to get your hands round the triggers of the guns. Your legs were virtually locked in one position – you couldn't stretch them more than an inch or two without hitting the metal sides or the pedal that turned the turret.'[58]

There was almost as much difficulty for those going further up the plane, since they had to negotiate the long passage of the rear fuselage above the bomb bay, then climb over the waist-high mass of the main spars connecting the wings. 'You had very heavy clothing, were wearing a harness and carrying a parachute. It used to be very difficult. It would exhaust me to be quite honest,' said John Duffield, a flight engineer with 103 Squadron.[59] The stations of the pilot and the flight engineer were beside each other in the cockpit at the heart of the Lancaster. The pilot sat in a high, adjustable seat with an armoured back on the left-hand side of the cockpit, with his parachute pack serving as a seat cushion. In front of him was a standard control yoke for the elevator and aileron control, with rudder pedals at his feet. To his right were the four throttle levers and propeller-control speed levers. On the instrument panel, the markings and needles were painted with radium so that they were illuminated in the dark. The engineer on his right had only a basic fold-down stool. On the starboard wall in front of him was a panel with mounted gauges for electrical charge, oil pressure and temperature, engine coolant temperature and fuel volumes, in addition to controls for the fuel tank selection.[60] 'From an engineer's point of view, the Lanc was a good aircraft,' wrote Joe Nutt of 97 Squadron. 'Everything could be handled without stretching and the automatic boost control relieved one of the need for constant throttle pushing.'[61]

Behind the pilot and engineer, the navigator sat at a desk in his own curtained office facing port, surrounded by his instruments and charts and working by the light of an anglepoise lamp. One odd feature of the Lancaster navigator's cabin, compared to that of the Halifax, was the absence of any pigeonholes, which meant that violent evasive action could cause mayhem as papers and equipment were strewn across the floor. Further aft was the wireless operator's compartment, the warmest part of the plane. Indeed, it was so warm that the operator sometimes ended up working in an open-necked shirt and battledress. Above him was an astrodome through which he could both take star shots for the navigator and also act as a lookout for enemy fighters when he was not engaged with his sets. Down some steps at the front, in the Perspex nose of the Lancaster, was the bomb aimer's compartment, whose large transparent dome had the advantage of a panoramic view and the disadvantage of leaving the aimer with a sense of raw exposure. During the bombing run over the target, the bomb aimer lay on his front looking through the sight. Otherwise, he would move into the gun turret and keep a lookout, while manning the two Browning guns in the nose, though in practice frontal attacks were extremely rare. 'I don't recall ever firing my guns whilst on ops,' recalled Tom Wardle.[62] At the moment of take-off, because of the risk of a crash, the bomb aimer was meant to take up a position beside the engineer rather than stay at the front, though in practice few did so.

With all the crew settled at their stations, the pilot then led the final checks on the plane. The trolley accumulator was hauled into position. The next stage was graphically described in the memoir of R. E. Wannop:

> I slide open my side panel:
> 'Ready for starting, engineer?'
> 'All set, skipper.'
> I leaned out and shouted to the ground crew:
> 'Ready for starting – clear of props.'
> 'OK, skipper – port inner.'
> There was a quiet whirring sound as the electric starter commenced to turn the great prop. My right hand, resting lightly on the throttle, was ready to catch her the moment she fired. A roar, and she started.[63]

The rest of the engines were run up, the night air filled with the deafening sound of the Merlins being revved first to 1,500 rpm to check the magnetos and then to 3,000 rpm to check boost. All the instruments were tested, allowing any faulty generators, magnetos or plugs to be changed. The pilot also went round each crew member in turn to check that the intercom and oxygen supply were working properly. It was impossible, however, to fully test the radio-telephone set before take-off because radio silence had to be maintained. At the same time the gunners loaded the Brownings by placing the ammunition belts in the breach, ensuring that the safety mechanisms on the guns were switched to 'safe'. As tail gunner Frank Broome explained: 'Once loaded, all four guns were cocked, fired on "safe" and re-cocked. The guns were ready to be put on "fire"; each Browning now had a live round in each breachblock.'[64] There was one key administrative procedure to be completed once all the final checks had been done: the pilot's signature on Form 700, which had been filled in by the ground crew. Known in the RAF as 'the Bible', Form 700 indicated the pilot's acceptance of the plane as airworthy. This was not just a matter of clerical bookkeeping. As John Holmes, a senior maintenance officer, revealed, Form 700 encapsulated a heavy responsibility: 'You could easily be sending seven men to their deaths. It only needed a slight slip and we're all human. So I've sat and worried some nights for a very, very long time.'[65] With the engines now running, the job of getting the pilot to sign involved another obstacle course, according to fitter Stephen Rew. 'One of the ground crew grasps the foolscap booklet, which contains the 700, runs through the blustering gale of the slipstream to the door, reaches up and opens it, and scrambles inside. He makes his way over the main spar to the cockpit, fumbles with a pencil and shouts, "All OK?" The pilot nods, glances at the refuelling certificate and serviceability log, signs and returns them. The mechanic retraces his steps down the fuselage, jumps into the gale and closes the door.'[66]

The Lancaster was now itching to move. The pilot gave a signal to the ground crew to pull the chocks away from the front of the wheels. The men rushed forward and heaved at the great wooden blocks holding the aircraft in place. The pilot released the brakes, opened the engines slightly and then, almost imperceptibly, the Lancaster started to move forward from dispersal, joining the procession of other black silhouettes taxiing along the perimeter track towards the take-off point at the head of the runway. The pilot Jack Currie felt that during the process of taxiing:

> the Lancaster wasn't quite at her best. You had to negotiate a narrow, winding perimeter track, which might be more than a mile long if you were starting from the upside of the airfield, to reach the take-off point. You turned by gunning the outer engine on the side away from your turn, and straightened up by giving the opposite engine a burst, but there was a lot of inertia and you had to anticipate each turn by ten or twenty degrees, depending on your speed. You were supposed to taxi at a fast walking pace, but that wasn't easy to judge, sitting twenty feet above the ground. It was best to keep a steady grip on the brake lever, in case she tried to run away with you.[67]

A queue of Lancasters began to form at the marshalling point, each one a few yards behind the other. Near the edge of the start of the runway stood a black and white caravan, from which the airfield controller governed the movements of the aircraft with his large Aldis lamp. A green flash represented his signal to move onto the runway and take off. Beside the caravan a crowd of well-wishers invariably gathered, made up of the station commander, the chaplain, ground crews, ancillary staff and WAAFs. Harry Yates, in Lancaster *S-Sugar*, recorded the scene before a twilight take-off for France, as the green light of the controller sent off the bombers one by one:

> We tagged on to the queue of Lancasters, dramatic in the fading light, engines throbbing, moving slowly towards the take-off runway. The moment came nearer. The pilot in front of us opened his throttles and thundered away. I turned to the strip and ran up the engines on full brakes, checking things one last time. *S-Sugar* shook and strained. The seconds dragged out until the control caravan gave us our green. I released the brakes and we were away. We were going to war.[68]

At the signal, 30 tons of heavy bomber started hurtling down the runway, Merlin engines pulsating at 3,000 rpm, until the take-off speed of about 100 mph was approached. 'Tension was probably at the highest level at that time, prior to leaving the ground. Once the Lancaster was at full power on take-off, carrying a full bomb and fuel load, there was little chance of stopping her on the main runway. It was almost a life and death situation,' wrote tail gunner Frank Broome.[69] It took all the skill of the pilot and his engineer to keep this mighty beast under control, delicately balancing the engine power and rudder control to ensure that the plane did not swing violently to the left as it sped down the concrete.

Jack Currie wrote of how he performed the task with an instinctive co-ordination and calmness on his first-ever flight as a Lancaster pilot:

> I held the rim of the control wheel in my left hand, and opened the throttles with my right, leading with the thumb on the port outer lever to counter the tendency to swing left. I released the brakes, and Lancaster ED414 lurched forward. I kept my eyes on the white-painted centre line of the runway and continued to push the throttle levers up the quadrant until the port outer lever met the gate that marked full take-off power. As I brought the other three levers up to the gate, I kept a forward pressure on the control wheel to lift the tail off the ground. With the rudders up in the slipstream, it was easy to keep her straight. I brought the control wheel back gently as she gathered speed. There was plenty of runway still ahead when I felt her wanting to get airborne and gave more strength to the backward pressure on the wheel. She let go of the ground immediately.[70]

Currie had adopted the approved method of take-off, but others, like the crew of Doug Tritton in 49 Squadron, used a more unorthodox approach. 'The book specified that you should stand with your brakes on, open up to zero boosts, release your brakes and gradually run forward, opening the throttles. What we used to do was stand at the caravan, open up until we were underway and then let the brakes go. We were effectively over-riding the brakes. We would then go off considerably faster than most people did – and with considerably more noise.'[71]

For those in other positions on the Lancaster, the take-off could be an exhilarating if punishing experience. Joe Williams, the 625 Squadron rear gunner, recalled that 'at about 95 to 98 mph the tail would do a little dip and we would come off the runway. When the throttles were fully open at take-off, such was the force of the slipstream that the tail, which had been sitting on the ground, came up and the fuselage was horizontal. Suddenly you're eight feet off the ground in the rear turret. It was quite a long run on maximum boost.'[72] At the opposite end of the plane, bomb aimer J. W. Walsh of 619 Squadron wrote this account of take-off. 'We surge forward, the four Merlins thundering in full bore and we hurtle into the blackness of the night and follow the aircraft in front. I know now why people like to go to those stupid, mad, helter-skelter rides at theme parks and funfairs. I used to get the same incredible elation at take-off when one is a few feet off the ground, travelling at great speed and lying flat with one's head in a Perspex dome.'[73] In another typically striking passage, Stephen Rew gave the perspective of the ground crew, highlighting his emotional connection both with the plane and the airmen:

> Each ground-crew watches anxiously as their own kite turns to the runway and lines up. The slim shape seems to be quivering like a highly-strung hunter at a meet. A short burst of power on each engine in turn to clear the plugs, a flash of green from the control caravan and slowly the engine-note, previously inaudible among the others, becomes a thunderous roar, the kite quivering excitedly, as she is held by the brakes against the thrust of the engines. The brakes come off and she starts to roll, slowly at first, then faster, as the engines are opened up to full power in a full-throated triumphant chorus, the sequel to the solos they have sung while being run up. The dark shape alters as the tail comes up and she thunders, bouncing and rocking down the runway. For an agonising moment she is lost to sight against the darkening background at the far end of the airfield. I don't think anyone will ever forget the feeling of relief as she re-appears above the trees against the twilit sky, her wheels already up, climbing steadily and turning to port, and is soon lost among the other kites in the gathering darkness.[74]

But sometimes the agony was not followed by relief. The combination of darkness, tension, the power of the Lancaster, the weight of the load and the complexity of manoeuvres meant that take-off was one of the most dangerous moments on any sortie. Getting an aircraft weighing around 68,000 pounds airborne was filled with risks, and it was inevitable that disasters happened due either to technical faults or human errors. When they did, the consequences could be devastating, as Bill Jones, the intelligence officer, found one day at Kirmington, Lincolnshire, in April 1944, when a Lancaster taking off for France suddenly swung off the runway and burst into flames. There was a huge explosion as six tons of high explosive blew up, leaving a crater 15 feet deep and 50 feet in diameter on the runway. Jones was in the Kirmington control at this moment. 'I just fell flat on my face when the bomb exploded. It was my first experience of such an event and it was truly awesome. It was even more awesome when I looked up and saw a large object flying in my direction. In the dusk I could not readily identify the object until it hit the ground some 50 yards away. It was one of the Lancaster's Merlin engines.' It was later estimated that the blast had ejected 500 tons of earth from the crater.[75]

Ricky Dyson, a rear gunner, was on a sortie to Munich in November 1944 when his Lancaster crashed in the Leicestershire countryside just moments after take-off. 'I was sitting in the turret one moment, listening to the airspeed called out and then all of sudden I could see a glimpse of trees and hedges when this huge bang occurred. I was knocked out and when I came to I was encircled by noise and flames.' As the fire crept closer to his turret, he managed to smash his way through the Perspex with an axe and climb out. 'All around me was an inferno. There was ammunition going off in all directions, bottles exploding, bombs exploding. It was a terrible sight. I ran for my life towards a hedge but found I couldn't vault it. I looked back and heard the screams, screams of people being burnt alive.'[76] Dyson ran back and managed to drag the skipper to safety. Four of the other crew died that night. The sheer numbers of aircraft taking off over Lincolnshire and East Anglia also made collisions inevitable. On a maximum-effort raid, involving more than 600 heavy bombers, there would be an average of about eight collisions. Nature could bring her own hazards, as rear gunner Frank Broome recorded in his diary about a take-off at Scampton, Lincolnshire, in November 1944:

> We took off about 14.30 and as we went along the runway, about 200 to 300 seagulls suddenly arose and we flew into them at 110 mph. The view

from the tail was tragically spectacular! The Lancaster's airscrews were chopping four whirling tunnels right through the seabird flock. Over the roar of the engines I could hear the screams of distress and the thump of bird's bodies as they hit the runway. For the seagulls it was a scene of complete disaster and devastation. We inside the Lancaster were luckier. We managed to clear the ground and get the undercarriage up! The Perspex nose was damaged. Some of the crew up front were covered in blood and feathers. We made one circuit of the drome and landed safely.[77]

The damage to the Lancaster was considerable, with Perspex panels cracked, a propeller spinner broken and dead birds inside the radiators. The flight had to be cancelled.

For those that made it off the runway and into the sky, the ordeal was only just starting.

6

'The light is so bright that it hurts'

'THE LANCASTER LOOKED good from every angle,' wrote the pilot Jack Currie, 'strongly shaped and well-proportioned. In flight, she appeared both powerful and balanced. Some aeroplanes seem to lean forward anxiously as they fly, others to be protestingly pushed along from behind, but the Lancaster rode the air easily and steadily.'[1] The grace of the Lancaster was one of its most arresting features. Despite its weight and vast bomb load, it never lost its elegance. Its aesthetic dignity, so impressive as it waited at dispersal or queued for take-off, was just as evident in the air, when it sailed with a reassuring smoothness over the clouds or through the velvet sky, displaying its attractive lines as it gently banked one way, then the other. Roy Chadwick's daughter once spoke of her father's 'intimate love of line and beauty',[2] and those qualities shone through his design. Indeed, 'beautiful' was the word frequently used by the aircrews to describe the plane. 'The Lanc was a lovely aeroplane: beautiful, almost faultless,' said Peter Huggins.[3] When Peter Russell was first sent on a conversion course to train on Lancasters, he was inspired to write: 'On the ground it had beauty, a purposefulness, more than any I had seen before. In the air it was a delight.'[4]

But the apparently effortless movement of the plane belied the demands on the seven men of the aircrew throughout an operation, as they dealt with the complexity of the sophisticated, four-engine machine and the lethal threat from the enemy defences. A ten-hour flight to Germany involved an array of continual and heavy duties, including scanning the sky for night fighters, balancing the fuel supplies, synchronizing the engines, navigating the route, preparing to bomb the target, communicating with the base and controlling the plane through endless hazards. All this had to be done in a bitterly cold, noisy and claustrophobic environment. It was inevitable that exhaustion should set in after long periods of intense concentration, as rear gunner John Toombes described: 'You had to keep your eyes peeled and not allow your mind to drift. I was concentrating the whole time because if I allowed myself to be lulled into false security, then I was going to suffer and so would the rest of the crew. I could be pretty tired at the end of ops.'[5] Canadian pilot David Day recorded how he actually fell asleep after a trip to a synthetic oil plant in southern Germany: 'I was extremely tired on the way back. On a trip, you're always weaving, so the ground defences cannot predict where you will be if they are tracking you. But on this occasion, I had dozed off and so had my navigator, so he hadn't given me my change of course. We were over Karlsruhe and they got us and hit us. The tail was peppered. We were damned lucky not to be shot out of the sky.'[6]

No other British services personnel during the Second World War faced the same relentless level of sustained pressure as that experienced by the airmen of Bomber Command, 44 per cent of whom were killed in action during the war. The nearest physical and mental equivalent to bombing Germany was service in the trenches of the western front during the First World War, though Air Vice Marshal Harris's losses were proportionately even higher than those of Field Marshal Douglas Haig. In fact, Bomber Command's casualty rate far exceeded the overall army death toll of 9 per cent in the First World War. The Charge of the Light Brigade is seen as one of the most reckless and irresponsible ventures in British military history, yet the death toll amounted to 17 per cent of the total number of horsemen who took part. Heavy-bomber squadrons, with an average loss rate of 4 per cent for every sortie, would equal that after four operations. The burden on the pilots was summarized by Air Marshal McNeece Foster, the head of Bomber Command training, who wrote: 'I met on close terms many bomber pilots during the war. Some emphasized that it was not the flak or the risk of enemy fighter attacks which told most on their nerves. Rather it was the strain of flying by night hour after hour over enemy territory, responsible for their crews and for finding their targets, often under the most appalling weather conditions. Always there was the knowledge that they might be shot down at any moment by an unseen foe without a chance to lift a finger in defence.'[7]

The stress hardly eased from the moment a Lancaster sortie began. In the seconds after the plane lifted off the runway and began its ascent, tremendous concentration and sometimes physical effort was required by the pilot and engineer to ensure that the 30-ton Lancaster sustained its climb. For pilot John Whiteley, 'the important thing was to make sure that you built the speed up to a minimum of 135 mph because if you had engine failure below 135 mph the chances are that you would crash because you hadn't got sufficient flying speed. But once you'd got up to 135 mph, you had sufficient speed to climb away on three engines.'[8] As the Lancaster took to the air, the wheels kept revolving, which could lead to oscillation in the engines and cause mechanical damage. To prevent this, the pilot touched the brakes to stop the wheels turning, then the engineer retracted the undercarriage, the wheels making a dull thud as they folded into the engine nacelles. When the undercarriage was locked down for landing or take-off, a green light shone on the instrument panel, switching off once the wheels were locked up At the same time, the engineer brought in the wing flaps, which in their lowered position at 15 to 20 degrees helped to give the necessary lift to the plane on the runway. The dual working of the pilot and the engineer in this crucial period was depicted by Lancaster navigator Don Feesey on one of his flights. 'The tail began to lift and the plane began to climb at about 110 knots. The pilot needed all his strength to pull back the control column for the climb, so the engineer placed his hand over the pilot's on the throttles, and between them they eased the lever through the gates to get maximum thrust for the ascent. With the enormous weight, only a shallow climb was possible without stalling. To assist the climb, the engineer retracted the undercarriage and the wing flaps.'[9]

Having started the climb, the bombers then steadily moved south towards occupied Europe or eastwards out to the North Sea. The experience of heading away from the base was well-described by Peter Russell of 625 Squadron in an account of his first trip to Germany:

> Left wing down, right wing up, we banked round in part of a left-hand circuit. Below us the faint lights that marked the runway and the edges of the perimeter track were tiny pinpoints of amber and blue, and the green light, about every two minutes, flashed from the caravan at the runway's downwind end as the remainder of the nineteen aircraft of 625 squadron on the night's battle order followed. We were to fly south, down England, climbing as we went.[10]

Though the Lancasters queued up for take-off in procession, they did not fly in formation in night attacks on Germany. In the darkness, without even navigation lights as a guide, the risks of collision made such an approach impossible. Moreover, such a tactic was redundant, since the principal aim of a formation was for the bombers to provide mutual protection to each other. This was the thinking on which the US daylight bombing strategy was based, with the unity of the flying unit and the strength of the defensive firepower meant to act as a deterrent to German fighters. In contrast, the key form of protection for the Lancasters was lack of visibility in the darkness. The planes therefore flew in a loose bomber stream rather than a tight pattern. But even in the absence of a formation, the stream still needed to ensure that a concentrated force was gathered over the target. Concentration of attack was one of the central principles of Harris, for this, he argued, was the only way to overwhelm both the defences and the emergency services, especially the fire-fighters. Furthermore, it was always easier for the German searchlights and flak to pick up bombers that had strayed from the main group. So the Lancaster crews had to follow the course and timings set out at the briefing, sometimes assisted by the guidance of sky flares dropped along the route by Pathfinders out in front. Each Lancaster was allocated a height band and a time slot within the bomber stream to minimize the risk of collision. With hundreds of planes taking off from bases all over Lincolnshire and East Anglia for a raid on Germany, it was not always easy for some of the older Lancasters, which could struggle with the climb, to achieve their desired altitude.

Arnold Easton, a navigator with 467 Squadron based at Waddington, adopted an unorthodox approach when his elderly *F-Freddie* Lancaster was sent on a mission to Germany:

> Once we had taken off, I took over complete control of where the aircraft was to go. *F-Freddie* was an old machine and its climbing rate was not as good as on a new aircraft. I used to organize what I called a radius of action out over Wales, which meant that, after we took off, instead of flying all round Waddington and round Lincoln, I would give the skipper a course out to Wales, so we would be clear of all the other aircraft, and then I had to work out what time we had to turn back to set course to join up with the rest of the stream so we would be at bombing height over the French coast. That was a manoeuvre that took a little bit of working out. Some of the pilots did not like doing that.

But, as Easton explained in reference to a big raid on Stuttgart, manoeuvring into place on the bomber stream was vital to achieve results. 'It was rather remarkable to see the bombers flying off in all different directions and at a set time they would all gradually turn on the one course and off they would go. It was really a tremendous sight. You have to appreciate that on that Stuttgart raid there were 600 aircraft and they went through the target in three waves of five minutes. So you cannot just fly willy-nilly around and then assemble yourself on way to the target over enemy territory.'[11]

Once a Lancaster went above 8,000 feet, each airman had to use his oxygen, which was connected by a line from his mask to the aircraft's main supply kept in 15 cylinders in the main stowage in the centre part of the fuselage. Ron Smith, a rear gunner with the Pathfinder force, noted of this moment: 'As the ground disappeared in the murk, I could see scores of aircraft climbing slowly upwards, silhouetted against the light in the sky above. Fastening my oxygen mask, I adjusted the flow, feeling a slight light-headedness as my brain adjusted to the pure oxygen. The freezing air began to penetrate through the bulk of my layers of clothing.'[12] If an airman had to move around the plane, then he disconnected the line and used a small portable oxygen bottle that lasted about ten minutes. Once flying at high altitude, the loss of oxygen could be extremely dangerous, leading to disorientation, unconsciousness and even death. Rex Oldland, a flight engineer with 455 Squadron, recalled the night his skipper lost his oxygen tube. 'He started to act like a drunk driver. The aircraft began to wallow all over the sky and he went chasing searchlights, laughing his head off and making a hell of a noise. I spotted his tube hanging down so I fixed it up and he was all right.'[13] To deal with the oxygen problem and give the Lancaster much greater altitude, there had been plans in early 1942 to develop a Lancaster with a pressurized cabin, following the successful experiments with a pressurized Spitfire. But the Air Ministry recognized that the size of the Lancaster and the multiplicity of controls, pipes and electric wires meant that sealing the cabin would be a far bigger job than was required for a one-seater figher.[14] As the scheme was further considered, it was realized that a pressurized Lancaster would involve the removal of the front turret, an airtight bulkhead by the main spar, thermal insulation and a special tail turret fitted with its own air supply, though these difficulties were not felt to be 'insuperable' and Avro was asked to proceed with laboratory tests on the best method of sealing.[15] Optimistically, the Air Ministry predicted that a pressurized Lancaster with Merlin XX engines could reach 27,000 feet with a full load and 36,000 after releasing its bombs, whereas a plane with the advanced Merlin 60 was forecast to have an absolute ceiling with a full load of 35,000 feet. This was, however, a figure still below the maximum altitude of the German Me 109. Towards the end of 1942 the Ministry decided to abandon the idea of pressurization because, as a report from the Directorate of Operational Requirements put it, 'There is little value in this project. The aeroplane will fly neither high enough nor fast enough.'[16]

Almost as vital as the oxygen supply was another lifeline attached to the mask. This was for the intercom system, which allowed the aircrew to speak to each other above the roar of the Merlins. Without the intercom, they were all but mute. Indeed, even with their helmets, the noise fatigue from the engines left some Lancaster airmen with a legacy of partial deafness in later life. 'We were drowned in sound. You could drop something and not hear it,'[17] said flight engineer Doug Tritton. Though the intercom enabled all seven crew members to communicate, most pilots banned idle chatter, as the Dambuster pilot Les Munro explained: 'I suppose in a way you could describe my plane as a flying morgue, complete silence sometimes for long periods of time, broken only by the navigator advising changes of course. I was a strong believer that the intercom should always remain clear for urgent instructions and directions in the event of fighter attack or other abnormal happenings.'[18] Like so much else inside the Lancaster, the functioning of the intercom was occasionally at risk in sub-zero conditions. But the solution lay in the imaginative use of condoms, as George Luckraft, a Lancaster wireless operator explained: 'We never had intercom failure caused by the diaphragms of the microphones freezing up, thanks to a WAAF who told me to go to the guard room and buy nine French letters: one for each crew member's mask, one for the spare mask – and another one for myself! She showed me how to cut out a square of rubber from each one, which was then stretched over the diaphragm and the top of the microphone was screwed back on again. It then became moisture proof and never froze up.'[19]

Compared with what was to come, the journey over the English coast and the Channel was relatively peaceful. Some crewmen even had time to appreciate their surroundings as the Lancaster sailed up towards 20,000 feet, especially if they had taken off in summer when the sun was just about to go down and the colours of the sky were made all the more dramatic by the nocturnal trial which was soon to follow. 'We broke cloud into the glory of a late summer evening,' wrote flight engineer Norman Ashton of a trip to the Ruhr. 'A few scattered tufts of medium cloud picked up the rays of the reluctantly setting sun and tossed them to us in an assortment of reds, golds and violets. The sky, blood-red where the sun blazed angrily on the devouring horizon, was mellowing from its familiar azure to a dark blue in which the first stars had already begun to twinkle.'[20] Most of the time on a sortie, though, the aircrews were too preoccupied with their duties to engage in such reveries. In fact, many of them welcomed the heavy demands of their roles as a distraction from thinking about the dangers they faced, so different to the hours of contemplative waiting on the ground. 'At the beginning, you tensed up and I guess I was petrified at times, but once you were airborne you were too busy. Really, you had not time to get frightened,' said Eddie Dawson, a flight engineer with 625 Squadron.[21]

For engineers like Dawson, their job largely consisted of monitoring the performance of the engines and the fuel systems, leaving the pilot free to concentrate on instruments and flying controls. They had a thorough technical understanding of the Lancaster, their lengthy training including spells at the Avro and Merlin factories, as well as instruction from ground engineers. The Merlin was not, of course, infallible, but even its failures could demonstrate the remarkable qualities of the Lancaster, as Basil Oxtaby found when three of his engines began to overheat dramatically on a trip back from France. Having stopped the three engines, he still managed to get back to England on one. Ensuring that the Lancaster had enough fuel for its journey was a key task for the engineer. This involved a regular check of the consumption and a careful switchover from one tank to another so that the engines were always kept supplied. He also closely watched the temperatures of the engines, using a small electrical control to operate the radiator flaps which managed the airflow in each engine. Another duty was to synchronize the Merlins so they were working in rhythm together. An engine out of synch would send a noisy vibration through the aircraft and, according to engineer Cyril Jewitt, 'there was nothing worse on a long flight'.[22] Such synchronization was carried out by gently adjusting the throttles or the pitch of the propellers until all the engines sounded 'like the beat of a single pulse', in Jack Currie's phrase.[23] In addition, the engineer was responsible for feathering the airscrew of an engine that failed. Achieved by shutting the fuel cock, closing the throttle and pressing a feathering button which locked the airscrew, this was vital because a propeller swinging round like a windmill not only created drag but more importantly could cause severe damage and even fire with its friction. If an engine did burst into flames, from either breakdown or enemy action, then the engineer switched on the Graviner extinguisher, which used nitrogen gas to eject methyl bromide into the nacelle. The methyl bromide had an intense cooling effect on red-hot metal, and just one ounce of the chemical could choke 10 ounces of flaming petrol. But often in battle, the inferno across the wings and fuel tanks would be too advanced for Graviner to have any effect. Nevertheless, the overall excellence of both the Merlin and the Lancaster's airframe made the engineer's role easier than it might have been.

The Lancaster pilots, sitting beside the engineers, carried a special weight of responsibility and were therefore always the captains of the aircraft, regardless of their rank or experience. Uniquely in the armed services, it was a regular occurrence for officers in roles like gunner or wireless operator to be commanded by an NCO, though in practice aircrews paid no attention to formal hierarchy within the plane. There were occasional demands within government to make all pilots automatically officers but these were resisted by the Air Ministry, partly on the grounds of the cost of increased salaries, partly because a commission was meant to denote a gift for leadership rather than a reward for a specific role. But whatever the arguments over rank, there is no doubt that pilots were a special breed of men, whose job required fortitude, authority, calmness, patience, technical awareness and aerobatic skill. Such qualities were described by Harry Irons, a rear gunner with 9 Squadron, in a tribute to his pilot Dick Stubbs:

> Stubbs had the two necessary ingredients for a successful Lancaster pilot. He had reactions like lightning, so when we saw a fighter he was into his evasive action before we'd half got the order out. And he had ice instead of blood. We were running into Germany one night with a full bomb load and all four engines cut out at once. Stubbs said, 'That's a nuisance, four engines gone', or words to that effect. We dropped like a stone and I think Tom (Partington, the engineer) must have blanked out because he didn't do anything. So Stubbs said, very calmly and quietly, 'How about changing the fuel tanks over?' which Tom did. The engines all started again and we carried on as if nothing had happened. Stubbs was only three or four years older than me but he seemed more, a lot more, like he'd had ten years experience of this terrible job.[24]

But Bomber Command rarely became too sentimental about the pilots. Harris often feared that, when it came to recruitment, the heavy bombers received lower priority than the fighters and hence attracted a lower calibre of trainee. One example he cited was the case of Sergeant Cavaneu, a Canadian undergoing bomber training, who had displayed such lack of responsibility in the air that his past record was investigated. It turned out that he had initially undergone fighter training, but his Chief Inspector had reported: 'Unsuitable as fighter pilot and recommended to be transferred to bombers. The pilot needs strict supervision in both the air and on the ground.' To Harris the case was 'a further manifestation of the archaic, fantastic and persistent idea that people not good enough for fighters are good enough for bombers'.[25] Harris's most severe condemnation of the standards of pilots came in a letter to Peter Drummond, the Air Member for Training. Never published before, its contents would have come as a shock to many of the men under his command. 'Only the cream of pupil pilots should be allowed to proceed as captains of heavy bombers,' he told Drummond in December 1943, 'yet as you will see, the precise opposite still persists. You have not far to seek the cause of some of the avoidable heavy bomber crashes in view of the fact that these aircraft – the most vital element in the war and the sole raison d'etre of a separate air force – are manned, and always have been manned, by the lowest strata of skill.'[26]

Other positions in the Lancaster did not quite carry the same responsibility, but were still crucial to operations. The wireless operator, sitting behind the cockpit and facing the navigator's station, had in the words of Bruce Lewis, 'a lonely existence, mentally isolated from other members of the crew for long periods of time when he strained to listen through the static in his headphones for faint but vital signals'.[27] The routine of the wireless operator was outlined by Kenneth Grantham, who served with 35 Squadron based at Graveley:

> We listened out to Group broadcasts every twenty minutes. They would come through with a message, the call sign of the group sending station and then a number, just a single digit. That digit was used to check on the wireless operator when he got back that he had in fact been listening to Group broadcasts and not the BBC. A typical call sign, sent in morse code, would be 8LY, that is 8 Group in Graveley, followed by 7. If you were getting just the call sign and the number, you knew they had no message to send to you. If they had an instruction, they would send more – for instance one night when we had set off for Germany, we were half-way across the North Sea when I tuned into the Group broadcast. The decoded message said, 'Return to base.'[28]

Grantham was full of praise for the standard of technology, particularly the Marconi radio set. 'The previous sets were extremely primitive. You actually had to change coils and crystals. This was a hell of an advance, very clever stuff.'[29] When not tuned into his equipment, the wireless operator assisted the aircrew by scanning the skies from the astrodome above his compartment, while he also played a crucial role if a severely damaged Lancaster was returning to base, when he could tune into an emergency frequency to guide the aircraft home.

In night flying, there was no job more essential than that of the navigator, on whom rested the responsibility for finding the target. Even with the advent of Gee, and later a host of other technical aids, the navigator's role always required a clear mind and a high degree of mathematical ability. When electronic instruments failed or had been blown up, the navigator had to rely on dead reckoning or guidance by the stars, something that required both imagination and precision. Noble Frankland, who later became a brilliant historian and Director of the Imperial War

Museum, confessed that his training in navigation was 'academically the most difficult thing I have ever tackled'.[30] Another Lancaster navigator who became an internationally renowned academic, Frank Musgrove, gave this interesting description of his work with 149 Squadron:

> Over black-out Britain and Europe, the navigator probably never saw the ground between take-off and landing. He probably never even looked – there was no point. Conventional map reading was impossible: at more than 20,000 feet, four miles above the ground, even on a clear moonlit night, there would be few landmarks down below that could be easily identified . . . Map reading skills were useless and in fact I never carried a detailed topographical map, like an Ordnance Survey map. My basic tool was an 'empty', very parsimonious Mercator's chart [a nautical chart with longitude in parallel lines, named after Gerardus Mercator], an outline map without any distracting detail, on which the route to the target, fixes and air positions could be clearly marked.[31]

When Gee was operating, it was the duty of the navigator to get a fix every six minutes to check that the Lancaster was on course for the target, though from early 1943 the Pathfinders and sophisticated radar devices, of which the most important was a ground-recognition system called H2S, played an increasing role. The Pathfinder leader Don Bennett once said that: 'Pilots were merely chauffeurs to get the really important people, the navigator and bomb aimer, there.'[32]

The bomb aimer came into his own once the Lancaster approached the target to begin its bombing run, for in those moments he was essentially in charge of the plane. Before then, in his vantage point in the front turret, he would help the navigator with course directions or assist in scanning the sky for fighters. As the Lancaster bomb aimer Miles Tripp wrote in his memoirs, his role was 'a jack of all trades – front gunner, second navigator, understudy pilot and map reader'. Tripp also described the cramped nature of the bomb aimer's compartment:

> There wasn't sufficient space in which to sit and so I lay and my couch was the escape hatch. To my left was the bombsight computer box which was connected by two drives to the sighting head which was about eight inches away from my nose. The front turret was directly in front of, and above, the sighting head and it contained two Browning .303 machine-guns. To my right, and within reach of my hand, was the pre-selector box on which the order for releasing the bombs could be set and whether they were to fall singly or in salvo.[33]

There was no doubt that the two coldest, most isolated jobs in the Lancaster belonged to the mid-upper gunner and the rear gunner, who both had to keep themselves at the peak of alertness in looking for fighters while enduring conditions of almost inhuman frigidity. Contrary to what their titles implied, their main responsibility was not shooting at the enemy but looking out for enemy fighters and then warning the pilot of the threat so he could take evasive action. Remarkably, a large number of gunners completed their tour without ever firing their weapons, partly because of the fashionable Air Ministry theory that the Brownings should only be used as a last resort since the flash from the guns could reveal the Lancaster's position in the night sky. This was the very opposite of the aggressive US attitude toward daylight operations, where the gunners on the B-17 Flying Fortresses opened up against anything that came in sight.

The reluctance of Bomber Command to use the Brownings in an offensive mode led some to question why gunners were needed at all on the Lancaster, since, it was argued, their presence compromised the speed of the plane without adding notably to its protection. This was the unorthodox view held by Frank Musgrove, the cerebral navigator of 149 Squadron, who argued that in a straight fight against an Me 109 or Focke-Wulf 190, the Lancaster stood no chance, particularly in view of the plane's 'pathetic' armament. For Musgrove, 'air gunners were obsolete. They should have been long redundant and their turrets removed, making the Lancaster more streamlined, adding 50 mph to its speed.'[134] Some within Bomber Command felt the same way. The distinguished scientist Freeman Dyson, a member of the Operational Research Section, urged that gun turrets be removed altogether from the Lancaster, thereby greatly increasing the speed of the plane. His suggestion was based on his research which indicated that experienced crews were no better at surviving an operation than novice ones and that it was 'a matter of pure chance' if aircraft were shot down.[35] 'The basic trouble with the bombers was that they were too slow and too heavily loaded . . . Bomber losses varied dramatically from night to night. We knew that the main cause of the variation was the success or failure of the German fighter controllers in directing the fighters into the bomber stream before it reached the target. An extra fifty miles an hour might have made an enormous difference.'[36] But Harris refused to countenance any such idea. All three turrets had to be retained, he once said, because they had 'a good psychological effect on the crew'.[37] There was the additional justification that the two gunners acted as rearward lookouts for the plane, a role that could not be performed either by technology or other crew members. But it was precisely this function that made the gunners' job so draining, a constant fight against eye-closing tedium while they searched the darkness, endlessly moving their guns up and down and left and right.

The Pathfinder rear gunner Ron Smith, after a series of difficult sorties in mid-1944, wrote of 'his tired body' in its 'tiny capsule' as his Lancaster ploughed on 'through the seemingly impenetrable cold' of a grey swirling mass of clouds over France. 'I stared at the dirty white grey mist racing astern, emphasizing our speed and making me wonder how many long hours it would take to reach the target. Turning up the heat [on his inner suit] a little, I rubbed my gloved hands on my aching eyes – the lids heavy with sleep after the marathon of the previous week's flying.'[38] Bob Knights, one of the legendary pilots of 617 Squadron, adopted a vigorous approach to the dangers of his gunners falling asleep. 'I would have them on the go the whole time. I would have them looking round the whole time and not getting out of their turrets. I kept talking to them, making sure they would be keeping a lookout. I thought it essential that the crew should not be allowed to sit and relax. After all it was a battle, a battle to survive.'[39] But even with the toughest captains, some could not help but succumb, as the New Zealander Vic Viggers, a wireless operator recalled when he flew twice to Berlin with a dormant mid-upper gunner. 'That filled me with horror, flying with a bastard who went to sleep, especially a gunner. Anyway, we got back and I told the captain, "Get rid of that man." A few nights later the gunner was gone.'[40]

The burden on the crews was made all the heavier by the Lancaster's savagely cold and Spartan conditions. The inadequate heating was more than just a matter of comfort. Airmen's health was at risk. One gunner experienced a heating failure on his Sidcot suit and had to spend two days in hospital with frostbite. A member of 49 Squadron went into the rear of the fuselage without his gloves on, fell unconscious through lack of oxygen, and collapsed on his hands. The frostbite from touching the metal decking was so severe that he lost all his fingers. It was the rear gunners that had the rawest deal, not least because of the practice of removing one of the Perspex panels to provide a clearer view. 'The Perspex gradually disappeared until you were literally sitting outside. That was cold I can tell you! I just felt cold and uncomfortable, and I was afraid,' said Jim Chapman.[41] Another graphic example of the piercing chill was provided by Lancaster rear gunner Hal Croxon. 'If you touch anything up there that's metal, you freeze to it. Sometimes the clips on my oxygen mask would touch my cheek and that would give me frost burns on the cheeks and they would be there for two or three days.'[42] The primitiveness of the conditions was reinforced by the toilet arrangements. Towards the rear of the fuselage, there was an Elsan chemical lavatory but airmen were reluctant to use it. First of all, it was as bitterly cold as the rest of the interior, which meant that it presented a hazard to its users, as 115 Squadron navigator Jack West revealed in his private memoir. 'On one of the night raids I needed to go to the toilet to have a shit. I attached a small oxygen bottle to my clothing and with a small torch proceeded down the back. Unfortunately the toilet seat was made of metal and after a while, when I tried to rise, I left most of the skin from my bottom on the seat. I had got frostbite at 20,000 feet. It took four weeks before I was comfortable again.'[43] Another problem with the Elsan was that its position near the rear turret meant that five of the crew had to climb over the main spar section in the darkness to reach it, while the airmen also disliked leaving their stations when they were flying over occupied territory. This was particularly true of the skipper, since he was usually the only one qualified to fly the Lancaster and the automatic pilot, nicknamed 'George', was unreliable.

The Canadian pilot David Day explained why, in his view, 'George' was not of much assistance: 'The Air Ministry had never been very successful at producing an automatic pilot. In fact on all the Lancasters in our squadron, the automatic pilots were wired off – we couldn't use them. George just did not work. It was a very crude arrangement. The gyros which were incorporated in the equipment were air driven and you had to move a lever into one position where it spun up these gyros. And then you moved it into the second position where it was supposed to engage the auto-pilot. All it seemed to do was produce a vicious dive or a vicious climb or anything other than what you wanted it to do. They were more dangerous than their worth.'[44] The disconcerting results of using the automatic pilot were experienced by bomb aimer Miles Tripp on one occasion when his pilot decided to go to the Elsan, leaving the navigator in charge. It was, said Miles, 'a crazy request' for the navigator 'had never touched a control column in his life'. But the pilot assured him that 'the aircraft was on automatic pilot and was a beaut to fly'. But the moment the pilot began his journey down to the Elsan 'a fore and aft movement was instantly discernible; the aircraft might have been a dinghy gently riding an ocean swell.' The motion then became 'increasingly violent' and Tripp began to wonder whether the pilot 'would be able to scramble over the main bulkhead on his return journey. It was a tremendous relief to hear his voice on the intercom again and feel the aircraft respond to his sure touch.' Once the plane had landed, Tripp and the rest of the crew told the pilot that they could not go through a repeat performance, so they suggested that in future he use a pot.[45] The pilot agreed. In fact, this was the solution to the Elsan problem adopted by most crews, though some pilots took the direct route of simply peeing out the side window of the cockpit. A variety of receptacles were commandeered for this purpose, including bottles, bags and tins, often with makeshift funnels or pipes for ease of use. Airmen had to be careful about the pipes freezing, or throwing the urine out the window too casually in case it splashed into the Perspex of the cockpit or the mid-upper turret and froze there, restricting the vision. One of the worst experiences was suffered by Ronald Olsen, a pilot with 619 Squadron. On a flight back from Berlin in early 1944 he tried to use a system of a funnel attached to a container, and ended up with a nasty frostburn on his penis. The psychological shock of the injury was so severe that throughout the journey back to England he was under the delusion that he had been hit in the groin by shrapnel over the target and was bleeding down his leg. On landing, he was surprised to find there was no blood in his boot or flying gear.[46]

On their missions to the Reich, the Lancaster crews did not have to imagine any threat that awaited them once they crossed the coast into occupied Europe. If the planes had already been picked up by German radar, the flashes from the anti-aircraft batteries and the noise of the exploding shells made that all too clear. It was a terrible precursor of things to come. 'The flak on the Dutch coast was murderous, light flak from hundreds of guns. From a distance it looked like twenty firework nights all at once, purples, blues, yellows, all different colours,' said Harry Irons.[47] By the end of 1942, the Germans had developed a sophisticated network of fighter, searchlight and anti-aircraft defences along the northern coast of Europe. This system, stretching from the Baltic to northeastern France, was called the 'Kammhuber Line' after the German officer who oversaw its creation, General Joseph Kammhuber, appointed commander of the Reich's night-fighter force in October 1940. At first this defensive line was rudimentary. Its central feature was a chain of 'Freya' radar sets which had an impressive 100-mile range and could pick up the RAF bombers over the sea, thereby allowing the German controllers to send the night fighters in their direction. The limitation of Freya was that it could not detect the altitude of the bombers. Even so, it was more than a match for the sporadic, disorganized efforts of Bomber Command in the pre-Harris era. The vital advance in the development of German defences came in 1942 with the arrival of the giant Würzburg radar, over 24 feet in diameter, which could provide details of a flying bomber in every dimension. Using Freya and Würzburg in tandem, Kammhuber formed a long belt of more than 100 overlapping radar zones called *Himmelbetten* (literally 'sky beds') along the coast, each covering airspace for a radius of about 20 miles, the range at which the Würzburg worked best. Within every radar box, there was a Freya set to give an early warning of the bombers and two Würzburg sets, one to monitor the RAF bombers at close range, the other to guide the night fighters. The radar information was relayed to the control room in each *Himmelbetten* sector, where the movements of both bombers and fighters were plotted on a large screen. Watching the action unfold, the German controllers had two related objectives. They could either seek to trap the British heavy bombers in a cone of searchlights, making them easier prey for the anti-aircraft guns, or they could direct a night fighter onto the tail of a bomber. When a German fighter came within two miles of a bomber, its own airborne Lichtenstein radar, which had also been brought into service in 1942, could take over in mounting the attack at close range. What made the flak and the searchlights all the more deadly was that they too were controlled by the latest radar technology. Lancaster crews learnt to dread the searching blue beam of the master searchlight. Able to turn through 360 degrees, possessing an illumination that stretched for eight miles into the sky and guided by a Würzburg, the master searchlight could quickly latch onto an aircraft and then would be surrounded by the other beams, creating a lethal cone of bright light to be exploited by the flak guns. By 1943, the average large battery in Germany contained no fewer than 70 searchlights and 160 flak guns, and a third of all flak was 'predicted' – that is, guided by radar.

The principal anti-aircraft gun was the 88 mm, which shot a 16.5-pound shrapnel grenade about four miles into the air. On detonation, it exploded into 1,500 fragments flying in all directions.[48] Any aircraft within ten yards of the detonation point was likely to be badly damaged or brought down, though the Lancasters, with their ceilings at 20,000 feet were less vulnerable to flak than the Stirling and the early versions of the Halifax. Nevertheless it was nerve-racking to have to fly through this cruel symphony of shell-bursts and blinding lights. A flavour of the experience came from a live BBC commentary given by the renowned Welsh reporter Wynford Vaughan-Thomas, who bravely flew with a Lancaster crew of 207 Squadron on a trip to Berlin in September 1943. His vivid description of the sortie, all the more enthralling because it was recorded live, included this passage about flying over the enemy coast:

> Now and again, as we watch, we see a burst of flak, a bright light wink-ing among the concentrated beams. They have got every single searchlight you could imagine out there to catch us. We are coming up to them all the time, waiting for it. In a moment it will be our turn to pass through them. A dark shape is going out ahead of us, another Lancaster, to lead in. There goes the flak again, a winking burst up among the searchlights. They must be having a go at us all right. Away to port another constel-lation is coming up. They work in great groups, trying to stop and grapple you as you come in over the coast. All the time, they are moving in. It is disconcerting to see that welcome waiting for us. I am counting the time, watching the hand on my watch creeping round. I know that it will be our turn in exactly three minutes time. [*Pause*] In the cone of searchlights, they caught one of our aircraft. Up goes the flak around him, bursting in vivid flashes. Now there are winks from the ground below us. They may be after us, because the searchlights are starting to move away. They have left that other bomber and they are moving now slowly towards us, feel-ing for us all the time. They are pumping up the flak in a steady stream. You suddenly see a white flash on the ground, then just seconds later, there is a vivid burst among the searchlight cones. There goes the flak, bursting in that cone of searchlights, darting from vivid white pinpoints, moving all the time, trying to follow that bomber. Again they come bend-ing, the whole lot of them. They seem to bend towards us, following a master beam. We are moving away to starboard and it looks as if, this time, we've slipped through.[49]

In early 1942, a report from the Air Ministry downplayed the strength of German defences, claiming that the searchlights had 'proved a disap-pointment' and were 'mainly ineffective', while the flak, though it admittedly appeared 'formidable', had 'an accuracy nothing like what was expected'.[50] With the RAF being pummelled night after night by the advanced radar-led system, those words were soon to appear almost as absurdly misplaced as Stanley Baldwin's fatalistic belief that the bomber would 'always get through'. But there were two serious weaknesses in the Kammhuber Line, both of which Harris quickly recognized. The first was the inability of the *Himmelbetten* radar zones to handle more than one fighter interception at a time. As a result, the system could be over-whelmed by the sheer volume of the attacking force, hence Harris's determination to concentrate his bombers in large streams over a single target rather than disperse them. Indeed, the senior Luftwaffe staff officer, Generalmajor Herhudt von Rhoden, interviewed just after the end of the war, admitted that Harris's bomber stream had been crucial in over-coming the Kammhuber Line, which proved too inflexible: 'Once established, it was impossible to move the installations rapidly into other areas . . . The tactics of the RAF bomber stream considerably shortened the attack time and grouped the flying components. They did not allow a sufficient number of pursuit planes to be brought into a successful engagement.'[51] The second was that Britain's expertise in radar meant that German systems were constantly in danger of being rendered in-operable by counter-measures. The classic example was the use from mid-1943 of a system known as 'Window', consisting of aluminium foil strips which, when thrown from Allied planes, jammed the Germans' ground radar. Another device was 'Tinsel', which broadcast noise from a microphone inside the engine bay on a frequency set by the wireless operator in an attempt to drown out the communication between the night fighters and ground control, though 'Tinsel' was to prove less reli-able than 'Window'.

For the Lancaster caught in the cone of searchlights or the radar beam of a night fighter, considerations of technology were an irrelevance. The sheer intensity of the defences was brutally intimidating to those who experienced it for the first time, as Pilot Joe McCrossan did on a trip to the Ruhr in April 1943. 'It was absolute blackness, then as we approached the target I could see the searchlights waving and the yellow and with tracks of the light flak and I thought, "We'll never get through this."' McCrossan's Lancaster flew on, but the fear kept increasing: 'Light ack-ack shells were coming towards us at a rate of knots, glowing red, green and white, but fell short as we were flying too high. The heavy ack-ack, however, was very different as shells kept bursting around us making the Lanc rock and it was very, very scary.'[52] German glee over the fate of the British bombers was captured in the memoirs of Wilhelm Johnen, who flew an Me 110 and took part in the Battle of the Ruhr. 'Hundreds of searchlights went on, pointing their thin fingers at the enemy bombers. Thousands of flak salvoes flashed, forming a box barrage round the Ruhr . . . Pitilessly, the leading enemy machines were caught in the search-light beams. Their silver bodies glittered like bright fishes against the dark night sky. The flak would not let its prey out of its claws. The fate of the bomber was sealed. In a matter of seconds, flight direction, speed and altitude were worked out on the flak gunners' instructions and, hit by the next salvo, the bomber crashed with its load into the depths.'[53]

Some believed that the flak was even more intimidating than the threat of the fighters But this was not a view shared by Bob Knights of

617 Squadron. 'Flak appeared worse than it was. Obviously if you got close it made a lot of noise. The explosions could be terrifying. But night fighters were the real danger. In the darkness, one never knew where the nearest night fighter was. The last thing one wanted was a stream of cannon fire coming towards the plane because it might make a direct hit.'[54] Engagement with German night fighters showed the Lancaster at its worst and best: worst because its woefully inadequate armament put it at a gross disadvantage against the more powerful guns of the Luftwaffe; best because its remarkable manoeuvrability offered an escape route from the hail of bullets and shells.

All but the last versions of the Lancaster were equipped with three Frazer-Nash hydraulically operated gun turrets, which had been developed by the motor manufacturer and engineer Archibald Frazer-Nash. There was the FN type 5 in the nose, the type 20 in the rear and the type 50 for the mid-upper turret. The mid-upper gunner had a 360-degree field of vision but his Brownings were restricted in their movements by a fairing which prevented him from blowing holes in the tailplane or the wings when the guns were depressed. The rounds in their .303 guns were generally made up of 30 per cent incendiary bullets, 60 per cent armour-piercing and 10 per cent tracer. Though ball ammunition was occasionally used, it was really an anti-personnel type of bullet of little use against armour plate. Harris's frustration with the firepower of the Frazer-Nash gun turrets was one of the never-ending themes of his command, and it is an indictment of the Air Ministry that the necessary urgency or imagination were never shown to resolve the problem before 1945. 'The turrets simply could not be worse. Rear turrets in particular might just as well not be there,' Harris told Freeman in June 1943. 'I have harped on this theme until I am blue in the face at the Air Ministry and outside, but there is complete inertia, lethargy and lack of drive.'[55] A year later he told Portal he was 'in despair over this heavier armament business', since there was 'not only an entire lack of drive behind this requirement but the tacit if not explicit obstruction . . . It is fantastic that we have nothing but .303 at this stage of the war.'[56] As early as mid-1942, the Air Ministry began an attempt to re-equip the Lancaster with 0.5 cannon, but the initiative was hampered by problems over the increased weight and the redesign of the turrets, as well as lack of resources for development.

The contrast with German night fighters was striking. The twin-engined Junkers 88, for instance, was equipped with 20-mm cannon, each of which could fire 520 rounds per minute of explosive, armour-piercing shell tipped with incendiary which burned at 3,000 degrees for nearly a second. A mere 20 rounds of this deadly ammunition was enough to bring down a Lancaster. What is more the cannon had a range of almost 1,000 yards, whereas the maximum distance for the Browning was only 600 yards, so, in the words of Arnold Easton, a navigator with 467 Squadron, 'in daylight or bright moonlight, they could virtually have a stand-off and blow you out of the sky and you could do nothing about it.'[57] The knowledge that they had superior weaponry gave confidence to the German pilots in taking on the bomber stream, as shown in this passage by Wilhelm Johnen, who flew an Me 110 bristling with four cannon and two machine guns. Having already shot down two Lancasters during a raid on Berlin in September 1943:

> I spotted a couple of four-engined Lancasters directly above the target. After a short attack, the first bomber exploded and fell in burning debris through the clouds. The second banked steeply to starboard, trying to escape. The Tommies fired at me with all their guns, framing my aircraft with gleaming tracers. I pressed home the attack. The tail unit grew ever larger in my sights. Now was the time to shoot. The fire power of my guns was terrific. My armour-piercing shells riddled the well-protected wing tanks and the pilot's armoured cockpit. The tracers set fire to the petrol and high explosive shells tore great holes in the wings. It was no wonder that my fourth bomber that night crashed in flames.[58]

Interestingly, the Germans felt their job was made even easier by the RAF's policy of not opening fire except in moments of crisis. In theory, the determination not to reveal a plane's location with a flash from the .303 Brownings might have appeared sound. Indeed, Don Bennett argued in a tactical note to the Air Staff in September 1943 that greater readiness on the trigger would 'merely help the German fighters to find their quarries'.[59] But in practice this reluctance to fire only emboldened the Luftwaffe pilots. In any case a blue flame from the Lancaster's engine exhausts, sometimes visible on a moonless night from 800 yards, could give away the position of the aircraft more easily than a burst of the .303s. Though the Air Ministry later provided exhaust covers, many pilots disliked them because they reduced the Lancaster's speed by about 5 mph. In an interview after the war, the highest-ranking Luftwaffe night-fighter pilot, Major Heinz-Wolfgang Schnaufer, who was credited with the astonishing feat of having shot down 121 enemy aircraft, expressed his surprise at the attitude of the RAF gunners. 'The bomber's tracer or gun flash did not give away the bomber's position, and Schnaufer remembers only two or three cases when bombers have been shot down due to this,' recorded the notes of his interrogation by the Allies:

He said he rarely saw the bomber's tracer, and therefore it did not worry him unduly while aiming. He was of the opinion that the gunners did not fire nearly enough or soon enough. He was convinced that had the bombers fired more and used much brighter tracer, many of the pilots, the less experienced especially, would not have attacked. Schnaufer had been surprised twice by fire from a bomber which he had not seen and in each case the fire was accurate; these bombers he did not attack.[60]

But the Lancasters were not always in a defensive position. Men who were brave enough to confront a forest fire of guns and searchlights over Germany did not always forgo the chance to take on the night fighters if the opportunity presented itself. In one remarkable instance of courage, David Day actually gave chase to a Ju 88 while on a raid to the Mittellandkanal near Dortmund in February 1945. The mid-upper gunner saw the Junkers crossing the sky ahead of the Lancaster, but it did not look like it was

> going to attack. So I said, 'Let's chase him.' Off we went, giving chase. By this time, the bomb aimer had gone into the front turret and fired away. I thought I saw a flash on the side of the aircraft but that was all. We lost sight of it, resumed track and landed safely. Intelligence later reported that we had damaged the Ju 88. He wasn't chasing us – perhaps he was on a training exercise or had no ammunition, but we saw him. He was the enemy so we attacked, probably one of the few occasions when a Lancaster could claim to have damaged the enemy.[61]

The most deadly form of German fighter attack further exposed the inadequacy of the Lancaster's defensive armament. This was the practice known as 'Schrage Musik' (literally 'jazz' or 'oblique' music), first introduced in the autumn of 1943, in which the fighter crept up on the Lancaster from below and astern. Then, using upward-firing cannon, the plane let rip into the Lancaster's belly and the underside of the wings where the fuel tanks were situated. The removal of the ventral turret had meant that the Lancaster had a blind spot, so Schrage Musik was brilliantly effective. The RAF's heavy bombers felt the shells tearing through the airframe or saw the wings bursting into flames before they were even aware that a fighter was underneath. The element of surprise, combined with the construction of the Lancaster, made the results of Schrage Musik all the more devastating, as Squadron Leader Peter Russell explained: 'A short burst between the fuselage and an engine nacelle or between the two engines,' he wrote, 'put the bomber immediately into a spin. Even if the cannon did not sever the main spar, the petrol flowed across the red-hot cut made by the cannon shot and the Lancaster burned fiercely.

They were, after all, built of an alloy of aluminium and magnesium, and burned like paper. In those circumstances, no one ever got out.'[62] Schrage Musik was the brainchild of a Luftwaffe armourer, Paul Mahle. One morning Mahle had been working at the Luftwaffe weapons test centre at Tarnewitz on the German coast, when he saw a Dornier 217 twin-engined bomber equipped with upward firing guns to defend itself from Allied fighters. Mahle immediately thought that such an idea could be applied to the German night fighters, so he came up with his own impro-vised design using a platform of hardwood for the guns and a reflector sight mounted on the roof of the cockpit. The innovation turned out to be such a success when tried by some pilots against the RAF that it was soon taken up by the Reich Air Ministry. In the latter stages of the war, at least 50 per cent of all attacks on Lancasters were carried out by Schrage Musik.

The experience of being hit by Schrage Musik was undergone by Robert Gill, a gunner with 35 Pathfinder Squadron, during the return from a raid in France in early 1944:

> We were on our way back from the target the second time about ten minutes later we were hit from underneath by a fighter with Schrage Musik. I heard the thump, thump, thump of cannon shells, then the aircraft was alight in the wing and fuselage. The ammunition was going off and I lost my eyebrows and eyelashes and some hair and skin was burned . . . I went down to the fuselage door and kicked it but I couldn't get it open so I went forward over the main spar and through the open hatch at the front. Just after I left I saw the flash as the aircraft exploded and the wreck-age came down at Niewpoort, just across the river from Dunkirk. The pilot and gunner were still onboard.[63]

Gill himself, after landing in a field, was soon captured and spent the rest of the war in a POW camp.

Confronted by the alarming phenomenon of Schrage Musik, some initially refused to believe in its existence and sought alternative explan-ations for the sight of Lancasters suddenly blowing up in mid-air. One of the favourite theories was that the Germans had invented a new decoy weapon called the 'Scarecrow', a ground-fired shell that exploded in a ball of fire and was said to resemble a blazing bomber. The aim of the Scarecrow explosions, it was argued, was to spread fear among the heavy bomber crews by exaggerating the number of planes being shot down by flak or fighters. Many were firmly convinced that Scarecrows existed. Even Bill Jones, the Intelligence Officer at Elsham Wolds, Lincolnshire, whose job was to be ruthlessly analytical, claimed to have witnessed

Scarecrows himself on a flight to Berlin at 21,000 feet. 'Although they looked very frightening, the more experienced members of the crew with whom I was flying were not impressed.'[64] In reality, however, there was no such weapon. This was confirmed after the war by interviews with Luftwaffe chiefs and German battery commanders, as well as research in the German archives. The real confidence trick was perpetrated by the men of the RAF. Crews were desperately trying to find reassurance in the idea that the skies were not as dangerous as they appeared, while the Air Ministry and senior officers were willing to collude with this self-deception to keep up morale. As Lancaster pilot Harry Yates said of his own crew: 'The seven of us were willing believers. Psychological warfare was a lot friendlier than the real thing. If we had to get clobbered, we were only too pleased for it to be a spoof.'[65] In some cases, the Air establishment directly encouraged such thinking. Rear gunner Harry Irons told his Intelligence Officer that during a trip to the Ruhr he had seen 15 bombers go down. '"That's not right," he said, "don't go spreading rumours about bombers being shot down." I said I was just telling him what I saw. He said I'd seen decoys, Scarecrows. He gave me a right rucking.'[66] Occasionally, however, the senior personnel would admit the truth. On his return from the notorious Nuremburg raid of March 1944, when the bomber stream was ripped to shreds by German fighters, bomb aimer Dickie Parfitt told his Intelligence Officer that the sky had been full of 'spoofs'. The IO replied, 'They weren't spoofs. They were our boys.'[67]

One tactic used by Lancaster pilots to avoid Schrage Musik – and other fighter attacks – was to keep weaving during their flight to the target, banking to one side then the other so the crew could check what was below and prevent the enemy getting a fix on a steady position. It was impossible to do this during the actual bombing run over the target because the bomb aimer had to hold on to the exact same course, but otherwise weaving provided some form of protection. The squadron navigator Arnold Easton admired the skill of his skipper, Jim Marshall, in executing the move, which he believed acted as a deterrent to the fighters. 'Jim had that coolness that was needed by bomber pilots because those raids were very trying. Because of the blind spot underneath the Lanc, we had to do a banking search every so often. Jim turned that into a continual weave. If you were a night fighter and you saw a Lanc weaving all the time, you would assume that he had seen you. So you'd probably go off somewhere else. It did not make my life easy as a navigator, but Jim averaged out those courses remarkably well.'[68] Some senior officers in Bomber Command disapproved of the practice of weaving, claiming that it denied the gunners a steady platform for firing, an observation that only illustrated their lack of understanding of operations. Lancaster pilot Maurice Chick was once confronted by a new commanding officer who ordered him to stop weaving and instead 'fly straight and level'. Chick replied: 'With respect, sir, if you lay down this order you will lose most of your pilots,' to which the new CO accused Chick and his fellow pilots of cowardice.[69]

If the night fighters did come within closer range, it might be thought that the Lancasters were little more than sitting ducks, given the superior weaponry of the Luftwaffe. But that was not the case. For when any fighter was spotted astern, the Lancaster's magnificent aerodynamic qualities and strength of design enabled it to execute a manoeuvre that could be the means of the crew's salvation. This ploy was called 'the corkscrew' and it involved a sudden dive to one side followed by a twisting spiral in the opposite direction. Corkscrewing was dramatic and violent, testing to the limit the ability of the pilot, the nerves of his crew and the toughness of Avro's engineering. The entire fuselage shuddered and rivets screamed as the aircraft plunged at over 300 mph for almost 1,000 feet, then was wrenched into a steep climb. The manoeuvre began when one of the gunners saw a fighter astern and would then yell over the intercom, 'corkscrew port!' or 'corkscrew starboard!'. If a fighter was on the left, the shout would be for a dive to port. The pilot would then throw his control column to the left as far as it would go and plunge at 45 degrees with full left rudder on. It was a brutal, stomach-lurching moment, for there was no room for tentativeness by the pilot. Survival depended on the sharpness of his reactions. At the bottom of the dive, he would use all his strength to heave the controls to starboard and then soar upwards. He might have to repeat the corkscrew several times before he had shaken off the fighter, leaving his body covered in sweat, his arms aching, his crew feeling nauseous, and the aircraft in chaos, with equipment strewn about the fuselage. Navigator Tug Wilson recalled his skipper asking for a course after a successful corkscrew: 'What course? He'd just had us all over the sky and the instruments were all over the floor and he's asking what course. I'd say just keep going where you're going and when I've found my stuff in every corner of this bloody aircraft I'll try and work something out.'[70]

Even if the corkscrew did not throw off the German fighter, the violent sudden movement made the Lancaster a much more difficult target. In his post-war interrogation by the Allies, Major Heinz-Wolfgang Schnaufer admitted that 'when approaching from astern and below for an attack

with forward firing guns, if the bomber corkscrewed it was most difficult for the fighter to gather speed quickly enough to follow it down in
the initial dive'.[71] That was what Donald Falgate, a bomb aimer with 49
Squadron found when his Lancaster was attacked on a raid to Magdeburg
in April 1944. A Ju 88 came in from astern and caught the Lancaster
with its first burst, but no real damage was inflicted. The fighter came
round again but this time, 'despite making a very steep dive and opening fire, he missed us'. The Ju 88 pilot would not give up. 'He pulled and
positioned himself astern to come in for his third run. It was then that
our rear gunner called out, "corkscrew port, go!"' The Lancaster went
into a screaming dive to port, followed by the starboard climb, and it
kept doing that, 'down to the left, climb to the right, down to the left,
up to the right' so the fighter could not keep the plane 'dead in his sights.
You are a moving target all the time. We managed to evade him until
we got into the cloud . . . It was quite frightening, a very scary time.'
Falgate's aircraft completed its bombing and got home.[72]

But against the nimble German fighters, the corkscrew was no guarantee of success, as Rex Oldland of 455 Squadron found when his
Lancaster was on a raid against Mannheim in central Germany, and was
attacked by a German fighter. 'We went into a corkscrew manoeuvre, a
violent one . . . The wings were supposed to drop off at 300 mph but
they never did . . . The idea was that the pilot could not follow you easily.
But this night we did not get away. He followed us for about three quarters of an hour and he clobbered us good and hard, so much so that we
were forced to jettison our bomb load because it was obvious that we
were not going to get to the target.' The fighter attack knocked a huge
hole in the port wing, took the cowlings off one of the engines, and
smashed the starboard rudder. 'I was down in the nose the moment we
were hit and the nose started to fill up with smoke. I thought for a
moment we were on fire but we weren't. It was just where the cannon
shells had gone in . . . We were very lucky and managed to get home.
In fact, we twisted the fuselage because the corkscrew was so violent.
The plane was a write-off. It never flew again.'[73]

Apart from evading fighters, a version of the corkscrew could also be
used by Lancaster pilots in the event of being trapped in German searchlights. The trial of being 'coned' was one of the most petrifying that
heavy-bomber crews could endure, as the plane was filled first with
the blue light of the master beam, then with the blinding glare of the
rest of the battery. So ferocious was the illumination that the airmen felt
as if the protective cover of night had been exchanged for the raw exposure

of day, their sense of terror exacerbated by the knowledge that the search-lights could soon be followed by the thump of exploding shrapnel. 'You felt so horribly naked. You didn't know what is going to come up at you,' said Peter Huggins, a pilot with 57 Squadron.[74] According to pilot Bill Perry: 'You could almost feel the vibration of the big blue light it was that powerful.'[75] The chilling feeling of vulnerability mixed with anx-iety shook Peter Russell of 625 squadron when he was 'coned' on a trip back from bombing a synthetic-oil plant at Zeitz:

> Suddenly, instantaneously we were in blinding light. It is a horrible feel-ing, dangerously close to hopelessness. For we often had seen an aircraft coned, seen it diving and turning, just as helpless as a wounded bird in a cat's clutches, until *flash* a shell from co-ordinated gunfire, twenty rounds a minute . . . blew it to smithereens. We felt helpless, expecting the inevitable. The light is so bright that it hurts. The body feels ice-cold as if your blood has frozen. But, though blinded, you must try to escape, dive, twist and turn, and yet you cannot see your instruments. You hardly know which way up you are. Perhaps because of that, perhaps because I was flying so clumsily, the aeroplane might have been sideslipping fast and temporarily evaded the beam. Or perhaps those below found a better target. The beam swung away and I was left in dazzled darkness.[76]

In these moments of psychological agony, the instinct for survival was paramount. Many bomber airmen, with some sense of guilt, confessed to feelings of relief if they saw another Lancaster 'coned', for it meant that their own aircraft was less likely to be the focus of the searchlights given that the batteries could only concentrate on one plane at a time. Again, that is why the bomber stream was so important and why pilots were so anxious to avoid becoming stragglers behind the main force. In the mortal lottery of the air war, one crew's disaster was another crew's luck. Canadian rear gunner Clayton Moore admitted that, during participation in air raids, 'I was to become sufficiently callous as to rejoice at the sight of someone else being coned because we could be assured that most eyes (both friendly and unfriendly) were on the unfortunate sods in the cone.'[77] The searchlights' grasp of one Lancaster could even be tactically exploited by another, as Thomas Murray of 207 Squadron explained:

> I devised my own tactic for dealing with searchlights. The instinct, if you see a cone of lights with some poor devil in it and then another over there, is to fly in the black in the middle. But I said, 'Never do that. If there is a cone of searchlights get as close as you can on one side of it.' Because that means the battery has got two targets. You are also now prob-ably confusing the aiming system and you have a much greater chance of

penetrating. That reduced casualties a lot. The Germans could not bring their battery to bear on us.[78]

The other method, much closer to the corkscrew, was to throw the Lancaster violently around the sky, turning, twisting, climbing and diving in the hope of sliding from the searchlights' grip.

In his memoirs Harry Yates of 75 Squadron wrote a compelling passage about trying to escape from the cone when flying Lancaster *P-Peter* on a raid to the port of Bremen:

As if some invisible hand had thrown a switch, we were snared by a radar-controlled searchlight. Its blinding power flooded the cockpit, bluish white, the colour of fear. In a moment every available searchlight was swung on us. We were coned, naked and no doubt exposed to a thousand pairs of eyes on the ground watching, hoping for the first sign of distress. The batteries wasted not a second in pumping heavy shells up into the cone. There was no future for us as things stood, and only one possible way out. But even as I pushed the column forward there was a huge explosion under the aircraft. We yawed and shuddered to port. I was lifted into my straps and my hands left the column. Lumps of coarse metal followed the shockwave, peppering the kite from nose to tail. I grabbed at the column again and pushed P-Peter down into the light. Nothing fancy, I went for speed. But she felt soggy. We didn't break free and those damned gunners were throwing everything up at us. More metal rattled into the fuselage and wings. I was operating on luck and instinct. The intensity of the beam completely obliterated the instrument panel. There was no indication of attitude, altitude or airspeed . . . I stamped on the starboard pedal. What did it matter if the tailplane fell off? Barrelling downward at God knows what speed, P-Peter began to bank. The gravity felt savage. But the light did not follow. We were re-united with the darkness and we were free.[79]

7

'Like entering the jaws of hell'

NOEL COWARD'S PUBLIC image before the war was that of a refined, rather camp playwright and actor, with an acid wit and a mastery of the drawing-room farce. But this reputation concealed the powerful spirit of British patriotism that burned within him. He admired Churchill, loathed Chamberlain and despised his fellow entertainers who 'scuttled' off to Holywood as Europe was plunged into crisis in the late 1930s. Such was his devotion to his country that he even served as an under-cover agent for the Foreign Office. Though Coward was not cut out for intelligence work, the advent of war allowed him more scope to express this patriotic impulse, reflected in his famous propaganda film *In Which We Serve*. His admiration for the men in the front line was perhaps even more graphically demonstrated in his poem 'Lie in the Dark and Listen', which paid tribute to Bomber Command. Full of reverence for the aircrews, the lines also showed Coward's contempt for those who failed to appreciate the heroism of such men. The final stanza, with its tone of reproach, went as follows:

> Lie in the dark and listen
> City magnates and steel contractors,
> Factory workers and politicians
> Soft, hysterical little actors.
> Ballet dancers, 'reserved' musicians
> Safe in your warm, civilian beds.
> Count your profits and count your sheep
> Life is flying above your heads
> Just turn over and try to sleep.
> Lie in the dark and let them go
> Theirs is a world you will never know
> Lie in the dark and listen.[1]

As Coward recognized, the bomber crews went through a regular nocturnal ordeal that was far beyond the imaginings of the civilians at home. Whatever the politics or morality of the bomber offensive, the airmen themselves were engaged in acts of astonishing self-sacrifice unparalleled in any other British theatre of war. The experience of flying to the Reich was bruising enough, but it reached its traumatic crescendo over the target, when the intensity of ground fire was worsened by the requirement that the aircraft had to fly straight and level for accuracy of bombing.

Even before the bombers reached their objective, their flight had often been a perilous adventure. The flak and the fighters were the worst hazards, but there were others, such as risks of freakish weather, collisions and even fire from their own side. Both Harris and the crews frequently complained of the erroneous forecasts provided by Bomber Command's meteorological unit. In fairness, however, it was impossible to be too accurate without satellite technology or intensive reconnaissance. But the imprecision meant that heavy bombers could sometimes encounter appalling conditions which were almost as big a threat as the 88-mm German guns. 'If there was a storm in our way, we just had to blunder right through it. You could hear the ice flying off the propeller and hitting the fuselage,' said Joe Williams, a gunner with 625 Squadron. 'St Elmo's fire, static electricity in a storm, would play around the ends of the gun barrels. You could hold up your finger and it would leap from your finger to the structure of the turret. These were the sort of conditions we sometimes had to fly in.'[2] St Elmo's fire was also experienced by the crew of Bob Woolf's Lancaster, *J-Johnny*, during a storm on the way back from bombing a railway target in southern France. 'There were sparks everywhere and the exterior of J-Johnny was covered with blue flames. Aerials, guns and wings were brilliantly alight. The props were just four circles of flame. Visibility was almost zero though enough for us to see three aircraft hit by flak and go down very close to us. There were hailstones. Rain poured into the aircraft making the floor awash with water.' In this appalling weather, one of the leading Pathfinder bombers told the main force to switch on their navigation lights, since there would be no fighters in the vicinity. 'Immediately the surrounding sky was filled with red, green and white lights showing just how close and heavily populated the bomber stream was. It was terrifying. Surprisingly, later we learned that the attack had been quite successful. Not surprisingly, the hailstones had stripped the paint off our aircraft.'[3]

As Woolf mentioned, the Lancasters were rarely aware of each other's presence because of the darkness. But with hundreds of heavy bombers all moving in the same direction and without any lights, there were huge dangers of collision. The heavy bombers were given specific altitudes and timings for the trip, but such measures could not eliminate all the risks. 'You knew that all around you were dozens, scores of aircraft,' said Joe Williams, 'and yet you could not see them. The only indication was when one came extremely close. The aircraft would then judder and lurch as you went across the slipstream.'[4] The experience of going through another Lancaster's slipstream was, according to engineer Doug Tritton, 'a sudden bumping sensation, like hitting the rumble strips on a road or going over a sleeping policeman.' Even worse than the slipstream, said Tritton, was flying through the wake of a Lancaster that had been blown up by Schrage Musik, or flak: 'You see ahead of you this great mushroom of flames as it blows up and, of course, you are less than a second away from it.'[5] In the great mass of planes, near-misses were inevitable. With the bomber stream shrouded in blackness and all sound muffled by the combination of helmets and thundering Merlins, aircrews received no warning of the presence of another nearby Lancaster. On a return trip from the German oil plant at Bochum in central Germany, Peter Russell of 625 Squadron went through one such nerve-shredding episode. 'Suddenly, in a terrifying instant my windscreen was filled with the shape of an oncoming aircraft. Head-on collision! It was huge, lit by the flashes of flak and the light of the fires below. As I had just done, I threw the stick forward. As we went down, I saw its lit-up belly rush over my head. Arrrgh! A groan escaped me.' The rest of the crew joined in. 'Then there was absolute silence. A shocked silence.'[6]

Others were not so lucky. In the inky night sky, collisions could happen on any part of the route but were particularly likely at the moments when the bombers swarmed together: on take-off, at the rendezvous point, over the target and on landing. In any such tragedy, 14 men would have their lives swept away in an inferno of flame and disintegrating metal, without the enemy having fired a single shot. The sight of a collision could be shocking, as rear gunner Ron Smith found when he was sitting in his rear turret on the return from a raid on Stuttgart. Nearing the French coast, Smith saw 'quite plainly a Lancaster in all detail slightly below, moving slowly across our course. Then, as I moved the turret in the other direction, another Lancaster could be observed, equally plainly, sliding almost imperceptibly across the other's path. As they edged nearer each other, as if intending to formate side by side, I eased the turret dead astern, so that both aircraft were now centred in my view.' To his anguish, Smith watched as the gap between the planes kept narrowing. He still expected that they would pass by each other, because it seemed almost inexplicable that they were both oblivious to the other's presence. 'Suddenly I realized the truth and shouted out a useless warning. Then a mighty eruption, a fountain of flame and falling debris, the night air all around us as day, our own aircraft falling away, the skipper fighting for control as the blast all but turned us over.' Smith was badly shaken and continued to be haunted for some time by the incident. At night he replayed the tragedy, 'sickened and disgusted at the waste of war'.[7]

Some of the self-inflicted losses could be even more grotesque. In every war there are incidents of so-called 'friendly fire', where confusion, anxiety and the fog of battle result in forces attacking their own side. Bomber Command was no exception, though the reluctance to open fire undoubtedly reduced such casualties. Nevertheless, Lancaster crews occasionally found themselves under fire from other RAF aircraft, including Spitfires, Beaufighters and sometimes even other Lancasters. In fact there were rumours among the airmen that the Luftwaffe had a special unit that rebuilt British heavy bombers which had been shot down and then sent these refashioned planes, wearing RAF colours, into the midst of the bomber stream to cause havoc. This was, however, nothing more than the kind of excitable scaremongering to which all military personnel are prone during conflict. There was no such unit, as Major Heinz-Wolfgang Schnaufer confirmed in his post-war interrogation: 'No Allied type of aircraft were employed at night at any time. He thought that if bomber crews had reported this, it was probably due to friendly aircraft shooting each other. On one occasion when about to attack a Lancaster, another Lancaster shot at it and he sat off and watched both Lancasters shoot each other down.'[8] On one frightening night in early 1944, bomb aimer Les Bartlett, who carried out three operational tours in Bomber Command, endured both a near collision and RAF bullets, as he noted in his diary for 5 January. Coming back from Stettin on the Baltic coast, 'we had two narrow squeaks, both with Lancasters. The first Lanc suddenly crossed above us from port to starboard and nearly took our mid-upper turret with it. The second just appeared on the port beam and before we knew where we were he was blazing away at us. How he didn't shoot us down I can't imagine. It was point blank range.'[9]

Even when they crossed the English Channel the bombers were not necessarily safe, since the Royal Navy tended to open up against anything they deemed suspicious. As one member of 44 Squadron remarked after coming under fire on a training mission off the coast of Scotland: 'The Navy doesn't know its aircraft from elbow.'[10] The anti-aircraft batteries around the coast of England tended to be less trigger-happy, partly because all heavy bombers carried a transmitter in the wireless operator's compartment which sent out an Identification Friend or Foe (IFF) blip that could be recognized by British radar stations. The problem was that the IFF signal could also be picked up by the Germans, so bomber crews were meant only to switch it on when approaching home. But, as a result of another of those fallacious rumours that spread in wartime, there was a misguided theory that the IFF signal helped to jam the expected flak from the Germans. As a result, some crews left the IFF transmitter on all the time, thereby reducing their safety by opening themselves up to German interception.[11]

But all these tribulations paled beside the bombing run itself, the moment when the Lancaster fulfilled its essential purpose of dropping a large bomb load on the chosen target. The run-up to the release of the bombs encapsulated many of the most harrowing aspects of a sortie: the claws of the searchlight batteries searching the sky; the sense of sickness in the stomach waiting for the enemy; the blast waves from exploding shells; the raging fires on the ground below; the hidden menace of fighters at the rear or underneath; the horror of watching another Lancaster burst into flames and plunge towards the ground. But what made this all the worse was the sense that there was no means of escape. The Lancaster had to be kept on a straight line through this hellish scene without weaving or corkscrewing while the bomb aimer lined up the target markers in his sight, no matter how blinding the master beam or how close the flak. More defenceless than at any other time on a raid, the bomber had to maintain its course until its load was dropped. 'Once again I began to experience the now familiar and unpleasant feeling in the pit of the stomach, and the dryness of the throat as we began our run to the target . . . It was always a time of intense vigilance and tension, caused largely by the feeling of naked exposure one got when having to traverse an illuminated area which contained so much activity,' wrote Canadian rear gunner Clayton Moore.[12] Heading straight into a wall of flak and searchlights, the men's survival could appear almost impossible. Little wonder, then, the crews had such a dread of this section of the trip, when their lives seemed to hang in the balance.

'Suddenly we were over the Big City,' wrote Ron Smith of a raid on Berlin, 'and I was petrified by the ghastly panorama all round. After the long hours of searching the night sky from the coast to be suddenly propelled into a brilliant hell over Berlin produced a freezing of the mind. As I gazed in awe at the multiple unfolding horror I felt exposed and vulnerable. Flak sliced up through the broken illuminated clouds, ascending gracefully, to scream past the turret. A Lancaster slid across at right angles with a single-engined fighter just behind it, as if attached by an invisible thread. The city far below was bubbling and boiling, splashes of fire opening out as the blockbusters pierced the terrible brew.' The atmosphere of mounting tension inside the Lancaster on the approach to the target was highlighted by Frank Musgrove, the navigator with 149 Squadron, in his description of a raid on the Ruhr valley:

> Suddenly, we were in brilliantly illuminated space high above the Ruhr, with myriads of searchlights criss-crossing the sky. I took my portable para- chute down from its rack and clipped it onto my chest. I worked at my charts, calculating an up-to-date wind for the bomb aimer to set on his bomb-sight and a course to get us most directly out of the target area once the bombs had been dropped. Light flickered through the window of my curtained apartment, brilliantly but fleetingly illuminating my charts. We were flying bumpily, the pilot sweating and asking impatiently, 'How much longer?' The bomb aimer replied soothingly, 'Nearly there, steady skipper, steady.'[13]

Lying on his front in the Perspex nose of the Lancaster, the bomb aimer was the crucial figure in the run to the target. He effectively took over the management of the plane, constantly issuing orders to the pilot for minor adjustments in direction as he pressed his face against the bomb-sight to watch the markers move into the centre of his graticule before pressing the bomb-release tit. 'When I was doing the bombing run, the pilot had to do exactly as I told him,' explained bomb aimer Arthur Smith. 'He would see the target in front of him lit up by markers or if it was daylight he might see the actual target itself. I would start saying, "Right, steady, there's the target ahead," and I would guide him on to the target by saying, "Right, left, left, right", and he would guide the aircraft accord- ing to my instructions. According to the tone in my voice, he would know how much to turn it, because he had got so used to me in training.'[14] The bomb aimer was in the most exposed position looking right into the eye of the fiery storm, but, paradoxically, he was the one crew member who could detach himself from the violent action all around because he had to concentrate so intently on his job. As bomb aimer Rex Oldland put it, 'I was lucky, as the bomb aimer down the front, I had to forget everything else, take everything out of my mind except that little red spot on the ground in front. It was just between me and the pilot.'[15] Apart from the pilot, the rest of the crew were almost redundant during the run, something that only enhanced the sense of mounting anxiety. Larry Curtis, a 617 Squadron wireless operator, confessed that during the bombing run he used to cling to a metal pole near his cabin 'like grim death. I've always said that if anyone found that steel pole, they would find my fingerprints embedded in it. And I'm not joking.'[16]

The almost random quality of the early RAF bombing raids had been revolutionized from 1942 by the creation of the Pathfinder Force. By the middle of the war, the Pathfinders' navigation systems, aircraft and marking techniques had all become highly sophisticated. In addition to the heavy bombers, Don Bennett's force also used the unarmed Mosquito, whose tremendous speed, height and versatility made it ideal for advanced marking of a target with pyrotechnic indicators. To help the Pathfinders find the target, the unit also had other aids which proved more effective than Gee. One was H2S, which used radar technology to transmit an image of the ground onto a cathode-ray screen in the aircraft. The great advantage of H2S was that, unlike Gee, it was not limited in range by the curvature of the earth. But the dots that appeared on the screen could be difficult to interpret, and it was only really effective in differentiating between major geographical features such as lakes, rivers and coastlines. The second, even more beneficial aid was Oboe, which used two ground stations in England to transmit Morse code signals to the receiving aircraft, audible to the Mosquito pilot in his earpiece. If the plane was on course, the pilot heard a long continuous tone, like that of an oboe. Deviations from the course resulted in variations in the Morse signal. On the approach to the target, there would be a second signal, a series of Morse dashes followed by a series of dots. The cessation of the dots showed that the aircraft was right over the target. At that moment the target indicators were released. The disadvantages of Oboe were that it was limited in range, its transmitting stations could only serve a few aircraft on a raid and the plane had to continue along a straight course. But these factors were outweighed by Oboe's phenomenal accuracy when operated by PFF Mosquitoes over western Germany and France from January 1943, often reaching an average of less than 100 yards from the target.

The inventive mind of Don Bennett also ensured that the target indicators (TIs) themselves had greatly improved. In its most common form, the TI was a 250-pound bomb filled with 60 pyrotechnic candles, coloured green, red or yellow. It was burst by a barometric fuse, usually set to go off at about 200 feet. The ignited candles then cascaded to the ground, lighting up the aiming point for the heavy bombers. There were other types. Some TIs were sky-markers used in thick cloud, set to go off at anything from 3,000 to 10,000 feet to mark the target below, though they could be unreliable, as bomb aimer Andrew Maitland related: 'Often markers dropped in the correct positions above the clouds would tend to drift quickly in varying winds and of course the more they drifted the less accurate would be the bombs dropped through them.'[17] Later, much larger versions were carried in 1,000-pound bomb cases with 200 candles, which could light up a wide area for more than twenty minutes. Sky-markers were also dropped along the route, while decoy flares were unloaded to deceive the Luftwaffe into sending their fighters in the wrong direction, though equally the Germans became adept at using fake markers to lure the bombers away from the cities. Experienced Lancaster pilots, however, claimed that they could easily spot a German decoy because it burned with a slightly different colour. In using the TIs for bombing, Bennett devised three main marking techniques, each with its own code name. The first, called Parramatta after Bennett's home town in Australia, involved the use of ground TIs dropped by blind-marking aids like H2S and Oboe. The second, named Newhaven because Bennett's personal WAAF Corporal Ralph came from the Sussex port, was used in clear weather when the Pathfinders could identify the target visually. Sky-marking was the third technique, called Wanganui after the home town of the New Zealander Squadron Leader Arthur Ashworth, who had been a heroic bomber pilot and then became a key member of Bennett's Pathfinder staff. In practice, a combination of these methods was often used on any given raid, particularly because smoke from the bombing could obscure the original flares.

Another development adopted by Bennett from August 1943 was the introduction of a Master Bomber for each raid, an airman effectively acting as the Pathfinder leader. It was a daunting role, requiring extraordinary reserves of courage, authority and calmness. Only the very greatest pilots, like Leonard Cheshire and Guy Gibson, were cut out for such a job. Usually flying in a Mosquito but sometimes a Lancaster, the Master Bomber had to check that the flares were dropped accurately at the aiming point, then tell the main force to come in and start bombing on whatever coloured markers had been chosen for the target. 'Bomb on green TIs,' he might say over the radio. Throughout the raid, he had to keep circling over the target, often with flak exploding all around him, while he ensured that burnt-out TIs were replenished and that bombers were hitting with reasonable accuracy. The navigator and later historian Noble Frankland wrote of the experience of Cheshire's control of a raid: 'His cool, collected and precise instructions came through our earphones with the kind of tone one might have expected from someone seated in a comfortable arm chair telephoning from a drawing-room.'[18]

The interplay between Master Bomber, pilot and bomb aimer was well described by Roy Yule, the skipper of Lancaster *R-Roger Two* of 626 Squadron, in his recollection of a night raid on Kleve, central Germany, in January 1945. Approaching the target at 10,000 feet, Yule heard the Master Bomber, Wing Commander 'Tubby' Baker, ordering the main force 'to come below the cloud'. To comply with the order, Yule 'closed the throttles and put Roger Two into a dive, getting under the cloud and levelling off at 4000 feet. This turned out to be one hell of a bombing run. Over half of the main force did not come below cloud and bombed the fires and flares which could be seen through the thin layer. The 140 or so Lancaster pilots that did obey the Master Bomber converged on to the tight bunch of target indicators.' Yule's bomb aimer announced that the bomb doors were open. Then, seconds later, Yule heard the 'clear, casual voice' of Baker telling the Lancasters to 'bomb to the starboard of the red TIs'. Suddenly, Yule saw another Lancaster looming over his port side. 'Looking up into its yawning bomb-bay with its rows of 500 pound bombs and a cookie, I jabbed left rudder to clear it.' The bomb aimer, who had not seen the other Lancaster, 'had started his run-up patter giving me right, and shouted agitatedly, "Right, right, not bloody left!"' The scene ahead was fantastic. Red and yellow tracer shells were criss-crossing from the flak batteries outside the town. They seemed to be coming from eight different positions and looked like 20 mm and 37 mm, which are nasty blighters at the height we were at. Strings of bombs were falling through the cloud from Lancs above. Flashes from the exploding blockbusters on the ground were blinding. A stricken Lancaster crashed on its run-in blowing up with its full bomb load. Large columns of black smoke rose from the town to 3000 feet.'[19]

As the Lancaster approached the start of the run, the aimer fused the bombs by pressing the necessary switches on a panel in his compartment. Once the aiming point was sighted, he kept giving his instructions to the skipper so the plane would remain on course for the target. The bomb-sight itself was another part of the Lancaster's technology that had undergone radical improvement since the dark days of 1940. The original sight, called the Mark IX, was an inadequate piece of equipment, 'a Heath Robinson lash-up with a graticule sight that you laid on the target and dropped the bombs when the time seemed right', according to Jim Brookbank of 9 Squadron.[20] Harris himself complained to Portal in early 1942: 'Our present sights are impracticable junk. Under prevailing tactical conditions they exaggerate rather than resolve sight problems.'[21] The great advance came with the Mark XIV developed in 1942, a far more sophisticated sight

A Lancaster Mark III in flight. 'Some products of the hand of man have that uncanny capacity
to pull at the heart-strings, and the Lancaster was one such. Everything about it was just right.
Its muscular, swept lines were beautiful to look at,' said one Bomber Command pilot

The genius behind the Lancaster: Roy Chadwick of the A. V. Roe company, one of the most influential designers in the history of British aviation. His life was to end in tragedy

The twin-engined Avro Manchester proved to be a lethal failure, but from its basic design emerged the incomparable Lancaster

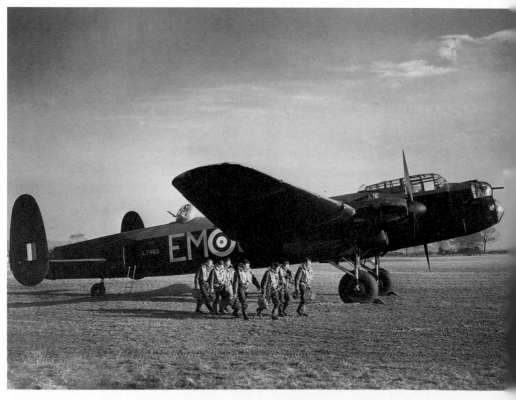

A gaggle of six Lancasters from 619 Squadron based at Coningsby, Lincolnshire

Three Lancaster Mark Is from 44 Squadron, the first RAF unit to receive the Avro bomber

Somehow eager, as if she wants to get at the enemy.' A Lancaster takes off at dusk, heading for the Reich

'Entering the jaws of hell.' A Lancaster landing using the FIDO system, which sent out jets of flame to light up runways and disperse thick fog

'It was great to breathe properly again . . . It meant we were alive,' said one Lancaster airman describing his relief on landing safely after a mission to Germany

Engine fitters working on one of the
starboard engines of a Lancaster
Mark I based at RAF Bottesford, near
Grantham

An RAF maintenance crew hoists a shot-up,
crashed Lancaster before taking it away for repair.
At the peak of the war, the Avro Repair Group
was putting more than 30 aircraft a week back
into the air

A shot taken at RAF Scampton, Lincolnshire, showing the personnel and equipment needed
to keep one Lancaster flying on operations, including aircrew, mechanics, WAAFs,
armourers, bomb handlers, fitters, AEC Matador petrol tender, mobile workshop and tractor
with loaded trailers

The pilot and flight engineer carrying out final checks before taking off on a raid in 1943

The loneliest job in the Lancaster: a rear gunner in his turret

From his Frazer-Nash FN50 turret, a mid-upper gunner of 57 Squadron scans the sky for enemy aircraft

Hauling a 4,000-pound 'Cookie' into a
Lancaster

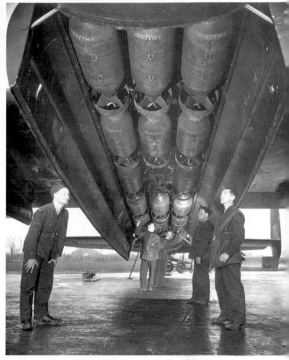

'Goddam, it's a flying bomb bay,' said an
American on seeing the Avro bomber for the
first time

A Lancaster of 467 Squadron being bombed-up by the ground crew

Left: A female Avro employee finishing the Perspex turret of a Lancaster. Women made up almost half the Avro workforce

Below: The assembly line at Avro's Woodford plant, near Manchester. Between October 1941 and March 1945, Woodford assembled 4,040 Lancasters – more than half the entire production run

that used a primitive but ingenious form of computer, operated by compressed air, to predict exactly where the bombs would land. The Mark XIV consisted of a large black box, about the size of a suitcase, situated at the left of the bomb aimer's compartment. Into this box the aimer fed the crucial data about the raid, such as the target's height above sea level, the weight of the aircraft and the terminal velocity of the bombs. Much of this information could be pre-set before the sortie. Then, at the beginning of the run, the navigator and skipper gave the aimer the final details of the course, like the altitude, wind direction and airspeed. Once all this data had been inputted, the aimer then turned to the bombsight itself. Tom Tredwell of 77 Squadron explained how it worked:

> The Mark XIV was a jump into a completely new age. We suddenly, for the first time, had a device which enabled us to look at both the bomb-sight and the ground at the same time. One of the problems with the old bombsight was that if you were looking at the bombsight itself, then you had to adjust when you wanted to look at the ground, which was 20,000 feet below. With the new type of bombsight this was completely over-come. You actually looked into a solid block of glass and, by means of a light source from over the top of your head, you saw reflected there what appeared to be a sword of red light. The idea was to guide the aircraft onto the target and get the target to slide down, in effect, the shaft of the sword until it met the cross section. And at the cross section you pressed the bomb release and away the bombs went. As far as I know, it was the best bombsight of the war.[22]

Apart from the ability to give a practical image of the aiming point on the glass screen, the other advantage of the Mark XIV was that, compared to other sights, it minimized the amount of time that the pilot had to fly straight and level, because its gyro stabilizers could take account of movements in the plane. The success of the Mark XIV provoked Harris into another of his regular grumbles against the Air establishment, which he felt was insufficiently energetic about installing the sight in the Lancasters. 'I must appeal to you about the Lancaster,' he wrote to Freeman in July 1943, complaining that the Mark XIV programme had fallen behind compared to the other heavies. 70 to 80 per cent of Stirlings and Halifaxes had been fitted with Mark XIV, but 'the Lancasters, which are our most efficient bomber potential, are only equipped to about 40 per cent and a backlog of some 500 Lancasters remains to be worked off . . . Please do your utmost to help us. It is no exaggeration to say that the provision of the Mark XIV sight has increased the effectiveness of the bomber offensive out of all recognition.'[23] There followed a dispute between Avro and the Ministry of Aircraft Production over where the blame lay for these delays. Avro claimed that MAP had been slow in ordering the parts, a charge fiercely denied by the MAP official E.C. Dearth. 'I can only say that the firm has been continually pressed by both my predecessor and myself throughout the past year to hasten the production of parts for this modification . . . From the point of view of results the response has been most unsatisfactory and I have not failed to tell the firm so.' Eventually Avro and MAP agreed on an accelerated programme for retrospective fitting of the Mark XIV in the Lancaster at a rate of 40 sets a week by September.

No matter how advanced its bombsight, the Lancaster still had to maintain a steady course during the climactic moments of the bombing run, as flak grew more aggressive. 'There is much activity ahead of us,' wrote bomber aimer J. W. Walsh of 619 Squadron in his account of a raid on Krefeld in western Germany. 'A solid wall of ack ack and searchlights appears stretching from port to starboard. It is a few miles ahead of us but it looks impenetrable. We are here to bomb Krefeld so we hold our course towards the heart of this deadly barrier. The Pathfinders are dropping brilliantly coloured target marker flares ahead and we fly straight and level through the heavy flak. I direct the pilot, "left, left – right".'[24] Above the roar of the Merlins, the habitual silence within the Lancaster's interior was now more intense than ever, only punctuated by terse exchanges between the bomb aimer and the pilot. The raging scene of searchlights and fires further induced an edgy taciturnity.

The 625 Squadron pilot Peter Russell, one of the most eloquent commentators on the experience of flying the Lancaster, wrote this passage about the astonishing vision of the target during the bombing run:

> As we came nearer, the flashing, star-filled arch of the sky broadened like a curtain and its white and yellow pattern, with orange too now, filled more of its space. From the wings of this vast proscenium searchlight beams now arose and groped about the sky above the target, swinging to the left and right, crossing and opening like giant scissors. Still nearer now, the curtain of exploding shells was not only in front of us, but to each side as well. They flashed at our height, just below us, just above us, lighting up the other aircraft nearby. Surely there was no possible way through. In the light of the explosions of the nearer ones I could see the puff of black smoke that followed instantaneously the white-shell burst. Suddenly, not far above us, an orange ball of fire appeared, then hung, then slowly fell. An aircraft had been hit. If the chaos in the air around us was like an evil fairyland, the scene below was fantastic. Fire raged over a large area, peppered with white explosions and lit every few seconds by a greater

flash, obliterating in its vicinity all other sight of the red and orange conflagration as 4000-pounders, 'cookies', one from almost every aircraft, fell into
the target area.[25]

Wynford Vaughan-Thomas, the BBC reporter who provided a running
commentary inside a 207 Squadron Lancaster on a raid to Berlin in 1943,
gave this glimpse of the experience of the run-up to the target:

> It is pretty obvious now, as we are coming in through the searchlight cones,
> it is going to be hell over the city itself. There is one comfort. It is going
> to be soundless because the roar of our engines is drowning every other
> sound. We are running straight into the most gigantic display of soundless
> fireworks in the world. We are due over our target in two minutes' time.
> Bill our bomb aimer is forward, he is lying prone over the bombsight and
> the searchlights are coming nearer all the time. There is one cone, split
> again and then it comes together. They seem to splay out, like the tentacles
> of an octopus waiting to catch you. Then suddenly they come together.[26]

Through this mayhem, the bomb aimer and pilot had to retain their
concentration. What was so striking about Vaughan-Thomas's broadcast
was the almost superhuman calmness within the Lancaster as the plane
flew over the target, the pilot opened the bomb doors and the bomb
aimer, continuing to give instructions, waited until the markers were at
the centre of the cross on his sight. The voices betrayed not a shred of
the anxiety the crew must have been feeling.

> 'Half a minute to go. OK, boys,' said the skipper, in a deadpan tone.
> 'Left . . . left,' said the bomb aimer, or bombardier as he was called on
> this aircraft.
> 'Hello, bombardier, ready when you are, bomb doors open.'
> 'Steady . . . steady . . . bit longer yet. Steady . . . level a bit. Steady, bombs
> going. One, two, three, bombs still going.'[27]

The entire effort of Bomber Command was crystallized in the single
moment that the aimer pressed the bomb tit and released the Lancaster's
cargo. All the work, from the planning at High Wycombe to the fuelling
of the tanks across eastern England, culminated in that one, split-second
movement of a gloved thumb, sending more than 12,000 pounds of explosives and incendiaries into the heart of a German city.

Because of the understandable desperation to leave the target area,
some bomb aimers dropped their load a fraction too soon, an error that
was to become a common feature of raids over Germany. Called 'creepback', this practice was so widespread that Pathfinders sometimes adopted
the technique of leaving the TIs marginally beyond the actual aiming

point, recognizing the inevitability of bombs falling short. Bomb aimer Campbell Muirhead recorded in his diary his own method of dealing with the problem, having been told by his Wing Commander of the detrimental effects of creepback:

> One kite, he said, does it, then another, and before you know it, the entire effort of the operation is nullified. The suburbs of the target area have been pranged and the principal object of the raid has escaped virtually scot free. I must admit that, once or twice, I've been sorely tempted to press that button just that split second too soon and when that happens I tell myself to count to three. Which I do, as slowly as I can manage. By the 'three' the target is exactly on the cross and my sighting is bang-on. I think it is better to be a half-second late in pressing the tit than being half a second early. If you over-shoot slightly others, sighting perhaps on the fires you raise, will plank their loads reasonably accurately.[28]

On the release of the bombs, the Lancaster leapt at the sudden reduction in its weight, jumping 'as if you'd hit a bump in the air,' according to the 15 Squadron pilot Leonard Miller.[29] There was almost a sense of liberation as the plane shot upwards once the bombs had gone and the bomb doors were closed. The instant increase of manoeuvrability after the bombs' release was what impressed American pilot Robert Raymond. 'There is a slight upward lift and the plane becomes light and easy to handle again. Everyone feels better after they've gone, even though we're still over the target.'[30] For Rex Oldland, a bomb aimer with 455 Squadron, the biggest sense of relief came from the closure of the bomb doors, though he saw that this was more psychological than practical. 'We always felt very vulnerable once the bomb doors were open. Stupid really, because the bomb doors were only an eighth of an inch of metal. They would not stop anything.'[31] But on rare occasions, when a really heavy bomb load was dropped, the relief could be replaced by embarrassment, as revealed by the private memoir of Jack West, a navigator with 115 Squadron, who in December 1944 was sent on a mission to drop a massive 12,000 pounder on Oberhausen in the Ruhr. Without a nose cone or tail, this vast cylindrical monster was constructed by simply bolting together three cookies. 'The bomb was released right on target,' wrote West, 'but what happened next was truly unbelievable because the loss of weight from the aircraft rocketing upwards at least 1000 feet was at such a rate that every opening in the human body evacuated. Noses and eyes bled, ears popped and some crew members experienced a bowel movement.'[32]

Yet even after the bomb release, the ordeal of the Lancaster crew over the target was not quite completed, because the plane had to continue flying straight and level for another thirty-six seconds in order for photographic evidence to be captured of the individual bombing effort by each aircraft in the raid. When the first bomb fell, the electrical circuit in the Lancaster's bay also released a 4.5-inch photoflash, full of about 20 pounds of aluminium powder, which gave out nearly 200 million candle-power as it exploded, sufficient to light up the target and the surrounding sky. At the same time, a camera in the nose of the plane automatically took a sequence of photographs of the bombs' impact on the target. Once the cycle was completed, the bomber aimer would tell the skipper, 'Photos taken,' and the Lancaster could begin its escape from the target. The photographic requirement had two objectives: first to provide detailed evidence of the results of an attack, helping RAF intelligence in future raids; second, to confirm that the heavy-bomber crews had actually gone for the target and not dropped their bombs in open countryside or the North Sea.

But many crews loathed the dictates of Bomber Command on this issue. For a start, they feared that the flash itself, with its explosive power, added to the dangers of a sortie. Though problems with the flash were rare in practice, they were not unknown. 'I had a nasty experience on a raid to Nuremburg,' recalled pilot Peter Huggins. 'There was a lot of opposition but the worst thing that happened to me was that I had a photoflash go off straight in front of me from an aircraft above which practically blinded me. I lost my vision for a few moments. I had to rely on the engineer in the next seat to give me instructions, right or left.'[33] Flashes were also known to explode occasionally inside the fuselage or hang up in the flare chute, the latter occurrence presenting a risk on landing. But far worse was the stipulation that the pilot keep flying straight after the bombs had gone, something that increased the danger to the aircraft in the flak-drenched skies.

Bomber Command's willingness to lengthen the bombing run partly because of its lack of trust in the integrity of crews caused offence to men like rear gunner Clayton Moore, who in his memoirs wrote that the wait for the camera to function on his first trip to Hamburg was a 'long, nail-biting ordeal' while 'all hell was breaking loose around us', with 'flak shells bursting all over the place, causing the Lancaster to wallow drunkenly each time one got a bit near'. Moore admitted that 'a small number of crews were not keen to attack their objective, and some ingenuity had gone into the perfection of ploys which were designed to cheat the system'. But he believed 'these crews were very much the minority and their existence did not warrant the exposure of honest men to unnecessary danger'.[34] Such an argument held little sway with either the staff of Bomber Command HQ or with Harris, who treasured his photographs of the raids on Germany.

Apart from the photoflash, there were other hazards that could exacerbate the stress of the bombing run. One was the attitude of certain ultra-conscientious bomb aimers who would insist on their plane going round again if they could not get the markers in the cross of their bomb-sight, usually because of smoke or because the Lancaster had been thrown off course by evasive action. After braving the savagery of the German defences once, it was understandable that crews were reluctant to put themselves through the trial a second time, and any bomb aimer who insisted on such a course by calling out 'dummy run' could trigger a wave of vocal antagonism. Given that the RAF was committed to area rather than precision bombing, such a demand for pinpoint accuracy could be seen as smacking of self-indulgence. In addition to the greater exposure to the flak caused by a second or third run, there was also a much greater danger of collision when a Lancaster had to turn and rejoin the oncoming wave of heavy bombers. On his very first operational trip to Germany, Donald Falgate of 49 Squadron made the pilot go round three times, a decision he put down to his own naivety. 'I won't repeat what was said over the intercom from various crew members. At the time I did not appreciate the hazard of going round again . . . and on the third run I managed to convince the pilot to keep the aircraft sufficiently stable so I could get a good line up on the markers.'[35]

Gerry Murphy, an aimer with 101 Squadron, recalled the abuse he had to endure: 'One night on a bomb-run, the target was not quite in the bomb-sight and I automatically called, "Dummy run!" There was no response for a moment and then I heard the voice of the rear-gunner over the intercom: "Who is the dim-witted b— who just called a dummy run?" This was followed by ribald comments and improper suggestions by other members of the crew. A couple of nights later during an op the skipper called me on the intercom and did not receive a reply. My oxygen tube had got fouled. The skipper realized what had happened and asked the engineer to check and then the comments started. "Leave him and we'll have no more dummy runs!" "Let the b— die and we'll live longer."'[36] So exasperated was Jack Currie with a new bomb aimer on his crew during a flight by *C-Charlie Two* to Berlin that he simply refused to comply. He recounted their exchange as follows:

Bomb aimer to pilot: 'Are you ready to commence the bombing-run?'

'Ready? I've been ready and waiting for the last ten minutes!'

'Thank you, pilot, I am satisfied that the bomb-sight is levelled and all stations selected.'

'Get cracking, then.'

'Thank you, pilot. Commencing bombing run now. Right . . . steady. Left, left . . . steady. Right a bit . . . steady . . . steady.'

My God, I thought, it's really going to happen, he's going to say 'back a bit'. But there was worse to come.

'Right . . . steady. Right . . . steady. Right . . . right . . . dummy run!'

I sensed, rather than saw, the flight engineer stiffen in horror beside me. I spoke as calmly as I could.

'You don't do dummy runs on Berlin. Let 'em go.'

'But . . .'

'Let 'em go.'

I felt Charlie Two lift as the high explosive tumbled out of the bomb bay and my heart lifted with her.[37]

But sometimes, due to mechanical failure, the bombs did not fall out. Such an eventuality mainly arose when components froze in high altitude, locking some of the bombs in their cradles. Alternatively, some bombs might be slow to leave their mounts and would be trapped in the bay once the doors closed. It was highly dangerous for a live bomb still to be inside the aircraft, especially if it was rolling around, for one sudden movement against the detonator would instantly blow it up. Aware that any 'hang-up' (a mechanical failure to release the bomb) could be deadly, the aimer had the duty to go along to the bay, open a small inspection panel, and shine his torch inside to check that the bombs had gone. If any were still there, the pilot had to open the doors as quickly as possible and let them drop, with the aimer using the bomb tit again on stubborn devices if necessary. But errors inevitably arose due to the pressure on the crews at the intensity of the run. On a raid to Flers in Normandy in June 1944, bomb aimer Campbell Muirhead forgot to carry out his inspection until the plane was well on its way back to England. 'When I slid back the panel and shone the lamp into the bay, there they were: three 500 pounders, rolling about the bay of the floor.' He screamed at the pilot to open the doors, which was quickly done. 'And three bombs dropped through the night on to somewhere in France. I hope it was a French field which received them – not some innocent French village. But I shall never know. It's something I refuse to think about.' When he returned to his compartment, the pilot asked: 'What the fuck happened there?' Muirhead struggled to give an answer but believed that 'when I pressed the tit, these three bombs had come slightly adrift from their cradles, but not sufficiently to free them: then the movement of the Lanc had gradually eased them away from the cradles and on to the bomb bay floor. Where, all fused, they rolled around waiting for something to detonate them, such as violent corkscrewing to evade a fighter.' On landing, Muirhead asked the armourers to check all the release mechanisms on the cradles.[38] Rear gunner Alfred Watson's Lancaster crew from 567 Squadron had a more vigorous response when they dropped a hung–up bomb over the English Channel. 'I yelled. "I can see the surf below me. Give it a couple of minutes and then let her go." Well, we are just off Calais, and the bomb is dropped with a bloody great splash. Then the bloody heavens opened. We had dropped it in the middle of the bloody Channel Fleet and of course they thought it was bloody Germans. They gave us a really rough time.'[39]

Perhaps the most frightening experience of all was to look up and see another Lancaster directly above, with its bomb doors open ready to drop its load. At 30 feet away, the cavernous bomb bay of the plane never seemed larger or more well-stocked than at such moments. The Lancasters had their own timings for bombing, but changing wind directions or mechanical problems, combined with the sheer number of aircraft over the target in darkness, meant that a perfect schedule was never feasible. 'I have seen a rear turret sliced off an aircraft by a cookie dropped from above,' said John Smith, an air gunner with 625 Squadron. 'One night I thought the same was going to happen to us. We were on our bombing run and as I looked up, directly above us was another Lancaster with its bomb bay doors wide open. I could see it as clear as day. I couldn't shout out a warning as we had to stay straight and level, but I can tell you that for those few seconds I wasn't looking for any fighters, I was looking to see if the bomber was going to drop his bombs on us.'[40] Fortunately, Smith's plane escaped the bombs.

Not so lucky was the Lancaster of navigator Frank Musgrove during a raid on Homberg, central Germany, in November 1944. Just as Musgrove's plane was approaching the target, a Lancaster moved over-head with its doors open:

> To my horror I saw the bombs beginning to fall – vast ungainly canisters falling in slow motion. They couldn't possibly miss our aircraft. But they did. One fell on one side of the fuselage: it seemed only a foot or so clear, but a third seemed to be falling in slow motion directly towards the rear gunner's turret. It missed the turret and the gunner and struck the tailplane;

it was, of course, fused, but it did not explode. However, it took a large section of the tailplane away. The aircraft was destabilised and with ten tons of bombs on board we went into a sickening dive through a great barrage of flak.

The pilot pulled the Lancaster out of its dive at 12,000 feet and even managed to get back on the bombing run, drop the bombs on the target and return home, though Musgrove felt that throughout the journey, 'I expected to fall out of the sky at any moment.'[41] A much worse fate was suffered by John Duffield, a 103 Squadron engineer, and his crew on a sortie to Turin in February 1943. Usually Italian trips were seen as much easier than German ones but not in this case:

> We were just turning off to clear away. All of a sudden I heard this awful battering noise. What had actually happened is that another aircraft had dropped its bomb load on us. So we had run into a stream of incendiaries. I don't know what he thought he was bombing because we were a minute clear of the target so he wasn't bombing that. All the engines stopped. I heard the pilot say, 'We've had it. You'd better jump.' I was very lucky. I had my parachute with me. So I made my way to the rear door. But I couldn't open the door, no way. The aircraft started to twist and I thought I'd better brace myself somewhere. I put my back against the bomb compartment on the fuselage floor and braced myself there. The aircraft was spinning like mad by this time. I was just stuck there with the force of the spin.

Suddenly the spinning stopped. As the aircraft levelled, Duffield stood up, made his way to the rear door and leapt out. Unfortunately, his harness was too loose and the jerk of the opening parachute ripped into his groin. The pain was 'something to be believed, agonizing'. He landed with a terrific thump, limped to a nearby farm and was soon arrested by the Italian army. He spent the rest of the war as a POW. The mid-upper gunner and pilot were both killed in the crashed Lancaster, having failed to escape.[42]

If the Lancaster managed to make it through the run without being hit by flak, cannon or bombs, the skipper or some other crew member might shout over the intercom: 'Let's get the hell out of here.' The navigator would then give a course for England and the Lancaster started its homeward journey. There was still danger from the German defences, especially the fighters, but the risks had been considerably reduced because, without its heavy bomb load, the Lancaster could fly more quickly. A palpable sense of relief swept through the crew as the plane climbed and increased its speed. The worst was over. Concentration had to be maintained but some of the nervous tension had evaporated. 'At last we enter the wall of darkness,' wrote Pathfinder gunner Ron Smith, 'and looking back I can see the brilliant red and pyrotechnics as more Pathfinders release their loads . . . Out into the black void again, every turn of the propellers taking us nearer salvation and away from the clutches of the lurking fighters'.[43]

Once the Kammhuber Line and the northern European coast was passed, the atmosphere grew more relaxed inside the Lancaster. Don Charlwood, a 103 Squadron navigator, said that he always felt 'a sweet satisfaction' once he gave the skipper the Estimated Time of Arrival (ETA) for the English coast. 'Future danger does not exist. We have come through tonight. We have done what we set out to do; there are no men on earth better than these men beside me.'[44] No longer sickened by nerves, airmen could undo the straps on their masks, consume their rations, have a coffee or even listen to some music, though the last activity was officially forbidden because radio silence was meant to be maintained. The feeling of a reward after an ordeal was well conveyed by Joe Williams of 625 Squadron. 'Coming back over the North Sea, the wireless operator sometimes used to tune into a bit of dance music We heard it on the intercom. That would be nice. The wireless operator would come down the fuselage, bringing a flask of coffee. I would turn my turret onto the beam and I had a little sliding window on the port side. I could open this and he would pass the coffee through.'[45] Even more unauthorized than music was smoking in the plane, though plenty of airmen indulged in the habit once the plane had descended enough for them to switch off their oxygen, as Ken Parfitt, a navigator with 97 Squadron, recalled. 'On the way back we would light up cigarettes. It was against the rules, of course – just to my left was a little fuel cock which was constantly dripping on the floor. But it seemed a minimal risk compared to what we had just been through.'[46] The crossing of the North Sea and the English Channel had its own risks, not only because of German fighters but because of the Royal Navy. Flight Lieutenant J. S. A. Marshall of the Royal Australian Air Force recorded in his log book a tragic moment on returning from a trip to Argentan, Normandy, in June 1944: 'On crossing the channel the Navy (ours) shot down a plane (Lanc) about 200 yards on our port. Trigger happy bastards.'[47]

There was no illicit smoking, music or swearing at the navy on Wynford Vaughan-Thomas's flight back for the BBC from Berlin aboard *F-Freddie* in 1943. Nevertheless, with his journalistic skill and the authentic recording of the airmen's voices, he revealed the mood of happiness in the aircraft as the journey approached its end:

There it goes, our first sight of England, just a little light from a beacon, flashing at us from the darkness below. After the giant glare of lights we left behind in Berlin, it seems small and frail. But everyone on board *F for Freddie* is mighty glad to see it. Con our navigator has got out the goodies that we were not able to tackle during the hectic hours over Germany. We are cracking open our fruit juice. Someone has got his mouthful of chocolate and Scottie the engineer, who is just ahead of me, is pouring out from his thermos a cup of hot tea. We have got our oxygen masks off. There is a sense of freedom throughout the whole of *F-Freddie*. Ken our skipper has just said over the intercom:

'Boys, we won't be the first home, but we're damned glad to be home at all.' (Skipper continues after pause) 'Hello, bombardier, English coast should be coming up now. Will you tell me when you cross it?'

'OK, I'll let you know . . . I can see it coming up ahead.'

'Thank you.'

'Nav lights on, skipper.'

'OK, navigator, nav lights on.'

Bomb Aimer: 'We should be over it in a few seconds. There it is. Good to see old England again.'

Skipper: 'Yes, after that trip, boy, that's a sight for sore eyes, that is.'

Navigator: 'ETA at base: 15 minutes.'

'OK, navigator, thanks very much . . . Hello, engineer, skipper here. How's the petrol going? Are we doing all right?'

'Oh yes.'

'Everything running OK?'

'Just lovely.'

'Good show, boy.'[48]

For all such elation at reaching England, the Lancaster crew still had to find their own airfield and bring the plane in to land, not an easy task in darkness and often foul weather. In fact, despite the loss of weight in bombs and fuel, landing was more complex technically than taking off because of the difficulty of judging height and avoiding other bombers in the circuit. On a return from Germany, once the plane passed the English coast from the North Sea, it was usually about ten minutes from its base in Lincolnshire or the Fens. Guided by Gee and the navigator's expertise, the pilot then looked for his own airfield's red beacon, which flashed an identification signal during the hours of darkness. Once that was found, he called up Flying Control over the radio-telephone (or r/t), gave the squadron call-sign and his plane's name, and then asked for permission to land, or 'pancake' as it was called in RAF parlance. If there were several aircraft returning from the raid and seeking to land, the Flying Control operator, usually a WAAF, told the Lancaster in response to join the circuit flying over the base at a prescribed height. Calm and reassuring, the sound of the Flying Control WAAF over the r/t always had a special appeal for airmen. 'I am sure that those girls were chosen because of their gorgeous voices,' was the view of Group Captain Jack Goodman of the Pathfinder Force.[49] As the Lancaster took its place in the circuit, gradually descending in a spiral, the engineer put down the undercarriage and the flaps. At about 1,000 feet, with its predecessor now clearing the runway, the plane was given permission to land by Flying Control. A final exchange was made with the WAAF and the pilot used the navigation lights to flash confirmation of the plane's identity in Morse code. Taking careful account of the wind direction, the pilot lined up the Lancaster with the white marker lights either side of the runway, and began the approach at around 120 mph before slowing to 100 mph as the wheels touched the ground.

Jack Currie described those final moments of the descent: 'The Lancaster swung towards the runway lights, crabbed down the approach, and swept across the threshold. The throttled engines coughed, the rudders twitched the nose straight down the runway's centre-line, the wheels flirted with the concrete, kissed, withdrew and finally embraced.'[50] The sight and sound of the Lancasters coming in to land was conveyed by rear gunner Ron Smith, recalling a night when he was off duty and was walking along the airfield's perimeter track. 'The familiar beat of the Merlin engines stopped me in my tracks, to stand and listen intently. The distant throb became a constant roar, as the blackness gave way to a glow across the airfield, the runway lights spacing out the distance. A change in the engines' note as the pitch altered for landing, the dark shape winking out the lights temporarily, showing its slowing progress as the engines cut to the backfire of exhausts.'[51]

The return of the Lancasters led to a burst of activity from the ground crewmen on duty, who were only able to take a fitful doze while waiting for their aircraft to come back. Engine fitter Stephen Rew, attached to 44 Squadron based at Waddington, left this account:

> The scene outside appears to be chaotic. Red, green and white navigation lights and behind them patches of blackness, black even in the darkness, revealing the presence of an aircraft, seem to be everywhere, while flashes of blue torchlight reveal the presence of the ground-crew men. The air is full of the sound of engines, some idling and some being given bursts of throttle to swing the aircraft round. The pilot identifies his plane by flashing the navigation lights. The ground man gives the pilot a mental pat for remembering and flashes back on one of his torches. As his plane approaches,

he starts to wave both torches in circles, indicating 'straight ahead'. As the aircraft comes closer, he holds his left hand still, waving with his right. The aircraft swings uncertainly to starboard, and then he guides it in with both torches. The aircraft stops with a hiss of brakes. One by one the four engines rustle into silence, and there she stands, noticeably higher off the ground than before she went, looking somehow tired but cheerful, like a man after a game of rugger. The ground crewman drags the heavy chocks into position in front of the wheels. He fetches the access ladder from the tent and waits for the door to be unlocked. It opens after a few minutes and the dim interior lights reveal the figure of one of the gunners, looking huge and unnatural in his yellow buoyancy suit. The gunner scrambles down the ladder, followed at intervals by the others. The nav lights are extinguished, and finally the engineer followed by the skipper make their way down.[52]

In addition to the white runway marker lights, the RAF had developed another useful tool to guide the plane down, a set of coloured lights by the runway which showed whether the Lancaster was on the correct glide path for landing. Hugh Parrott of 582 Squadron explained: 'Landing at night could be relatively easy. You had a glide path indicator: red if you're too low, green if you're right, yellow if you're too high. So all you had to do was line the plane up with the runway, and keep it in green on the GPI.'[53] That was why pilots sometimes talked of approaching 'in the green', as engineer Norman Ashton put it of a smooth landing with *W-William* at Elsham Wolds: 'Nicely "in the green" and lined up beautifully on the runway, with flaps fully down, I cut the throttles back as we wafted over the boundary and *William* sank to the tarmac with scarcely a shudder.'[54] But landing was not always a straightforward exercise, particularly if the weather was poor or the plane was damaged. Fog, so common in the bleak Fenlands and the coast throughout the winter months, was the worst menace, enshrouding airfields in a thick blanket which could make it impossible to see either the glide path indicator or the runway lights. In these extreme circumstances, pilots were literally flying blind into their bases, without any real idea of their direction.

The mounting catalogue of deaths and accidents forced Bomber Command and the Air Ministry to put forward two potential solutions to the problem of landing in fog. One was the Standard Beam Approach (SBA), which, not unlike a short-range version of the Oboe target finder, employed beacons in line with the runway to emit a series of signals in Morse code, telling the pilot if he was on track. A series of dots or dashes warned him that he had strayed to one side or the other, while a steady tone showed that he was on course for the runway. Using his altimeter to adjust his height, the pilot could then descend onto the runway. That was the theory, but in practice SBA proved difficult to operate success-fully. For a start, the Lancaster's standard altimeter was both unreliable and too imprecisely calibrated for effective use at low height, as revealed by the experience of Nick Knilans, an RCAF sergeant with 619 Squadron who once had to land in dismal conditions at Woodhall Spa after a raid on Hamburg. As he came in, unable to see the glide path indicator through the fog, his instruments showed he was at 1,000 feet. Suddenly the bomb aimer yelled, 'There's the ground.' Fighting desperately with the controls, Knilans managed to haul the Lancaster into the air, but not before it hit a gravel tip and sliced through some trees. When he had flown round again and then nursed the stricken aircraft onto the concrete, the alti-meter still read 960 feet. 'You son of a bitch,' he muttered to himself.[55] The SBA system itself required a lot of practice in realistic conditions, something that was difficult to achieve with the heavy demands on Bomber Command's resources and time. More importantly, it left a dangerously thin margin of error for an aircraft travelling at over 100 miles an hour, a speed at which a Lancaster could pass right across an airfield in less than thirty seconds.[56] Neither popular nor much used by crews even though it was installed on all airfields, SBA was operated in fewer than 8 per cent of landings in late 1943, and in the main Lancaster No. 5 Group the figure was just 0.99 per cent, according to a report by the Inspector General of Training. Gradually it was phased out in most Bomber Groups, after the Air Ministry had concluded, 'the SBA has not proved a practical means of landing in fog conditions with average operational crews'.[57]

The other solution was more radical. It aimed at dealing with the fog itself rather than merely trying to find a way to manoeuvre the plane through it. Winston Churchill was one of the driving forces behind this development, again displaying the phenomenal range of his military inter-ests. 'It is of great importance to find means to dissipate fog at aerodromes so that the aircraft can land safely. Let full experiments to this end be put in hand by the Petroleum Warfare Department with all expedition,' he wrote in September 1942 to Geoffrey Lloyd MP, the Minister for Petroleum.[58] Lloyd's Warfare Department, set up by the government to oversee the technical development of oil supply and weaponry such as flamethrowers, enlisted the help of a variety of scientists and engineers to come up with a practicable fog dispersal scheme. Some of the ideas were ingenious. A leading agriculturalist from Kent, Mr E. R. Mount, looked into the use of agricultural heaters employed for the prevention of frosts in orchards, while the chemical giant ICI conducted experiments with a

vast hot air blower installed on the back of a lorry, though this had no
real potential for Bomber Command because the lorry was so heavy it
could only be moved on a specially constructed road.

But the only realistic proposal was the system devised by the Anglo-
Iranian Oil Company (renamed BP in 1954), in which high-octane fuel
was pumped along a pipe pierced with burner holes. As the petrol vapour
spurted out through each hole, it was lit, sending a long jet of flame into
the air. The intensity of the heat and fire not only pushed some of the
fog away by causing the temperature to rise, but it also made the runway
visible to the bomber crew. Known as FIDO, short for Fog Investigation
Dispersal Operation, the system had an awesome rate of petrol consumption. On every hour of operation, FIDO swallowed 80,000 gallons of
fuel. But given the number of lives and machines that FIDO could save,
ministers knew that this was a price well worth paying. The first installation took place at Graveley in Cambridgeshire in January 1943, the
pipes laid parallel to the 1,000-yard-long runway. With characteristic
energy, the Pathfinder leader Don Bennett immediately arranged to test
the system himself once it was set up at Graveley. 'The glare was certainly
considerable,' he wrote 'but it was nothing to worry about and I expressed
the view that FIDO was a usable project and should be developed with
the utmost speed.'[59]

Following Bennett's approval, FIDO was installed in other Bomber
Command airfields. By the end of the war, 15 stations were so equipped,
the largest version being at Woodbridge in Suffolk, which had a massive
runway 3,000 yards long and 250 yards wide, and required four 350,000-
gallon tanks for its FIDO system. Crews soon came to appreciate the
benefits of the innovation, but few found FIDO as easy to handle as
Bennett had done. The roar of the burning petrol fumes temporarily
drowned out the sound of the Merlins and the rising heat caused turbulence in the air. Peter Russell of 625 Squadron felt it was like 'flying in
a vaulted cavern' with the walls on each side aflame.[60] To Pat Moorhead,
a navigator with 35 Squadron, the first time his Lancaster used FIDO
was 'like entering the jaws of hell'. Coming in to land in poor visibility,
his crew initially saw little, 'then gradually the elongated rectangle of the
runway began to show more clearly, with belching yellow flames and
swirling fog all around and above. The worst part was coming in over
the flames at the end of the runway and wondering whether the under-
cart would melt or buckle or go up in flames.'[61] The first sight of FIDO
in action proved too intimidating for Freddie Watts of 617 Squadron. One
foggy night, when he was returning from a raid on Stettin, he was ordered

to land at RAF Metheringham in Lincolnshire which was equipped with FIDO: 'I took one look and it seemed like Dante's Inferno down there, with all these aircraft coming in and the fires from FIDO burning along the runway. So I went back to a station I knew: Coningsby.'[62]

FIDO was described by some navigators as 'a salvation'[63] because at full blast its flames could sometimes be seen from over sixty miles away. But even on clearer nights and with the advantage of Gee, it was inevitable that some heavy bombers should be lost over England or the sea, especially after the disorientation and exhaustion of a long raid to Germany. In such circumstances, there was another ingenious device fitted to the heavy bombers to guide them to an RAF airfield in an emergency. This was the little-known 'Darkie' system which, in the words of WAAF flying controller Vera Jacobs, 'was a position fixing procedure using radio transmission so that the pilot of an aircraft who was lost could speak to us when over England and we could tell him where he was'.[64] The operation of the system was explained by Lancaster wireless operator Kenneth Grantham, who flew with 640 and 35 Squadrons:

> Not a lot of people know about Darkie these days, but it was very much used in the war. It was used on the VHF radio, which was operated by the pilot. That had four channels on it only, A, B, C and D. A was his airfield control tower, and D was Darkie, a pre-set frequency. And on every airfield in England there was a Darkie Watch in the control tower. If you got into trouble, and all your radio equipment was blown out, you could, via the intercom, tell the pilot to press button D and then you were on the Darkie Frequency. You could then call out, 'Hello Darkie, Hello Darkie, Hello Darkie,' and give the call sign of your home station. It only had a range of 10 miles. The nearest station would take over and give you instructions. He would say, for example, 'This is Manston' and would tell you to switch on your navigation lights. He then would instruct the Observer Corps and the searchlight batteries to look for you. If they detected you, the searchlight batteries would raise a light vertically and then would lay it along the ground and all you had to do was fly along that beam until the next searchlight picked you up. They could also send up Spitfires to guide you home.[65]

Yet all the technical aids could not prevent landing disasters becoming part of the fabric of Bomber Command. The fact that a crew might have survived a lethal barrage over Germany, only to crash on their own airfield, added to the terrible poignancy of such occurrences. Sometimes a hung-up bomb in the bay would be detonated by the impact of a touchdown. Often the Lancaster was too broken to survive the landing.

On his eighth sortie, rear gunner Clayton Moore went through a near-fatal ordeal when his Lancaster started showing the effects of flak damage. A heavy burst had already left holes in the fuselage, broken some of the instruments and forced the starboard outer engine to be feathered. Then, when the plane was in the approach for landing and the wheels had been lowered, there was 'an abrupt change in the note of the three remaining engines. There was a lot of popping and coughing taking place, and the aircraft at once swung sharply to starboard, seemingly out of control'. The pilot, unable to line up the plane whose engines and hydraulics had now failed completely, ordered his crew to brace for a crash. Moore felt the end had arrived:

'What a bloody awful way to die!' I thought, as I tried to prepare myself for whatever the event might bring. Having sensed that the moment of impact must be near, I forced my back hard against the turret doors, just as I felt the Lanc give a sudden judder, and I heard the sound of tearing metal from I knew not where. We were still in a nose-down gliding attitude, but we had hit something a glancing blow – probably a tree or a building. Then I felt the tailplane shake and vibrate violently and I was forced against the doors, only to be pounded relentlessly on either side of the head by the oscillating gun mounts. I instinctively raised my arms and clasped my hands behind my head to ward off the blows. Then we were hit once more, and I lost all sense of direction as I felt myself and my turret spinning through space at an alarming rate. There was just one more sickening impact amid all the turmoil and confusion. I felt a severe blow to the back of my head and this was accompanied by a sharp pain, the seat of which I was unable to determine. There was so much pain. Then the pain eased and there was nothing but nothingness: peace, silence, oblivion.[66]

But Moore and his colleagues survived this crash, and after a spell of convalescence in the RAF hospital at Rauceby Hall they were back on duty.

On other occasions the sheer volume of traffic at a darkened base, combined with poor weather conditions, made collisions almost unavoidable. One of the worst nights in Bomber Command's history occurred on 16–17 September 1943, known as 'Black Thursday', when 481 Lancasters took part in a heavy raid on Berlin. Returning to England in thick, swirling fog and icy damp, no fewer than 28 Lancasters crashed or collided or were abandoned by their crews by parachute after becoming lost and running out of fuel. Particularly badly hit were 100 Squadron based at Waltham near Grimsby, which suffered four crashes, and 97 Squadron, based at

Bourn in Cambridgeshire, which lost 7 of its 20 Lancasters to crashes and had to record another as missing. At the time, only three airfields were equipped with FIDO, including Graveley, which some of the returning bombers tried to reach, often in vain. One of them, *D-Donald* of 405 Squadron, crashed in a potato field after the plane ran out of petrol while attempting a second landing at Graveley in the atrocious weather. Five of the seven crew were killed instantly. The captain, Flying Officer B. A. McLennan, clung onto life for a few hours before dying in hospital. The sole survivor was Clair Nutting, who later gave this account: 'My own recollection of events after the crash is dim. We were stacked up over Graveley trying to get down and after one unsuccessful attempt to land on the beam, I think we went to come in again. We were very low, perhaps no more than 50 feet off the deck. When the aircraft crashed and the tail broke off, I was strapped in securely, braced against the guns. When my head struck the gun-sight, I was knocked out. I recall climbing out over the guns. Further on the aircraft was burning. Various fail-safe devices were blowing up.' Nutting then went to look for the other crew members. He found two, one of them dead, the other, McClennan, barely alive. 'When I went to move him I saw the bare bone where his leg was all but severed at the knee, so I left him. The next thing I remember was going into hospital with McClennan in the back of a van. He died, I was told, shortly after we got there.'[67]

Amidst such tales of agony, though, what so often stood out was the astonishing resilience of the Lancaster, able to survive the most vicious mauling and still able to land. In these traumatic episodes, Chadwick's design abundantly repaid all the faith that had been invested in it. Burst tyres, collapsed undercarriages, destroyed tailplanes, bullet-riddled fuselages, smashed hydraulics and shattered engines, all these proved to be obstacles that could be surmounted by the heroic warrior of the night skies. In an experience that was typical of the plane's ruggedness, one Lancaster in David Day's 50 Squadron, based at Skellingthorpe near Lincoln, managed to return to its home station after a raid on Duren in West Germany in November 1944, even though it had an enormous hole in its starboard wing having been accidentally bombed from above by another Lancaster. The bomb not only tore through the wing, but also pulled out a fuel tank and started a fire in one engine. At the height of the emergency, as the flames engulfed the wing and the plane went into a spiralling dive, the pilot told the crew to prepare to abandon the plane. But the rapid descent put out the fire, and when the pilot regained control, he cancelled the order to bail out. Despite the loss of height and extensive damage, the

Lancaster flew back without further incident and landed at Skellingthorpe. A similar ordeal was endured by Geoff King, a bomb aimer with 57 Squadron. Coming back over France from a raid on Frankfurt in March 1944, he suddenly felt 'a massive explosion' on the underside of the starboard wing. 'This virtually turned us on our back,' recalled King. As the plane continued on its homeward journey, there was a tremendous drag on the starboard side. The engineer picked up the Aldis lamp, shone it across the wing and saw that the undercarriage was hanging down. 'But what we did not realize was that the tyre had burst. The other disturbing factor was that the skipper could not identify whether the undercarriage was down in the locked position or not.' Having been diverted to RAF Syerston because of its stricken condition, the Lancaster then descended for landing.

> Our skipper came in with starboard wing high, having advised us to take up our ditching positions in case the whole thing collapsed. As we touched down, the starboard wing lowered and the tyre quickly wrapped itself round the oleo legs. But fortunately the legs remained upright. Before coming to a standstill we did a couple of ground loops. A ground loop is where the aircraft goes round in a circle uncontrolled on the ground. It just spins, making a hell of racket. We were flung about in our positions. Most of us were bruised or had slight cuts, but no serious injuries. As we came to a halt, the fire engine and ambulance were there, but none of us required any major attention. We crept out from the back of the plane and we thanked our stars.[68]

It was a feeling shared by crewmen throughout the bomber war.

For those that survived the sense of relief was overwhelming. They had taken another step towards the completion of their tour. They might still live to see the end of the war. 'On landing, that walk back to the Sergeants' Mess was so exhilarating that you never felt the cold, not even on a wintry morning in January,' said J.W. Henderson, a gunner with 619 Squadron. Another rear gunner, Bob Pierson, could not wait to get out of the aircraft once it had taxied into dispersal. 'The feeling was indescribable. We were supposed to stay at our posts until the skipper brought the plane to a halt but I was always straight out of my turret and waiting at the side door. I'd open it as we were taxiing off the main runway, just to get a bit of fresh air after all those hours in the sky. We'd been on oxygen the whole way and there was the constant stink from the Elsan toilet. It was great to breathe properly again. I gulped it in. It meant we were alive.'[69] For many the exhilaration was mixed with almost paralysing tiredness, as Chan Chandler described:

Round the peri-track to dispersal and brakes on, engines off for the first time in eight or nine hours. Those four bloody Merlins have shut up. You'd have been in a bloody funny state without 'em, wouldn't you? Stop bitching and get out there. Too tired – I'll sleep here. Oh fuck – there's bloody debriefing, isn't there? Almost too tired to open the turret doors. Crawl across the spar into the fuselage; legs won't work, have to crawl to the door and stick my feet out backwards. Jimmy the wireless operator guides them onto the ladder and helps me down. A flight van rolls up. We all fall into it and it takes us off to debriefing.[70]

Usually held in the station's operations room, the debriefing had little of the tension or asperity of the pre-flight briefing. The atmosphere of relaxation was enhanced as a WAAF or padre went round offering cigarettes and refreshments, which could be hot chocolate or sweet tea laced with rum. The officers who conducted the debriefing had a delicate line to tread. Using a standard questionnaire, they had to acquire as much information as they could about each crew's experience of the raid, from the strength of defences to the accuracy of the TIs, but they also had to be aware of the men's deepening fatigue. 'When a crew had flown for several hours over enemy territory, sometimes having been shot up by night fighters or plastered with anti-aircraft fire, the last thing they wanted was a sprog Intelligence Officer to interrogate them, especially if he was also clueless, asking them some forty questions and taking a very long time over it,' wrote Bill Jones, the Intelligence Officer at Elsham Wolds.[71] Though many crewmen struggled to remember the details of the raid, they mostly respected the job the interrogating officers had to do. Bob Knights of 617 Squadron thought that 'the process was pretty good. The Intelligence Officers were very discreet and kind about getting the facts. The CO was usually there, any hour of the morning. It was very thorough. There was an intelligence officer for each crew. They were interested in everything: what defences, fighters, flak were like, what you'd seen. You took it in turns and it lasted about 20 minutes.'[72]

But others had a very different reaction, regarding the whole debriefing procedure as a hostile test of the integrity of the airmen rather than an attempt to gather intelligence. Sid Pope, a wireless operator with 100 Squadron, had this fascinating view which contradicts any sentimentality about Bomber Command's unity of purpose:

Heartless is not the word to describe Bomber Command. Debriefing was the worst part of the whole set-up. You would fly for eight hours, and you'd come back, no tucker, all they'd give you was a cup of coffee and a sandwich. You weren't allowed to speak to anyone, not even other crews.

They took you into a special room where they had trained interrogators. They used to grill you. They'd asked you what you'd seen and then they would cross-check everything so they would have a full picture. We used to hate the debriefing. It was really worse than flying. They would fire questions at you, always trying to cross-check. Some people must have told terrible lies to cover up what they had done. I reckon only a third of pilots had the guts to go in and bomb the target, irrespective of what was coming up. The other two-thirds would drop their bombs anywhere and got the hell out of it. To cover up, they would say different things. That's why the interrogators did all this cross-checking. And it went on for an hour.[73]

Once the debriefing was over the crews went for their post-op meal, almost always consisting of bacon, chips and eggs. 'They'd drag themselves into the dining room,' recalled Aileen Walker, a WAAF waitress based at Waddington, 'flying boots undone, hardly able to walk upright and they'd flop into chairs. Tea and cigarettes, they mostly wanted. Some wanted their food right away, and one might say, "I want so-and-so's egg. He got the chop." You had to wonder how they could adjust their minds and be ready to do it again tomorrow.'[74] A luxury in wartime Britain, the fresh eggs and bacon were relished all the more because of the sense of relief at the end of the raid, as Frank Broome recalled. 'One often got the impression that it seemed all worth it just for the extra bacon and egg! It always worked wonders for tired, tense minds and bodies.'[75] Finally, perhaps with dawn beginning its rise in the east, the weary men could make their way to their Nissen huts. The final steps at the end of a long day after a trip to Berlin were evoked by flight engineer Norman Ashton. 'The sky was quite light . . . and early-rising farm folk were leisurely making their way to the fields. All was peaceful and normal. As I looked round, I found it hard to believe that only a few hours ago we had been over the Big City. How glorious to climb between the sheets! I never sat down on a trip and my legs had been taking the strain since the operational meal on the previous day. I felt so weary that I fell to sleep as soon as I laid my head on the pillow.'[76]

8

'Living under a sentence of death'

~~~

IN AN INTERVIEW after the war, former Lancaster pilot David Day recalled the moment of panic when he received a letter from the RAF in 1942 telling him he had been posted to Bomber Command: 'The pangs of fear went right through my body because it was a time when the losses were extremely heavy and it was frightening to think what I was destined for. I did have that horrible moment when I was first told. I thought, "Oh God no." I could see myself being shot out of the sky in no time at all.'[1] His fears were hardly unjustified. At the peak of the bomber war, when a full operational tour comprised 30 sorties, the average loss rate was 4 per cent. This meant that the average crewman had only about a 30 per cent chance of completing the tour. One training instructor, John Wynne, felt that he was doing little more than teaching young men to fly to their deaths. 'As a flight commander on a training unit, I knew that 70 per cent of my course would be dead in a few months and there was nothing I could do to change that. They had little chance of survival.'[2] Of the 125,000 men who served in Bomber Command, 55,573 were killed, 8,403 seriously wounded and 9,838 taken prisoner. For all its inherent superiority and the fierce advocacy it inspired from Harris, the Lancaster protected its men little better than other types. Out of a total of 7,377 Lancasters that went into service, 45 per cent or 3,349 planes were lost on operations, a statistic that tallies almost exactly with the overall loss rate in Bomber Command. In fact, Portal was so worried about the effect of the extraordinarily high casualty rate that he tried to restrict the circulation of figures on losses. 'Statistical information relating to the chances of survival of aircrews should be confined to the smallest number of people. The information can be so easily distorted and is then so dangerous to morale.'[3] But the Air Staff could not hide the grim realities from the squadrons. No official notices of losses might have been printed, but the information was all too easily available from newspaper stories, BBC reports and anecdotal evidence from crews. Moreover, the men could see with their own eyes the endless succession of empty places at the post-op breakfasts, the removal of personal belongings from lockers and Nissen huts, the constant arrival of new crews to replace the departed.

'There was no other body of fighting men so exposed to the statistics of death,' wrote Frank Musgrove. 'Death pervaded their lives through long years of training and then squadron service. The statistics of aircrew mortality chipped away at their courage long before they could become airborne over the Third Reich.' With his cool, analytical mind, Musgrove worked out that beneath the flux of numbers, every main force squadron in Bomber Command had a roll-call of approximately 900 deaths during the war, no matter what its aircraft or the nature of its missions. 'This is a basic structural feature of the bombers' war. Nine hundred men who served on a squadron would be killed. This was a mathematical certainty from which the young men who flew the bombers had no chance of escape.' There were two factors, Musgrove argued, that made this bearable. The first was that the incidence of death was fragmented. 'If thirty aircraft were lost in one night, an actual majority of the forty or fifty squadrons that took part in the raid would actually have lost none.' The second was the 30-sortie limit on the operational tour. 'A requirement of more than 30 missions, say 45 or 50, would have found very few aircrew volunteers.'[4]

Musgrove's second point highlights one of the most remarkable features about Bomber Command: every single one of its 125,000 recruits was a volunteer. Military conscription was introduced by Neville Chamberlain's government in the spring of 1939, but no one was ever forced to sign up with the RAF against their will. It might seem extraordinary that so many young men joined up, given the daunting odds against survival, but the values of patriotic duty and self-sacrifice had a powerful grip on wartime society, reinforced by Churchill's soaring rhetoric, official propaganda and pressure from peers. Moreover, the RAF had a glamour lacking in the other two forces. Aircraft exuded modernity and excitement, feeding the ambition to fly in successive generations of schoolboys from the 1930s and 1940s. Victory in the Battle of Britain added to the heroic image of the RAF. 'Once you were accepted you're with the elite because you had to be pretty good,' said Fred Stern, who volunteered in 1940. 'They considered you to be the cream of the nation. It was the proudest moment of my life to be accepted as aircrew.'[5] The sense that Bomber Command was the nation's premier fighting force was strengthened from early 1942 with the launch of the strategic offensive against Germany. While Britain suffered endless setbacks and humiliations on land and sea, newsreels and papers showed the heavy bombers taking the war to the heart of the Reich. Some volunteers, having lived through the Blitz, were motivated by a desire for revenge against Germany. Eddie Dawson, who was an ARP worker during the Luftwaffe's heavy raid on Hull in 1940 and had also lost his father at sea, became a Lancaster engineer with 625 Squadron. 'It was the only way we could attack Germany, otherwise we would have just sat there, taking everything that was given. I had relations who were killed in the services or the bombing at home. It is a natural thing. If someone is hitting me, I want to hit them back – hard.'[6]

For George Atkinson, a Lancaster bomb aimer with 7 Squadron, his religious faith brought a moral imperative to the cause of Allied bombing. 'I had great debate and reservations about joining because in principle I hate war. I am a Christian and I feel that there is a clash between Christianity and war. Having said that, I was very conscious of the way events were developing in Germany under Hitler, with the appalling way that he was dealing with the Jews. I came to the conclusion that we had no options but to stand up to the situation. So I felt I had to go into this, no matter how much I disliked it. The only alternative was domination by Nazi Germany.'[7]

On a more mundane level, there were advantages to serving in Bomber Command compared to other units. Unless taken prisoner, airmen did not have to endure months, even years away from home, like soldiers and sailors. They might go through traumatic experiences over Germany, but if they survived they were usually able to sleep in their own beds at night. They had better food, living conditions and entertainment than the infantry in Africa or the naval crews in the North Atlantic. The pay was higher in the RAF than in the army; a Lancaster airman could earn around 10 shillings a day compared to 3 shillings for a private. Alcohol and sex were readily available around the base. The view of Stephen Masters, a navigator with 622 Squadron, was as follows: 'I think the life of a bomber airman was preferable to that of a soldier. Yes, we were shattered when we returned from a raid, but we came back to a bed, to bacon and eggs, and we knew that our fighting for that day was finished. An infantryman didn't.'[8] George Bilton, a Lancaster engineer, said that he even 'enjoyed the life in Bomber Command. Admittedly it was dangerous, but it was a clean life. You came back to a clean bed and good food. You were given leave every six weeks. You were given extra rations when you came home. They looked after you. Discipline was not severe on Bomber Command squadrons.'[9]

The lengthy process of turning new recruits into fully trained bomber airmen began at one of the RAF reception centres established for those who passed the initial fitness, medical and academic tests organized by local RAF Aircrew Selection Boards. There was nothing remotely glamorous about these places. The conditions were primitive, the NCO instructors brutal. The centre at St John's Wood near Lord's Cricket Ground was particularly nasty, as revealed by this testimony from Peter Antwis, a Cambridge graduate who went on to serve as a Lancaster navigator. 'The flats at St John's Wood were filthy with neglect. The RAF corporals and sergeants in charge were animals who took sadistic delight in tormenting the "nancy boys" from "fucking universities". There followed three weeks of meaningless route marches through the streets of London, often at night with the rear rank man carrying a red lantern. There were minimum meals served from filthy kitchens and we washed our irons in buckets of greasy water.'[10]

After this dismal start, the recruits were then sent to one of the Initial Training Wings (ITWs) which were dotted around the country, mostly in seaside resorts like Eastbourne and Blackpool. Here they underwent their first instruction in airmanship, meteorology, Morse code and aircraft recognition, as well as endless physical drill and lectures on the dangers of sexually transmitted diseases. The recruits also did a few hours flying in a Tiger Moth so the instructors could ascertain the natural pilots. It was at the end of the ITW course that they were allotted their various roles within the bomber crew: pilot, navigator, engineer, wireless operator, bomb aimer and gunner. Such designations were not, however, fixed absolutely and airmen could be reclassified depending on their performance in more advanced instruction. Trainee pilots, in particular, were susceptible to being 'washed out' and ordered to retrain as navigators or bomb aimers if they failed to meet the necessary high standards.

Because of both Britain's poor climate and the RAF's limited resources, cadets were then sent overseas to carry on their training at one of the huge network of specialist flying schools across the Empire. Started in April 1940, the Empire Air Training Scheme reached its peak in 1943 with no fewer than 333 schools, 92 of them in Canada, and the rest in Rhodesia, South Africa, Australia and India. There were also five flying schools in the USA. After the damp gloom of bombed-out, blacked-out, heavily rationed Britain, the sunlit abundance of these overseas postings was a revelation to the Bomber Command cadets. Navigator Frank Musgrove was fortunate to travel to South Africa. 'There was swimming and tennis, abundant fruit, endless fried bacon and eggs, and gorgeous suntanned girls in swimming suits. Bomber Command was losing some of its appeal.'[11] It was not all fun. Trainees spent hours learning their specialist skills as they flew cross-country, usually in the utra-reliable Avro Anson, another of Chadwick's masterpieces. Lancaster navigator Noble Frankland described his spell in South Africa as 'intensive', for it required 100 hours of flying and tough examinations in navigation theory.[12]

Most Empire Air Training courses lasted twenty-eight weeks. On their return to England successful cadets had two more hurdles to clear in Training Command before they could formally be transferred to Bomber Command. The first was Elementary Flying School, where they rehearsed in the more difficult English conditions the skills they had learnt over-seas. If they performed satisfactorily, they moved on to the greater challenge of an Advanced Flying Unit, where the aim was to acclima-tize them to night-flying in the black-out. Noble Frankland said that though they were still using the now familiar Avro Ansons, this part of the training was 'a culture shock. My confidence in being a trained navigator evaporated into the dark night and I discovered that success depended on an intimate understanding between the pilot, the navigator and the bomb-aimer.'[13] What struck many trainees, however, was not so much the difficulties of night-flying as the wearisome, drawn-out nature of the induction process, which could stretch for years. The Air Staff often complained about the lack of personnel for the strategic offensive, yet there was an apparent lack of urgency in ensuring that recruits reached the bomber squadrons as quickly as possible. On his return from Canada, Donald Falgate, then a trainee bomb aimer, grew exasperated at being shuttled from one billet to another without any sight of a Lancaster. At one stage he had to stay in a Harrogate hotel 'with little or nothing to do for almost a month', then he was sent up to Perthshire for another bout of 'killing time'.[14] Navigator Donald Feesey was called up to the Aircrew Receiving Centre at St John's Wood in July 1942 yet, amazingly, by July 1944 he had still not set foot in a heavy bomber, having spent many 'demoralizing months with absolutely nothing to do'.[15]

Once all the initial courses had finally been completed, the recruits were sent to an Operational Training Unit, where they began their real preparation for bomber combat. It was at the OTUs that the individual trainees formed themselves into crews for the first time. After all the formality of the previous selection procedures and examinations, the nature of 'crewing-up' seemed strangely haphazard, even anarchic. There was no involvement from the senior commanders, no direction, no regi-mentation. Instead, the trainees were all taken to a large hangar or mess room, and just told to choose their colleagues to make up the five-man crew: pilot, bomb aimer, gunner, wireless operator and navigator. The engineer, who had to undergo specialized training, and the second gunner, would join at a later stage. Without any guidance or rules, the trainees had to rely entirely on their own gut instincts in selecting which group to join. Because intuitive emotional connection played such a large part, the process of 'crewing-up' was often likened to a large 'marriage market', to use the phrase of bomb aimer Miles Tripp, who wrote that 'the choice of a good flying partner was far more important than a good wife. You couldn't divorce your crew and you could die if one of them wasn't up to his job at the critical moment.'[16] Somehow, the embryonic crews gradually came together, united by shared interests, personality traits or simply mutual trust. Yet, as Bomber Command understood, the happy coalescence of airmen was not really that odd, since they had much in common. Most of them were in their early twenties, shared a desire to fly, had a steady temperament and were of above average intelligence. Hailing from either the Commonwealth or grammar schools, the vast majority of them had a healthy contempt for traditional class divisions and the old public school concept of aristocratic leadership.

With his keen sociologist's eye, Frank Musgrove summed up the character type who predominated in Bomber Command:

> They were mostly born between 1912 and 1922; the oldest would be about 27 when the war began, the youngest (like me) about seventeen. They were rigorously tested by the RAF, but they were all in the first instance self-selected . . . They were of high intelligence and in very good physical shape. In fact, they were, for the most part, the eleven-plus scholarship boys, the 10 or 12 per cent of their age group who had passed their exams and entered the state secondary grammar schools. They were diligent, highly conscientious, inwardly motivated; they could be relied upon to do their homework and were seldom a 'discipline problem' . . . They were a new twentieth-century meritocratic elite, the product of a first-rate system of secondary school education, humane and broadly based . . . The challenge called for great technical skill and quick intelligence as well as high courage. As pilots and navigators they were tailor-made for the job. They were often afraid and reluctant to carry on, but the vast majority did. They did not need leaders or formal structures.[17]

It was inevitable, however, that this method of self-selection did not always work. Under the strain of operations, some crews found that they could not gel. Friction developed. The trust so essential for operations was replaced by suspicion, even antipathy. Some crews simply refused to continue flying with a pilot in whose ability they had lost faith. New

Zealander Bill Wilson and his colleagues walked out on their Australian pilot after he had twice crashed on landing. 'We declared that we would not go up with that Aussie again,' said Wilson. When the station commander almost accused them of cowardice, they said they were quite willing to fly with another pilot, so the commanding officer took over the role of pilot himself.[18] Lack of fighting spirit was the reason Terry Kearns, a New Zealand pilot with 617 Squadron, was determined to be rid of his engineer: 'He was frightening the daylights out of us and upsetting the crew. He was not doing his job properly as part of the team. Even on the ground, he had a funny way with him. You could not get to the bottom of him. He did not have the same feelings, attitude of mind as we did.' The squadron commander agreed to provide them with a new engineer 'and he turned out to be marvellous. He did what he had to without any prompting. Even when the flak started, he was unperturbed.'[19]

The OTU syllabus was demanding. Airmen received lessons in aircraft layout, dinghy drills, low-level flying, fuel systems, gunnery practice, bombing procedures and parachuting. A minimum of 80 hours flying had to be undertaken, most of it in elderly two-engined Wellingtons. Once the OTU course was finished, the cadets moved to the Heavy Conversion Units (HCUs) at which they finally learnt to familiarize themselves with the four-engine heavy bomber. But because Lancasters were in such demand in the front-line squadrons, not all crews were able to train on them for a significant period. Instead, many of them had to learn the heavy-bomber techniques on Halifaxes and Stirlings. All too predictably, the question of the provision of training aircraft led to a rumbling dispute between Harris, who wanted to minimize the number of Lancasters at HCUs, and certain members of the Air Staff and Bomber Command who felt it dangerous not to provide recruits with sufficient instruction on the Lancaster itself.

Throughout his time as Commander-in-Chief, Harris was always looking for ways to increase the size of his Lancaster force. The transfer of planes from training to operational duties was one route he exploited. In late October 1942 he told Portal, 'I have decided to replace as many Lancasters as possible in conversion units with Halifaxes. This will allow two frontline Halifax squadrons to be converted to Lancasters.'[20] At this stage Portal welcomed such a move: 'I am entirely in favour of your proposals to put as many extra Lancasters as possible in the front line. So long as this change results in an increase in bomb delivery and fewer casualties, I am sure that no one could have an objection to it.'[21] In the middle of the following year, the phased withdrawal of the obsolescent Stirling from the front line gave Harris a further opportunity to transfer more Lancasters out of the Heavy Conversion Units and into the squadrons. He proposed that the Stirling be used as the basic four-engined trainer in most of the HCUs alongside the Halifax, providing recruits with a minimum of 40 hours training in the air. At the same time three separate 'Lancaster Finishing Schools' should be established, one connected to each of the three Lancaster Groups, to give recruits familiar with the Halifax or Stirling brief experience of the Avro machine. Harris suggested that ten hours flying in the Lancaster would be adequate on this final part of the conversion course, with a further five hours of check flying once the pupils had reached the operational Lancaster squadrons.

But Ralph Cochrane, the cool-headed commander of No. 5 Group, was deeply concerned about this plan, warning that the amount of train- ing on the Lancaster would be too limited. He told Harris in August 1943 that he felt 'very strongly that Lancasters must be used in training' at Heavy Conversion Units. Though he recognized 'the desire that Lancasters should concentrate on bombing', he feared there was 'a danger that crews will not be properly trained in tactics' at the HCUs. He went on: 'When I became AOC of 5 Group I was determined to improve training. We are now getting results. The number of crews lost in their first five sorties has fallen. If you insist that I must cut down the amount of Lancaster flying in conversion units, then all this tactical training, which has been built up with so much thought and effort, will have to be scrapped and tactical training and experience must be given in squadrons, where it could not properly be supervised.'[22] Showing that imperious streak which made him such a tough Commander-in-Chief, Harris told Cochrane that there was no alternative: 'The plain fact of the matter is, however, that we are defin- itely short of Lancasters in the operational groups. No prospect of saving aircraft in the more distant future can therefore compensate for the lack of them at present and during the next two or three critical months of the war. You must therefore come into line.'[23]

By the mid-autumn, however, Cochrane felt even more disturbed about the inadequacy of Lancaster training, as the number of accidents increased and the skills of crews failed to improve. On 24 October he wrote to Saundby, Bomber Command's Senior Air Staff Officer, to urge that Harris's proposals be modified. What he suggested was that more second-rate airmen should be weeded out at the OTU stage before they were allowed to convert to Lancasters. 'I am getting a proportion of crews whose ability to operate successfully on Lancasters is in doubt,' he said. Standards of instructors also had to be raised, he argued. 'There are still a number of instructors who are not really fitted for the task and who would have been discarded had it been possible to obtain replacements. An amalgamation of the best Stirling and the best Lancaster instructors would result in an immediate raising of the standard of the crew product.' Above all, he believed that the proposed time spent on Lancaster instruction at the Finishing Schools had to be increased, for ten hours flying was simply not enough for the final Lancaster conversion. Pilots, he wrote, had to be tested to 'ensure that they are thoroughly at home in the aircraft when things go wrong and can compete with three or two engine flying, with over-shooting and so on'. He concluded that 'the increase of even a few hours would have a considerable effect and increase the chances of survival during the first few sorties'.[24]

But Harris continued with his scheme, arguing that the benefits of putting more Lancasters in the front line outweighed the disadvantages. 'I am well aware of the difficulties which will have to be surmounted in turning the Stirling into a satisfactory basic four-engined trainer for the production of Lancaster crews, but having given the question the fullest consideration, I am of the opinion that they can be overcome without any ultimate loss of efficiency. The consequence of strengthening the Lancaster front-line effort will more than compensate for any additional complications experienced in the operational training organisation of this Command.'[25] With an air of complacency Harris even claimed that new arrangements would decrease the number of accidents. 'All the early four-engined flying is carried out on the Stirling and the Halifax, and crews will not fly the Lancaster until they have completed 40 hours on other types of aircraft. This will reduce the amount of flying that is done on the Lancaster in the training stage and any crew who has flown a Halifax or Stirling for 40 hours should find absolutely no difficulty in transferring to the Lancaster which everyone agrees is very much simpler for the pilot and flight engineer.'[26]

But as the scheme was implemented in November 1943, Harris's bold assertion was challenged by the Air Ministry, whose investigators were troubled by the 'excessive' number of training accidents in the Lancaster. The only explanation, said the accident investigation team, was that pupils were sent off to fly solo in Lancasters too early, having had insufficient dual-control instruction aboard the plane. In a report for the Air Ministry, the team said that this happened partly because of the increased pressure from the operational squadrons for replacement crews, and partly because of the 'failure among instructors to realize that the ability to fly a Halifax does not necessarily imply ability to fly a Lancaster' even if 'the second type is actually easier to fly than the first'. Having garnered the views of many instructors at the Heavy Conversion Units, the investigators stated that 'the general view seemed to be strongly held that the period allowed for the second conversion to the Lancaster was not long enough. Some even asserted that the intermediate period on a Halifax was actually a disadvantage and that it was easier to convert a pupil direct from a Wellington to a Lancaster than from a Halifax.' The report concluded that instructors should be made more aware of the solo danger, that dual instruction had to be increased and that 'Special care should be given to the second conversion and the Halifax or Stirling periods should not be regarded as a complete substitute for an equivalent Lancaster period.'[27] This last point was borne out by the Canadian pilot David Day, who trained on Stirlings before going to a Lancaster Finishing School:

> I did not get on with the Lancaster to start with. I had been flying the Stirling, which had a poor reputation. The Stirling was a huge aircraft with a weak undercarriage. If you landed in a cross-wind you were likely to wipe the whole thing off and land on your belly. The secret of landing a Stirling was to come in a little faster and land on the wheels, rather than making a three-point landing—as we had been trained to do. When I got onto the Lancaster, I tried to fly it the way I had been flying the Stirling. I was really crashing the thing into the ground. It took me a long time, but the instructor was very patient and I got the hang of it, though I was still banging them in.[28]

Armed with the information in the accident investigators' report, Air Vice Marshal A. J. Capel, the head of Bomber Command training, urged that the number of flying hours in the finishing schools be increased from ten to thirteen. But Harris, determined to prioritize front-line aircraft, refused to move and for the rest of the war the standard flight period at the Lancaster Finishing Schools remained at ten hours. The only changes in the organization were a gradual expansion in the number of Lancasters at the three finishing schools, up from 45 in December 1943 to 54 in early 1944, and the addition of a fourth school purely for the Canadian No. 6 Group. But by the time the Canadian Finishing School was established, in December 1944, the other three had started to be wound up. The tremendous strain on the Lancaster squadrons had eased by late 1944, due both to a fall in casualty rates as the Allies gained air superiority over Europe after D-Day and the growth in Lancaster output from the factories. As the availability of Lancasters improved, so increasing numbers of pupils could be directly trained on them at the HCUs without having to go through the elaborate, sometimes counterproductive, two-stage process of conversion.

Given the brutal pressures of the bomber war, especially in the winter of 1943–4, whatever Lancaster training scheme was devised by Harris was bound to carry severe risks. It was not possible to instruct tens of thousands of young men for combat in night-flying in the damp, blacked-out conditions of England without a high casualty rate. Nor should the quality of the training itself be dismissed, since most instructors were highly conscientious. Danny Boon, who did his heavy conversion on a Halifax before going to a Lancaster Finishing School, said: 'By the time I had finished I could fly a Lanc quite easily. The training was really good. On our dinghy drill, for instance, we could sit in a Lanc and get out in 25 seconds. It stood us in good stead during several emergencies in our career.' On Boon's first sortie, he found that the training had been 'a great help' in calming his nerves. 'Everyone was on top of the job and we were ready for what we had to do.'[29] Nevertheless, there was something tragic about the loss of so many trainees who had not even seen action, and instructors who had managed to survive the hell of an operational tour. Altogether 5,327 Bomber Command airmen were killed in training accidents, almost 10 per cent of the total deaths, and another 3,113 were seriously injured. On some OTUs the death rate reached an astonishing 25 per cent.

Inexperience and misjudgements in night-time conditions played a huge part, as did the ageing quality of the training Lancasters themselves. 'In training all the aircraft we had flown in were clapped out and the instructors were a bit wary of them falling apart,' said Edwin Watson, an engineer with 630 Squadron.[30] The need to keep pushing trainee crews to the limit could also be a lethal factor. On one of his first flights at a Lancaster Finishing School, rear gunner Clayton Moore had this heart-stopping experience. 'We were being instructed in diving turns by a Canadian pilot who was being rested after completing a tour on ops. The Lancaster we were flying that day was fitted with dual controls and it turned out to be fortunate for us that it was.' Moore's own pilot had executed some

> fairly severe corkscrews at a signal from me and I was impressed by his handling of the new aircraft type. Not so the instructor. 'Look buddy,' he shouted with impatience, 'when one of yer gunners tells ya to dive to port, get the Goddam nose down and go!' At this, he thrust his own control column hard against the instrument panel, thus setting in motion a number of hitherto unexpected high jinks. The engineer, who had been standing behind the two pilots, soared into the top of the cockpit canopy before

coming down across the throttle bank, pushing all four levers through the gate. I banged my head against the top of my turret and the Lancaster went into a vertical power dive. Meanwhile, back in the cockpit, it was taking the combined strength of four men to pull us out. As we began to level, I sensed the sky beginning to turn grey and I saw a large chunk of something go hurtling past on my left. I was already reporting this to the flight deck when we finally resumed level flight and went screaming out across the Nottinghamshire landscape at a height of about 200 feet.

Moore was later told, once the plane had landed, that the air speed indicator had 'gone off the clock' during the dive, and the object he had seen flying past the turret was the dinghy stowage hatch, ripped off by the violence of the plunge.[31] At times the forcefulness of the instructors could verge on reckless bullying. One trainee crew at the Heavy Conversion Unit at Lindholme near Doncaster found that during a cross-country flight in bad weather their bomber would not climb to the required safe height. So they returned to base, where their commander refused to believe their story about defective engines and ordered them to take off again. The next morning, the wreck of the plane was found strewn across a Scottish mountainside.[32]

It was not just the pupils who suffered. Operational crews also had to carry out regular training flights throughout their tour, as well as mock combat exercises known as 'fighter affiliation' in which they tested their skills in evading attackers. Carried out against Spitfires, these fighter affiliation exercises could be highly dangerous. Wireless operator Reg Payne and bomb aimer Les Bartlett were part of a 50 Squadron Lancaster crew that took part in such a training exercise against a Spitfire over the Lincolnshire countryside on 12 February 1944. For half an hour both planes circles and dived, then, after a brief pause, the Spitfire spiralled down once more to attack. Payne recorded what happened next: 'At the word "go", the Lancaster started its corkscrew but during its first dive to port a sudden explosion came from the port outer engine and in seconds was a mass of flames.' The Graviner extinguisher system failed to dampen the fire. The pilot, Michael Beetham (later Sir Michael Beetham, Marshal of the RAF) gave the order for the crew to prepare to abandon the aircraft. As smoke began to pour into the cabin, parachutes and harnesses were adjusted by all the airmen − except one. The engineer had boarded the plane without his. 'I remember him saying in the crew room that as it was only a training flight he wouldn't bring his,' wrote Payne. Doomed by his insouciance, the tragic figure had to stay with the burning plane. The position was now hopeless. The pilot gave the order to bail out.

Bartlett was the first to go. 'I fixed my parachute pack on to my harness, whipped off my helmet, opened the rear door, pegged it back and out I went. I distinctly remember having no sense of falling whatsoever and when I could no longer hear the roar of the engines I pulled the ripcord. With a crack like a whip, my "chute" opened, my harness took the strain and my fall to earth was checked. From then on I seemed to be just suspended in a void and not descending at all.' Bartlett looked round and could see the Lancaster going into a steeper dive. Other parachutes now followed. 'In a short space of time I was through the cloud layer and the earth began to creep up to meet me. At 1000 feet I realised I was heading for a canal. Wearing no "Mae West" and not being able to swim, I tugged the appropriate side of my "chute" and cleared it with yards to spare.' Soon afterwards he came down in a ploughed field.[33] Payne was the last to go, but he found some difficulty in escaping the Lancaster, which was now burning badly:

> I made an effort to roll out sidewards but was blown back in by the slip-stream. My second attempt was more successful and I found myself falling towards a cloud layer 3000 feet below the aircraft. By this time I was frantically tugging at my parachute release, which had no effect, and added to this a white mist was swirling around me so I knew I had reached the cloud layer only 3000 feet from the fields below. Terrified, and with tears filling my eyes, I prayed desperately to God to help me as I felt sure I had only seconds to live. Some instinct told me to re-examine my parachute pack and to intense relief I saw it was one of the four carrying handles I was gripping and not the release ring. Immediately I pulled at the release ring and was overjoyed to see the white silk passing over my head as the parachute opened with a crack. I was amazed at the silence around me. A black rainbow of smoke showed clearly the descent of the Lancaster, which was now a raging ball of fire, and above it part of the port wing was falling like an autumn leaf.[34]

The Lancaster fell to the ground at the RAF East Kirby airfield in Lincolnshire, killing the engineer and several members of another crew who had been on board to take part in the exercise.

If they came through their training unscathed, the crews finally made it to the front-line squadrons. But the battle to conquer fear now intensified as operations began. No one could escape the shadow of mortality that loomed over every Bomber Command station. Even the most courageous airmen had a knot in their stomach at the thought of carrying on for night after night in a pitilessly hostile environment. As a newly trained Lancaster pilot, Robert Wannop was all too aware of his feelings of anxiety when he arrived on his base for the first time from the railway station, noting in his journal: 'My thoughts during the journey to the camp were very mixed. How would I make out? Was flak very deadly? Would I be able to set an example of courage to the crew if called upon? Had I the guts? I remember sitting there in the cold silence, muttering a prayer, asking for courage. It was only one of many that followed.'[35] Fear was woven so deeply into the fabric of life in Bomber Command that Lancaster bomb aimer Miles Tripp called it 'The Eighth Passenger', a term that he also used as the title of a memoir of his RAF service. In that book, he wrote with candour about an attack of nerves he experienced on operations. On one daylight flight in Lancaster *A-Able* to Cologne late in the war, he admitted that his

> uneasiness became acute as we flew towards a fierce flak barrage and a Lancaster ahead went down in a cartwheel of flame. Almost at once *A-Able* was raked with flak and again we heard the sound of an explosion followed by the metallic noise of shell fragments raining on to the fuselage. But no vital points had been pierced and we flew on and dropped our bombs. I was still clutching the bomb release when a delayed wave of shock made my body almost unbearably hot with prickling heat and my face felt as though it was being jabbed by a hundred pins. Gradually the stinging heat disappeared but then my body started to tremble and I couldn't control the shaking of my legs. Any residual dreams of glory faded and forever vanished in the daylight over Cologne. From now on survival dominated my thoughts.[36]

Miles Tripp's own pilot George Klenner, a tough Australian, confessed that he was 'afraid' on all his operations, but added 'a man would have to be stupid or a liar that under those circumstances claimed to be without fear'.[37] Some unfortunate airmen could not always conceal from their colleagues their reaction to terror. Navigator Reg Davey recalled one man who came on a trip with his crew as 'a spare bod' on 'a nasty raid to the Ruhr'. After the Lancaster landed, 'we could smell he had messed his trousers. Despite popular belief, that was most unusual.'[38] With commendable honesty, mid-upper gunner John Pearl admitted that on one of his early trips to Germany in March 1945 he completely went to pieces. 'I suddenly became petrified and really fell apart. I couldn't keep still, my arms and legs were shivering and the rest of me trembled uncontrollably. I said nothing, and got rid of it eventually. I gritted my teeth, clenched back my fists, clung to my guns and forced myself to get back to normal and for the rest of the trip I was all right.' Pearl explained that on future trips he overcame the threat of emotional meltdown with a remarkable act of self-discipline. 'I got over it by deliberately scaring myself for five minutes every time after getting into the aircraft, then gradually shutting down the fear by sheer will-power. Once I got it out of my head I was all right and when we reached the target I was on a high.'[39]

A few rare souls actually revelled in operations, through excitement or a desire to smash the Reich or sheer camaraderie, and volunteered for all the sorties they could. Bomb aimer J. W. Walsh of 619 Squadron was actually disappointed when the war in Europe was over because he had not completed his tour, and therefore asked Bomber Command, unsuccessfully, if he could serve in the Far East. 'My time with 619 squadron was the most enjoyable period of my life. I thoroughly enjoyed what I was doing but what was doubly rewarding were the people in whose company I was fighting the Germans,' he wrote later.[40] But that was distinctly a minority view. As Joe Williams, a gunner with 625 Squadron put it: 'Watching an aircraft going down is not a pretty sight, and you know that young men are dying a horrible and terrible death. You cannot be blasé about that.'[41] Most airmen regarded their operational tour as a difficult task they had to complete, and they did so with a spirit of grim determination, counting down every sortie until the liberating figure of 30 was reached. Yet the mood tended to fluctuate with burgeoning experience. Harold Davis, a pilot with 101 Squadron, argued that attitudes towards survival went through three distinct phases. 'There were the first six to eight trips, when everything is new and you're scared all the time. You don't know what's coming and you're still learning. After this, from say ten to twenty trips, you feel you know it all and take it just as another job of work. The old fears are still there but you are settled well in the groove. When you only have five or six trips to go, you begin to think, "Will I or won't I make it?" Each trip becomes a strain towards the end.'[42]

Air crews developed mechanisms, both psychological and physical, to cope with the unbelievable strain they had to endure for months on end. One of the most common was a sense of detachment, a spirit of fatalism towards the butchery of war. This outlook was most graphically manifested in the way that the emotional focus of each crew was often on its own tightly knit circle, with many airmen largely unconcerned with the fortunes of other crews or the wider squadron. Such insularity was summed up by Joe Williams. 'A plane went missing. The next day, there would be, in its place, another aircraft, another crew. The squadron was always up to strength. The missing men were soon forgotten. They were forgotten because – I suppose this reflects the crewing-up procedure – as a crew you were a group of friends. You drank together, had all your fun together, you didn't mix much with other crews. So when one crew dropped out of the picture, it really didn't make much difference.'[43] For Victor Wood, a Dublin-born pilot in 12 Squadron, isolation was the best way to deal with the emotional turmoil of squadron life. 'My crew and I were very introverted. Some crews mixed socially with others, but I more or less told my chaps that I didn't want us to do that. We went out as a crew and we did not make a lot of friends. We had enough to worry about without dealing with the grief of losing a close friend.'[44]

Another widely used stratagem was simply to ignore the mathematical laws of probability. Crews found comfort in the belief that disaster would befall others, not themselves, an attitude encapsulated by flight engineer Doug Tritton of 49 Squadron. 'We had heavy losses on the squadron, 907 throughout the war. But you always had the foolish confidence that it was going to happen to someone else. You were conscious that you were living under a sentence of death, but you could not be morbid.'[45] In a world dictated by cruel fate, the resort to superstition was widespread and understandable. It has been estimated that 80 per cent of airmen carried some sort of lucky charm or enacted a fixed pre-flight ritual, urination on the wheels being the most common. One Lancaster bomb aimer, Vernon Wilkes, recorded how his crew always insisted that the rear gunner, Danny Driscoll, spit on the rudder before take-off:

> On one occasion I remember we were about to take off and the skipper asked Danny over the intercom if he had spat on the rudder. Danny replied that he had forgotten! The skipper immediately slammed on the brakes and told Danny to get out and do it! Because of the slipstream from the running engines the spittle was difficult to direct on to the rudder so Danny had to direct it through cupped hands . . . In the meantime the flying control couldn't understand why our Lancaster was holding up the whole squadron's take-off and was frantically flashing green lights at us. The skipper had to respond and start taxiing, causing Danny to have to run alongside and struggle to jump the four feet up into the rear fuselage entry. The mid upper gunner managed to heave him in as we continued to take off. Danny made sure this never happened again and all our following take-offs went smoothly.[46]

Solace was also found in organized religion, and most of the larger bases had an Anglican padre and a Catholic chaplain who held regular acts of worship. 'Lots of chaps went because they thought their next trip might be the last,' said Harold Davis.[47] The private power of prayer helped Larry Curtis of 617 Squadron. 'I think I got used to the idea of being killed. I did not go to any religious services, but I got on my knees in my own room and prayed there. It is a very personal thing.'[48] Belief in divine intervention, however, could be sorely tested in the heat of combat, as demonstrated by this mordant exchange that took place in a Lancaster of 101 Squadron during a raid over France in early 1944, when the crew of Doug Todd was accompanied by the sanctimonious and unpopular station commander. As shells from German night fighters rocked the aircraft, the rear gunner called up over the intercom, 'Toddy, Toddy, the bastards are everywhere!' The commander now decided to come onto the intercom: 'Never fear, rear gunner, never fear, the Lord is with us.' To which the rear gunner replied: 'He might be up your fucking end but there's no sign of him down here.'[49]

Release from the strain of operations was also sought on a less elevated, more earthy level. Wild mess-room antics, juvenile pranks, heavy drinking and sexual indulgence were all valves that could release some of the exhausting tension that enveloped a bomber station. 'You were just so highly strung,' said Lancaster pilot John Gee. 'You tried to calm down, but you had to let off steam. You would have a number of beers and get yourself into a state where you could go to sleep. That was how you got over it. You were just glad to have got back and survived.'[50] Airmen who had been sweating in concentration and fear over Germany could be found the next evening playing indoor rugby with a tin tray, or drunkenly singing raucous songs, or burning newspapers, or erecting inverted pyramids by balancing wooden chairs on top of each other. 'The mess was full of airmen singing *This Old Shirt of Mine* and some without a stitch on. WAAFs went about their usual jobs pretending not to notice what was going on,' wrote Fred Mills of a scene at 7 Squadron.[51] Indeed, the WAAFs were often on the receiving end of bawdy masculine bravado, as aircraftwoman Morfydd Gronland recalled of life at Scampton: 'The sergeants' mess doors would burst open and the aircrew would swarm in, shouting boisterously. We young WAAFs had to endure a barrage of good-humoured banter: "How's your sex-life?" "I dreamed of you last night." "Please serve us in the nude." Then someone would ask, "What's the collective noun for WAAF's?" And a chorus would answer, "A mattress." But we took it all in good part because we knew the great strain they were under.'[52]

Harris tried to foster a climate of tolerance towards the bomber crews in recognition of the special burdens that were placed on them. Though he sought strict discipline in any matters relating to flying, he believed that more leeway should be allowed in other fields, and he had a particular dislike of petty regulations of the kind that prevailed in the army, another legacy of his gruelling infantry service in southern Africa. A letter he wrote in May 1944 to the bomber station commanders summed up his attitude. 'I have always considered that the strain imposed by sustained bomber operations requires that aircrew personnel should enjoy the maximum amount of freedom from restraint and should be relieved, as far as can be done without loss of efficiency, of routine station duties,' adding that 'the last thing which I would wish to do would be to impose on aircrew personnel an irksome regime of inspections, parades and "spit and polish".'[53] The issue of air force discipline was seen at its most controversial on the question of sex. Given the combustible mixture of a highly charged emotional atmosphere, a relaxed regime for the testosterone-fuelled crews, the presence of tens of thousands of unmarried young women in the WAAF and the nocturnal attractions of nearby towns and cities, it is hardly surprising that Bomber Command had by far the highest incidence of venereal disease of any part of the RAF, despite the lectures that trainees were given. A report commissioned for the Air Ministry in January 1944 showed that in the previous year there had been 43.9 cases of VD per 1,000 aircrew, compared to only 24.1 in the aircrews of Coastal Command and just 11.2 in the ground crews of Bomber Command. The Air Ministry's Morale and Disciplinary Committee wondered 'whether this was connected with the stress and strain of the increased intensity of bomber operations', but no action was taken.[54] A proposal to hand out free condoms was rejected, as were attempts to clamp down on all-ranks dances at bomber stations, which had attracted the disapproval of some moral crusaders within the Air Ministry. But for most of the men – and quite a few of the women – on the bomber stations the advent of greater sexual freedom was a source of pleasure rather than concern. When WAAF radio-telephone operator Pip Beck first arrived at Waddington, one of her colleagues told her: 'You'll have a good time here. You can have a different boyfriend every night if you want to – it's wizzo.'[55] For bomb aimer J. W. Walsh, the search for romantic liaisons was a coolly rational decision driven by the exigencies of wartime. 'Reflecting on my first few operations, I came to the conclusion that my experience of life was very limited and my chances of survival very small. Since I was surrounded by many friendly, fun-loving, fine young women I made up my mind to redress the balance.'[56]

The use of sex as a form of therapy to escape the horrors of war was consciously recognized by Peter Russell, a Lancaster pilot with 625 Squadron, who was gloriously unashamed about the promiscuous side of his life at Kelstern in Lincolnshire. 'I thanked God for the gift of sex, which we who operated from home-based stations could thankfully receive, unlike those poor devils who flew or fought in the jungle, who could only dream of it.' In his memoirs, Russell admitted that in 625 Squadron he was sometimes 'shit-scared' since it was 'a severe strain to have to steel oneself to fly yet again, straight and level, defenceless and without hesitation, through an anti-aircraft barrage'. But he 'knew that a girl, if she wanted to, could put me right. I knew that the kind of magic that a woman can give a man comes not in the ecstasy but in the peace that follows.'[57]

Even in the relatively liberated culture of Bomber Command, there was one unfortunate type of potential partner that most airmen tried to avoid, not because of any failings in her character but merely because she was seen as a harbinger of bad luck. Known as 'a chop girl' or 'jinx girl', such a woman was said to doom the life of anyone who became involved with her, and by extension she could exert the same unintentional curse over the rest of the crew. In Miles Tripp's squadron there was a 'chop girl' whose previous five boyfriends had all been killed in action. When his skipper, George Klenner, shared a dance with her at one function, Tripp was mortified. 'It was ridiculous but until we had flown and returned safely from the next operation, I was worried lest some supernatural influence working through the medium of a pretty cookhouse WAAF might be stronger than the crew's skills and the other imponderables of survival.'[58] Yet it was inevitable that, in the context of the appalling casualty rate, these superstitious prophecies could sometimes turn into reality. In September 1944 Tom Burnard, a flight engineer with 622 Squadron, was at a dance in his base of Mildenhall in Suffolk when he saw a stunning blonde WAAF arm in arm with a flight lieutenant from another squadron. All too aware of Burnard's longing gaze in the direction of the beauty with the film-star eyes, his skipper warned: 'Don't have anything to do with that girl, Tom.' In fact, Burnard was already aware of her reputation. 'She was a smasher, but was known at Mildenhall as The Chop Blonde and we all steered clear of her. Every man in whom she had shown an interest had been killed on a bombing raid. Someone later told the flight lieutenant who laughed it off, saying, "Well, if I die tomorrow, my wife will get a decent pension."' The next morning Burnard was flying on a major daylight raid to Calais. The smitten flight lieutenant was in another Lancaster on the left of the formation. As the raiders crossed the Essex countryside, Burnard watched in anguish as the flight lieutenant's Lancaster, almost in slow motion, seemed to lose its sense of direction and then fly into the path of another bomber. The two planes were crushed together, and fell to the ground in a single, disintegrating, exploding mass. All 15 men on board were killed. Burnard was haunted by the memory. 'At other times I had seen our bombers blowing up a few yards away in great orange balls of flames, but nothing affected me so deeply as the collision of those two Lancasters. I knew both crews.'[59] The blonde 'chop girl', it seemed, had struck again.

Neither sexual relief nor beer-sodden oblivion could wipe out the life-threatening realities of the bomber offensive. Masculine bravado might be a distraction, but the painful job still had to be done, and the struggle almost always took its toll, no matter how brave the airmen. Indeed, sometimes the longer that crewmen had been on operations, the worse became the physical symptoms of their anxiety. John Duffield, a flight engineer with 103 Squadron, had this memory of one of his crew: 'People would be tense, especially after the briefing where you learnt of the target. The wireless operator was the most tense because he was on his second tour. He was very nervous during operations. He used to shake a little bit, he used to sweat very easily and his voice was clipped, not like in normal conversation.'[60] Bomb aimer Thomas Tredwell experienced his own symptoms of strain. 'Apprehension came out in the form of tics, usually under the eye. You would get a little pulse beating there. Sometimes it happened that it wasn't visible, but you could feel it. I must admit that towards the end of that tour I had a non-visible tic which I could feel, and this we were told was due to the accumulation of tension.'[61]

But the leaders of Bomber Command were worried that the pressure of operations would lead to far more than just mere tics or heavy perspiration. What really troubled them was the prospect that large numbers of airmen might be intimidated into failing to carry out their duties with the required single-mindedness. This was why they persistently talked about the importance of a 'press-on' spirit on bomber operations and were so ruthless in dealing with the slightest hint of cowardice, called in the RAF 'Lack of Moral Fibre' (LMF). Discipline might not have been rigorously enforced about dress codes or sex, but the need for perseverance towards the target was a different matter. The perception of a lack of bravery was treated like a dangerous contagion that had to be instantly expunged before it might spread to the rest of the squadron. Any crew that aborted its mission before bombing the objective immediately aroused the suspicion of station commanders, no matter how serious the mechanical or technical problems in the aircraft that prompted an early return. In a letter to Harris in May 1943, Ralph Cochrane of No.5 Group revealed this climate of official distrust: 'I have discussed the problem with Station Commanders and find that in their view the weaker brethren generally make themselves known by an early return and that those who get to the target area generally attempt to drop their bombs on a target indicator.'[62]

One of those who found himself classified as potentially one of 'the weaker brethren' was Ronald Olsen, a pilot with 619 Squadron, on his very first sortie, a trip to Leipzig on 20 October 1943:

> We were on our way over the North Sea. The rain was belting down. It was a pitch black night and you could see nothing outside the aircraft at all. The instruments I was flying on were fed from a pump which was attached to the starboard engine. There was another on the port engine. So there were two pumps which would drive compressed air to the instruments, like the artificial horizon. One of the pumps failed so I did the obvious thing and switched to the other one. That failed as well. So my blind flying instruments were gone. The weather was shocking. I did not know if I was upside down, or turning or what I was doing, because the artificial horizon had gone, the gyro had gone. I had not had sufficient training to fly on turn and bank alone. So I decided we would ditch the cookie in the North Sea and return.

But the next morning, the Wing Commander virtually accused Olsen of LMF, claiming that he had turned back when he didn't need to and that the chance of both compressed air pumps failing was almost 'impossible'. Eventually the pumps were sent back to the manufacturer where it was proved that they were indeed both faulty. 'But this took some while. All the time I was under a cloud. And when my story was confirmed, I did not get an apology.'[63] In a similar incident, engineer Doug Tritton of 49 Squadron found that the compasses had failed on his Lancaster during a trip to Berlin. 'We returned to base, having dropped the cookie in the sea. That was called a boomerang raid, not completing the mission. When you did that, you got a very, very cold reception. The immediate suspicion was that you have abandoned your trip for cowardice. They took the navigator's log and went through it with a fine toothcomb. Our explanation was accepted and we were not disciplined. But they were very cold about it.'[64]

For all the concern about 'the weaker brethren', the actual number of cases of LMF in Bomber Command was extremely small. According to the historian John Terraine, only 0.3 per cent of the total aircrew who served in the RAF during the war were officially classified as demonstrating 'Lack of Moral Fibre'.[65] Though the Ministry of Defence has said that there are no detailed figures available, an Air Ministry survey in 1945 indicated there were in total 2,726 cases of LMF during the war, of which probably around 1,200 were in Bomber Command, a rate of around 200 cases a year. This would mean less than 1 per cent of all who flew with the Command were formally found guilty of cowardice, a moving tribute to the overwhelming heroism of the airmen. What kept the incidence so low was that they dreaded the charge of cowardice even more than German fighters or ack-ack guns. Cases usually involved a clear-cut refusal to continue flying on operations or to carry on to the target. Thomas Murray, as Wing Commander of Lancaster 207 Squadron, had a case that could not have been more straightforward: 'I had a New Zealander, a flight sergeant who refused to fly. I had him off the station within 24 hours. He seemed very confident, self-assured. He was not a nervous wreck, but he just said that he would not go on flying, said he did not want to get killed. I did not have much sympathy for him because he did not appear to be under a great strain and had not been on operations for very long on his first tour. I spoke very quietly, telling him that I held him in "contempt".'[66] Ted Mercer of 83 Squadron had to take over a crew whose pilot had been taken off flying duties because of LMF. 'When he saw the target in the distance lighting up and things going on he turned round and came back. He was probably getting more and more scared of his job every time he went up. He just wasn't cut out for it. I had no ill feelings against him. I just thought, "Poor sod".'[67] Resorting to alcohol was another desperate tactic, according to bomb aimer Arthur Cole:

> In our own crew, we had a mid-upper gunner who was turned out of the crew and classified LMF. He was perfectly all right as an individual but he was 35 and I don't think he could handle the tremendous strain of operations. Eventually his nerve cracked and he started to drink far too much. I heard my name being called at midday and in the middle of four Nissen huts I found him crawling on his hands and knees, hopelessly drunk. A few questions at the bar, not at all open, revealed that he had been deliberately getting drunk. So I had to disclose to my pilot what had happened and there was no way we could take him on the raid that night. Our main feeling was one of regret. He was replaced by a seasoned gunnery leader. Everyone only had so much courage to give and you never knew when yours would run out.[68]

Others tried to evade operations over Germany by persistently inventing mechanical faults with engines and equipment, one reason why early returns were treated with such suspicion. J. W. Henderson of 50 Squadron recalled an incident when one pilot notified the watchtower that he could not take off as he had magneto trouble. This pilot, on four previous occasions, had taken off but had never reached the target before returning to base. On hearing this, Wing Commander Russell (the squadron commander) got in his car, went round to the dispersal point where the aircraft was standing. Once there, he questioned the pilot on what was wrong. Then he said that in his opinion there was nothing wrong and ordered him to take off. The pilot refused to do so. Russell then called the RAF Special Police and put him under close arrest.[69]

Russell flew the Lancaster himself and returned safely to base. The pilot was convicted of LMF and expelled from the squadron in disgrace. Little sympathy was shown by Jack West towards an engineer in his crew who tried to avoid flying by faking an injury on the ground at the Lancaster dispersal point. 'He arranged with the engine fitter that he would casually walk out to the aircraft whilst morning engine checks were being made. The skipper was subsequently told that the flight engineer had walked under one of the gantries and at a given signal the fitter deliberately knocked off a cowling so that it hit him and he fell to the ground. It was alleged that he enacted various symptoms, the main one being that he had lost his memory and didn't know where he was.' The engineer was charged with LMF and moved to a detention unit. Intriguingly, this engineer telephoned West in the 1980s, having obtained his number, and asked to meet him. 'I refused. I strongly believed that he had planned his so-called accident for weeks because he was afraid of flying.'[70]

When an airman was charged with LMF, the station commander usually tried to deal with the case as briskly and discreetly as possible to prevent any controversy on the base. The great bomber pilot Leonard Cheshire, who was to show the depths of his compassion after the war in his work with the disabled, wrote that his aim in LMF cases was 'to act quickly, either getting rid of the person or taking my own line with him before others got to know what was afoot'.[71] Once the station commander decided there was a case to answer, the culprit was sent to the Aircrew Disposal Unit at Kersley Grange near Coventry, where his actions were assessed by a board of officers, advised by psychiatrists. Any officer or NCO found guilty was usually stripped of his rank, reduced to the status of Aircraftman Second Rank (AC2), the lowest in the RAF, and either forced to carry out menial duties, such as toilet cleaning, for the rest of the war or transferred to another armed service. Occasionally, the ceremony of stripping an airman of his rank would take place in full view of the rest of the squadron, in order to serve as an example to others. Bomb aimer Campbell Muirhead witnessed just such an event at his base of Wickenby, Lincolnshire, in May 1944, as he recorded in his diary in June. It was

> a sad, sad sight. We were well away from the action so I couldn't hear exactly all of what was being said. But I certainly could see it being done. This sergeant had refused to fly on an op. He had been accused and found guilty of LMF. There he was standing out in front, all on his own, in full view of every person on the unit, to be stripped of his wings, followed by his sergeant's tapes (they would all be unstitched beforehand). Reduced from sergeant to AC2 in the space of a minute. One crew member says he feels sorry for him, another that it serves him 'bloody well right, that the RAF had spent a packet on training him and that the time to chicken out was before you find yourself in the kitchen'. Maybe they're both right. If the chap had done say, 15 or 20 ops and his nerve had failed him, well it was a raw deal he'd got. But if it was after only his second or third op, well, what could he have expected.[72]

If there was a hope of rehabilitation the LMF airman was sent to one of the two RAF Aircrew Correctional Facilities at Sheffield, or Eastchurch on the Isle of Sheppey in Kent, both of which ran hard, physically exhausting regimes.

The need for sanctions against those who refused to fly was recognized by the airmen themselves. As Lancaster pilot Harry Yates put it: 'No crew could afford to have one of their number snap on board and plunge everything into hysteria and chaos.'[73] But many in Bomber Command thought that the whole policy of LMF was far too cruel and insensitive, since it neither took account of the airmen's volunteer status nor the merciless nature of the bomber offensive. Such critics could point to the example of the American 8th Air Force, which adopted a more liberal approach, though its daylight bomber war against the Reich was just as savage. Air Gunner Derek Jackson went so far as to suggest that 'grading a man LMF was a scandal. These men were all volunteers and if they lost their nerve, well, it could have happened to any of us. I think they should have simply been taken off ops and posted away, not disgraced and sent to do menial jobs or kicked out. Perhaps some of the people who judged these men should have tried it out for themselves. Halfway through our tour the navigator told our pilot that he could not go on, but the pilot had a word with him and he stayed with us. He was as sick as a dog before every op, but he kept going and finished the tour – and that took real guts.'[74]

But the RAF chiefs were not as vicious as was sometimes claimed. They recognized that some men were unable to fly, not because of any cowardice, but simply because they had suffered a nervous breakdown, Bomber Command's equivalent of shell-shock. What they needed therefore was medical support, not punishment. From 1942 to 1945, 8,402 men were classified as suffering from some form of neurosis. Many were discharged into civilian life. Others were looked after in the RAF rehabilitation centre at Matlock in Derbyshire, a place where Lancaster engineer Dennis Wiltshire was taken after experiencing a complete blackout on a raid to Cologne, when the front of the plane was peppered by flak and the bomb aimer killed. 'There was a terrific gale blowing through the front of the kite which made it difficult to stand up and the pilot was in the throes of making a left-hand turn with seventy or eighty other aircraft. I got back into my seat and then I felt absolutely terrible. The skipper asked me, "Are you all right?" I didn't say anything. I just put the thumbs up. I don't know what happened. I've been told that I took my harness off, got out of my seat and walked aft. Apparently I fell over the main spar span and the navigator came to help me. He spoke to me, but I didn't answer him. I couldn't talk to hm. I have no further recollection of that flight.' Wiltshire was propped up by the navigator on the deck by the main spar. When the Lancaster landed he was first placed in his station's sick quarters, and then, having failed to improve, transferred to Matlock. There he remained unconscious for several more days until a nurse dropped a metal dish on the floor and he suddenly woke up, screaming: 'There's another poor sod going down. Look at the flares! Look at the flares!'[75] He underwent intensive tests and the latest psychiatric treatments, but there was little chance of recovery. He was invalided out of the RAF.

The only surprise was that it did not happen more often.

9

'It was a real beaut to fly'

━━◆━━

IN HIS MEMOIRS Sir Arthur Harris wrote of the start of 1943: 'At long last we were ready and equipped.'[1] He had considered 1942 largely as a year of preparation in building the forces of Bomber Command. Now he believed he was in a position to launch an all-out offensive against Germany. The Lancaster was, inevitably, at the centre of his plans, since it was the only heavy bomber in which he ever had any faith. Though the government were still not producing enough for his liking, they were now coming out of the factories in substantial numbers. In January 1943 Lancaster output from the main Avro plants reached a rate of 100 a month for the first time, with another 60 a month emerging from the two 'daughter' firms of Metropolitan-Vickers in Manchester and Armstrong Whitworth in Coventry by mid-summer. During 1943 Lancaster deliveries from Avro reached a total of 1,293 planes, and the two other factories turned out 660. In addition, towards the end of the year, the first Lancasters began to emerge from the massive Castle Bromwich factory in Birmingham.

The year 1943 also saw the arrival in England of the first Lancasters produced in Canada. The initial contract to build the Canadian Lancasters had been given to the National Steel and Car Corporation, which also had a contract for the Westland Lysander. But in 1942 the Canadian Government grew increasingly concerned about the ability of the Corporation to fulfil the terms of the agreement. There were continual delays at National Steel's Ontario factory as the sheer size of the Lancaster production process, which involved 500,000 manufacturing operations and 55,000 separate parts, proved daunting for an inexperienced firm with a largely unskilled workforce. In September the government took over the Ontario plant and set up its own state-run firm, Victory Aircraft Ltd, to carry out the contract. A Lancaster (R-7257) was flown over from England to act as a model for Victory's production line. After some difficulties with labour shortages, the nationalization ultimately proved successful. The first Lancaster rolled off the production line in August

1943, less than a year after Victory Aircraft had been created. By the end of the war, 430 Canadian Lancasters had been built. To distinguish them from the British-built versions, they were known as the Mark X, though in practice they were largely the same as the Mark III with its Packard-built engines, since spare parts had to be interchangeable with the British types. As they arrived in England, all the Mark Xs went to the Royal Canadian Air Force No. 6 Bomber Group, which had been established in January 1943. The move to form a separate Canadian group had been partly driven by pressure from the Ottawa Government, seeking recognition for the contribution of its homeland towards the RAF: over half of all the Dominion pilots came from Canada. There was also pressure from the RCAF itself which felt its authority was undermined by continually having to submit to British orders. Fearing that this might lead to demands from other Dominions for their own separate groups and thereby weaken Bomber Command's unity, Harris initially disapproved of the idea. But having spent some of his formative years in Rhodesia, he was also a strong admirer of Commonwealth airmen, who made up over 40 per cent of Bomber Command's crews by 1943. So he accepted the establishment of RCAF No. 6 Group without the obstreperousness that usually accompanied any Air Ministry decision he opposed.

Nevertheless, his usual prickliness could not be entirely hidden, and questions about the supply of Lancasters were the means of expressing some of this pique. In September 1942, when Victory Aircraft was about to be set up, Harris protested to Portal about plans to equip the planned RCAF No. 6 Group with Lancasters, when so many other units needed them. 'I fail to see why we should give people who are determined to huddle into a corner by themselves on purely political grounds, the best of our equipment at the expense of British and other Dominion crews. To rob our own crews of their expectations of Lancasters for that purpose is to add injury to the original political insult.'[2] Portal replied that he had spoken about the issue to the Vice-Chief of the Air Staff, Sir Wilfrid Freeman, who had 'given a ruling that the Canadians are not to get more Lancasters than they are producing in their own country'.[3] The production of the Avro York, a transport derivative of the Lancaster, was the cause for another eruption by Harris against the Canadians the following year. The York had been under development at Avro since 1941 to fulfil the RAF's chronic need for a long-range military transport, and the first prototype had successfully flown in July 1942. But production of the aircraft proceeded extremely slowly, partly because of the ferocious opposition of Harris, who loathed any distraction from the offensive against Germany and wanted all Avro's efforts concentrated on the Lancaster. In an attempt to boost production, the government considered asking Victory Aircraft to undertake some of the manufacture of the York, a proposal that sparked the inevitable blast of fury from Harris. 'This of course can only be done at the expense of potential Lancaster production', he told Portal. 'I understand that a potential factory for the purpose is already nearing completion next door to the Canadian Lancaster factory. Yet at the same time the Canadians come imploring me for a bigger share of Lancasters. I hope if you get the opportunity you will make it clear that the best way to get more Lancasters for the Canadian Group is to produce more and stop messing about with the non-essentials in a bare-faced and anyhow futile effort to secure the post-war civil aviation position at the expense of the vital war equipment of the moment.'[4] Harris's intervention achieved the result he wanted. Though Victory Aircraft tooled up for the York, only one was ever built in Ontario.

The depth of Harris's attachment to the Lancaster was graphically highlighted by his loudly voiced contempt for the entire York project. For him, there could be no compromise about the need to step up the bombing of Germany. The very idea of using a version of the Lancaster as a transport aircraft or troop carrier struck him as absurd. 'The production of the Lancaster, which is our best bomber, the only one really adequate for its work, is being interfered with by the conversion of a considerable number of them to transport duties,' he complained to Freeman in September 1942. 'If the equipment of airborne troops with aircraft is to be seriously considered it must await the day when the provision of up-to-date types for bombing, such as the Lancaster, is adequate, and obsolete types, such as the Wellington or the Halifax, can be offered for conversion to this task.'[5] In another missive to Freeman, he reiterated that if the Air Staff insisted on a heavy transport, then the answer was to convert the Halifax, 'which in my view is unlikely to remain fit for use as a bomber under tactical conditions likely to prevail in a year or 18 months' time'.[6] But in his wish to see the York abandoned, Harris was up against two determined opponents. One was the Avro company, which saw the York as a means not just to greater security of orders but also to future diversification into large-scale civil aviation once the war was over. Moreover, the innovative spirit of Roy Chadwick was intrigued with a new project now the Lancaster was an assured success. To meet the specification as an aircraft capable of carrying troops, freight or passengers, he had to make a number of changes to the Lancaster's design, the most important of which were a larger, flat-sided fuselage with a stronger underside and the placement of the wing high on the fuselage because the position of the huge main spars in the Lancaster was unsuitable in a transport plane. In turn, this meant that the fuselage was much nearer the ground, while a central fin was also needed for directional stability. Even in the face of Harris's disapproval, Chadwick was keen to continue, the earlier tortured saga of the Lancaster's birth serving as a source of inspiration. 'Leave it to me. We got away with the Lanc, so we'll do the same with a transport. Press on with the design,' he told his staff.[7]

The other supporter of the York scheme was Portal, who wanted Avro to be given a contract for 200 of the aircraft to be built by early 1944, even if this meant a reduction in Lancaster output. In a memorandum to Churchill in September 1942, he set out the case for the York, arguing that a conversion of the Lancaster was the only realistic way to provide the RAF with an economical transport aircraft. He admitted that the design and manufacture of the York would lead to 'some reduction in the weight of our bomber offensive next year' but such losses would be offset by 'greater strategic mobility'. This was precisely the sort of thinking that Harris could not abide, believing that the only theatre of war that mattered was the German one. Portal then addressed the question, which Churchill had raised with him in a previous conversation, as to why the Halifax rather than the Lancaster could not be converted, particularly as he admitted 'the Lancaster is our most effective bomber'. But, said Portal, 'the great advantage of the Lancaster transport is that it is ready now and production can start this year. The order for 200 should be finished by March 1944. Messrs Handley Page are considering a transport version of the Halifax but this will not be ready until the end of next year and so could do nothing to fill our need during 1943. The project could not therefore be regarded as an alternative to that of the Lancaster. For 1943, it is the Lancaster transport or nothing.'[8]

Like Harris, Churchill had his grave doubts about this diversion from the Lancaster programme, particularly as Portal had been pressing him so hard since the spring of 1941 for an increase in the bomber offensive. 'I am not at all convinced by this argument,' he told Portal, and asked for more detailed figures of the effect that the York would have on Lancaster production.[9] Portal tried to reassure him that 'only four Lancaster squadrons would be lost by December 1943, and the loss would be reduced to nothing before September 1944 owing to the completion of the order.' In any case, he promised, plans by MAP to expand industrial capacity would eventually make up the difference.[10] With some reluctance, Churchill agreed to the order for 200 Yorks. But production moved more slowly than Portal envisioned, and by the end of 1943 just five Yorks had been produced. Only another 40 were built in 1944, when the first full York squadron operated in Transport Command. It was not until 1948 that the original York contract was completed. As it turned out, the Douglas C-47, known in Britain as the Dakota, largely fulfilled the RAF's transport needs. Harris had been correct in seeing the York as a wasteful distraction from the bomber offensive, for at the very moment when Victory Aircraft in Canada was gearing up to build the York, Freeman was urging an increase in Lancaster output, claiming that 'we need in the United Kingdom every Lancaster that can possibly be produced'.[11] Similarly, when the Australian Government asked Churchill for a squadron of Lancasters in mid-1943 for bomber operations against the Japanese, Portal told the Prime Minister to reject the request. 'As you know every Lancaster is wanted for Bomber Command and will pull its full weight here.'[12] In fact, in successfully urging the rejection of Australia's appeal, Portal mirrored exactly Harris's attitude about the need to concentrate everything on the bomber offensive against Germany. The RAF 'could not possibly give' Australia any Lancasters, he said, because 'every heavy bomber we make is going into the bomber offensive on Germany. The Battle of Germany is a battle like no other. Our casualties are rising and the German defences are being strengthened all the time. We owe it to our heavy bomber force to give them the greatest possible support and reinforcement.'[13] But such words directly contradicted what he had said to Churchill about the York.

The energy and resources expended on the York were aggravating enough to Harris, but a much deeper sense of frustration was caused by the continuing failure of the Air Ministry to dump the Halifax and switch all heavy-bomber production to the Lancaster. Throughout 1943, barely a month passed without Harris launching into another epistolic tirade against the Halifax and a paean to the Lancaster. For him, the issue was simple: the Lancaster was easily the best plane in his Command, so its output should be maximized, even if the changeover meant a temporary drop in the overall deliveries of the heavy bombers. The government, the Ministry of Aircraft Production and the Air Staff took a very different view. Part of their unwillingness to switch Halifax production to the Lancaster was based on a concern about the immediate diminution of the bomber force because of the time needed to retool the aircraft factories. The idea of the change, said an Air Staff paper of November 1942, was 'on the face of it attractive. The loss would, however, be very considerable. The switch of all Halifax firms would probably take from mid-1943 to mid-1945 and the loss over the two years might be as much as a 1000 bombers with a possible further loss after the latter date.'[14] Within official circles there was also a belief that the Halifax could be so radically improved that it might begin to match the Lancaster. This faith in the Halifax's future was not entirely misplaced, for the prototype of the Mark III, equipped with powerful Bristol Hercules engines, had shown genuine potential. Yet there was also a deep contradiction in the opposition to Harris. On the one hand, the Air Staff and MAP claimed that, for the sake of numbers, they had to maintain the production of an aircraft which they admitted was patently inferior to the Lancaster and was verging on obsolescence at the start of 1943. On the other hand, having wailed about the production difficulties of a switch to the Lancaster, they then kept hankering after new, bigger and longer-range types, such as the Vickers Windsor, built to specification B3/42, or even an anglicized version of the vast new American heavy-weight, the Boeing B-29.

To be fair to the Air Staff and MAP, none of these questions were straightforward in 1943, since there could be no confidence as to when the war might end, what technology the Germans might produce or how the Allies would fight back against Japan in the Pacific. Nor did the combustible personality of Arthur Harris assist in the openness of debate, since he was inclined to be savagely dismissive of any opinion but his own. He opened 1943 as he had ended 1942, challenging the Air Staff's refusal to switch from the Halifax to the Lancaster and questioning the statistical basis of the decision. His Command's growing experience of raids over Germany only further emboldened him. 'Too much time has already been lost in putting these measures into effect and I must urge that the necessary decisions are taken without further delay,' he wrote to Freeman on 8 January 1943.[15] But the Air Staff refused to budge. Ralph Sorley, the Assistant Chief in charge of Technical Requirements, told Harris that the whole question had been examined thoroughly and it 'would not be practicable to change over and at short notice to Lancaster production' because of 'the loss of output' and the 'hundreds of sub-contractors' involved. But as well as trumpeting the potential virtues of the Halifax III, Sorley tried to mollify Harris by promising him 'that the development of the Lancaster had not been overlooked'. There was, he said 'a planned programme for improvement' which included the installation of the new two-speed, two-stage supercharged Rolls-Royce Merlin 60 series.[16] This engine gave an aircraft a much higher ceiling and had already proved an outstanding success in the Spitfire Mark IX. In the

Lancaster, said Sorley, the two-stage supercharged Merlin could potentially raise the maximum cruising height to 30,000 feet. This was no hollow promise, for in August 1943 Avro was given the contract to build three prototypes for this advanced new version of the Lancaster, initially called the Mark IV. With a wingspan widened by nine feet, large new fuel tanks installed to raise the capacity from 2,154 to 3,580 gallons, a redesigned nose, 0.5-calibre guns installed and the all-up weight raised to 75,000 pounds, the Mark IV was a radical change from the previous three versions of the Lancaster, so radical that soon after its maiden flight in June 1944, the Air Ministry decided that it could no longer be called a Lancaster and so renamed it the Lincoln Mark I. But it was never to see wartime action, the first production Lincolns only reaching a front-line squadron in August 1945.

None of this carried any weight with Harris in early 1943. He wanted immediate action on the Lancaster and Halifax, not distant pledges for the future. He told Sorley that he 'was not in any way impressed by your letter', arguing that the increase of 30 mph in the top speed of the Halifax III still left it 'far behind the Lancaster in every way. There really isn't any comparison – the Lancaster is an aeroplane and the Halifax a failure.' He then launched into a vituperative attack on the whole policy of the Air Staff. 'Why we go on producing such an aircraft I cannot understand. If my suggestion made last August, that all production of the Halifax should be stopped and turned over to the Lancaster, had been followed, we should now be much nearer having good Lancasters in place of the bad Halifax.'[17] This latest outburst from Harris provoked exasperation at the top of the Air Staff when the letter was circulated. Increasingly fed up with the Bomber Command chief, Sorley told Portal in a handwritten note that he preferred not to reply, since a response would just open up 'a ding-dong correspondence'.[18] But Portal was all in favour of taking the verbal battle to Harris, especially since he felt that Harris was exaggerating the inferiority of the Halifax compared to the Lancaster. 'I should go on at him!' he told Sorley. 'This is another cause for pleasure. In February, Halifaxes dropped 108 tons for every one lost, against 30 tons average for October–December 1942. The February Lancaster figure was only 21 tons (or 20 per cent) better.'[19] Encouraged by Portal's support, Sorley wrote back to Harris, saying that he was 'disappointed by your letter, because at no time was I comparing the Halifax with the Lancaster, which we all know is better. I know of no way of waving a wand to convert the "Cinderella" Halifax into the "Fairy Princess" Lancaster, and other than the efforts which are being made to turn over

Halifax production, there is no more that can be done to meet your wishes in this respect. In the meantime, however, it seems to me that the recovery of the Halifax from the position it was in last September to the present one seems to me deserving of more pleasure than you express.'[20]

While the row over the Lancaster versus the Halifax continued to simmer through the spring of 1943, the Air establishment was also looking in a very different direction: at the creation of a new bomber more advanced than the Lancaster. Sorley believed that the future lay on the other side of the Atlantic, in the giant B-29 whose prototype was being tested in early 1943. 'From our point of view, the B-29 remains the only prospective replacement type which can be introduced to follow the Lancaster,' he wrote.[21] In June, Portal led discussions about the possibility of building a British version of the B-29, and it was agreed that an Air Ministry delegation should go to America to investigate 'anglicizing' the long-range 'Superfortress'. But the difficulties of adapting the B-29 for night bombing from England proved insurmountable and the plane was never used in the European theatre, concentrating its efforts in the Pacific. By the late autumn of 1943, with the tide of the war beginning to turn in the Allies' favour, opinion in the Air Ministry and MAP came to see that the real hope for the future lay in the Vickers Windsor and the Lancaster Mark IV rather than a vast new heavy bomber.

True to his majestic nature that had once advocated a six-engined heavy bomber, Churchill was concerned at this failure to match the Americans. He told the Minister of Aircraft Production, Sir Stafford Cripps, that he was disquieted because 'we have no really heavy bomber under development. The Vickers Windsor will not really be much larger – though we must trust it will be better – than the improved Lancaster which will come into production at the end of next year. In the meanwhile, the Americans have the B-29 already in production with an all-up weight of 120,000 lbs. . . . Ought we not to be looking forward to making aircraft of a similar performance?'[22] In reply, Cripps pointed out that there were disadvantages to massive bombers. 'They involve locking up a great number of man-hours in one aircraft, which may be lost in a single blow . . . The enemy will probably be able to inflict relatively higher losses against a small number of big machines than against a much greater number of comparatively small ones. Saturation of the defences has, it is believed, been the tactical policy of Bomber Command.' In addition, warned Cripps, there was the problem of facilities for very large bombers. 'Many of the airfields suitable for the Lancaster and the B3/42 would not permit a machine two or three times larger to take off or land safely. For example the new civil airport at Heath Row designed to accommodate aircraft of the size now being developed in the USA will cost over £10 million.' After noting that the B-29 is 'still in the experimental stage', he asserted that the Windsor and the Lancaster Mark IV were 'the best that could be brought into service in time to affect the future course of the war'.[23]

Like a bloodhound in pursuit of his quarry, Harris refused to be distracted by this speculation from his present goal of terminating the Halifax programme. In another missive to Sorley in April, he complained that the Mark III was still 'hopelessly inferior to the Lancaster in speed and altitude', with a ceiling 1,500 feet below the Lancaster II. To pursue the present Halifax III project, he argued, is 'to embark on an inexcusable waste of manpower and materials. I realize my proposals involve some sacrifice in the numerical output of aircraft. This must in my view be accepted.'[24] The Air Staff refused to accept Harris's assertions about the weakness of the Halifax III. Air Vice Marshal John Breakey, who had succeeded Sorley as the head of Technical Requirements, told Harris that the Halifax III had an excellent rate of climb and a maximum speed just 2–3 mph lower than the Lancaster.[25] Harris fell uncharacteristically quiet during the high summer of 1943, when he was preoccupied with overseeing some of Bomber Command's most famous raids, including the bombing of Hamburg and the attack on the Peenemünde rocket station on the north-eastern coast of Germany, but he blazed forth again in the autumn on his favourite subject, telling Portal in early September: 'I hope that once and for all the opposition of Handley Page will be dispensed with by the simple, obvious and essential step of getting rid of Handley Page. We may then begin to get somewhere.' Harris even described the Halifax as a menace to the men of his Command. 'You will recall that the Halifax, on a long haul, carries only half the load of the Lancaster, while putting at jeopardy the same crew. Their crews moreover take more training than Lancaster crews. Furthermore, by reason of their shorter range, the use of the Halifax frequently forces us to make the Lancasters take shorter and more dangerous routes to and from distant targets in order to keep both types "in the stream" for mutual cover.'[26] He wrote in the same tone to Sir Wilfrid Freeman on 8 September, warning that the Halifax 'is of little use for war purposes now and will be of no damned use for war next year' and expressing the hope that 'the Lancaster is being given absolute preference with all manpower and materials at the expense of Halifax production.'[27]

But the two leading figures on the Air Staff had no intention of yielding any ground. Freeman told Harris that 'the fundamental fallacy of your letter is that you assume we could give you better equipment than you are getting at present. You appear to take no account of the practical difficulties of production.' Freeman repeated the claim that not only would a changeover have taken two years but would have led to a loss of more than 1,000 bombers. With barely concealed menace, he warned that if Harris did not want his Halifaxes, then they could be taken from Bomber Command and handed over to Arthur Tedder, the Commander of the RAF in the Mediterranean theatre, who could use them 'for striking at Germany from the south, from my point of view a very satisfactory solution'.[28] Portal then added the full weight of his authority, stressing that Harris should not undermine his airmen's fighting spirit by his continual wails about equipment. 'The morale of your crews is bound in the end to reflect your personal attitude.'[29] Harris was never a leader to be cowed by his superiors. The dispute rumbled on through the autumn, with figures bandied about comparing the performance of the Halifax III with the Lancaster, the Air Staff talking up the Handley Page plane, Harris talking it down. Indeed, Harris went so far as to say that, for all the vaunted improvements in the Halifax, he 'would rather have one Lancaster than three Halifaxes in 1944'.[30]

Despite the accusation from some in the Air Staff that Harris 'appears to be overstating his case',[31] there was overwhelming evidence of the Halifax's inferiority compared to the Lancaster. On almost every criterion, the Lancaster was better, from speed and bomb load to range and rate of climb. It could carry more fuel, 2,154 gallons compared to the Halifax's 1,802, and, being a more streamlined aircraft, had a lower rate of consumption. Reflecting Avro's time-honoured belief in making it simple, the Lancaster was also a cheaper and easier aircraft to produce. According to MAP, the labour required to build 100 Halifaxes could build 120 Lancasters, a point that rather undermined the constant assertion about the disastrous potential loss in production from a changeover.[32] Intriguingly the most powerful voice in support of Harris's case was that of Syd Bufton, who had become the Air Ministry's Director of Bombing Operations in March 1943. Ever since Bufton had first entered the Bombing Operations Directorate in late 1941 after a distinguished spell as a squadron leader, his relationship with Harris had been volatile. They had frequently clashed on major questions of policy and Harris instinctively resented any interference from the Ministry. He once complained that Bufton had been 'a thorn in our side and the personification of all that is un-understanding and unhelpful in our relations with the Air Staff. For these reasons his very name has become anathema to me and my senior staff here.'[33] Yet Bufton, clear–sighted and independent, had no interest in turf wars or personal quarrels. His only concern was to improve the efficiency of RAF bombing, hence his passionate belief in the creation of Pathfinders. In this case, his assessment of the Lancaster's superiority was exactly in line with Harris's view. Unlike the rather artificial tests that some of the Air Staff used to justify their claims about the Halifax III, Bufton looked at the outcome of actual raids against Germany over the previous ten months.

In a paper he submitted to Portal in December, Bufton revealed that Halifax losses per sortie exceeded those of the Lancaster by 56 per cent, and that the Lancasters dropped on average 9,634 pounds per attacking aircraft compared with 5,631 pounds for the Halifaxes, 'that is each Lancaster dropped 75 per cent more bombs than the Halifax'. The vulnerability of the Halifax was just as obvious: '17 personnel were lost per every 100 tons of bombs dropped by Halifaxes. The corresponding figure for the Lancaster was 6. Thus the Halifax for a given tonnage is nearly three times as expensive in crew personnel as the Lancaster.' Bufton also pointed to the much lower operational height of the Halifax, 18,000 feet compared to 22,000 feet for the Lancaster, which seriously restricted its capability. Like Harris, Bufton had little faith in the Halifax III. 'The indications are that operationally it will not show any material improvement.' The Lancaster, argued Bufton, remained in a different league. It was 'faster, has a higher ceiling and greater endurance and can deliver a much greater bomb load. It is easier to fly and more easily mastered by new crews. Owing to its smaller losses, the average experience of Lancaster crews will continue to be higher than in the case of the Halifax.' Departing from the rigid establishment line, Bufton asserted that the gains from the switchover could balance out any fall in output. 'We could afford to make the change at some reduction in the total number of bombers produced, as the tonnage of bombs delivered at the target would by no means fall in proportion to the loss in total production. We should, at the same time, make great economies in crew personnel and training.'[34]

For all the certitude of Bufton and Harris, it is interesting that the men of Bomber Command were much more divided about the merits of the two heavy bombers. The statistics might have been sending out a clear message about the inadequacy of the Halifax, but many aircrews were attached to it and some even preferred it to the Lancaster. One of those who most strongly valued the Halifax's qualities was Wing Commander James Calder. With wide experience of wartime operations, having flown over 40 different bomber types and served for a time as

Harris's personal pilot, Calder deeply admired the robustness of the Halifax:

> I preferred the Halifax. When the shit started flying, the Hali was the thing to be in. It was better than the Lanc, oh Christ yes. It was better at with-standing damage, better to manoeuvre. You could tear the wings of a Lancaster before a Halifax would even start twitching. It was a beautiful aircraft to fly, not land, it was a bastard to land – and that's when all the trouble occurred. Yes, the Halifax would not go as far or carry as much as the Lanc, but if I was in a scrap, I know which aircraft I would rather be in. I once had three fighters coming at me over Berlin, and I would not have survived in a Lanc, oh Christ no.[35]

Other airmen also appreciated the bigger interior of the Halifax compared to the narrow confinement of the Lancaster. The Halifax, said Tom Wingham of 102 Squadron, was 'a lot more comfortable than the Lancaster for the crew. We had more space and you could move about freely'.[36] For Tom Tredwell, a bomb aimer with 77 and 10 Squadrons, the absence of the Lancaster's main spar was a relief. 'The Halifax was a very comfortable aircraft, better than the Lancaster, bigger and with more crea-ture comforts. It did not have that infamous Lanc main spar which ran right through the fuselage. That was quite a thing. It was not relished by anybody. It could be an obstacle course, especially at night. I had a great affection for the Halifax. While it was always in the shadow of the Lanc, anyone who had flown on the two for any length of time preferred the company of the Halifax.'[37] The spaciousness of the Halifax was not just a matter of comfort. Combined with larger escape hatches, it also allowed crews to exit the Halifax more easily than the Lancaster. The hatches on the Lancaster were just 22 inches wide, compared to 24 inches on the Halifax, and this meant that, in an emergency, the Lancaster was actually more of a death trap than the Halifax. Amidst all the data showing the inferiority of the Halifax, there is one other statistic that stands out: 25 per cent of Halifax crews who were shot down survived, compared to just 15 per cent of Lancaster crews.

Freeman Dyson, the scientist who worked in Operational Research for Bomber Command, believed that this showed the streak of indiffer-ence in Harris towards the fate of his crews:

> I shared an office at Command headquarters with a half-Irish boy of my own age called Mike O'Loughlin . . . One of the things that Mike was angry about was escape hatches. Every bomber had a trap door in the floor through which the crew was supposed to jump when the captain gave the order to bail out . . . A far larger number died because they were

inadequately prepared for the job of squeezing through a small hole with a bulky flying suit and parachute harness, in the dark, in a hurry, in an airplane rapidly going out of control. The mechanics of bailing out was another taboo subject which right-thinking crewmen were not encouraged to discuss . . . Mike spent two years in a lonely struggle to force the Command to enlarge the Lancaster hatch.[38]

In Harris's defence, it should be said that, far from being indifferent, he too was seriously concerned about the hatches on the Lancaster and regularly badgered the Air Ministry about the problem throughout the war, though he found change as hard to accomplish here as he did on other issues. After only a few months of taking office, he complained to Sorley of the Lancaster's 'inadequate escape hatches' and said 'that the sickening regularity with which these shortcomings repeat themselves in new types certainly indicates that we should tighten up the whole methods of controlling manufacturers and designers'.[39] One of the very last letters he wrote as Commander-in-Chief in June 1945 was to call for a 'drastic overhaul of the present facilities for escape' in the Lancaster, whose record of saving their crews when downed was, he admitted, 'appalling'.[40]

Contrary to the scepticism of Bufton and Harris about the Halifax III, some of those who flew this new version regarded it as an enormous improvement, particularly because of the big increase in power from the four Bristol Hercules engines. Replacing the Merlin with the Hercules engine, said pilot Jim Porter of 10 Squadron, was like 'putting a fifth engine in the plane', making it 'every bit as manoeuvrable as the Lancaster'.[41] But the enthusiasm for the Halifax should not be exaggerated. Despite all the affection it engendered amongst its users, it was in reality no match for the Lancaster in the key task of bombing Germany. Most aircrews were willing to put up with the defects of the Lancaster, like its lack of space, in return for its much greater overall performance, which meant that it had more chance of delivering its cargo and of escaping from the target. 'It was absolutely wonderful flying the Lancaster,' recalled John Sanders, a pilot with 49 and 617 Squadrons. 'We proved a couple of times that it would take a tremendous beating and still fly. I did have the opportunity to fly the Halifax during training and to me there was no comparison between the two aircraft. Although the Halifax was a good rugged plane, it had not got the feel of the Lancaster.'[42] The Lancaster's smoothness was what impressed Harold Davis, a pilot with 101 Squadron. The Halifax, said Davis, 'was rather heavy' but 'the Lanc was much lighter, you did not need so much muscle. It was a real beaut to fly and everyone seemed to like it. There were no bad characteristics, no bad reputation followed it anywhere.'[43] The same inclination towards the Lancaster could be found among ground crews, since maintenance was more straightforward on the Avro plane, as explained by engine fitter Stephen Rew, who was transferred in 1944 from Elsham Wolds to the Halifax station of Riccall in Yorkshire:

> The Halifaxes themselves were infinitely more difficult to work on than Lancasters, and suffered far more snags. The exhaust system was a horror compared to that of a Lancaster. On a Lanc there were separate stub-pipes from each cylinder, so that if one cracked, it only meant undoing four rather inaccessible nuts, replacing the stub and refitting the nuts. On a Halibag, however, all the stubs ran into one pipe so that when the thing cracked – when, not if – one had to undo 24 very inaccessible nuts, replace whichever half of the assembly was cracked and reassemble the whole thing . . . On the credit side, it must be said that the aircraft was more roomy, rather better finished, and far more solidly built, which was why their performance was so far inferior, because of the extra weight from the battleship-like construction. All in all, however, for us ex-Lanc types, the expression 'From Hull, Hell and Halifax, good Lord deliver us,' took on a new and very real meaning.[44]

No matter what the opinions of fitters, crews, Bufton or Harris, the Air Staff was not to be deflected from its course. The longer the debate went on, the more unrealistic became the chances of a switch-over from the Halifax to the Lancaster. With the Ministry of Aircraft Production warning in December 1943 that it would take '16 months to produce the first Lancaster after the order to change from one type to another',[45] the first planes would not emerge until the summer of 1945, when the war in Europe was likely to have finished. So the status quo was maintained. Despite all the talk from the Air Staff about the need to increase Lancaster output, there was not even much attempt to turn over the former Stirling plants run by Short Brothers in Rochester and Belfast to Lancaster production. The only major expansion centred on the former Vickers Armstrong factory at Chester, which had previously turned out the Wellington but from mid-1944 started producing Lancasters. Otherwise, Harris lost his long battle. At two Air Staff conferences in late December 1943, it was confirmed that there would be no wholesale changeover away from the Halifax. These meetings even crushed the lingering hope that there might be a less drastic switch, namely by diverting labour and materials from Halifax to Lancaster factories. The benefit of such a move, Freeman told his colleagues, 'would be very limited since an increase in production of Lancasters could only take place if there were more jigs and tools and an adequate supply of skilled labour'. But this could not happen in 1944 since the 'skill in the aircraft industry was going to be more diluted than ever; moreover the direction of the labour from one factory to another would produce more labour troubles.'[46] In the end pragmatism triumphed over radicalism. Harris never got the Lancaster force that he wanted.

Yet for all the tempestuousness of this debate, Harris and the Air Staff had exactly the same outlook on the pursuit of the air war. The discussion had been entirely predicated on the belief that the predominant role of the RAF was to conduct area attacks on Germany through concentrated streams of heavy bombers. The Air Staff and Harris had been arguing only about different equipment to achieve the same end: the wholesale destruction of German industry and the mass slaughter of German civilians. Whatever bomber they advocated, they shared the united goal of dropping the maximum possible tonnage of incendiaries and explosives on the Reich's urban areas. No alternative was even considered, such as switching over some output to the Mosquito or developing a long-range fighter escort to enhance precision-bombing capability. Inflexible and uncompromising, Harris showed his disdain for anything beyond heavy bombing in his grotesquely misjudged dismissal of the Mosquito. The aircraft, he warned in 1942, would suffer 'a still grimmer fate than has always been the lot of such naive attempts to produce an aeroplane so much faster than anything the enemy possesses that it requires no armament. It will go down in history in consequence as a second "Battle" as far as bombing is concerned.'[47] The strategy of pulverizing the Reich by night from heavy-bomber stations in eastern England had been agreed in 1942, and there was no deviation from it in 1943. The only change was an intensification of the offensive as more aircraft, personnel and equipment became available.

The heightened tempo of the bomber offensive in 1943 took place against the backdrop of growing military success by the Allies across North Africa, the Mediterranean, Italy and the Atlantic, as well as the victories by Russian forces against the Wehrmacht on the eastern front. With the Germans in retreat for the first time since the start of the war, pressure began to build on Britain and America to open up a second front in Western Europe to hasten the downfall of the Reich. Both Stalin and the US Government were keen for a full-scale invasion in 1943, but Churchill was anxious to avoid this eventuality, haunted by memories of Gallipoli in 1915 and the fiasco of the Dieppe raid in August 1942, when an Allied landing party was swiftly defeated in its attempt to seize the

French port. In the absence of an attack on land, Churchill presented the bomber offensive as a form of second front in the air, an approach that perfectly suited Harris and Portal, for it effectively put mass bombing at the centre of the Allied military strategy. In his thought-provoking book *Why the Allies Won*, Professor Richard Overy wrote a vivid account of Churchill's visit to Stalin in August 1942, when the Soviet leader kept up his demand for a second front and all but accused Britain of cowardice. Attempting to convince Stalin of Britain's resolution, Churchill told him of the plans to step up the bombing offensive. Stalin, who had been frosty up to this point, now warmed to Churchill, urging the RAF to bomb German homes as well as factories. As the American envoy Averell Harriman reported to Roosevelt: 'Between the two of them, they soon had destroyed most of the important cities of Germany.'[48] It was partly this summit that led Churchill to throw his weight behind the bomber expansion programme from late 1942, despite his doubts, regularly expressed to Portal and Sinclair, that bombing was the only way to win the war.

At this stage of the war, Portal himself did not have any reservations about the bombing strategy. He told Churchill in November that an Anglo-US force of between 4,000 and 6,000 heavy bombers could drop 1.25 million tons of bombs on Germany between January and December 1943. Such a rate of devastation, he said, would result in the destruction of 6 million German homes, 25 million Germans rendered homeless, and 'civilian casualties estimated at about 900,000 killed and 1,000,000 seriously injured'. In conclusion, he argued that 'an Anglo-American force of the size proposed could reduce the German economic and military strength to a point well below that at which the Anglo-American invasion of the continent would become possible'.[49]

But this was little more than wishful thinking at the end of 1942. The US Army Air Force, with its Liberators and Flying Fortresses, was only just starting to arrive in England in significant numbers. Furthermore, the Americans had a very different approach to that of Bomber Command. The 8th Air Force, led by General Ira Eaker, rejected the concept of area attacks and instead maintained a strategy of trying to hit specific military and industrial targets through precision assaults. Such methods could only be undertaken by day, which meant the USAAF bombers were more open to attack by Luftwaffe fighters. Indeed, Harris thought that the Americans were indulging in dangerous folly by abandoning the cover of night. 'God knows I hope you can do it,' he said soon after Eaker arrived in England, 'but I don't think you can. Come join us at night.

Together we'll lick them.'[50] The Americans stuck to daylight bombing, but not because of any moral scruples about area bombing at night. Indeed, the use of atomic weapons on Japan in 1945 showed that the USAAF could be just as ruthless as the RAF. The real reasons were twofold. First, they held that precision bombing was a more militarily effective way of weakening the enemy. As the General of the US Air Force Hap Arnold put it: 'Indiscriminate widespread destruction of enemy industry is simply a waste of effort. Examination of any national economy will disclose several specific industries or other national activities without which the nation cannot effectively carry on modern warfare,' a statement that was diametrically the opposite of Harris's own thinking.[51] Second, the Americans believed that if Germany was to be defeated, the Luftwaffe fighter forces would have to be confronted both in the air and on the ground rather than avoided. Even if it led to horrendous losses in 1943, this strategy would ultimately prove more sound than Bomber Command's, since the crucial turning point in the air war occurred when the USAAF began to overwhelm the German fighter defences.

The American reliance on day attack, so foolhardy in the eyes of Harris, meant that their bombers had to be far more heavily armed than the RAF's. Thus the B-17 Flying Fortress had almost five times the hitting power of the Lancaster Mark I for the same all-round field of fire. Compared to the Lancaster's inadequate Brownings, the Fortress had up to 13 machine guns of 0.5-inch calibre, including two in a ventral ball turret, precisely the sort of protection that would have made the Lancaster less vulnerable to Schräge Musik.[52] Given the 8th Air Force's growing use of extensive facilities across southern England from late 1942, its presence could have been a recipe for serious conflict with the RAF. That harmony was maintained was in part down to the close relationship and mutual admiration between Eaker and Harris, who was far more accommodating towards the American than he was towards most of his RAF colleagues. When the USAAF senior officers first needed a headquarters in England, Harris went out of his way to secure the use of Wycombe Abbey Girls School for them, near Bomber Command's own HQ. The well-appointed but rather incongruous setting for the USAAF led to one bizarre incident on the first night that the Americans stayed there. Soon after most of the men had retired to their quarters, a loud ringing sound could be heard echoing through the wood-panelled walls of the school. It was discovered that by the side of every bed in the erstwhile dormitories was the notice: 'If you need a mistress in the night, ring twice.'[53]

More importantly, the disparity in method meant that the two air forces, at least in theory, complemented each other. To accommodate their radically different approaches, Eaker and Harris evolved the concept of bombing Germany 'round the clock', a strategy that was to become known as the Combined Bombing Offensive. This was first put forward by Eaker at the Casablanca Conference in January 1943, when Churchill met Roosevelt to discuss the Allied campaign for the coming year. Churchill's central aim at Casablanca was to secure a postponement until 1944 of the invasion of France. He succeeded in this goal, Roosevelt accepting his case for the Allied attack to be concentrated on the drive through Italy and an increase in the bomber offensive. In return for the postponement of the invasion, Churchill agreed to drop his proposal that the Americans should abandon day bombing and join the RAF in night attacks on Germany. On his arrival at Casablanca, Churchill was convinced that day bombing was doomed, but Eaker produced a well-argued paper which played up to British sensibilities and stressed that the Germans would have to double their defences under the weight of a dual attack. 'Give us our chance and your reward will be ample – a successful day bombing offense to combine and conspire with the admirable night bombing of the RAF to wreck German industry, transportation and morale – soften the Hun for land invasion and the kill.'[54] Churchill was won over, and the 8th Air Force continued its daylight bombing strategy. The actual directive drawn up at the Casablanca Conference told the RAF and the USAAF commanders: 'Your primary aim will be the progressive destruction and dislocation of the German military, industrial and economic system, and the undermining of the morale of the German people to a point where their capacity for armed resistance is fatally weakened.'[55] Following this opening, the directive set out a list of targets that the two air forces should prioritize, starting with naval submarines and bases, followed by the Luftwaffe and the German aircraft factories, and then other key industrial objectives, including oil plants and ball-bearing factories. In practice, this list was only of interest to the Americans. Contemptuous of 'panacea' targets, Harris barely even paid lip-service to it and just carried on with area bombing, for which the preamble of the Casablanca directive appeared to provide some justification.

The vagueness of the Casablanca document suited Harris, in that it did little to restrict his freedom of action. But over the coming months, Eaker produced a much more detailed plan, giving exact figures on the amount of destruction he expected to achieve in Germany through a carefully organized programme of attacks. Originally called the 'Eaker

Plan', this document went through a lengthy process of negotiation, during which it was turned into the 'Pointblank' Directive. It was presented to the Washington Conference of May 1943 and approved by the Allied political and military leadership. 'Pointblank' became the basis of the Combined Bombing Offensive, which formally began after the directive had been sent out to the RAF and 8th Air Force on 10 June 1943. Once more, however, the detailed instructions in the directive related more to US daylight bombing than to RAF night bombing. Reflecting the detail of the Eaker Plan, Pointblank listed 76 precision targets to be attacked within six vital industries, and even specified the levels of hit accuracy that should be achieved by the bombers. Though the directive reiterated the opening statement at Casablanca about the need to undermine 'the morale of the German people', perhaps its most crucial aspect was the priority it gave to reducing 'the material effectiveness of the German fighter forces'.[56] For all the high-level discussions in Washington, Harris did not allow Pointblank to influence his strategy in the slightest. He just pressed on with city bombing regardless, claiming that Pointblank gave him 'a very wide range of choice and allowed me to attack any German city of 100,000 inhabitants'.[57] In fact, Pointblank itself all but acknowledged that Harris would go his own way: 'This plan does not attempt to prescribe the major effort of the RAF Bomber Command. It simply recognises the fact that when precision targets are bombed by the 8th Air Force in daylight, the effort should be complemented and completed by RAF bombing attacks against the surrounding industrial area at night. Fortunately, the industrial areas to be attacked are in most cases identical with the industrial areas which the British Bomber Command has selected for mass destruction anyway.'[58]

In practice, the idea of 'round the clock bombing' existed largely on paper. There was nothing much 'combined' about the bomber offensive in 1943, since each air force pursued its own course. Apart from the raid on Hamburg in July, it was not until 1944 that 'round the clock bombing' was implemented. In fact, the obvious lack of real unity was something that troubled General Hap Arnold, who urged in the spring of 1943 that the two bomber forces should be integrated. 'The increasing complexity of their operations would appear to me as soon to be beyond the capabilities of the commanders, in person, to co-ordinate,' he wrote.[59] But he found little backing from either the politicians or the military leaders for his stance, and at the Washington summit his proposal was rejected.

One of the reasons Harris was in a strong enough position to resist infringements of his autonomy was that, since the start of 1943, Bomber

Command had enjoyed increasing success in its campaign against the Reich. After the dark days of 1940–1, area bombing finally appeared to be inflicting real damage on Germany, leaving the Nazi regime shaken. The second front that Churchill promised Stalin in 1942 started to become a reality, as Albert Speer, the Nazi Armaments Minister, admitted after the war: 'The real importance of the air war consisted in the fact that it opened a second front long before the invasion of Europe. That front was the skies over Germany. The fleets of bombers might appear at any time over any large city or important factory. The unpredictability of the attacks made this front gigantic; every square mile of territory we controlled was a kind of front line.'[60] The growing power of Bomber Command was reflected from the start of the year, when Lancasters made a total of 1,260 sorties in January compared to 753 in the previous month. On the night of 16–17 January, Lancasters took part in their first full operation against Berlin, 'The Big City', when 190 of them bombed the German capital. 'Congratulations on the greater success of last night's attack on Berlin,' Sinclair telegraphed Harris. 'It was almost miraculous to get away with the loss of only one Lancaster, especially as it seems clear from the German wireless as well as reports of your own crews that you hit Berlin harder than it has ever been hit before.'[61] During February and March, as well as attacks on big cities like Cologne, Essen, Nuremburg and Düsseldorf, heavy raids were launched against U-boat pens in the ports of Wilhelmshaven and Hamburg.

An account showing the precariousness of such attacks and the resilience of the Lancaster was given by J. W. Henderson, a rear gunner with 50 Squadron, who took part in a crisis-strewn raid on Wilhelmshaven. 'About one hour after leaving Flamborough Head, the two pipes in my gun turret broke loose, the inlet pipe and the outlet pipe. Oil went gushing up to the roof of the turret and back down on top of me and I was saturated with hot oil.' Despite his predicament and the fact that he had to operate his Brownings manually, he told the pilot that he was willing to carry on. But almost immediately after bombing the target, the Lancaster was coned by two sets of searchlights at 8,000 feet and the flak guns opened fire. 'To get out of trouble, the pilot had to dive. Immediately I heard him scream at the engineer, asking for help to pull the stick back as he had lost control. When he and the engineer managed to pull out of the dive, it was just in time. We were so near the sea that it looked as if the rear turret was going through the water like a motorboat.' Then, as the Lancaster flew low over the North Sea, it was attacked by flak ships. 'They all turned on their searchlights and opened up with a hail of light flak, pom-pom guns and machine-gun fire. It was just like getting sprayed by a hosepipe. We were so low that you felt you could have put your hand out and plucked the pom-poms out of the sky. How we were not shot down I do not know. We were raked from front to back. Bullets and shells appeared to go right through the plane.' Battered and off course, the pilot had to use the Darkie system once he reached the English coast. 'That call was used only in real emergencies. We asked permission to land at the nearest airfield.' On arrival at this base, the crew were met by transport and taken to the sergeants' mess. 'I was absolutely saturated in oil and when I took all my flying gear off, including my boots and socks, I was still leaving my oily footprints on the floor.' The next morning, the crew had to wait for spare parts to patch up their Lancaster. After the repairs were carried out, they returned to the 50 Squadron base at Skellingthorpe. 'I was never so pleased to strip off and get into a hot bath.'[62]

As he stepped up the offensive, Harris was seeking all the time to improve the effectiveness of his force, not least through the introduction of new technological aids to improve navigation and give greater warning of fighter attacks. In the case of the Lancaster, by far the most important change was H2S, the ground-imaging system that was first employed in Bomber Command by Stirling and Halifax Pathfinders in a raid on Hamburg on 30 January 1943. H2S used a narrow rotating beam to scan the ground below the aircraft, and then the radar reflections were fed into a receiver, which showed the results as a grainy picture on a cathode-ray tube. The breakthrough that led to this invention occurred in November 1941, when a Blenheim navigator on a trip back over the English coast noticed that if the radar on his air interception set was pointing at the ground, he could see an outline of the Isle of Wight. This discovery was reported to the Telecommunications Research Establishment, whose scientists, headed by Sir Bernard Lovell, were able to develop a functioning ground search radar, the equipment fitted in a dome underneath the fuselage. It is one of Bomber Command's legends that the system was given its name after Lord Cherwell came to the TRE station in Swanage, in Dorset, to examine an early model. When asked what he thought of it, he replied, 'It stinks.' At this disparagement, the scientists decided to call it H2S, this being the chemical code for hydrogen sulphide, which smells of rotten eggs.[63] There was initially some resistance within the Air Ministry towards fitting H2S in Bomber Command's planes, because of fears that a downed aircraft with a set onboard could give away the RAF's secrets. But Churchill quickly overruled such opposition.

Even so, installation was a slow process, and Harris complained to Churchill in April 1943 that only Halifaxes and Stirlings in the PFF squadrons had so far been equipped with the system. The delays, he said, were the responsibility of Avro: 'There has been inordinate delay in fitting the Lancasters and that delay is being perpetuated. I was originally promised eight fitted Lancasters by the end of March. I have not got one yet. I am now promised 15 by the end of April but I am informed by my own staff that as matters progress it looks as if we shall be lucky to get more than six by then.'[64]

But Sir Bernard Lovell of the TRE presented a completely different picture, recalling that Chadwick had been fully co-operative and that the blame lay with the government for not pushing through the orders:

When I first met Chadwick in the spring of 1942 at the Avro works in Manchester, I did not expect a pleasant encounter since I had to persuade him to design a large cupola to protrude underneath the belly of his beautiful Lancaster bomber. I had already faced Mr Handley Page with the same problem. He had raged and said it would spoil the performance of his bomber and was reluctant to do anything until informed from high level that it was better to drop a few bombs in the right place rather than waste the entire load – which had so far been the case. Chadwick's reaction was entirely different. He was anxious to help so that his Lancasters could operate with the maximum efficiency and he had the wisdom to realize that maximum altitude and speed were only part of the equation of getting the bombs on to the assigned target, so the meeting which I had expected to be a stormy one turned out to be calm and helpful.[65]

Lovell said that Chadwick came up with a successful modification and was disturbed at the low priority given to the installation programme. But it is also true that from early 1943 Chadwick was overwhelmed with work in preparing for the Dambusters raid. Wherever the responsibility lay, the H2S Lancasters did not finally go into operation until August 1943, initially with the Pathfinders to assist with blind marking and later with the rest of the main force.

Opinion about the practicality of the H2S was decidedly mixed among the aircrews. Because they required no wireless or radio transmitter and were not affected by the curvature of the earth, they could operate anywhere in Germany. But their pictures were difficult to decipher, which meant that a high degree of expertise was required. Bob Knights of 617 Squadron said that 'it just gave you a shadow. I remember I was on the force when it first came out and they did a survey of aeroplanes crossing certain points and they discovered that the planes with H2S were just as far off track as those without it. It would certainly pick out large towns but you should not be over large towns unless you are going to bomb them.'[66]

But others found H2S more valuable, especially when an improved device was introduced from November 1943, operating on a much shorter wavelength and so providing a more accurate picture. Bomb aimer Thomas Tredwell explained that experience was the key to using it. 'I liked it very much. H2S gave you a bearing and a direction but the special radar maps that were prepared for us showed the outline of the various towns and the coastlines that we could expect to see. On the coastline, it did not differentiate between high and low tide which meant that, at low tide, the shape of a headland could be completely changed. As far as the shape of towns was concerned, it did not really help at all. All that really mattered was the relative size of the town. What you had to do was associate the bigger blobs with the smaller ones and try and fix up a pattern as you saw it on the radar screen. You could often get a fix short of the Ruhr on towns ten or fifteen miles away and by means of triangulation you could establish pretty exactly where you were.'[67]

One of the themes of the air war between the RAF and the Luftwaffe was that every technological advance was almost invariably followed by a counter-measure. So it was with H2S. The fears of the Air Ministry were realized in early 1943 when two H2S-equipped Pathfinder bombers were shot down over Germany. On examining the captured sets, the Germans were at first amazed at the RAF's ingenuity, but then they turned the discovery to their advantage, developing their own Naxos system which could home in on the H2S signal, thereby revealing a bomber's position. At its best, Naxos had a huge range and could sometimes even detect the bombers warming up in England. But it was also fragile and prone to breakdowns. In an attempt to counter the Germans' tracking devices, the RAF came up with their own technology which could warn a crew of German attacks. The first such development was called Boozer, which could detect the radar signals given out either by the night fighters or the predicted flak guns. If a Lichtenstein-equipped enemy fighter was approaching, a red light would flash in the pilot's cockpit. If the bomber was being tracked by a radar-controlled battery on the ground, then Boozer illuminated an orange light. In both cases, the pilot was meant to have the chance to take evasive action before the enemy opened fire. But the problems with Boozer were that it could easily be swamped by the German Naxos and it could not detect any fighters that were not using airborne radar.

A more successful British innovation was Monica, an active radar that used an aerial in the tail of the rear turret and transmitted a signal for a range of about 1,000 yards in a 45-degree cone. Any plane that came within this radar cone would reveal its presence to the pilot and the rear gunner by a series of bleeps in their headphones. Having seen the device under development in 1942, Harris was immediately enthusiastic and pushed the government to order 2,000 Monica sets. When one of the government's scientific advisers, Sir Henry Tizard, warned that Monica might be bleeping all the time because it could not distinguish between friend and foe, Harris replied: 'The necessity for Monica is that it is not humanly possible for rear gunners to remain constantly on the qui vive [to be alert] throughout a long operation. That does not mean they cannot constantly come to attention and investigate a Monica alarm be it caused by friend or foe. I regard Monica as being a first essential in the reduction of the casualty rate amongst the night bombers.'[68] Inevitably there were delays about the installation of the 2,000 sets, which was carried out by Avro and Armstrong Whitworth in Coventry, and throughout the spring Harris badgered MAP to speed up the programme. In June he was told that the first Lancasters with Monica would arrive from Armstrong Whitworth in July, news that prompted the sardonic comment to Freeman: 'Always late and often never with that firm.'[69] But Monica did not live up to Harris's expectations because, all too predictably, the Germans came up with their own night-fighter device, Flensburg, which could home in on Monica signals. Meant as a means of protection, Monica had been turned into a tool for the enemy.

Apart from developments in technology and the expansion in Lancaster numbers, Harris kept trying to improve his bomber force in other ways. One was by making sure that all his group commanders fully subscribed to the policy of area bombing. Aggressively independent himself, he could brook no independence in any subordinates. In a dramatic instance of this trait, he sacked the Commander of the Lancaster-led No. 5 Group, Sir Alec Coryton, in February 1943 after the two of them had clashed over the conduct of the German raids. Coryton felt that Harris was taking too many risks with the lives of airmen. Harris believed Coryton had demonstrated neither sufficient respect for his authority nor sufficient ruthlessness in the use of the Lancasters. In his letter summarily removing Coryton from his post, Harris wrote: 'I am not prepared to bear further the perpetual and persistent disputes which have characterised your relations with my operational staff.' The next passage encapsulated Harris's whole outlook, mixing personal toughness with a recognition of the barbarity of war.

'You are soft-hearted. You cannot bear the thought of casualties to your crews. But you have no monopoly in this. I only hope that you may never have on your head and on your conscience the load that lies on mine.'[70] Coryton's place was taken by Ralph Cochrane, the former head of No. 3 Group, who combined an aristocratic Scottish background and a distant manner with uncompromising resolution and efficiency. Harris was far more in tune with chiefs like Cochrane and Don Bennett, leader of the Pathfinders, who shared his ferocious determination to keep pounding Germany harder, whatever the cost. Indeed, in his endless quest for improvement, Bennett could be extraordinarily harsh about the abilities of the airmen in Bomber Command. Reviewing the work of the Pathfinder Force during its first nine months of operations, Bennett told Harris: 'The term "operational accuracy" is a smug expression used by all-too-many of the so-called "experienced crews". These so-called experienced crews are those brilliant young men who, before the days of the PFF, were perfectly happy and satisfied that all was well when they were getting 3% of the bombs on the built up area. They are the curse of Bomber Command.' Bennett felt that 'the entire aircrews' of Bomber Command 'should be given a mental "kick in the pants" of the severest order' and, in particular 'the experienced ones should be made to realize the extent of their inability in the business of night bombing'.[71]

The remorseless focus of Bennett and Harris on sharpening the bomber offensive was also reflected at this time in their joint fury over an article that appeared in the official RAF magazine *Tee Em* in February 1943. Against all the advice that was instilled in the bomber pilots about flying straight and level during the bombing run, this piece advocated '90 degree turns' as the way to avoid predicted flak.[72] Bennett sent a copy to Harris with the words: 'The attached article might well be regarded as an attempt to sabotage our bombing offensive.'[73] Harris then took up the matter with the Air Member for Training, Guy Garrod, telling him that the article had to be 'fundamentally repudiated' and adding that he could 'imagine no better method of ensuring that no bomb ever hits its objective than by executing the idiotic antics recommended'.[74] Garrod's solution was for Bennett to write a response, explaining the correct methods to use. Bennett agreed. His subsequent article stressed it was useless having 'the best aircraft in the world, carrying enormous bombloads', if crews just 'flung away their bombs uselessly' once they got to the target. The suggestions about making violent turns on the bombing run were not just counterproductive but physically 'impossible', he argued, so the only way to hit the target was to 'reduce our evasive action to the bounds of sanity. However strong the urge, captains must restrain themselves. They must do their jobs.'[75] Though he agreed with the words, this right of reply was not good enough for Harris, who instituted a temporary ban on *Tee Em* from all bomber stations.

From March 1943, the men of Bomber Command needed all their perseverance. The offensive now reached a new level of intensity through an unremitting concentration on Germany's industrial heartland of the Ruhr valley. This pounding attack became known as the 'Battle of the Ruhr' and its weight demonstrated the growing confidence, numbers and sophistication of Bomber Command. At the beginning of March, Harris now had a daily front-line operational force of around 300 medium and 660 heavy bombers, of which a third were Lancasters. The Battle started on the night of 5–6 March, when 394 heavy bombers carried out an assault on the mighty Krupps engineering works in the heart of Essen in western Germany. In a tactical approach that was to set the pattern for the heavy-bomber offensive into 1944, the raid was led by Oboe-equipped Mosquitoes of the Pathfinder Force, which laid down yellow markers on the approach to the target, and then dropped red flares on the aiming point itself at the centre of the Krupps complex. The aiming point was further highlighted by green target indicators left by the backers-up from the PFF. The main force now followed up, with the 145 Lancasters making up the last wave of the bomber stream. Demonstrating their awesome capacity, they dropped 88 4,000-pound cookies, 470 1,000-pounders, 713 general-purpose 500-pounders and 804 cannisters of 4-pound incendiaries. Despite some incidence of creepback, the attack on Essen was regarded as an enormous success. Photographic reconnaissance showed that 50 per cent of bombs had landed within a mile of the aiming point, a huge improvement on the figures in the Butt report, and 15 per cent of the Lancasters had hit the aiming point itself. A full 160 acres of the town were wiped out, 700 houses destroyed and 30 per cent of the Krupps works badly damaged.[76] Harris could not conceal his exultation at the devastation. 'It will in due course take precedence as the greatest victory yet achieved on any front,' he said in a telegram of congratulations to his groups. 'You have set a fire in the belly of Germany which will burn the very black heart out of Nazidom and wither its grasping limbs at the very roots. Such attacks which will continue to a crescendo will progressively make it more and more impossible for the enemy to further his aggressions or hold where he now stands.'[77]

Even the German High Command was shaken. Josef Goebbels, who in 1940 had ordered the creation of false fires in Berlin to exaggerate for propaganda purposes the RAF bombing threat, now found that enemy havoc had become a terrifying reality, as he recorded in his diary. 'For months the working population has had to go out into air-raid shelters night after night, and when they come out again they see part of their city going up in flames and smoke. The enervating thing about it is that we are not in a position to reply to the English. Our war in the East has lost us air supremacy in essential sections of Europe and we are completely at the mercy of the English.'[78] A visit to the remains of the Krupps works shocked Goebbels. 'The city of Krupps has been hard hit. The number of dead, too, is considerable. If the English continue their raids on this scale, they will make things exceedingly difficult for us. The dangerous thing about this matter, looking at it psychologically, is the fact that the population can see no way of doing anything about it.'[79]

Bomber Command did continue on this scale against the Ruhr. Three further heavy attacks followed in the week after the first big raid on Essen. In April the offensive moved to another level, thanks to the increasing numbers of planes coming off the production line. For the first time, the number of Lancasters employed on an assault passed 200, the largest being the 215 that took part in the attack on Duisburg in western Germany on the night of 26–27 April. In May the total number of Lancasters on some raids reached over 300, with 343 attacking Dortmund, western Germany, on the night of 23–24 May for just 8 losses, a reflection of how the mix of technology and tactics was currently overwhelming the Germans. By now the Lancasters were not just the predominant element of Bomber Command attacks, they were also becoming the premier heavy bomber in the Pathfinder Force, superseding the Halifax and Stirling. On the Dortmund raid, three Lancaster Pathfinder squadrons, 83, 97 and 156, took part for the first time, and the quality of the marking was highly praised by the crews. Two nights later, another massive raid took place involving over 300 Lancasters, this time flying to Düsseldorf. Lancaster engineer Norman Ashton was one of those who took part: 'The effect of that first glimpse of a town undergoing the agony of a saturation raid was shattering. The fierce red glow of bursting bombs, the white shimmer of incendiaries, the brilliant glare of the target indicators, the blinding flashes of the photo flares, and the whole witches' cauldron of fire and belching smoke was like all hell let loose. My mind was bludgeoned by the impact of it all.' But his plane made a good run-up and dropped the bombs on the target. 'The aircraft shuddered as the bombs left the racks. Bill [the navigator] gave us a course and we turned for home.'[80]

Again there were only nine Lancasters lost on that Düsseldorf raid, a casualty rate of 2.7 per cent, far less than the normal Bomber Command average of 5 per cent and reinforcing Harris's point about the plane's effectiveness compared to the other heavy bombers. But it should not be thought that these raids were in any way straightforward for the Lancaster. Because of its economic importance, the Ruhr was the most heavily defended area of the Reich. Even if the German night fighters were not yet available in either the dangerous numbers or quality that they would be later in the year, the flak was still intimidating and dangerous. For navigator Peter Baker: 'The Ruhr was one of the worst targets. You were flying over enemy territory from the coast and there were searchlights and fighters and so you had a fairly hectic couple of hours' run in over this part of the country to the target. Once you got over the target it was even worse. The flak was intense, the searchlights and fighter activity was intense. In fact, as you ran up to the target, at times you wondered how you'd ever get there, far less get back.'[81]

The experience of being coned over the Ruhr was described by Peter Johnson, a pilot with 101 Squadron, who took part in a 292-strong Lancaster raid on Wuppertal at the end of May:

> One or two searchlights picked us up, then they all joined in from all over the sky. I couldn't see a thing, it was so bright. I just let my seat down and dived and weaved in and out. It wasn't a question of diving towards the lights because I didn't know where they were coming from. The only thing I could do was to check my instruments to make sure I wasn't upside down or whatever. I could smell the bursting flak. We were terrified. We bombed at 14,500 feet instead of 20,000 and we had to climb to get there because we'd dived to get out of the lights. Afterwards the navigator's log book showed we'd been coned for eight minutes. We'd been peppered, the Heywood compressor [a pump for the pneumatic system] was damaged and a piece of canopy disappeared from flak. All the maps were blown off the navigator's chart table by the draught and ended up at the back of the Elsan. We had to find our way home by the Pole Star, leaving it always on my right so that we knew we were heading west. When we got back we had no brakes because of the compressor damage.[82]

James Arnold, a wireless operator with 49 Squadron, was more unlucky when he was hit by fighters during a raid on the industrial centre of Oberhausen in June. Both starboard engines were knocked out and the plane rapidly began to lose height. 'We didn't have much power and to maintain height I was throwing extinguishers and everything I could out of the escape hatch.' The plane was too low for him to bail out. 'Suddenly

I heard this swishing sound and it was us going over the top of some woods at Oosterbeek near Arnhem. I came to outside the aircraft, which was going up in flames with a terrible noise. In my confused state, I tried to get back in for safety, but it was too high.' Arnold knew that few of his comrades could have survived. He limped to a nearby farm but was soon picked up by the Germans.[83]

The Oberhausen raid was one of the last of the Ruhr campaign, before Bomber Command turned to preparations for an even bigger battle over Germany. Overall, the RAF had flown 43 major operations over targets in the Ruhr, with 18,506 aircraft dispatched at a loss rate of 4.7 per cent. Within the context of the area-bombing strategy, the raids could be seen as a success in terms of civilian and industrial devastation. About 21,000 Germans were killed, and large swathes of cities like Wuppertal and Duisburg were reduced to ruins. Harris called the battle 'an impressive victory', and there was no doubt that the realities of war had been brought home to millions of Germans for the first time. Various German newspapers at the time testified to the deepening anxiety within the Reich. 'No one will deny that the nervous strain is tremendous, particularly for those in western districts, and it often approaches the limits of endurance,' reported the *Kelnische Zeitung* on 10 March 1943, while the *Bremer Nachrichten* admitted that an air attack meant 'an incomparably greater nerve strain than heavy fighting at the front'. Beyond the Reich, Josef Stalin expressed his pleasure that Churchill's promise of an aerial second front was starting to be fulfilled. 'Every blow delivered by your Air Force to the vital German centres evokes a most lively echo in the hearts of many millions throughout the length and breadth of our country,' he wrote in a telegram to Harris after another raid on Essen at the end of April.[84]

But by far the most spectacular raid of the Ruhr campaign was also one of the smallest. And it was an attack that would secure the name of the Lancaster in history.

IO

'What the hell do you damned inventors want?'

~~~

THE IMAGE OF Wing Commander Guy Gibson, VC, DSO, DFC was forever cemented in the public imagination by the performance of Richard Todd in the 1955 film *The Dam Busters*. Dashing, courageous, modest and unflinching, Todd's Gibson was the epitome of the gallant RAF officer: the resolute stiffness on his upper lip, the warmth of patriotism and comradeship in his generous heart. Todd was able to bring such conviction to the role because not only was he a fine actor but also he had a valiant war record himself, having served as an officer in the King's Own Yorkshire Light Infantry and as a paratrooper at D-Day on 6 June 1944. And his portrayal of Gibson was no piece of nostalgic myth-making. Gibson was a truly heroic figure, with almost superhuman bravery, diligence and skills as a pilot. When Harris wanted him to take command of a Lancaster squadron in early 1942, he wrote to Sir John Slessor, then Head of No. 5 Group: 'He was without exception the most full out fighting pilot in the whole of 5 Group in the days when I had it. Not content with doing more operational flying than anybody else, he used to go out on additional nights just for fun . . . You will find him absolutely first-class.'[1]

By March 1943, as the preparations for the famous raid on the dams in the Ruhr valley began, Gibson had flown an astonishing 173 operational sorties in a variety of aircraft, including the Lancaster and a number of fighters. In the same month, the citation for his award of a bar to his DSO spoke of 'his outstanding determination to make every sortie a success. By his skilled leadership and contempt for danger he has set an example which has inspired the squadron he commands.'[2] Despite his diminutive 5'6" stature, which meant that he was rejected by the RAF for being too short when he first applied, Gibson exuded charisma and natural leadership, as was shown in the physical description of him by his great friend and fellow Lancaster pilot David Shannon: 'The stance is aggressive – legs, knees and calves well braced, hands in trouser pockets or folded across the chest. The facial expression appears mildly pugnacious, with the lower jaw pushed forward and teeth clamped. But the clear eyes are a give-away, ever ready to break into a grin.'[3] Even during the war, he was by far the most famous pilot in England, his youthful face constantly in the press, his celebrity exploited by politicians and RAF chiefs for propaganda campaigns.

Yet Gibson was a far more complex personality than the iconography suggested. For all the public admiration he inspired, he was not universally popular within the RAF. Whereas Shannon called him 'a fantastic character, one of the finest leaders I have ever met',[4] others found him arrogant, opinionated and often rude. He was a stickler for petty rules, showed little concern for the ground crews and could be contemptuous of those he did not regard as his equals. On one occasion he reacted with fury after an RAF messenger failed to respond with sufficient swiftness to his summons. When he demanded an explanation from this messenger, whom he mistakenly called 'George', the man replied, 'My name's not George.' This only heightened Gibson's anger: 'If I call you bloody George, you are George.'[5] Some of Gibson's perceived impatience could be put down to his perfectionism, for in every squadron he set a painfully high standard and knew that discipline was one of the keys to survival. Strong-willed himself, he could not tolerate any hint of weakness in others. When the Gee set on one of his squadron's Lancasters blew up shortly before take-off, Gibson simply told the crew: 'You've got four good engines, you'll bloody well go and bomb Germany.'[6] Larry Curtis, a wireless operator with 617 Squadron, said: 'You could not help but be impressed by the tremendous record that the man had. I found him likeable, hard but very just. You could not really ask for anything more than that. If he asked you to do something, you did it. He had a hard manner, that of a real professional airman.'[7]

But, for all Gibson's disciplinarian tendencies, he could also be volatile and was prone to savage migraine headaches. He suffered violent mood swings, often plunging from euphoria into depression. Despite the enormous responsibilities he shouldered, he could be curiously naive about anything outside flying. His devotion to operations almost amounted to an addiction. According to one of his biographers, Richard Morris, he had a death wish and never believed that he would survive the war. This toughest of officers once broke down in tears in the arms of a girlfriend, overwhelmed by the exhausting butchery of war. Indeed, his relationships with women reflected some of the awkwardness and self-absorption of his character. His marriage to former actress Evelyn Moore descended into permanent emotional conflict, and after his death in 1944 she complained that she 'never really knew him. He kept his innermost thoughts to himself. His first love was the Air Force and he was married to whatever aircraft he happened to be flying at the time. I only came second.'[8]

Gibson's traits of isolation, self-will and inner turmoil stemmed partly from his unorthodox background. It is an intriguing fact that, like Sir Arthur Harris, he was born into an imperial civil service family, for his father, Alexander Gibson, was a government engineer in India, where Guy was born in 1918. But again, just as with Harris, there was nothing comforting about this superficially privileged upbringing. His parents' marriage was deeply unhappy and in 1924 they separated, Nora Gibson returning to England with the children. Guy was sent to a succession of boarding schools, the last of which, St Edward's in Oxford, was also the alma mater of Douglas Bader, the renowned legless fighter pilot. On leaving school, Guy was determined to join the RAF and, with typical persistence, he was finally accepted in 1936 after his initial rejection. As he forged ahead in his air force career, his mother's life fell apart after the split from her husband. She sank into chronic alcoholism and promiscuity, becoming such an embarrassment to Guy that he refused to have any contact with her. Her end was tragic. In November 1939, after another spell in a sanatorium in an attempt to conquer her drink problem, she took up residence in a boarding house in Kensington. There she accidentally set fire to herself, dying from her burns a few weeks later. She was only forty-six. Gibson refused to attend her funeral.

In his three years of RAF service until 1939, Gibson had given little inkling of the brilliance that was to come. Some of his commanders even described him as nothing more than an ordinary pilot. But the onset of war brought out the best in him, as he demonstrated his incredible fearlessness in the face of the enemy. He served first in Bomber Command, flying 37 sorties in Handley Page Hampdens and winning the DFC, then moved on to Bristol Beaufighters, in which role he won a bar to his DFC. He also gained a reputation as a womanizer, despite his marriage to Evelyn in November 1940. According to RAF rumours, 'he spent more time in bed with other chaps' wives that he ever did in the air'.[9] After a frustrating spell as an instructor once his night fighter tour was finished, he was rescued by Harris, who put him in charge of 106 Lancaster Squadron based at Coningsby. He was there for eleven months, during which time he pushed his squadron to new levels of efficiency. Edward Johnson, a bomb aimer with 106 Squadron, recalled Gibson's leadership: 'He wasn't a bully or a show-off but he liked things to be done right and he also liked you to keep fit (sometimes a sore point) with runs round the aerodrome and so on. After a night out on the tiles these weren't frightfully popular – but I think he was on the right lines. He was strict about work, but he was a great mixer – not so much during the working day but always at night – he could sup his ale with anybody.'[10] Gibson's exceptional leadership meant that in early 1943, when the Air Staff were first considering the daring raid on the dams in the Ruhr valley, he was the obvious choice to head the operation. On him would lie the responsibility for organizing the most incredible feat of low-level precision bombing ever seen in aviation history.

It was the Lancaster, with its immense lift capacity and unrivalled manoeuvrability, that made the Dambusters raid possible. As long ago as 1937, the Air Ministry had recognized the strategic importance of the large dams in western Germany which provided the water supplies for the Ruhr industry, generated hydroelectric power and protected against flooding. On the list of targets drawn up by the Ministry were three of the biggest dams: the Mohne, constructed in 1913 with a 2,133-foot-long curved wall of granite masonry blocks, holding 176 million cubic yards of water in its reservoir; the Eder, built between 1908 and 1914, its reservoir containing 264 million cubic yards of water; and the Sorpe, opened in 1935, the smallest in capacity at 94 million cubic yards but the one with the biggest, most solid wall, a vast 226-foot-high earthen embankment built around an inner concrete core. If this trio of dams could be breached, argued the Ministry, then devastation of almost Biblical proportions could be inflicted on German life, from the breakdown of industry to the destruction of the transport system. The problem was how. In the late 1930s no conventional bomb dropped on such a structure would do much more than chip at a parapet even if it scored a direct hit. In any case, from overhead, the target would be far too narrow to be attacked with any hope of accuracy. Nor were torpedoes any use. They were rendered impracticable by heavy nets drawn across the front of each dam.

But there was a scientist working on a solution. Just as Guy Gibson almost seemed like the archetypal RAF officer, so Dr Barnes Wallis lived up to the classic image of the other-worldly inventor. Shy, white-haired, somewhat eccentric, he brought a highly original, probing intellect to aeronautical engineering in his role as the assistant chief designer at Vickers Aviation. It was Wallis who had pioneered the R100 airship and, using this technology, developed the geodetic construction method for the Wellington, whereby a lattice structure of metal beams on the fuselage provided the bomber with strength, durability and lightness, though the fabric covering and the complexity of manufacturing meant that the geodetic process had little long-term potential in production. A unique insight into Wallis's character and methods can be found in a taped interview with Norman Boorer, a draughtsman who worked alongside him at Vickers at Weybridge, Surrey, and assisted in the work on the Dambusters:

> He was a good engineer, who insisted on quality in his work. He reckoned he could do anything he wanted to do if he gave enough thought to it, provided he did not upset any basic laws of physics. He did not let problems stand in his way. He could not abide criticism. He knew what he wanted and there were some senior figures who became his enemies pretty quickly because they were apt to criticize or tell him he should be doing something different. It was difficult working with him. You had to have a tremendous amount of patience. He could be a very cheerful, pleasant and thoughtful man at certain times, but at other times, he could be very awkward.[11]

But Wallis was not a reclusive loner. Happily married, he had a family of four children, to which he and his wife good-heartedly added two orphaned nephews from 1940. 'Always working, often abstracted, he was frequently absent from the daily round of chat, laughter and games which large families enjoy,' his daughter Mary recalled. 'But when he did join in, it was lively and great fun. Even in the darkest days, he would burst into cheerful, spontaneously made-up doggerel verse.'[12]

Brimming with innovations, Wallis began thinking from late 1940 about ways to breach the dams with airborne weapons. One of his first ideas was the use of a 10-ton 'earthquake' bomb which, if dropped into the reservoir within 150 feet of the dam wall, could crack the structure. Since there was no bomber that could carry such a load, Wallis proposed designing his own six-engined plane, called the Victory. But this proposal failed to win the approval of the military planners, who decided it was an extravagant diversion from the real war effort. Wallis had to come up with an alternative. He was fortunate that just at this moment other dam-breaching tests were being conducted by a team headed by A. R. Collins, an expert in concrete engineering at the Road Research Laboratory. In a series of experiments using dam models, Collins found that the destructive effect of an underwater explosion was far greater if the bomb were in direct contact with the wall so the water did not absorb the shock waves from the blast. This discovery meant that, in theory, it would be feasible to use a much lighter bomb, one that could be carried by the current generation of RAF aircraft. The crucial question was how such a bomb could be dropped against the structure beyond the torpedo netting booms before sinking below the surface.

Aware of Barnes Wallis's work, the government put him in contact with Collins and the two men exchanged their analyses of the dams project. With characteristic ingenuity, Wallis came up with the concept of a spherical bomb which could be released with mechanically-induced backspin at a low level by an attacking aircraft about 500 feet from the target. Like a stone flicked over water, the backspin would make the bomb bounce several times until it reached the dam wall, and would then, in accordance with Collins's findings, be detonated at a predetermined height by a hydrostatic fuse. According to Norman Boorer, the theory of backspin was inspired both by Wallis's interest in naval history, when he found that Horatio Nelson's ships used to try skimming their cannon balls off the water into the enemy, and by his design colleague George Edwards's interest in cricket:

> Wallis had studied old naval cannonball techniques, where the bomb was fired on a low trajectory and bounced, giving it more range. In his experimental work, he also found that backspin would allow it to bounce two or three more times. George Edwards, who was working closely with Wallis, was a very good cricketer – he could probably have been a county cricketer if he had not been a designer. He was a fine spin bowler and he explained that if you spin it backwards it will shoot and if you spin it forwards it will dig in. There was the other point that when the bomb hit the dam, if it were spinning backwards, it would hug the face and roll down, whereas if it were spinning forwards there was a chance it would climb up over the top of the dam.[13]

Energized by the support of Collins, Wallis constantly experimented on bombing trajectories at his Surrey home, an old washtub, a catapult and a set of children's marbles serving as his equipment. 'We gathered round the elderly galvanised washtub, filled to the brim,' recalled Wallis's daughter Mary, 'and helped my father shoot marbles from a large wooden catapult over the surface of the water, measuring the hops. "Playing marbles" became my mother's explanation for his incessant activity in the following months.'[14]

In May 1942 Wallis presented a paper with his proposal for a bouncing bomb to the government's scientific advisers, Sir Henry Tizard, then Chairman of the Aeronautical Research Committee, and Professor Patrick Blackett, the eminent physicist based at Manchester University. They were both so impressed that they authorized trials to be conducted at the National Physical Laboratory at Teddington, using scale models of the bomb fired by catapult across the water of a 640-foot ship tank. Held between June and September 1942, these tests attracted the interest of the top brass at both the Air Ministry and the Admiralty, who saw the potential in attacking enemy ships, particularly the *Tirpitz*, with the revolutionary torpedo. Further confirmation that the bouncing bomb was a practical proposition came when Wallis and Collins embarked on even bigger experiments in August at the disused Nant-y-Gro dam near Ryader in mid-Wales. Employing a 500-pound mine suspended from a scaffold, they found that the explosive charge, detonated at 30 feet below the surface, punched a hole in the dam's wall. On this basis Wallis and Collins estimated that a Torpex bomb, weighing about 6,000 pounds and placed in the right spot, would be enough to smash through the Mohne dam. The transport of such a weapon was easily within the capability of the Lancaster.

The time had arrived for airborne tests. Six half-size prototype mines were built of varying surfaces and material: smooth, ribbed and wood. Meanwhile a Wellington bomber was fitted with a special spinning apparatus in its fuselage, the mechanism having first been tested on the ground for stability. The first trial took place on 4 December 1942, when the modified Wellington, flown by Vickers's chief test pilot Joseph 'Mutt' Summers, took off from the Dorset airfield of Warmwell and headed for the coast at Chesil Beach. Lying on his front in the bomb aimer's position in the nose was Barnes Wallis, ready to press the tit at the right moment. He later described the experience as 'rather exciting',[15] but the result was disappointing as the experimental bomb shattered on impact with the water. Wallis ordered the casing to be strengthened, but the outcome of a second trial on 12 December was little better, with neither of the two prototype mines bouncing. Renewed trials at the start of 1943 with different bomb casings continued to be plagued by failures, yet Wallis remained undaunted, certain that his idea was viable. Finally, success came on 23 January when the Wellington, flying at 283 mph and an altitude of just 42 feet, released the wooden-clad spherical bomb revolving at 485 rpm. It bounced 13 times. Further tests were even more fruitful, one prototype bouncing no fewer than 22 times, another reaching a distance of 1,315 yards. After this breakthrough, Wallis was more determined than ever to secure agreement for the full-scale development of the bouncing bomb, two versions of which he was now planning: a large one, code-named 'Upkeep', to be delivered by a modified Lancaster against the dams, and a smaller one, called 'Highball', to be dropped by a Mosquito against German ships.

Armed with film footage from Chesil Beach and Teddington, as well as detailed reports from all the trials, Wallis engaged in a frenetic round of meetings, conferences and phone calls to win over the top politicians and military. The quest was governed by a sense of mounting urgency, for RAF Intelligence reported that the water levels in the reservoirs of the upper Ruhr would be at their peak in mid-May as a result of the winter and spring rains. The date of 26 May was deemed by the RAF to be the last possible day on which an effective mission could take place before the water level began to fall. Failure to act by this looming deadline would mean either postponement for months or even the abandonment of the whole project. Wallis, who had already shown remarkable assiduity in advancing the scheme, told the Air Staff on 5 February that if his plan were approved 'we could develop a large sphere to be dropped from a Lancaster bomber within a period of two months'. He also downplayed the extent to which Lancasters would be diverted from the main bomber offensive. By employing a detachable rig for carrying Upkeep, modifications to the Lancaster, he promised, would be 'small and the aircraft can be restored to their original use after having achieved this particular object in a few days'.[16] But most voices within the Air establishment were sceptical. Some said the Chesil Beach tests provided no hard evidence that a real bomb could work against a German dam of the size of the Mohne. Others argued that the timetable for production of the bombs was simply impractical. There was also concern about putting another burden on Roy Chadwick and Avro when the Lancaster programme was already under intense pressure as a result of the Casablanca directive.

It was perhaps inevitable that the fiercest critic of the whole idea was Arthur Harris, filled with his scathing disdain for so-called 'panacea targets' and anything that took his beloved Lancasters away from the job of pounding the German cities. 'If I could send 1000 bombers to Germany every night, it would end the war by the autumn,' he told the *Daily Express* at this time.[17] On 14 February, having attended an Air Ministry meeting on the project, Robert Saundby, Bomber Command's Senior Air Staff Officer, gave Harris a written outline of Wallis's plans for Highball and Upkeep, explaining that in the latter case 'a special modified Lancaster' would be used to deliver a 10,000-pound mine at one of the Ruhr dams, and adding that one squadron would have to be nominated for the task. In a livid handwritten response, Harris called the proposal 'tripe of the wildest description. There are so many ifs and buts that there is not the smallest chance of its working.' He urged that every effort be made to stop the Air Staff 'putting aside Lancasters and reducing our effort on this wild goose chase'. The war, wrote Harris, 'will be over before it works & it never will'.[18]

But Harris's view was becoming a minority one. The extraordinary persistence shown by Wallis had started to win round official opinion, as the scepticism of earlier in the month was replaced by mounting enthusiasm. Harris was appalled when he learnt of the growth in support for Wallis's bouncing bomb. On 18 February, he sent off another of his thunderous letters to Portal, though he seemed unable to grasp the difference between the maritime Highball and dam-busting Upkeep:

> All sorts of enthusiasts and panacea-mongers are now careering round MAP suggesting the taking of about 30 Lancasters off the line to rig them up for this weapon, when the weapon itself exists so far only within the imaginations of those who conceived it. I cannot too strongly deprecate any diversion of Lancasters at this critical moment in our affairs on the assumption that some entirely new weapon, totally untried, is going to be a success. With some slight practical knowledge and many previous bitter experiences on similar lines, I am prepared to bet that the Highball is just about the maddest proposition as a weapon that we have yet come across – and that is saying something. The job of rotating some 1200 pounds [Harris missed out a zero] of material at 500 rpm on an aircraft is in itself fraught with difficulty. The slightest loss of balance will just tear the aircraft to pieces and in the packing of the explosive, let alone in retaining it packed in balance during rotation, are obvious technical difficulties. I am prepared to bet my shirt: a) that the weapon itself cannot be passed as a prototype for trial inside six months; b) that its ballistics will in no way resemble those claimed for it; c) that it will be impossible to keep such a weapon in balance either when rotating it prior to release or at all in storage; d) that it will not work when we have got it . . . Lancasters make the greatest contribution to our bomber offensive, which we have to carry on so continuously against such great odds. The heaviest of these odds arises from the continual attempts to ruin Lancasters for some specialist purpose or to take them away for others to use.[19]

In his reply, Portal explained that all the Air Staff had agreed so far was that three Lancasters be prepared for the Upkeep modifications. He accepted that the bouncing bomb 'may come to nothing' but it was worth conducting a trial in the Lancaster to see if it could work. 'I can assure you that I will not allow more than three of your precious Lancasters to be diverted for this purpose until the full scale experiments have shown that the bomb will do what is claimed for it. I shall ask for the necessary conversion sets to be manufactured but there will be no further interruption of supply of Lancasters to you until it is known that the difficulties to which you refer have actually been overcome.'[20] Thankfully, for the sake of the Dambusters, Portal did not fulfil this pledge of giving only limited support to the scheme.

Soon after this exchange, Barnes Wallis called on Harris at Bomber Command Headquarters in High Wycombe as part of his continuing campaign to win backing for Upkeep. He found Harris as hostile as ever. 'What the hell do you damned inventors want? My boys' lives are too precious to be thrown away by you.'[21] Still mistakenly focusing on Highball, the naval bomb, he railed at the pointlessness of attacking German shipping. Even after watching the film of the experiments at Chesil Beach and hearing Wallis's explanation of how Upkeep could destroy the Mohne, he refused to give any indication that he would change his mind. But, largely due to the influence of Portal, who told colleagues he wanted to see 'every endeavour' in preparing the Lancasters,[22] the tide was now running swiftly against Harris.

On 26 February a crucial conference was held at the Ministry of Aircraft Production to discuss Upkeep. In addition to representatives of MAP and the Air Staff, among the others present were Wallis, Sir Charles Craven of Vickers and Roy Chadwick, who had been given little information about Upkeep but was never one to quail at a challenge. Chadwick was asked directly at the meeting if he would be able to modify the Lancasters by the extremely tight deadline of 26 May, when the reservoirs would be at their fullest for the last time before the autumn. With barely a moment's hesitation, Chadwick said: 'Yes, we will do it, if Vickers take the responsibility for the attachment arms and the driving mechanisms of the mines.'[23] Wallis looked relieved. Later he wrote to Chadwick: 'If at that fateful meeting on 26th February you had declared the task impossible to fulfil in the given time, the powers of opposition were so great that I should never have got the instructions to go ahead. Possibly you did not realize how much hung on your instantaneous reaction, but I can assure you that I nearly had heart failure until you decided to join the great adventure.'[24] Sir Charles Craven, on behalf of Vickers, agreed to the demarcation, with his engineering group instructed to manufacture the Upkeep apparatus and the mine itself, while Avro would make all the necessary alterations to the plane. As to the numbers, the meeting decided that three full Lancaster Upkeep prototypes would be produced as soon as possible, and 27 more aircraft would be equipped before the May deadline. The Dams raid was on. Upkeep was to be given the highest priority. After all his exertions over the last year, Wallis later confessed after the conference he felt 'physically sick because somebody had actually called my bluff' and he realized he had such a short time 'for making good all my claims'.[25]

The RAF now had an absolute maximum of three months to prepare for its audacious mission, which was given the code name of Operation Chastise. There were two strands to the preparations: the technical, and the operational. In his drive to win support, Wallis had deliberately under-stated the problems of modifying the Lancaster, even claiming that Upkeep could be carried in detachable cradles that could be fitted or removed in a couple of days. But the reality was very different. The apparatus required was far too complex and the necessary stability too demanding for such a primitive modification. Moreover, the full-size Upkeep bomb existed only as a sketchy paper plan and had never been tested. With his usual energy, Chadwick got to work immediately on the drawings for the dam-busting plane, which was officially called the Type 464 (Provisioning) Lancaster. Originally it was planned that most of the modi-fications would be carried out by an Avro team working at the Vickers base in Weybridge while the Upkeep apparatus was fitted, but it soon became clear that the scale of the task meant that this was impossible. The work was therefore transferred to the Avro plant at Woodford in Manchester, where Mark IIIs were taken off the production line at random and converted into Upkeep carriers. Doug Godfrey, an Avro fitter, described the mood in the workforce. 'We knew the Lancasters we started working on were for a special raid but didn't know what. We worked 12 hour shifts, seven days a week to get them ready. The atmosphere was exciting, electric.'[26]

The main changes to the standard Lancaster included a deeper bomb aimer's blister in the nose, the removal of the mid-upper gun turret to reduce the amount of drag, the replacement of bomb doors by front and rear fairings, and the installation of the V-shaped support brackets with pivots, built by Vickers, to hold Upkeep in place. The action of pressing the bomb-release tit opened the two arms and let the bomb fall out of their grip. On the starboard bracket there was a belt connected to a Vickers Janny variable-speed hydraulic motor, which was originally designed for the steering gear in submarines. This motor was situated in the forward bomb bay and kept Upkeep spinning at the necessary 500 rpm. When the Avro modifications were completed to the first Type 464 Lancaster, it was flown on 8 April to the Royal Aircraft Establishment at Farnborough for tests by Vickers on the carrying gear.

Since the vital conference of 26 February, Wallis had been working about ninety hours a week on all aspects of the project, including the bomb itself. His central base was, rather incongruously, the Burhill golf course in rural Surrey, to which the Research and Development team of Vickers had been dispersed after a heavy air raid on Weybridge in 1940. In fact, the beautiful Silvermere lake, between the 17th and 18th holes, was used for some of the early tests on the bouncing bomb in 1942. In a characteristically British example of wartime expediency, the squash court at Burhill was used as the Vickers drawing office, with a huge drawing board 20 feet long and 7 feet wide to accommodate the design of Upkeep. Vickers draughtsman Norman Boorer, who was intimately involved with Upkeep, recalled the intimidating nature of the ground tests on the spinning apparatus: 'A spinning bomb in an aircraft has a tremendous gyroscopic action. We had a big steel rig – I designed it – on which to test Upkeep. It was frightening, actually, watching this enormous great 78-inch ball spinning round at 500 revs on this rig. Had it come off, I am sure it would have ploughed through the hangar doors and on through the trees.'[27]

Boorer also incurred the wrath of Wallis during the tests of the carrying gear at Farnborough. He had designed the heavy wire sling which was meant to haul the sphere into the two calliper brackets, but on that crucial day in early April, the Vickers team found that the ends of the sling would not fit through the required spaces, as Boorer explained: 'I got a call from Barnes Wallis at Farnborough and he was as irate as anything. "I don't know what you're thinking of, Boorer, but we can't get that bomb into the bomb bay. Come over here immediately." So I got a car to take me to Farnborough. There they were trying to get the bomb from the trolley into the Lancaster for trials. "Look," he said, "there's your wire, there's the bomb bay. But the wire won't go up there." ' What had happened was that the manufacturers had ignored Boorer's careful design of the spliced ends of the wire, designed to go round 90 degrees, and instead had just fitted hard, standard catalogue items that had no flexibility. 'So you had a straight wire rope with two dirty great big stiff ends to it. And of course it was those two stiff ends that wouldn't go round the corner. I had designed it to be soft.

'Sorry, Mr Wallis,' I said, explaining that the fault lay in the manufacture.

'Well, what are you going to do about? We've got to get this bomb in the Lancaster today.'

'I'll go and find a sledgehammer.'

Which I did. I came back with the hammer and said, 'You'd better not look while I do this.' I got the sledgehammer and just belted these fittings and bent them, which is something you shouldn't do unless you properly heat-treat them. But it was an emergency. There was nothing else I could do. So I belted them round, and sure enough, we got the bomb into the bay.[28]

While Wallis and Chadwick were presiding over the technical side, Arthur Harris oversaw the organization of the force that would carry out Operation Chastise. Contrary to claims from his supporters, Harris did not always accept orders once they were clearly given. Throughout 1943 he blithely ignored the Pointblank Directive which was meant to prioritize attacks on German fighter forces and the aircraft industry. Even more graphically, from late 1944 he was in a position of near open mutiny against Portal over the direction of strategic bombing. But in this case he co-operated fully with the Air Staff once Operation Chastise was approved. He instructed Ralph Cochrane, the new commander of No. 5 Group, to create a new squadron especially for the mission, with Guy Gibson as its chief. Cochrane immediately summoned Gibson to 5 Group's headquarters in Grantham, Lincolnshire:

> 'How would you like the idea of doing one more trip?' he asked Gibson.
> 'What kind of a trip, sir?'
> 'A pretty important one, perhaps one of the most devastating of all time. I can't tell you any more about it now. Do you want to do it?'[29]

Gibson said he would. For the next few days he was given no information about either the target or the nature of the mission. His sole instruction was to start assembling his own special squadron, which was at first simply called Squadron X but was soon renamed No. 617.

Squadron X was to be based at Scampton in Lincolnshire, and it was here that Gibson started work on choosing his crews. Cochrane had given him a free hand in selection, a unique privilege for someone of Gibson's rank. The only stipulation, said Cochrane, was that he should pick 'the best'.[30] It later became part of Dambusters legend that 617 Squadron was entirely made up of brilliant veterans, a belief fuelled by Gibson's own claim in his autobiography: 'I had picked them all myself because from my personal knowledge I believed them to be the best bomber pilots available. I knew that each one of them had already done a full tour of duty.'[31] As historian John Sweetman pointed out in his excellent history of the raid, this was far from the case, for the sheer scale of organizing an entirely new squadron at short notice meant that Gibson had to be assisted by other officers at Scampton, including the station commander Charles Whitworth. 'Not all the pilots were personally known to Gibson.

Aircrew ages ranged from twenty to thirty-two. The majority were not decorated (including six of the pilots); and far from having finished two operational tours some had not done one. Many who would fly to the German dams in May 1943 had completed fewer than ten operations against enemy targets and some of the flight engineers were actually on their first.'[32]

Yet there could be no dispute about the high calibre of the 617 Squadron pilots who gathered at Scampton in the last weeks of March. The 21 came from all parts of the globe. The Englishmen included Old Etonian Henry Maudslay and the long-serving Melvin Young, who had read law at Oxford, rowed in the Boat Race, flown 65 sorties and acquired the nickname 'Dinghy' after he had once come down in the North Atlantic and spent 22 hours in his inflatable life raft. A particular favourite of Gibson's was John 'Hoppy' Hopgood, whom he described as a man of 'no nerves' and 'the best pilot in the squadron'.[33] From New Zealand came Les Munro, from America Joe McCarthy and from Canada Lewis Burpee. But it was the Australians who provided some of the most distinguished leaders. Among them were Gibson's close friend Dave Shannon and the devoutly Christian teetotaller Les Knight, who 'kept himself away from the coarser side of life' but 'could fly the ass off a Lancaster', according to his bomb aimer Edward Johnson.[34]

Above all there was Harold 'Micky' Martin, who along with Gibson and Leonard Cheshire was one of the three great bomber pilots of the war. Cheshire himself said of Martin: 'As an operational pilot I consider him greater than Gibson and indeed the greatest that the Air Force has ever produced. I have seen him do things that I, for one, would have never looked at.'[35] Like Gibson, Martin had a streak of fatalism, convinced that he would die on operations 'sometime'.[36] Born in Sydney in 1918, he was the son of doctor and, as a brilliant young horseman, enlisted in the Australian cavalry before serving on the crew of an ocean liner. When war broke out, he joined Bomber Command and quickly demonstrated his boldness and skill by flying at low level on sorties in defiance of all regulations. Despite official disapproval of his methods, he was awarded the DFC in 1942. The devotion that Martin could inspire was demonstrated by the testimony of Larry Curtis, who served with him as a wireless operator in 617 Squadron: 'It gives you an idea of the esteem in which I hold him that I named one of my sons after him. He was without doubt the best pilot that I ever flew with. He inspired confidence. I never worried, and I flew on most of his raids. I have been with Micky Martin – and Dave Shannon – where they have thrown Lancasters around like toys. They have landed in the most terrible weather conditions. They were just good pilots, natural flyers.'[37] Engine fitter John Elliott, who served as a ground crewman in 617 Squadron, had this memory of Martin: 'Some people may have said he was a daredevil, but I would say he was extremely efficient, especially in low flying. I saw him one day in a Lancaster fly between a control tower and a hangar. We were in the control tower and we were actually looking down on the top of his Lancaster as he flew through between us and the hangar. He could not have been more than twenty feet off the ground.'[38] But not everyone treated 617 Squadron or their own credentials with reverence. When Flight Sergeant Hughie Hewstone was told that his crew was 'the backbone' of the squadron, he replied: 'If we're the backbone, I reckon we're close to the arsehole.'[39]

Operation Chastise remained shrouded in mystery when the crews arrived at Scampton. The men were only told that they would soon have to undertake intensive low-level training in Lancasters. 'There was no inkling of what was going on. There were lots of rumours as to what the target might be,' said bomb aimer Edward Johnson, 'most of them more terrifying than it turned out to be in the end. One was that we would be going to the U-boat pens to toss bombs into their engines and blow them up internally since we did not seem to be doing much damage externally.'[40] But Gibson was partially let into the secret on 24 March, when he travelled down to the Burhill Golf Club to see Wallis. At first Wallis was rather nervous about explaining the Upkeep scheme, largely because an administrative oversight meant that Gibson had not yet been given complete security clearance, but he soon overcame such hesitations, though he never mentioned the target itself beyond saying that the mission would be over water. He showed Gibson the Chesil Beach and Teddington footage, and explained how the bouncing bomb would work. Gibson was amazed when he saw the film of the Wellington releasing the mine from 200 feet. 'I expected to see the aircraft blown sky high. But when it hit the water there was a great splash and then – it worked. That's all I can say to describe it – just that it worked, while the aircraft flew over serenely on its way.'[41] Throughout his talk Wallis emphasized the importance of the Lancaster. He told Gibson that he had been contemplating attacks on major structural installations for some years, but at first 'there wasn't an aeroplane with a high enough performance to carry the load at the required speed. Then along came the Lancaster bomber, and the problem was solved.' To modify the Lancaster for Operation Chastise, he explained, 'Avro's are doing a great rush job to get the special fittings put on. I believe they're working 24 hours-a-day.' Wallis then turned to Gibson and asked him if he could fulfil the requirements needed to make the attack successful, flying at roughly 240 mph at 150 feet above smooth water before releasing the bombs to an accuracy within a few yards. 'I said I thought it was a bit difficult but worth trying,' Gibson wrote in his account.[42]

The pace of preparations now began to speed up. Soon after his return from Burhill, Gibson took a Lancaster to the Derwent reservoir to try flying at the required height over water in darkness. It was even more dangerous than he feared, and he almost hit the surface on one run. Having survived, he was then summoned to see Cochrane, the clipped martinet who commanded No. 5 Group. Cochrane now gave Gibson the full details of the mission, showing him scale models and reconnaissance photographs of the Mohne and Sorpe dams. But Gibson could not pass any of this information on to his men. Using standard, unmodified Lancasters, they were instructed to practise flying in formations of three at 200 feet, and then, when they had become proficient at that, to go down to 150 feet. Many of the pilots found it exhilarating to be encouraged to fly so low, even if the altimeters on the Lancaster were unreliable at such a height, but for other members of the crew the experience could be more traumatic, as rear gunner Grant McDonald recalled. 'At that time Bomber Command had been attacking targets from higher and higher. We had all been stacked up at 20,000 feet and above. Suddenly it was low level and quite alarming in the rear turret, watching the ground go by so quickly. You heard a lot about people flying under high-tension wires and so on. Some aircraft suffered damage through hitting the tops of trees.'[43] While the crews undertook their training, the vital trials of Upkeep in the first modified Lancaster began at Reculver Bay on the north Kent coast. This spot, which was overlooked by a Norman abbey, had been chosen in preference to Chesil Beach, partly because it was more secluded and therefore offered more security, and partly because the two towers of the medieval church could serve as a useful aiming point.

On the morning of 13 April, the Vickers test pilot Maurice 'Shorty' Longbottom took off from the nearby RAF base of Manston and swept over the coast, his Lancaster carrying a mock-up sphere made from a compound of cement, cork and concrete enclosed in a metal drum within a wooden shell, and packed to the equivalent density of a 9,000-pound Torpex mine A small crowd, including Gibson and Wallis, stood in front of the Norman towers of Reculver Abbey, binoculars at the ready to watch the scene. Flying at 270 mph towards the shore and with the hydraulic motor spinning Upkeep at 300 rpm, the Lancaster released the mine at around 250 feet. An almost audible groan of disappointment swept through the crowd as the sphere broke up the moment it hit the water. Already used to setbacks, Wallis now ordered that the emergency work be undertaken at Manston to strengthen Upkeep's casing. At the same time, he instructed Longbottom to fly much lower on his next test, no more than fifty feet. It was early evening by the time the second mock-up was ready. Dusk was beginning to spread across the bay as the sound of the Merlins could be heard in the distance. Just after seven o'clock, the Lancaster came roaring across the water and dropped the bomb, sending a huge fountain of spray into the air. Again the casing was torn apart, one large splinter even damaging the Lancaster's elevator, but this time the inner drum bounced on for some distance. There was now a glimmer of hope.

Encouraged by this portent of success, Wallis pressed on with the trials of Upkeep. Paradoxically, the break-up of the second sphere had revealed the way forward. As George Edwards of Vickers explained, when the outer sphere shattered, 'the metal drum that was inside was left spinning on its own. It travelled along quite nicely as a cylinder.'[44] It looked as if a cylindrical shape without any wooden casing was more effective than a spherical one, and this was confirmed by subsequent tests on a full dummy version. On 28 April, a bare steel cylinder, rotating at 500 rpm when it was dropped from the Lancaster, bounced seven times over a distance of 670 yards. In further trials over the next few days, the cylinder gave what Wallis called 'a very good performance'.[45] By the beginning of May he was certain that the bomb could work. The final version of the Upkeep mine that emerged from the trials comprised a cylinder 50 inches in diameter and 60 inches in length, with a metal case ⅜ of an inch thick. Inside the cylinder, which Dave Shannon said 'looked like a huge oil drum, a most cumbersome-looking thing',[46] was an explosive charge of 6,600 lbs Torpex, itself a compound of TNT, hexogen and powdered aluminium. The detonators were three hydrostatic pistols, each containing a charge of Tetryl to activate at a depth of 30 feet. The total weight of the mine was 9,250 pounds.

Apart from the superiority of the cylinder, the other key finding of the Reculver trials was that the ideal height and speed at which to drop the mine was 60 feet from a Lancaster travelling at 232 mph. For the 617 Squadron crews, who still knew nothing of the target, these requirements only reinforced the pressures of training. They practised all over the country, over reservoirs, rivers, canals and rolling fields, getting used to the feel of the plane at such a low level. 'It was frightening at the beginning but it is surprising how accustomed you become to these things after a few efforts,' recalled bomb aimer Edward Johnson:

> You adjust yourself and begin to think of it as normal. We did not think of it as hazardous. The training to me was interesting to the nth degree. You could feel yourself progressing, starting high, getting lower and lower, getting into low-level formation flying, which in itself was quite hair-raising at the beginning. There was nothing boring at all about it. The practice did not really involve a lot of bombs. We dropped a few practice bombs at Wainfleet Sands in the Wash but our training was mainly concerned with practising the positioning of the aircraft, getting it in the right place to release the bomb.[47]

For 617 Squadron engineer Ray Grayston, these high-pressure training runs highlighted once more the sturdy qualities of the Lancaster. 'It's amazing to me that the Lancaster stayed in one piece, the way we had to fly it. When you look at how modern aircraft structures are made, there's no comparison at all. It was quite an easy machine to manoeuvre. The wings flapped about a lot and the engine flopped up and down a lot.'[48]

As the training progressed, a host of practical difficulties became apparent, most of them relating to the Lancaster's equipment which had never been designed for such exquisitely accurate bombing. Yet they were all overcome with the same spirit of ingenuity that Barnes Wallis showed in advancing the dams project in the first place. The biggest problem, said Gibson, was how to maintain exactly the right height over the water, for the Lancasters' standard altimeters were simply not precise enough. Various methods were tried. One was to tie a heavy weight to a long wire of exactly the required length and then trail it beneath the aircraft. The theory was that when the weight hit the water, the pilot would feel a sudden jerk, indicating that the plane was at the right height. But this idea proved impracticable because the weight swung wildly behind the Lancaster. It was the Ministry of Aircraft Production's Director of Scientific Research, Ben Lockspeiser, who came up with a cunning solution. A pioneering scientist who was once described as surveying 'the world with a benevolent but quizzical air, through wire-rimmed spectacles',[49] Lockspeiser had already invented a chemical method for de-icing the wings of aircraft. He now suggested that the Lancaster's altitude be measured by the use of two Aldis lights, which could be installed underneath the plane and set at just the right angle so their beams would converge at 60 feet.

Successful tests of the innovation were carried out at Farnborough and then the spotlights were fitted to the Type 464 Lancaster, one behind the nose, the other at the rear of the bomb bay, both of them configured to send twin beams which would join on the water just forward of the leading edge of the starboard wing. The convergence could be viewed by the navigator from the Lancaster's Perspex blister on the starboard side of the cockpit. It was a simple but brilliant idea, which transformed the job of the pilot, even if its application was rather intimidating at first. As Dave Shannon explained, the navigator, or sometimes the wireless operator, would keep saying 'down, down, down' until the beams met. 'We actually found that flying over the water we could be very much more accurate over still water than we were over the runway. It was very successful but it was hellish low, I don't mind saying, especially in the first runs that we made with this – one thought that the chap calling out "down, down, down" was never going to stop. But once we got the feel of it, it was perfectly all right.' The crucial skill was to balance the height with the correct speed, and that required another, far less dramatic innovation, said Shannon. 'We had to carry out quite of lot of practice using the spotlights because it did become absolutely essential that the bombs, when they were released, had to be released at 232 mph. So what we did was that on the air-speed indicator, we made a little red mark against the 232 so that when the needle came round we could see that.'[50]

Just as the standard altimeter was insufficiently accurate for low-level bombing, so was the usual bombsight, even in its advanced Mark XIV form. Again, simplicity was the answer to the problem. Wing Commander W. L. Dann from the Aircraft and Armament Experimental Establishment came up with a seemingly primitive device which enabled the bomb aimer to release Upkeep at precisely the right moment. Using reconnaissance photographs, Dann calculated the distance between the two sluice towers on the Mohne dam. He then used this information to construct a triangular wooden bomb sight, with a handle at its apex and a nail each at the other two points. Holding this sight in one hand, the bomb aimer looked through his eyepiece and when the two nails at the base of the triangle lined up with the two towers, he pressed the bomb tit. After the Dann sight was successfully tested on the Derwent dam, Barnes Wallis embarked on studies of distances between landmarks on the Eder and the Sorpe so sights could be developed for those two dams. But the device was not universally popular among crews because the movement of the aircraft at low levels meant that it was difficult to hold the sight steady on the approach. As a result, aimers came up with their own stratagems. Edward Johnson said that he did not use the Dann apparatus 'at all' because he found it 'clumsy and inconvenient and not very accurate'. So he developed his own technique, 'using a long piece of string, fastened each side of the clear bombing panel, and some clear marks on the panel itself in grease pencil. It worked very well because I had a bigger triangle than the official one and it was stationary rather than having to be held'.[51] Several other measures were taken to improve accuracy and training. Gibson and Cochrane had decided the maximum amount of moonlight would be necessary for the raid in order to enhance visibility. Because of the extremely tight schedule, however, there were simply not enough nights in which the crews could practise moonlit techniques, so the only answer was to create artificial moonlight in the cockpit during the day. The first attempts at this, through the use of tinted goggles, did not work because the pilots found they could hardly read their instruments. More successful was the synthetic aid called 'Two Stage Amber', by which the cockpit windows were fitted with blue Perspex screens and the pilot wore amber goggles. 'The effect was quite eerie,' said Dave Shannon. 'One had a strong desire to tear off the goggles and see what the hell was happening. But on overcoming that urge one realized that it offered a pretty fair comparison with moonlight flying.'[52]

Another vital move was the improvement in communications so that Gibson could liaise with all his other pilots. In Bomber Command, the radio and wireless were generally only used for take-offs, landings and the receipt of Group messages at predetermined times. Gibson needed something far more extensive and, through the influence of Charles Whitworth, the AOC at Scampton, he had the Type 464 Lancasters fitted with the VHF equipment which was normally reserved for fighters. George Chalmers, one of 617 Squadron's wireless operators, was impressed with the VHF. 'These Lancasters were kitted with very good wireless equipment with a long range – I've used the equipment in the UK and called up Malta in my time. So the range was pretty good.'[53] To avoid chatter or misunderstanding over the VHF system, Gibson ordered that the crews use simple language backed up by certain code words or letters that he devised. For instance, X was the Mohne, Y the Eder and Z the Sorpe. 'Dinghy', Melvin Young's nickname, meant that the Eder had been breached, 'Goner' that the bombs had been dropped and 'Nigger' that the Mohne had been broken – this last a reference to the name of Gibson's beloved black Labrador, who had become quite a character around Scampton with his devotion to his master, and his fondness for beer.

The deadline for the raids was fast approaching, with Wallis increasingly concerned that the water levels in the Mohne and Sorpe reservoirs would begin to drop towards the end of the month. An additional factor was that the best moon conditions would occur on the night of 16–17 May, making this by far the most suitable date for the attack. So intense was the pressure on Gibson that he developed a boil on his face, but he could only laugh at the RAF doctor who told him to take a complete rest. Yet there were still hesitations at the highest political and military levels. The Ministry of Economic Warfare felt that the Sorpe dam was by far the most important target, and advised that the destruction of the Mohne and Eder would produce only limited results. But however justified this warning, it ignored the reality that the Upkeep bomb was unsuitable for destroying the colossal earthenware mound of the Sorpe. Another note of caution was sounded by the Admiralty which felt that the Upkeep dams raid would be futile without a simultaneous Highball attack on the *Tirpitz*. Once it became clear that Highball would not be ready before 16 May because of the concentration of Wallis and the RAF on Upkeep, some of the senior naval staff sought to block Operation Chastise, fearing that the unsuccessful use of the bouncing bomb might compromise its future deployment against the German navy. At one stage, the deadlock seemed so serious that the Dams raid might have had to be postponed. But Sir Douglas Evill, the Vice-Chief of the Air Staff, made a last-minute appeal to Portal, who was then at the Washington summit with Churchill and the other military leaders, finalizing Pointblank and the Allied strategy for 1943. In his minute to Portal, Evill stressed the viability of both Wallis's bomb and the operational techniques of 617 Squadron, which had now undergone more than 2,000 hours' training and dropped 2,500 practice bombs. Portal and the Chiefs of Staff in America immediately overruled the naval opposition by authorizing that Operation Chastise should proceed immediately.[54]

In anticipation of this decision, the Upkeep bombs started to arrive at Scampton on the night of 13–14 May, ready for installation in the Type 464 Lancasters. Originally, it was planned that 20 aircraft would take part in the raids, with a crew spare in case of an emergency, but one of the planes was too badly damaged in a final training flight to be made serviceable for the operation. Even at this late hour, none of the air or ground crews knew the target, and security was tighter than ever around the base. 'Security was as tight as a drum,' said Dave Shannon. 'No telephoning out, all mail censored. One poor chap phoned a girlfriend and was reported by the telephone operator. He was sent packing. There were no more breaches.'[55] The engine fitter John Elliott gave this account of the atmosphere at Scampton as the tension built up:

> It was really hard work, some of the hardest work that I ever did in the air force. When the operational aircraft had arrived, we knew something really special was going on because they were modified. We had never seen Lancasters like them before. They had two great arms, one either side of the belly of the aircraft. When they eventually brought these cylinder bombs up to the aircraft, they were winched up in between these two arms. Then the arms were closed together, and there were two pads which fitted into either side of the frame. It was such a peculiar set-up and a peculiar-looking weapon. It was like the front of a steamroller, that's what it looked like. There was a drive on one side to spin it, and obviously by then we realized it was going to be something a bit spectacular.[56]

Some ground crews nicknamed the Type 464s 'abortions' because someone joked that with the bomb doors and mid-upper turret removed 'it looks as if the Lancs have had abortions'. Alternatively, once Upkeep was installed, the same wag said 'they looked like pregnant ducks'.[57] The next morning, 15 May, Bomber Command and 5 Group sent through the orders to Scampton confirming that Operation Chastise would be held the following night, 16–17 May. Gibson spent much of the rest of the day drawing up the full battle order and informing those closest to him, like 'Hoppy' Hopgood and 'Dinghy' Young, of the target. That night personal tragedy struck Gibson when his Labrador Nigger was hit by a car outside the gates of Scampton and killed instantly. Gibson admitted that he was 'very depressed' by the incident because he and the dog had been devoted to each other but he never let his professionalism waver for a moment. He carried on with his preparations, kept the loss quiet for fear that the men would think it a worrying omen and gave orders that Nigger should be buried at midnight on 16 May, just at the moment when Gibson would be crossing the enemy coast.

On the evening of 15 May a hushed sense of expectation had descended on Scampton. Some of the men took sleeping pills, while others fell into an immediate slumber, exhausted by the weeks of the rehearsals. The next morning a reconnaissance aircraft reported that the weather forecast was good, the dams' defences had remained unchanged and the water levels were perfect for the attack. There could be no turning back now. Gibson then called the pilots and navigators into a lengthy briefing lasting over two hours, at which they were shown scale models of the three targets and given the planned routes. The men were instructed to memorize as much as they could of the targets but they remained sworn to secrecy. In the late afternoon the Tannoy at Scampton crackled into action, summoning the rest of the airmen for a full briefing at six o'clock. 'The boys came in hushed,' wrote Gibson, 'having waited two and a half months to hear what they were going to attack. There were about 133 young men in that room, rather tousled and a little bit scruffy and perhaps a little old-looking in spite of their youth. But now they were experts.'[58] Some of the airmen were surprised at the sight of the white-haired, rather shy figure standing on the platform beside Gibson, as wireless operator George Chalmers recalled: 'I turned around to my colleague and said, "Who's the bloody civilian up there?" and he said, "That's Barnes Wallis." "Barnes Wallis? What does he do?"' Chalmers soon found out as Wallis, with a scholarly but benign air, explained the purpose of his bomb and the importance of the dams to German industry. To navigator Harold Hobday, he 'came across as a very kindly man – very dedicated, frightfully clever – but rather a fatherly type. We were very impressed with him and thought he was a marvellous man – everybody did.'[59]

Gibson and other officers then set out the full operational details, including timings, the route, the weather forecast and the method of attack. The men were told that the 19 Lancasters would take off in three waves. The first, comprising nine aircraft and led by Gibson, would attack the Mohne and, once that was breached, move on to the Eder. The second, consisting of five Lancasters, would have the twin duties of attacking the Sorpe and also creating a diversion with flares and Very lights to draw away the German fighters. Finally, the last five, taking off two hours later than the first two waves, would act as an airborne reserve to support the attack on the big three dams or any hit on any other more minor targets chosen by Bomber Command. Filling in any gap left by the first two formations, they would be told their objectives once Gibson had seen how the operation was unfolding, another reason why VHF radio was so crucial. According to the memory of bomb aimer Edward Johnson, there were very few questions once the senior officers had finished speaking. The widespread feeling was one of shock mingled with relief. 'We were a bit overawed at what the target was. It had come completely out of the blue and no one had the slightest inkling. It took a bit of time to digest what exactly was going on. After the briefing, we were all asking each other, "What did you think of the target?" But in most cases it was a sigh of relief that it did not seem as dangerous as some of the others we were thinking about.'[60]

While the 133 airmen went for the traditional pre-op meal of bacon and eggs, the final tasks were performed on the 19 Lancasters: filling up their tanks with 100-octane fuel and loading the ammunition for the Brownings. Even when all the planes were ready, the ground crews were still not informed of the purpose of the raid, as fitter John Elliott remembered. 'We did not know on the evening of the raid what the actual target was going to be. Cochrane came to our dispersal before they took off and said, "I realize how difficult this has been and the work you have had to put in. I hope in the morning you will consider it has all been worth it."'[61] In the crew room, the airmen said little as they changed into their flying gear before being taken out by trucks to dispersal. The nervousness was even greater than was usual for a Lancaster operation. 'It was not like an ordinary operational scene,' wrote Gibson, 'all the crews on this occasion being aware of the terrific task confronting them. Most of them wore expressions varying from "don't care a damn" to the grim and determined. On the whole I think it appeared rather reminiscent of a crusade.'[62] Once they had clambered on board, the engines were started up, ready for the take-off from 9.30 p.m. It was a beautiful, warm early summer's night and a large crowd had gathered at the caravan by the runway, waiting expectantly for the green Aldis lamp to send each plane hurtling along the runway. Among the crowd was the 617 Squadron adjutant Harry Humphries: 'The dramatic part is when it's silent, then they open the throttles and start the engines and start waddling along to the take-off point – that's the exciting part. They took off in formation, very, very low – and that was a tremendous sight. I knew it was going to be a historical night.'[63]

The second wave of Lancasters actually took off first on the evening of 16 May, since its pilots had to go a longer, more northerly route over the Dutch island of Vlieland, compared to Gibson's formation which was due to cross the Dutch coast further south at the Scheldt estuary. The aim of the split was to confuse and divide the German fighter defences. As it turned out, the second wave paid a heavy price for the course it had to take. Flying low to avoid radar, one plane was shot down when its navigator became lost and flew into heavy flak. Once over occupied territory, another struck high-tension cables and plunged to the ground in flames. Unfortunately the Upkeep bomb, whose fail-safe destructive timer was only activated by release, remained intact so its secrets swiftly fell into German hands, exactly as the Royal Navy had feared. Another pilot from the formation, Geoff Rice, misjudged the height as he flew towards the Dutch coast, going down too low. His mine touched the water and though he pulled up with full boost, the violent movement tore the Upkeep bomb away from its brackets. He had no alternative but to head back to base. Also returning prematurely was the Lancaster of Les Munro which came under fire over the island of Vlieland. As Munro recalled: 'We were flying at 240 mph and I would have been at 70 or 60 feet when we were hit over Vlieland on the port side of the aircraft. The intercom immediately went dead. I felt the thump of the shell. The damage from that shell exploding blew a hole in the side of the aircraft where the squadron letters were, but didn't cause much damage to the other side and no damage to the rear gunner and his turret.'[64] Without the ability to speak to his crew over the intercom, Munro knew there was no point in continuing the mission. The only plane out of the second formation to continue with its mission was that of the American Joe McCarthy, who had been half an hour late in taking off because his designated Lancaster had developed an engine coolant leak and he had to switch to another aircraft just before take-off.

Gibson's first wave, flying in three vics (V formations) at just over 200 feet across the North Sea and Holland, had fared much better along its route. Though some heavy flak was encountered from the Kammhuber Line on the coast, none of the aircraft were hit. Nor were the fighters much of a threat, said Dave Shannon: 'I believe there were plenty of fighter aircraft about but of course we were down on the deck and the fighter aircraft didn't really know whether we were enemy aircraft or their own. It's too low level for the fighters to operate, to come down there.'[65] It was not until the formation had crossed the German border that the first casualty occurred when Bill Astell's Lancaster was hit by flak, plunged out of control and smashed into an electricity pylon, killing all seven members of the crew.

At 00.20, a few minutes after Astell's plane had gone down, Gibson arrived at the Mohne Lake. 'Then we saw the dam itself,' he wrote. 'In that light it looked squat and heavy and unconquerable. It looked grey and solid in the moonlight, as though it were part of the countryside itself and just as immovable.' Almost as soon as he arrived, the flak guns from the sluice towers and nearby hamlets opened fire. By now the rest of the first wave were arriving. Gibson circled the lake, surveying the defences and the landmarks while maintaining contact with the rest of the crews. Then he swept round, ready for the first attack. The hydraulic motor began to spin Upkeep. The engineer pushed the throttles fully forward. The navigator switched on the spotlights. The bomb aimer held up his Dann sight and was relieved to see the two towers of the dam gradually moving into line as the aircraft sped towards its target. Shells and tracer were now pouring from the German guns. Gibson later admitted that he needed all his nerve to hold the plane steady under fire. 'This was a horrible moment. We were being dragged along at four miles a minute, against our will, towards the things we were going to destroy. I think at that moment the boys did not want to go on. I did not want to go on.'[66] But he overcame his fear. The Lancaster was skimming over the water, flying at 60 feet. At exactly the moment the bomb aimer saw the nails on his Dann sight cover the towers, he pressed the tit. Rotating backwards at 500 rpm, Upkeep fell from its arms, bounced across the lake, sank to 30 feet and then exploded, stirring up the water into a maelstrom and sending a plume over 1,000 feet high. Gibson, who had by now flown over the dam wall, looked over his shoulder and half expected to see a violent torrent gushing into the valley. But instead the water began to settle. The dam had remained intact. The planned method was for the Lancasters to make their attacks at three-minute intervals so the disturbance could subside. This only put more pressure on the aircraft as they had to keep circling over the lake waiting their turn as the flak continued to pour into the night sky.

The next to try was Hoppy Hopgood in Lancaster *M-Mother*. The plane began to roar at 230 mph towards the dam, but just as the aimer prepared to release, anti-aircraft fire burst through the wings, hitting two engines and the petrol tank. In the mayhem, the bomb fell fractionally late, bouncing over the parapet and demolishing a power station beyond. As the flames gripped Hopgood's Lancaster, he desperately struggled to gain height so the crew could bail out. Miraculously, two of the men made it before the plane crashed to the ground and exploded. Hopgood himself, who died instantly in the conflagration, had confessed to Dave Shannon before take-off that he did not think he would make it, a rare instance of anxiety from a man so usually nerveless.

After these two abortive attempts and the loss of four other aircraft from the intended Sorpe attack, Gibson realized that the Dams raid was at an increasing risk of failure. Showing those gifts of intrepidity and coolness that marked him out as a unique leader, Gibson now took a decision that was to transform his squadron's fortunes. He called up Micky Martin to attack next, and then told Martin that he would fly alongside him to draw away the anti-aircraft fire and confuse the German gunners. The ruse almost worked, as Martin's Lancaster, though damaged by flak, dropped its mine accurately and again, the huge jet of water could be seen shooting from the end of the reservoir. But once more, the wall remained intact.

Exactly the same happened with the next mine, which was dropped by 'Dinghy' Young. When the water subsided, the Mohne dam was still standing. A sense of despair was now creeping into the formation. 'We began to wonder if this thing was going to work. They'd dropped a few and nothing had happened except tremendous explosions which were quite spectacular,' said Edward Johnson, who was in Les Knight's crew waiting to attack.[67] The sense of anticlimax was shared in the Operations Room at Scampton, which had been in constant VHF communication with Gibson. Waiting by the radio for messages were Cochrane, Wallis and Harris, who despite his earlier opposition to Chastise, had made one of his rare station visits because of the importance of the raid. Wallis later admitted that he could feel Harris and Cochrane 'looking suspiciously at me' every time the news was transmitted of another failure.[68]

The fifth attempt was now made by David Maltby in Lancaster *J-Jig*. At 0049 he raced over the water and then the aimer pressed the Upkeep release at precisely the right moment. At first it was hard to see anything through all the spray and the smoke from the burning power station. Gibson was so certain of another disappointment that he instructed Dave Shannon in *L-Love* to start preparing for his run. Suddenly the sound of crumbling masonry could be heard echoing through the valley. 'I could not believe my eyes. I heard someone shout, "I think she's gone! I think she's gone!" . . . There was no doubt about it: there was a great breach 100 yards across, and the water, now looking like stirred porridge in the moonlight, was gushing out and rolling into the Ruhr Valley towards the industrial centres of Germany's Third Reich.'[69] As the thunderous flood-tide descended on the countryside, sending up vast clouds of steam, Gibson ordered the wireless operator to transmit the exultant message of 'Nigger' to Scampton.

A German perspective on the Mohne assault came from Unteroffizier Karl Schutte, commander of the gun crew on the north tower of the dam. He later recalled how the night of 16 May had seemed 'very quiet', then suddenly the silence was broken by the 'noise of engines growing nearer'. He picked out a 'speeding black shape' in the darkness 'thundering like a four-engined monster between the two towers and over the wall at a height of 20 metres, spitting fire and almost ramming the defence post with its tail. Moments later there was a horrendous explosion and a 300-metre column of water thundered into the air from the lake.' Schutte's crew were amazed at the spectacle, but still tried to keep their fire focused on the bomber. More Lancasters swooped down, their spot-lights helping the German gunners with their aim. But the force of the

British planes appeared overwhelming. 'One couldn't take it any more, as the roar of the engines combined with the sound of our own fire and explosions, which doubled as they echoed round the valley and appeared to come from all sides.' Pointing to the wisdom of Gibson's decision, Schutte continued, 'We no longer knew which aircraft we should engage first, as the four-engined monsters were flying together to attack.' Then the fifth bomber came in, just as the ammunition ran out. 'It was child's play for him now. The aircraft was close enough to touch — I believe to this day that I could see the outline of the pilot in his cockpit. But our guns were silent.' Then Schutte saw the dam starting to collapse. 'The water gushed unstoppably through the breached wall into the valley and the air was so full of spray that practically all visibility was gone. The swooping aircraft turned away. They had done their job.'[70]

The months of training had been rewarded. The genius of Wallis had proved all the sceptics wrong. But the night's work was far from finished. Two other dams were still standing. Gibson now instructed Martin and Maltby to return home, their bombs now gone, while Shannon, Knight and Maudslay were ordered to head for the Eder, with 'Dinghy' Young acting as his deputy leader. The Eder dam, though of less economic importance to the German economy, was a more difficult target than the Mohne, because it was situated deep in a valley surrounded by pine forests. Less than a mile opposite the dam was a steep rocky mountainside, which meant that an attacking Lancaster had to make a diving approach, fly level at 60 feet, release its bomb and then make a sudden steep climbing turn to the right. The only advantage of this difficult terrain was that, unlike the Mohne, the dam itself was poorly defended because the Germans appeared to believe that no bomber could physically attempt an assault. Indeed the geography did initially appear too daunting. Dave Shannon made no fewer than four dummy runs before Gibson ordered him to take a rest, Henry Maudslay taking his place. But Maudslay found it equally difficult and made two dummy runs before his third attempt appeared to end in tragedy. Released a fraction late, his bomb hit the parapet of the dam and sparked a huge, yellow-flamed explosion which caught the underside of the Lancaster just as it tried to climb out of the valley. The plane staggered through the air and then was never seen again. There is some dispute over what actually happened next. There are claims that Maudslay's badly mauled Lancaster managed to scrape out of the valley and head for home, only to be shot down by flak on the German border with Holland. But Edward Johnson, who had a clear view of the scene from his bomb aimer's position in Les Knight's Lancaster, was certain that Maudslay crashed into the cliff face opposite the dam. His bomb 'actually hit the top of the dam and went off with a terrifying flash. We could see his aircraft silhouetted against this light. Gibson could see the same, and he called up almost immediately after the explosion and said, "Are you all right, Henry?" There was quite a time when nothing was said, then all of us were sure that we heard Henry saying that he thought he was all right, in a very weak voice, shaky, not at all like himself. But the aircraft went on and we thought it crashed into this mountain. We saw a second explosion which we felt sure was Henry Maudslay.'[71]

Whatever the grisly fate of this crew, the fight had to continue. Gibson now called up Dave Shannon again, who made another dummy run and then, on his next attempt, got in exactly the right position and released his mine, prompting the same huge vertical deluge that the crews had seen at the Mohne. But still the Eder remained standing. Then the austere Les Knight came in. After one dummy run, Knight made an almost perfect approach. His aimer, Edward Johnson, described the scene:

> I could clearly see the towers and I was quite happy with my bombsight and position and everything. I released the bomb and I forgot all about it because we seemed to be flying directly into this large piece of land which was only just across the river from the dam. In the front of the aircraft it is quite a terrifying experience to see this lump looming up at high speed. I was very anxious that the pilot should get the stick right back and get over the top, which he did. He pushed the throttle right through the emergency gate to get the max power. We skimmed over the top of this hill, in which we were sure we had seen Maudslay crash shortly before. I did not actually see the dam burst because I was out of sight of it, being in the front of the aircraft. But it was obvious what had happened from the noise from the rear gunner and everyone else who could see anything. They were all going mad on the intercom because the wall at the centre of the dam had fallen. The water was absolutely pouring out, down this narrow river, causing a tidal wave. Now we forgot all about safety, and going home. We were trying to follow the water down the river to see what happened. It was such a terrifying sight, really. We could see cars being engulfed. Then Gibson called up, 'It is all right boys, you are having a good time, but we still have to get back to base. Let's go.' We all left.[72]

Even now Gibson did not give up. There was one more dam, the Sorpe, to crack and he flew there to oversee the last part of Chastise. But the number of men available was dwindling rapidly. McCarthy of the second wave had reached the target and dropped his mine on the Sorpe reservoir. Despite another awesome swelling of water, so expansive that the rear gunner thought at one moment he was drowning, the Sorpe wall stood firm. The back-up third wave, which had left Scampton after midnight and had been ordered by Gibson to attack the Sorpe, had also run into deep trouble. One Lancaster was downed by ground fire near the German-Dutch border, another nearer the target. The plane captained by Cyril Anderson became lost and found its rear turret unserviceable, so it returned to Scampton with Upkeep still on board. A fourth Lancaster, captained by Bill Townsend, was ordered by 5 Group Headquarters to hit the minor Ennepe dam, which it did without any results. The only Lancaster in the third wave to reach the Sorpe was that piloted by Ken Brown, but again, though there was the usual huge explosion of water, the wall remained intact. Wallis, who before the raid had privately expressed fears about the durability of the Sorpe's structure, had been proved correct. For many of those that survived, the journey homewards was anything but straightforward, as they again had to encounter vicious flak from the German batteries along the route. Ken Brown had part of the side of his Lancaster blown out by anti-aircraft fire over the Zuider Zee, and decided that the only way to escape was by flying lower even than the maximum depressed level of the German guns. Sadly, the crew of 'Dinghy' Young's Lancaster did not make it, as they were shot down over the Dutch coast.

Altogether, 8 of the 19 Lancasters that set out from Scampton did not return. Fifty-three airmen lost their lives, a loss rate of 40 per cent, eight times the highest normally accepted level of casualties. Barnes Wallis was in tears as the death toll became apparent, while 617 Squadron adjutant Harry Humphries recalled that when he walked over to the Flying Control tower 'my worst possible estimation was insignificant compared with the shock I received. Eight blanks on the blackboard. It was hard to accept.'[73] When the airmen returned and were met at dispersal by Cochrane and Harris, their natural elation was tempered by depression at the numbers declared missing in action. The mix of relief, triumph and sadness lent a slightly manic edge to the celebrations in the mess into the early hours, as Edward Johnson recalled: 'We were a bit shattered at the losses but we had somehow expected they would be high. We stayed up late. There was a good deal of boozing. I have not the faintest idea what time I went to bed but it would have been a long time after breakfast.'[74] The next day, there was a sense of numbness on the base, particularly amongst the ground crew and support staff. 'The following days were a nightmare. We were still shattered by the terrible losses but gradually we began to adjust to the squadron routine,' said aircraftwoman Morfydd Gronland.[75] Most of the airmen, used to the brutal lottery of war, were more stoical. 'I suppose we had become hardened to loss,' said Dave Shannon. 'We could shrug it off. We had to, otherwise we would never have flown again.'[76]

But stoicism soon began to turn to pride, as the exploits of 617 Squadron reached public consciousness. The story of Gibson and his men made perfect material for the papers and newsreels, always searching for acts of unique heroism against Germany. 'Huns get a flood blitz. Torrent rages along the Ruhr,' proclaimed the *Daily Mirror*. Carried away on a tide of enthusiasm, the *Daily Telegraph* exaggerated the extent of the destruction: 'With a single blow RAF has precipitated on Germany what may prove to be the greatest industrial disaster yet inflicted on Germany in this war. A force of Lancasters, loaded with mines and specially trained for the task, early yesterday morning attacked and destroyed the great dams on the Mohne and Sorpe rivers, tributaries of the Ruhr, and also the dam on the Eder river. Two walls of water sweeping down the Ruhr and Eder valleys are carrying all before them.' The news also created an impression in America, where there had been some doubts about the bomber offensive up till then. In a report that was more accurate than the *Telegraph*'s, the *New York Times* declared: 'The RAF has secured another triumph. With unexampled daring, skill and ingenuity it has blasted two of Germany's important water dams which are vital parts of the whole industrial and transportation system of west Germany.'

Gibson and the men of the Dambusters quickly became national heroes. The tale of the RAF smashing through the vast block of the Mohne dam seemed almost a national metaphor for Britain's increasingly confident struggle against the once-impregnable Reich war machine. The King and Queen visited Scampton to meet the crew. Honours were showered on the participants, Gibson receiving the Victoria Cross and 33 other airmen gallantry decorations. Roy Chadwick was not forgotten and was awarded the CBE. Politicians were keen to add the lustre of the raid to boost the war effort. In a speech to the US Congress, Winston Churchill referred directly to Chastise: 'The condition to which the great centres of German war industry, and particularly the Ruhr, are being reduced is one of unparalleled devastation. You have just read of the destruction of the great dams which feed the canals and provide the power to the enemy's munition works. That was a gallant operation, costing eight of the nineteen Lancasters employed but it will play a very far reaching part in reducing the German munition output.'[77] On 21 June, 617 Squadron travelled to London for the investiture of Gibson and the other decorated crew members at Buckingham Palace the following day. There was a mood of celebration the whole way down on the train, fuelled by the crates of beer that had been brought on board. After the Royal ceremony on 22 June, a lavish party was hosted by Avro in the Hungaria restaurant, neither the menu nor the drinks paying obeisance to wartime rationing.

The Dams raid was undoubtedly an enormous propaganda triumph. At a stroke it raised the morale of both Bomber Command and the British public. But whether it actually caused any serious damage to German industry has long been a source of historical controversy. There was no dispute that the breaches in the Mohne and the Eder caused immense devastation in their immediate aftermath. The flooding spread for miles, uprooting trees, ripping through homes, villages and towns, killing livestock and people. Eleven factories were completely gutted and another 114 badly damaged. The final confirmed death toll reached 1,294, almost 600 of them forced labourers or prisoners-of-war. Nearly 3,000 acres of farmland were ruined and 25 road bridges were washed away. Gas, electricity and water supplies were temporarily disrupted, while steel production fell in the Ruhr because of the lack of water for the cooling process. Albert Speer, the German Minister for Armaments, later said that though a breach in the Sorpe would have represented 'a complete disaster', the Dams raid was nevertheless 'a disaster for us for a number of months'.[78]

But in the longer term, the results were more mixed. With his characteristic flair for organization, Speer began working on repairs to the dams immediately, and by September the holes in both the Mohne and the Eder were closed. By the end of the year, steel production from the Ruhr actually exceeded the output of 1942. Speer said he was surprised that the RAF did not return while the repairs were undertaken, a point with which Dave Shannon agreed. 'Talking with hindsight, and it's easy to say after the event, but the Germans were able to rebuild the dams with much more speed and rapidity than had been thought by the pundits back at home . . . I think perhaps if Bomber Command had gone back the following night or within a very short space of time . . . and blown away the foundations when the water had gone, there was no way that the Germans could have rebuilt those dams'.[79] But the completeness of the restoration should not be exaggerated. Because of the extensive damage, the dams could not be fully repaired until after the war, and never operated at their full capacity until 1946–7. Twenty thousand workers had to be diverted to the Ruhr from building defences on the Dutch and French coasts, something that was to play a crucial role on D-Day. In addition, research by the Cambridge historian Richard Evans indicates that the raid may have had more industrial consequences than previously thought. Evans has argued that before Chastise, arms production had been growing at an average of 5.5 per cent per month since 1942, but now growth stopped altogether. Similarly, steel production fell by 200,000 tons in the second quarter of 1943, ammunition quotas had to be cut and aircraft production stagnated until March 1944.[80]

The most powerful British critic of the Dams raid was, intriguingly, Arthur Harris himself, something that has been overlooked in previous histories. He had never believed in the value of Chastise, and he continued privately to view the attack as an indulgence even after glory had been heaped on Gibson and the 617 Squadron crews. In one telling letter of December 1943 to Norman Bottomley, the Deputy Chief of the Air Staff, he wrote: 'For years we have been told that the destruction of the Mohne Dam alone would be a vital blow to Germany. Both the Mohne and the Eder Dams were destroyed and I have seen nothing, either in the present circumstances or in the Ministry of Economic Warfare reports, to show that the effort was worthwhile except as a spectacular operation.'[81] For Harris, the entire project summed up the pointlessness of panacea targets compared to area attacks. He was still keeping up the same refrain towards the end of the war, when he told Portal: 'The destruction of the Mohne and Eder dams was to achieve wonders. It achieved nothing compared with the effort and the loss. Nothing, that is, but a supreme display of skill, gallantry, devotion and technical ingenuity. It appears that the vital industrial water supplies sprang in fact from wells in the Ruhr which could not be depleted unless the dams were kept out over a matter of years, drought supervened and the whole water table of the Ruhr could thereby be lowered. Another afterthought: the material damage was negligible compared with one small area attack.'[82]

Harris produced no figures to back up his claims, and the same point could be forcefully made about his obsession with area bombing, which, for all its carnage, never seemed to undermine German output to the extent that he promised. More importantly, in his fixation with dropping maximum tonnage on urban areas, he failed to understand the lessons that the Dambusters had taught about the astonishing accuracy, manoeuvrability and versatility of the Lancaster. Even if the breaches of the two dams did not have the long-term economic effects that the government hoped, the raid still showed what a truly remarkable plane Chadwick had built, able to fly steady at just 60 feet, soak up punishment and still drop a five-ton bomb to an accuracy of a few feet. As Barnes Wallis put it in his generous letter to Chadwick barely a week after the raid: 'No one believed that we should do it. You yourself said that it would be a miracle if we did and I think the whole thing is one of the most amazing examples of team-work and co-operation in the whole history of the war. May I offer you my very deep thanks for the existence of your wonderful Lancaster, for it was the only aircraft in the world capable of doing the job, and I should like to pay my tribute of congratulation and admiration to you, the designer.'[83]

11

'A sea of flames!'

━━━◆━━━

IN HIS HEARTFELT letter of congratulations to Roy Chadwick after the
Dams raid, Barnes Wallis wrote: 'Let us hope that the future will hold
for us another terrific adventure in which we may join, though I fear no
such spectacular target remains to be brought down.'[1] In some respects
Wallis was right. The circumstances of Gibson's mission had been unique.
Never could another precision attack be mounted on such a scale against
a major target with the same element of surprise. Upkeep was not used
again in the war, despite the fact that 58 of the mines had been built by
the time of Operation Chastise. Two had been lost in live trials at Reculver
in Kent, and 17 dropped over Germany. The remaining 39 went into storage
at Lossiemouth. Occasionally plans were drawn up for other Upkeep raids
by 617 Squadron, which on Harris's orders had stayed together as an elite
unit after May 1943. Dams in northern Italy, a nickel production site in
Finland and the dam across the River Roer in Holland were all considered as potential targets but were ruled out, either because of logistical
difficulties or because other types of bombing were seen as more effective.
To prevent the risks of explosions through deterioration at the Lossiemouth
dump, the unused Upkeeps were jettisoned in the North Sea between
March 1945 and November 1946, flown there by the last serviceable
Lancasters able to carry the mines. The final Dambusting Lancaster was
declared surplus to requirements in July 1947 and reduced to scrap.

A second Dams raid might have been impossible, but another spectacular attack was not. Soon after Chastise, Bomber Command embarked
on planning a colossal urban assault, one that would be sufficiently devastating to inspire feelings of defeatism in the German military and terror
in the German public. The bombing of Dresden in February 1945 has
gone down in history as the most brutal and destructive action by Bomber
Command during the war, regarded by many as an act of unethical
savagery inflicted on a largely innocent civilian population. But in truth,
the horror of Dresden paled beside the awesome conflagration created
by the RAF at Hamburg in late July 1943. The attack on the northern

German port was the quintessence of the Trenchard doctrine, area bombing at a new level of destructive power. Fed by over 9,000 tons of bombs, the firestorm that engulfed Hamburg was the most deadly of the European war, turning whole streets and neighbourhoods into boiling cauldrons, sending howling winds through collapsing buildings, reducing bodies to nothing more than charred stumps. Those who witnessed the terrifying scenes on the peak night of the Hamburg raid on 27–28 July said that it was like a vision of hell, so all-consuming were the violent flames, so scorching was the heat. For some Hamburg residents, the sound of the tornado ripping through the city, mixed with the exploding bombs, evoked thoughts of the Devil himself. Fredy Borck, who was an eleven-year-old girl at the time of the raid and had taken shelter in an underground cellar, later recalled how 'an inhuman screeching and groaning came from the walls. We screamed along with it, screaming out in our terror! We lost all self-control, crouched on our benches, cowering together with our heads between our knees to cover our ears.'[3] From the air, the sight of the city ablaze was stupefying, as Flight Lieutenant A. Forsdike recorded. 'The burning of Hamburg was remarkable in that I saw not many fires, but one. Set in the darkness was a turbulent dome of bright red fire, lighted and ignited like the glowing heart of a vast brazier. I saw no streets, no outlines of buildings, only brighter fires which flared like yellow torches against a background of bright red ash. Above the city was a red misty haze. I looked down, fascinated but aghast, satisfied yet horrified. I had never seen a fire like that and was never to see its like again.'[2] If the Dams raid demonstrated the Lancaster's capability for precision bombing, then the Hamburg raid confirmed its unique bomb-loading quality. Only Chadwick's design, with its huge bay, could have inflicted the overwhelming destruction that Hamburg experienced on those volcanic summer nights in 1943.

Situated on the estuary of the River Elbe, Hamburg was an obvious target for Bomber Command. Its geographical position near the North Sea meant that relatively little flying over enemy territory was involved in a raid. Moreover, the outline of the Elbe showed up clearly on the Lancasters' H2S screens, though the city lay just outside the range of Gee. Hamburg was also one of Germany's leading industrial centres, home to a population of 1.7 million people and some of the Reich's biggest manufacturers, including the shipbuilding giant Blohm und Voss. Twice the size of Rotterdam, it was Europe's second-largest port after London. Throughout his time as Commander-in-Chief, Harris had ordered regular assaults on the city. The third operational raid ever carried out by Lancasters against Germany was a flight to Hamburg on the night of 8–9 April 1942. Other far bigger raids followed such as the 72 Lancasters that attacked the city on 9–10 November 1942, the 135 on 30–31 January 1943, and the 149 on 3–4 March 1943. But Harris and the Air Staff had always hankered after something even more formidable. In fact, Harris had originally chosen Hamburg as the target for the very first 'Millennium' raid by 1,000 bombers in May 1942, but the city was reprieved by poor weather and the RAF was ordered instead to hit Cologne.

During the spring of 1943, Portal reminded Harris of the importance of the northern port. 'If you can pull off an 800 raid on a place such as Hamburg, I shall be delighted.'[4] In contrast to his attitude towards Chastise, Harris had not the slightest hesitation about throwing his full energy into planning the attack on Hamburg. What he envisaged was not just a raid, but a systematic campaign over several nights and days, with the support of the Americans, to reduce Germany's second city to a state of near desolation. This was the co-ordinated 'round-the-clock' bombing which the Pointblank directive had proposed in May but had not yet been put into action. Now, in the improved weather of the summer and against a less demanding target than either Berlin or the German cities deep in the Ruhr, was the opportunity to try the new approach.

Hamburg might not have been as dangerous as some other cities but it could never have been described as an easy target. It was the second most heavily defended city in Germany after Berlin, protected not only by the Kammhuber Line on the coast but also by its own huge arsenal of radar-controlled master-searchlights and anti-aircraft guns. 'Hamburg was not a target that was liked,' said bomb aimer Tom Tredwell, 'we certainly expected to be battered by flak'.[5] But a technological break-through offered Bomber Command a tremendous advantage over the German defences, rendering them almost useless against the bomber. Called 'Window', this device was astonishingly simple, consisting of nothing more than a bunch of metallic strips, each of them with coarse paper on one side and thin aluminium foil on the other. Thrown from the planes in sufficient quantities, Window created false blips on the German Würzburg and Freya screens. To the radar operators, it appeared as if thousands of bombers had suddenly filled the sky, making it impossible to detect the real planes amidst the sea of moving dots. Window was not actually a new development by the time its use was first agreed in the summer of 1943, but had been pioneered in early 1942 by the brilliant physicist R. V. Jones, who proved that the system could be effective in disrupting radar.

Despite Window's obvious promise, powerful voices were raised within the government against its deployment, based on the fear that the Germans could discover its secret and then adopt a similar method on raids against England. One of the strongest opponents of Window's operational use was Sholto Douglas, head of Fighter Command, who relied on radar to guide his fighters in defensive combat against the Luftwaffe. Another powerful objector was Dr Robert Watson-Watt, the inventor of radar. In the cynical words of Professor Jones, Watson-Watt was pained 'to think of radar being neutralized, even German radar'.[6] Watson-Watt's attitude was reflected in a letter to Harris written in late May 1942, soon after tests had proved Window's practicability. Having warned of the risks of higher casualties in Britain 'by stimulating the enemy to use Window effectively against us', he concluded that its 'use against the enemy should be withheld until i) the casualty rate shows a significant rise or ii) we have an exceptionally difficult major operation specifically suited to Window or iii) we have a countermeasure to Window used against us.'[7] Harris had already heard about Window's potential in reducing bomber losses by weakening the enemy's defences and had little truck with such caution, believing that Fighter Command and Watson-Watt had exaggerated the Luftwaffe's ability to mount a serious offensive against England. He told Sir Wilfrid Freeman, Chief Executive of the Ministry of Aircraft Production: 'It is generally wise when you think of a weapon first to use it first. Otherwise you lose all chance of profit before the enemy, as he will, thinks of it and gets it into service. This weapon is adjudged to be of benefit to the bomber. The bomber crews have more to face than anyone else in the war. They should be given all reasonable preference. But because we are defensively minded – and that never yet won a war – everyone else always gets preference over the bomber.'[8] Harris's pessimism was proved correct. The Air Staff refused to sanction Window throughout 1942. Surprisingly, Harris did not push for it in the autumn with anything like the vigour he showed on other issues, apparently believing that the concentrated bomber stream was already achieving considerable disruption of the German defences.

But by mid-1943 the Air Staff's policy could not be sustained. Broken on the eastern front, beaten in Africa and on the defensive in southern Italy, the Luftwaffe was in no position to mount anything more than light sporadic raids on southern England. Meanwhile, Bomber Command's casualties had continued to rise inexorably during the Battle of the Ruhr. One estimate held that the introduction of Window could lead to a 35 per cent reduction in Bomber Command's losses. In addition, the fears about secrecy had become an irrelevance, since RAF intelligence reported that the Germans were 'certain' to be already aware of the Window principle.[9] Indeed, German scientific experts had actually been experimenting with a version of their own called Duppel. It is a rich irony that Göring, adopting the same outlook as Sholto Douglas, was deeply perturbed by the successful tests of Duppel, terrified that the RAF might learn from the Luftwaffe the secret of how to crack radar defences with metallic strips. He immediately ordered General Wolfgang Martini, the German Head of Signals, to cease all research on Duppel, hide the files in a safe and prevent, on pain of death, any talk about the project. Nevertheless, even with the risks of German retaliation having largely evaporated, the Air Staff still hesitated. In June, a new argument was formulated to justify a delay, with claims that nothing should be done to endanger the RAF tactical forces operating in Sicily and the Mediterranean in support of the army and navy. Surprisingly, even Churchill's spirit of adventure seemed to desert him. 'This is one of those cases,' he told Portal on 2 July 1943, 'which ought to be proved three-ply before the plunge is taken. You must excuse my being cautious, but I feel it my duty to be completely convinced.'[10]

The issue then went to a crucial meeting of the Chiefs of Staff on 15 July, attended not just by the military chiefs but also Churchill and his Minister for Home Security, the Labour MP Herbert Morrison who conjured up menacing imagery of a renewed Blitz by the German bomber force, stressing that it was his duty to safeguard the civilian population of Britain. The matter would have to go to the Cabinet, he said. But Churchill, emboldened by the recent success of the Italian invasion, refused to back him. The issue was too technical for the Cabinet, he argued, and in any case priority must be given to reducing Bomber Command's losses. Having told the Chiefs of Staff of his willingness to shoulder responsibility for any losses at home if Britain's defences were neutralized, he concluded the meeting with the words: 'Very well, let us open the Window.'[11]

The actual metal strips of Window, measuring six inches long and an inch wide, were produced on heavy printing presses by the Sun Engraving Company, which had wide experience of war work for the government. Once trimmed they were put in bundles of 2,200, held together with elastic bands. Twelve bundles formed a Window parcel. A Lancaster would often carry 50 of these parcels on a trip over Germany. There were plans to develop an automatic mechanism to feed Window out of the aircraft, but MAP warned in 1943 that it would take at least 18 months to complete, so the task of throwing out the bundles usually fell to the bomb aimer or the wireless operator. Timed by stopwatch, he was meant to dump them at the rate of one a minute. Initially, they were dropped down the plane's flare chute near the rear of the fuselage, but later Lancasters had their own Window chute on the starboard side of the bombing compartment. Lancaster navigator Frank Musgrove felt a great deal of sympathy for anyone given this duty. 'This was repetitive, menial work – a labouring job performed by an RAF commissioned officer for hours towards the target and then for hours on the return to base.'[12] The Lancaster's interior, already cramped, was made even more uncomfortable by the piles of Window parcels lined up along the fuselage. Furthermore, the process of hurling the bundles into the night sky could also create difficulties. Sometimes they would blow back into the Lancaster, filling the aircraft with metal strips. One mid-upper gunner was injured when the engineer forgot to remove the elastic strap from the bundle. Pulled by a fierce draught, the solid lump of foil strips crashed into the gunner's face and, as he fell, blood pouring from his wound, he accidently grabbed one of his Brownings and let off a couple of hundred rounds. Fortunately his facial injury was not serious. On other occasions the bundles would fail to open properly and would smash into other aircraft, damaging aerials and Perspex. The paper side of the strip had a black coating, so if it blew against any of the turrets it would leave a dirty smear, restricting the vision of a gunner. For all such problems, the paraphernalia of Window could have its novel uses, as bomb aimer Donald Falgate explained: 'The bomb aimer's compartment was literally lined with parcels and parcels of these strips of metal – at times you could only just get into it. I found it rather convenient, after I had turfed out a parcel, to wrap myself up in the brown paper as an extra protection against the cold. It was quite useful for insulation. I did this many nights, despite having an electrically heated suit under my outer flying suit. Boy it was cold.'[13]

With Window sanctioned at the highest level of government, Harris was ready to proceed with his ambitious plan to destroy the heart of Hamburg through four massive raids by the RAF, supported by USAAF daylight attacks on the port's shipyards. In keeping with the spirit of Biblical destruction that sometimes infused Harris at moments of high intensity, he decided to call the assault Operation Gomorrah. In this narrative of vengeance, the people of Hamburg were about to reap the whirlwind for the sins of the Reich, with Bomber Command acting as the terrifying instrument of retribution in sending down 'brimstone and fire' from the sky. (Genesis 19, 24: 'Then the Lord rained upon Sodom and Gomorrah brimstone and fire from the Lord out of heaven.') On the morning of 24 July 1943, Harris held his usual nine o'clock conference in the Operations Room at High Wycombe. Bomber Command's Meteorological Officer Magnus Spence reported that, after several days of heavy cloud, the weather over Hamburg had radically improved. Gomorrah could go ahead that evening. Harris sent out the order for the stations to prepare. It was to be the biggest collective effort in Bomber Command since the Millennium Raids of early 1942. Despite the size of the force, the plan of attack was simple. Between 9.55 p.m. and 10.30 p.m. that night, 791 bombers including the Pathfinders were to take off from airfields all over the east of England, made up of 354 Lancasters, 246 Halifaxes, 125 Stirlings and 73 Wellingtons, the predominance of the Lancaster reflecting its overwhelming superiority in altitude and bomb-carrying. The plan was then for the planes to merge in a huge stream over the North Sea and head towards Hamburg, guided by yellow marker flares on the route. At one o'clock on the morning of 25 July, the Pathfinders would drop red and yellow target indicators to illuminate the aiming point. Two minutes later the first planes of the main force would start bombing. The attack would be made in six waves, each comprising between 100 and 120 bombers Each wave would have about eight minutes to clear the target, which meant every 60 seconds around 16 bombers would be flying over the aiming point.

The scale of Gomorrah added to the sense of nervous anticipation that always enveloped a station on the night of a big raid. As darkness fell, the Lancasters taxied from dispersal to the head of the runway, waiting for the green light from the controller. The first Lancasters to take off were the Pathfinders of 7 Squadron from Oakington in Cambridgeshire. Within two hours nearly 800 bombers, flying between 13,000 feet and 23,000 feet and using Gee at the limit of its range, had converged at the assembly point over the surging black waters of the North Sea. The bombers then turned towards Heligoland, the heavily fortified island on the approach to the River Elbe. Just before passing Heligoland, the Lancasters began disgorging their bundles of Window strips. Then using their H2S sets, they flew over the coast and along the Elbe towards Hamburg.

The bomber crews had expected to encounter the usual heavy fire from flak and fighters as they reached enemy territory, but to their amazement the bombardment never materialized. Window had worked more successfully than even its most enthusiastic supporters had predicted. The intricate web of German defences, so reliant on the Würzburg and Freya radars, was thrown into total chaos, overwhelmed by the little metal strips descending from the bombers at 300 feet per minute. Some of the search-lights swayed across the sky like a gang of drunks, unable to focus on anything. In the operations rooms around Hamburg, the radar screens showed nothing but a general fuzz. It was just as frustrating for the German fighter crews, whose Lichtenstein radar guidance system was also knocked out by Window. One Luftwaffe pilot, Peter Spoden, testified to his panicky confusion. 'It was a huge shock. Suddenly we were blind. All our radar equipment just tinkled. The ground control could no longer tell us anything.'[14] Back in Berlin, General Kammhuber himself was in despair at the breakdown in his cherished system. 'The whole defence system was blinded at a stroke.'[15]

For the RAF, witnessing the impotence of the once fabled flak guns, the new sense of invincibility was exhilarating, as Sergeant Len Bradfield, a bomb aimer with 49 Squadron, recalled: 'It was absolutely fantastic. We came up the Elbe and could see the river quite clearly. The radar-controlled master blue searchlights were standing absolutely upright and the white ones were weaving around, just searching . . . We were quite early in on the second wave and the fires were just beginning. The target had been very well marked with red and green TIs. It was the only time on any bomb run I was able to have twenty seconds completely unimpeded, without being stalked by flak.'[16] Thomas Tredwell was impressed that Window was just as effective as his commanders had promised at the pre-flight briefing. 'It proved to be exactly as we had been told. As we were dropping the Window through a chute and it was spreading out below us like confetti, it really worked beautifully. We were able to go across, bomb our target without any particular trouble whatsoever and come back as if it had been an uneventful trip.'[17]

With the German guns and fighters groping helplessly in the darkness, the first raid on Hamburg on 24–5 July was one of those rare occasions when a military operation is executed almost as the commanders had planned it. Only 45 of the 791 bombers made abortive sorties. The weather was even better than forecast. The attack began right on schedule at 12.57 a.m. when the first yellow and red markers were dropped by the Pathfinders on the aiming point. As the main force swept over the target, the Pathfinders kept replenishing the blazing light of the target with green markers. Inevitably, there was the usual problem of 'creepback' as the attack developed, with successive bomb aimers releasing their loads further and further away from the aiming point. By the end of the raid, the fires created by the incendiary bombs stretched back seven miles along the approach to the target. Even so, there could be no dispute that Hamburg had taken a fearful pounding. A total of 2,400 tons of bombs, including 350,412 individual incendiaries, had fallen on the centre of the city and its suburbs. Numerous factories, civic buildings and residential streets were reduced to nothing but glass and rubble. The Hamburg fire brigade was overwhelmed by the blazes started by incendiaries, its task made all the harder because the water pressure was low in the dry peak of summer. The public was dumbfounded at this unprecedented onslaught, which seemed to open a dark new chapter on the German home front.

A vivid description of the attack was provided by Johann Johannsen, who manned a flak battery near the aiming point:

> With incredible swiftness, the disaster was suddenly upon us. Before and behind our battery heavy chunks of metal were striking. Howling and hissing, fire and iron were falling from the sky. The whole city was lit up in a sea of flames! With dogged fury we remained at our guns, exposed to the raging force of the attack. Everyone looked for something to hold on to, so as not to be hurled down by the pressure of the exploding bombs. Every now and then I chanced another look over towards my house. I skipped a breath – a column of fire shot up high – everything was in flames.[18]

The combination of the summer heat and the ferocity of the incendiary fires was so lethal that it led to surreal, unearthly weather conditions over the city. Professor Dr Franz Termer, the director of one of Hamburg's museums, watched the inferno from his home in the western suburbs:

> On a wide horizon, from north to south, a single fiery glow; above this, while we had a clear starry sky over us, an enormous cloud whirled and billowed upon itself over the city, reaching to the sky with sharp, threatening edges. I was reminded of a volcano eruption and, to strengthen this, the phenomena it caused were similar to an eruption. Because of the hot air, which rose and then cooled and condensed in the upper atmosphere, a downpour fell over Hamburg from the 2000-3000 metre high cloud of smoke . . . In Hamburg the rain mixed with ash and created a thick black mud, as we know of volcanic eruptions – a mixture that covered everything, distorted people's faces and matted their hair.[19]

Fifteen hundred people were killed that night in Hamburg, a toll three times higher than in Coventry in November 1940. But this was only just the start of the devastation.

Apart from the savagery of the fires, what made the first raid on

Hamburg remarkable was the low number of Allied casualties, far below the usual for a raid on Germany. Just 12 of the bombers failed to return and only 33 were damaged, a tribute to the power of Window. Invigorated by this achievement, the Allies gave Hamburg no respite. During the day on 25 and 26 July, the American 8th Air Force made two heavy attacks on the city. These were followed up at night by light Mosquito raids aimed at disrupting the emergency services. Then on 27 July, Harris launched another bomber armada at the German port. A total of 736 aircraft, including 356 Lancasters, flew to Hamburg, this time adopting a north-easterly approach but again using Window strips. The results were even more catastrophic than on the previous raid, partly because the Pathfinder marking was more consistent and partly because a greater proportion of incendiaries were used, Harris having been taken with how well the city burnt on the previous raid. For once there was little 'creep-back'. A massive concentration of bombs fell in the Billwarder district, almost half the aircraft dropping their loads within three miles of the aiming point.

As high explosives ripped apart buildings and created sweeping draughts through the streets, the incendiaries spread their flames across the ground. By 1.20 a.m. a raging firestorm had started to engulf the city, its howling force whipped up by the freakish weather conditions over the city. The sultriness of an unusually dry, hot summer had created a pocket of warm, unstable air directly above Hamburg, its heat intensified by the glowing fires and smoke particles caused by the first RAF and USAAF raids. As the historian Keith Lowe put it in his magnificent study of the bombing of Hamburg, this pocket, surrounded on all sides and above by colder air, was like 'a huge pressurized balloon, sticking up some 10,000 feet' and ready to be exploded by another sudden rise in temperature.[20] That is precisely what now happened. The flaming mass of incendiaries sent the warm air soaring thousands more feet into the sky, creating a vacuum at ground level which was filled by rushing, thundering winds. Gusting at over 170 mph and accompanied by a diabolical roar, these tornadoes not only fanned the flames but also scythed through almost everything in their path. Trees were uprooted, roofs torn off buildings, people hurled through the air. The fire and wind fed one another in an orgy of destruction. It was the most savage firestorm in history, not so much Gomorrah as the Apocalypse. People burned to death in the streets from sheer intensity of the heat. Trams and trains buckled and collapsed. The asphalt of roadways turned to boiling liquid. One nineteen-year-old milliner described seeing 'people on the roadway, some already dead, some still lying alive but stuck in the asphalt . . . Their feet had got stuck and then they had to put out their hands to try to get out again. They were on their hands and knees screaming.'[21] Thousands were asphyxiated by lack of oxygen or died of smoke inhalation as they sought shelter in underground cellars. Those who made it to rivers or canals fared little better, for the deadly heat continued to suck oxygen out of the air, while the fire was even spread across water surfaces by exploding oil tankers and the debris of burning coal barges. Hermann Kroger, the leader of a fire-fighting team at a factory in Wendenstrasse, described how the storm started as 'a shrill howling in the street. It grew into a hurricane so that we had to abandon all hope of fighting the fire. It was as though we were doing no more than throwing a drop of water onto a hot stone. The whole yard, the canal, in fact as far as we could see, was just a whole great massive sea of fire.'[22]

The boiling inferno below was an awesome spectacle to the men of Bomber Command. 'It was like flying into a holocaust. It was awful, just one huge fire,' said Maurice Flower.[23] One Pathfinder pilot, Trevor Timperley of 156 Squadron, was so shocked by the sight that he kept demanding his navigator join him in the cockpit to witness the firestorm. 'The blaze was unimaginable. I remember saying to the navigator, who was always engrossed with his charts: "For Christ's sake, Smithy, come and see this. You'll never see the like of it again." I had to tell him about three times. "Do come and bloody well have a look at it." I was astounded that anyone would not wish to see such a spectacle. There were solid flames. It looked as though the whole ground was ablaze.'[24] Timperley admitted that the devastation provoked troubling questions about the morality of the bomber offensive, and his views sum up the feelings of most of these courageous men:

> Hamburg raised for me for the first time the ethics of bombing because the casualties from the fire were so high. At the time I took the view that the so-called civilian was part of the German war machine. To call a woman a civilian and a non-combatant was untrue, because she could be working in a factory producing ammunition. The same could be said of anyone else working in the shipyards or transport. They were all part of the Germans' wholehearted effort. The only ones you are left with are children, and they are the most difficult of the lot. They were not involved, so you were left with a terrible feeling about them. But the Germans did have a chance to evacuate them from big cities and obvious targets. So to an extent the Germans put their own children in the front line. I still think the greatest war crime of all would have been to lose the war. There was not any alternative to defeating the Nazi regime.[25]

The next morning, much of Hamburg was a wilderness of death and chaos. The smoke was so thick that it blotted out the sun. There were corpses everywhere, many of them little more than twisted, blackened remnants of humanity. Other bodies lay in a mass of congealed fat. Occasionally, to the anguish of the rescue parties, a naked figure, charred beyond recognition, might give a faint agonized sound of life. Because of the complete breakdown in all administrative machinery and the subsequent mass evacuation of the city, it was impossible to put a definite figure on the number of people who died in Hamburg on the night of 27–8 July. The total number killed in the Hamburg campaign has been estimated at 45,000, including 21,000 women and 8,000 children, and the vast majority of these casualties occurred in the firestorm. But statistical inexactitude could not disguise the hammer blow that the Reich had suffered. A wave of panic swept through the German High Command. In his diaries Goebbels called the aftermath of the second raid 'the greatest crisis of the war' and warned that the Germans faced problems that were 'almost impossible of solution'.[26] Albert Speer expressed his fear that six similar raids on other German cities would bring the entire armaments industry to a halt, though Erhard Milch, the State Secretary for Air, regarded this as complacent. 'We have lost the war,' he cried.[27] For the first time, civilian morale in Germany showed signs of cracking, the sense of despair fuelled by the vast evacuation of the homeless to other German regions. According to intelligence reports from the SS, the refugees' testimony of the devastation inflicted by the RAF had caused a 'shock-effect and huge consternation' across 'the whole territory of the Reich'.[28] One Hamburg resident Mathilde Wolf-Monkenburg confessed that 'we have lost courage and are filled only with a dumb kind of passive apathy'.[29] Some were not so passive. A few brave souls, feeling they had nothing to lose, dared to voice their open defiance of the Nazi Party. Amidst the wreckage of her home, one woman yelled at a group of Nazi guards: 'You pigs! It's all your fault.'[30]

In contrast to the despondency in Germany, the mood in Britain was more positive than it had been at any time since 1939. Bomber Command really seemed to be turning the tide. Cinema audiences cheered as a British Movietone newsreel reported: 'Hamburg – second city of the Reich – is being liquidated in a series of attacks by the RAF. Germans call these attacks terror raids. They must certainly be terrifying to Hitler as he watches factory after factory, city after city going up in smoke.'[31] For the *Daily Express* Basil Cardew reported on the growing confidence at the Lancaster bases. 'Never has Bomber Command's morale been higher.

The men know they are winning a great strategic battle.'[32] The high spirits reflected the continuing low casualties as a result of Window. On the second Hamburg raid, just 17 bombers had failed to return out of the 777 despatched, and only 49 were damaged. Yet Bomber Command's apparently insignificant losses concealed a worrying reality. For amidst the fiery carnage of the second raid on Hamburg, the Luftwaffe was developing a new tactic to fight back against Window, one that would ultimately spell disaster for Bomber Command. The tragic irony of Window was that it gave the RAF an overwhelming short-term advantage over the Reich's defences, but its deployment inspired the Germans to create a much more flexible and dangerous fighter system, which would eventually begin to wreak havoc in the heavy-bomber streams. Those who had cautioned against the use of Window, fearing that it could be counterproductive, turned out to be correct, though not in the way that they imagined.

What Window had exposed was the rigidity of the Kammhuber Line, whose elaborately constructed network of fighter 'boxes' was both too reliant on radar-led ground controllers and too restrictive of night fighter pilots' initiative. The procedures, demarcation lines and technology had almost become ends in themselves rather than tools with which to help the fighters. German night fighter pilot Peter Boden gave this insight into the limitations of the box system during the first Hamburg raid. 'I remember the terrible fires but at that time we had tactics that were completely wrong. We were given boxes, areas of sky 150 kilometres by, say, 200 kilometres and there we had to stay. I was over Greichwald and because the fires were so terrible, I could see the silhouettes of the four-engined aircraft over Hamburg, but I was not allowed to leave my box. We were shouting, "We must go to Hamburg, we can see them, we can see them!" But we were not allowed.'[33]

Window liberated the Luftwaffe from the failing prison of the Kammhuber Line. Its entire edifice crumbled the moment its radar became inoperable. One German officer quick to seize the opportunity for an alternative approach was Major Hajo Hermann, a former bomber pilot serving on the Luftwaffe staff. Since March 1943 Hermann had been conducting experiments in the use of single-engine day fighters on freelance operations at night. His theory was that the light from marker flares, fires and searchlights would be enough to illuminate the British heavy bombers without having to resort to radar. Effectively, German fighters would roam the skies on their own looking for their prey, the antithesis of Kammhuber's system. It was a tactic known as 'Wilde Sau' (Wild Boar)

and, after the disaster of the first Hamburg raid, the Luftwaffe was willing to try it in action against a full bomber stream. A few of Hermann's
Wilde Sau aircraft operated against the RAF on the night of 27–8 July,
returning Bomber Command pilots reporting that, to their surprise, they
had seen Focke-Wulf 190s and Messerschmitt 109s in the night skies. It
is likely that Hermann's fighters accounted for the small increase in casualties over the first raid. But it was when Harris ordered a third massive
attack on Hamburg, on 29–30 July by 777 bombers, including 355
Lancasters, that the new Wilde Sau tactic really made itself felt. After the
first two raids, many of the bomber crews were expecting an even easier
trip, now that so much of Hamburg lay in smouldering ashes. But just
the opposite was the case. Completely fearless, the German fighters tore
into the heavy bombers as soon as the Pathfinders had dropped their
markers. A total of 27 RAF aircraft were shot down, 11 of them Lancasters.
Bill McCrea, a 57 Squadron pilot, recalled the new terror that the maraud-
ing fighters could provoke:

> The journey across and above a blazing Hamburg was one of the strangest
> I have ever undertaken. No one fired at us, no fighter attacked us, no
> searchlight pointed in our direction. But as I turned away after dropping
> our bombs, I have never felt so exposed and so vulnerable All I could do
> was fix my eyes on the darkness beyond the fires and pray that we would
> reach that darkness before we were spotted by a fighter. Although we
> managed to fly without incident, one of our colleagues was not so lucky.
> I watched as a bomber just ahead and slightly below was subjected to a
> series of attacks from a fighter. It burst into flames and soon commenced
> its final fiery spiral into the earth below.[34]

An account of taking down a Lancaster of 460 Squadron during this
third raid was given by Oberleutnant Joachim Wendtland, a fighter-control
officer who flew in an Me 110 as an observer with the renowned pilot
Hauptmann Prinz zur Lippe-Weissenfeld in a freelance operation against
the bomber stream. 'The dark shape of the four-engined aircraft was
clearly visible against the night sky above us. It was a Lancaster. The pilot
hit his left wing with his first attack and burning pieces of it flew off.
The pilot was a little disappointed that the bomber was not shot down
by this first attack. He had wanted to show me how to hit it between
the two engines and finish it off quickly. The Lancaster kept straight and
level all the time, without any evasive action.' So the Me 110 now made
a second attack. 'Prinz zur Lippe used his special method. He slid under
the bomber, pulled up the nose suddenly, fired a burst and dropped away
quickly in case the bomber blew up. It didn't although pieces were still

falling off it. We attacked again. The bomber still did not explode.' The German fighter now came in for another attack. 'This time, his wing started burning after only half a second. We saw the Lancaster go down into a wood near a railway.'[35] Despite the German fightback, however, the further damage inflicted on Hamburg was considerable. One resident, Luise Solmitz, said the scene in her street, when she emerged from her shelter, was a 'fantastic drama . . . a lonely blazing hell, filled with flames raging with their own life. Later only the bunker shafts were aglow, the shops were black, dead caves. At the end the flame was burning blue. During the daytime the air was shimmering with heat.'[36]

If the third Hamburg raid was not the unqualified success of the first two, the final raid, on the night of 2 August, turned out to be a disaster, thanks mainly to Harris's mix of impatience and misjudgement. As the fires in the city still glowed, he was determined to finish off the job with another devastating onslaught. But after the heat of July, the weather now turned against him. Reconnaissance Mosquitoes reported in the early evening that there was a danger of a possible storm that night, but Harris ignored the warning and dispatched 740 bombers, with 318 Lancasters again the dominant force. The weather was just as bad as the grimmest forecasts. Conditions were appalling over the North Sea as the bombers flew into a gigantic storm cloud over 20,000 feet high, its edges lit up by flashes of lightning. The storm then worsened over the coast, as the aircraft faced the threats of static electricity, gale force winds and ice on the wings.

Engineer Norman Ashton of 460 Squadron wrote in his memoir of the desperate battle by his Lancaster *W-William* against the elements:

> As we stooged along little blue lights of static electricity began to dance across the framework of our cockpit windows . . . Suddenly a terrific flash split the darkness, followed by several more at short intervals. The 'front' was beginning to show its teeth! The static increased in severity and when I looked out of the windows I saw a fantastic sight. Each propeller track formed a huge foot-thick circle of vivid blue light; guns, aerials, windows and air-intake grilles flickered with gremlinesque lights and from each wing tip a vicious, yards long, blue electric flame licked back into the slipstream.

The Lancaster roared on, but now ice started to form on the wings and the airframe. The ice became heavier and the Merlins throbbed out of synchronization as *W-William* lurched about the sky. 'We tried everything but the port engines got worse every minute and the airframe was shaking like a leaf in the wind. The situation was rapidly getting out of hand. A few miles short of the target, *William* gave a convulsive shudder, turned over on to his port side and then fell clean out of the sky.' But in a cool manoeuvre Ashton and his pilot managed to regain control of the Lancaster. First they jettisoned the bomb load. Then they feathered both port engines and increased power on the starboard ones, before heaving back the control column so the plane came out of its plunge. Having set course for home, they managed to restart the port engines over the North Sea and returned to base with the *W-William* intact.[37]

The Lancaster flown by Jack Currie suffered even more drama when it was held in the icy grip of the storm. 'I could see nothing through the window, nothing but a blue infernal glow. I heard no engines, only roaring wind and savage thunder-claps For the first time in the air, I felt impotence and with that, a sudden prick of panic.' Weighed down by ice, his Lancaster suddenly stalled and Currie barked the warning over the intercom: 'Pilot to crew, prepare to abandon aircraft.' But the plunge had the effect of loosening some of the ice and at 8,000 feet Currie was able to bring the aircraft back to level altitude. The violence of the spinning dive, however, had torn off both ailerons. By clever manipulation of the throttles to adjust the power in the engines, Currie was able to turn round the aircraft and stagger towards home, despite the heavy damage to the plane. Increasingly short of petrol, the Lancaster made it to the Lincolnshire coast but now came the hardest part. 'I began to consider how I might make a landing. I had heard no precedent for landing a Lancaster without aileron control.' Because of the tremendous risk, he gave the crew the option of bailing out, but they showed their faith in him by staying. He justified their loyalty by making a remarkably smooth descent onto the runway, his performance hailed as a 'magnificent show' by his station commander.[38] The same words could not be used of Bomber Command's organization of this fourth raid. A total of 30 aircraft had been lost, fewer than half of the bombers reached their target and 106 of them had dropped their bombs into the sea. Yet even in these dire circumstances, 1,426 tons of bombs had still been dropped on Hamburg.

Operation Gomorrah had come to an end. It had left much of Germany's second city in ruins. The stench of decay and burnt flesh was everywhere. As the sewage and refuse systems broke down, plagues of rats infested the streets, feasting on the piles of rubbish and waste. Bodies had to be dragged from cellars, canals and the streets 'No flight of imagination will ever succeed in measuring and describing the gruesome scenes of horror in many buried air raid shelters,' wrote the Police President of

Hamburg.[39] Four huge mass graves were dug by workers from concentration camps, guarded by SS troops who kept drinking alcohol to cope with the putrid smell. At first the death toll was put by the German authorities at over 100,000, but 45,400 is now the widely accepted estimate. Less than 1 per cent of the casualties were caused by the two daylight American raids. According to the US and British post-war surveys, 61 per cent of Hamburg's living accommodation and half of its commercial buildings were razed to the ground. The catalogue of obliteration included 22 transport depots, 112 Nazi Party offices, 12 bridges, 5,000 retail stores and 80 military installations. The morbid gloom emanating from Hamburg was reinforced by the mass exodus of frightened people in the aftermath of the raids. 'It was the most pathetic sight I have ever seen,' recalled Margot Schulz, who lived on the route out of the city towards Berlin. 'They were in their night dresses, half-burned sometimes . . . You have to imagine the hysteria, with some of the people burnt and crying. It went on for days. It was just endless.'[40] Around 1.2 million people left Hamburg in the wake of the attack.

It seemed impossible that life could carry on in Hamburg. Indeed some in Britain, like the Pathfinder leader Don Bennett, felt that the moment had come to push for a negotiated surrender, given the scale of the disaster inflicted on the Reich. That was never even a remote possibility, since Churchill and Roosevelt had agreed at the Casablanca conference in January 1943 to demand the unconditional surrender of the Axis powers. But the view, promoted by the Joint Intelligence Committee, that Germany was about to break like in November 1918 was a dangerous fallacy. The truth was that, for all the human suffering, the wider military and industrial consequences of the Hamburg campaign were less far-reaching than Bomber Command imagined. The infrastructure of the city itself proved astonishingly resilient. Within days of the fourth raid, the roads had been opened again, and by the end of November, 80 per cent of gas, water and electricity services had been restored. Astonishingly, at the end of 1943, 91 per cent of the aircraft industry was operating at its pre-July capacity, while U-boat production had risen to 80 per cent of its previous level. Even British post-war surveyors admitted that the devastation had 'only an irritant effect on German production'.[41] The almost miraculous recovery of Hamburg and the lack of real impact on the German industry pointed to the strategic flaw at the heart of Harris and Portal's policy of area bombing. It was of little use wiping out vast numbers of civilians if Germany continued to retain the military and industrial capability to wage war. This is what had occurred at Hamburg. The vast concentration of bombs had fallen on residential districts, while some industrial quarters, including the ship-yards, emerged relatively unscathed. The Prussian soldier and historian Carl von Clausewitz, perhaps the most influential of all military theor-ists, had argued that victory in war required 'direct annihilation of the enemy's forces',[42] a doctrine to which Pointblank adhered in its injunc-tion to destroy the Luftwaffe fighter forces. Harris rejected that approach and the men of Bomber Command would pay a heavy price for his stubbornness.

The firestorm at Hamburg was the result of a unique set of circum-stances which could never be repeated again during the war. One was the introduction of Window, giving the bombers brief supremacy of the air before the Germans changed their tactics. Another was the unusual weather conditions over the city at the height of summer. A third was the geographical location of the port. But for all the debate about strategy, the Lancaster had yet again demonstrated its stunning power and bomb-loading capacity. More than half of all the planes that flew on the four raids to Hamburg were Lancasters, and on the last raid the 318 Lancasters were left to go it alone through the electric storms because the inferior altitude performance of the Stirlings, Halifaxes and Wellingtons could not cope. Another awesome display of the Lancaster's unique qualities was given just a few weeks after Gomorrah in an entirely different type of raid, when a force of 597 heavy bombers, including 324 Lancasters, attacked the German experimental weapons establishment at Peenemünde, a remote peninsula on the Baltic coast. If Hamburg showed the Lancaster at its most devastating, the Peenemünde raid showed the plane at its most incisive, flying at a low level against a narrow target.

The German research station at Peenemünde, north of Stettin, had been opened in 1937, and by 1942 work was well-advanced on the V-1 pilot-less flying bomb and the V-2 rocket, which were being developed for a long-range aerial assault on Britain. British intelligence had been dimly aware of Peenemünde during the early years of the war, but it was not until March 1943 that the station's importance was fully grasped, when two German commanders, Generals Wilhelm von Thoma and Ludwig Cruewell, who had been captured during the North African campaign, were secretly recorded in a prison camp near London talking about the V-1 and rocket programmes. Von Thoma even whispered his surprise to his colleague that he had heard no explosions in London, having expected the V-1 onslaught to have started by now. The British Government swung into action, appointing the Tory MP Duncan Sandys to investigate the truth behind the generals' conversation. It could, after all, be a hoax, argued Churchill's adviser Lord Cherwell. But reconnaissance by Mosquitoes confirmed the existence of the site. Sandys submitted his report to the War Cabinet, which authorized a heavy attack on Peenemünde.

In league with Ralph Cochrane, the Commander of 5 Group, Harris drew up the plan for the raid, which was to incorporate four key innovations. The first, and perhaps most important, was the use of the 'Master Bomber' technique, in which the raid leader orchestrated the entire operation by circling over the site and guiding the crews to the target. The method had been evolved by Guy Gibson on the Dams raid, but this was the first time it had been tried on such a big scale. The man chosen for the Gibson role was Group Captain John Searby, a calm, naturally authoritative and highly experienced Lancaster pilot who had joined the RAF as an engineering apprentice and had served under Gibson. The second innovation was the use of a significantly improved marker bomb, a 250-pound case packed with impregnated cotton wool which ignited at 3,000 feet and burned on the ground as a bright red fire. It was easy for bomber crews to identify but difficult for the Germans to simulate. The third was that there would be three aiming points rather than one, a reflection of the precision nature of the raid. These covered the quarters for the scientists and workers, the rocket factory and the experimental station. As the raid developed, some of the Pathfinders, under Searby's guidance, would have to shift the marking from one point to another, hence their designation for the raid as 'Shifters'. The fourth innovation was the adoption by some Lancasters from No. 5 Group of the 'time-and-distance' method of bombing, in which the bomb aimer did not rely on visual target indicators at all. Instead, co-operating closely with the pilot and the navigator, he calculated the time it would take the plane, travelling at a fixed speed, to fly from a certain reference point on the ground to the target. Having worked out this figure and ensured that the plane was moving at the correct speed and in the right direction, he counted down the time to cover the distance and pressed the bomb release at the required moment. The great advantage of time-and-distance was that it could be used no matter how poor the visibility over the target, but it was also highly risky because there was so much scope for human error. Ralph Cochrane was a strong advocate of the technique and pressed Harris to use it for the whole raid, but Harris, feeling that it was too experimental for such a vital operation, only agreed to a compromise by which the 5 Group Lancasters in the final wave would attack by time-and-distance.

On the night of 17 August, three waves of 596 bombers in total, of which 324 were Lancasters, took off in bright moonlight for Peenemünde and followed a straight route to the peninsula over the North Sea and Denmark. To evade radar Searby, accompanied by the leading Pathfinder Lancasters, flew over the sea at no more than 200 feet. As they headed to the isolated target, there was little flak or fighter resistance, though the Germans on Peenemünde began to send up a smokescreen to hide the station. But this action could not prevent the first Pathfinders laying down the red spot markers with great accuracy. At 02.00 the first of the main force bombers went in from 8,000 feet to attack the living quarters of the 20,000 Peenemünde staff. 'As we approached, we were pointing straight at the centre of the fires which had started – and still no fighters! There was heavy calibre flak, exploding far too high for our bombing height, but quite a lot of light stuff,' recalled flight engineer W. L. Miller of 460 Squadron. 'Over the target, we were being kicked about in front and underneath, mostly by exploding "cookies". My God, I now knew what a fly feels like being dangled over a coal fire on which chestnuts are roasting. Below was just a jumble of fire and wreckage.'[43] As the first wave completed the bombing of the accommodation blocks, the Pathfinder 'Shifters' started to mark the V-2 rocket factory ready for the second wave. Some of the green target indicators went astray, but the reds accurately fell on the buildings. 'I can hear Searby now calling out: "Don't bomb the greens, you're dropping in the sea, bomb the reds, bomb the reds,"' remembered Alec Flett of 460 Squadron.[44] Bill Griffiths, an engineer with 115 Squadron, was exhilarated by the experience: 'We had to go real steady for about four minutes. We saw the buildings below and it gave me a lot of pleasure to hit those fucking buildings. It really did. "Bombs gone": "Right, we got the bastards," I thought. There was a bit of flak but it was so exciting going in.'[45]

The first two waves had been lucky to escape the attention of the German fighters, which had initially been drawn to Berlin by a diversionary raid mounted by Mosquitoes. But when the German ground control saw through Bomber Command's deception, the fighters were immediately dispatched to Peenemünde, where they confronted the third wave, made up of Halifaxes and No. 5 Group Lancasters attacking the experimental block with the 'time-and-distance' method. Hajo Hermann's new Wilde Sau freelance technique of using day fighters as night marauders was particularly deadly, as Sergeant Patrick Barry, a rear gunner with 467 Squadron, recalled. Just as his Lancaster was turning from the target, it was attacked by an Me 109. 'It was an explosive and confused situation. It happened so quickly and dramatically. Cannon fire ripped in from the 109. There was an explosion inside the bomber. The fighter came up, exposing his belly and I got a burst in before my hydraulics were destroyed and the turret immobilised. Everything went haywire. The ammunition started exploding in the ducts, the damned aircraft was on fire and in a mad screaming dive at a sharp angle. It was, I thought, a death dive.' Barry was in agony, his face lacerated by shards of Perspex and blood pouring from a wound in his leg. 'A feeling of calm acceptance washed over me. It was extraordinary. I have never since experienced anything like it. But it was a unique situation. I sat there, completely relaxed, waiting to die.'

But the pilot, an Australian called Warren Wilson, was not ready to give up. He pulled the Lancaster out of its dive, then ordered two of the airmen to put out the fire. Oblivious to their own safety, the two men turned on the raging flames with fire extinguishers and even their gloved hands. Once the fire had died down, they then hauled Barry from his shattered turret, cut off his blood-soaked boot and injected him with a heavy dose of morphine. The Lancaster limped over the Danish coast, across the North Sea and, under Wilson's expert handling, landed at Bottesford in Leicestershire. The plane was so badly damaged that it was sent back to Avro for rebuilding. As for Barry, he was brought into Bottesford sick quarters and was in such a poor condition that he was given the last rites by a Catholic chaplain. But he survived, was awarded the DFC and had his leg rebuilt by plastic surgery. A fragment of shrapnel always remained lodged in his skull.[46]

The Peenemünde raid was also the first time that the Germans used the deadly tactic of Schrage Musik, where fighters equipped with upward-firing guns slid undetected below the heavy bombers and fired into their undersides. The experience of being hit without seeing any fighter perplexed the bomber crews, as Sergeant R. Garnett, a rear gunner in 467 Squadron described: 'We were hit, just a very gentle judder, but the speed of the aircraft was affected. The sensation was as though the aircraft had hit a very big cloud of cotton wool. We saw no tracer. That was a complete mystery to we gunners. We couldn't see how an aircraft could be hit by invisible fire like that. Then immediately a real stream of fire and sparks came back past my turret from the port wing. It was just like a real gunpowder plot night, just like a bonfire being lit. The pilot told us to get out at once. I heard him asking for someone to pass his parachute.'[47] But even with this new tactic, the German pilots did not have it all their own way, thanks to the courageous skill of the RAF crews and the resilience of the Lancaster.

Unteroffizier Walter Holker described one attempt to bring down a Lancaster, after sending a Halifax to its doom:

> We climbed up again and found another (bomber) immediately – a Lancaster this time. I think this one had seen us because he started his weaving, evasive manoeuvre. It was difficult to get under this bomber when he was flying in this way so I maintained a steady course and waited for him to cross over the top of me. I fired when he did so but my first shots went behind him. I corrected by dropping my nose a little and the next burst started hitting him in the left wing. But he responded by putting his nose up and his tail gunner opened fire on me. He was a really good shot. One of his bullets hit the portable oxygen bottles that our third man – the extra lookout – needed. The bottle exploded. I don't know what happened next. I wasn't able to think very clearly. I found later that I had got three bits of metal in the back of my head and about forty in the rest of my body.[48]

Bomber Command suffered far higher losses at Peenemünde than on any of the Hamburg raids. Of the 40 bombers that failed to return, 23 were Lancasters, the vast majority of these losses incurred during the last wave. The missing rate of 6.7 per cent was far above Bomber Command's sustainable average. While this might have been acceptable for such a special mission, the impact of both Wilde Sau and Schrage Musik were worrying portents for the future. Despite the heavy losses, Bomber Command deemed the raid a tactical success. Almost 1,800 tons had been dropped on the target, destroying the main buildings, drawing offices and living quarters. Over 600 workers were killed, among them several key scientists. Moreover, the tactic of the Master Bomber, heroically executed in this case by John Searby, had proved highly effective, and Cochrane's time-and-distance method had been of crucial assistance for the third wave just when smoke and flames were obscuring the markers. But again, just as with Hamburg, the long-term results were more mixed. The damage to the experimental stations and the rocket factory at Peenenünde was not as terminal as first appeared, and the base rapidly returned to full operations. The process of recovery was further accelerated by Albert Speer's highly efficient dispersal organization for German industry, which meant that there was little chance of knocking out a key element of the production process in one blow. In fact, it has been estimated that the V-2 rocket programme was only delayed by two months and the V-1 programme was barely affected at all.

The offensive against Germany was the dominant theme of the bomber war throughout the summer of 1943, but Harris, with some reluctance, had to continue with mine-laying sorties and missions to Italy. The crews generally saw the trips to Milan, Genoa and Turin as a relief from the strains of flying over Germany, since the Italian defences were so much weaker and Mussolini's regime was crumbling. Indeed, the heavy-bomber assaults on the northern cities played a useful role in turning the public mood against Il Duce and forcing Italy out of the war by September 1943. Taking part in a raid on Turin on 12 July by 295 Lancasters, wireless operator Les King recalled that the opposition from the Italians 'was laughable in comparison to the Ruhr. When we arrived the first bombs were falling and the Italians' searchlight system collapsed, as if they'd lit up their own city to help us identify the target. The Italians as an enemy were not exactly a brave force, but this was pathetic, ridiculous. In consequences, the ack-ack was negligible and no losses were incurred by our squadron, although one Lancaster iced up while flying over the Alps and had to return earlier.'[49] A total of 792 people were killed in the raid. But the moral dimension of bombing northern Italy troubled Don Charlwood, a navigator with 103 Squadron, who was plunged into introspection by the ease of a raid on Turin:

> As the first aircraft neared the target, the cone of searchlights sprang angrily into action. At the same time the air was filled with the smoke of shells. But when the first bombs fell, a strange thing happened. For a few moments the searchlights sought for aircraft, then, as though the defenders had been called to some more urgent duty, the beams stopped moving. Some remained pointing upward, some at acute angles, some almost horizontal. The whole scene had taken on the immobility of a picture. At the same time the flak almost ceased. We looked down incredulously. Under the light of the moon the city was mercilessly exposed – houses, churches, gardens, even statuary along the streets. The crews wheeled and dived, exulting as the Germans exulted over lightly defended Britain in 1940. And yet, perhaps the minds of the attackers would have been easier if the Italians attempted to defend their city. As it was, we blew women and children to pieces, unopposed by their men.[50]

But these trips in mid-1943 were not entirely free from danger, especially because heavy German reinforcements, including fighters, had moved into Italy to halt the northerly advance of the Allies. On the raid against Turin on 12 July, for instance, 13 Lancasters were lost. Seven Lancasters were shot down on a raid to Milan on 15 August, one of them a plane flown by Jack Sullivan. Engineer Ken Harvey recalled the incident:

We thought it would be a piece of cake, being an Italian target. We were obviously in the wrong area at the right time. We were on our way to Milan with a full bomb load and the fighter came from nowhere underneath. He hit a magnesium flare and the back of the aircraft was an inferno. The roaring flames were just behind me and I was virtually blinded by the glare. It was impossible to see what was happening behind me. Jack Sullivan ordered a bail-out. I can't understand why only I and the bomb aimer got out. The pilot seemed to be the only one left in the aircraft and he was trying to hold the controls as best he could. He was magnificent. He saw me and shouted, 'Get out.'

Harvey was leaning over the escape hatch, when suddenly the Lancaster went into a spin and he was thrown against the roof. He thought he was doomed but then the Lancaster twisted violently again. 'I fell and went straight through the escape hatch. I pulled the ripcord straight away and almost immediately afterwards saw the aircraft hit the ground.'[51] Harvey had landed in a tree near a German airfield and though he managed to get down, he was arrested the next morning and spent the rest of the war as a POW in Germany.

Harris had never been enthusiastic about the Italian raids and had only conducted them under political pressure from the Air Staff. There was, however, one Italian adventure that seized his imagination, even though it ran counter to all his instinctive loathing for 'panacea' targets. Flushed with the success of 617 Squadron, Harris was looking for another daring mission for Gibson's 'old lags', as he called them. Reviving an idea he had first contemplated in 1942, Harris came up with the extraordinary proposal that the Dambusters men could be used to assassinate Mussolini either in his residence or in his office. On 11 July he wrote to Portal, setting out a scheme, under the code name Audax, by which 12 Lancasters would be 'routed across France under the cover of darkness and then would attack the Palazzo Venezia and the Villa Torlonia at 0930, before going on to North Africa'. The Lancasters would each be carrying a 1,000-pound general-purpose bomb fused with a three-second delay.[52] Portal was enthusiastic and took the idea up with Churchill, writing to him on 13 July:

> Harris has asked permission to try to bomb Mussolini in his office and to bomb his residence simultaneously in case the Duce is late that morning. The plan was made last year but was turned down because of the ban on bombing Rome at that time. Harris would use the squadron of the Lancasters (617) which made the attack on the Dams. It is manned by experts and is kept for special purposes of this kind.[53]

Churchill passed the correspondence on to Anthony Eden, the Foreign Secretary, who found little merit in the proposal. 'The chances of killing Mussolini are surely very slight,' he told Churchill:

> and those of 'shaking' him not much better. If we fail to kill him, we shall certainly not do his reputation any harm. We may even raise his stock of waning popularity. Meanwhile, we will have incurred the odium of knocking the older part of the city about and causing civilian casualties without achieving any military result My advice is to lay off the present proposal because the target is too difficult a one to warrant the attempt on military grounds and because on psychological grounds it could be exploited to our disadvantage unless 100 per cent successful.[54]

It was a veto that Churchill fully supported. 'I agree,' he wrote back to Eden.[55]

The swift downfall of Mussolini rendered the whole project an irrelevance. From September 1943, the Reich was to be Bomber Command's sole enemy. And the battle was about to become even harder.

12

'At the machines all the time'

~

AIRCRAFT MANUFACTURING WAS Britain's largest industrial concern during the war, employing 1.8 million people at its peak in 1944, a reflection of the importance of the bomber offensive. At the centre of this vital industry was the manufacture of the Avro Lancaster, which by the middle of the war had become the RAF's most important plane. Building the Lancaster was a mammoth task. Each aircraft consisted of 55,000 separate parts, excluding nuts, bolts and rivets. To produce one, an estimated 500,000 different manufacturing operations were involved, taking up to 70,000 man-hours, which compared to 15,200 hours for a Spitfire. Nearly ten tons of light aluminium alloy were consumed in building each plane, the equivalent of 11 million saucepans. A Lancaster required 7,140 square feet of floor-space to complete and needed the same manufacturing capacity as that needed for 40 basic motor cars. The factory cycle from raw material to finished aircraft took about ten weeks. In 1943 prices, each finished plane cost approximately £42,000 to build, including the engines, landing gear and flying systems, though it is telling that, thanks to Avro's efficiency, the outlay on the Lancaster's airframe was substantially lower than the Halifax's. According to a 1944 report by MAP, the Lancaster Mark III's airframe cost £17,000, excluding profit and tools, whereas the Halifax figure could be as high as £28,000.[1] This difference reflected the ethos of Avro, which held that simplicity of production was a key element of good design. As a result, the structure of the plane was divided into 36 components which could be built individually on different sites around the factory and then put together on one final assembly line. The fuselage, including the bomb doors and the rear turret, was broken into seven sections to permit the separate production of each unit. Similarly, the complete span of the wing was divided into 14 segments, the most important of which was the centre section where the main spar booms were attached to the load-bearing longerons and the floor of the fuselage, forming a single sturdy unit at the heart of the plane.

The technical journal *Aircraft Manufacturing*, which ran a four-part series on the detailed construction of the Lancaster in early 1943, was full of praise for Avro's approach: 'Much of the success which has been achieved in the large-scale production of the Lancaster is due to the very thorough pre-production system of organising labour, equipment and material supplies. The basis of the system is the careful planning of the manufacturing programme right down to the smallest detail.[2]

Once all details of planning and ordering had been completed, the work of making the parts and constructing the plane began. Again the scale of the enterprise was striking. Many sheet-metal parts were moulded to the correct shape on a massive 6,000-ton John Shaw hydraulic press, which had previously been used to make newspapers. The main spar booms were channelled out and milled from solid bars on special cutting machines built for Avro by the firm of Watkins Ltd. Even the Lancaster wing tip, usually a minor component on other aircraft, required three sub-assemblies in its construction. As the separate sections were finished, they were then brought together to create unified major parts, such as the rear fuselage or the starboard wing. As the assembly progressed, the crucial equipment was installed, like the wiring, the instrument panels, the oil tanks, turrets, canopies and rudder pedals. Then the final assembly took place as engines were fitted and the wings, tail unit and fuselage sections were joined to form the complete aircraft. At the main Avro base in Manchester, the components were built at the factory in Chadderton and then transported by lorry and trailers on a 16-mile journey to the massive plant at Woodford, which by August 1943 had three assembly tracks each a quarter of a mile long. Between October 1941 and March 1945, Woodford assembled 4,040 Lancasters, more than half the entire production run. Other factories in the Lancaster group, like Avro's at Yeadon in Yorkshire or Vickers' at Chester, carried out their own final assembly. The last stages of the production process impressed a reporter from the *Aeroplane* magazine:

> And so the Lancaster begins to take shape on the final assembly floor – the product of many dispersed shops reaching one of many assembly plants. The machine begins to assume its huge size, towering on its wheels – each 5 feet 6 inches in diameter – 20 feet above the floor. A thing that strikes one immediately is the huge single-bomb compartment, 33 feet long, under the fuselage, closed only by two great doors curved to follow the lines of the fuselage itself. The simplification to two doors, which can be opened hydraulically in five seconds, is typical of the simplicity in design on which Mr Chadwick insists and contributes largely to the speed of production.[3]

Demand for the Lancaster had led to a phenomenal growth in the size of the Avro operation. In the late 1930s, the firm had been based at Newton Heath, with assembly and flight testing carried out at Woodford. But the substantial contracts for both the Manchester and the Anson meant that Avro needed more floor-space, so under the aircraft expansion programme the government gave a grant of £1 million to build a new factory at Chadderton. The new plant, with an attractive art-deco frontage, was certainly an impressive building, but the pressures of war meant that it was not big enough to meet the government's production needs. Instructed by the Air Ministry to build another, even larger factory, Roy Dobson chose the site of Yeadon in Yorkshire, previously used for the Leeds/Bradford municipal airport. Contractors worked through the winter of 1940–1 and the Avro Yeadon factory opened in February 1941. At the time Yeadon was the largest factory under one roof in Europe, standing 740 feet high and taking up 1.5 million acres of floor-space, twice the size of Chadderton. The plant incorporated several advanced features, including an American-style heating and ventilation system and a well-appointed canteen with seating for 7,000 workers. The machine shop was the most up-to-date in the country, its centrepiece an 8,000-ton hydraulic press known as the 'Manipulator'. But the really interesting physical aspect of Yeadon was the method used to camouflage the buildings. Dobson brought in expert designers from the film industry and, on their advice, earth was banked at 45 degrees against the walls to eliminate shadows, while the flat roof was laid out with replica fields, farms, a pond and even dummy animals to blend in with the surrounding countryside. The effect, achieved at a modest cost of £20,000, was so convincing that even Allied pilots struggled to locate the Yeadon runway.

But even the advent of Yeadon was not enough to ensure that the supply of Lancasters could meet the RAF's demand for them. So other firms and plants, most of them part of the giant Vickers-Armstrong armaments and aviation conglomerate, had to be enlisted for Lancaster production, becoming part of 'the Lancaster Group' under the auspices of Avro. Among these companies were Vickers at Chester, which delivered a total of 235 aircraft between June 1944 and September 1945, and Metropolitan-Vickers of Manchester, which produced its first Lancaster in January 1942 and altogether turned out 1,080 Avro planes, reaching its peak at 45 aircraft a month in October 1944. There was also a trio of Lancaster 'daughter firms' in the West Midlands: Armstrong Whitworth of Coventry, which delivered its first Lancaster in August 1942 and attained an impressive peak rate of 75 machines a month in October 1944;Vickers at the huge Castle Bromwich plant, which built 300 Lancasters at an average rate of 15 a month, and Austin Aero at Longbridge, which made 330 of all types from March 1944 until the end of 1945. Like Chadderton, Longbridge did not have adequate assembly and testing facilities, so the Lancaster components built at Austin were taken to the large hangar at the Elmdon airfield (now Birmingham International Airport) to be put together.

As the parent firm, Avro was responsible for supplying all the drawings and modification details to the contractors, as well as ensuring other aspects of Lancaster production ran smoothly. The Lancaster Group first met formally on 9 September 1941 under the chairmanship of Roy Dobson, and subsequently met monthly under C. H. 'Ted' Fielding, Avro's Assistant General Manager, though at major meetings with government ministers and senior MAP officials Dobson took the chair. Daunted by the scale of the task it had undertaken, the Vickers management at Castle Bromwich wanted the Lancaster Group to have a more formal structure, with direct, centralized control exerted by Avro over the whole organization. But Dobson was strongly opposed to such an idea, on the grounds that it would require 'an extremely large staff in Manchester' and would slow down the circulation of information.[4] So the loose structure remained, and over the next four years it generally worked satisfactorily. Liaison officers from the daughter firms were based at Chadderton to keep abreast of the latest technical developments in the Lancaster programme, and Avro's supervision of drawings was so efficient that almost 100 per cent of the parts made were interchangeable within the group, a vital factor when so many Lancasters had to undergo major repairs. Towards the end of the war, MAP paid tribute to the management of Avro: 'The Lancaster Group, as controlled and co-ordinated by A.V. Roe, has been a unique success from the production point of view. At all times the Group has worked together amicably with A.V. Roe's accepting the fullest responsibility and recognition of their position as the parent firm. Over the period of the Lancaster Group, there have been many occasions where it has been necessary to do something urgently to meet a shortage at one or more of the daughter firms or to get a modification introduced, etc, and these have been thrown on to the resources of A.V. Roe who at all times have responded most satisfactorily.'[5] By the end of 1943, the Lancaster Group was turning out over 170 Lancasters a month. Early the following year monthly output had reached 230 planes and in September 1944 the Group reached its wartime peak, delivering 281 aircraft.

There was another crucial way that more Lancasters were put into service. In addition to overseeing production through the Lancaster Group, Avro also ran a Repair Group to salvage badly hit or crashed planes. Aircraft that had sustained only light damage, such as flak holes, could generally be repaired at the bomber stations. If the ground crews needed spare parts, they sent a telegram to Avro for the immediate dispatch of the required item. If the damage was more serious, then the plane was transported by road to the Repair Group's main depot at Bracebridge Heath in Lincoln, which had been the site of an aerodrome in the First World War. At Bracebridge, the Lancaster was split into its main sections and then the damaged components were sent for reconstruction to subcontractors, of which Field Aircraft Services Ltd. at Tollerton near Nottingham was the most important. The most vulnerable parts were the two bomb doors, which had to endure both flak and belly landings when the undercarriage failed.

Thanks to the foresight of Roy Chadwick, who was instrumental in creating the Repair Group, Avro had built up large stores of spare parts to maintain the Lancasters in service. One of those who worked at Bracebridge Heath was Eva Feulou, who was called up at the age of twenty in 1942. 'I wasn't very strong but they never bothered to give me a medical. We had to do men's work dismantling crashed aircraft. I was given a hammer and chisel and told to remove all the rivets from the outside fabric of a Lancaster bomber. I was a novice and all I did was cause a lump on the side of my hand. A married woman who worked part-time showed me how to handle the chisel and then I had to use a punch through every hole to release the fabric.' Her early efforts were not rewarding. 'My foreman had a word with me and told me I was like 10 men; 9 dead and 1 unconscious. What a compliment.' Later she was employed on cleaning up Lancasters, less physically exhausting but still tiresome work. 'The only thing I enjoyed was being lifted in and out by an airman – especially if he was handsome.'[6] Her war ended when she was hospitalized with a bad chest, due, she thought, to the heavy-duty cleaning fluids she had to use. But generally the operation, which included almost 3,000 personnel and a network of working parties around the country, worked with high efficiency. Once the parts had been fixed, the plane was reassembled at the Avro base of Langar in the East Midlands and sent back to the squadrons. The process generally took about three months. It is another testament to Chadwick's genius and the simplicity of his design that three-quarters of all the Lancasters taken to Bracebridge returned to front-line service, a total of 3,816 planes. At the peak of the war, the Repair Group was putting more than 30 aircraft a week back into the air.

The fulfilment of the Lancaster programme required an enormous workforce, dominating the wartime labour market in the way that the Lancaster airfields dominated Lincolnshire and the Fens. Avro itself had almost 40,000 employees at the height of Lancaster production, including 11,300 at Chadderton, 10,240 at Yeadon and 5,100 at Newton Heath. But that was only a fraction of the personnel connected to the manufacture of the plane. The aviation historian Francis Mason estimated that, taking into account subcontracting, there were 1.15 million people involved in building the Lancaster, a figure that accounts for more than half the number employed in the entire aircraft industry in wartime Britain, though many of these people would have been simultaneously working on components for other aircraft. No other single industrial product in British history, not the Spitfire, nor the Mini, nor the Dreadnought battleship, ever acquired such an immense workforce in its manufacture. Everything about the Avro operation was large. Geoff Bentley, who started working at Chadderton in 1942 as a fourteen-year old boy, recalled that 'it was a hell of a factory. You could see the Lancasters for miles, fifty of them lined up at a time. Chadderton was a lovely building at the front, with a beautiful big reception and staircase, a bit like a film set. But the factory was so noisy. The pop riveters would be going all day. I worked for a time in the pressing shop and when those massive presses dropped down, the whole place shuddered.'[7] Again the sense of size was reflected in the work on the aeroplane itself. Joe Munns, a specialist engineer, said that 'the largest job was working on the jig for the Lancaster wings. The blueprint was so big that we had to spread it out on the floor and crawl about it on our hands and knees until we found what we wanted.'[8] Lyndis Winterbottom, who worked at Yeadon, always remembered the intimidating size of the Lancaster's wheels, thanks to one incident on the shopfloor. 'One day we had to flatten ourselves against the factory wall and literally hold our breath for one of the great wheels had come loose from the trolley taking it for a fitting to the Lancaster. It crashed through the doors and out into the field.'[9]

The performance of Avro was all the more impressive given that a large proportion of the workforce was unskilled, around 70 per cent in the Manchester factories and almost 85 per cent at Yeadon. This was partly because so many women, without any industrial experience, had to be recruited for the aircraft factories. Overall, about 46 per cent of the Avro workforce was female, but this figure rose to 60 per cent at Yeadon.

According to Sophie Pape, who started work at Woodford in March 1942, 'the presence of women employees caused some disquiet amongst the predominantly male workforce. On my first day I and two other girls had to wait whilst the union officials met to consider the reaction of their members to our arrival. After a number of hours, our jobs were finally allocated. I was sent to work on the shopfloor where the Lancaster bombers were assembled. As my small stature was ideal for working in restricted spaces, I joined the team who fitted oxygen systems in the aircraft.' Sophie Pape admitted that she was 'very quiet and shy' when she began and found the prospect of working at Avro 'rather daunting at first', but two other senior male workers helped her to become confident in the technicalities of her job.[10] 'Each oxygen system required around nine pipes of various shapes, a length of pliable hose, two valves, a number of clips and screws and an accumulator. The pipes were covered in green "dope" paint [a type of heavy lacquer used to protect the aircraft's fabric surfaces]. I had to remove small sections of paint to facilitate good connections with the half-circular jubilee clips which were used to secure the pipes inside the aircraft. The hose and accumulator were fitted in the nose of the plane. When there was a shortage of components I did other tasks such as pop riveting – attaching the "skin" of the plane to the fuselage – or attaching the rubber seals to the undercarriage of the plane prior to it being attached to the fuselage.'[11] The hours were long at Avro and the conditions often tough. The average working week for men lasted 61 hours, and 55 for women, but at times of peak demand it could be even longer. Joe Munn's hours at Yeadon in early 1944 were from 7 a.m. to 7 p.m. six days a week, and that did not include his lengthy journey of ninety minutes to the factory. 'When I think back to those days now, I don't know how we managed it. It was all work and sleep, nothing else.'[12] The pay was hardly generous. An unskilled female worker in 1943 earned a basic wage of 22 shillings for a 47-hour week, plus overtime on Saturday and Sunday, an incentive piece-rate payment and a 16-shilling 'cost of living bonus'. Male unskilled workers received 34 shillings as their basic wage, plus overtime and a 22-shilling weekly bonus. Skilled workers generally were paid double the rate of the unskilled.[13] Lilian Grundy, who was conscripted into the aircraft industry and worked ten hours a day making bolts for the Lancaster, had a grim picture of life at Newton Heath. She said that she

> never enjoyed working there and would rather have been called up to the forces. The factory had dreadful conditions. It was an old building, put up in World War One and it had a stone floor, no sunlight and was freezing

in winter. It was like going into a dungeon and the noise was horrendous. We worked long hours for peanuts under bad management. They
had you at the machines all the time. If you went and sat down, the chargehand would soon order you back to the machine. Even when you went
to the toilet, they were watching. We had to buy our own uniforms. There
was a female chargehand who used to come round and if I did not have
every curl under my hat, she'd shout and bawl at me, saying it was for my
own safety.[14]

Even more unpleasant was the experience of working in the dope
shop of the Avro factories. Because of the strength of the dope, employees suffered headaches and bad chests, as Margaret Westropp recalled of
the shop at Yeadon. 'The fumes were really bad. It was tiring, hard, smelly
work but the worst thing was going down that slope into the factory
each morning knowing that you wouldn't see daylight till goodness knows
when.'[15]

But life at Avro was not all dismal toil. There was a spirit of camaraderie in large parts of the workforce, the food was reasonable, and the
management laid on sports clubs, a Christian fellowship and entertainment in the canteens, such as boxing matches, big bands and variety
shows. George Formby, Gracie Fields and band leader Joe Loss all
performed. Sophie Pape recalled how 'on Sunday mornings a group at
one end of the hangar would start to sing a hymn and soon the singing
spread until it was like a Mexican wave of sound – we all knew lots of
hymns and so the singing lasted for hours. A very happy memory.'[16] With
the full-hearted co-operation of Harris, Freeman organized morale-
boosting visits and talks for the Avro workers by the Lancaster airmen,
Guy Gibson inevitably being the star draw after the Dambusters raid. On
visits to Woodford and Yeadon, the airmen brought their Lancasters with
them, giving the workers a chance to see the planes in their full operational finish, as Lillian Grundy recalled: 'When the Lancaster flew
overhead, it was amazing to watch. I felt very proud to have helped build
it. I could have screamed, "There you go, you little belter." '[17] Mrs Grundy
also recalled the wonderful sense of belonging when the Avro managers
announced that the invasion of France had started. 'I had my head down
in the canteen, trying to get some sleep. Then one of the bosses came
in and said, "I'm very pleased to tell you that this has been D-Day." We
all hammered the tables and banged our feet on the floor. You couldn't
hear a word. Then he said, "Let's wish all our boys the best of British."
Then someone else said, "Let's say a prayer for them. God bless the boys."
It was a beautiful moment. I'll remember it for the rest of my life.'[18]

Sir Stafford Cripps, the dynamic but ascetic Minister for Aircraft Production from 1942, was also a regular visitor to the Lancaster plants. For all his executive abilities, Cripps's puritan eccentricities were never far from the surface. Whenever he went on his factory visits, he always brought a brown cardboard box which contained his vegetarian meals, while, as a socialist radical, he also had a fondness for addressing shopfloor workers as 'comrades'. Occasionally, his exhortations could strike a jarring note, as in a broadcast where he complained of those who 'voluntarily absent themselves, causing unnecessary delays in production or who, in other ways, hold back the flow of aeroplane production.[19] A less admonishing tone accompanied the visits to the Avro sites by the King and Queen. In March 1942 they went to Yeadon, where two of the Lancasters on the production line were named *Elizabeth* and *George* in recognition of the visit. Later that year they were taken around Avro's Manchester factories. As *The Times* reported: 'They saw many thousands of men and women at work and they had a chat with Mr Roy Chadwick, the designer of the Lancaster bomber. In their conversations with Mr Roy Chadwick and Mr Roy Dobson, the King and Queen impressed both these experts with their technical knowledge of many varieties of aeroplanes. Mr Chadwick has been connected with the manufacturing side for over thirty years and when the Queen heard this she exclaimed, "Thank God we have got men who have devoted their lives to aviation."' The Queen then asked about the plane she had christened *Elizabeth* earlier in the year. 'She was informed that it had unfortunately been lost. Mr Dobson asked her not to worry too much as there were plenty of other Lancasters now. The King was informed that the Lancaster on which he had written the name *George* was still flying.'[20]

The greatest distraction from the Avro production line came in the form of sex. In the factories as much as the bomber stations, the advent of war brought a new freedom from traditional morality, especially for young women. The intermingling of thousands of male and female workers created unprecedented opportunities for liaisons, while the tension of war, the implementation of a night shift seven days a week and the absence of husbands on overseas service added to the erotic charge. Sophie Pape, newly married herself, worked alongside a quiet but good-looking bachelor called Fred. 'He was very handsome. I was often asked his name and girls working nearby sometimes made an excuse to ask his advice so they could engage him in conversation.' Joseph Barry, who started work as an apprentice at Chadderton, was amazed at how forward some of the women at the factory could be. 'In one job, when I had the duty of collecting some tools, there would be girls saying as I passed, "Come round here," trying to get me to go with them behind their machines. Some even started to take off their overalls.'[21]

The mood in the Yeadon factory could be equally adventurous. 'It might be hard to believe,' said Evelyn Fitzgerald, 'but there were a lot of babies born at Avro and there were a lot of abortions too. I can tell you if the lads from the Air Force had known what had gone on in some of their Lancasters – and not just on the night shift either – they would have been really surprised. Some babies were started in them and a few were born in them too.' This kind of ardour could even cause damage to the aircraft. Alf Harris recalled how a colleague, 'who always fancied himself', tried to show off to a girl from another department by inviting her inside a Lancaster. 'Not content with a kiss and cuddle, he had to take her into the cockpit and, no doubt trying to give the impression that he knew how to fly the thing, it wasn't long before he pulled the wrong lever. You could hear the sound of the collapsing undercarriage above the machinery. There was hell to pay.'[22] But many of the relationships formed at Avro were deeper and more tender. A significant number of 'Avro sweethearts', as they were known, went on to have happy marriages. Lillian Grundy had her own deeply romantic experience while working at Avro. Her boyfriend had been taken prisoner at Dunkirk and she had become engaged to him by proxy. From his POW camp in Germany, he was able to send via the Red Cross the money for her to buy an engagement ring. He also sent a letter, telling her to place the ring on her finger on Christmas Eve when the moon was full, so that, even though they were divided by war and geography, they could be united in spirit. 'We will be looking up at the same moon then. Put on the ring and I'll be with you,' he wrote. She did so and, at the appointed time, she went into the garden of her cottage to gaze up at the moon. 'I felt his arms around me,' she said. Their devotion was not in vain. After VE day, he returned to England to start a new life with Lillian.[23]

The influence of the emotional and sexual turmoil should not be exaggerated. The Lancaster factories were generally efficient, and the performance of the workforce attracted regular plaudits from politicians and military leaders. Cripps told the press in March 1944 'during the last 12 months the number of man-hours of work required for the manufacture of a Lancaster has fallen by 38.2 per cent and this reflects good work on the part of everyone'.[24] This was no mere act of political bombast. Outsiders without a vested interest were also impressed by the Avro operation. E. W. Walton, a representative on Roosevelt's European mission, made a tour of Manchester in July 1943 and reported favourably that the 'tempo of work at Avro seemed very good'. The equipment, he said, was not 'so elaborate as that in North American factories' but the 'final results are good'.[25]

Yet this was hardly the complete picture. No workforce the size of Avro's could be entirely free of idlers, troublemakers and incompetents. One buffoon at Yeadon plunged the main assembly area into darkness by firing off a missile from a home-made catapult that he had made for his son. The weapon was stronger than he expected and the projectile hurtled into the mercury vapour lights. Unsurprisingly, the offender was deeply unpopular with the men who were working 20 feet up on the Lancaster's wings. Some irresponsible workers at Woodford had the habit of filling up their cigarette lighters by dipping them into the Lancaster's fuel tanks. That practice ceased after one of them lit up while he was casually walking away from the plane. A spark ignited the fumes and the aircraft exploded. The miscreant survived, but was instantly sacked by Avro.[26] Nor was diligence universal. Clare Hollingworth worked as a riveter at Chadderton putting the fins on the Lancaster, and though she was in her own words 'a little toughie', she sometimes needed the help of her male colleague to finish the job. But his attitude to work was exasperating. 'He was bone idle. Quite frankly, he slept on top of a cabinet in the toilet during the night shift. It took most of one evening to build a Lancaster fin. My mate would get all the stuff from the store: the ribs, the rivets and so on. Then he would set up the jig and just disappear. I was amazed with him at times. If I needed him I'd have to send for him from the toilet. He was quite pleasant when he came back, said he'd had "a nice sleep".' He was able to get away with it, according to Clare Hollingworth, because there were fewer supervisors at night and some of the men, who took it in turns to have a nap, also covered for each other.[27] In the Midlands, Harry Errington, an operative at the Austin factory, was surprised at the lackadaisical attitude of many of his colleagues. 'At the end of the evening shift, what I did not understand was a queue of people waiting at the machine to clock off. Often they would be waiting for more than five minutes. There was a war on and they should have worked until their time was up. Every day I always felt the same. As soon as the time approached, they'd queue up to clock off. That was the majority of people in the factory. I could not say anything to them because I was the last one in. There were a lot of old timers who did not seem to worry much about the war.'[28]

The worst labour problem lay in industrial relations. It now seems almost incredible that there could have been strikes during the war, when the Blitz spirit was meant to be all-pervasive in British society and thousands of young men were sacrificing their lives in the RAF. But that is what happened in mid-1943 and 1945, as the aircraft factories were plagued by sudden rashes of wildcat actions and walkouts. The government ensured that news of such troubles was kept out of the papers for fear of undermining morale, and the incidents have rarely been referred to in any other bomber histories, precisely because they do not fit the cheering wartime narrative of national unity. But records in the National Archives and first-hand accounts expose the reality of simmering unrest. The first strikes at Avro began on 5 June 1943 at the small, outlying factory at Middleton in Manchester, when part of the night shift organized a sit-down protest in one of the machine shops in a dispute over piece-work prices. At the same time, assembly and flight-shed inspection personnel told management that they would limit their working hours to pursue a pay claim. At the end of the month, some operators at Newton Heath walked out over the sacking of an 'inferior worker'.[29] These three stoppages died down almost as soon as they had started, but a far bigger strike began at Woodford on 27 July, involving 1,400 employees, lasting 8 days and losing a total of 77,000 man-hours. Further sporadic disputes followed in August and September. The most drawn-out one occurred at Chadderton where workers on the fuselage section adopted go-slow tactics over a new method for sinking rivets into the Lancaster's fuselage, a technique that was regarded by the strikers as a threat to their piece rates. Avro management told MAP that the attitude of the strikers was pig-headed. The men had demanded a piece-work rate on the basis that the new riveting procedure took 312 hours, but 'we could not accept this as we know it to be an unfair price as the job can actually be done by experienced people in under 110 hours'.[30] Eventually a compromise was reached, much in the workers' favour, and the dispute ended. Interestingly, the main trade union in the industry, the Amalgamated Engineering Union (AEU), rarely lent its backing to the strikers, and in many cases shop stewards appealed for a return to work. Despite the lack of official backing, discontent rumbled on through the autumn. There were other stoppages at Metropolitan-Vickers, Chester and Castle Bromwich, sometimes over the pettiest of causes such as the appointment of a new foreman. But apart from the big dispute at Woodford, the industrial action never encompassed a wide section of the workforce in 1943. Dick Marsh, a draughtsman who worked at Chadderton, had little time for the protests. 'Some people were always griping. There were no really prolonged strikes but there were a lot of threats and sabre-rattling. Considering there was a war on, quite a few bolshie people worked at Avro and a lot of communists. The chap in front of my desk was a communist: a very nice chap but a dedicated communist. He always thought we should be doing more to help Russia.'[31] Sophie Pape, based at Woodford, confessed that she found the mood ugly. 'I carried on working as I was not a union member. Crossing the picket line was scary. My family worried about me.'[32]

A surprising feature of the strikes was the limited effect they had on long-term output. At one stage, in September 1943, Freeman was worried that the Lancaster programme might be seriously undermined, but it turned out there was no such problem, as a MAP report for 2 October demonstrated. 'In the strike at AV Roe's assembly shops at Woodford, 76,633 man hours were lost and as the assembly time for a Lancaster is 3000 hours, one would expect there to be a loss of 25.5 aircraft in the assembly line through Woodford. On the other hand, this loss had already been made up in actual practice. These figures are quoted to show the fallacy and difficulty of approaching the question from the angle of actual losses.'[33]

Another potential threat to Lancaster production, that of German bombing against the Avro factories, hardly materialized during the war, largely because the Germans had no strategic air force in the west after June 1941 and could only mount infrequent raids by fighter bombers. Yeadon was never hit, nor was Woodford, and there was only one minor raid on Chadderton. This took place on Easter Monday, 23 April 1941, when a single Ju 88 flew at low level over the site and, with a display of accuracy that would have provoked the grudging admiration of Don Bennett, dropped four bombs directly on the main factory. There was a unit of the Home Guard on the roof which manned a small-calibre machine-gun post, but the Ju 88 managed to escape easily. Fortunately, because of the Easter break, the factory was largely deserted, but the physical damage was extensive. 'It was a right shambles. There was such a mess. Some of the assembly bays were wrecked,' said Harry Tulson, who worked at Chadderton on the Lancaster wing's centre section.[34] The worst impact was at the stores, where one exploding bomb scattered millions of rivets of all sizes across the wide floors. It seemed that it would be an almost impossible task to collect and sort them out, but then, with that gift for innovation which made Avro so effective, one manager suggested that they ask the pupils and teachers at the local blind school to help. This was done, and the blind volunteers did a superb job in sorting out the rivets purely by feel.[35] Despite the absence of any further German attempts at raids, Harris regularly complained to the Air Ministry about the lack of adequate defences at the Lancaster factories. He told Sir

Norman Bottomley, the Deputy Chief of the Air Staff: 'I think we were being very complacent. The air offensive against Germany is now catastrophic for them and I am sure they will realize sooner or later – and probably sooner – that their best and indeed their only chance of reducing it is to attack the factories. We can assume for certain that they know precisely where they are.'[36] He also urged Trafford Leigh-Mallory, the head of Fighter Command, to provide more fighter cover over the factories. But Leigh-Mallory and the Air Staff were dismissive of his warnings, claiming, with some justification, that major raids were 'unlikely' and a big increase in defence would 'only indicate the importance of the installations'.[37] There was a certain irony in Harris complaining to the Air Staff about the risks of precision mass-bomber raids against targets in England, when his area strategy was founded on the impossibility of mounting just such raids against targets in Germany. Indeed, aircraft factories were the sort of 'panacea' objectives that always aroused his fury.

There was another, far more isolated but infinitely more dangerous menace to Lancaster production during the war. This came from saboteurs working inside the aircraft industry or on the bomber stations, who through mental derangement, treachery or bitter grievance were determined to undermine the war effort by putting aircrews' lives at risk. Thankfully such cases were extremely rare, but they undoubtedly did occur. Sophie Pape recalled that 'during my time at Woodford there were two instances of sabotage, when electric cables were cut through overnight. I don't think the culprits were ever found.'[38] One culprit who was caught was a disgruntled workman at Castle Bromwich. In June 1944, some wires in a Lancaster had been severed and the Vickers management called in the Military Branch at Scotland Yard. A watch was mounted at the factory and, after two further incidents, the offender was apprehended. But the historian Bruce Robertson argued in his 1964 study of the Lancaster that the problem of sabotage may have been more widespread. He pointed to a string of unexplained accidents, such as the crash of a 101 Squadron Lancaster in November 1942 when the plane appeared to explode in mid-air during a routine flight over Wales. Just as disturbing were a series of what Robertson called 'mysterious' crashes over the summer of 1943, most of them involving planes from training units. Yet no evidence of sabotage was ever found by the authorities, despite a tightening of security around the air bases, and the fact that the crashes were spread all over the country made it less likely that criminals, traitors or foreign agents were responsible. The sheer inexperience of young pilots flying a 30-ton aircraft was a more likely explanation.[39]

The completion of the Lancasters was not quite the end of the production process. Before they could be flown to the squadrons, they had to be tested for their airworthiness. This was a job carried out by the brave group of company test pilots, who had to put every Lancaster through a rigorous examination. The most famous of them was Alex Henshaw, who before the war had been a record-breaking aviation pioneer. Employed by Vickers as the Chief Test Pilot at Castle Bromwich, he was renowned for his extraordinary aerobatic skills, once bringing the centre of Birmingham to a halt during a fundraising aerial display by flying in a Spitfire at high speed down the main street below the skyline. Testing the Spitfire took up the bulk of his time at Castle Bromwich. He flew over 2,000 of them, more than any pilot, but he also regularly applied his unique talent to the Lancaster. His combination of daring, self-assurance and split-second reactions enabled him to fly the Lancaster almost as if it were a Spitfire, executing dives, climbs and rolls that tested the structure to its limits but ultimately proved the brilliance of the design. 'The Lancaster was a beautiful aircraft to fly and I can think of no other large four-engined machine that gave the pilot so much satisfaction,' he once wrote. The test procedure 'followed a similar pattern to the Spitfire, but took longer and naturally was more cumbersome in operations both in the air and on the ground'. Its elements included a full-power climb to 15,000 feet, a 'simple part of the exercise' but vitally important because 'so many irregularities could easily be overlooked, perhaps with severe repercussions at a later date under severe combat conditions. Even if only one of the four engines failed to give the correct power at the right rate of consumption during a long raid over enemy territory, the risk to pilot and crew would be something they did not deserve.' There would be a host of other checks on temperatures, pressures and calibrations in the cockpit, and then a level speed run at 10,000 feet at full throttle and maximum revs of 3,000 rpm. Accurate recordings of the speed were made and any vibration from the engines or propellers was carefully monitored. Finally, a dive was carried out to maximum speed and revs to an indicated speed of 3,700 rpm, which resulted in a 'deafening throb'. During the dive 'the ailerons would be carefully but firmly operated for signs of over-balancing, lightness of control and lateral stability. The rudders would also be tested for directional response and accuracy.' This was the standard exercise for testing a production Lancaster.

But on certain occasions, usually when he was putting a plane through a special examination at A&AEE at Boscombe Down, Henshaw performed the astounding manoeuvre of deliberately putting the Lancaster into a roll, something that he agreed was 'much more spectacular' than rolling a Spitfire:

> Although the change in power-to-weight ratio was more obvious and helpful as the Lancaster became inverted, I did not at first find it easy to keep the machine within the fine limits required, as the controls had far less sensitivity than on a fighter. I discovered that the most accurate and sensitive method was to leave my glove on the shelf forming the instrument panel. Then, as the machine became inverted, the trick was to keep the glove floating gently up and down on the panel and suspended in mid-air, rather like a ping-pong ball on a jet of water. It was really very safe, simple and easy to manoeuvre, imposing no excessive loads, but it did require careful and experienced handling.

The experience of inverting the Lancaster could disconcert fellow passengers, as one of Henshaw's co-pilots, the Czech Venda Jicha, found when he failed to catch the signal that the roll was about to start. 'I shall never forget the look of amazement on his face as he peered at the ground from upside down, with his feet gently lifting from the well floor from time to time.' The combination of the Lancaster's reliability, Henshaw's skill and the presence of four engines meant that he rarely had any dangerous incidents. One time, a dinghy blew out of the aircraft in a power dive and remained stuck in the tailplane, but once it had been torn away Henshaw was able to fly as normal. On another occasion, in dismal weather, deepening gloom and a strong wind, he misjudged his approach to Castle Bromwich and touched down in some nearby sewage beds before lumbering into his own airfield. The fact that he never suffered a structural failure was, he believed, a tribute to Avro: 'For a heavy bomber in that period of aerodynamic development, I think that the controls and behaviour of the Lancaster under full load and operational long-range wartime conditions made it the best bomber in the Allied forces.'[40]

One crew at Woodford were not as fortunate as Henshaw. In the only fatal casualty of the Lancaster testing regime throughout the war, Sid Gleave and his flight engineer Harry Barnes were killed on 11 September 1944 when their plane failed to come out of a power dive but instead ploughed into the ground. Through a subsequent investigation, it was found that the fabric covering on the elevators had been torn off. In response to this tragedy, Roy Chadwick instructed that extra wooden ribs be added to strengthen the elevator. Avro engineer Sandy Jack, who was deeply shaken by the deaths of his two colleagues, later said, 'in retrospect, I regret it did not occur to me before the accident just how vulnerable the fabric-covered elevators actually were. All who flew Lancs knew that at high speed in a dive they became progressively heavier to pull out by use of the control column, but they could be controlled easily and positively by the trimmer wheel.' But as Jack recognized, the 'development of the Lancaster was a continuous course of improvement in the light of operational experience'.[41]

The final task in the process was the delivery of the Lancasters from the factories to the squadrons. In order to conserve RAF resources in the operational squadrons, this was done by personnel from the Air Transport Auxiliary, an organization set up by the government in 1939 on the initiative of Gerard d'Erlanger, a merchant banker and director of British Airways. At first it was intended that the ATA would carry only mail and medical supplies, but the wartime demands on the RAF meant that ferrying aircraft became its primary role. By 1944 the ATA was a key part of the war effort. With its unofficial slogan 'Any Aircraft, Anywhere', the service had more than 1,300 pilots at 14 ferry pools across the country, supported by nearly 3,000 ground staff. The aircrews largely comprised flying enthusiasts who were unable to join the RAF because of age or physical fitness. One-armed, one-legged and one-eyed airmen all served, many of them showing amazing determination to overcome their handicaps. During the war over 300,000 aircraft of more than 130 different types were delivered to the front line, among them the Lancaster. Paul Longthorp, who worked for the Blackburn Aircraft Company at the start of the war, and then qualified as an engineer for the ATA in 1943, recorded the thrill of flying in the Lancaster for the first time, alongside the experienced Australian ATA pilot Geoffrey Whitner:

> He took the time to show me round the Lancaster. He was incredibly generous, showing me what was needed. After all the checks were done, I got into this gorgeous bomber, which I will remember to this day as my first love. With a clatter, we started the engines. We taxied down the runway as if we were flying in a big greenhouse. And these beautiful, paddle-bladed Merlins were clattering away, a lovely sound. With a rush, the plane was airborne. I thought to myself, 'This is the aeroplane for me.'

Longthorp revelled in the smoothness of the plane as it sailed over the Pennines towards Coningsby before starting its descent. 'The gear was lowered on command. Flaps were positioned at 20 degrees. The aircraft was slowed. I checked the fuel system had been set correctly. We swept on down to the runway and landed. Finished. My first flight in a Lancaster. That started my love affair. From then on I did perhaps 50 Lancaster ferry flights over to the East Coast.'[42]

The only women pilots to fly the Lancaster during the war belonged to the ATA. Initially there had been some hesitation in government circles about allowing women to serve in the air, but a mixture of pressure on resources and d'Erlanger's enlightenment soon overcame such prejudice. The women's section of the ATA was headed by the formidable Pauline Gower, one of Britain's first female commercial pilots. Under her leadership 166 women flew with the service, among them Lettice Curtis, a cool, unemotional but brilliant pilot who in 1943 became the first of her gender qualified to fly four-engined bombers. The excitable press coverage given to Lettice Curtis's achievement reflected the belief, still widespread in mid-war, that heavyweight planes were somehow beyond the capabilities of a female pilot. Rosemary Rees, another ATA airwoman, remembered an argument with an RAF wing commander who expressed surprise when she told him she was about to ferry an Avro plane. 'He said it was so heavy compared with my five foot three and seven stone weight. I pointed out that I was not proposing to attempt to carry it after all, but on the contrary to make it carry me.' Rees admitted that taxiing a four-engined bomber in a strong wind could take some strength, but, she said, 'the controls of a big aircraft were not at all heavy in the air'.[43] The superlative ease of the Lancaster was what impressed pilot Margaret Gore, who joined the ATA in June 1940 and worked at the Hamble ferry pool on the south coast. Gore began her heavy-bomber duty with Halifaxes, and she recalled that on the first occasion she had landed one, an Air Chief Marshal on the base grumbled: 'By God, I've seen everything now.' Soon, Gore had moved on to Lancasters. 'They were the nicest of all, nicer than the Halifax, they were lovely. There is something about a plane which is very difficult to describe; some are just nicer to fly than others. They handled better and the layout was more convenient. I also preferred it to the Fortress, which I had to fly out of Hamble occasionally. The Fortresses were much more complicated because everything in the American machines was electrical, lots of little switches. And the Fortresses were more lumbering than the Lancaster. The Lanc was like an eager horse wanting to gallop off.'[44] Reactionary outbursts at the female ATA pilots were far outweighed by the sense of admiration that they inspired, as engineer Frank Iredell recalled of a trip to the East Midlands, when a young woman, 'more or less a girl', flew a Lancaster that needed to be modified by Rolls-Royce. 'Conditions were very, very bad. Visibility at Radford airport near Rolls-Royce was extremely poor. Anyway, she circled round and made a perfect landing. And when she got out, all the mechanics gave her a big cheer. It seemed so remarkable that this tiny pilot could get this big aircraft down under such conditions. They did not really expect us to bring the plane in at all.'[45]

The arrival of a fresh new Lancaster on the bomber base usually led to a surge of elation among the airmen, mixed with a sense of relief that they might now stand a better chance against the defences of the Reich. Harry Yates of 75 Squadron recalled the feelings of excitement when 'our own beautiful, matt black' Lancaster was delivered. 'The cockpit was pristine. Not an inch of Perspex or a single dial harboured a scratch or a smear or a speck of dust. Every Lancaster cockpit smelled good. But there was an indefinable and delicious scent of factory newness about this one. It had yet to be anointed with the unmentionable filth that was apt to swill around during a bad trip, of course, or the kerosene with which the erks disinfected it the next morning.' Yates settled into his seat and reached forward to the column, then, with his right hand, down to the four throttles. It felt exactly right to him. The difference between a new machine and 'an old warhorse' was evident as soon he took to the air with his crew. 'She was taut and responsive, a lovely aircraft. I couldn't ask for more – except, of course, that she should be lucky.'[46]

Before each new Lancaster went on operations, the riggers gave it the last finishing touch by painting its individual emblem on the fuselage just below the cockpit. The artwork encompassed a wide range of imagery, from boxing kangaroos to barrels of beer. After each sortie, a falling bomb was also painted on the side of the aircraft. In keeping with its name, 9 Squadron's Lancaster *J-Johnnie Walker*, serial number W4964, which flew over 100 operations and was not retired from RAF service until 1949, carried the famous symbol of the Johnnie Walker Scotch whisky company, a jaunty red-coated gentleman with monocle, top hat and cane. Appropriately enough for such a long-serving aircraft, the slogan of the Johnnie Walker company, 'Still Going Strong', was painted just below this sign. In solidarity with Britain's Soviet ally, Lancaster *U-Uncle,* known as 'Uncle Joe', which flew with 44 and 463 Squadrons, had a caricature of the Communist leader Josef Stalin beaming out from a red star. A particular favourite of many crews was an image of Jane, the clothes-shedding heroine of the *Daily Mirror*, who gave a literal meaning to the term 'strip cartoon' and spent most of the war in various stages of undress. The logo on *J-Jane* of 61 Squadron, for instance, portrayed her in fully nude glory reclining on a bomb. Nudity also featured for a time on one of the most famous Lancasters of them all, *S-Sugar*, serial number R5868, which now resides in the RAF Museum at Hendon having lasted through most of the war from 1942 until VE Day. The first image on *S-Sugar*, when the plane was with 83 Squadron, was of a red devil thumbing its nose while dancing in flames, a reference to the German legend of Faust who sold his soul to Mephistopheles. When the Lancaster moved to 467 Squadron, this was painted out and replaced by a naked female kneeling in front of a bomb. But once *S-Sugar* approached the landmark of 100 sorties, the station commander Group Captain D. Bonham-Carter decided that the unclad woman was inappropriate for such an august, venerable aircraft: 'Because it's rude and Sugar will be publicised so much, it will upset the Archbishop of Canterbury,' he said.[47] So the nude was replaced by the words spelling out Göring's notorious boast: 'No enemy aircraft will fly over Reich territory,' a prediction whose foolishness became more apparent with every passing night.

13

'A calculated, remorseless campaign
of destruction'

~~~

THE HOUR OF reckoning had arrived for Sir Arthur Harris. His absolute faith in the supremacy of the heavy-bomber offensive was about to be put to the ultimate test. Throughout the first four years of the war, he had argued that the only route to victory was through the destruction of Germany's leading cities by area bombing. In the autumn of 1943, he had the chance to justify his belief. He had the resources to launch an all-out offensive against the urban infrastructure of Germany, focusing on the greatest target of them all: Berlin, the 'Big City'. Until this moment, he had felt restrained by the limited number of Lancasters, the demands of the Air Staff for attacks on other 'panacea targets' and the lack of effective navigation aids. But now almost everything was in place. His planes were equipped with Gee and Window, while H2S had been installed in all Pathfinders and was being extended to all main force Lancasters. The Pathfinders themselves had evolved sophisticated new tactics and marking techniques. With the ageing Wellingtons and Stirlings now being withdrawn from operational service over Germany, Lancasters increasingly predominated in the heavy-bomber force. By October, Harris had 30 front-line Lancaster squadrons and the plane was emerging from the factories at a rate of over 160 a month, supplemented by the first deliveries from Victory Aircraft in Canada. As demonstrated by the rows over the Halifax and the training units, Harris never felt that he had enough of the Avro machines, but even so, from November 1943 he was able to launch major attacks on Germany by over 400 Lancasters, the figure rising to over 550 in February 1944 and above 600 in March. In what was to become known as the 'Battle of Berlin', though the geographical spread was much wider than the name suggested, he dispatched no fewer than 14,582 Lancaster sorties against Germany, half of them against the German capital.[1]

At the start of the campaign, Harris was unshakeable in his conviction that this phase of the bomber offensive would win the war if the government and the Americans gave him their full support. Repeated area attacks on the scale of the devastation of Hamburg, he claimed, would bring the Reich to its knees, obviating the need for any Allied invasion of the Continent. He told Portal in the middle of August: 'It is my firm belief that we are on the verge of a final showdown in the bombing war and the next few months will be vital. Opportunities do not knock repeatedly and continuously. I am certain that given average weather and concentration on the main job, we can push Germany over by bomb-ing this year.'[2] In a famous letter to Churchill on 3 November 1943, he predicted that his bombers would exert a decisive influence if he was backed by the US 8th Air Force. 'We can wreck Berlin from end to end if the USAAF will come in on it. It will cost us between 400–500 aircraft. It will cost Germany the war.'[3] There was no chance of the American bomber crews joining in the full assault on Berlin. They were neither trained nor equipped for night bombing, and the casualties on daylight raids would have been bloodily prohibitive. Indeed, just at the time when Harris was gearing up for the campaign, the USAAF was scaling back its daylight operations, following disastrous losses on a raid against the ball-bearing factories at Schweinfurt in central Germany in October 1943, when no fewer than 198 bombers of 291 were shot down or damaged. It was the Schweinfurt catastrophe that led senior USAAF leaders to rethink their tactics, recognizing that even the heavily armed Flying Fortresses could not defend themselves against the Luftwaffe fighters by day. The only solution was to start using fighter escorts. In the long-range P51 Mustang the Americans had the perfect interceptor for operations on Germany. Though the Mustangs first started to arrive in England in October 1943, they were only available in sufficiently large numbers to head a renewed US air offensive from February 1944, by which time the British campaign had already been going on for three gruelling months.

Schweinfurt had done nothing to dent Harris's confidence. To him, the mass slaughter was only proof of the folly of daylight attacks and panacea targets. Even after it became obvious that the Americans would not be joining the Berlin offensive, he retained his unshakeable trust in his night-bombing strategy built around the Lancaster. Indeed, his devo-tion to the Avro plane even led him to tell the Air Staff that the Lancaster on its own could bring about the surrender of Germany by April 1944. In a detailed memorandum to the Air Staff of 7 December 1943, writ-ten after the first five raids of the Battle of Berlin, Harris said that over the next four months the RAF would be able to destroy 40 per cent of the built-up areas of major German towns if the bombing efficiency and factory output of 1943 were maintained. The Lancaster, he explained, was now responsible for 76 per cent of the weight of bombs dropped on Germany, and that ratio would rise as the Stirlings were transferred to the Heavy Conversion Units and the Halifaxes were increasingly excluded from the more difficult missions. With surprisingly detailed forecasting, Harris calculated that in the first months of the New Year, 1944, he would have 40 Lancaster squadrons, each of them carrying out 85 sorties a month, or 3,400 sorties a month by the heavy-bomber force in total. Based on an average bomb load of 9,730 pounds per Lancaster and allowing for a rate of 7 per cent early returns, this implied that 13,850 tons of bombs would be dropped on Germany every month, enough to bring about the defeat of the Reich. 'From this it appears that the Lancaster force alone should be sufficient, but only just sufficient to produce in Germany by April 1st 1944 a state of devastation in which surrender is inevitable.' It was a remarkable statement of belief in Chadwick's design, and in stressing the need to keep up Avro production and the installation of the latest navigational equipment, Harris reiterated the crucial importance of the Lancaster. 'It is therefore obvious that the success of the bombing offensive depends on the Lancasters and that their production and protection from avoidable loss are more important than anything else for the purpose of winning the war quickly.'[4]

In Harris's mind, the Lancaster and the bomber offensive had reached a position of intense symbiosis. The only purpose of the Lancaster, he believed, was to carry out saturation bombing of Germany, while such bombing could be effectively performed by no other plane except the Lancaster. At Bomber Command's headquarters in High Wycombe, such thinking was no doubt obvious. Yet there were alternative missions for the Lancaster, as highlighted in the Dambusters raid and other special operations like Operation Robinson, when the Schneider armament works at Le Creusot had been daringly attacked in October 1942. Or there was Operation Bellicose in June 1942, when the old Zeppelin works at Friedrichshafen near Switzerland were hit by 56 Lancasters and 4 Pathfinders; the planes then flew on to the Allied airbase at Maison Blanche in Algeria where they were refuelled before the return flight to England, during which they bombed La Spezia in Italy. Such tactical flexibility and imaginativeness could have exploited the qualities of the Lancaster as well as giving more support to other armed forces. The infantry, for instance, often complained of the absence of backing from the RAF during their long struggle northwards through Italy. Similarly, Arthur Tedder, the Deputy Supreme Commander of the Allied forces at D-Day, demonstrated later in the war how expertly the Lancaster could be used to disrupt transport networks, energy plants and communication links.

But this was of no concern to Harris. He had fixed his strategy and was sticking to it. Any diversion from the German cities was regarded by him as a waste of time. He therefore paid no heed to Air Ministry entreaties that he should use precision Lancaster attacks to bomb key industrial targets, such as the Schweinfurt ball-bearing plants. In July 1943, when presented with an Air Staff note which informed him that the vital importance of 'the ball bearing industry' in German aircraft production 'has long been established to the satisfaction of the British and American air staffs', he wrote on the paper in his hand: 'But not to mine.'[5] Later in the year, when the Deputy Chief of the Air Staff Norman Bottomley again urged him to bomb Schweinfurt, Harris launched into a tirade against the whole concept of panacea targets, which he mockingly said were nothing more than an alien conspiracy to undermine the war effort: 'You must excuse me if I have become cynical with regard to the continual diversions of the bomber effort from its legitimate role in which, as we all know, it has inflicted the most grievous and intolerable damage on Germany.'[6] Again, in October 1943, when the Air Ministry had asked Harris to see General Adolphe Sice of the Free French Army to discuss the possibility of dropping supplies for the Resistance, Harris was at his most dismissive: 'It seems to me that the feeding of a few ragged tailed Frenchmen at the expense of bombing Germany would be a poor exchange indeed – though I am surprised at nothing.'[7] In the same way, despite the fact that not a single Lancaster had been lost on Operation Bellicose to Friedrichshafen and Algeria, Harris rejected out of hand the idea that this kind of 'shuttle run' across the Mediterranean could become a feature of Bomber Command's work. He told the Air Staff that the logistical demands of such an approach would require a duplicate organization to the one in eastern England, which was simply unfeasible. But the relish with which he dismissed the idea pointed to his unwillingness to even consider it properly. Some, like the Chief of Staff Sir Alan Brooke, thought that Harris had slid into a cocoon of self-deceit. In a diary entry for 13 October 1943, Brooke wrote sarcastically after seeing Harris at a Whitehall meeting: 'According to him, the only reason why the Russian army has succeeded in advancing is due to the results of the bomber offensive! If Bomber Command was left to itself it would make shorter work of it all.'[8]

Yet for all the exasperation in official circles with Harris, he was not dissuaded from proceeding with the Battle of Berlin. There were a number of reasons for this willingness to accept his strategy, whatever the doubts. One was that as a result of decisions taken by the War Cabinet and Chiefs of Staff in 1941 and 1942, the heavy-bomber war had developed a vast internal momentum of its own which it would have been difficult to reverse. Much of the domestic industrial effort was now geared towards bomber production. The huge expansion of the airfields, the recruitment of an army of WAAFs for the bomber bases, and the Empire Air Training Scheme added to the pressure to stick to the same air policy. There was also the feeling that Harris, for all his blinkered stubbornness, might be right. The fiery destruction of Hamburg had sent a shockwave through the Reich, creating the hope that a succession of similar assaults on Berlin could topple the Nazi regime. A British intelligence report from late 1943, now in the Syd Bufton papers at the Cambridge University archives, circulated the testimony of 'a reliable source' within Germany as to the terror caused in urban areas by RAF incendiary bombs: 'Owing to the panic caused by the continually bursting bombs the population in general has not dared to go up immediately to the attics or the top storeys of buildings to extinguish the flames. Thus the fires have been able to get a firm grip on the buildings and as most inner walls in Germany are made of wood, the fires have quickly spread to the entire building. The fire brigades have not been able to cope with all the fires at once.'[9] Crucially, Harris could rely on the support of Winston Churchill, whose belligerent spirit was stirred by the thought of the Reich capital in flames and whose negotiations with Stalin had presented the bombing of Germany as a 'second front' in the air. The military historian Basil Liddell Hart, a passionate critic of Churchill, wrote that 'Winston is pinning all his faith on the bomber offensive now. The devastation it causes suits his temperament and he would be disappointed at a less destructive ending to the war.'[10] Throughout 1942 and much of 1943 Churchill sent regular messages to Portal asking Bomber Command to step up its attacks on Berlin, seeking an even stronger offensive against Germany. In June 1943 he asked why the number of heavy-bomber sorties 'should be so low', forcing Portal to defend Harris from charges of over-caution, not something of which he was usually accused. 'I hope your comments to do not indicate any lack of confidence in him or any doubt that he has done, and will always do, his best to deliver the maximum weight of bombs on Germany.'[11] Nor could other politicians and military leaders ignore popular opinion, which was strongly behind Harris in his desire to take the bomber war directly to Germany.

This public attitude, partly forged as a legacy of the Blitz, was re-inforced by acclaim in the press and the BBC for the heroic men of Bomber Command. Wynford Vaughan-Thomas was one correspondent who captivated BBC listeners with his report from inside a Lancaster of a raid on Berlin. Another, even more famous, reporter who did the same was Richard Dimbleby. In early 1943 he accompanied a crew in Lancaster *W-William* to the 'Big City' to see for himself 'the wonderful work of the men of the Royal Air Force'.[12] Polls showed the vast majority of the British people in favour of area bombing. Newspapers acted as both a barometer and a conductor of the public mood. On the eve of the Berlin campaign, the *Daily Mirror*, by far Britain's biggest-selling paper, gloried in the thought that Germany's 'arsenals and war-making centres' were now facing 'emasculation' as the bomber offensive intensified, while the *Daily Telegraph*, in concentrating its ire on the Führer, adopted the quasi-Old Testament tone occasionally favoured by Harris: 'He who took up the sword will perish by the sword. And the flames in which he swore he would convulse the world in his fall will be the flames of Berlin and the cities of Germany.'[13] The press also heightened public affection for the undoubted star of the offensive: the Lancaster bomber.

That affection was demonstrated in March 1943 when huge crowds gathered in Trafalgar Square for the start of a nationwide initiative called 'Wings For Victory' to raise funds to build heavy bombers. The show-piece of the Trafalgar Square event was a Lancaster, *O-Orange*, a veteran of 27 operations with 207 Squadron, which stood overlooking the lions at the bottom of Nelson's column and attracted the admiring looks of a vast flood of visitors. Over one million people were estimated to have visited the square on the day of the launch, 'the biggest crowd since the Coronation' said the *Daily Express*. The initiative raised £13,250,000, enough to build 315 Lancasters. The specialist press joined in this adula-tion, the usually restrained *Aeroplane* magazine describing the bomber as 'the Hammerer of the Huns'.[14]

From August 1943, Harris started increasing the number of operations against Germany, hitting a wide range of targets across the Reich. Berlin itself was attacked three times between 23 August and 4 September. Over 300 Lancasters took part in each raid and altogether 54 of them were lost during the three nights, an ominous casualty rate of 5.5 per cent. All told, Bomber Command flew 1,719 sorties to Berlin in this period and the overall loss rate was even higher, at 7.7 per cent. Other cities bombed included Stuttgart, Brunswick, Leipzig and Nuremburg. Ken Dagnall was a bomb aimer with 9 Squadron which took part in an attack on

Nuremburg on the night of 10–11 August, when his Lancaster was badly hit by a Ju 88 in the middle of its bombing run. The mid-upper gunner, Dicky Lynham, was killed instantly. But Dagnall, with great presence of mind, leapt up from his position as soon as he had pressed the bomb release tit, grabbed the guns and blasted at the Ju 88 flashing past. 'The fighter was swinging from side to side,' recalled Dagnall, 'and all those instructions we'd had about getting your target in the sights were a load of rubbish. I tried to imagine the fighter's flight path. I aimed for the sky where I hoped he would turn up, and he flew right through my bullets.' Dagnall hit the Ju 88 on the starboard engine, then watched as the German fighter plunged from the sky with black smoke pouring from the wing. But his own Lancaster was in 'a hell of state', much of its equipment unserviceable. Even more frighteningly, the bombs had not fallen, because the release mechanism had been damaged in the attack. On the journey back the plane was sinking fast. 'We threw everything we could out into the sea, including the bombs which were stuck and had to be released by hand.' The Lancaster scraped in to land at the Sussex fighter base of Tangmere. 'I walked back through after we'd landed and saw Dicky. He was splattered all around inside the aircraft.' Dagnall then stepped out through the rear door. 'What we had been through must have hit me because I was standing there in a daze. A ground crew flight sergeant came up to me and gave me my first taste of counselling. He belted me across the face and said: "Sergeant, get on with your job! You're all right." I felt so ashamed.'[15]

It was during a raid on Düsseldorf, on the night of 3–4 November, that one of the most astonishingly courageous actions in the history of Bomber Command took place, when Bill Reid of 61 Squadron managed to press on to the target and return home despite appalling injuries and severe damage to his Lancaster. In many ways Reid was typical of the best of the breed that made Bomber Command: modest, brave, highly skilled and unwaveringly determined. The son of a blacksmith, he was born in Glasgow in 1922 and joined the RAF as soon as he left school, undergoing most of his training in Canada before he received his wings in June 1942. True to his resolute nature, Reid was keen to go on operations as soon as possible, but because he was such an accomplished pilot the RAF persuaded him to become a training instructor for a spell, the promise of future service in the Lancaster used as an inducement. As Reid explained, 'After OTU, I was offered a post as a crew instructor. I wanted to go on ops, but my Wing Commander said, "Well, I can guarantee you a Lancaster posting if you do stay and do these three months."

At the time there were still a large number of Stirling and Halifax postings and we all knew the Lancaster was the best. So that persuaded me to stay and do a bit of training.'[16] Bomber Command kept its promise and, following his spell as an instructor, Reid was posted to 61 Squadron at RAF Syerston in Nottinghamshire.

The November flight to Düsseldorf was his tenth Lancaster operation, and the drama started almost as soon as the plane crossed the Dutch coast. Flying at 21,000 feet, Reid's Lancaster came under attack from a Messerschmitt 110, cannon shells ripping through the aircraft and shattering the Perspex canopy. Severe damage was done to the port elevator, both turrets, the instrument panel and the hydraulic system. As Reid recalled:

> I felt a terrific bang on my face. The windscreen had been shot away. I thought at the time it was predicted ack-ack, much more accurate than normal flak with searchlights. Later I learnt from the rear gunner that the fire actually came from a fighter. The rear gunner should really have said at the time right away 'Dive starboard, dive port' if he had seen it. Whether he had just seen it disappearing, I don't know. But he should have told me to dive right away. I was wounded in the forearm, shoulder and head, and the plane had gone out of control temporarily. During that time to regain control, I probably lost about 2,000 feet. Having levelled out again, I checked up with the crew to see if they were all right. Although I had been hit in the shoulder, I just felt a numbness, as if I had been hit with a hammer, not painful.[17]

Not wanting to undermine morale, Reid refused to tell the rest of the crew that he was seriously wounded, his head and shoulders full of shell fragments, his face lacerated with Perspex fragments. He merely asked the navigator for a new course and continued flying towards Düsseldorf. 'I had no windscreen in the front. In some ways this was lucky because my head had been cut up and it was bleeding pretty badly but the cold air coming in – it was minus 20 – froze it up quickly, like you do with a cold compress. It stopped bleeding so this helped. I could see. We did not normally use our goggles because they steamed up. The windscreen was quite big in the Lancaster because you had to see out, to see your enemy. It was pretty cold, this was the main thing.'[18]

A few minutes later the Lancaster came under fire again, this time from a Focke-Wulf 190. Cannon shells exploded all over the aircraft. Both Reid and the engineer were badly injured. The navigator was killed and the wireless operator mortally wounded, though throughout the flight Reid was not aware of the extent of these casualties. He only thought that the navigator must have collapsed in shock. On the plane itself, now riddled with holes, the intercom had been shot away, the oxygen supply cut, the master unit for the gyro compass blown apart and the port elevator destroyed, so Reid, the engineer and the bomb aimer, who had come back from his compartment to help, had to hold the stick right back, as if taking the plane into a climb. It was a draining task, for both Reid and the engineer had sustained injuries to their arms. The surviving crew also had to rely on the emergency oxygen supplies kept in small bottles. In the mayhem the Lancaster had lost another 2,000 feet, as Reid struggled to regain control of the aircraft. Yet still he refused to turn back. Without a navigator or compass, he now guided the plane by the Pole Star. He later said that the question of turning back 'never occurred' to him. 'It was not a "press on regardless" feeling. It was just the fact that the four engines were still flying. If I'd had any engine cut I would have said to myself, "Well, I can't get any further." Another factor was that had I turned back, there were another six or seven hundred planes more or less on the same track, spread eight or ten miles broad and maybe four to six thousand feet deep. I would have been turning back right into them.'[19]

Thanks to Reid's cool leadership, the Lancaster reached the target, Düsseldorf, and moved in for the bombing run. 'I watched for target indicators, opened the bomb doors, and kept the plane as steady and level as I could. You feel the bombs going down, because there is about 12,000 pounds in the aircraft. You hold up for 25 or 30 seconds to take your picture. I think that this is one of the things they made the fuss about, because we had a picture of the actual target, after all that had happened. As soon as the picture was taken I turned off and began to head for base. I could still fly, holding the stick back.'[20] The return to England was a struggle, as the tattered Lancaster limped through flak, its speed slowed even further by drag caused from the open bomb doors which could not be closed because of the breakdown in the hydraulics. Reid went through periods of semi-consciousness as his wounds reopened and the emergency oxygen bottles ran out. But he was determined to keep going, partly through a selfless concern for his comrades. 'One of the things I remember feeling on this particular trip was that we had to get back because there were wounded on board and we had to get hospital treatment.'[21] Then, over the North Sea, another crisis arose, when all four Merlin engines suddenly cut out. For a moment it seemed as if all Reid's valiant efforts had been in vain. 'Normally the engineer tried to keep the petrol tanks fairly even, so if a tank was hit you would not lose half your petrol. You kept them even on the way to the target and on the way back. But he had forgotten to switch over the tanks so the engines had just run out. But the Lancaster was a wonderful plane. It had no vices and it just settled in the air. He switched over the petrol and the props started up again.'[22]

With all four engines working again, the Lancaster reached England and Reid prepared to land at the nearest base, which was the USAAF heavy-bomber station at Shipdham in Norfolk. With no hydraulics, the engineer had to use the emergency air bottle to put down the under-carriage, while Reid lowered the flaps. 'My head started to bleed again, which looked a bit rough for the others. But I said I was all right. We came in and as we landed, the legs of the undercarriage collapsed and we went along on our belly for maybe fifty yards and then came to a stop and switched off the engines to keep the fire hazard down. It was then that I knew the navigator had been killed because he had slid forward beside me, lying on the floor.' The Lancaster airmen were pulled out of the plane and immediately taken to hospital, where the wireless operator died two days later. The rest of the men survived and, with the fortitude characteristic of Bomber Command, returned to operations. All of them were awarded gallantry medals, Reid the deserving recipient of the Victoria Cross, one of the ten Lancaster airmen so honoured during the war. His citation read:

> Wounded in two attacks, without oxygen, suffering severely from cold, his navigator dead, his wireless operator fatally wounded, his aircraft crippled and defenceless, Flight Lieutenant Reid showed superb courage and lead-ership in penetrating a further 200 miles into enemy territory to attack one of the most strongly defended targets in Germany, every additional mile increasing the hazards of the long and perilous journey home. His tenacity and devotion to duty were beyond praise.[23]

For all their trauma, these autumn raids were only a rehearsal for the main offensive, Harris's much-trumpeted 'Battle of Berlin' which he prom-ised would finish off Germany before the spring. The big assault began on the night of 18–19 November, when 416 Lancasters were dispatched to Berlin, followed by four more heavy raids on the capital before the end of the month, all of them with a minimum of 350 Lancasters. Superficially the sheer size of the bomber force and the tonnage of bombs appeared to have shaken the German High Command. 'Hell seems to have broken loose over us,' wrote Goebbels in his diary after the second raid and, four days later he was moved to claim: 'Conditions in the city are pretty hopeless.' After the last November raid he privately expressed his admiration for the RAF: 'The English aimed so accurately that one might think spies had pointed their way.'[24] Swiss intelligence submitted reports to the Air Staff indicating that the first raids had undermined production and morale, while in London the Air Secretary Sir Archibald Sinclair indulged in one of his periodic bursts of sycophancy towards Harris: 'My warmest congratulations to you and to all ranks serving under your command on two crushing attacks upon the Nazi citadel. Berlin is not only the home of all Prussian militarism but it is also the greatest centre of industry in all Germany. The most convincing measure of their success has been the huge deployment of the enemy's resources for its defence.'[25]

Yet Sinclair's telegram to Harris inadvertently exposed a fundamental problem at the centre of the Berlin campaign. The 'huge deployment' of German defences around Berlin was no indicator of the RAF's ascendancy. On the contrary, the strengthened array of flak and fighters demonstrated the ferocity of the battle in which Bomber Command was now engaged. Since Hamburg, the Reich had become well prepared to deal with the bomber offensive. On the ground, there was a continuing increase in the number and power of the anti-aircraft batteries. The output of heavy flak guns rose from 6,864 in 1943 to 8,402 in 1944, allowing a 22 per cent increase in the number of heavy batteries within Germany. Similarly, the production of light flak guns went up over the same period from 35,580 to 50,917. In addition, there was a significant rise in the supply of searchlights and an expansion in the number of personnel operating the ground defences, particularly through the recruitment of women and young people. It has been estimated that by the spring of 1944, there were some 111,000 German women working in the defence batteries.[26] The air defences had also been significantly strengthened. By the turn of the year 1,500 day and night fighters were available in the front line.

Just as importantly, the introduction of new tactics and equipment since the collapse of the Kammhuber Line in July 1943 had made the Luftwaffe more lethal in combat. In place of the former rigid 'boxes', the fighters were free to roam the skies, aided by advanced radar devices. Major Hajo Hermann's single-engined Wilde Sau (Wild Boar) Gruppen, which had made their first appearance at Hamburg, were joined by the new Zahme Sau (Tame Boar) units. Whereas Wilde Sau relied on pilots with airborne radar to find their own prey, Zahme Sau was essentially a new type of ground control system, which used radar and beacons to guide two-engined Me 110s and Ju 88s into the heart of the bomber stream. The technical breakthrough that made Zahme Sau possible was the development of a type of radar called Lichtenstein SN-2, which was impervious to jamming by Window. SN-2 first began to be installed in German fighters in November 1943, adding a new edge to the Luftwaffe's night-fighting armoury. As a radar, it was not nearly as precise as the increasingly ineffective Würzburg system, but it could deal with far more aircraft at any one time. The key to the success of the Zahme Sau technique lay in finding the RAF bomber stream, and here the German defences were aided by tracking devices like Naxos and Corfu, which could pick up H2S signals emanating from the British aircraft.

Once the general direction of the stream had been ascertained over the North Sea, the Zahme Sau fighters took off en masse and were directed by continuous ground control commentary to radio beacons that were thought to be in the bombers' flight path. Sometimes they would circle the beacons, waiting for further instructions or a sighting of the bombers. On other occasions, they would fly long distances through the night sky, moving from one beacon to another as the direction of the RAF bomber stream unfolded. The Me 110s and Ju 88s could often sense they were near to the bombers from the huge amount of air turbulence caused by the slipstream of hundreds of 30-ton aircraft. Alternatively, some of the night-fighter pilots found they could glimpse the bombers from vapour trails or exhaust stubs or the silhouettes outlined against marker flares. Once the night fighters were close, they would slide into the stream, position themselves underneath the Lancasters and then use Schrage Musik upward-firing cannon to cause mayhem, the shells all the more deadly because their explosive arrival was rarely anticipated. Many of the Lancasters caught just went up in a ball of flames. Sometimes the crew was lucky enough to bail out, as rear gunner Jim Chapman found when his plane was hit by Schrage Musik over Germany in February 1944:

> There was nothing happening in our vicinity to suggest we were likely to be under attack, then suddenly I'm gazing out the back, operating my turret and I hear a noise at the back end of the Lancaster. I can only describe it as like somebody rattling a dustbin lid. That was followed by a glow from underneath the rear end of the aircraft. It wasn't until then that I realized we were under attack. I realized this noise was his cannon fire. The mid-upper gunner had picked him up as well and within seconds the captain was ordering, 'Bail out!' Those were the words I never wanted to hear.

As fire swept through the fuel tanks and the Lancaster fell through the sky, Chapman leapt out the escape hatch. All the crew survived and became prisoners-of-war, except the eighteen-year-old flight engineer, who in his panic jumped from the aircraft without his parachute.[27]

On many raids the German fighters covered the last part of the bomber stream's flight path with flares, making the planes an easier target against the blinding light and removing the cover of darkness which had been the whole point of a night offensive, as bomb aimer J. W. Walsh recorded in his private memoir: 'Each time we go to Berlin the number of bright white flares greatly increases. When we enter this enormous sphere of white light it is like stepping on to a brilliantly lit West End stage. Perhaps it is more like the Christians entering the Roman Amphitheatre to face the lions. Certainly for me it has a theatrical quality of great drama. We are aware of the lurking fighters and the flak is very accurate.'[28]

The reinforced German defences inflicted heavy losses on the bomber stream right from the start of the campaign. On their flights lasting almost nine hours, the Lancasters were now more vulnerable to attack than at any stage since their introduction to Bomber Command in December 1941. In a characteristically memorable passage in the official history of the bomber offensive, Noble Frankland, himself a former Lancaster navigator, wrote of how the Avro planes struggled in the new environment:

> Belching flame from their exhausts as well as radar transmissions from their navigational and fighter warning apparatus made them all too apparent to those who hunted them. Once engaged in combat, they had little chance of victory and not much of escape, while the large quantities of petrol, incendiary bombs, high explosives and oxygen with which they were filled often gave spectacular evidence of their destruction. Outpaced, outmanoeuvred and outgunned by the German night fighters in a generally highly inflammable and explosive condition, these black monsters presented an ideal target to any fighter pilot who could find them.[29]

During the raid on Berlin on 26–27 November, 29 Lancasters were shot down, and 37 on 2–3 December. The overall loss rate on the first raid of December had reached an unsustainable 8.7 per cent, causing a rising tide of apprehension among the crews. 'Lying in the nose of a Lancaster on a visual bomb run over Berlin was probably the most frightening experience of my lifetime,' said R. B. Leigh, a bomb aimer with 156 Squadron. 'Approaching the target, the city appeared to be surrounded by searchlights and the flak was always intense. The run-up seemed endless, the minutes of flying "straight and level" seemed like hours and every second I expected to be blown to pieces. I sweated with fear and the perspiration seemed to freeze on my body.'[30]

A vivid contemporary description of the nerve-shredding dangers faced by the bomber crews over Berlin was provided for American listeners by the celebrated broadcaster Ed Murrow, who flew with Lancaster *D-Dog* on the fateful night of 2–3 December. In those measured tones which had first won international fame during his broadcasts from London in the Blitz of 1940, he recorded his impressions of the 'orchestrated hell' that was Berlin. About 30 miles from the target, Murrow heard the bomb aimer say over the intercom 'target indicators going down'. At the same moment, 'the sky ahead was lit up by bright yellow flares. Off to starboard, another kite went down in flames. The flares were sprouting all over the sky: reds, greens and yellows. And we were flying straight for the centre of the fireworks. *D-Dog* seemed to be standing still, the four propellers thrashing the air, but we didn't seem to be closing in. The cloud had cleared and off to starboard a Lancaster was caught by at least fifteen searchlight beams. We could see him twist and turn and finally break out.' Then suddenly the cabin of *D-Dog* filled with 'unhealthy white light'. Murrow's own plane had been coned. He watched as the skipper jammed the control column forward and to the left. 'We were going down.' Murrow could see the fingernails of the pilot

> turn white as he gripped the steering wheel. And then I was on my knees, flat on the deck, for he had whipped the *Dog* back into a climbing turn. The knees should have been strong enough to support me but they weren't and the stomach seemed in danger of letting me down too. I picked myself up and looked out again. It seemed that one big searchlight, instead of being 20,000 feet below, was mounted right on our wing tip. *D-Dog* was corkscrewing. As we rolled down on the other side, I began to see what was happening to Berlin. The clouds were gone and the sticks of incendiaries from the preceding waves made the place look like a badly laid out city with the streetlights on. The small incendiaries were going down like a fistful of white rice thrown on a piece of black velvet.

The corkscrew continued and Murrow was thrown to the other side of the cockpit. 'There below were more incendiaries, glowing white and then turning red. The cookies, the 4,000-pound high explosives, were bursting below like great sunflowers gone mad. And then as we started down again, still held in the lights, I remembered that *Dog* had still had one of those cookies and a whole basket of incendiaries in his belly. And the lights still held us, and I was very frightened.' Finally *D-Dog* escaped the cone, and as the plane levelled out, the skipper and bomb aimer dicussed the bombing run. 'A few seconds later, the incendiaries went and *D-Dog* seemed lighter and easier to handle.' Murrow began to breathe more easily as the skipper turned away from the target. 'Then there was a tremendous whoomp and an unintelligible shout from the tail gunner and *D-Dog* shivered and lost altitude. I looked to the port side and there was a Lancaster that seemed close enough to touch. It had whipped straight under us, missed us by twenty five, fifty feet. No one knew how much.' Moments later, *D-Dog* was coned again and the skipper had to ram the throttles home as he went into another corkscrew. Soon the Lancaster escaped and the plane was back on course for England. A few flak shells burst around the plane but the pilot assured Murrow they were 'not very close. When they are near, you can smell them.' Without further trouble, the Lancaster reached England. Towards the end of his report, Murrow explained that two of his colleagues from the American press had been shot down in Lancasters over Berlin on the same raid, covering the same story. 'Men die in the sky while others are roasted alive in their cellars. Berlin last night was not a pretty sight. This is a calculated, remorseless campaign of destruction.'[31]

The problem for Bomber Command was that so far the campaign was proving insufficiently destructive. The hopes of another Hamburg firestorm had not materialized. Contrary to Sinclair's hollow exultation, Harris's bombast and Goebbels's melodramatic pessimism, the early raids had inflicted nothing like the damage claimed. Marking was often poor. H2S was an inadequate aid over a vast, built-up area. On some attacks, bombs were scattered over a 30-square-mile area, with the result that the fires were isolated and did not create the sort of conflagration that would sweep through a city. Albert Speer, more balanced than Goebbels, wryly commented that all the raids did was to improve production efficiency by demolishing some of the administrative buildings of the Nazis' central bureaucracy.[32] Looking back on the Battle of Berlin, the Pathfinder leader Don Bennett later told Harris that some of the blame had to be attached to the bomber crews themselves, who he claimed had shown insufficient resolution in the face of the enemy. 'There can be no doubt,' he wrote, 'that a large number of crews failed to carry out their attacks in their customary determined manner.' He pointed to reports from Pathfinder crews which 'consistently showed that the amount of bombing on the markers which they dropped was negligible. I feel quite sure in my own mind that many bombs were wasted en route in an effort to increase aircraft performance and that, unfortunately, the Command suffered from many "fringe merchants".'[33]

Bennett was a tough leader, but this was little short of a calumny against men who, like the British soldiers in the First World War, displayed an astonishing spirit of self-sacrifice against overwhelming odds in carrying out an ill-conceived strategy. As the broadcast of Ed Murrow or the example of Bill Reid demonstrated, there was no taint of pusillanimity within the ranks of the heavy-bomber crews. Bennett's unjust charge ignored the realities of the campaign. The bombers were not achieving their objective because the very idea of wiping out Berlin before the spring of 1944 was absurd. Such a goal ignored the strength of the German defences and the geographical layout of Berlin itself, with its wide avenues and parks which prevented fires spreading and assisted the fire brigades. As the scientist Freeman Dyson put it, 'the city is more modern and less dense than Hamburg, spread out over an area as large as London with only half of London's population; so it did not burn well.'[34] Bennett's accusation also paid no heed to the poor weather that invariably descended on northern Europe in the depths of winter. With only two airfields equipped with the petrol-burning FIDO landing system, it was impossible for heavy Lancaster raids to be mounted in foggy conditions. Indeed, for a fortnight from 2 December, Bomber Command mounted no trips to Berlin at all. The next one, on the night of 16–17 December, was to turn into one of the darker episodes in Bomber Command's history, when thick mist covered East Anglia as the Lancasters returned and 28 of them crashed or collided in attempting to land, 25 already having been shot down over Berlin.

The wintry conditions of December 1943 also made life difficult for the ground crews on the bomber stations. Stephen Rew, a Lancaster engine fitter at Coningsby, looked back on those bleak months with a shudder:

> It was not everybody's idea of fun, standing on a trestle about ten feet up, in a biting east wind and an icy penetrating drizzle, which sooner or later found its way down your neck, no matter how you tried to stop it, wearing an oilskin coat which kept some of the wet out, but which hampered your movements, with the rain gradually soaking through the legs of your overalls and trousers and down into your gumboots.

In the freezing dampness the Lancasters had to be covered with a thick canvas to protect them from the weather, but again, this could be an awkward procedure, especially in a stiff breeze when the canvas acted like a sail. 'One fitter climbed on the engine, unfolded the canvas and then the man on the ground tied the sides with greasy chords. Then he had to repeat the operation for the rear turret, mid-upper, nose and cockpit. When doing the cockpit, the man was more than 20 feet off the ground. One ground crewman suffered a broken leg, after being blown off the cockpit-canopy. If anyone thinks life dull and unexciting, I recommend that he finds a Lancaster on a dark and windy night and puts the covers on.' In addition to clearing ice and snow off the Lancaster, one job Rew particularly loathed was the application of the de-icing fluid to the plane's wings and tail unit. 'This was horrible, thick, sticky stuff, about the consistency of butter, but much stickier and coloured a sort of greyish brown and as it had to be smeared on by hand, one's condition after applying it can well be imagined. It was amazing how big a Lancaster seemed when it came to applying this stuff.'[35]

The sense of gloom over the campaign was matched by growing political controversy about the area-bombing strategy. Voices were now raised in Parliament, in parts of the government and in intellectual circles about both the moral and military soundness of indiscriminate urban attacks. Such voices had largely been muted in the first year of Harris's tenure, as Britain remained on the defensive and Nazi tyranny seemed all-conquering. But as the Germans retreated and the scale of the bombing offensive dramatically increased, more doubts were expressed. One of the most powerful critics was Richard Stokes, the Labour MP for Ipswich, who condemned attacks on civilian centres as 'morally wrong and strategic lunacy'.[36] Stokes was no pacifist. As a gunner major in the First World War, he had won the Military Cross and the Croix de Guerre, but he was convinced that bombing operations should focus on targets of military importance. On 1 December 1943, after the first four raids of the Battle of Berlin, he asked Sir Archibald Sinclair in the Commons: 'Within what area in square miles was it estimated that the 350 blockbusters recently dropped on Berlin fell?' Sinclair refused to answer the question, claiming that the information would be 'of value to the enemy'. This provoked Stokes to respond: 'Would not the proper answer be that the Government does not dare give it? Does not my Right Honourable Friend admit by his answer that the Government is resorting to indiscriminate bombing including residential areas?' Sinclair now denied the charge, claiming that government policy was only to hit 'vitally important military objectives' in Germany.[37] Other dissenting figures joined in the condemnation. Sir Basil Liddell Hart, the military historian, warned of the folly of a 'mad competition of mutual devastation',[38] while Bishop George Bell of Chichester questioned whether the government had lost its sense of proportion and respect for the law in attempting to obliterate whole towns. However, there was little sign of public opinion showing the same concern. One study by the research group Mass Observation found that only one in ten Londoners disapproved of the bombing of

Berlin. In condemning the intervention by Richard Stokes, the *Sunday Dispatch* captured the public mood. 'Those MPs who appear to regard the German civilians as their constituents can be assured that the British public is not shedding any tears over the suffering of German cities.'[39]

Mounting distaste within parts of the political establishment could also be articulated behind the scenes. When Harris had declared after the second Berlin raid that the campaign would continue 'until the heart of Nazi Germany ceases to beat',[40] the Tory grandee Lord Salisbury, Leader of the House of Lords and Dominions Secretary in the Cabinet, felt moved to write to Sinclair, saying that Harris's proclamation

> gives one a shake. This would seem to bring us up short against the repeated Government declarations that we are bombing only military or industrial targets. Perhaps that is all that Harris contemplates and I shall be delighted if you tell me so. But there is a great deal of evidence that makes some of us afraid that we are losing some of our moral superiority to the Germans and if Harris means not merely that the incidental casualties to women and children cannot be avoided, but also that the residential heart of Berlin is to cease to beat then a good many people will feel they have been let down, though in writing this I speak in the name of no Committee. Of course the Germans began it, but we do not take the devil as an example.[41]

As he had done in the Commons, Sinclair denied that there had been any shift in government policy towards indiscriminate bombing. With the classic politician's gift for dissembling, Sinclair said that while he had never denied it would be possible to achieve the destruction of the German military and industrial system 'without inflicting terrible casualties on the civilian population of Germany', he assured Salisbury that the government had always 'adhered firmly to the principle that we would attack none but military objectives'.[42]

This was the deceitful line that Sinclair, the Air Staff and other government figures publicly maintained throughout the war, pretending that mass attacks on residential quarters were never part of the air strategy. But the scale of the raids meant that such a stance was scarcely credible. With typical cunning, Portal tried to resolve the contradiction between official rhetoric and bombing reality by claiming that 'the whole of a city is a military objective'.[43] But Harris had no time for such sophistry, which he believed was counterproductive. The attempt to conceal the truth about the killing of civilians as a deliberate war aim, he argued, only served to undermine the morale of his men and the strength of the offensive. What he wanted was far greater candour about bombing policy instead of the usual denials and evasions. In a letter that demonstrated both his raw honesty and his famous ruthlessness, Harris told Portal and Sinclair on 25 October:

> The aim of Bomber Command should be unambiguously and publicly stated. That aim is the destruction of German cities, the killing of German workers and the disruption of civilized community life throughout Germany. It should be emphasized that the destruction of houses, public utilities, transport and lives; the creation of a refugee problem on an unprecedented scale and the breakdown of morale at home and at the battle fronts by fear of extended and intensified bombing are accepted and intended aims of our bombing policy. They are not by-products of attempts to hit factories . . . It should be made clear that the destruction of factory installations is only part and by no means the most important part of the plan. Acreages of housing devastation are infinitely more important.

This eagerness to downplay 'the obliteration of German cities and their inhabitants', he said, did nothing to assist the bomber crews in their difficult task. 'Our crews know what the real aim of the attack is. When they read what the public are told about it, they are bound to think (and they do think) that the authorities are ashamed of area bombing. It is not to be expected that men will go on risking their lives to effect a purpose which their own Government appears to consider at least as too disreputable to be mentioned in public.'[44]

But the Air Ministry refused to give Harris the unequivocal declaration that he wanted. He was told that all the official statements could only emphasize 'an obvious truth, ie, that the widespread devastation is not an end in itself but the inevitable accompaniment of an all-out attack on the enemy's means and capacity to wage war'.[45] Harris was still dissatisfied. The German economic system, he wrote on 23 December 1943 to Portal and Sinclair, 'includes workers, houses and public utilities and it is therefore meaningless to claim that the wiping out of German cities is not an end in itself'. Harris then reiterated his conviction that 'the cities of Germany including their working populations are literally the heart of Germany's war potential. That is why they are being deliberately attacked.' He went on:

> Unless my interpretation is accepted without ambiguity or evasion on the issue, it is clear that our crews are being sacrificed in a deliberate attempt to do something which the Air Council do not regard as necessary or even legitimate, namely to eliminate entire German cities. It is not enough to admit that devastation is caused by our attacks, or to suggest that it is incidental and a rather regrettable concomitant of night bombing. It is in

fact produced deliberately and our whole Pathfinder and navigational technique is primarily designed to promote it. Failure to assert it openly will inevitably affect adversely the morale of crews and I would urge that this rather than the appeasement of sentimental and humanitarian scruples should be our primary consideration.

Showing some prescience, Harris warned that if the Air Ministry continued to 'shroud war objectives in obscurity' then this would 'inevitably lead to deplorable controversies when the facts are fully and generally known', precisely what did happen after the war when the role of Harris and Bomber Command became the subject of the most bitter debate.[46] But the Air Ministry never gave Harris the frank statement he wanted.

Harris was perhaps exaggerating the effect of Air Ministry pronouncements on the morale of the airmen. Most of them were so involved in the task of surviving from week to week that they did not pay much attention to the niceties of debates about strategic policy or morality. In a contemporary account written in 1943, Squadron Leader A. J. Brown wrote: 'It always surprises me how little interest the majority of flying personnel in the mess take in the BBC bulletins, the newspapers or the progress of the war generally. The noise of their talk drowns the announcer's voice and for the most part they seem completely apathetic about the progress of the war. One airman said, "We have given ourselves to the country, and we can't do anything more about it anyhow, so why worry."'[47] There was a studied indifference, even cynicism towards the outpourings of politicians and the top brass. Trevor Timperley of 156 Squadron recounted an embarrassing occasion before a raid on Germany in late 1943 when Sir Archibald Sinclair turned up at the base of Warboys in Huntingdonshire to give a morale-boosting speech after the briefing. 'It was not very popular. People did not like this sort of thing. It was a waste of time. Between briefing and going out to the aircraft, people wanted time to themselves rather than listening to politicians.'[48]

On the issue of bombing cities, most crews just regarded it as part of their work, a job that had to be done. It was not their role to question the targets they were given. As Lancaster pilot Harry Yates put it: 'If every briefing had required us, in the official euphemism of the time, to de-house the civilian population, it would have made no difference. We would have gone out and done our duty just the same.'[49] In any case, the crews largely shared the view of the British public that the Germans got what they deserved for starting the war and pursuing it so aggressively. That was a view summed up by Arnold Easton, an Australian navigator with 467 Squadron: 'Having seen the devastation of the cities in England, particularly London, I couldn't help but feel that the Germans had it coming to them. Hitler had to be put back in his box. He had his dagger at England's throat. Whatever had to be done, had to be done.'[50] The fact that the area bombing was usually carried out at high altitude also helped airmen to divorce themselves from the devastation on the ground. 'The casualties did not worry me at all. I did not feel a thing, actually,' said Bert Wolstenholme, a wireless operator with 115 Squadron. 'We did not see it with our own eyes. We were not looking at dead bodies. We were up there at about 20,000 feet.'[51] But it also must be said the Reich was the most bitter foe in the darkest war ever to consume humanity, and, like all Britons, the bomber crews knew that the German people had not just voted the Nazi Party into power but had supported the advent of war with exuberant relish. It was therefore understandable that for some airmen, like flight engineer Danny Boon, a vengeful animosity towards the Germans infused their missions. 'I was taught when I was eighteen that all good Germans were dead ones. That was the theme of the war, that the Germans are horrible people.'[52]

Yet when they were not embroiled in the heat of conflict, most airmen were intelligent and humane enough to have their qualms about the policy of area bombing, even if they felt it was justified. In moments of contemplation, the very concept of deliberately attacking civilians was bound to trouble the consciences of many. Having entered the Lancaster on his first flight to Berlin, in November 1943, Les Bartlett of 50 Squadron felt so moved by the forthcoming ordeal that 'in spite of the unsuitable surroundings I said a prayer to ask for forgiveness for killing so many human beings with the dropping of my bombs'.[53] Bomb aimer Campbell Muirhead, who generally had a breezy, gregarious approach to life in a Lancaster crew, wrote this entry in his diary after a visit to the Ruhr: 'I could not help staring at the fires burning below, which, even from 19,000 feet one could see clearly . . . That really was widespread area bombing. What is now referred to as an "area bash". Some of my load must have fallen on houses, maybe even on air raid shelters as well. A faint niggling at the back of my mind: how many women and children had I killed simply by pressing that little tit? No point in deluding oneself over that – one had killed people.'[54] Thomas Murray, a pilot with 207 Squadron and never an admirer of Harris, had more than a 'faint niggling' about area attacks: 'As the German defences grew, we were hitting wider targets, just trying to hit the middle of the town or city, really only bombing civilians. I didn't like that.' Murray was relieved in 1944 when he was transferred to 138 Squadron, flying Stirlings for the Special Operations Executive which co-ordinated espionage and the movement of secret agents behind enemy lines. 'I preferred SOE work because you weren't burning cities. It was an awful business, setting old towns alight, seeing houses burning. I never really believed in the bombing but you had to do it. And it was the only thing we could do, I suppose. But with the SOE, you were giving something to help and getting a result.'[55]

Even in the pit of winter, as the losses mounted, Harris remained convinced that the Berlin campaign would ultimately succeed. 'It is surely impossible to believe that an increase by more than half of existing devastation within four months could be sustained by Germany without total collapse,' he wrote at the end of December 1943.[56] Certain that he could achieve such a result he intensified the bombing in the New Year. On the very first night in 1944, 421 Lancasters flew to Berlin, sustaining 29 losses or 6.9 per cent of the force. Six other raids followed on the capital during the month, in addition to major attacks on three other German cities. On the night of 27–8 January 1944, over 500 Lancasters took part in a single raid for the first time, though the losses were, once more, significant: 34 of the 515 planes were shot down, a rate of 6.6 per cent.

Bomb aimer Les Bartlett took part in one of those January raids, as he recorded in his diary: 'The fireworks started. We were about forty miles from the target and the familiar red Very signals from fighter to fighter were everywhere in the sky. As we were in the fifth wave of the attack practically the whole main force was ahead of us and I could see combats taking place in every direction.' Disconcertingly, the German fighters had laid a path of flares along the bombing run, 'making the whole area as bright as day'. But Bartlett's Lancaster carried on towards the aiming point. Getting the target in his bombsights, Bartlett 'could see numerous fires and one particularly vivid explosion which seemed to light up the whole of Berlin with a vivid orange flash for about ten seconds. At the critical moment I yelled the now familiar "bomb doors open", followed by "bombs gone" and "bomb doors closed".' Just as the crew left the target, they saw a Ju 88 straight ahead attacking another Lancaster. Almost as soon as the skipper's words were out of his mouth, Bartlett was up in the front turret 'blazing away. After this for about thirty seconds it did a slow turn to port, then spiralled down to earth.'[57] After taking down this fighter, Bartlett's crew successfully headed home for England.

In a crisis where a Lancaster crew had to bail out, the airmen either went through the narrow hatch at the bottom of the bomb aimer's compartment in the front or the door at the rear. But for any of the airmen it could often be extremely difficult even to reach one of the hatches. Smoke or flames might be filling the fuselage, while the search in the darkness for parachutes could be a desperate one. Even worse, the massive g-forces in a violent dive could pin an airman to the walls. On a raid to Cologne, Hugh Parrott, a wireless operator with 582 Squadron, found that he and the mid-upper gunner were so paralysed that they could not move towards the hatch when the order was given to bail out. 'The Lancaster started spinning. We, at the back, were flung to the floor and we could not move. The centrifugal force was simply too great. There we were. We went down with the plane. My foot was caught in a step at the back, which may have been a stroke of good fortune. Because when we crashed into the ground and I was flung forward, my trapped leg must have absorbed some of the energy. What happened was I cracked my head on the side, broke my back and smashed my leg up. I passed out and when I recovered consciousness, I was lying upside down on the roof of the Lancaster'.[58] Parrott spent much of the remainder of the war in a German hospital, undergoing a series of operations on his legs before being transferred to a POW camp. If an airman did make it to the escape hatch, the ideal routine for bailing out was, according to wireless operator Fred Gardiner, 'to kneel on the sill of the door, roll into a ball and go out head first in order to avoid hitting the tailplane which was just behind the door'.[59] Those who found themselves dangling in the sky were immediately struck by the echoing silence after the tremendous, continual roar of the Merlins inside the Lancaster. 'When the parachute opened it gave me a hefty blast in the crotch. But then it was marvellous really. It was lovely and quiet after all the turmoil in the aeroplane,' said Charles Marshall, whose 460 Squadron Lancaster was set ablaze on a raid to Hanover in October 1944.[60]

If they landed safely, the airmen had little chance of escaping Germany. Most were picked up within hours, their crashed Lancaster often giving away their location. Once captured, they were first taken for interrogation at the Dulag Luft transit centre run by the Luftwaffe near Frankfurt. Then they were incarcerated at one of the Stalag Luft POW camps for airmen, the most famous of which was Stalag Luft III, from where 76 British and US airmen escaped in March 1944 through tunnels they had elaborately constructed. All but three of them were recaptured and, on Hitler's personal orders, 50 were executed, most of the rest sent to concentration camps. The heroic episode was later turned into the epic film *The Great Escape*.

One of those who ended up as a POW was Frank Waddington, a navigator with 7 Pathfinder Squadron. In a subsequent interview, Waddington admitted that he came to dread the trauma of operations to Berlin, 'fretting and sweating and getting more and more terrified'. On the base he drank 'like a fish' so he could overcome his anxiety and get some sleep. On the night of 20 January 1944, his worst fears were realized. Just after the Lancaster had released its bombs over the aiming point, it was hit by a fighter, the cannon shells raking through fuselage and wings. The engines stopped almost immediately. The skipper gave the order to bail out:

> I think I grew up in the next moments. Whilst I had been drinking to get to sleep, thinking about this incident, when it had actually happened, I was so calm. There was no panic, no shouting or pushing. I knew what I had to do. I put on my parachute. I went forward through the curtain. To my surprise, there was no one there. The pilot had gone. I don't blame him. But I had always imagined that the pilot would stay until everyone had got out. I got into the cockpit and I could see that the control column was pressed right forward. So I leant over, got hold of it to try and pull it so that the Lancaster would straighten up. We were going down head first. I could not shift it. Then, just as I stood there, the plane suddenly exploded. I don't know who had actually got out through the escape hatches. I remember as plain as anything going through an opening in the disintegrating plane. And I am out in the night sky.

As he fell he pulled the ripcord, and with 'an almighty jerk' it opened. Waddington landed in a Berlin street. 'My first thought on landing was, Thank goodness that's over. What I meant was that I did not have to go on operations any more. I was so frightened.' Then to his horror he remembered that 2,000 tons of bombs were about to start falling on Berlin. So he took some hard backing from his parachute, put it over his head and curled up as tightly as he could against a street wall. 'Then there was the shattering noise of the bombs. The earth was shaking. It was terrible, though none fell near.' When the raid finished, he was approached by some German citizens, who took him to a police station. There one policeman 'rushed at me and started punching me. I could not do anything. I stood there with my eyes down. I felt utterly humiliated, really.' The beating stopped and he was taken to a cell:

> Then a Gestapo officer came in. I thought he was about to shoot me but he spoke:
> 'English or Canadian?'
> 'English.'

'Do the English usually murder women and children?'
'Not as a rule.'

After further interrogation, Waddington was then taken through the city to the mainline railway station. 'It was terribly exciting because you could see all the damage, really you were pleased about that. We got to a big railway station. We were surrounded by Luftwaffe guards. All the people were showing their hostility towards us, poking their umbrellas or spitting at us. We were very pleased to have the guards to protect us.' After a long train journey through the night, he arrived at Dulag Luft.[61]

The numbers of British airmen shot down remained high through February and the first weeks of March 1944 as the German night fighters grew more assured in their tactics. In a raid on Leipzig by 561 Lancasters on 19–20 February, 46 of them were lost, a rate of 8.2 per cent. Another 29 out of 554 Lancasters were shot down five nights later in a raid on Schweinfurt, a loss rate of 5.24 per cent. Harris's belief that Germany would be broken by the end of March now belonged to the distant realms of fantasy. 'The losses were becoming increasingly unacceptable,' wrote Ron Smith, a rear gunner in 156 Squadron, who recalled that at one briefing, when Berlin was announced again as the target, 'a groan of disbelief from a hundred throats filled the room'.[62] The campaign that was meant to be the ultimate vindication of area bombing had turned into a gruesome war of bloody attrition. An aerial Battle of the Somme was now taking place over Germany. Morale in the squadrons was badly shaken by the grim toll. One rear gunner in 44 Squadron was so reluctant to go on a sortie to Frankfurt that he sabotaged his Lancaster by taking an axe to the oil feed pipe to his rear turret. He was convicted of LMF and sentenced to two years' hard labour. Dick Raymond flew to Berlin on 15 February, after being badly injured the previous November when a Lancaster exploded on his base and he was hit by debris. 'To be honest, after what had happened with the explosion, the smell of an aircraft nearly made me vomit. It was shocking to re-enter a Lancaster. The survival rate in those days was so low you felt you were almost under a death sentence.'[63]

Thanks to the skill of his pilot, Arnold Easton, a navigator with 467 Squadron, was lucky to live through a raid in March over Stuttgart, when 29 of the 616 Lancasters were shot down. During the bombing run, Easton's job as navigator was to go into the astrodome and look straight up to check that no plane was directly above ready to bomb:

The target was brilliantly lit when we approached, with the fires burning. We were going in at 20,000 feet and silhouetted against the glowing cloud.

All of a sudden the rear gunner screamed, 'Dive, skipper, dive.' The skipper put the control column forward and he applied left rudder. My feet were in mid-air. Tracer shells were coming all around me. One hit the starboard wing and blew a big hole in it. The German fighter swooped away, after the mid-upper gunner reckoned he got a burst into him. We were diving down at a speed in excess of what was permitted in a Lancaster. The skipper was diving so fast that he could not physically lift the elevators to bring it out of the dive. So he used the trimming wheel beside him, trimmed that round and that meant that the little tab on the elevators was wound down. The air going up, hitting that little tab, helped him to raise the elevators. So he trimmed it out of the dive.

The plane then moved in for the bombing run and then managed to limp back to England, having survived another fighter attack.[64]

The mayhem that an expert German fighter pilot could cause in a bomber stream was described by Luftwaffe radar operator Feldwebel Ostheimer, who flew in a Ju 88 with Major Prince Heinrich zu Sayn Wittgenstein, holder of the Knight's Cross with oakleaves after gaining 79 victories in the night skies. On 21 January he and Ostheimer took off from Stendal near Berlin. 'At about 22.00 hours I picked up the first contact on my search equipment,' wrote Ostheimer:

> I passed the pilot directions and a little later the target was sighted: it was a Lancaster. We moved into position and opened fire, and the aircraft immediately caught fire in the left wing. It went down at a steep angle and started to spin. Between 22.00 and 22.05 hours the bomber crashed and went off with a violent explosion. Again we searched. At times I could see as many as six aircraft on my radar. After some further directions the next target was sighted: again a Lancaster. Following the first burst from us there was a small fire and the machine dropped its left wing and went down in a vertical dive. Shortly afterwards I saw it crash. It was some time between 22.10 and 22.15 hours. When it crashed there were heavy detonations, most probably it was the bomb load.

Two more Lancasters were shot down in plummeting balls of flame. Ostheimer found another Lancaster on his radar and Wittgenstein moved in for his fifth kill of the evening. Then something different happened. 'We were again in position and ready to shoot when, in our own machine, there were terrible explosions and sparks. It immediately caught fire and began to go down.' Ostheimer managed to bail out but Wittgenstein was killed in his own aircraft. It seems that he was hit from below by a Lancaster climbing from behind.[65]

The shooting down of Prince Wittgenstein proved that the Lancaster was not totally defenceless. Neither the Me 109 nor the Fw 190 were built as night fighters, and the Ju 88 and Me 110 were comparatively slow, as they had shown in their disastrous performance in the Battle of Britain. Moreover, the German losses on several fronts over the previous five years meant that the number of pilots with experience was dwindling. The steady drumbeat of death also sounded over the Luftwaffe squadrons during the long months of the bombing campaign, intensified from February with the entry of the lethal American Mustang in support of the USAAF daylight raids. In January 1944, the Luftwaffe lost 233 planes and 133 of its personnel were killed. In the following month 309 German planes were lost and 171 crewmen died. Nor were advances in technology and tactics all one-sided. During the Battle of Berlin, Bomber Command introduced two key innovations. The first, installed in Mosquitoes and later in certain Lancasters, was a new navigational and blind-bombing aid called G-H, which was in essence a combination of Oboe and Gee. Like those two devices, G-H was linked to ground stations in England, but the crucial difference was that the transmitter for sending out target-finding signals was now carried in the aircraft. A cathode-ray tube indicated that the plane was right over the target when the two lines of blips came together on the screen, showing the exact moment for the bombs to be released. The twin advantages of G-H were, first, that more than 100 aircraft could operate the system simultaneously, and second, that it had greater range than Oboe.

For bomb aimer Miles Tripp, the introduction of G-H meant that he was 'a doomed species'. As he wrote, 'When using G-H the navigator would give a count down and tell the bomb aimer when to press the bomb release and thus the skill of bomb-aiming was reduced to pressing a button which could have been pressed by anybody.'[66] The invention was first used in October 1943 and though it only played a small part in the Battle of Berlin, its potential was obvious. From mid-1944 it became a vital part of Bomber Command's armoury. In later daylight operations, when the Allies had gained air superiority over Germany, two yellow bars were painted on the tail fins of Lancasters with this equipment. The aircraft without G-H would then formate on the G-H leader, dropping their bombs when he dropped his.

The other significant device was a sophisticated cathode-ray tube radio receiver called Airborne Cigar, or ABC, which could lock on to the control transmissions of German fighters and disrupt them. Developed by the Telecommunications Research Establishment under Dr Robert Cockburn in the summer of 1943, the ABC equipment, fitted within the

Lancaster's cabin, enabled a German-speaking operator to find the relevant frequency of the Luftwaffe night fighters. He could then use his powerful transmitter either to jam the ground-control instructions or, in a suitably convincing German voice, issue his own false instructions. Bomber Command was so impressed with Airborne Cigar that in October 1943 a special unit of Lancasters was established at Ludford Magna in Lincolnshire to accompany all major main force raids. Named 101 Squadron, it started with 36 front-line planes, reaching a peak of 42 plus four reserves. Ferguson Smith, one of the early recruits, explained how the system worked: 'This device had a cathode ray screen and it was tuned into the frequencies used by the German night-fighter controllers. Once you had identified one of the controllers giving instructions, a blip would come up on your screen and then you jammed the commentary by pressing a button. At the receiving end, the Germans heard a screech. We were given instruction in the jargon of the night-fighter controllers. It was not hard to find because it was a fairly narrow band. It was like tuning a radio with a dial.'[67] The special ABC Lancasters still carried a heavy bomb load, though the maximum had to be reduced by 1,000 pounds because of the weight of the equipment. Externally, they were distinguishable by the three large transmission aerials they had installed, two in front of the mid-upper turret, and another in the nose, in addition to a small dorsal reception aerial. They also differed internally in carrying an eighth crew member, the German-speaking radio operator. The Luftwaffe initially were infuriated at the disruption to their running commentaries for the fighters, so essential to the Zahme Sau (Tame Boar) method. As Ferguson Smith put it: 'Certainly you could hear the frustration of the controllers. If you lifted the jamming for a second, you could hear them complaining.'[68] Luftwaffe stations resorted to ineffective countermeasures like changing the frequency, to which ABC could easily adjust, or, according to Sam Brookes, a 101 wireless operator, 'having their instructions sung by Wagnerian sopranos to fool us into thinking it was just a civilian channel and not worth jamming'.[69]

But, as with so many breakthroughs in the technological war, ABC carried the risk of heightening the vulnerability of its users. With some experience the German fighters learnt that they could detect the 101 Squadron bombers from the ABC signals, and so they could deliberately target them. During the first ten weeks of the Battle of Berlin, 101 Squadron lost 21 aircraft and 168 crew members. Ferguson Smith was one of those who came under attack during the raid on Berlin on 20 January 1944:

We were about half an hour away from the target when the aircraft was peppered with cannon fire. We could feel it right through the plane. It was like something from an old-fashioned western, where the stranger comes into the bar and fires off two six-shooters and everyone dives under the table. There's always glass shattering behind the bar. The sound of shattering glass was exactly what I heard in that aircraft. I was jamming at the time. The shells got the rear gunner and the mid-upper gunner. I was hit and there was damage to the steering. I was wounded in the back, the chest, the leg and the bottom. I was flung down to the back of the aircraft with the impact of the shells. The next thing I knew the aircraft was in a dive towards the ground. I did not know if it was a controlled dive or if this was it. Then I was flung against the main spar as the plane pulled out. I could feel the stickiness of the blood on my skin. By the time I crawled to wear my chute was and hooked it on I realized that the plane was under control and it had been a deliberate, evasive dive. I managed to tell the pilot I was OK but that the ABC had been shattered.

Both the gunners were killed, but the skipper managed to bring the badly damaged Lancaster home to Ludford Magna. Smith spent a month in hospital, having 'a whole lot of shrapnel' removed from his body, and was then told to go back on operations with 101 Squadron.[70]

Despite the constant threat of attack, Airborne Cigar remained in service from its inception throughout the war. But by the end of March 1944, the Battle of Berlin was drawing to a sorry close. With the loss rate well above 5 per cent, the campaign was simply unsustainable. Bomber Command had neither the men nor the planes to keep enduring such casualties. Furthermore, the pressure on the airmen was unremittingly brutal. 'The Battle of Berlin did cause morale to sag,' said Joe Sherriff, a wireless operator with 57 Squadron. 'Crews were weary and angry, strained and much more fearful of their next trip than usual, cursing 'Butch' Harris for his unrelenting demands and his apparently uncaring attitude towards his own men. The results didn't appear to come anywhere near justifying the loss and hardship.'[71] Harris himself, despite all his stubbornness, knew that he could not continue at the same level. On the night of 24–5 March he dispatched the last big raid to Berlin, 577 Lancasters as part of a force of 811 aircraft. Once more savage casualties were inflicted by the German fighters and flak. A total of 9.1 per cent of all the RAF 'heavies' were lost, and 8 per cent of the Lancasters. Navigator Bob Brydon of 630 Squadron was one of those hit:

We were high at 22,000 feet but the flak was more accurate than I had ever known it and with frightening regularity we felt bursts juddering our aircraft. We were weaving through the sky, changing height and direction every fifteen seconds or so, but though we must have made their predicted fire difficult we never shook off the searchlights . . . The inevitable happened. There was an extremely loud bang and a lot of crunching, and the Lancaster seemed to rear up. Afterwards I learned from the mid-upper gunner that the starboard fin and rudder had been shot clean away. The pilot tried to hold her steady but it was impossible and on the intercom he shouted to us to abandon.[72]

Brydon leapt out, parachuted, and having landed, was taken prisoner the next morning.

It was on this final raid to Berlin that one of the most incredible bail-outs in the entire history of the war occurred. Rear gunner Nick Alkemede was flying in the 115 Squadron Lancaster *S-Sugar* when the plane came under attack from a Ju 88. After cannon shells had torn through the starboard wing and fuselage, the plane began to burn badly and smoke filled Alkemede's turret. The pilot gave the order to bail out. To his anguish, Alkemede realized that because of the flames, now licking the rear of the aircraft, he could not reach his parachute, which was stashed in its usual place in the fuselage. When the fire reached his turret and his oxygen mask started to melt, he was faced with a terrible dilemma: remain in the aircraft and be burned alive, or jump out from 18,000 feet without a parachute. He chose the latter, swinging the turret round, opening the doors and falling out backwards into the cold night sky. Descending at about 120 mph, he blacked out before he reached the earth. Unconscious, he had apparently been spared the awareness of an agonizingly painful death. Yet by some miracle, as his limp body plummeted to the ground, its fall was broken by the dense branches of a pine forest and then by a snowdrift. Astonishingly, when Alkemede regained consciousness three hours later he found that he was still alive. The worst of his injuries came from the fire rather than the fall. He had burns to his legs, face and hands, but the only result of his 18,000-feet plunge was a strained back, mild concussion, a twisted knee and a deep splinter in his thigh. Unable to move, he was soon picked up by the German home guard, who handed him over to the Gestapo. After a spell in hospital, he was taken to the Dulag Luft for interrogation. The Germans refused to believe his outlandish tale and suspected him of being a spy, which meant that he faced execution. But, on Alkemede's insistence, the wreckage of his Lancaster was investigated by the Luftwaffe and there, amidst the twisted metal, were the remnants of his parachute. His story had proved true. He spent the rest of the war as a much-fêted POW.

The Battle of Berlin ended on a far less uplifting note. On the night of 30–31 March, Bomber Command endured the worst night in its history, when a heavy raid on Nuremburg ended in a near massacre in the sky. The mission was uncharacteristically badly planned at High Wycombe, for the planes had to make a long, straight journey of more than 250 miles from Belgium over German territory and two fighter beacons until they reached the turning point northeast of Frankfurt, making them easy prey for the Luftwaffe. Furthermore, there was bright moonlight that night and little cloud cover was predicted for the route, though there was a forecast that the target itself might be obscured by cloud. In fact, the conditions seemed so favourable to the defences that it was widely assumed the raid would be cancelled. But Harris, still determined to inflict as much damage as he could by the start of April, pressed ahead, even after warnings from some navigation leaders about the route and the potential lack of high cloud cover. Robert Saundby, Harris's Deputy C-in-C, later admitted that 'we were most surprised' when Harris did not cancel.[73] The results fulfilled the darkest expectations. A total of 781 heavy bombers took off from their bases in the east of England at nine o'clock, 569 of them Lancasters, but the raid soon ran into trouble. With high winds blowing across northern Germany, the bomber stream became hopelessly scattered across the route. Great masses of thick cloud descended on Nuremburg so that the marking was wildly inaccurate or indiscernible, so most crews that made it to the target had to bomb using the primitive method of Estimated Time of Arrival, or ETA.[74] Only 500 tons of bombs fell on the city itself, causing little real damage because there was no pattern of concentration. By far the worst destruction was experienced by the bombers themselves. Aircrews were shocked at the continual sight of great balls of fire lighting up the sky as the bombers were systematically shot down, as Freddie Watts, a pilot with 630 Squadron recalled. 'It was the duty of air gunners to report any explosions or planes going down, so the navigator could log them. After the gunners had reported something like twenty going down, I told them not to report any more because I did not think it was doing very much for the morale of the crew.'[75]

Another airman on that trip, Basil Oxtaby of 467 Squadron, described how 'it was common to see four or five Lancasters or Halifaxes going down in flames, sometimes with three or four engines on fire, exploding on the ground. That made it even worse because when the aircraft exploded, there was a pool of light for hundreds of yards and the fighters above could see bombers silhouetted against that light. We tended to corkscrew most of the time rather than waiting for the gunners to give instructions. It was a pretty exacting trip.'[76] The Germans were exultant at their manifest superiority. The journalist Werner Kark, flying with the crew of an Me 110, wrote this account for his newspaper *Oberdonau Zeitung:* 'Our target comes into sight for a fraction of a second. Our pilot fires a long burst. Blood-red flashes streak from the barrels of our cannon. The shells hit his starboard wing, tear it off. For an instant the wreckage fills the air, then the bomber goes down vertically and hits the ground. There is a ball of fire on the earth, a thick black cloud of smoke from the explosion.'[77]

Harris was later to admit that Nuremburg was 'the one real disaster' of his time as chief of Bomber Command.[78] Of the 569 Lancasters sent to the city, 69 were lost, a casualty rate of 12.13 per cent. A total of 369 Lancaster crewmen were killed and another 101 made POWs. The Halifax crews fared even more badly, enduring a loss rate of 16.98 per cent. It was a harrowing climax to the Battle of Berlin. Even Harris now recognized that continuing with mass raids on Germany would end up destroying his own force. In justification for the campaign, he could point to the heavy damage done to Berlin and other cities. In the capital itself, almost 27 per cent of its built-up area was destroyed, most of its factories were hit at some stage, 10,305 people were killed and 1,500,000 people made homeless. Wider German production and supplies of personnel to the armed forces were put under tremendous strain by the needs of defence and reconstruction work. Erhard Milch, the Armaments Chief of Staff, told his staff in February 1944: 'Everyone should pay a visit to Berlin. It would then be realized that the experience we have undergone in the last few months cannot be endured indefinitely.'[79] But that second sentence of Milch's could also be applied to Bomber Command. The damage to Germany had only been achieved at a terrible cost and had not come close to Bomber Command's goal of overthrowing the Reich by air assault alone. According to research by Martin Middlebrook, in the 19 major raids over Berlin between 23 August 1943 and 24 March 1944, 421 Lancasters were lost during over 8,000 sorties, a loss rate of 5.2 per cent, and 2,461 Lancaster airmen were killed. Interestingly, Middlebrook's studies provided graphic confirmation that though the Lancaster was more resilient than the Halifax in the air, the chances of survival were far worse in a Lancaster because of its huge load and poor escape hatches. The percentage of Lancaster airmen who survived being shot down during the Berlin raids was just 19.2 per cent, compared to 35 per cent in the Halifax. Moreover, the number of airmen surviving from the average seven-man Lancaster crew shot down during the Berlin campaign was 1.3, a figure that reached 2.45 in the Halifax.[80]

But the overall picture could hardly be more grim for Bomber Command. The early winter months of 1944 had been the most bloody of the war. Over 180 bombers had been lost on the last two raids against Berlin and Nuremburg. A total of 1,529 airmen had died in February, another 1,880 in March. The verdict of the official historians was damning. 'The Battle of Berlin was more than a failure. It was a defeat.'[81] A drastic change in strategy was needed, whether Harris liked it or not.

14

'The supreme operation for 1944'

◆～～

THE FAILURE OF the Battle of Berlin was a crisis for Harris. His entire strategy of area bombing by night had been found wanting. Further mass attacks would result only in the devastation of his own force by German night fighters. Yet the stubborn determination which had made him such a powerful commander in 1942 now meant that he refused to learn the lessons from this setback. Instead of changing his policy, he continued to argue for a mass offensive against the German cities. To the obvious objection that this would result in carnage for his Lancaster crews, his answer was to provide them with cover from Mosquito escorts.

It was this demand for fighter support that led to a vicious row between Harris and Portal, marked by complaints of disloyalty and even a threat to resign. Harris's position in the spring of 1944 was gravely weakened, not just by the failure of the Berlin campaign but also by his reluctance to give his full co-operation to the preparations for Operation Overlord, the code name for the invasion of France. It was obvious in the opening months of 1944 that Overlord would dominate the Allies' strategic thinking, but Harris, to the exasperation of other US and British military chiefs, was dismissive of the idea that Bomber Command should have any role in the build-up to D-Day. In his myopia, he held tightly to his belief that the sole purpose of his force was to attack urban Germany. The rest of the war was almost an irrelevance for him. 'My only fear – and it is a very substantial one – is that we shall be diverted from our proper job of hitting the Germans where it hurts,' he told the American Assistant Secretary for Air R. A. Lovett in late January 1944, when the plans for Overlord were first being drawn up. Harris went on to warn that if the heavy bombers were diverted into 'Overlord and assorted panacea targets', then 'we shall fail to finish the job this spring', thereby enabling the Germans to increase their defences and drag on the war for years.[1]

By now Portal was increasingly frustrated with Harris's leadership of Bomber Command. The Chief of the Air Staff's faith in the area offensive had been badly weakened by the long, dark months of heavy losses for poor results, while Harris's obstinacy about Overlord had been a continual source of aggravation during crucial months of discussions with the Americans. Furthermore, the US 8th Air Force was starting to achieve a dramatic impact against the Luftwaffe with their new, radically different strategy of massive daylight attacks, accompanied by the Mustang, Thunderbolt and Lightning fighters, and directed specifically at aircraft factories. The twofold aim was to undermine production and to draw the Germans into the air, where they would be no match for the deadly American planes. This was the very opposite of the British and previous US air strategies, where everything was done to avoid the Luftwaffe. But the new US approach fulfilled the Clausewitz doctrine that victory could only be achieved through the 'maximum use of force' against the 'substance of the enemy's strength'.[2] It was Henry 'Hap' Arnold, the Commanding General of the USAAF, who summarized the new policy with brutal simplicity: 'Destroy the Enemy Forces wherever you find them, in the air, on the ground, in the factories,' he told his European air chiefs.[3] The US bomber raids, which reached their zenith in the 'Big Week' of 20 February, inflicted crippling losses on the Luftwaffe and the German air industry. 'Each incursion of the enemy is costing us some 50 aircrews. The time has come when our weapon is in sight of collapse,' said the Luftwaffe Fighter Leader Adolf Galland.[4]

Against this background, the government was in no mood to be receptive when, in the spring of 1944, Harris made another plea for the Halifax to be phased out in favour of the Lancaster. The experience of the Battle of Berlin not only reinforced his disdain for the Handley Page machine but also provided him with an explanation for failure. In a letter to Portal of 28 March, he claimed that the Halifax had sustained a 30 per cent higher loss rate than the Lancaster during the campaign, while also undermining Lancaster operations: 'Halifax IIIs are deliberately and necessarily used in a manner which enables them to obtain more protection from the Lancasters than they provide for the Lancasters. Viz, the Lancaster having a higher ceiling than the Halifax gets a lot of protection from Lancaster Window, and the Lancaster comparatively little from the Halifax Window. Furthermore, as far as possible, the Halifax III is wrapped up in the Lancaster stream, so that the Lancasters take the brunt in the vanguard and the rearguard. On distant targets the Lancasters have often to be put at extra risk by using shorter and more dangerous routes in order to enable the Halifax III to get there and back at all.' Harris concluded, 'Nothing we can reasonably do to rid ourselves of these obsolescent planes as soon as possible should therefore be undone.'[5] Harris's opinion was backed up by a study from researchers at the Air Ministry's statistical section, published on 2 April 1944, which showed that the Lancaster was also far more economically efficient in terms of weight of bombs dropped. The analysis revealed that, between December 1943 and March 1944, the average life of a Halifax was 13.9 sorties and, with a bomb load of 1.61 tons, this implied an average life load of 22.3 tons, whereas the life of a Lancaster was 19.4 sorties and, based on a load of 3.95 tons per sortie, its average life load was 76.6 tons. 'The operational value of a Lancaster is at present over three times greater than that of a Halifax III. The cost in man hours of the Halifax is rather greater than that of the Lancaster. The crew is the same in both. Thus the economic superiority of the Lancaster is, if anything, more marked than its operational superiority.'[6] The Air Staff were well aware of these figures but they still clung to the view that the loss of production from a switchover would be too great. In a clear summary of their position, Portal told Harris on 7 April 1944, that he was 'fully alive to the superiority of the Lancaster', but the reduction in bomber output from the switch 'would have been prohibitive' before the end of 1945. He stressed, however, that the Lancaster still heavily predominated. 'Deliveries will still be in the ratio of four Halifaxes to seven Lancasters at the end of this year, although the proportion of Lancasters will continue to increase until the end of 1945.' Portal then looked more broadly at the nature of bomber production and the progress of the war. 'It is very unlikely that we or any other country shall ever be in the happy position of being able to equip our bomber fleet completely with one type of the highest performance, or that we shall be able to scrap one type immediately it is surpassed in performance by another. It seems that we must always have at least two types in service, the latest and the obsolescent, unless we are willing to see our offensive virtually peter out with the introduction of each new type. There is every hope that the German Air Force will be so weakened by the fighting this year that the Halifax can be retained as a front-line bomber into 1945, if necessary, but if this hope is proved false and the Halifax is outclassed, we must limit our first-line operations to the Lancaster.' The Halifax would then be used only for mining, second-line targets and training, suggested Portal.[7] The campaign to switch production was over. For the rest of the war, Harris continued to grumble about the Halifax, but he never again pressed the case for change.

It was immediately after this debate that a far more explosive row between Harris and Portal occurred, this time over the question of fighter support for the night-bombing offensive. In a letter to Portal of 7 April, which crossed with the Air Chief's reply of the same day about Lancaster production, Harris demonstrated an almost wilful blindness to what was happening in the European air war. He began by claiming that day bombing as practised by the 8th Air Force 'is not a very serious menace to Germany. Its effect on morale as compared with night bombing on a large scale is known to be slight, while its influence on production is not likely to be very great.' In any case, argued Harris, factories could be rebuilt whereas 'factories without cities are valueless'. But even with such scorn, Harris had to admit that his own strategy was not working. 'The cost of attacking targets in the Berlin area under weather conditions that give good prospects of accurate and concentrated bombing is too high to be incurred with any frequency.' The solution, he said, lay not in copying the Americans but in providing cover for the Lancasters. 'It is impossible to deal with the situation by turning to day bombing with fighter escorts since even the Lancaster would be incapable of operating in formation above 18,000 or 19,000 feet. At this height, flak would be lethal and would more than compensate for the losses which the fighter escort might be expected to save. The only remedy therefore is the provision of fighter support on a substantial scale.'

Harris then told Portal that 'a total minimum of ten night fighter Mosquito squadrons should forthwith be placed at the disposal of 100 Group to satisfy this requirement'. The 100 Group was a special-duties unit set up in November 1943 to utilize Mosquitoes in conducting electronic warfare against the Luftwaffe. Now Harris envisaged it as a major support arm for the continuation of the Lancaster night offensive. There was a self-defeating inconsistency behind his stance. The whole point of night bombing was that darkness was meant to provide cover for the 'heavies'. If it were now so dangerous that it could not be sustained unless fighter escorts were provided, its very reason for existence was undermined, and so were Harris's arguments against a day offensive. Nor did Harris help his cause by the imperious, belittling manner in which he pressed his case. He warned that if the Air Staff withheld 'protection from our bombers', it would be 'a further instance of the defensive-mindedness at a point in the war at which it is surely agreed we must be prepared to accept reasonable risks in order to deal decisive blows'. He concluded on an outrageously self-pitying note, which took no account of the massive logistical, military and industrial muscle put behind the bomber war. 'The fact is that support for the Bomber Offensive within our available resources has all along been on low priority compared especially with defence against comparatively non-existent menace and almost against any and every other fancied or real requirement.'[8]

Normally so emollient, Portal reacted furiously to this missive. Having accused Harris of being 'unfair', he wrote that 'it seems to me your habit of throwing blame wherever possible has entirely defeated your sense of logic'. He added that Harris's claims of a lack of priority given to Bomber Command were 'utterly contrary to the truth. As long as I have been here I have striven to give the bomber offensive the highest priority in aircraft, men and equipment and I know the Air Staff have done the same.' He urged that Harris 'display towards the Air Ministry and towards me the same loyalty in these matters which you no doubt expect from your own subordinates when you have to disappoint them'.[9] Harris was so rankled by the charge of disloyalty that, in an extraordinary move, he offered Portal his resignation. 'You infer that I am lacking in loyalty to you personally. That is untrue. For twenty years or more you have had no more loyal supporter than I. But I do not regard loyalty as in any way involving an automatic and unquestioning acceptance of your ideas and still less the ideas or rulings of every or any junior officer on your staff. If in these circumstances you have no confidence in my loyalty I must ask you to relieve me of the onerous duties of my Command at the earliest opportunity which serves the interest of the country.'[10] The threat to resign was a sudden escalation of a dispute that had essentially started about the provision of fighter cover for Lancasters. There is no doubt that Portal took Harris's words seriously. He had in the past thought about moving Harris, the first time in the summer of 1943 when he considered him for the post of Commander of the Allied Expeditionary Air Force in preparation for Overlord, a position that eventually went to Leigh-Mallory, and the second in December after Harris had rejected Air Ministry requests to mount an assault on the ball-bearing factories at Schweinfurt. 'I do not regard a night attack on Schweinfurt as a reasonable operation of war,' he had told Bottomley.[11] Such had been Portal's frustration then with the recalcitrant attitude of Harris that in January 1944 he had actually consulted Bufton, the Director of Bombing Operations at the Air Ministry, as to whether Harris should be moved. With a fair-mindedness that Harris rarely displayed to others, Bufton urged that Harris should retain his command, largely because the Battle of Berlin was about to enter its crucial phase. Now that the battle was over, Portal would have been perfectly justified in transferring Harris. After all, Hugh Dowding was forced out as Fighter Command chief in 1940 after victory in the Battle of Britain. Harris was now tainted by failure.

But Portal did not have the necessary cold instinct to be a butcher. For all his strategic thinking, political gifts and high intelligence, he lacked that streak of ruthlessness that makes the truly great leader. Confronted with a direct challenge from Harris and his offer of resignation, he faltered and adopted a newly conciliatory tone. 'I have always valued your loyalty to me in the sense in which you use the word, and it is not in question now,' he told Harris on 16 April, going on to express the hope that he could establish 'the same relations' between Bomber Command and the Air Ministry 'as we enjoy with all other commands'. He promised 'that the request for Mosquitoes will be decided entirely on its merits'.[12] With an undeniable air of triumph at having seen off the Chief of the Air Staff, Harris in response launched into another tirade against the Ministry. 'I am afraid that it is inevitable that Bomber Command should be less tractable than other Commands. We always have been and still are the milch cow, and unlike other Commands, have been in direct action with the enemy concurrently and continuously throughout the war. With the best will in the world, I cannot help resenting bitterly the sacrifices we are called upon to make in order to meet the requirements of others.' He then produced a litany of perceived failures by the Air Ministry to meet his needs, including the lack of effective turrets for the heavy bombers and delays over the introduction of a practicable bombsight. 'In much the same way, I have long appealed in vain for adequate night fighter support for my operations but so far have received a negligible response.' He concluded: 'I do not enjoy these repeated controversies and I shall be greatly relieved if a more helpful attitude throughout the Air Ministry renders them unnecessary in future.'[13]

If Portal had accepted Harris's resignation, the course of the European war might have been different. It would probably have been several months shorter, given that Bomber Command would have concentrated on targets of real military and economic value instead of relentlessly aiming for nothing more than urban devastation. Indeed, bomber pilot and 617 Squadron commander Leonard Cheshire, who performed his greatest heroics in 1944, later argued that after the Battle of Berlin Harris should have been replaced as the head of Bomber Command by Ralph Cochrane, commander of No. 5 Group, whom he regarded as a more flexible, effective leader. Like Guy Gibson, Leonard Cheshire achieved national glory in 617 Squadron as a brilliant, dynamic pilot, but he was completely different in looks and personality. In contrast to Gibson's stockiness, Cheshire was tall, lean and angular. Whereas Gibson was impatient and often aloof, Cheshire was even-tempered and unreserved. His fearlessness never came across as arrogance but instead was a source of reassurance to his crews. 'I never recaptured with any other captain the queer confidence he gave me,' said

George Roberts, who flew with him in the early part of the war. 'The question, "Will we get back?" never seemed to arise, as it did soon afterwards when I flew with another crew.'[14] Cheshire had not a shred of social superiority, and he could often be found having tea with erks at dispersal or a smoke with canteen staff in station kitchens. Fitter Laurence Scott said of his decency: 'He gave us all the feeling that we were important and could be trusted, and I'll never forget what the trust meant. Regardless of what early hour he got back from the Ruhr or anywhere else, he would invariably let the crew truck go when he'd climbed out. Then he'd sit down beside the aircraft, thank us, hand round his cigarettes and start describing what had happened. We felt part of the outfit. Often he'd pass round what was left of the flying rations, talking all the while like an excited youngster back from his first film rather than a bone-weary skipper who'd probably gone through hell for seven hours in a cramped cockpit.'[15] Once criticized for drinking with his crew in a saloon bar reserved for officers, Cheshire replied: 'If I am good enough to fight and fly with these men I am good enough to drink with them.'[16]

Yet Cheshire's warm-hearted attitude never appeared to undermine his natural authority, as Bob Knights of 617 Squadron recalled: 'He had an aura, this ability of leadership that made everyone else seem rather small. In fact I hero-worshipped him. I thought he was the most marvellous man, and he was very conscious of the people on the squadron. He made a big effort to know people's names on the squadron, their background and their relationships with other people.'[17] Another 617 Squadron pilot, Arthur Poore, was equally impressed by his gift for leadership, as well as his lighter, more gregarious side:

> He was a wonderful man and a remarkable pilot, an amazing leader. Everyone loved him and would do anything for him. He had that presence. He would give the impression in the briefing that this particular raid was the most important event of the whole war. He had a magnificent white poodle by the name of Simon. Cheshire used to delight in showing us his famous trick with the dog. He would get the dog to stand in front of him and he would say, in sombre voice, 'Simon, what would you do if Hitler invaded this country?' Simon would lie down, close his eyes, and be perfectly still, feigning death. 'Right Simon, what will you do when we win the war?' And Simon would get up and dance on his two hind legs, right round the room, much to the delight of the rest of the squadron.[18]

In his youth, Cheshire had given some indications of his future strength as a leader. Born in 1917, he was the son of an Oxford don and attended the public school of Stowe. As a student at Oxford reading law, he worked hard academically but also gave vent to an extrovert, rebellious streak, indulging in pranks, building up debts, drinking heavily and driving cars at dare-devil speeds. But the biggest legacy of Oxford was the kindling of his devotion to flying. He joined the University Air Squadron in his first year and, on graduation, accepted a permanent commission in the RAF. After initial flight training he was posted to Bomber Command, unlike most of his Oxford contemporaries who became fighter pilots. When some of them expressed sympathy that he was destined for the less glamorous branch of the RAF, he replied: 'Nonsense. There are nineteen of you but only one of me – and they will hear of me.'[19]

Cheshire soon lived up to those words. By 1941 he had won the DSO and a reputation for unique courage. At the same time, he had contracted a rather unorthodox marriage, having fallen for the wealthy American actress and divorcee Constance Binney while he was in the USA ferrying planes in the spring of 1941. On his return to Britain in July, he was transferred to 76 Squadron, flying Halifaxes as part of the bomber offensive over Germany. He later said that he never felt 'squeamish' about the area-bombing strategy. 'On the actual attack, we were far too concerned with getting through the defences and dropping the bombs to think about the people on the ground. Besides bombing is a cold, impersonal game. You are so far removed in distance and vision from the people you are attacking that you don't really think of it in terms of human beings.' But he did have some doubts as to whether it was the right approach militarily. 'I don't think I was ever actually against area bombing as such, but I was inclined to think that, at least at times, precision bombing was more valuable. Once we discovered that we could do precision bombing, I'm sure that we thought in terms of factories to be destroyed and not homes.'[20]

It was in 617 Squadron that Cheshire really began to perfect the art of precision attacks by heavy planes. After the Dambusters raids of May 1943, Harris had ordered the retention of the squadron for special missions, but it had enjoyed only limited success, Gibson himself having been taken out of 617 Squadron to conduct propaganda work for the government. Two attacks on Italian power stations in July 1943 achieved little damage, and an attempt to breach the banks of the Dortmund–Ems canal in September ended in bloody failure. During that raid, the 617 Lancasters carried a new weapon, the 12,000-pound high-capacity blockbuster, but it did not help them achieve their objective. The first attempt at the canal, on the evening of 14 September, had to be aborted because of appalling conditions over the target, but sadly, on the way back, David Maltby's

Lancaster flew into the slipstream of another aircraft and crashed into the North Sea. Although Maltby's body was recovered, nothing of the rest of the crew was ever found. Even worse followed the next night, 15 September, when the squadron tried again. Approaching the target at barely 100 feet, the Lancasters came under ferocious bombardment from anti-aircraft guns as the planes struggled to find the canal in poor visibility and the absence of accurate marking. In the appalling weather and heavy flak, four of them went down near the target and another, flown by Dambusters veteran Les Knight, hit some trees, sustained serious damage and then, as it tried to struggle home, went out of control.

Bomb aimer Edward Johnson, another veteran of the Dams raids, was in the front of the plane as the incident unfolded: 'All of a sudden I was confronted with a hillside covered in trees at a much greater height than we were flying. I called out on the intercom, "For God's sake, Les, pull the stick back." He had only just seen the trees at the same instant as me.' The Lancaster sliced through the tree tops, damaging the oil coolers under the two port engines and smashing the rudder. As the engineer feathered the engines to prevent them bursting into flames, the rest of the crew chucked out equipment to lighten the plane. With all the power on one side, the pilot now had great difficulty in controlling the Lancaster. The crew had a conference and agreed to try and reach the Dutch border before bailing out. 'It was a brave decision on the pilot's part because he was going to have the greatest difficulty getting out.' The plane was taken to 1,000 feet and Johnson was the first to jump. 'I did not follow the parachute procedure of counting to ten and pulling the ripcord. I jumped out and pulled immediately because we were so near the ground. We were so near the ground you would not have thought the chute had time to open. But it did and I made a fairly good landing in a ploughed field.' Johnson managed to evade capture and, after a long adventure through Holland, Belgium and France, where he was helped by the Resistance, he made it to the Spanish border and then Gibraltar, before embarking on the journey back to England. Tragically, Les Knight did not have time to bail out before the plane crashed. His self-sacrifice was characteristic of Bomber Command's spirit, as shown by this tribute from his wireless operator, Bob Kellow: 'He kept that damaged aircraft flying straight and level so that we, his crew, would have a chance to live by parachuting to safety, but in doing so, he gave his life for us.'[21]

The Dortmund-Ems had been a disaster for 617 Squadron, which for a time was known as 'the suicide squadron'.[22] Wireless operator Larry Curtis admitted that 'after Dortmund-Ems morale slumped quite badly because those were rather staggering losses for our squadron'.[23] Spirits were hardly raised when an attempt by 617 Squadron to demolish the Antheor viaduct on the vital railway link between southern France and Italy also ended in failure. But the following month, Harris sent Cheshire to take command of the squadron. It was a move that would transform the fortunes of the squadron, once Cheshire had the chance to implement his radical new ideas on bombing tactics. But first he had to learn to fly the Lancaster, for the bombers he had previously flown were the Whitley, the B-24 Liberator and the Halifax. After his initial spell of instruction he said: 'What a beautiful plane she is. She handles more smoothly than anything I've ever flown.'[24] As well as a new commander, 617 Squadron also acquired the sophisticated new Stabilised Automatic Bomb Sight (SABS), which was the brainchild of Air Ministry expert Squadron Leader Arthur Richardson, known as 'The Talking Bomb' because of his depth of knowledge on the subject.[25] His new device, highly advanced for its time and utilizing primitive computer controls, enabled the Lancaster to bomb with great accuracy when flown correctly. As the aircraft began the run, the aimer fed into the computer the necessary information, such as altitude, speed, barometric pressure, distance to target and wind-drift. The pilot had to fly on exactly the right course, while the aimer aligned the target in his sight. When he had a precise fix on the target, he flicked a switch and the SABS took over, tracking the aircraft to the target and passing a constant flow of information to the instrument panel in the cockpit so that the pilot could make the required minute adjustments in directions. At the right moment over the target, the SABS automatically released the bombs.

Richardson came to Scampton in a Lancaster fitted with SABS to show the men of the squadron how it operated. During a practice session on a bombing range at the Wash, they were astonished at their own accuracy once they had become acquainted with the sight. From 20,000 feet, the average error was less than 100 yards. Bob Knights, one of 617 Squadron's pilots, was deeply impressed:

> This bombsight was quite uncanny provided that you flew the aeroplane well. I can remember when we first flew with practice bombs, Richardson set a very small limit, less than twenty yards, I think. I said, 'No way will we ever be able to get near that.' Richardson replied, 'You can with this bombsight.' I remember the first few bombs we dropped. They were extremely close. I was absolutely thrilled with this. Also Leonard Cheshire kept a very good eye on people joining the squadron to see that they did do it accurately. He set very high standards because he was a very fastidious man.[26]

Though the SABS was a tremendous innovation, it was, inevitably, more difficult to use on operations than in training. Its main drawback was that a long, straight run was needed to line up the target, during which the pilot had to fly absolutely steadily at the right height and speed, not easy in a night sky filled with flak, fighters and the slipstreams of other bombers. Nor was the SABS any better than previous bombsights when marking was inaccurate or cloud cover heavy.

The limitations of the SABS were exposed on Cheshire's first major operation as Wing Commander, when a second attack was made on the Antheor viaduct in southern France on the night of 11–12 November. Again 12,000-pound high-capacity bombs were used, but the bombers found it difficult to ascertain the target against the glare of the German searchlights. Even the three bombs that did land within 100 yards of the structure were not enough to bring it down. Further precision attacks in December and January on V-1 rocket sites had little success, largely because the marking by the Pathfinder squadrons had been poor. But one attack, against the site at Freval in northern France, proved more effective when Cheshire and his deputy leader, Dambusters veteran Micky Martin, dived to 400 feet to mark the target. This time the Lancasters placed the 12,000-pounders right on the site, destroying it completely. Cheshire now thought he had the tactical solution. Marking from high altitude in darkness could never be wholly reliable, he believed, so the alternative was for the Master Bomber to fly low and drop the target indicators from no more than a few hundred feet. This technique of low-level marking required incredible courage and iron self-control by the Master Bomber, but those were qualities that Cheshire never lacked.

With the approval of the No. 5 Group Commander Ralph Cochrane, Cheshire tried out the new method in an assault on the French Gnome-Rhône aero-engine works at Limoges, 200 miles south of Paris, on the night of 8–9 February 1944. Because he wanted to avoid killing French civilians, he flew very low over the factory three times to warn the workers to leave. Pat Moyna of the RAF film unit, who flew in Cheshire's Lancaster, recalled:

> We went in very low. I heard Cheshire say that he had time in hand to warn the 500 women workers on the night shift. We could see the moon behind the cathedral on the banks of the river. The clouds were breaking up at the right moment. Twice the Lancaster swooped in a shallow dive above the factory, seeming almost to scrape over the roof at 50 feet. 'Keep a look-out for the girls. Tell me when they clear out,' called Cheshire. On

a third low warning run, someone said, 'There they go skipper, hundreds of them, streaming to the shelters.'

Cheshire now dropped his markers in the centre bay of the workshops, causing a light so dazzling that Moyna thought the Lancaster had caught fire.[27] Cheshire then climbed to 5,000 feet and called in the main force with the code word, 'Commando, markers dead centre'. The very first Lancaster, flown by Dave Shannon, dropped its 12,000-pounder directly on the markers. The next to bomb was Bob Knights, whose 11 1,000-pounders fell along the western edge of the factory. According to Cheshire's own contemporary report, 'during the next eight minutes, seven more loads fell in the target with only one outside and some 150 yards to the west'.[28] Having supervised the completion of the bombing, Cheshire flew down to low level to machine gun the target and allow the RAF film unit to photograph the wreckage. Though heavy smoke made photography difficult, 'it was very apparent that great damage had been done to the entire factory and that only the north-western sheds were still standing,' wrote Cheshire.[29] The low-level marking, combined with the crews' greater experience of the SABS, had been a dramatic early triumph. Having looked at the reconnaissance photographs, Portal wrote to Harris: 'The very severe damage caused by so small a number of aircraft is most remarkable and I should be grateful if you would convey my warmest congratulations to this squad on the extreme accuracy of the bombing.'[30]

After this success, Cheshire decided it was time for another attempt at the Antheor viaduct on the Marseilles-Genoa railway. But this was a much more difficult target than the Limoges factory. The viaduct itself was just ten yards wide, beyond the margin of error even on Richardson's SABS. In addition, the previous attacks meant that the Germans had heavily reinforced the flak defences. Because of the long distance to the south of France, which for the Lancasters was the limit of their petrol endurance, 617 Squadron were required to operate from Ford in Sussex. As a backup, Cheshire had asked permission to land at the US base in Sardinia, where the planes could refuel before returning to Britain. 'This permission was refused, categorically and without qualification,' recorded Cheshire.[31] At 21.45 on the night of 12 February, Cheshire and Micky Martin took off from Ford and set out for France in icy cloud. The main force followed twenty minutes later. But when the two leaders arrived at the target, they found defences even stronger than they feared. The flak was so intense that it was almost impossible to make a run to drop their markers. In one attempt Micky Martin almost got through, but just at the moment the bomb aimer Bob Hay was about to release the markers, anti-aircraft shells ripped through the nose and wings of the Lancaster. Bob Hay was killed, the engineer was injured and two engines were put out of action. Trying to control the stricken aircraft, Martin called up Cheshire to tell him that he was going to try to reach an Allied base in the Mediterranean.

Larry Curtis was Martin's wireless operator on that flight. 'I remember the rear gunner saying, "It's getting wet in here," because by this time we were heading out to sea from the viaduct. That was the only time I sent an SOS. I am pleased to say the replies came back straight away.' Having been told by the USAAF to head to Sardinia, Martin instructed Curtis to go to the bomb aimer's compartment, for at the time the crew did not know that Bob Hay had been killed:

> When I got there, I reported back that he was unconscious but seemed to be warm, but I had not realized that he was wearing his electrically heated suit. Then I found that he'd got a big hole in his chest and another in his head. I gave him a shot of morphia but he may have already been dead by then. We had no real training in first-aid. The flight engineer had been hit in the leg. The remarkable thing was that, while all this was going on and we were trying to get across the sea to Sardinia, everyone was so efficient. It must have been the mark of a well-trained crew. Everyone did the job the way it should be done. I was very proud to be one of its members. When we got to Sardinia, we found that the ammo had exploded in the front turret, part of the radio had been damaged and the throttle cables had been frayed by flak, which made it difficult for the pilot, to say the least.[32]

While Martin headed for Sardinia, the rest of 617 Squadron continued its mission. Eventually Cheshire managed to drop his markers, but they fell on the beach about 100 yards in front of the bridge. He called up the main force and instructed them to overshoot the markers, but none of the Lancasters were able to make a direct hit. At 01.35 Cheshire ordered them to return to Ford. In his report of the raid, he could not conceal his anger at the intelligence and support he had been given. 'The information on the enemy defences was inaccurate so that the plan was not adequate to meet the opposition actually encountered. Insufficient petrol could be carried to allow enough time over the target to enable the leader to change his tactics.'[33]

Better results were achieved with the low-level marking technique in other raids in February and March, as 617 Squadron was deployed against northern French targets in the run-up to D-Day. An aero-engine factory in Albert was destroyed by extremely accurate bombing, after markers had landed in the middle of the target. 'This was a highly successful attack on a heavily camouflaged target, which will not produce any more engines for the Hun,' wrote Cheshire.[34] A raid on the Pouderie Nationale munitions works in the Dordogne, southern France, on 18 March was equally successful in terms of accurate marking. One 12,000-pounder landed in an ammunition dump and, as Cheshire noted, 'caused an explosion which lasted at least 15 seconds and which could only be described as fantastic'.[35] Other French installations badly hit included an aero-engine factory at Lyons, an aircraft repair plant in Toulouse, marshalling yards around Paris and an airbase at Versailles. But Cheshire, the supreme perfectionist, was still not satisfied with the standard of marking. Even at low levels, accuracy could remain a problem. A raid against a needle-bearing works at St Etienne on 10–11 March highlighted the difficulties. In his report to Cochrane, Cheshire described how in poor weather he made five level runs over the factory, but 'even from a height of 200 feet, it was impossible to see the works until they were directly underneath the plane'. In consequence, on the sixth run he 'came in at 500 feet and when the factory appeared beneath the plane, he pushed the stick forward and dived to it. Unfortunately, the majority of the incendiaries skidded and overshot the road west of the factory. He then called upon the deputy leaders to drop their incendiaries from low level, undershooting the markers by fifty yards. Owing to a misunderstanding, the first two aircraft undershot by 400 to 600 yards and unfortunately started a bigger fire than on the factory itself.' Not surprisingly, Cheshire had to send a message back to Scampton, 'deeply regret, attack unsuccessful'.[36] Cheshire decided that part of the trouble lay in the Lancaster itself. With the SABS bombsight, it had shown it could carry out highly accurate precision bombing.

But Cheshire increasingly felt that, for all its agility as a heavy bomber, the Lancaster was too cumbersome and large for the highly specialized task of low-level marking. So he switched aircraft once more, this time to a Mosquito. With his usual determined flair, he had soon mastered the skill of flying the wooden fighter/bomber, renowned for its manoeuvrability and quicksilver speed. Cheshire also made another innovation. Always intrigued by new technology, he paid a visit to the south coast to meet Flight Lieutenant Noel Holland, the senior controller of the Beachy Head radar stations for Fighter Command. Holland told Cheshire that his radar equipment could reach 200 miles into France, thereby providing advance warning of night fighters in the area. Cheshire was fascinated, and, backed up by Cochrane, arranged for his Mosquito and all 617 Lancasters to be fitted with crystal pick-ups and the latest VHF sets, so that Beachy Head could give complete radar cover on their future raids.

Revelling in his new plane and equipment, Cheshire stepped up the precision attacks against French targets. But his most startling achievement came over German soil on the night of 24 April, in a raid that he regarded as his 'greatest single triumph of the war'.[37] Supported by Lancasters from 83 and 97 Squadrons, 617 Squadron embarked on the long journey to Munich in southern Germany to destroy the city's rail marshalling yards. Despite a ferocious barrage from Munich's anti-aircraft defences, Cheshire flew towards the target, put his Mosquito into a dive at almost 400 mph and dropped his red spot flares accurately on the aiming point before pulling out sharply at 500 feet. Three accompanying 617 Squadron Mosquitoes were equally accurate in their marking. Continuing to circle over the target at 1,000 feet while flak burst all around him, Cheshire then called in the main force to take up the bombing. Even when his Mosquito was coned and hit by shell fragments, he carried on circling to ensure the main force Lancasters hit the target. As Cheshire recorded, the attack was unprecedented in its accuracy. 'The spearhead that the squadron provided gave the main force the opportunity for which they had waited so long – an unmistakable and accurate marker and they were quick to make the most of the moment. The bombing that followed was remarkably concentrated and far in advance of any bombing of a major German target in the past.'[38] Five months later, Cheshire, having completed 100 sorties, was awarded the Victoria Cross for his sustained bravery during his bombing career. His citation highlighted this raid as a classic example of his 'cool and calculated acceptance of risks'. What he did at Munich, was 'typical of the careful planning, brilliant execution and contempt for danger which has established for Wing Commander Cheshire a reputation second to none in Bomber Command'.[39]

The Munich raid had taken place against the backdrop of a far-reaching organizational change within Bomber Command. Inspired by Cheshire's leadership of 617 Squadron and frustrated by the performance of Don Bennett's Pathfinders during the Berlin campaign, Ralph Cochrane had long been pressing for the creation of a separate Pathfinder force within his own No. 5 Group. Cold, hard and a tough disciplinarian, the Honourable Ralph Cochrane was not an easy man to like. His upper-class background as the son of a Scottish peer had given him little social charm. 'He was a lean cadaverous man who did not suffer fools gladly. He was severe, used to terrify his junior officers. He terrified me every time I saw him,' said Bob Knights of 617 Squadron.[40] But his ruthless efficiency appealed to the air chiefs, particularly Harris, who had been his superior in Iraq in the 1920s and at the Directorate of Plans in the 1930s. Indeed, Harris once felt moved to describe him as 'a genius', telling Portal in November 1944: 'He is an absolutely outstanding commander. In the past six months his Group has been twice as effective as any other group in the command although I do not consider that by average or high standards my other Group commanders are inefficient.'[41] Never enamoured of the Pathfinder concept, Harris was only too willing to grant Cochrane's request for his own force. At the beginning of April he therefore ordered that two of the Lancaster Pathfinder squadrons, 83 and 97, be transferred from Bennett's No. 8 Group to No. 5, along with 627 Squadron. In effect, Cochrane's Group had been turned into its own independent air force, while the prestige of the Pathfinders had been undermined.

Bennett was outraged at the 'great damage' done to his force and approached Saundby, hoping to halt the change. But, according to Bennett's account, Saundby 'simply shrugged his shoulders and said that he and Cochrane had once been flight commanders together, under Bert Harris, in the Middle East and that the same situation had then prevailed. Cochrane could do anything and the Commander-in-Chief would always support him. Any attempts to convince the Commander-in-Chief that Cochrane could ever be wrong were inevitably doomed to failure.'[42] Despite Saundby's warnings, Bennett took his grievance directly to Harris, writing to him in late May 1944 that 'this detachment has been taken as a slap in the face for the PFF force and it has therefore had a slightly adverse effect on PFF morale. It has also had an adverse effect on the Blind Marking abilities of the two squadrons detached.' He continued, 'the diversion of strength to 5 Group has already caused a tremendous amount of difficulty and embarrassment. The AOC of 5 Group has himself told me that it has always been his policy to shout the loudest in order to get what he wants. I would most respectfully urge you to judge this experiment and the question of its termination in the light of what is right and wrong in actual fact and not merely on vague claims and loud assertions.'[43] Harris did not budge, and the success of Cheshire's methods only strengthened Cochrane's position. When Bennett again asked for the return of 83 and 97 Lancaster squadrons in late June 1944, Cochrane strongly objected: 'The two squadrons have been doing splendid work and have fitted themselves into the Group organisation. I would therefore be very sorry to see this organisation broken up especially as the team is still gaining in experience and efficiency.'[44] Harris in early July replied that he had 'no intention of returning these squadrons to the Pathfinder Group'.[45]

Having established his new elite force, Cochrane then proposed a new marking technique, one that would overcome the problems caused by smoke and fire obscuring the target indicators. In league with the ever resourceful Cheshire, he introduced a method called 'off-set marking' into 5 Group, by which the Pathfinders deliberately dropped their markers slightly away from the target, then the Master Bomber told the main force pilots to make the necessary adjustments to compensate for the gap between markers and the aiming point. In this way, the illumination of the target indicators remained undiminished during an attack. The method achieved a significant improvement in results during its first month of operation. The average margin of error of 5 Group fell from 680 yards to 285 yards.[46] One sophisticated version of 'offset-marking' allowed for the bomb aimer to get the TIs in his sight and then the Lancaster made a time-and-distance run from them, the bomb aimer using a stopwatch to count down the seconds towards the exact moment of release. Donald Falgate, a bomb aimer with 463 Squadron, explained: 'Once those markers went down, the Master Bomber would go in and assess their accuracy. Then, if he were happy, on the r/t he would call in the main force. We then made a run onto the markers. Once I got the centre of the markers in my sights, I made a timed run of so many seconds. Each aircraft was given a set heading and on your heading you released your bombs. If you can imagine anything from 200 to 500 Lancasters coming in, all making timed runs on a heading, you could get a carpet of bombs falling over the target. We got quite remarkable results through this technique.'[47]

But the new techniques were not infallible, nor was Cheshire's remorseless quest for pin-point accuracy universally welcomed. Any delays in marking or any technical problems in communications could mean that the main force bombers had to circle over enemy territory, feeling exposed to fighters or flak while waiting for orders from the Master Bomber. As Geoff King, a bomb aimer in 57 Squadron, put it: 'It was quite an effective method but it did create its own hazard, because once these flares illuminated, obviously you were silhouetted above the burning flares. So for that short time you were in the target area, you were very vulnerable.'[48] One pilot, who wished to remain anonymous, told Cheshire's official biographer Andrew Boyle: 'We objected to Cheshire's perfectionism. He lost all sense of time in his efforts to provide the best possible point of aim and kept heavily loaded bombers hanging about as easy meat for German fighters. Surely no raid was so important that more than 40 bombers could be sacrificed against one small target.'[49] Such concerns reached their peak in a big raid on the night of 3–4 May against Mailly-le-Camp southeast of Paris, where there was a large Wehrmacht depot. Led by 14 Mosquitos, 348 Lancasters started taking off at 21.30, each of them carrying a 4,000-pound cookie and 16 500-pound general-purpose bombs. Ominously, just like on the night of the Nuremburg raid, bright moonlight filled the sky over northern Europe. The problems began almost as soon as Cheshire dived to mark the target. Unhappy with his accuracy, he called on fellow 617 Mosquito pilot Dave Shannon to correct the marking. By now, the first wave was beginning to approach the target. Cheshire wanted to call the Lancasters to bomb but, to his anguish, the main force leader, Wing Commander Charles Deane of 83 Squadron, found that he struggled to issue instructions over the r/t because the VHF channel was jammed by an American ground station back in England which was broadcasting on the RAF's authorized frequency. According to some accounts, the US transmissions largely consisted of dance band music.

In the mood of increasing confusion, as the main force pilots waited for their orders, the German night fighters gathered, their task made all the easier by the bright moonlight. Dennis Goodliffe, an engineer with 101 Squadron, believed that the delay in calling in the bombers 'gave the fighters free range in a shooting gallery. A number of pilots who were being attacked while orbiting the markers were shouting things to the Master Bomber such as "Pull your finger out, we're dying here."'[50] All coherence had been lost, and some of those who could get through on the r/t vented their fury at the leaders. Another 101 Squadron crewman, rear gunner Tom Welsby, remembered: 'One Commonwealth pilot on our squadron called up twice, "Hello Master Bomber, can we come in and bomb?" and the reply came back, "No do not bomb, continue circling." He asked again and this time the reply came, "No, continue circling, what would the Germans think of the RAF?" The pilot replied, "Fuck the RAF, we're coming in."'[51] Some who had flown on the Nuremburg raid felt that Mailly-le-Camp was even worse. 'The fighters were there, waiting for us before we got anywhere near the target,' said Frank Belben of 9 Squadron. 'It was terrible. You could see the aircraft going down all around you in flames and you'd see when they hit the ground and exploded. Terrible. There were fires burning all over the place and not from bombs, from our aircraft.'[52]

Unlike Nuremburg, the raid was not entirely in vain. Once communications were re-established and the bombers hit the markers, more than 1,200 tons of explosive descended on the German camp, reducing it to rubble. A total of 220 Wehrmacht soldiers were killed, another 150 wounded and 37 tanks were destroyed. In truth, however, that damage was achieved at the appallingly high price of 42 Lancasters. The sense of shock at the loss rate of over 11 per cent reverberated back to the bomber bases in England. Stephen Rew, the fitter at Coningsby, gave this typically moving account of his personal sense of grief when the Lancaster to which he was attached, G-George, failed to return:

> The Lancs started coming back. The sergeant went through their letters. C-Charlie, M-Mother, F-Freddie. Gradually silence fell as, one after the other, boys returned with their torches and snag sheets, said goodnight and cycled off to supper and bed. Still no news of George. The Sergeant rang Woodbridge, which had a long runway. We reckoned two o'clock would be the end of her fuel. Never have the hands of a clock moved so slowly, the seconds ticking away reluctantly, like water dripping from a leaky tap. The hands crawled to half-past two. Finally it was reported that George was officially missing. There was no use hanging about the office. On my way back to the billet I felt an unreasoning hatred for every damned aeroplane I saw. Why couldn't it have been that one, or that one? Why George?

The next morning Rew received confirmation that his beloved Lancaster had gone down over Mailly-le-Camp.[53]

The flawed assault on Mailly-le-Camp was part of the build-up to Operation Overlord, the invasion of France that the Allies had been planning since early 1943. The role of Bomber Command had long been the subject of deep controversy among the politicians and military, Harris clinging to the belief that his sole contribution to the build-up to D-Day should be the area bombing of Germany. But the British and American chiefs could not possibly accept such isolationism from the operation, given the huge resources that Harris controlled. In early January 1944 Harris was directly pressed to set out his views on how Bomber Command could assist in Overlord. He did so in a paper, dated 13 January 1944, which summarized his views about the air offensive. Paradoxically, in his determination to limit his Command's involvement in D-Day, he ended up exaggerating the weaknesses of the bomber force and downplaying its ability to hit targets accurately.

He opened his paper by explaining that 'the heavy bomber force has been developed as an independent strategic weapon. Its task is the destruction of the enemy's industrial centres and to carry this out it has been equipped with highly specialised aircraft and evolved a similarly specialised and complex operational technique and economy.' Harris argued that, in planning for Overlord, this specialization 'constitutes an unavoidable limitation on the tasks which can be undertaken'. He then ran through a lengthy checklist of all the problems the heavy bombers would encounter if used for any purpose other than the bombing of Germany. The bomber force was 'trained to operate at night only', he argued, and could not fly in formation. Every operation required lengthy preparations. 'Some seven daylight hours are the minimum necessary between the decision to bomb a given target and the take-off of aircraft to attack it.' The bomber force could mount an absolute maximum of eight full-scale raids, or 5,000 sorties, every month, he claimed, and it would be 'impracticable' to deploy it against railway communications. Then Harris turned to the consequences of ceasing the bomber offensive. He warned that the Reich would be freed from the burden of defending its territory and therefore 'the vast resources in fighters, flak and searchlights and their crews would automatically be released for us in the relatively small invasion area'. With his usual myopia, he said that the offensive had been the key factor in the Soviet Union's advance. Abandoning the night attacks would mean the revival of the Reich's military strength and morale. 'What the Russians have done and what we ourselves hope to do on land is fundamentally made possible only by the acute shortage of manpower and munitions which strategic bombing has produced and by the pre-occupation of nearly three-quarters of the enemy fighter forces with the defence of Germany. There could be no greater relief afforded Germany than the cessation or any ponderable reduction of the bombing of Germany proper. The entire country would go wild with a sense of relief and newborn hope and get down to the prosecution of a purely land war with renewed determination and every hope of success.' He concluded with what amounted to a restatement of his unbroken faith in the classic Trenchardian doctrine: 'It is clear that the best and indeed the only efficient support which Bomber Command can give to Overlord is the intensification of attacks on suitable industrial centres in Germany as and when the opportunity offers.'[54]

But to those planning the invasion Harris's paper was an unconvincing statement of dogma, supported by neither operational evidence nor any recognition of the wider military needs of the Allies. In separate responses in late January 1944, the policy makers at the Air Staff and the Allied Expeditionary Air Force (AEAF), commanded by Leigh-Mallory, powerfully demolished all Harris's arguments. On the claim that the bomber force was suitable only for bombing Germany, the AEAF wrote that 'it is not clear why targets in France should be any less suitable than industrial centres in Germany', while the Air Staff pointed out that the purpose of Bomber Command's technological evolution had been to 'enable the force to place its bombs accurately on the desired target' regardless of its geographical location. The two organizations were equally dismissive of Harris's professed concerns about the weather and daylight flying. The AEAF argued that, because of the shorter range to France, forecasts were likely to be more accurate and weather conditions less important. The Air Staff referred to Bomber Command's high-profile daylight attacks to distant targets like Milan, Le Creusot and Augsburg. Harris's argument about the maximum number of sorties carried no weight, since the shorter journeys to France 'will allow a considerably greater number of sorties to be carried out', reaching at least 7,300 per month. The Bomber Command chief was also accused of exaggerating the preparations needed for bombing raids. 'It is not true to say that the target cannot be altered during the period of seven hours without involv- ing a new start and consequent further delay. In bombing by marker technique the target can be changed at short notice.' Moreover, Harris was at risk of 'belittling' the accuracy that could be achieved by his bomber crews with their advanced equipment. Above all, through his focus on area bombing against Germany, he had shown no understanding of the importance of Overlord, whose failure 'would result in far graver reper- cussions than a temporary cessation in the bombing of German centres'.[55]

In trying to uphold his usual strategy, Harris was confronted not just by Portal and Leigh-Mallory, but also by Arthur Tedder, whom Eisenhower had appointed the Deputy Supreme Commander of the Allied Expeditionary Force in December 1943. Clear-sighted, authoritative and intellectually gifted, Tedder had none of Harris's separatist contempt for the other armed forces. As he had showed in his campaigns in North Africa and Italy, where his calm leadership won Einsenhower's admir- ation, he believed that air power had to be integrated into the overall military campaign. His task now was to decide how best to deploy the British and American bomber forces in weakening the German defences across northern France and the Low Countries before the D-Day inva- sion. He saw that moving reinforcements and supplies would be vital for the Wehrmacht. The bombers, therefore, could play a vital role in destroy- ing the Germans' logistical support.

From January 1944 Tedder began to work up a detailed plan to smash the Germans' transport network by hitting railways, bridges, canals,

Bundles of 'Window' are released by a 101 Squadron Lancaster during Operation Hurricane, October 1944. 'Window' consisted of thin strips of foil which could disrupt the German radar system. This Lancaster also carries 'Airborne Cigar', another jamming device

A Lancaster of 617 Squadron drops the 22,000-pound 'Grand Slam' bomb during an attack on the Arnsberg Bridge, March 1945. The 'Grand Slam' was by far the heaviest bomb used in the Second World War

A Lancaster silhouetted against the fire-lit sky over Hamburg during a raid on the night of 30–31 January 1943

A Lancaster of 514 Squadron bombs an oil storage depot at Bec d'Ambes, near the Garonne estuary, France, August 1944

Above left: Wing Commander Leonard Cheshire, one of the most remarkable bomber pilots of the war. 'Everyone loved him and would do anything for him. He had that presence,' said a fellow officer

Above right: Sir Arthur Harris, architect of the bomber offensive and passionate advocate of the Lancaster

Right: Sir Charles Portal, Chief of the Air Staff, who clashed bitterly with Harris towards the end of the war over the direction of the RAF's bombing strategy

Barnes Wallis: inventor of the bouncing bomb. The detailed plans for the bomb were drawn up in the squash court of a Surrey golf club

One of the specially modified Lancasters of 617 Squadron conducting tests on the Upkeep bomb at Reculver Bay, near Margate, shortly before the Dams raid

'It looked like a huge oil drum, a most cumbersome-looking thing,' said Dambusters hero Dave Shannon of the Upkeep bomb

Dambusters leader Guy Gibson and his crew board their Lancaster before the most historic air raid of the Second World War, 16 May 1943

'I think she's gone.' The Mohne dam is breached. But in his correspondence, Sir Arthur Harris wrote that the raid 'achieved nothing'

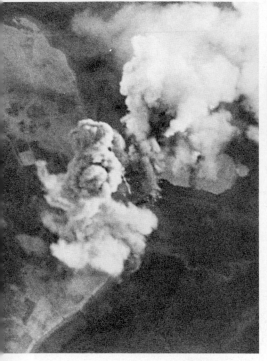

Above left: 'By God, she's had it today.' The *Tirpitz*, pride of the German fleet, sunk by Lancasters of 617 Squadron, 12 November 1944

Above right: After the most infamous RAF attack of the war, Dresden lies in ruins: 796 Lancasters took part in the assault on the east German city on the night of 13–14 February. Controversy about the raid lingers to this day

Left: From destruction to salvation: a Lancaster delivering food supplies to the starving Dutch people during Operation Manna, May 1945

Ushering in a new era: a Lancaster Mark III refuels a Gloster Meteor, the first operational jet of the RAF, August 1949

The astonishingly durable Avro Shackleton evolved from the Lancaster. It is a tribute to Roy Chadwick's original design that the plane remained in RAF service until 1991

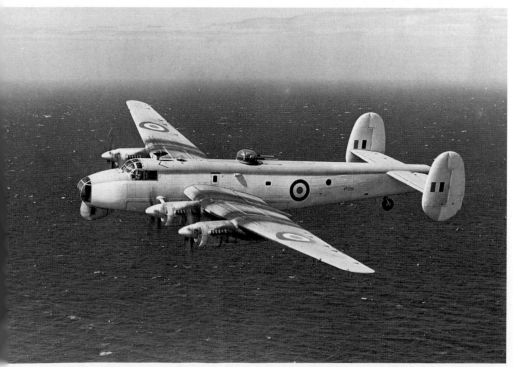

A post-war Lancaster in its all-white colours. The renowned bomber served largely in maritime reconnaissance in the years after 1945. The last of the type retired from the RAF on 15 October 1956

marshalling yards, depots and junctions. In drawing up his Transportation Plan, Tedder was strongly supported by Leigh-Mallory, whose early thinking had also focused on the railways, and Professor Solly Zuckerman, one of the government's chief scientific advisers. An eminent zoologist before the war, Zuckerman had become an expert analyst on the effects of bombing. At Tedder's request, he conducted a detailed study of the Allied invasion of Sicily and southern Italy in 1943, where the army had been given strong support by the Allies' tactical air force, and found that 'assaults on a limited number of railway centres had virtually paralysed the system'.[56]

But before his plan could be implemented, Tedder faced a large obstacle in the truculent form of the AOC Bomber Command. During the discussions over his appointment as Deputy Supreme Commander, Tedder had been warned by Eisenhower that relations with Harris might be difficult. In a note of one of their conversations, Tedder recorded that Einsenhower believed the RAF bomber chief was 'by way of being something of a dictator who had very much the reputation of not taking kindly to directions outside his own command. Eisenhower saw rocks ahead. Bomber Command had a tremendous and greatly responsible role to play in Overlord. If Harris chose to be difficult in his relations with the Air Ministry, there might well be endless scope for friction. I did my best to reassure Eisenhower by telling him that I was quite certain that if Harris were given specific orders to carry out specific jobs, he would do them loyally.'[57] But Tedder's early hopes were misplaced. Harris was as recalcitrant as ever. 'I am afraid that, having started as a confirmed optimist, I am steadily losing my optimism as to how this is all going to work,' Tedder told Portal at the end of February. 'The only sign of activity from Harris's representatives has been a series of adjustments to the records of their past bombing statistics with the evident intention of demonstrating that they are equipped and untrained to do anything except mass fire-raising on very large targets'.[58] Almost as obstinate as Harris was Carl Spaatz, the US commander of strategic forces in Europe, who resented the idea of taking orders from Leigh-Mallory and believed that he should be free to press on with the bombing of German aircraft factories and oil plants.

More fruitless meetings on the Transportation Plan were held throughout February, Harris maintaining that the bomber offensive over Germany would soon emerge as 'a winning factor'.[59] Zuckerman tried to puncture such delusions by pointing out that 'all the available evidence showed that what the bomber offensive would achieve between March and May 1944 would be a seven per cent reduction in the enemy's overall output'.[60]

Harris was not inclined to show much respect for what Zuckerman said, describing him to his American friend R. A. Lovett as 'a civilian professor whose peacetime forte is the study of the sexual aberrations of higher apes'.[61] Even the success of Cheshire's low-level raids, especially the spectacular assault on the Limoges aero-engine factory, would not shift Harris. In an attempt to break the deadlock, Portal decided to put Harris's protestations to the test. On 4 March he ordered Bomber Command to attack six French marshalling yards over the next three weeks. Contrary to all Harris's claims, the experiment was highly successful. 'The results proved beyond peradventure that Harris had underestimated the skills of his crews,' wrote Tedder.[62] Yet even now Harris still refused to move, telling Portal that he must have 'full discretion as to what German target I shall attack on any given night'.[63] But the worsening losses in the Battle of Berlin had weakened the strength of his position. At a crucial meeting attended by Eisenhower and Portal on 25 March, the day after the disastrous raid on Berlin when 44 Lancasters were shot down, the Transportation Plan was finally agreed by the military chiefs, Eisenhower telling his commanders that the 'greatest contribution they could make' to D-Day would be that they 'hinder the enemy's movement'.[64]

Now a new stumbling block emerged. The plan, which centred on the bombing of 74 key rail centres in France and Belgium, needed political as well as military approval. At the meeting on 25 March, Leigh-Mallory had raised his concern about the potential number of French civilian casualties, saying that he 'did not want to go down to posterity as the man who killed thousands of Frenchmen'. At this remark, Harris is reputed to have growled: 'What makes you think you're going to go down to posterity at all?'[65] But the politicians, including Winston Churchill, shared Leigh-Mallory's anxieties about French casualties. They were particularly shocked by a paper produced by the Bombing Operations Director Syd Bufton on 5 April, which predicted devastation on an epic scale because accuracy could not be guaranteed. Having warned that the 'large majority of bombs will always fall outside the marshalling yard areas', he said that attacks on the 74 rail centres could result in 'a total of 160,000 killed and seriously injured'.[66] Bufton had his own axe to grind, since he believed that Tedder's Transportation Plan was 'a national disaster' and far more could be achieved at less cost by bombing bridges in France and oil plants in Germany.[67] He therefore had a vested interest in presenting the scheme in the most negative light. Effectively he was following the same line as Harris, implying that aircrews had neither the skills nor the equipment to carry out precision bombing.

As a passionate Francophile, Churchill baulked at such carnage among innocent French citizens, and at a meeting of the Defence Committee on 5 April 1944 he refused to give his full approval to the Transportation Plan. All Churchill would accept was an 'experimental application' of the plan, by which targets were limited to those where the risk of civilian casualties was small.[68] This decision meant that Tedder had to undertake a substantial reworking of the target schedule, something that pleased Harris who sensed that he might now be able to concentrate on the offensive against Germany. Mistakenly interpreting the delay in the plan as a sign of Tedder's support for his case, Harris told Lovett: 'Tedder has entirely sound views about the importance of strategic bombing and there is no fear that he will agree to it being abandoned in favour of slogan and panacea even if others should try to revise the monkey fancier's plan in its original form.'[69]

But Harris was deluding himself if he thought he had been reprieved. Eisenhower and Tedder were not prepared to abandon a plan that they considered absolutely essential to the success of Overlord. Harris was therefore instructed to embark on night attacks against certain selected targets in France including Lille, Tours and St Cyr, using the Lancasters of Cochrane's No. 5 Group. Meanwhile Tedder's staff produced their own revised analysis of the potential casualties, based partly on the results of these early April raids and the previous ones in March. This information was passed to Portal who told Churchill that 'so far 549 civilians have been killed and 873 injured in 11 out of 13 attacks on French railway targets.'[70] From those figures, it was estimated that the likely casualty total from the Transportation Plan would be no higher than 10,500 killed and 5,500 seriously injured. But this was still too much for Churchill, who hesitated to give his approval and, with an uncharacteristic lack of decisiveness, allowed Cabinet and committee discussions to drag on for weeks. 'Another terrible meeting from 10.30 to just on 1 a.m.,' wrote Sir Alan Brooke after yet another delay, 'at a time when we are within five weeks of the attack and definite decisions are required.'[71]

But Eisenhower and Tedder were not prepared to wait. In a bold move on 17 April, they issued their directive to Spaatz and Harris authorizing the implementation of the Transportation Plan. 'Our re-entry on the continent constitutes the supreme operation for 1944. All possible support must therefore be afforded to the Allied Armies by our Air Forces to assist them in establishing themselves in the lodgement area'. To get round the political difficulty, the directive explained that 'it is understood that the political aspects of this plan, as affecting the French, will be kept under continuous supervision'.[72] In fact, Churchill was to continue his opposition almost until D-Day itself, deploring the killing of French civilians and arguing that the destruction of railways was an irrelevance, since the capacity of the French network was 800 trains a day and the German army used only 10 per cent of that number. At one stage he even sent a telegram to Roosevelt urging him to intervene to suspend operations against French targets, but the US President replied that the decision was a military one and must be left to the military commanders. It was a sign of Churchill's waning influence, squeezed between the mighty superpowers of the USA and USSR, that his objections to the Transportation Plan carried so little weight.

Having received the directive, Harris buckled down to the job with a vigour that surprised his commanders. He still hankered after a full-blooded offensive against Germany and continued to mount regular attacks against targets in the Reich, but, after all his protests, he displayed little reluctance in hitting the French railways as well. This was partly out of professional pride: having been given a direct order, he wanted to carry it out to the best of his ability. Furthermore, he had enormous respect for Eisenhower, who had a unique talent for gaining obedience from the most wilful subordinates. Even Field Marshal Montgomery, notorious for his opinionated contempt for other military leaders, was quietly respectful towards Ike. Professor Zuckerman was impressed by Harris's attitude, recording in his diary: 'The amazing thing is that Harris, who was even more resistant than the Americans to the idea of AEAF domination, has in fact thrown himself whole-heartedly into the battle, has improved his bombing enormously and has contributed more to the dislocation of enemy communications etc. than any of the rest.'[73] The directive gave Harris 37 of the 74 targets in the plan, the others being allocated to the US 8th Air Force under Jimmy Doolittle and to the AEAF under Leigh-Mallory.

Harris began work immediately with an attack by 202 Lancasters on the night of 18–19 April against marshalling yards at Juvisy near Paris, followed the next evening by the dispatch of 247 Lancasters to La Chapelle just north of Paris. The attacks on the French railway system continued in the rest of April and throughout May. The damage became increasingly extensive as the raids intensified. One report on Radio Paris in late May reported: 'The French railway system is in complete chaos. The Allies have successfully pulverised into rubble whole marshalling yards. They have destroyed countless locomotives and have made scores of railway stations unusable.'[74] A picture of the scene on a typical French raid was provided by Bill Jones, the intelligence officer at Elsham Wolds, who flew in a Lancaster to Rouen in April:

> The bombing started and yellow flashes on the ground showed where the bombs were landing – right on the target. The red and green target indicators were now cascading in rapid succession and thick smoke was beginning to cover the area. But I could see the railway marshalling yards and the river quite clearly through the smoke because of the intense illumination due to the markers. It was a fantastic sight to me and, although I flew on a number of ops after this, I never failed to be fascinated by the spectacle of the TI markers, the bomb bursts and the explosions which sometimes accompanied a particular cluster of bombs.[75]

After the Berlin campaign, these raids were regarded with relief by the crews. 'In and out in ten minutes, a smoothly run operation,' said Denis Burns, a navigator with 106 Squadron, of the attack on Juvisy.[76] After one 'straightforward' raid to Bernaville in Picardy on 2 June, bomb aimer Campbell Muirhead wrote in his diary: 'the more of those "easy efforts", the happier we'll be.'[77]

Harris considered at one stage ruling that each French trip should only count as a third of a normal sortie towards the completion of a full operational tour. He told Norman Bottomley, the Deputy Chief of the Air Staff, that short-range missions to 'lightly defended targets in France' were in 'no way comparable to those associated with long-range targets in Germany'. Harris further warned that, because the trips were so much shorter and more frequent, there was a danger of experienced crews finishing their tours too early.[78] But there was fury in the squadrons at this proposal. Crews who had gone through the hell of bombing the Reich felt that they deserved some reward, as Saundby informed Harris: 'There is evidently real feeling among Lancaster and Halifax III crews that as they carry the weight of attack on Germany they should be allowed to offset this by counting full marks for operations against more lightly defended areas.'[79] After the blood-stained fiasco of Mailly-le-Camp on 3–4 May, Harris quietly dropped the proposition. What made his proposal all the more untenable was that any sortie, no matter how short, remained dangerous, since the Germans still had around 350 fighters in northern France, while the flak defences in occupied territories were far from negligible. Twelve Lancasters were shot down in a raid on Lille on 10–11 May, five on a trip to Bourg Leopold in Belgium the following evening.

Alf Ridpath, a pilot in 49 Squadron, was one of those who came under fire during the Bourg Leopold raid: 'We thought it was going to be a cake walk. It was only a short trip of two and three-quarter hours.' The

Lancaster was on its way home after being ordered not to bomb because of the difficulty in marking the target when, over the Dutch coast, there was 'a crash, bang wallop as this fighter attacked from below. A cannon shell went right through the rear gunner's parachute stowed behind him, another burst through the Elsan toilet and there was chemical fluid all over the floor. The pilot, Alan Edgar, immediately put the aircraft into a dive, we opened the bomb doors and let the bombs go. I think the night fighter thought the bombs were us going in and that's why he didn't come back.' But the aircraft was now 'in a terrible state. There were dozens of holes in it. All aileron control had been lost and the aircraft kept pitching up then diving, like a bucking bronco. It took the pilot, the flight engineer and the bomb aimer on the controls together to try to get it level. The pilot had his leg round the control column trying to hold it back. They got a rope round the column eventually. There was surplus oil on fire in the fuselage. I stamped on the flames in my flying boots and the mid-upper gunner, Johnny Watters, came out of his turret and beat them with his gloves.' So serious were the fire and the damage that the crew had a vote as to whether to bail out and they decided to stay. In a characteristic tale of resilience, the Lancaster made it back to England, even though, in Ridpath's words, 'it was riddled like a colander'.[80]

For all such threats the bombing turned out be superbly effective. By 3 June the British bombers had attacked every one of their allotted targets. A total of 54,869 tons of bombs had been dropped, of which the Lancasters contributed 33,090 tons. The devastation inflicted on the railway system in France and Belgium was extensive. As Charles Carrington, the army's chief liaison officer at Bomber Command headquarters, noted: 'A glance at the map demonstrated that every important railway junction through which supplies and reinforcements could reach Normandy had been severely damaged if not destroyed. The task was declared complete when a railway desert had been created.'[81] According to military intelligence reports, the Germans had counted on 48 trains a day for supply and re-inforcement. By D-Day the capacity of the lines was reduced to six trains a day. A message sent on 3 June by an officer on the staff of Germany's commander in the west, Generalfeldmarschall Gerd von Rundstedt, reported that 'the railway authorities are seriously considering whether it is not useless to attempt further repair work', such was the intensity of the Allied bombing.[82] The architect of the Transportation Plan, Arthur Tedder, felt vindicated. 'Within the Seine-Loire area, the railways were almost paralysed,' he wrote, 'and only one division, whose move originated within the area, used rail transport to any appreciable extent. Even then our bombing on the trains of leading units obliged them to detrain and cost serious losses in equipment and ammunition. Armoured vehicles were obliged to progress as best they could by road, a process which often damaged them seriously before they reached the battle area.'[83] Interrogated after the war by the Americans, Hermann Göring paid this tribute: 'The Allies owe the success of the invasion to the Air Forces. They prepared the invasion. They made it possible and they carried it through.'[84]

In the final days before D-Day, Bomber Command pulverized the German defences along the coast. Altogether almost 1,700 sorties were flown by Lancasters in 30 separate attacks on gun emplacements and batteries. In an attempt to deceive the Germans into thinking that the invasion would take place in the Pas de Calais region, three times as many bombs fell east of the Seine as they did to the west. Sensing that the invasion was imminent, none of the Lancaster crews knew the exact date. Danny Boon, a flight engineer with 625 Squadron recalled that:

> on the night before D-Day, we were allocated to take out some gun emplacements at St Martin. We thought, 'this is a cushy type of raid, just going to the coast of France.' We had no idea that the offensive was about to start. Coming back in the early morning, I saw this massive array of ships. I remember seeing a hospital ship with a big red cross, cruisers and battleships. It looked like an armada. We thought, 'Crikey, that's a big convoy.' We found it strange that no one fired at us. When we woke up later, we found that D-Day had started. The reason they did not tell us was because if we had been shot down, we might have told the Germans. They kept us completely in the dark.[85]

Another Lancaster engineer, Rex Oldland of 405 Squadron, was in a raid sent to wipe out nine coastal batteries on the early morning of 6 June:

> We had no knowledge of D-Day the night before. I remember we were awakened at half past one in the morning for briefing and got airborne sometime after three. Eight of the batteries we destroyed completely and the ninth could only be operated manually. It was a filthy night, raining very heavily. The cloud was right down on the deck. We attacked at just over 4,000 feet, which was as low as we dared to go with a 4,000-pounder. Any lower and we would have been damaged by the blast. It was just getting daylight when we left. I was down in the nose and I could see feathers in the water. They did not look like the white crests of water you usually see. There were a lot of them. We had a pair of night glasses and I found they were ships as far as the eye could see, just thousands of them.

We were flying at about 7,000 feet so we had a good view . . . That was it, D-Day. We were a bit miffed because we had not been told about it but looking back, it was quite sensible. At the interrogation we said that we had not seen any ships so we got our own back.[86]

During the night before the invasion, the Lancasters of 617 Squadron performed one highly unorthodox operation as part of the elaborate plan aimed at deceiving the Germans into thinking that the Allied assault was about to take place in the Pas de Calais region, far to the east of the Normandy beaches. This sophisticated ruse, code-named Operation Taxable, involved two waves of Lancasters flying in a box formation 12 miles abreast and 4 miles deep at exactly 180 mph, each dropping a bundle of Window strips every five seconds. Each wave completed an elongated orbit over the coast, moving southwards in unison at 2,500 feet, then gently swinging round to return northwards before starting another circuit. Using a constant stream of Gee fixes, each Lancaster orbit started marginally nearer the French coast than the previous one, thereby giving the impression on the German Würzburg and Freya radar screens that the advancing planes were a naval fleet moving across the sea at eight knots. To succeed, Taxable required the highest levels of accuracy and concentration from the crews, for the bomber formation had to be kept on its course for eight hours while 30 orbits were completed. Such precision was only possible with intensive training throughout May, some of it off the Scottish coast, some off Flamborough Head, East Yorkshire, as Air Ministry experts worked out the exact measurements of speed, turns and Window drops to create the illusion of a moving convoy.

On the night itself, the first wave of 617 Lancasters, led by Leonard Cheshire, took off at 19.00 hours for the eight-hour mission. Each Lancaster was fitted with two lots of navigation equipment, two pilots, two navigators and two crews, because it was recognized how tiring the operation would be. 'The pilots had to fly exact courses with exact timing by the navigator,' recalled John Sanders, a pilot with 617 Squadron. 'After forty minutes of this, we would change seats and the other pilot would take over.'[87] Another 617 Squadron pilot, Malcolm Hamilton, remembered the split-second timing required in difficult conditions. 'We would go down towards Calais and each time we would go eight seconds further than the last time. We would go round and back on another course, dropping Window. You would turn round and come down and each time you extended the leg a little bit further. The weather was filthy. It was drizzling and there were high winds so the navigator had to work very hard to keep you on course.'[88] The 617 Lancaster crews were under extreme pressure throughout these eight hours, having been warned that their performance was crucial to the D-Day operation.

But no mistakes were made. The 617 crews succeeded heroically. It is impossible to tell how much direct influence Operation Taxable had on the response to the invasion, for German communications had been so badly damaged in the last month, but certainly there was no recognition in the Wehrmacht's High Command that a spoof had been perpetrated. For more than two days, the German military leaders were convinced that the Normandy landings were just a diversion, with the real invasion about to take place in the Pas de Calais. The great irony of the success of air operations at D-Day and in the weeks before was that it exposed how wrong Harris was in his claim that the heavy-bomber force was capable only of urban saturation bombing. Cheshire's spectaculars at Munich and Limoges, the precision achievement of the Transportation Plan and the clinical efficiency of Operation Taxable showed that the Lancaster was capable of much more than the limited role to which Harris had assigned it. As Charles Carrington, the army liaison officer at High Wycombe succinctly put it: 'By the accuracy of his railway attacks, Harris had destroyed his own argument for area bombing.'[89] On another level, the triumph of D-Day represented an even deeper setback for Harris. He had always maintained that the war could be won by bombing alone. The first troops to arrive in Normandy were the ultimate refutation of that cherished theory.

15

'Get on and knock Germany finally flat'

IN THE IMMEDIATE aftermath of D-Day, as Bomber Command continued to pound the German defences and communications, the Lancaster
acquired a fearsome addition to its arsenal, a new weapon that emphasized both its unique loading capacity and its ability to carry out precision
bombing. The 12,000-pound 'Tallboy' was another creation from Barnes
Wallis, who had long been privately working on the development of a
new generation of heavyweight, aerodynamic bombs. In 1941 Wallis had
written a paper entitled 'A Note on a Method of Attacking the Axis
Powers' in which he argued that a massive bomb, weighing ten tons and
exploding underground, would create shock waves sufficient to destroy
the foundations of a substantial enemy target. He even came up with a
preliminary design for an enormous 50-ton aircraft to drop this 'earthquake' bomb from 45,000 feet. Still living in the age of the Whitley and
the Wellington, the government thought the idea technically unfeasible
and tactically unsound since the loss of just one of these huge bombers
would represent a crippling blow to the RAF. The idea was not pursued.
But then the success of the Dams raid gave Wallis a new credibility
in official circles. Operation Chastise, wrote Wallis, 'tended to establish in
the minds of the C-in-Cs such as Sir Arthur Harris and CE Sir Wilfrid
Freeman an impression of the rightness of the lines on which I argued
when writing "A Note on a Method of Attacking the Axis Powers".'[1]

In July 1943 Wallis was urged to revive the earthquake bomb project.
While he continued working on his plan for a ten-ton monster, which
was to emerge towards the end of the war as the awe-inspiring 'Grand
Slam', he more rapidly developed a five-ton version, code-named 'Tallboy'.
It was the most advanced British bomb of the war thus far. There had
been other 12,000-pounders but they were essentially cylindrical bins
packed with explosive. Due to its aerodynamic shape, long tail fins and
thick steel casing, the Tallboy combined the shattering power of a very
large blast bomb with the penetration of an armour-piercing bomb.
Reaching a terminal velocity of 3,700 feet per second, the Tallboy was

capable of making a crater that would have taken 5,000 tons of earth to fill. Because of its unique qualities, its production was a demanding process, requiring costly raw materials and precision engineering by hand. But the priority attached to the project by the government meant that progress was swift. The prototype was ready for inspection in the autumn of 1943, and by the following summer the first Tallboys were delivered to the elite 617 Squadron, whose Stabilised Automatic Bomb Sights (SABS) could provide the necessary accuracy to exploit the new bombs to their fullest potential. Once so doubtful of the practicality of Wallis's ideas, Sir Arthur Harris was enthusiastic about the weapon: 'This remarkable bomb was a contradiction in terms; it could penetrate twelve feet of concrete or pierce any ship's armour, but whereas most armour-piercing bombs have so thick a case that they contain little explosive, this one carried terrific power. It was ballistically perfect and had a very high terminal velocity; it could therefore be aimed with great precision.'[2]

The awe that the Tallboys could inspire among the airmen was revealed in the testimony of Don Cheney, a Canadian pilot in 617 Squadron, who watched them arrive at Scampton. 'A convoy of large, flatbed lorries arrived at the squadron, each loaded with long, tapering shapes carefully covered by heavy canvas. All hands followed the lorries in great haste and excitement, thinking that we were receiving a squadron of "knocked-down" Spitfires intended to provide us with fighter cover during daylight operations. Not so! To our amazement the largest, most aerodynamic projectiles we had ever seen or even imagined were quickly unloaded and stowed in the bomb dump.'[3]

The campaign to smash German communication and transport links provided the ideal opportunity to use Tallboy for the first time. As the invasion unfolded, the French Resistance and British Intelligence had reported to Allied headquarters that the Wehrmacht was planning to move a Panzer division to Normandy on a railway which passed through a tunnel near the town of Saumur in the Loire valley. On 8 June the Lancasters of 617 Squadron were loaded up with their Tallboys and, following the lead of Cheshire in his Mosquito, took off for northwestern France. Cheshire found the target easily, dropping two red spot flares at the entrance to the tunnel. Then the rest of 617 Squadron moved in, each Lancaster's SABS releasing the bomb automatically. Clouds of smoke and falling earth filled the air around the tunnel as the Tallboys pulverized the ground. Reconnaissance photographs taken the next day showed that almost all the bombs had fallen on the markers, creating huge craters where there had been a railway. The greatest damage, however, came from a Tallboy that had burst through the hillside and brought the roof of the tunnel crashing down. The railway line was not used again during the war.

After this initial success, the Tallboys were used against a wide range of French targets over the summer of 1944, including heavily concreted submarine pens at Brest, Lorient and St Nazaire, and torpedo E-boat bases at Le Havre and Boulogne. These last two raids involved Lancasters with conventional bombs as well as the Tallboys. A total of 221 Lancasters flew to Le Havre on 14 June, and 155 to Boulogne the following day. These were the first major Bomber Command operations mounted over occupied territory in daylight since 1941, a reflection of the growing confidence among the Allies and the increasing weakness in the German defences on the French coast. Flight engineer Ken Down of 550 Squadron recalled:

> We were very surprised when we were woken up early for a day raid. We wondered what was going on. When we went into the briefing there was some sort of apologetic remark about this being Bomber Command's first daylight raid for some time but 'never mind', it would be good experience. In fact, we were thinking the losses might be quite high. Nobody expressed it but you thought it was likely to be a bit dodgy. Just before the target, there was a lot of flak coming up to port as we cruised along and I thought, 'I'm glad I'm not going there.'

But then Down's pilot had to change course to reach the target. 'Oddly enough we sailed right through without being hit. Going in to the target, when I saw 617 Squadron's bombs explode it was as if the whole surface had erupted. We hadn't been told anything at the briefing about the Tallboy bombs but when I saw them go in it was obvious that this was something special. We went in to bomb ourselves, then we were away back over the sea without problems.'[4] Again footage showed that severe damage had been sustained by the E-boat pens, while not one Lancaster had been shot down.

But Malcolm Hamilton's Lancaster *G-George* came very close to being destroyed, as he later recalled: 'We went into the target and immediately the flak started. The first shot burst under the Tallboy, and then the Tallboy deflected it into the aircraft and we lost our hydraulics. But the bomb aimer's voice was still coming, "Steady, steady."' More shots went through the Lancaster. One bent the bomb doors. Another broke the lock on the starboard undercarriage, causing the wheel to come down. 'That caused drag, pulling us to the right. The damaged bomb door was also pushing us to the right so I had to adjust my trim. The plane was still on its twelve-mile bomb run. The next shot went straight through the starboard middle tank and we lost 140 gallons of high octane fuel, which sprayed out over the rear gunner through the clear vision panel.' But still Hamilton kept on course for the target before the SABS automatically released the bombs:

> I remember that it felt like a fortnight but it was only about fourteen seconds. The bomb aimer shouted, 'We've hit it', and just as he said that, the nose of the aircraft blew off. The hatch had gone and the whole of the glass nose had gone. A terrific draught came in and it blew all the navigator's papers everywhere. It also caught a load of Window. The bomb aimer was writhing around in agony. The crew tried to help. The engineer said, 'I don't know what he's making all that fuss about, he's only got a small hole in his leg. We tried to put a tourniquet around it but he wouldn't let us.' By this time I was totally engaged with flying the aircraft. We were sinking, although we had climbing power on. It was chaos with the drag, the undercarriage down, the draught, and the bomb aimer, who in his writhing had kicked the centre pedestal on which I had the controls for the pitch and throttles. I shouted, 'Take him back, get him on the rest bed.' By this time we had come across the channel and we were down to about 3,000 feet.

Expecting that he would have to ditch in the English Channel, Hamilton sent out a distress call and an air-sea rescue boat was launched. But, as so often in the war, the battered Lancaster managed to pull its crew home, reaching RAF West Malling in Kent which had a grass airfield:

> As I landed on the grass, I think I did one of the smoothest lands I had ever done. At least it felt like that because I was dead scared of the under-carriage collapsing. I had all the boys in crash positions. The only way we could get the undercarriage down was to use the emergency air bottle because the hydraulics had gone. We blew it down and we managed to get the undercarriage to lock. I could not get the whole flap down. I knew I was going to come in fast but I also knew that the grass would pull us up. As I landed, I saw the fire engine coming along with all these blokes in their fire suits, their helmets on and carrying long poles with hooks on – to hook us out of the flames, I suppose. Someone came to the front of the aircraft, looked up through the hole and said, 'God, how the bloody hell did you get this thing back?[5]

The bomb aimer was taken to hospital, where doctors found he had 27 pieces of shrapnel in his body between his chest and his legs. But, along with his Lancaster and his crew, he survived.

Lancasters were also used in Operation Crossbow, the campaign to destroy the Germans' long-range V weapons. In response to Overlord, the Germans had been firing V-1 flying bombs towards London and Antwerp from sites in the Pas de Calais region and the Dutch coast. Once launched, these deadly unmanned bombs could only be brought down by fast fighters like the Spitfire or the Typhoon, but the Lancasters, both with Tallboys or conventional bombs, played a role in trying to obliterate any site or storage depot revealed by intelligence or reconnaissance. Two such attacks, each by over 200 Lancasters, were made on the nights of 4 and 7 July on the huge storage facility at St Leu d'Esserent, near the River Orne where the flying bombs were stored in a network of underground caves before being moved to the launch sites. The tactics and hazards of a typical V-1 raid were well described by John Gedney, a flight engineer with 156 Squadron:

> We were using a new technique because the sites were so hard to pick out – well camouflaged and hidden. So the method was for the Lancaster stream to be stepped, one behind the other and when you saw the bombs going from the one in front, then you opened your bomb doors. The idea was to get the bombs going in a big mass. Then, as we flew, we saw a Lancaster directly above us, with his bomb doors open, ready to bomb. At that very moment a lump of flak smashed through the windscreen, and hit the pilot, knocking his helmet and leaving him covered in blood. I thought that the Lanc above was about to drop his bombs on us. So I got hold of the wheel and steered the plane away, while calling on the bomb aimer to get rid of the bombs. I steered her out of the way, away from the flak, then the pilot was playing hell up because he couldn't see anything for blood. We had a flask of cold tea and I washed his face with that and my own dirty handkerchief. We now set course for home. And the pilot was able to carry on.[6]

It was a daylight attack against a V-1 storage site at Trossy-St-Maxim in the Pas-de-Calais region on 4 August that brought one of the ten Victoria crosses won by Lancaster airmen during the war. Canadian pilot Ian Bazalgette of 635 Squadron in the Pathfinder Force was nearing the target when his Lancaster came under heavy anti-aircraft fire. Both starboard engines were put out of action, fire broke out in the fuselage and the bomb aimer was badly injured. Nevertheless, he carried on to the target, dropping his markers accurately. Turning away, the Lancaster now lost one of its port engines as the flames grew fiercer across the wings. The mid-upper gunner collapsed, overcome by the fumes from the fires. At 1,000 feet and with no hope of regaining altitude on a single engine, Bazalgette gave the order to bail out. The four uninjured crewmen grabbed their parachutes and left, but Bazalgette refused to abandon his Lancaster with two stricken comrades on board. Instead he tried to land in a field. With superb airmanship, he skilfully managed to avoid a small French village in his path, then he brought the aircraft down. Descending in his parachute, wireless operator Chuck Godfrey watched the plane touch the grass: 'I could see it all. He did get it down in a field but it was well ablaze and with all the petrol on board it just exploded.'[7] Bazalgette and the other two men were killed instantly. He was posthumously awarded the Victoria Cross, his citation stating that 'his courage and devotion to duty were beyond praise'.[8]

Just as threatening for the Allies was the V-2 rocket programme which had survived the Peenemünde assault in 1943 and was in the process of acquiring its own bases and depots ready for an all-out attack on England. Again the Lancasters played their part in attempting to reduce the V-2 infrastructure. One of the most crucial anti-V-2 raids took place on 19 June, when 19 Lancasters of 617 Squadron, equipped with Tallboys and led once more by Cheshire, attacked a massive concrete storage bunker built into the hillside at Watten near St Omer, not far from Calais. For once, Cheshire failed to mark the target, when his TIs failed to ignite, but his deputy Dave Shannon dropped his red spot fires accurately and then the Lancasters swooped on the site, among them the aircraft piloted by Malcolm Hamilton. 'There was a huge dome of concrete with a hole in the middle. What we did was to fly at 500-feet intervals so that we would not get in each other's slipstream. We circled round and as soon as the markers went down, we all turned in. We came in like the spokes of a wheel. All the bombs went down and all you saw was this huge mushroom cloud over what had been the target. When we got back to base, the Mosquitoes told us it had been destroyed.'[9] Soon after this sortie Cheshire completed his 100th mission. On the orders of Cochrane and with some reluctance, he was posted to other, non-flying duties 'for a rest'.[10]

In addition to these special operations, the Lancasters undertook a huge number of other sorties during the Battle of Normandy. They were dispatched to attack road and rail targets, enemy troop concentrations, military barracks, radar installations and fuel depots. In the week immediately after D-Day, the Lancasters flew 2,689 operational sorties, of which 1,856 were flown against road and rail targets. The effect on Germany's logistics was outlined in a report from the Reich Air Ministry which warned on 13 June: 'The raids carried out in recent weeks have caused the breakdown of all main lines; the coastal defences have been cut off from the supply bases in the interior, thus producing a situation which threatens to have serious consequences.'[11] A total of 77 Lancasters were lost during these raids, one of them piloted by Canadian Art de Breyne of 419 Squadron.

On the night of 12–13 June, de Breyne's plane was among 40 Lancasters of RCAF No. 6 Group sent to bomb the railways at Cambrai in northern Picardy. It was expected to be a low-key trip, but on the approach to the target his Lancaster was hit by Schrage Musik. Both engines failed in the port wing and fire engulfed the fuselage between the mid-upper turret and the tail. Realizing the situation was hopeless, de Breyne gave the order for the crew to bail out. But as the mid-upper gunner, Andrew Mynarski, made his way to the rear escape door, he saw that his close friend rear gunner Pat Brophy was trapped in his turret. The cannon shells from the Ju 88 had put the turret's hydraulic gear out of action and the manual gear had been broken by Brophy in his desperate attempt to escape. With astonishing selflessness, Mynarski fought his way through the blaze to rescue his comrade, first trying to open the turret doors with an axe and then, when that did not work, with his hands. By now the conflagration had started to burn his own clothing and parachute. Recognizing that the task was futile, Brophy urged his friend to save his own life. Mynarski reluctantly went back through the fire to the escape hatch. As a last gesture to the trapped gunner, he turned towards him, stood to attention in his flaming clothing and saluted before jumping out of the aircraft, which was about to enter its final dive. Mynarski fell to earth with his parachute and clothes in flames. He was soon found by some Frenchmen who had seen the Lancaster hurtling to its doom. He was still alive but died from his wounds shortly afterwards. In a strange twist of fate, Brophy survived the crash, and when he was released from his POW camp at the end of the war, he testified to Mynarski's bravery. On 11 October 1946, Mynarski was posthumously awarded the Victoria Cross, the citation for which read: 'Pilot Officer Mynarski must have been fully aware that in trying to free the rear gunner he was almost certain to lose his own life. Despite this, with outstanding courage and complete disregard for his own safety, he went to the rescue. Willingly accepting the danger, Pilot Officer Mynarski lost his life by a most conspicuous act of heroism which called for valour of the highest order.'[12]

In the subsequent weeks the bomber raids on France became increasingly more effective, aided by a new high definition of H2S, and the far greater accuracy that could be achieved by both Oboe and G-H operating at short range. Furthermore, as the number of daylight raids increased, the Lancasters received fighter cover from the RAF for the first time in the war. 'The Spitfires were a very reassuring sight and would accompany you to the target,' said Bob Knights of 617 Squadron. 'They would hang around and see you were all right. Once the invasion was underway the German radar defences began to crumble. Then we could go on raids to the channel ports without much fear of fighters.'[13] Bomb aimer Campbell Muirhead wrote in his diary after a raid on Trossy-St-Maxim on 3 August that, though the flak had been heavy, causing 'several ugly, big holes' in his Lancaster, there had not been any enemy action in the air: 'no wonder with all those Spits milling around the sunny, summer sky desperate for a fight'.[14] The confidence of Muirhead's crew over France was reflected in an incident during a raid on a V-1 site near the small port of Wissant near Calais, when the pilot put the Lancaster into a dive so that the gunners could strafe the German flak posts near the site. 'I held off as long as possible and then opened up with my twin Brownings, keeping the trigger pressed and taking a chance on their jamming,' recorded Muirhead. The skipper even dived several more times so that the rear and mid-upper gunners could let rip. And, naturally, we didn't mention this little bit of what might be termed "free entertainment" at de-briefing. Certainly not: they view that kind of thing somewhat sourly – you might lose one of their precious Lancs.'[15]

But even with such air superiority, these raids over France were not without their significant risks, especially because of the heavy flak barrage that the anti-aircraft guns could mount over key targets. A dramatic account of the experience of flying through such flak was recorded in the diary of David Scholes, who joined the Royal Australian Air Force at the age of just twenty and completed his training at the Lancaster Finishing School at Woodhall Spa in July 1944. Posted to 61 Squadron, he had his first operation on 24 July when he was sent to bomb an oil storage plant at Donges. 'Great strings of yellow cascading, illuminating flares go down as the Pathfinders locate the target. Over the VHF the controller and the deputy can be heard. We turn towards the target. Other Lancasters are around us, their four silver exhausts showing up.' But then, after dropping the flight-path markers, the Pathfinders appeared to struggle to hit the aiming point:

> We are almost there and still no marking down. There is nothing that can be done but orbit. This is an awful business – hundreds of aircraft circling, waiting to bomb and no one can see anyone else. The collision risk is very great. Another aircraft narrowly misses us and passes overhead. The greens are down at last. The Controller calls us in with 'Tally Ho' and to bomb

the greens. We go on the run up, the sight is terrific. Searchlights come up from nowhere. We are at 9000 feet. We weave violently towards the markings. Flak is coming up now. I see a Pathfinder coned below and to port and they are giving him merry hell, however, he escapes – good show! Now we are almost there. Never have I experienced such a feeling of tense excitement as this. The whole sky is lit up with weird lights – just like a ten times glorified Henley Night. Bombs burst with vivid white flashes. Flak is all around and light flak, like snakes, comes up to meet us in long red streams. One feels like a sitting pigeon, so exposed, or like a man walking across Piccadilly with no trousers on would feel. At length the bombs go and they create shudders as they leave the carriers. Away we go again, weaving violently with much power on. We narrowly miss being caught in the fork of two probing searchlights, as we run out of the target. On we go straight up to the coast inland. 'Well, we are OK so far', is the way I feel. Eventually we reach the French coast again after what seems like hours and hours.

Scholes's plane made it safely back to England.[16]

Navigator Peter Antwis was less fortunate when his crew took part in an attack on an oil storage depot at Bordeaux in southwestern France on 13 August. During the bombing run, he stood in the astrodome of the Lancaster to check there were no aircraft above. 'We continued steadily on course for the target. Suddenly we were in the middle of black balls of smoke. They were bursting with fierce red flashes and I could feel and hear their explosion.' He heard the bomb aimer call out 'bombs gone' over the intercom.

> The Lanc shook again. Angry chunks of metal ripped up through the floor of my office. My parachute was thrown out of its stowage and my spare oxygen bottle was flung backwards. There was another group of four explosions. Through the starboard window I saw the inboard engine burst into flames. A hole opened up beside my seat and my parachute popped open in the corner. We banked away from the target. The engine fire fizzled out. A scalding hot stream of glycol sprayed in through one of the holes and across my chest as the plane came round towards the coast.

Then the bomb aimer found that the bombs had not released over the target because the doors, having suffered flak damage, would not open. The Lancaster would have to go around again. 'There was a howling gale blowing straight through from end to end of the fuselage and it stank of petrol and glycol.' The aircraft was now yawing up and down as the pilot, Peter Lorimer, fought with the controls. He gave the order to bail out.

The airmen went out in an orderly manner, then it was the turn of Peter Antwis, who had bundled up his semi-open chute.

> I sat on the edge of the hatch and looked down to the river, a couple of miles below. I wrapped my arms around my parachute. Peter was still struggling with the controls when I went out. The slipstream was ice cold. I tumbled slowly and opened my arms. The bundle I was clutching burst open into a beautiful white canopy and the harness cut into my crotch and my chest and I floated. I looked all around. I saw woodland below. Our Lancaster was doing the most extraordinary things. I saw two more parachutes but there was no sign of Peter Lorimer. The plane turned steeply and flew straight back towards us, smoke and flames trailing behind it. Less than a mile away from me it suddenly climbed, half turned away in a kind of roll and at the top of the climb it stalled, and dived 1000 feet into the trees.

Still not knowing what had happened to the pilot, Antwis had barely time to hide his parachute before he was captured by the Germans, taken to a Luftwaffe base and then a POW camp. Amazingly, it was to be forty-nine years before he found out that Peter Lorimer had escaped just before the plane crashed into the forest. Having been asked by Antwis to provide his account, Lorimer recalled that after the crew had bailed out,

> I eased the pressure on the controls but the nose came up rapidly and the speed dropped away. I realized that I was rapidly running out of height so I unbuckled and headed for the front hatch. By the time I pulled myself out of the front hatch the aircraft was stalling and had dropped the starboard wing about 45 degrees. I saw the tail go between my legs and opened the parachute. I reckoned I was between 1000 and 1500 feet above the ground, facing south.[18]

He managed to come down in the forest without injury and, unlike the others, he evaded capture and reached the American lines.

It was during another raid on France that New Zealander Nick Williamson, a pilot with 75 Squadron, inadvertently became the first man to land a Lancaster in occupied Europe during the war. On 30 June he took part in a daylight raid by 150 Lancasters on the crossroads at Villers-Bocage in Picardy, where German armour was massing to attack. As he approached the target, his Lancaster was hit by flak and the engineer Pat McDevitt was badly injured. 'A shell exploded very close and a piece of flak the size of an apple went between my back and the seat. I sat back and there's McDevitt with the white bone of this knee exposed and blood pumping out. He just looked at me. I can still see his eyes, like a spaniel asking for help.'[19] The other crewmen could not stem the blood, so just after bombing, Williamson decided to peel away from the bomber stream and try to land in a makeshift fighter airfield. Despite the narrowness and shortness of the airstrip, he brought the plane down successfully and stopped it with a gentle ground loop on a rough area. As Williamson climbed out of the plane, he heard a local fighter commander lecturing his pilots: 'Don't complain to me about this strip. If a Lancaster can get down, you should have no trouble.' McDevitt was taken to a field hospital, where he was treated immediately and made a swift recovery. Two days later he was ready to return with Williamson's crew. A large contingent of British troops lined the runway as the mighty plane taxied into position on the tiny airfield, whose boundary was marked by a large fence. Having loaded up the Lancaster with wine, cognac and captured German souvenirs including a swastika flag and even a Spandau machine-gun, Williamson prepared for take-off. 'Bomb aimer Graham Coull held the throttles back while I revved her on the brakes and then let her go. By God those Merlins were magnificent bloody engines. We cleared the fence and she was up.'[20]

Williamson's raid was one of the eight that Bomber Command undertook against enemy concentrations of troops during the Battle of Normandy. Harris had never considered the Lancaster a tactical bomber, and certainly did not envisage the plane's deployment on the battlefield in support of Allied infantry against the German ground forces. Not least of his concerns was his fear that the bombing would be insufficiently accurate and could thereby present a risk to the Allied armies. But the Supreme Headquarters of the Allied Expeditionary Force (SHAEF) required Bomber Command to perform this tactical role when German resistance seemed too stiff for other methods to be successful. 'We would never have attempted the invasion of the Continent without overwhelming air power, and it was because we had that power that the initial assault was successful,' wrote Leigh-Mallory. 'We must use air power to get the Army forward if they can't do it on their own, and I repeat it looks to me, unfortunately, as though they can't.'[21] The first such raid took place just thirty-six hours after D-Day when 202 Lancasters attacked German troops and armour gathered in the Forêt de Cerisy, about 15 miles behind the enemy front. The raid was deemed a success. The next, even bigger assault was on 7 July against Caen, where German troops were dug in heavily and had slowed the advance of General Montgomery's Anglo-Canadian 2nd Army, which had been expected to capture the city soon after D-Day, a failure for which he had come in for heavy criticism. To achieve a breakthrough, Montgomery asked for the help of Bomber

Command. Tedder had grave doubts. Sensing that 'the army did seem prepared to fight its own battles', he warned that acceptance of this demand would only encourage the soldiers to make 'endless vague' requests for support.[22] But he was overruled by Eisenhower and the raid was authorized. On the evening of 7 July, 467 RAF heavy bombers, 283 of them Lancasters, took off for Caen. In less than forty minutes most of the northern part of the city was reduced to rubble by 2,276 tons of bombs.

Soon after the raid Montgomery sent a generous telegram to Harris: 'We know well that your main work lies further afield and we applaud your continuous and sustained bombing of German war industries and the effect this has on the German war effort. But we also know well that you are always ready to bring your mighty effort closer in when such action is really needed and to co-operate in our tactical battle. When you do this, your action is always decisive. Please tell your brave and gallant pilots how greatly the Allied soldiers admire and applaud their work.'[23] For all such words of praise, the bombing did not achieve its goal of helping Montgomery to make rapid progress. 'The grandiose operations of 7th/8th July were a disappointment and not helped by Monty's exalted claim of victory,' wrote Charles Carrington, the army's liaison officer at SHAEF.[24] Indeed the rubble and craters in the roads may have held up the 2nd Army, confirming Professor Zuckerman's view that it was 'idle to expect the best the air can provide by calling in heavy bombers as a frill to a ground plan already made'.[25] Tedder also feared that the failure to capitalize on the bombing pointed to a worrying hesitancy in the British army, which bred an over-reliance on backing from the air. As evidence for this thesis, he later quoted a German military intelligence document which was captured during the Battle of Normandy. 'A successful break-in by the enemy is almost never exploited to pursuit,' said the paper, adding, 'the British infantry rely largely on the artillery and air force support. In the case of well-directed artillery fire by us they often abandon their position in flight. The enemy is extraordinarily nervous of close combat. Whenever the enemy infantry is energetically engaged, they mostly retreat or surrender.'[26] Tedder's view was backed up by Robert Oxland, a senior Bomber Command officer who toured the site and told Charles Carrington on his return: 'The soldiers he spoke to in France were so ashamed of themselves when they saw the Lancasters flying through the flak, whereas they took cover when a single machine gun opened fire.'[27]

Montgomery's frustration led him to call for an even bigger raid, to which SHAEF agreed. This time it was a joint US-British operation involving no fewer than 1,567 heavy bombers and 349 medium bombers. A total of 568 Lancasters, on their biggest raid since the Berlin campaign, were ordered to attack four specific areas around Caen, among them Colombelles. Donald Falgate, a bomb aimer with 463 Squadron, was one of the airmen who flew to Colombelles:

> It was the first attack I made in daylight conditions, so I could see the target, which was a very large steelworks where the Germans had dug themselves in. We were the first aircraft to bomb. It was quite something to see the bombs going down and actually hitting the target. I had not actually seen that on any of the night raids. Because the raid was low-level and the steelworks were so big, there was no way you could miss. I could see all the German tanks entrenched. It was very satisfying to see the stick hitting them. The opposition was insignificant.[28]

Altogether 7,700 tons of bombs fell on Caen, leaving most of the city obliterated and between 1,500 and 4,000 French civilians dead. As Falgate's testimony demonstrated, the German troops also took a battering. Many of those who were not killed outright were left in a state of shock by the remorseless pounding. One group of German soldiers could not walk in a straight line when captured. Another was stone deaf for twenty-four hours. The Wehrmacht commander in Normandy, Gunther von Kluge, who had taken over from von Rundstedt on 2 July 1944, wrote to Hitler soon after the second Caen bombing: 'The psychological effect of such a mass of bombs coming down with all the power of elemental nature on the fighting forces, especially the infantry, is a factor which has to be taken into very serious consideration. It is immaterial whether such a carpet catches good troops or not. They are more or less annihilated and, above all, their equipment is shattered.'[29]

Yet even now, Montgomery's progress remained slow, as the Germans regrouped south of the city. When Operation Goodwood, the code name for the seizure of Caen, ended on 20 July, two days after the bombing, the Allies had gained just seven miles for the loss of 4,011 men. When he heard this news, Harris ruefully commented that he had dropped an average of a thousand tons of bombs to advance the army one mile, and at that rate it would take him 600,000 tons to get them to Berlin.[30] Nevertheless, SHAEF persisted with the tactic, not least because it was showing signs of breaking German lines elsewhere. On 30 July, 462 Lancasters attacked a German armour concentration at Caumont in Picardy. Another 613 took part in four attacks in support of Canadian troops seeking to outflank the Germans and trap them in the Falaise Gap in Normandy. A total of 613 Lancasters took part in the raid on Falaise on 7 July, the biggest number since the Berlin campaign. Given the propinquity of the Allied army to the Wehrmacht, accuracy of marking and bombing was essential to avoid self-inflicted casualties. But in the fog of battle it was not always possible to achieve this. On 14 July, in a second huge raid over Falaise, 77 Lancasters ended up bombing short of the Germans. Some 65 Canadian troops were killed and many more wounded as some Lancaster bombs fell on their lines. Navigator Jack West of 115 Squadron took part in this injurious operation:

> We arrived over our target just after midday and saw what we thought was a gathering of tanks and infantry. The pilot gave orders to dive down using the front turret guns first and then using the rear and upper turrets. We levelled out at 200 feet and I noticed that there was a lot of waving from the troops on the ground, whilst the wireless operator was taking a coded message which meant Abandon Mission and Return to Base. It seemed that most of the aircraft ignored this command and completed their mission before returning to base where we were told that we had not 'wiped out' a German panzer division but instead had almost 'wiped out' an army of Canadian soldiers.[31]

Harris was appalled and ordered an immediate investigation. The subsequent report he wrote for Tedder and Leigh-Mallory, based on the findings of this study, made interesting reading. He opened by stating that the previous operations in support of the armies in France 'had been outstanding successes', despite the fact that 'the heavy bomber force is trained primarily to operate in darkness' and that such raids carried 'the grave risk of some bombing going astray and taking effect upon our troops'. Harris elaborated on some of the difficulties faced by the crews on daylight tactical assaults. 'The pilot in a heavy bomber has a very limited view of the ground. Such as he has he is unable to take advantage of in an operation of this description because the whole of his time and attention is taken up in listening to his navigator's and air bomber's instructions while controlling his aircraft, keeping on the correct course and avoiding collisions in the high concentration of aircraft which the methods of bombing and considerations of enemy opposition make essential.' He further pointed out that the navigator, in his compartment, had no view of the ground at all, while bomb aimers were not trained for map reading in daylight. Not always as respectful of his men as he claimed after the war, Harris then took an extraordinary swipe at the calibre of bomb aimers. 'Air bombers as a whole are by no means of outstanding intelligence. They are in the main selected as such because, although passing other standards for aircrew, they are the least likely to make efficient pilots or navigators.' Experience was also lacking in the crews, he added, because of the 'exceedingly high' casualty rate.

Harris then turned to the circumstances of the raid of 14 July. The main problem had arisen because some of the Lancasters confused the Pathfinders' own target indicators with the yellow markers used by Allied troops to show their own location. Harris complained that he had never been given any information that such ground markers were used by the Allied soldiers, a serious oversight since 'these yellow flares, smokes and strips are laid in the form of a cluster and thus they resemble the pattern of target indicators on the ground'. Harris also admitted, however, that other Lancasters had simply bombed the wrong targets because their navigation and timing had been poor, and there was 'a sheep-like following on of some crews misled by those preceding them'. He concluded that ground troops 'must be given orders to use no pyrotechnics likely to be confused as target markers', while he also said that action would be taken to ensure that all crews on close operations carried large maps and photographs of the target.[32] As a result of the Falaise tragedy, the squadron and flight commanders implicated were forced to relinquish their commands and acting ranks. Furthermore, two Pathfinder crews were expelled from the force and were reposted to ordinary crew duties. But Falaise marked the end of the Lancasters' tactical operations in support of the army in Normandy. From then on the job was largely done for the RAF by Typhoons, Tempests and Spitfires. Looking back on these operations, Portal later told Tedder that he did not feel they had been essential, and their real effect had been to demoralize the army by encouraging a mistaken reliance on heavy-bomber support. Tedder agreed and said that the army had been 'drugged with bombs'.[33] The one benefit, from the airmen's viewpoint, was the low casualty rate of just 0.35 per cent. Only 20 Lancasters were lost during these interventions.

For Bomber Command the final phase of the French campaign was the drive to bomb the enemy garrisons out of the northern ports of Le Havre, Boulogne and Calais. Said by British Intelligence to be held by 11,000 German troops, Le Havre was continually hammered by six Lancaster raids on successive days between 6 and 11 September. The attack on 10 September was particularly savage, as 522 Lancasters dropped 2,647 tons of bombs, including several Tallboys. 'A damn fine show,' recorded the Australian David Scholes in his diary. 'Never have I seen such vivid proof of the awful destruction caused by a concentrated high explosive attack. Columns of smoke billow up to a great height while the bomb flashes are quite distinct through it. The ground waves, too, are easily seen.

Nothing could live through such bombardment or, if one did survive, one would be insane for life. Never shall I forget this.'[34] Nor would the French civilians. When British troops entered Le Havre after the surrender of the German garrison on 11 September, it turned out that, contrary to intelligence reports, few soldiers were actually billeted in the town. But a probable total of 3,000 French men, women and children had been killed, more than five times the death toll from the German bombing of Coventry. British intelligence seemed at fault in misjudging the size of the German garrison. Bomber Command's warnings to the local population, either by leaflet or radio, appeared to have been inadequate. The assault on Le Havre stood in graphic contrast to the efforts made by Leonard Cheshire at Limoges in February to protect French lives during a raid. In his memoirs bomber pilot Harry Yates of 75 Squadron faced up to the carnage of Le Havre with both honesty and a sense of perspective. 'The young men in their Lancasters were not the villains of the piece that September afternoon, much less butchers. The three thousand lives were not lost to wickedness. Wherever the blame actually lay, the real culprit was incompetence . . . mundane, tiresome incompetence. And that is what makes this event so poignant and inadmissible.'[35] During September, Calais and Boulogne were also subjected to heavy raids (if not on the scale of Le Havre). In both towns the Germans had surrendered by 1 October. Again the cost to Bomber Command was minimal compared to the Berlin raids. Out of 3,761 sorties flown by Lancasters on the French ports, only 15 aircraft were lost.

By the end of September 1944, with most of France liberated, SHAEF had relinquished control of Bomber Command. After five months under Eisenhower and Tedder, Harris had regained the independence he always treasured. Yet throughout the period, he had surprised all his colleagues with the enthusiasm he showed for Overlord. As Eisenhower put it in a letter to General George Marshall, the Army Chief of Staff: 'In view of the earlier expressed fears that Harris would not willingly devote his Command to the support of ground operations, he actually proved to be one of the most effective and co-operative members of the team. Not only did he meet every request I ever made upon him but he actually took the lead in discovering new ways and the means for his particular types of planes to be of use in the battlefield.'[36] In October, Harris was awarded the Legion of Merit for his services to the Allied cause in Operation Overlord. A strong admirer of Eisenhower, Tedder and the Americans, Harris was gratified. Eisenhower, he wrote, was 'a wise and immensely understanding man', whose leadership gave him his only moments of calm during his years in charge.[37] But what annoyed him was that similar recognition was not given to the bomber crews for their role in D-Day. He protested to Portal about the 'grave injustice' of failing to give 'adequate or even reasonable credit to the RAF' for their efforts in the invasion.[38] Part of the blame, he thought, should be attached to the Air Ministry's Publicity Office, working in collaboration with the Admiralty. He told Sir Douglas Evill that he was 'appalled at this Air Ministry attitude towards the press because the entire world is quite certain by now that everything is done by the Americans except when the British Navy or Monty's Army chip in. We can't get a darn thing out except what we work out ourselves.' Evill replied blandly: 'I don't think our activities are badly represented in the press at all.' This only provoked Harris to another paroxysm. 'All we get is suppression of the RAF's achievements and glory for RN. It is a blatant put up job. It is a question of telling the ruddy Admiralty where to get off. We won't stand for it.'[39]

Harris was only gearing up for a much bigger fight with the Air Staff, one that would consume him almost until the end of the war. Throughout the French campaign he had been yearning to return to the bomber offensive against Germany. In fact he had not completely ignored the Reich since the disastrous raid on Nuremburg on 30 March. Though Overlord took absolute priority and dominated his Command's operations until October, he was still able to mount occasional raids against Germany. In April attacks were made against Cologne, Essen, Düsseldorf and Brunswick.

On the night of 26–7 April, a raid by 215 Lancasters on Schweinfurt led to one of the most astounding acts of bravery during the entire war. Sergeant Norman Jackson, an engineer with 106 Squadron, was sitting beside his pilot after a successful bombing run when suddenly their plane came under attack from a Ju 88. The stream of shells started a fire in the starboard wing close to the main inboard fuel tank and Jackson himself was thrown to the floor, suffering shrapnel wounds in his right leg and shoulder. Despite his injuries, he told the captain that he was willing to try to put the fire out by climbing onto the starboard wing with a hand-held extinguisher. The skipper gave him permission. Jackson then began to haul himself through the tiny escape hatch in the canopy over the pilot's head. Before he climbed out fully, he pulled the ripcord on his parachute back so that other crew members could hold onto the rigging lines as he made his way over the fuselage and onto the wing. Overcoming the tremendous buffeting induced by the plane travelling at 200 mph,

Jackson managed to reach the fire and get it under control. But just at this moment, the German night fighter attacked again. The Lancaster shook as more shells poured into its structure. Hit in the leg again and badly burnt, Jackson lost his grip and fell off the wing. His crewmates, seeing him tumble, let go of the parachute lines and he plunged towards the earth. Fortunately his parachute, though full of blazing holes, managed to bring him down safely. But he was in a terrible state because of burns to his eyes and arms and bullet wounds in his leg. In severe pain, he crawled to a nearby farmhouse, where he was taken prisoner and then sent to the Dulag Luft for interrogation. There followed a ten-month spell in a German hospital, where he made a partial recovery though he never regained the full use of his hands. Of the rest of his crew, four others bailed out when the flames spread through the Lancaster, but the skipper and rear gunner went down with the plane. At the end of the war, when all the survivors had been repatriated, Jackson was awarded the Victoria Cross. 'To venture outside, when travelling at almost 200 miles an hour, at a great height and in intense cold, was an almost incredible feat,' read his citation. 'By his ready willingness to face these dangers he set an example of self-sacrifice which will ever be remembered.'[40]

Other occasional attacks on Germany followed during the five months that Harris was under the command of Tedder and Eisenhower, some of them involving significant numbers. A force of 629 bombers, including 519 Lancasters, made a successful attack on the Kiel canal on 23–4 July, losing only four aircraft, and two big raids on Stuttgart were made before the end of the month. Though the Luftwaffe forces had been weakened by the American day offensive in the spring, which had targeted not only fighters and aircraft factories but also oil supplies, they still represented a formidable foe. As Campbell Muirhead wrote in his diary after his first sortie to the Reich that summer: 'So bloody different. It made one feel we'd simply been playing at the game up until now. Indeed, compared to this, all those previous efforts over Occupied Europe seemed like little picnics, events you looked back upon with something akin to pleasure (if you can equate dropping bombs with that word).'[41]

The severe threat that the Germans continued to pose was described by Richard Smith, a navigator with 7 Squadron who took part in the raid on Stuttgart on 28 July. With the Lancaster heading towards the target, he wrote,

> the bomb aimer was lying prone over his bombsight and also pushing out handfuls of Window. Window was carried in small packets and stacked by the bomb aimer's position over the lower escape hatch. Suddenly there

was an explosion on the starboard side. Also a tremendous racket as the
gunners fired their eight Browning machine guns causing empty .303
cartridges to cascade from the mid-upper turret and rattle against the inside
of the fuselage. Also there was a lot of noise over the intercom as the
gunners called for evasive action. The aircraft dived violently to starboard
and I watched the navigator's altimeter record a loss of 4000 feet. The
aircraft filled with smoke and the captain gave the order to abandon.

As one of the engines burst into flames, Smith went for his parachute
and made for the escape exit at the front, but he found the hatch was
blocked by piles of Window parcels. 'The bomb aimer was desperately
flinging the parcels out of the way and they were bursting open as he
flung them. Suddenly the hatch came open and a blast of freezing air
blew through the opening carrying with it masses of strips of tin foil. I
was standing in a direct line with the blast and was covered with the
stuff.' But by now the skipper had regained control of the aircraft, and
the engineer had put out the fire in the inner starboard Merlin with the
Graviner system. Flying straight and level, he cancelled the order to abandon the plane. Continuing towards the target would have been useless,
however, because the bomb doors would not open, the gun turrets could
not be operated and many of the navigational aids were unserviceable.
Using only the main compass and dead reckoning, Smith gave a course
to take the Lancaster over northern France. Once the English Channel
was reached, the bombs were jettisoned. The Lancaster then limped over
the English coast. Moments later, the wireless operator got through to
the controller at RAF Manston in Kent. 'Dawn was breaking and we
could see we were above a sheet of unbroken cloud. I can remember the
controller's words, "All right lads I will find you a home."' He gave a
course for Bradwell in Essex, on the other side of the Thames estuary.
'The cloud began to break up and the north-coast of the estuary came
into sight. There ahead was an airfield and they were giving us a welcome
green light . . . The pilot made a rather heavy but safe landing. The screech
of the tyres as we touched down was the most beautiful sound we had
ever heard.'[42] Yet again the Lancaster had proved its toughness. It was this
resilience that so often was a source of reassurance to crews during their
dark nights over Germany.

As he prepared to resume his full offensive against Germany, Harris
now had at his disposal a bomber force of unprecedented size. The rise
in factory output, the drastic fall in losses over France compared to Berlin,
and the efficiency of the aircrew training scheme across the empire had
all combined to give him resources far beyond anything he had enjoyed

in early 1944. By October he had a front-line operational force of 1,400 heavy bombers available on a daily basis. Altogether, there were now 51 Lancaster squadrons in service, providing a total of 1,200 planes. Bomber Command itself was now an enormous organization, employing at its peak 230,000 people in aircrews, ground crews, ancillary staff, training and security. The civil-engineering requirements alone of building the bomber stations with 2,000-yard runways were colossal. 'Did you know that one of your bomber aerodromes involved 300,000 yards of concrete for runways, perimeter track and dispersal points,' Christopher Courtney, the Air Member for Supply and Organisation, said rather plaintively to Harris in March 1942.[43] During the war the government spent over £200 million on hard surfacing for the airfields, almost all of it to meet the needs of the heavy bombers. A workforce of 60,000 men was annually needed during the mid-war years just for this task. Another indicator of the size of Bomber Command was the vast petrol supply network to keep the heavy bombers flying. In Lincolnshire, for instance, the tankers fuelling the bombers filled up at the Stow Park Fuel Distribution Depot, which held 8,000 tons in underground storage. In turn, Stow Park was supplied by rail from the Misterton Depot in Nottinghamshire, which had a capacity of 80,000 tons and was kept replenished by a pipeline from the Stanlow refinery in Cheshire.[44]

The question in the autumn of 1944 was how the gargantuan weapon of Bomber Command should be used. For Harris, the answer was simple. He wanted nothing less than a return to mass area bombing, laying waste to as much of urban Germany as possible. Anything apart from factories and residential districts he regarded as 'panacea targets', while precision bombing was dismissed as 'impracticable' for a host of reasons, including the weather, the difficulties of flying at night and the strength of German defences.[45] This was Harris at his most blinkered, retreating into his siege mentality without the influence of Eisenhower and Tedder. The co-operative leader of the summer had been replaced by the stubborn chief of the disastrous spring campaign. Never overburdened by doubt, Harris adhered to his view that area attacks were the only route to victory. 'On the one side I saw certainty of success, and on the other side many chances of failure,' he wrote.[46] There was something almost jealous about the possessive way he guarded his commitment to the area-bombing strategy, voicing his protests at any attempt to stop 'the offensive for which we had worked for five years'.[47] Once more, this narrow stance did a disservice to the Lancaster and its crews. In his rigid attachment to his own creed, he appeared willing to ignore not only the lessons of the

French campaign, which had confounded his predictions of inaccuracy, but also the increasing weakness of the Third Reich, now crumbling in the wake of defeats on every front. To Harris, the technical improvements over the last year in Lancaster operations, like the SABS, the Tallboy bomb, better markers and the GH navigational device, were reasons why area bombing should be more effective, not a justification for a change in strategy.

Harris's continued belief in such bombing was illustrated by a number of devastating urban raids he dispatched in August 1944, such as the attack by 189 Lancasters on medieval Königsberg in East Prussia on the night of 29–30 August, when 134,000 people were 'dehoused' by the weight of 480 tons of bombs dropped on the centre of the city. The German-Jewish author Michael Wieck, a native of the city, later wrote that 'the people of Königsberg will never expunge these nights of terror from their memory'.[48] Little more than a week earlier, 217 Lancasters had bombarded the port of Bremen. Ils Mar Garthaus, a ballet dancer with the Bremen company, called this raid 'a total disaster for the city'. In her memoir of life in Germany at this time, she left this memorable description of the bombs falling near her flat:

> A stream of enemy bombers made their way through a barricade of search-lights raking the sky, causing the ground to tremble with the sound of their passage. Flak bursts of red, yellow and white travelled up shafts of light hitting their target and moving beyond . . . Then a mine came down close by and every one of us made for the door, where another mine, or the pressure of it rather, swept us down the stairway. Stumbling down ahead of us were the two French girls who helped in the kitchen in the restaurant below. 'Cheri, Cheri!' Their screams mingled with the spine-chilling whistle of the falling bombs, as stark naked they ran after their lovers, nightly visitors from a labour camp in the vicinity. When it was all over but for the candelabra flares hanging above the chaos I felt I had survived a game of Russian roulette.'[49]

The Air Staff had once been almost as enthusiastic as Harris about area bombing. Back in 1941 Portal and Sinclair had been the loudest advocates of such a strategy. But all that had changed by the autumn of 1944. No longer did the doctrine of saturation attacks hold sway. Three factors had led to this change in outlook. One was the failure of the Berlin campaign. Another was the success of Operation Overlord. But third, and most important, was the dramatic impact of the American daylight offensive against German oil supplies, which General Spaatz had conducted intermittently from April. Even with the heavy distractions of D–Day, the US bombing of oil refineries, pipelines and storage facilities was badly disrupting the German war machine. As the aviation historian Dr Alfred Price noted: 'During the spring and summer of 1944 German production of oil plummeted and, by design, the plants that were hardest hit were those producing aviation fuel. Compared with an output of 175,000 tons of aviation fuel per month in April 1944, before the campaign began, they turned out 35,000 tons in July, 16,000 tons in August and a mere 7,000 tons in September.'[50] Shortages of high-octane fuel badly undermined the Luftwaffe's training programme for fighter pilots, who had to undergo much of their instruction in simulators and thereby went into the air lacking any real experience. The introduction of the revolutionary jet fighters, the rocket-propelled Me 163 and the more effective twin-engined Me 262, was also disrupted by dwindling oil stocks. British intelligence from the Enigma code-breakers at Bletchley Park, Buckinghamshire, further confirmed how decisive the attacks on oil installations had been.

Impressed by the results achieved by the Americans, the Air Staff began to see that oil could be a central theme of the bomber offensive. An Anglo-American oil targets committee, made up of representatives of the two air forces, had been established in July, and during August Syd Bufton, the Air Ministry's Director of Bombing Operations, pushed for oil targets to be made 'the over-riding priority' of the Allied offensive. 'Shortage of fuel rather than a shortage of aircraft or aircrews promises to be the immediate factor in GAF (German Air Force) operations,' declared a paper written by Bufton and his US counterpart, Air Vice Marshal D. Colyer. In this document they were particularly critical of the attack on Bremen, claiming it had been a 'misdirection of effort'.[51] Portal was won over by their arguments. On 9 September, travelling aboard the *Queen Mary* to the Allies' Conference in Quebec, he drew up a report which stated: 'It has been abundantly clear over the past few months that the enemy is faced with an increasingly critical situation in regard to his oil supplies. To exploit his difficulties, it is essential that the attack on his resources be pressed home at maximum intensity and on the widest scale possible. Any relaxation in the tempo of our attacks against oil installations will provide opportunity for rehabilitation and dispersal.'[52] The Quebec summit backed Portal's approach, with the result that on 25 September Norman Bottomley, Deputy Chief of the Air Staff, issued a directive to Harris confirming that the 'first priority' of the renewed bomber offensive should be the oil campaign. The 'second priority' was the German rail and waterborne transport system, including canals, motor production plants and depots. Flushed with the success of his Transportation Plan in France, Tedder regretted that communications had not been named as the central objective of Allied bombing, but Portal warned him that 'it would be dangerous to apply wholesale to Germany the lessons of France'.[53] Nevertheless, Germany's transport infrastructure was remorselessly attacked over the coming winter, especially by the Americans. The effect on the Reich was all the more damaging because the dispersal of production meant that German industry was heavily dependent on transport links.

The real hostility to Bottomley's directive came from Harris, who claimed that the concentration on oil would allow Germany to rebuild her industry and armed forces. 'We should now get on and knock Germany finally flat. For the first time, we have the force to do it. Opportunities do not last forever and this one is slipping,' he told Churchill on 30 September.[54] He showed what he thought of the oil plan in his actions as much as his words. During the summer, Bomber Command had occasionally lent support to the American offensive against oil plants. In fact, between July and September, 11 per cent of its sorties had been aimed at oil targets, but in October this figure fell to just 6 per cent. For the remainder of the year, only 14 per cent of bomber missions went to oil installations, 58 per cent to cities.[55] Area bombing had returned with a vengeance. In the last three months of 1944, 14,254 sorties were mounted against the major industrial centres like Essen, Düsseldorf and Cologne, and 60,830 tons of bombs were dropped.

Ian Dunlop, a navigator with 635 Squadron, gave this description of Cologne at the height of a raid by 435 Lancasters, on the night of 30–31 October. 'It was an absolutely staggering sight. The only thing you could see was the river running through it. The rest was simply fire. Navigators operated behind a curtain. Having been so careful not to let any light in, I drew the curtain back and it was like daylight outside, with searchlights, lights from flares, fighter flares, light from fires. It was absolutely incredible. There was no point in having a curtain there at all.'[56] In the space of just twenty-four hours over 14–15 October, Duisburg west of Essen received a greater weight of bombs than fell on London during the entire war up to that time. Rear gunner Frank Broome of 626 Squadron took part in that raid and gave this account: 'We could hear the Master Bomber on the VHF quite clearly, "Calling Main Force – bomb the centre of the red TIs." The instruction was repeated throughout the attack. The Master Bomber's voice seemed very calm and unruffled. You would have thought he was sitting in a deck-chair at the seaside, perhaps calling to the newspaper boy or ice-cream vendor. Instead he was flying a Lancaster round and round a heavily defended target at 8000 feet or less.' Broome's Lancaster completed its run and the bomb load was released. 'I didn't see the cookie but I saw the incendiaries, blowing away behind and beneath us. They looked just like a gigantic box of matches being opened upside down in a gale.'[57]

The excitement and fear that a Lancaster raid could generate at this time were captured in the diary of John Byrne, a young wireless operator from Liverpool who was filled with hatred for Germany and littered his entries with references to 'the filthy Hun'. On 4 November his plane was part of a force of 336 Lancasters that attacked Bochum east of Essen in the dusk:

> The bomb aimer saw one of our kites fall in flames and hit near the target area. From 1930 to 1955 we were all scared to death. The target was a blazing inferno. More than one hundred searchlight beams penetrated the moonlit skies to cone our bombers. Flak was heavy and it seemed an absolute impossibility to get through without incident. The bomb aimer was giving his instructions to the Skipper. 'Right – steady.' The mid upper gunner was reporting other aircraft flying above us. I incidentally counted about 50 bombers clearly visible in the moonlight about 1000 feet above weaving to evade flak and fighters and searchlight beams. We all waited for 'bombs gone' but to our dismay got 'hang-up'. God. We would have to go in again. I couldn't help thinking – but no! – after about five minutes the bombardier reported 'bombs away OK'. So I turned in the astro-dome to look at the target. Red TIs were going down. Smoke was thick and a thousand coloured and yellow lights marked the place where our beautiful bombs had fallen. The target was left well and truly pranged.[58]

Allied air superiority meant that the losses over Germany in these autumn raids were far lower than earlier in the year. In October, for example, just 0.8 per cent of the bombers sent to German targets were shot down. This was not to say that the Lancaster crews were not still in significant danger as they flew over the Reich. The reckless courage of the Luftwaffe's dwindling number of pilots was astonishing, while Germany still had 50,000 heavy and light anti-aircraft guns. On a trip to the Ruhr in September, Harry Yates's Lancaster *R-Roger* came under severe anti-aircraft fire just as it left the target:

> A tremendous explosion ripped at the air in front of me The entire nose section of the Lancaster disappeared, taking with it the front gun turret . . . Then the Perspex windscreen disintegrated before my eyes into a thousand dancing fragments of silver. They were organised on the gale and

flung full in my face. Everything disintegrated into chaos. I was in darkness. My senses were disorientated by shock and pain – most of that from
what felt like dozens of blades slicing into my eyes. A roaring wall of icy
air pressed so hard against my face that I was fighting to draw breath.

By now the Lancaster was plunging through the sky. Yates somehow
had to bring it back under control. He knew he had to find the steering column. 'I groped forward, locked my hands on it and pulled. The
effort brought me to my normal consciousness and razor-sharpened the
pain. But through the seat of my pants I could feel R-Roger pulling out.
She appeared to respond well. As the airspeed moderated I tried to open
my eyes. It was an unequal struggle against the gale but there was light
at the end of the darkness.' Yates then had his wounds tended by his engineer, who told him that the Lancaster had suffered little damage beyond
the nose section. Slowly his eyes began to function again. He took the
Lancaster down to 5,000 feet so the cold was more endurable, but the
loss of height made little difference. 'Airspeed was 200 mph, still a hell
of a blast through the nose and windscreen apertures. I couldn't stop my
teeth chattering. My fingers had lost all feeling.' Yates lost height again,
crossing Holland at just 500 feet. Fortunately *R-Roger* was not picked up
by any of the anti-aircraft guns.

On reaching Cambridgeshire, the Lancaster was given priority for landing by flying control at its base of Mepal. Yates was now filled with
concern. Not only could he barely see the instrument panel, but he
wondered how the noseless Lancaster would handle at low speed. 'I need
not have worried. This was the indomitable R-Roger bringing us home.
She put up with my split-arse circuit (flying parlance for no circuit at
all) and she remained a lady while Tubby called out the altitude and held
the throttle closed and we waited, finally, for the wheels to touch.'[59] Yates
had to undergo several agonizing operations to remove the splinters from
his eyes but made a full recovery and was back with his squadron before
the end of October.

Lancaster crews also had to deal with the new menace of the Me 262.
The jet fighter, capable of a maximum speed of 559 mph, was not available in anything like the numbers the Reich High Command had hoped,
partly because of production difficulties with the turbojet and partly
because Hitler had interrupted the plane's development by his insistence
it should have a bombing capability, something that was to prove impossible. Moreover, when the Me 262 did enter service, its operations were
restricted by the chronic fuel shortages. At the turn of the year petrol
was so precious that the jet fighters had to be towed out to the runways,

and because no other method of haulage was available, cows had to do the job. Even so, its arrival marked a leap forward in military technology, spelling doom in the long term for piston-engined aircraft. For those unlucky enough to encounter an Me 262 in action, it could be a traumatic experience. Bill Hough of 582 Squadron was piloting his Lancaster over Belgium towards the target of the town of Heimbach when one of the gunners yelled over the intercom the instruction to corkscrew starboard as a pair of Me 262s attacked.

> His words were lost in an almighty clatter and bang, the second aircraft firing its four cannon from a range of about 500 yards, the rear gunner firing back and hits being registered on our port wings and engines. The first aircraft went underneath us and the second flew over the top at a tremendous speed . . . Black smoke, presumably from the fuel tanks, poured from the wing and the port outer was quickly enveloped in flames. Fire extinguishers were operated up front and we went through a shallow dive but the fire only seemed to intensify, although the aircraft was still being held steady.[60]

The mid-upper gunner had been killed by the Me 262's shells, but the rest of the crew managed to bail out and, after being picked up by American troops, made it back to England.

But the Me 262 was not invincible against the Lancaster. It is another tribute to the agility of the Avro machine that it could emerge victorious from a duel with the German jet fighter, as F. W. Walker of 428 Squadron recalled:

> On 4th November we were flying an op against Bochum, an oil target, when an ME262 was spotted by the wireless operator, off to one side and above at a range of 1200 yards. It looked like a blot trailing vapour and according to our rear gunner, Ben Rakus, was moving faster than anything he had ever seen. Ben gave me the word to corkscrew, and the jet shot over to our other side before closing in to 500 yards. We then took further evasive action, throwing the aircraft about, while Ben went to work with his guns, hitting the jet alongside the fuselage and wings, giving it another burst as it peeled over and dived towards the ground, where several bombers saw it explode. This was the first time a heavy bomber shot down one of these jets, so they were vulnerable.[61]

Yet the fact that the Lancaster was confronting the Me 262 at all was another indirect sign of the Allies' growing dominance of the air. For the jet operated only during the day, having never been conceived as a night fighter and possessing far too much speed to creep up on a bomber. Mass daylight sorties over the Reich had been unthinkable since 1940 and, as

Harris never tired of saying, his entire force had been built and trained for night operations. But the decline of the Luftwaffe fighter force, so badly mauled by the Americans, gave the freedom to operate by day without disproportionate risks. During October, Bomber Command flew no fewer than 4,500 daylight sorties and the loss rate was only 1 per cent, only marginally higher than the overall rate of attrition. Some Lancaster aircrews had mixed feelings about flying over Germany by day, the greater vision and ease of navigation balanced by the sense of exposure and vulnerability. In particular, the sight of hundreds of other Lancasters in the bomber stream could accentuate the fear of collisions, as navigator Ian Dunlop recalled: 'I preferred operating at night. In daylight, you're out in a stream of aircraft, constantly jockeying about to try to get out of people's way to avoid a mid-air collision. As soon as it gets dark and you cannot see another aeroplane you settle down and fly straight. You feel as if you're the only one there. I liked that much better.'[62]

But Dunlop's view was a minority one. Most airmen were relieved at a daylight raid, even if the concentration of bombers over the target could seem hazardous. 'Daylight raids were better,' said Jack Thornton of 7 Squadron. 'They were not anything like as fearsome as night raids. You could see everyone around you. The only snag was that at night you were spread out more. Going over the target in daylight, everyone congregated together and nobody wanted to be on the outside because of the fighters coming in.'[63] An interesting summary of the benefits, and some of the disadvantages, of daylight bombing was provided by engineer Norman Ashton of 103 Squadron:

> Everything seemed so easy in the broad light of day; no pre-flight checks with feeble-rayed torch, no stumbling about the aircraft in pitch darkness, no grim lonely stooges to and from the target, no searchlights probing the sky like a dentist searching for a bad tooth, and no struggling to fight off the effects of fatigue during the early morning hours . . . Even the flak over the target area seemed quite friendly, for the grey-black puffs of smoke were ridiculous when compared with the angry flashes to which I had been accustomed.

But there were other aspects of night flying that Ashton missed, such as 'the glowing stubs and flaming exhausts of the Merlins; there was always something exciting and comforting about those outward signs of hidden power.' He also recognized that the cover of night had lulled him into a false sense of security about the distance from fighters and other bombers. On a daylight raid against Cologne, when his pilot performed a 'dog-leg' manoeuvre over the target after arriving too early and needing to lose some time, Ashton was shocked to be confronted by the main force as his Lancaster turned. 'It was an appalling sight. Seven or eight hundred aircraft bore down on us like a vast swarm of bees; the confounded things were all over the place and we must have bagged a record number of near misses before finally straightening out.' Yet at night his skipper had executed just such a turn without causing such a scare. 'We had known full well that the area was infested with aircraft but "out-of-sight" was blissfully "out-of-mind" and phenomenal avoidances have been few and far between. It seemed queer that one had to do a daylight operation before one could fully appreciate the enormous risks of a night operation.'[64]

The RAF's growing ascendancy in the air, far from uniting commanders, was the cause for greater friction, as the exasperation of the Air Staff deepened over Harris's refusal to put the weight of his vast force behind the September directive. But Harris was unrepentant, continuing to maintain that area bombing was the most effective policy. Having claimed that Bomber Command had 'virtually destroyed 45 out of the leading sixty German cities', he said he wanted to keep up a rate of devastating two and a half cities a month. 'There are not many industrial centres of population now left intact. Are we going to abandon this vast task, which the Germans themselves have long admitted to be their worst headache, just as it nears completion?' he asked Portal on 1 November 1944.[65] The problem was that Portal did not believe Harris's strategy would bring about a swift completion of the war. 'At the risk of your dubbing me another "panacea merchant",' he replied on 5 November, 'I believe that that offensive against oil gives us by far the best hope of victory in the next few months.'[66] Harris responded the next day, denying that he had failed to recognize 'the urgency and effectiveness of the oil plan', though he rather contradicted this point by casting doubt on the intelligence which had formed the basis of the plan. In addition, just as he had initially done in reaction to Tedder's Transportation Plan, he downplayed the effectiveness of his heavy bombers and exaggerated their operational difficulties. Among the problems he raised were prevailing weather conditions, clarity of orders and physical geography: 'the oil targets are small and usually outlying,' he complained.[67] With excessive forbearance, Portal tried plaintively to reason with his self-willed bomber chief in a further letter of 12 November:

> You refer to a plan for the destruction of the sixty leading German cities and to your efforts to keep up with, and even to exceed your average of two and a half cities devastated each month. I know that you have long

felt such a plan to be the most effective way of bringing about the collapse of Germany. Knowing this, I have, I must confess, at times wondered whether the magnetism of the remaining German cities has not in the past tended as much to deflect our bombers from their primary objectives as the tactical and weather difficulties which you described so fully . . . If I knew you to be as whole-hearted in the attack of oil as in the past you have been in the matter of attacking cities I would have little to worry about.[68]

Not all Harris's loudly expressed anxieties about oil raids were specious. There were genuine problems with reconnaissance, the worsening weather at the depths of winter and the risk of wasting bombs on plants that had already been put out of action. But to Portal and the Air Staff, such difficulties were all the more reason to intensify the campaign, not give it up. Destruction had to be maximized to prevent the Germans rebuilding their supply lines. For a few weeks Harris appeared to accept Portal's request and the weight of bombs dropped on the German oil industry increased significantly, up from 3,653 tons in October to 13,030 tons in November. Overall, the proportion of attacks on oil installations rose from 6 per cent to 24.6 per cent. But then, in December, Harris slid back into his old ways, becoming more recalcitrant than ever. The last months of war would become the backdrop for the most bitter of all quarrels between Harris and Portal.

16

'The *Tirpitz* was doomed'

⬤━ ～

IN JUNE 1944 Harris had written to Portal: 'Personally I think it is important that we should investigate every method of boosting the Lancaster as quickly as possible, every source of 12,000 pound bombs and most vital of all, every possibility of expediting the fitting of heavier armament to our bombers.'[1] The concern about the Lancaster's defences was a perennial theme of Harris's command, and his demand for heavier armament led to more friction with the bureaucracy of the Air Ministry. His annoyance was not without some justification, for the officials showed a surprising lack of initiative on this question. It had taken Avro barely six months to move from the Manchester to the Lancaster prototype, yet, despite the repeated complaints from Harris, the .303 Browning remained the standard Lancaster weapon throughout the war, even after daylight operations had resumed in mid-1944. In mitigation, the officials recognized the gun's weakness but argued that the capacity of the turret manufacturers was stretched to the limit in the peak years of the war, so the sudden introduction of major modifications would have led to delays on the production line, a similar argument to the one used to reject a switch from the Halifax to the Lancaster. They further pointed out that it was not just a simple matter of changing the calibre of the guns. A different design of turret could also affect the Lancaster's weight and centre of gravity, with the result that further changes would be needed to the plane's airframe.

Even in 1942, during the aircraft's first full year of service, the Air Staff had expressed the need to introduce a 0.5-inch gun turret 'into the Lancaster as soon as possible'.[2] The identification of inadequacy in the .303 led to a full-scale conference at the Air Ministry in Whitehall on 12 January 1943, chaired by Air Vice Marshal Ralph Sorley, the Assistant Chief of the Air Staff in charge of technical requirements. Opening the meeting, Sorley said that the ideal armament for the Lancaster would be two 20-mm guns in the mid-upper turret, two 0.5-inch guns in the tail and two .303 Brownings in the nose. There was general consensus in favour of this, except from Sir Melvill Jones, the distinguished Cambridge professor of aeronautical engineering and the Air Ministry's expert on air gunnery. Professor Jones 'expressed some doubt whether the 20mm was justified unless the 0.5 could not be expected to penetrate the armour of enemy fighters. In his opinion, the lightest calibre capable of penetrating enemy fighter armour should be chosen for its advantages in weight and duration of fire.' But Sorley countered that the 20-mm gun had 'far greater damaging power' and in any case, the Germans were bound to improve their fighter armour over the coming years. Sorley concluded the meeting by reiterating that 'a clear decision' was needed immediately on introducing the new 20-mm mid-upper turret and 0.5-inch tail guns. 'He wanted to be sure that everyone present was in complete agreement before that decision was taken so that there would be no obstruction at a later date to its early implementation.' He further stressed that 'the highest priority should be given to the Lancaster programme and every effort should be made to introduce the mid-upper and redesigned tail turrets in a year's time. If this programme fails or is unduly delayed the armament of the Lancaster would be obsolete and this would have serious repercussions.'[3]

Those were fine words but they proved difficult to translate into reality. In fact the 20-mm gun turret never appeared on any operational Lancaster during the war. The first to use it was the Avro Lincoln, as the Mark IV Lancaster was officially redesignated in August 1944 because of the major changes in its structure compared to the previous three Lancaster types. One of those changes was a strengthened undercarriage to cope with the new heavyweight turret. But VE Day had long passed before the Lincoln arrived in the squadrons. The Lincoln also had two 0.5-inch Browning heavy machine guns in its rear turret and in this respect the plane was not such a radical advance on its predecessor, for 0.5-inch guns had already been installed on some Lancasters before May 1945. The saga of their introduction was a tortuous one. As the months passed by in 1943, there was little sign that the Air Ministry would meet Sorley's deadline of introducing a redesigned rear turret within a year. Harris had long been certain that the Air Ministry's approach would not yield results quickly enough. As he asked Sir Wilfrid Freeman: 'Will you really start a riot on this particular subject because, try as I may, I can get no signs of life out of the Air Ministry and in the present organisation of the armament side, I cannot even find anybody to shout at.'[4] With typical contempt for officialdom, Harris decided to embark on his own quasi-freelance operation for gun-turret production, based within Bomber Command. This was done through his close relationship with the small Gainsborough firm of

Rose Brothers, which had a wide array of manufacturing experience ranging from tobacco-packaging machinery to motor cars. The head of the company, Alfred Rose, had won an enviable reputation for his willingness to accept production orders no matter how difficult they were to execute, since he cared more about high standards of craftsmanship than making a profit. It was when he was head of No. 5 Group in 1940 that Harris first approached Alfred Rose, seeking his assistance in creating improved mountings for the guns of the Hampden bomber. In his memoirs, Harris described how his frustration with the Air Ministry forced him to go down this avenue. 'I had not served 25 years without knowing that it is quite impossible to get anything drastic done through the proper channels within a reasonable time.'[5] Along with one of his senior station commanders, Edward Rice, later the head of No. 1 Group, Harris headed into the Lincolnshire countryside to pay a visit to Rose. It was, said Harris, a 'typically English family firm' which could 'do anything without a fuss and with a comparatively minute staff in the design and drawing office'.[6]

Rose had done an excellent job on the Hampden mountings, so when Harris was becoming exasperated with the slow progress on the 0.5-inch guns, he and Rice again turned to Rose and the Gainsborough firm. As in 1940, the request was unofficial, but Harris believed that he could force the Air Ministry into giving an order to the Rose company if its prototype 0.5-inch gun turret were of an acceptable standard. His prediction was correct. When the Ministry of Aircraft Production first heard about the project in early 1943 it offered to supply draughtsmen, but Alfred Rose, in his spirit of independence, turned down that overture, relying instead on the technical advice of Air Vice Marshal Edward Rice. He did, however, accept help with raw materials. Then in June 1943, at another major planning conference at the Air Ministry, Harris pressed the case for the new Rose-Rice turret, which featured two 0.5-inch Brownings and a much wider field of view for the gunner. Having told colleagues with his usual forthrightness that 'existing turrets were useless for night operations', he stated that 'the best hope of achieving the desired result in the near future was the Rose turret and asked for an assurance that all possible assistance was being given to the designer. The turret, which had the gunner in front of the guns, showed promise of meeting Bomber Command requirements admirably.'[7] Sorley pledged that there would be no obstruction placed in the way of Alfred Rose, but he stressed 'it would be two or three months before the turret would be ready for firing trials. If successful, it would then have to go for official trials, including air firing tests. It was unlikely to be in production, therefore, for about nine to twelve months.'[8]

But, even after giving qualified backing to the Rose-Rice turret, the Air Ministry and MAP felt that they could not rely solely on the efforts of a small Lincolnshire firm. The manufacturers Nash and Thomson, which produced the current armament for the Lancaster, were therefore encouraged to continue with the development of their own 0.5-inch turret, the FN82. Indeed, the Air Staff estimated that the FN82 would end up in service more quickly than the Rose version. In an optimistic report of July 1943, Sorley told Evill that all Lancaster production from Castle Bromwich could incorporate the FN82 by May 1944, followed by Austin and Vickers in July, Armstrong Whitworth in October, and then a gradual changeover could be made at Avro. 'We can hope to have sufficient turrets available to equip total Lancaster production by March 1945,' he declared.[9] In addition to the FN82, there was another, more intriguing, rear turret being developed at this time by Nash and Thomson. At the Telecommunications Research Establishment, a team headed by the Cambridge physicist Philip Dee had been working since early 1943 on a blind-firing system code-named Village Inn, in which a radar device installed in the rear turret could guide the four .303 guns in the direction of an enemy fighter. Village Inn used some of the same technology as the Monica system, which had given Lancaster crews early warning of an aircraft approaching from the rear. The disadvantage of Monica was that the German pilots could pick up the signal. Thereby it almost became a tracking device for the Luftwaffe and in mid-1944 it was withdrawn from service. But Village Inn, also known more technically as 'Automatic Gun Laying Turret' (AGLT), was a great advance on this, exploiting radar for an offensive purpose by enabling the gunner to shoot accurately even if he could not see the enemy in total darkness.

In the AGLT, or Village Inn, system, a radar scanner was fitted in a small dome just below the rear turret gunsight. This scanner fed signals via a transmitter in the navigator's compartment onto a cathode-ray tube beside the gunner. In turn, the image from the tube was then projected onto his gunsight. If a German fighter came near, it would appear as a blip on the screen and then as a green spot on his sight. All the rear gunner had to do, therefore, was rotate his guns until the spot was right in the centre of his sight. Then he knew the enemy plane was in range and he would open fire. One obvious problem was the risk of shooting down another Lancaster rather than a Luftwaffe fighter. But that obstacle was overcome by the simple measure of installing in the nose of every

Lancaster a pair of infrared lamps which sent out a morse-code signal to indicate that the plane was friendly.

Initial tests on Village Inn during 1943 were promising. According to a report by the Bomber Development Unit, the system 'appears able to pick up another aircraft at about 1400 yards range and to hold that aircraft until it is within 150 yards. The radar automatic ranging device appears most satisfactory.'[10] The Ministry of Aircraft Production was so impressed that it placed an initial order for no fewer than 3,000 AGLT sets. But this was never a realistic programme. The system's technology was so sophisticated that serious difficulties were found in its service-ability when it was used on an experimental basis by 460 Squadron in the summer of 1944. The infrared lamps proved unreliable, which meant, in Harris's words, that gunners 'were loath to fire blind at what they thought might be friendly aircraft'.[11] Two improved versions of AGLT were developed but by the end of the war they had only been installed on four squadrons. Similar problems were encountered on an even bigger scale with the two 0.5-inch gun programmes. Harris kept up the pressure for the Rose turret during the autumn of 1943, telling Evill that he was 'convinced we should go into production with it at once. I do not even think this is a gamble as I am confident of Rose's ability to make a good job of it'. But, more widely, Harris was concerned at the 'unsatisfactory state armament development in the Air Force', which he now blamed on the lack of a director in the Air Ministry with sole responsibility for pursuing the weapons programmes.[12] Air Commodore A. R. Wardle of the Directorate of Operational Requirements attempted both to excuse the present and provide reassurance for the future. What 'must be borne in mind', he wrote, 'is the present saturation in the aircraft and armament industries to meet the very heavy commitments already placed on them by the heavy bomber re-armament programme. Further work could only be undertaken at the expense of existing modifications.' The armament of the Lancaster IV, soon to be called the Lincoln, was proceeding satisfactorily, he promised, though its weight was 'very considerable and a year ago was thought to be the maximum which the Lancaster would ever be capable of carrying'.[13] But the Lincoln, which was not due off the production line until spring of 1945, was not the present concern of Bomber Command.

The continuing delays in the two 0.5-inch gun programmes through early 1944 drove Harris to fury. 'I confess that I do not know what the programme is and I am no longer interested in programmes,' he told Evill in July 1944. 'The programmes we have had in the past bore no relation whatsoever to reality and I believe nothing until the stuff is delivered on the doorstep. We are in for a first-class catastrophe in both morale and in keeping up to date in the war unless something drastic is done and done at once with the turret and armament business. The present organisation is achieving nothing and by the time we get the .5 guns they will be so hopelessly out of date as to be of little improvement for the purpose in view.' What was needed, he said, was 'a large clear-out of the incompetents and deadheads who have been strangling armament development and production ever since the dim ages, many of them having been there through the entire period'.[14] It was true that the FN82 schedule had become hopelessly bogged down due to limited production capacity and frequent changes in design, as attempts were made to incorporate new types of belt feeds and sights. But the Rose turret had not progressed as smoothly as Harris had hoped. In certain early firing trials, the turret shook violently, which Harris confessed to Portal was due to 'poor workmanship in regard to tolerances in the base ring'.[15]

Eventually the teething problems were resolved, and in June 1944 the Air Staff ordered that the Rose turret go into production, with orders placed for 600. Once the first of them emerged hand-made from the Gainsborough works, Harris was exultant at what he saw as a personal triumph over Whitehall bureaucracy. In a letter to Evill in August 1944, he recalled the previous discussions at the Air Ministry on the subject of the 0.5-inch guns. At one such meeting, he wrote, 'of the sixty present about 99 per cent appeared to be there for the sole purpose of asserting that there were no additional resources and that nothing whatsoever could be done to speed matters up. In complete despair after this meeting, I went away and found unoccupied resources for the manufacture of our own .5 turret which is now arriving at a rate which will shortly be one a day, and in the meantime the Air Ministry and Ministry of Aircraft Production programme has, as usual, fallen flat on its back.'[16]

It was a truth that the air establishment could not deny. The FN82 was delayed so much that the first one was not even forecast to come off the production line until January 1945. Harris may have been wrong on bombing strategy, but he had shown a greater grasp of the technical and production realities than many of the Whitehall officials. 'The original forecast of one year from the word go to commencement of production was unduly optimistic,' wrote Sorley to Portal in July 1944. 'The magnitude of the task of re-arming the whole of our rapidly expanding heavy bomber force was underestimated and the available design capacity in the turret industry was inadequate to meet these great new commitments in addition to other essential current work such as the modification of existing turrets to improve the gunner's view and the introduction of AGLT.'[17] Rather unconvincingly, Sorley also tried to pin some of the blame on Harris for his demands for turret redesigns to improve the gunner's view. The serious delays in re-equipping the Lancaster led to talk of desperate interim measures, for the Rose programme was not enough to fill the gap. At one stage, on the suggestion of his American friend Bob Lovett, Harris took up the idea of using in the Lancaster surplus 0.5-inch gun turrets intended for the Boeing Liberator. But tests carried out in Northern Ireland showed that the Lancaster would need major changes to its hydraulic and electricity systems, as well as the fuselage, before it could accommodate the Liberator turrets. 'The job is impossible without a great deal of modification to the aircraft,' Harris told Portal. 'Attempts to install it may lead to delays in the Lancaster programme so it appears impracticable and must be dropped. Our own turret programme seems to be falling further and further behind.'[18]

The autumn of 1944 had arrived and still little progress had been made. 'While the Air Ministry and MAP have consistently adopted a non possumus attitude to our repeated requests for expedition in the production of .5 armament,' Harris told Sorley in October, 'this Command, of its own resources, has had designed, produced and put into action the thoroughly satisfactory Rice-Rose .5 tail turret. The whole matter has reached a first-class scandal and I have now to request an investigation for the purpose of bringing to book those who have contributed to this deplorable state of affairs.'[19] A few days later he complained to Portal about 'the lack of drive' in MAP and the absence of 'goodwill' towards Rose. 'The incompetents who have failed us all along on this turret programme can still sleep securely in their appointments.'[20] For Harris there were two other benefits of the Rose-Rice turret, apart from its higher calibre guns. First the gunner had a better all-round view, and second he could escape more easily in an emergency. Instead of having to pick up his parachute from the fuselage, rotate the turret and then open the doors at the back, as on standard Lancasters, all he had to do was open a Perspex panel at the front, lean forward and roll out, since he had enough space to wear his parachute. But for the Air Staff, the serious drawback of the Rose-Rice turret was the hand-made method used in its manufacture. Harris might have described the turrets as 'beautifully designed'[21] but the fact was that they could not be produced quickly enough nor were their parts interchangeable. The Air Ministry warned that 'if mass production of the Rose turret were to be achieved, it would be necessary for completely new drawings to be produced and the job to be properly tooled up'. This process, it was estimated, could take another nine months.[22] Furthermore, the Rose-Rice turrets were not nearly as reliable as Harris claimed. One study by Ministry researchers showed that 60 per cent of them had suffered stoppages to their guns in action, compared to 23 per cent for the standard .303 Brownings. On the other hand, the study also revealed that Lancasters fitted with the Rose-Rice turret were half as likely as standard Lancasters to be attacked by fighters. 'This may be accounted by the increased field of view from the turret which would assist evasion from attacks,' concluded the report, thereby upholding one of Harris's key arguments.[23]

In November 1944, at yet another conference to discuss heavy-bomber armament, the Air Staff tried to make the best of a bad job. It was agreed that the Rose-Rice order of 600 should be completed, the turrets to be installed retrospectively on Lancasters in No. 1 Group, that the FN82 should be fitted 'to the greatest extent possible' in new production aircraft once it was available in January 1945, and that a programme of retrospective fitting of the FN82 should also begin next year on all operational Lancasters which were not scheduled to have the Rose turret.[24] Such decisions made little difference. Only 400 Rose-Rice turrets were ever built and even fewer FN82s were fitted to wartime Lancasters.

It is impossible to escape the conclusion that the turret programme would have been pursued with far greater energy and efficiency if it had been in the hands of Avro. There is a dramatic contrast between Roy Chadwick's phenomenal achievement in adapting the Lancaster in just a few weeks for the Dams raid, and the years of elongated debate and excuses over the 0.5-inch gun armament programme. Sir Douglas Evill admitted that 'Bomber Command undoubtedly has reason for disappointment in the rate at which new equipment has been provided to the heavy bomber squadrons', which he said was 'due to the fact that MAP have not succeeded in producing capacity for the design and production of turrets to enable those to keep pace with urgent tactical developments'.[25] The failure of the Air Ministry and MAP would have been even more serious had Allied air superiority over Germany in late 1944 not greatly reduced the threat from Luftwaffe fighters. One of the few figures to emerge with any credit from this sorry business was Harris himself. In his vociferous determination to improve the Lancaster's defences and means of escape from tail turrets, he contradicted the accusation that he was indifferent to the fate of his men, a charge reflected in the bitter words of one of his pilots, Ken

Newman: 'I came to the conclusion that the Commander-in-Chief and his staff at Bomber Command – and Churchill too, come to that – regarded us as expendable. I don't think that the top brass had any respect for us, none at all.'[26] The desire to preserve his bombers was, of course, a key part of Harris's campaign, but his concern for the aircrews was all too obvious in his correspondence. The fight for better turrets also highlighted the attention he gave to every aspect of Lancaster operations. The sweeping questions of strategy did not prevent him dealing with a wide range of detailed, often technical issues. In the last part of the war, he could be found addressing the merits of different cranes for bomb-loading, the inspection routine for Mark XIV bombsights, the composition of incendiary bombs, the servicing of Merlin engines, the supply of tyres, the production of marker flares, repairs to troublesome carburettors and the position of the engineer's gauges in the Lancaster cockpit.

One typical example of his thoroughness occurred in February 1945 with Don Bennett, the commander of No. 8 Pathfinder Group, over the new standard drills for handling Lancasters, which tended to vary between groups. Bennett was strongly of the opinion that the pilot should operate the flaps and the engineer the undercarriage. 'Both controls are situated near each other and although of slightly different design, both have an up and down actuating movement. Thus, if any one person is in the habit of operating both controls the time eventually will come when he accidentally operates the wrong one,' he told Harris. 'Moreover, the flap control on a Lancaster is very quick acting and has immediate serious effects on the flying characteristics of the aircraft. Such a quick and vital control should definitely be under the direct operation of the pilot himself. If it is given to the flight engineer and he makes a mistake, then it is generally too late for the pilot to save the situation.'[27] Harris received this letter on the day he ordered the raid against Dresden, the most controversial of all Bomber Command attacks. Yet he still found time to enter into a deep analysis of the issue, speaking to other officers and asking for information. He replied on 19 February 1945, telling Bennett that after consultation with group commanders and a study of accident reports: 'It has now been decided that the Lancaster drills will make the pilot responsible for the flaps and the flight engineer for the undercarriage. This will become the standard procedure.'[28] Given his workload, it is little wonder that Harris took only two weekend holidays during the whole of the war.

All this Trojan effort was directed to Harris's single goal of reinforcing the bomber offensive against Germany. That remained his unrelenting focus right until the end. Almost everything else was regarded as a distraction. When the Churchill government considered lending support from the air to the heroic Warsaw uprising against German occupation in September 1944, a rebellion that sought to exploit the German retreat from the eastern front in the face of the Red Army, Harris was uncooperative. Sinclair then took up the cause of the Polish rebels, urging Harris to consider whether there was anything he could do, even on a small scale. 'I fully realize the difficulties and I have been explaining to the Poles what a different thing it is to drop bombs from 20,000 feet on Königsberg from dropping containers on Warsaw.' But he hoped that Harris might be able to drop 'a few loads' and thereby give 'the moral encouragement which might prolong the defence till the Russians break through'.[29] The idea of using his Lancasters to drop supplies from a low level was impracticable, Harris said: 'I am not prepared to hazard my aircraft by dropping these containers from a low altitude. Each Lancaster can carry fourteen containers and as far as it is possible to estimate such a thing, I doubt if more than five to 20 per cent of the containers that are taken off from this country will fetch up within the town of Warsaw.' After predicting that losses could reach 15 per cent, he declared to Evill, 'I do not consider this task can be considered an Operation of War and the results that are likely to be achieved, assuming that 100 aircraft were sent, would be infinitesimal and would be most unlikely to influence the position in Warsaw.'[30] Having made his position clear, Harris received no orders to help Poland.

But he could not dismiss every plan that did not involve pulverizing urban Germany. As Operation Overlord demonstrated, Harris did not enjoy total independence over the use of his bomber force. As well as the strategic offensive against the Reich, therefore, he also had to dispatch his Lancasters on other operations across northern Europe throughout the autumn. In the build-up to Operation Market Garden in September 1944, the failed attempt by Montgomery to seize the bridge over the Rhine in the Dutch town of Arnhem, Bomber Command was required to undertake a series of daylight attacks against Luftwaffe fighter bases in Holland, Belgium and northwest Germany, but this was largely irrelevant to the brutal conflict on the ground. Another more successful raid, on the northern coast, was the bombardment of the strategically important Dutch island of Walcheren, which stood at the mouth of the Scheldt Estuary. Heavy gun batteries, radar, flak and a large garrison meant that the Germans had turned the 90-square-mile island into a fortress, with the result that the Allies could not easily use the port of Antwerp, which they had liberated on 9 September 1944. During the course of the next month, the Lancasters mounted nine raids against Walcheren, the biggest of them by 336 planes on 11 October. Altogether 8,970 tons of bombs were dropped on the island in 1,436 sorties. A vivid description of one of these raids was written by bomb aimer Miles Tripp, who, despite the flak, was relieved to attack a purely military target:

> The Lancasters went in low against light anti-aircraft fire. I saw some emplacements lying at the top of a narrow beach and gave Dig [Tripp's skipper] corrections until the concrete ramparts were drifting straight and fast towards the bombsight graticule. Eleven 1000-pound bombs and four 500-pound bombs swung down in a forward curve. For a moment I thought the dark cluster was going to fall short and curl into the sea, but the bombs cleared the water and seemed to race up the beach before exploding directly on the emplacements. This was the bomb-aimer's ideal target: a military objective with no danger to civilians and everything staked on a direct hit because anything less would have been a complete waste of time and money.[31]

The bombing badly weakened the defences in preparation for the invading British and Canadian forces, though there was still a fierce land battle before the Germans surrendered on 8 November.

By far the most spectacular of Lancaster operations in late 1944 occurred not in the cruel battlefields of continental Europe but in the chilly fjords of Scandinavia. For more than two years the British Government had been desperate to sink the *Tirpitz*, Germany's largest battleship. Displacing 43,000 tons, with a crew of 2,400 and a range of 9,000 miles, the *Tirpitz* was regarded as a constant threat to Allied shipping. Churchill told the RAF that her destruction was 'a prize to be won beyond compare', which would 'alter the balances of naval power all over the world and would immediately change the course of the war'.[32] From early 1942, the *Tirpitz* spent most of her time in Norwegian waters, a potential menace to the Arctic convoys heading for Russia. On Churchill's orders, the Royal Navy and RAF made persistent efforts to wreck her. The most daring was an attack in September 1943 by British midget-class submarines, which managed to evade a minefield and dodge nets to place explosive charges against the side of the *Tirpitz*. So severe was the damage that it took the next six months for the Germans to repair her. But she had survived and by April 1944 she was roaming the seas again. Efforts to sink her were now heightened by the navy and the Fleet Air Arm but they had no success, partly because the *Tirptiz's* armour plating was so thick, extending to 15 inches in places, and partly because her smokescreen system was so effective.

It was time to turn to Bomber Command. In the armour–piercing Tallboy bomb, the heavyweight Lancaster and the highly skilled 617 Squadron, the RAF had the ideal instruments for the task. Harris might have been expected to show some reluctance to take on this job, since the *Tirpitz* could be seen as the ultimate 'panacea' target. In fact, he said he was 'quite willing' to mount an attack, provided it did not interfere too much with the offensive against Germany.[33] Part of his motivation was a desire to give more proof to his frequently voiced claim that bombers were far more lethal than warships. He dismissed the naval war as a 'fantastic' conflict between 'dinosaurs',[34] and once told his mentor Lord Trenchard in September 1943 why, in strictly mathematical terms, Lancasters were more destructive than the navy's newest vessels. 'Between five and six Lancasters can stow the same amount of explosive (with a radius of action of 500 miles) as one of our latest capital ships. Whereas the average naval gun has to be relined after firing approximately 100 rounds representing 4500 pounds of explosive, a Lancaster will deliver during a normal life of, say, 30 sorties, 250,000 pounds of explosives.'[35] The sinking of the *Tirpitz* would be the ultimate evidence of the triumph of the bomber over the battleship.

But it would not be a straightforward operation, for at the beginning of September 1944 the *Tirpitz* was anchored in Kaa Fjord in the far north of Norway inside the Arctic Circle. A Tallboy-armed Lancaster was incapable of covering such a vast distance, so Bomber Command devised a plan in which the Lancasters would break up the journey by using a base in Russia as a refuelling point. Code-named Operation Paravane, the attack was to be led by 617 Squadron, supported by 9 Squadron. On the transfer of Leonard Cheshire to non-flying duties in June 1944, Willie Tait, a taciturn but iron-willed Scotsman, had become commander of 617 Squadron. He lacked Cheshire's charisma, but he was still a leader of great resourcefulness and courage, flying over 100 missions and, uniquely in the RAF, winning three bars to his DSO. 'He had a very distinguished career but he did not project himself in the same way as Cheshire. He was a very shy man, very shy,' said Bob Knights of 617 Squadron.[36]

Accompanied by a 463 Squadron Lancaster from the No. 5 Group film unit, 38 Lancasters from 617 and 9 Squadrons were due to take part in Operation Paravane, 24 of them carrying Tallboys and the rest loaded with an ingenious mine called the 'Johnny Walker'. This explosive device, powered by a compressed hydrogen system and weighing 500 pounds, was to be dropped in the water where it would sink to about 50 feet, then the gas pressure would send it to the surface. If it did not hit anything, it sank again, moved horizontally underwater about 30 feet, then rose upwards once more. The idea was that it would keep up the cycle of sinking, moving and rising until either the gas ran out or it hit something, preferably the underside of the *Tirpitz*. But not many of the aircrews were impressed. Mick Maguire, a pilot with 9 Squadron, said that 'if by some remote chance one of them had hit *Tirpitz*, the armour plating would have shrugged it off. It had a very small charge. I thought they were a bloody waste of time and it would have been far better to have all the Lancs carrying Tallboys.'[37] Carrying so much fuel and such a bomb load meant that the Lancasters with Tallboys would be taking off at 68,000 pounds, 5,000 pounds over the maximum specified take-off. Yet none of them encountered any trouble when they embarked on the long journey to Russia on 11 September 1944. The plan was to land at the remote Soviet station of Yagodnik, an island on the Dvina river near Archangel. There they would refuel before heading the 600 miles on a northwesterly course to Kaa Fjord. The crossing of the North Sea was largely uneventful, except for one Lancaster whose Tallboy became loose in the bomb bay and had to be jettisoned, forcing the crew to return to England. As the other Lancasters continued towards Russia, they crossed northern Scandinavia without much incident. It was exciting for the crews, having endured more than five years of the blackout in Britain and occupied Europe, to see lights blazing in neutral Sweden amid the snowy wastes under a silvery moon. 'It was like fairyland,' recalled Malcolm Hamilton, a pilot with 617 Squadron.[38] The problems for the raiders began when they reached Russia on 12 September. The weather worsened. Navigational aids proved unserviceable and maps were out of date. Wireless operators had been provided with the wrong call signs for the Russian radio beacons. The pilots and navigators had to fly by dead reckoning, and inevitably the two squadrons became scattered in the thickening cloud. Six of them had to make crash landings, having run out of fuel after being in the air for over twelve hours. Thomas Andrew, an engineer with 9 Squadron, recalled: 'The cloud was right down on the ground, the visibility was terrible and we could not find the Russian base. But we did see an airfield, with no runways, and we had to land there because of the lack of fuel. But we touched down far too late and ended up in a vegetable field, with the aircraft on its nose, tail in the air and four bent propellers. We got out as quickly as we could because we were worried about fire or the bomb exploding.'[39]

When the crew were safely on the ground, they were met by some Russians and, after a meal, taken to Yagodnik. Having become lost over a 'vast area of pine forest', Pilot Tony Iveson of 617 Squadron also had to make an emergency landing in an unknown airfield, but his was more successful. The Russian reception party, however, did not seem too welcoming. 'They were a villainous-looking lot, unshaven, wearing German greatcoats. We felt that they might have cut our throats for sixpence.' But their hospitality belied their appearance. Iveson's crew were put on a lorry, taken to the nearest town and then introduced to the local army major. 'He asked us where we had flown from. When I pointed out on a map that we'd come from Lincolnshire, he could not believe it.' On the instructions of the major, the Lancaster was refuelled, and Iveson managed to find his way to Yagodnik.[40] Larry Curtis was another who was forced to land away from the designated base. 'The weather was awful. We were down to a few hundred feet, trying to pick up a land-mark which you couldn't because of bad visibility. We had made up our minds to ditch in one of the rivers about 60 miles from Archangel. We had got rid of the escape hatches on the top. Unfortunately, when we had done this all the engine covers flew out, as did the maps. We were just about to ditch when we saw another Lanc. We presumed he knew where he was, and he thought the same of us. But eventually we saw a field that looked like it might have been an airstrip. It was actually near a Red Army camp.' The two Lancasters landed. Their Russian hosts got through on the army radio to Willie Tait, who, with characteristic bril-liance, had managed to find Yagodnik and had been the first to arrive. Tait flew over in a Dakota with a large supply of petrol in ten-gallon drums, which were used to refuel the two Lancasters. 'We filled up our planes. Then on take-off, with the weight of the bomb and the very short runway we hit some trees and damaged the engines.' But they made it to the base.[41]

It was a reflection of both the crews' skills and the endurance of the Lancaster that most of the aircraft made it directly to their destination in spite of the filthy weather conditions. The runway at Yagodnik was marked by two lines of sailors standing to attention and, according to the testimony of Freddie Watts of 617 Squadron, there was also a Russian band present. 'On our arrival, the band was playing *The Lambeth Walk* in front of a big banner which said, "Welcome The Glorious Flyers of the Royal Air Force".'[42] The generosity of spirit was not matched by the facilities. The aerodrome was basic, with little equipment. The crews were quartered in some Nissen huts and on an elderly paddle steamer on the river. The boat was so full of lice that, after their first night sleeping there, the airmen were covered in blotches. 'We woke up to find armies of red bugs marching across our bunks. One of our gunners said that he felt the communist bugs were very well-disciplined because the only member of our party they did not bite was our Commanding Officer,' recalled Tony Iveson.[43] That morning an American liaison officer arrived by Dakota with a fumigator and disinfected the steamer. The airmen had no trouble after that, which was a relief because their stay at Yagodnik was longer than expected, since it was impossible to mount the raid on the *Tirpitz* immediately. The first problem was that the weather remained poor. Every morning a Mosquito flew over Kaa Fjord and then returned to Yagodnik, firing a red Very light to indicate that conditions were still unfavourable. But even with better weather, it would have been difficult to mount a raid because so many of the Lancasters needed running repairs after their long flight and awkward landings, a laborious process given the lack of tools and materials. Some of the spares had to be cannibalized from other Lancasters which were too damaged to make it to Norway. Equally difficult was the job of refuelling the planes because the tanks at the airfield were far smaller than expected and had to be frequently resupplied. It took over sixteen hours to fill up all the serviceable Lancasters.

The RAF crews tried to occupy their time while they waited, and the Russians did their best to entertain them by, for example, playing football.[44] Activities in the evening usually revolved around showings of long-winded Soviet propaganda films or, more enjoyably, alcohol-fuelled mess dinners and dances at the all-ranks club to which local Russian girls were invited. Thomas Andrew had these memories of those few days on the base: 'We were well-treated, well-fed, though the meat was always goat. We saw them killing goats on the station. But they were very security conscious at night. We did not know what else went on at the base. Two of our chaps went one night to get some blankets from a Lancaster and were fired at by Russian soldiers.'[45]

At last, on the morning of 15 September the Mosquito signalled with a green Very light that the skies over Kaa Fjord had cleared. A total of 27 Lancasters were on standby, refuelled and loaded with their bombs, seven with the 'Johnny Walkers' and the rest with the Tallboys. The Lancaster with the No. 5 Group film unit was also ready. At 9.30 a.m. the aircraft took off from Yagodnik, Willie Tait once more at their head. Since surprise was so essential to prevent the Germans putting up a smokescreen, the Lancasters flew at low level across Sweden and Norway, hoping to avoid radar. It was only at the last moment that they climbed to gain bombing height. But their precautions were in vain. 'As we flew in towards the fjord,' recalled commander James Bazin of 9 Squadron in a BBC interview just after the raid, 'I could see the smokescreen starting. They must have heard our engines but the ship was still visible. My Lancaster, O for Oboe, was one of the first aircraft to make the bombing run. We met a considerable amount of inaccurate flak from the heavy guns which were situated around the fjord. As we were about to bomb, my bomb aimer reported that he was unable to see the ship.' Bazin decided to go round and try to make a second run. This time he and the bomb aimer noticed that the flashes from the guns of the *Tirpitz* could be seen through the smokescreen, making a useful target indicator. 'We bombed on the centre of the flashes.'[46] Larry Curtis was in one of the Lancasters following Bazin. 'It was a beautiful day and as we got nearer the target we could see the Tirpitz quite clearly but then the smoke canisters started to work. A couple of us managed to get a run-in at the ship and drop our bombs but by the time the last aircraft had gone the thing was completely covered and I think people aimed at the flashes from the battleship's guns. We did not know whether we had hit it or not.'[47] Once the smoke became too thick, the Lancasters returned to Archangel, some of them with their Tallboys still on board. It is a tribute to the Lancaster crews' respect for Air Ministry property that they refused to be extravagant in their use of Barnes Wallis's expensive bomb. 'We were never criticized for bringing back Tallboys because they were so valuable,' said John Sanders of 617 Squadron.[48]

On their arrival at Yagodnik the crews were unsure of the outcome of the raid. 'When we got back we were greeted by the Russian band but we had to wait for news from the reconnaissance Mosquito. It came back and told us that the Tirpitz was still there which absolutely broke our hearts,' recalled Larry Curtis.[49] The despair was, in fact, misplaced. The *Tirpitz* might still have been upright in the water, but it had sustained considerable punishment. One Tallboy had hit the ship near the prow, making a huge hole and causing 1,500 tons of water to flood on board. Other near misses had sent shockwaves big enough to damage her engines. As predicted, however, the Johnny Walkers had achieved little. The RAF did not know it at the time, but the *Tirpitz* was so badly mauled by the Tallboys that it was reclassified by Admiral Karl Dönitz, commander of the German navy, as no longer fit for duty. In its stricken state, barely able to move, it was towed southwards along the Norwegian coast to Tromsø, where, on Hitler's orders, it was to be converted into a floating coastal defence battery. Unaware that their mission had essentially been a success, the airmen of 9 and 617 Squadrons prepared to return to England. Before they did so, the Russians generously laid on a banquet at the main hotel in Archangel, featuring copious quantities of vodka and a performance of Russian opera. The next day, with several men nursing their hangovers, it was back to Britain. John Sanders recalled the startling results of using Russian aviation spirit for the trip home, because normal 100-octane fuel was in short supply:

> When you took off in a Lancaster with 100-octane fuel at full power you got sheets of bright blue flame, about a yard long, out of all the exhausts. But with this Russian stuff you got a red flame. And you could smell the lead in the cockpit. Apparently when we arrived back at Woodhall, on the ground they heard the noise from the Lancs and thought, 'Good grief, what's happened here?' Every single plug on all the engine mountings had to be changed because they'd all been burnt with this dreadful petrol.[50]

Amazingly, there had not been one casualty on the mission so far, despite the poor weather and the flak from the *Tirpitz*. On the return trip, however, one of the Lancasters crashed in Norway, killing all 11 men on board.

Fearing that they had failed to inflict mortal wounds on the *Tirpitz*, the Lancaster crews felt that 'we were due to meet again', to use the phrase of Tony Iveson's.[51] But before another mission could be undertaken against the ship, 617 Squadron was required for two more special operations in Germany. The first was another attempt to smash the Dortmund-Ems canal, this time using the more lethal Tallboys, the previous raid with conventional bombs having ended in failure in September 1943. Carried out on 23–4 September by 136 Lancasters, again led by Willie Tait, the raid was successful in achieving a breach in the canal, causing the water to drain away for a six-mile stretch, but 14 Lancasters, more than 10 per cent of the force, were lost. The second was a daring attack on the Kembs dam, just north of the Swiss border at Basle. The dam, situated on the Rhine, held a huge quantity of water, and the Allies feared that if American and French troops advanced into the valley, they could be swamped should the Germans open the floodgates. So the aim was to launch a pre-emptive strike, destroying the locks of the Kembs dam so the water would be released before any Allied forward movement. The plan was for the Lancasters of 617 Squadron to attack in two separate waves. One would attack from the west, dropping its Tallboys from 8,000 feet. The other, flying in at very low level from the east, would drop their Tallboys, with thirty-minute delay fuses, against the sluice gates. The attack would be supported by rocket-firing Mustangs whose objective was to distract the dam's anti-aircraft defences.

The raid was carried out in daylight on 7 October and both Lancaster waves reached the target on time, but the Mustangs failed to do so. The German guns could therefore concentrate on sending a hail of fire against the low-flying planes coming from the east. John Sanders was piloting the last of the six Lancasters in this wave:

> The fighters lost us on the final run into the target so we went in undefended. The first two aircraft were unscathed. The third was hit in the engines. The fourth got through. The fifth went in, just in front of me at 600 feet. I watched as shells were pouring into this Lanc. It rolled over, hit the ground upside down and then went skating through the forest. Pine trees were bursting into flames as it slithered along, a wreck of an aircraft. By now I was on my run in. I am convinced that when that crew died, it saved my life because the German gunners lost our plane through the intense pall of smoke. We went in with everything rattling. All the machine guns were going as we went in . . . 600 feet is a suicidal height against cannon fire. But we had to drop from that height because the experts had calculated that a Tallboy would have to drop its nose sufficiently far when it left the aircraft to enter the water without bouncing.

Because of the half-hour delay fuses, nothing seemed to have happened once all the Lancasters had left the target. But then, as plotted, the Tallboys exploded, ripping out the dam and flooding the countryside. 'So it did work,' concluded Sanders.[52]

Now it was time to finish off the *Tirpitz*, British intelligence still being unaware that the ship was no longer seaworthy. The move southwards to Tromsø had the great advantage of bringing the *Tirpitz* within the extreme range of the Lancasters, as long as the planes operated from Scotland and had additional 250-gallon fuel tanks installed in their fuselages. Bomber Command drew up a plan for 617 and 9 Squadrons to take off from the RAF base of Lossiemouth near Elgin, one of the most northerly bases in the mainland United Kingdom. The problem was that the runway at Lossiemouth was a fraction too short for a Lancaster carrying a Tallboy and an extra fuel tank. So several changes were made to the Lancasters. All extraneous equipment and armour plating were stripped out. The mid-upper turret was removed. More importantly, the normal Merlin 24 engine used on the Lancaster Mark IIIs was replaced by a Merlin 28, which gave more power on take-off.

A total of 40 modified Lancasters flew up to Scotland, the crews rested briefly and then, in the early hours of 29 October, they took off for Tromsø. 'With these new Merlins, our Lancasters leapt off the runway like Spitfires,' recalled Tony Iveson.[53] But this time the weather, rather than the smokescreen, was against them. 'I did see her for just a second or two, like a silver pencil. There was cloud coming in from the sea, which soon obscured her,' said Thomas Andrew of 9 Squadron. 'It was guesswork really. It was not possible to bomb accurately. She was firing, using her main armament. There were tremendous flashes down below but then even they became obscure, though we still felt terrific bursts above us.'[54] Despite the weather, Bob Knights of 617 Squadron thought his Lancaster had scored a hit on the *Tirpitz*. 'By the time our bomb-sight was ready to go, the bomb aimer said that the target was under cloud. But he told me it was a perfect run so we let the bomb go and I thought we had sunk it. The bomb aimer said that it went right down the side of the ship, putting it over at 90 degrees. But then it righted itself again and came up. We were rather disappointed at that.'[55] Indeed, the entire raid was a disappointment. None of the Tallboys found their mark and the Lancaster flown by Bill Carey of 617 Squadron, badly hit by flak, had to ditch in a lake in Sweden, though the crew eventually made it back to England. The Lancaster of Freddie Watts of 617 Squadron also sustained some damage to its undercarriage and had to make an emergency landing at RAF Sumburgh on the Shetlands.

By now the deep freeze of the arctic winter was approaching Norway. The days were becoming shorter, the weather worse. Bomber Command had only one more realistic chance to sink the *Tirpitz* before the spring of 1945. On 12 November Willie Tait led 31 Lancasters again to Tromsø from Lossiemouth. This time fortune favoured the bombers. The skies were clear. The Germans were caught by surprise with the result that the smokescreen began too late. Tony Iveson recalled how the raid unfolded:

> We all fell into place in the gaggle and started to climb up to 14,000–16,000 feet. The weather at 9 a.m. was absolutely perfect, no cloud, bright sunlight, gin clear. You could see for 100 miles. Suddenly, we saw the *Tirpitz*, black against the sea, ripples of fire as her guns went off. She used her big guns at maximum range, and when the shells went off there were slow, unfolding golden clouds, not just a flash of flak. Now we all felt there was no way she would escape. Conditions for our type of bombing were perfect. With the special bombsight, the Tallboy and the Lancaster, we all felt that the *Tirpitz* was doomed.

The bomb aimer fed the necessary information into the computer and soon the SABS took over:

> On came a red light, and 10 seconds later 12,000 pounds of Tallboy left the aircraft. If a bomb can be called beautiful, the Tallboy was that bomb. 21 feet long, a perfect streamlined shape, with the bomb section cast from

a single ingot of steel, you could feel the point in the palm of your hand. It had a terminal velocity of 4,000 feet per second. From the bomb plot, two Tallboys smashed into the *Tirpitz* and two were very near misses in the first seven bombs. Other hits followed and within five minutes she had capsized and lay bottom up, her masts grounded on the sea bed.[56]

There were probably at least three direct hits on the ship, one of which penetrated the main magazines. Bruce Buckham, who was captain of the 463 Squadron Lancaster carrying the film unit, captured the scene: 'We descended to about 2000 feet and the bombers were right overhead doing perfect bombing runs, bomb doors gaped open and glistening Tallboys suspended. Now they were released and to us they appeared to travel in a graceful curve like a high diver. I thought the first two were near misses and then Pow! A hit which was followed by two more in as many seconds.'[57]

On board the *Tirpitz* was Johann Troger, a twenty-two-year-old signaller. 'The ship seemed to leap out of the water when the magazine went up, making a huge hole through the side. There were men every-where in the water. It was bitterly cold and there was black smoke billowing over everything, then another bomb hit the waterline along-side. The suction pulled the ship sideways and stayed there for what seemed like a very long time but water was pouring in through the hole and suddenly she keeled over and slid bow first into the harbour sand.'[58] The crew of a reconnaissance Mosquito from 540 Squadron sent a message to Bomber Command HQ later that day, having photographed the *Tirpitz* at 11.50 a.m. There was, stated the report, a 'very large oil streak on the water. A large number of ships were standing around and the Tirpitz was upside down or on its side within the booms.'[59] In the much-reduced crew 700 German sailors were estimated to have been killed and another 100 were rescued from the water. Only one Lancaster was lost.

The threat posed by the *Tirpitz* in late 1944 might have existed more in the imagination of the government than in reality. Nevertheless, the navy felt sufficiently relieved by the demise of the battleship to transfer a substantial section of its own forces from Scapa Flow to the Far East. Within the RAF, Portal expressed to Harris his 'unbounded admiration' for the crews of 617 and 9 Squadrons, which 'have enhanced the fame of Bomber Command and the RAF throughout the world'.[60] Harris could not help crowing at the vindication of his belief in the supremacy of the bomber over the battleship, as he put it to his American friend Bob Lovatt: 'You can tell your sailor friends this, and tell them it from me to put in their pipes and smoke on: there is no ship yet built or ever to be built that will stand up to two hits from 12,000 lb bombs.'[61]

As 1944 drew to a close, Harris continued to seek vindication for the most powerful of all his theories: his faith in area bombing. During November he had complied, to a grudging extent, with the September directive, even claiming to recognize the efficacy of the plan to bomb oil installations. But by December he was sliding back to his cherished strategy of attacking cities. Far from accepting the importance of the German oil industry, he now directly challenged the priority given to its destruction, claiming that it was a waste of Bomber Command's resources and, in any case, the task was too big. The experts at the Ministry of Economic Warfare, he told Portal on 12 December, had never failed 'to overstate their case on "panaceas", e.g. ball bearings, molybdenum, locomotives, etc. in so far as, after the battle has been joined and the original targets attacked, more and more sources of supply or other factors unpredicted by MEW have become revealed'. He then argued that 'the oil plan has already displayed similar symptoms', adding he was sure 'there are dozens more benzol plants of which we are unaware and when and if we knock them out I am equally certain we shall eventually be told by MEW that German MT [Motor Transport] is continuing to run sufficiently for their purpose on producer gas, steam, industrial alcohol etc etc.'[62]

As with other strategic questions, such as the Pathfinders, the Mosquito and Tedder's Transportation Plan, Harris displayed woeful judgement about the oil industry. If he had pursued the oil plan with vigour, mobilizing the force at his command, it is probable that the war would have been won more quickly. For oil was no 'panacea' target. It was the central element of the Nazi war machine. The Germans themselves were surprised at the RAF's failure to mount an all-out effort against their oil installations. In his post-war memoir, Albert Speer said that with the lack of enterprise over the oil offensive 'the Allies threw away success when it was already in their hands',[63] while the senior Luftwaffe Commander Adolf Galland wrote that 'the most successful operation of the entire Allied stratecial air warfare was against Germany's fuel supply. Looking back, it is difficult to understand why the Allies started this undertaking so late.'[64] The answer was, of course, that the bomber chief had no interest in it. Even some of Harris's own men in the Lancaster squadrons came to despair of his outlook. 'I think we could have done more on the oil installations,' said Ian Anderson, a Pathfinder navigator. 'Then maybe we would have halted the war sooner than we did. If we had concentrated on oil it would have had a far greater effect.'[65]

That was the view of Portal, most of the Air Staff and Syd Bufton, the Director of Bombing Operations. Never a keen supporter of area bombing, Bufton was a passionate advocate of the oil plan by late 1944. His cool, analytical mind had no time for Harris's doubts and obstruction. In a letter to Portal of 21 December, he urged that oil had to remain 'the over-riding priority' and pointed out that 'by far the greater proportion of Germany's output is accounted for by a limited number of plants. Eleven synthetic plants in central Germany are producing 70 per cent of the enemy's current supplies of motor and aviation spirit.'[66] Backed up by Bufton's findings, Portal took on Harris again the next day, telling the bomber chief that he was 'profoundly disappointed that you still appear to feel that oil plan is just another "panacea". Naturally while you hold this view, you will not be able to put your heart into the attack on oil.' He then quoted Bufton's statistics on the central importance of the synthetic plants, concluding: 'there is no doubt in my mind that their immobilisation and the continued immobilisation of the remaining producers would represent by far the greatest and most certain contribution that our strategic bombers could make to the achievement of an early decision in the German war.'[67]

Portal's attempt to persuade his subordinate to fulfil orders only provoked Harris to new heights of ill-tempered recalcitrance. On 28 December he sent Portal a four-page, closely typed letter which amounted to a passionate defence of area bombing. 'In my view area attacks produce the best effect and on the entire war machine, whereas attacks on oil plants do nothing at all unless they hit the oil plant.' This was an argument that tried to make a virtue of inaccuracy, but the point ignored the Lancaster's increasing ability to hit even a narrow target. Turning next to the Luftwaffe's fighter forces, Harris showed an extraordinary reluctance to face the reality of what the US 8th Air Force and the Mustang had achieved in 1944 in comparison with the failure of the Berlin campaign. 'The attacks against German fighter forces and industry last year are an outstanding example of the futility of panacea seeking. After all that vast effort against the German fighter industry, the German fighter force finishes up at two to two and a half times as strong as when it started. The moral is that if you concentrate on a panacea the enemy concentrates on countering it. Yet nobody could say that every possible effort was not made, and brilliantly executed, in the best of conditions, to knock the German fighter forces out of the ground and their factories.' Here Harris was being disingenuous. One of the complaints against him was that, unlike the Americans, he deliberately refused to fulfil the Pointblank directive by making attacks on the Luftwaffe a priority. Yet, according to his logic, the Americans were at fault for concentrating on German air power rather than the cities. 'If, over that long period of attacks on the Germany aircraft industry, Eighth Bomber Command [US 8th Air Force] had instead joined with us in area bombing, what vastly greater effects would not have been achieved on the enemy's war machine and will to win the war as a whole.' In summarizing his position, Harris warned: 'Three years of bitter struggle have gone into area blitzing. All Germany openly bemoans it as their worst trial. We know that on more than one occasion they have nearly collapsed under it. As the programme nears completion we chuck it all up – for a panacea.'[68]

The core of the debate about the bombing strategy had now been reached. Harris remained a true believer, a committed disciple of Trenchard. But for Portal and Bufton, the lesson of 1944 was that area bombing was self-defeating. In a superbly lucid minute of 3 January 1945, Bufton used the narrative of the air war to refute Harris's arguments. There was no evidence to support the claim that Germany had 'nearly collapsed' under area bombing, he wrote. 'We know she was seriously alarmed by the Hamburg and the early Berlin attacks but this condition was probably far from collapse. She weathered successfully the storm of the subsequent Berlin attacks.' Harris's regret over the Americans' concentration on the German aircraft industry was dismissed as absurd, with Bufton pointing out that the situation would have been far worse if the US 8th Air Force had followed Bomber Command's example. 'Had the American Air Forces joined with Bomber Command in bombing cities instead of fighter production there is every possibility they would have been frozen out of the skies.' Warming to his theme, Bufton argued that Harris's whole area-bombing approach had been doomed to failure:

> Had Overlord not enabled us to advance to the German frontiers, it is probable that night blitzing of German cities would, by now, be too costly to sustain on a heavy scale. Thus it appears while area bombing, if it could have been continued long enough and with sufficient weight, might in the end have forced the enemy to capitulate, his counter-measures would have prevented us from maintaining such a policy to the decisive point. We would have been forced to precision attack to maintain the air situation needed to continue the offensive at all. The Americans did this for themselves with little assistance from Bomber Command. Under the cover of the resulting air situation, Overlord was launched successfully and night bombing was given a new lease of life. These are factors the Commander-in-Chief overlooks.[69]

In essence, said Bufton, there could be no area bombing without successful precision attacks on German air power. This was a point, interestingly, that Göring also made when he was first interrogated by the US army after his capture in May 1945. 'Without the American air force,' he said, 'the war would be going on elsewhere and certainly not on German soil.'[70]

Portal was in complete agreement with Bufton and used most of his text verbatim for the stiff reply he sent to Harris on 8 January. He concluded: 'The energy, resource and determination displayed by the enemy in his efforts to maintain his oil production must be more than matched by our determination to destroy it, and your determination matters more than all the rest put together.'[71] Simmering in fury, Harris sent another lengthy missive, this one stretching to five typed pages, in which he launched into another condemnation of precision bombing and claimed that the 'oil policy will not succeed'. He was dismissive of the argument that Bomber Command, in contrast to the 8th Air Force, had not significantly contributed to the decline of the German aircraft industry. 'I doubt if the Boche would so compare or classify the vast destruction of every conceivable type of basic and specialised industrial activity.' At the end of the letter, he called Portal's bluff by offering his resignation, just nine months after a previous such threat over fighter cover for the Lancasters. Describing his position as 'intolerable', he urged Portal 'to consider whether it is best for the prosecution of the war and the success of our arms, which alone matters, that I should remain in this situation'.[72] Once more, Portal meekly surrendered. In his reply he said: 'I willingly accept your assurance that you will continue to do your utmost to ensure the successful execution of the policy laid down. I am very sorry that you do not believe in it, but it is no use my craving for what is evidently unattainable.'[73] The Chief of the Air Staff had shown himself too supine in the face of Harris. Instead of acting like a limp suitor, 'craving' for Harris's agreement, he should have instructed him to obey his orders or face the consequences. It was an affront to all military discipline to retain in office a man who had challenged his authority at such length. In later years Portal said he never took Harris's threat of resignation seriously, and it would have been 'monstrously unjust to have tried to have him replaced' after all Harris had achieved over the years. But the truth was that Harris had proved himself to be the stronger leader.[74] Recognizing Harris's public stature through triumphs like the Dambusters raids and the sinking of the *Tirpitz*, Portal simply did not have the stomach for the controversy that would erupt if he dismissed the bomber chief.

It has further been claimed that Portal was afraid to act because Harris had the backing of Winston Churchill, but there is not any truth in this. In fact, Churchill was no great admirer of either Harris or area bombing, and strongly backed the plan to destroy oil installations, telling Portal in late January: 'In view of the great success of attacks on oil targets and their immediate effects, I trust they will not be neglected.'[75] Contrary to the suggestion of any closeness between the Prime Minister and the Bomber Commander, Harris once confessed in March 1942, in a rare admission of vulnerability, that he was intimidated by Churchill. Referring to a meeting at Chequers, Harris wrote that 'one is pushed and pressed and boxed into a corner in such discussions and in such circumstances by a past master in the art of the disembowelling process. Such occasions are normally concluded by the peremptory instruction to "write me a minute".'[76] But Portal was a more pliant figure to deal with than Churchill.

After the oil row was over, Sir Archibald Sinclair, the Secretary of State for Air, gave a shrewd psychological insight into Harris's mindset. In February 1945 Portal asked Harris to undertake a mission to Moscow in support of the Allied propaganda effort. Harris refused on the grounds that such a move might be taken as a signal of his support for the oil plan, a policy 'in which I do not believe'.[77] Portal abandoned the idea of the Russian trip, but passed Harris's letter of refusal to Sinclair with a note saying that the Bomber Chief 'is evidently under considerable mental stress'. Sinclair replied: 'Exquisitely right. I see what troubles his soul – our failure to go nap [a gambling term meaning to risk everything] on the policy of obliteration and that the laurels which he is receiving are for successes – Pathfinders, incendiary attacks, the oil plan – which are not of his design.'[78]

Harris's continuing emphasis on area bombing in the last months of the war has often been defended on the grounds that the strategy inflicted widespread devastation on German industry, forced the Reich to divert colossal resources into air defences and sapped the morale of the German people. All that is undeniable. By 1944 two million Germans were engaged in anti-aircraft duties, while vast construction efforts were needed to put production underground. As Professor Richard Overy has pointed out, anti-aircraft equipment absorbed a fifth of all ammunition production and two-thirds of radar and signals production.[79] In the last year of the war a third of all artillery production was devoted to anti-aircraft guns when such weaponry was in desperately short supply on both the western and eastern fronts. In 1942 German fighter production was barely half that of bomber production. By September 1944 three-quarters of aircraft production consisted of defensive planes, a development that, incidentally, prevented Britain from being subjected to any systematic raids after the Blitz of 1940–1. Twenty per cent of the non-agricultural labour force was required to deal with the physical devastation of the bombing: clearing rubble, laying track and repairing damaged structures. A study by the armaments minister Albert Speer calculated that by January 1945 the German economy had produced 25 per cent fewer tanks than planned, 31 per cent fewer aircraft and 42 per cent fewer lorries. Interrogated by the Allies just immediately after the surrender, the Luftwaffe commander Generalleutnant Joseph 'Beppo' Schmid said: 'I strongly decline to follow the judgement of those who maintain that the British night attacks did not have a decisive influence on the downfall of Germany. It may be right to say that the mass of British bombs did not hit the German war economy directly. But the systematic planning and continuity of those attacks increased their indirect effects, in particular in connection with the USAAF day attacks, to a quite unbearable extent. The success in target finding by night and in bad weather had increased to an astonishing measure by the autumn of 1944.'[80]

The bombing also meant deepening fatigue, gloom and misery for Germany's population. Families were broken up as over eight million children were evacuated. Basic foodstuffs were in short supply; sleep deprivation was widespread because of the constant air-raid sirens. 'The people are beginning to suffer from what is called bunker fever and inability to work. The faith in our leading men, including the Führer, is rapidly disappearing,' reported the Wuppertal SD [the intelligence branch of the SS] in January 1945.[81] Some of the public anger was turned on the bomber crews who had to bail out over Germany. One airman who landed in a field near Bochum just east of Essen in March 1945 was seized by a crowd and then beaten to death with a hammer. According to Professor Richard Evans in his magisterial study of the Reich at war, at least 350 Allied airmen were lynched in the last two years of conflict.[82] But the despondency more often translated into hatred for the Nazi regime than for the Allies. One study found that only a third of Germans blamed the Allies for the bombing, while half did not. An elderly Hamburg woman who worked in a hotel commented that 'the most remarkable thing one noticed when one sat in the air-raid shelter was how the people cursed the Nazis more and more as time went on, without inhibitions or reservations. Never was the cursing about England or America, always it was about the Nazis.'[83]

Yet for all the drastic fall in morale and output, the German armed forces kept fighting. That in itself was a comprehensive refutation of the Trenchardian doctrine that victory could be achieved by breaking the spirit of the enemy's population through aerial bombardment. Harris, too, in his fraught correspondence with Portal had spoken of destroying Germany's 'will to win the war'. The truth was that in a totalitarian dictatorship, filled with contempt for humanity or democracy, the will of the people was an irrelevance, as Norman Bottomley, the Deputy Chief of the Air Staff, recognized in a perceptive talk he gave to Bomber Command senior officers in late 1944: 'We have never before experienced a state so controlled and regimented by a political machine such as the Nazi party. Even when public morale is desperately low, general collapse can for a long while be staved off by a ruthless and desperate party system.'[84] Nor were the falls in production and the huge switch of resources to air defence a justification for mass area bombing. The same outcome, or even better, could have been achieved in 1944–5 with more focused attacks on specific targets, exploiting the Allies' air supremacy. Precision assaults, varied over Germany between Lancasters and Mosquitoes, would have made just as heavy a demand on the Reich's defences. The plane that destroyed the Mohne Dam, the *Tirpitz*, the Gnome aero-engine factory at Limoges, the Kembs Dam and the V-2 storage bunker at Watten was capable of so much more than just blowing up urban streets. Indeed, the Lancaster navigator Frank Musgrove argued in his memoir of his wartime service that:

> by 1944 area bombing should have been totally abandoned, Bomber Command drastically reduced in size and most of the aircrew and ground staff re-mustered or demobbed. A small bomber force would now engage in highly selective, pinpoint bombing of synthetic oil factories, steelworks, rocket-production plants and launch sties. Of course, events develop a powerful momentum of their own and become encrusted with vested interests; but it was now necessary to cut across the current of events and reverse it. What we actually experienced from mid-1943 was a massive failure in leadership: a palpable lack of imagination, of intellect and political will.[85]

Harris won his battle against Portal over oil targets, but by doing so he may have prolonged the war. The Ardennes Offensive, in the depth of the 1944–5 winter, when German forces almost broke through the Allied lines on the western front, would have been far more difficult to mount if German oil supplies had been more badly depleted. At the height of this battle, Harris wrote complacently to Lord Trenchard: 'It is a demonstrable fact that the armies in France had a complete walk-over from Brittany to the German borders owing to the effects of air attacks.' About 19,000 American soldiers died in the battle, and 1,400 British. The western front was some 'walk-over'.

17

'A pure morale air attack'

WAR IS A juggernaut that crushes moral scruples. In 1939 the Air Ministry refused to bomb Germany for fear of destroying 'private property'.[1] Yet within three years the government had developed its own clinical lexicon to describe the policy of urban devastation, built around terms like 'dehousing', 'index of activity' and 'Coventrate'. By 1944 the Allies had even developed a plan for the strategic employment of gas against the German population if Hitler resorted to chemical warfare. The plan, a copy of which is in the Bufton papers at Cambridge University, set out in precise detail the role of the Lancasters in such an attack, both in terms of load and targets. Fifteen cities were selected for the RAF to hit, including Essen, Cologne, Düsseldorf, Aachen and Gelsenkirken. 'It is recommended that the loads carried in these attacks should be in the overall proportions of 75 per cent mustard gas, 25 per cent High Explosive. The incorporation of 25 per cent HE is calculated to increase the effect of gas weapons by breaking the windows and water mains and by the creation of rubble which presents specially difficult problems of decontamination. The HE bomb craters will also indicate the gas bomb distribution achieved.'[2] Fortunately, this doomsday scenario never had to be enacted, but the very act of contemplating the use of mustard gas showed how far the Air Staff leaders had moved from their early, high-minded principles. With mass slaughter and destruction spreading across Europe, it was inevitable that there would be a diminution of the normal peacetime sensibilities towards humanity.

In this context, the Air Staff's preference for bombing oil installations over area bombing was not driven by any sense of morality but purely by a belief that the German oil industry was a more militarily efficient target. As the events of early 1945 demonstrated, they had no hesitation in ordering mass area attacks if they felt such saturation bombing would advance the Allied cause. This was particularly true of heavy assaults on transport systems and industry, the second priority, after oil installations, of the September directive and the strategy that Tedder had long espoused.

Railway stations, marshalling yards, factories and industrial plants were invariably situated in urban areas, so in practice the distinction between 'dehousing' and transportation or industrial bombing became blurred. Indeed, almost any area attack on a German town or city could be justified as an attempt to knock out its rail network or industry.

The Americans, who for so long had declared their reluctance to undertake area bombing, were drawn into the practice. The orders issued in October 1944 to the 8th Air Force by its commander General Jimmy Doolittle stated that 'no towns or cities in Germany will be attacked as secondary targets or last resort targets, targets of opportunity or otherwise', but then added a crucial qualification, 'unless such towns contain or have adjacent to them one or more military objectives. Military objectives include railway lines; junctions; marshalling yards; railway or road bridges or other communications networks; any industrial plant; and such obvious military objectives as oil storage tanks, military camps and barracks.'[3] It is impossible to conceive of any German town that would not have been covered by Doolittle's directive. In practice, the USAAF carried out just as much area bombing as the RAF in the last months of the war. The difference was that Harris was open about his approach. The USAAF chiefs hid their strategy behind euphemisms.

The irony of the Americans' slide into area bombing was that they had previously rejected such an approach partly on the grounds that their bombers, with their famous Norden sights, were capable of greater accuracy than the RAF's. But this turned out to be untrue. Thanks to the quality of the Lancaster, the skills of experienced aircrews and the sophistication of their Mark XIV and SABS bombsights, Bomber Command was actually capable of much the same levels of accuracy and efficiency as the USAAF. In fact, according to a study by the historian Ian Gooderson of bombing patterns in support of the Normandy invasion, 'The RAF method was slightly more accurate. Operational research proved that an RAF attack resulted in a pattern of bomb strikes much more dense at the centre of its objective than at the periphery, while a US bomber box achieved a fairly even density of strikes – to achieve the cumulative ground pattern of an RAF attack several boxes of US bombers had to have the same aiming point.'[4]

Far from declining as victory drew near and precision attacks became easier, saturation bombing actually increased in the winter of 1944 and spring of 1945. The Whig historian Lord Macaulay wrote in 1831 that 'the essence of war is violence. Moderation in war is an imbecility.'[5] There was certainly nothing moderate about Bomber Command's determination to flatten much of Germany's urban landscape, no matter how tenuous might be the link between a certain target and the overall military objective. In the last three months of 1944, a larger weight of bombs was dropped by Bomber Command than in the whole of 1943. The last nine months of war accounted for no less than 46 per cent of the entire tonnage of RAF bombs that fell throughout the war. In March 1945 Bomber Command achieved its highest monthly total weight of bombs delivered, 67,637 tons, a figure that compares to 20,149 tons in August 1943.

While the big centres like Essen and Dusseldorf continued to be hammered, Bomber Command exploited its air superiority to attack a growing list of other towns and cities, many of which had only the most limited industrial or military significance. On 18 October 1944, for instance, 128 Lancasters were dispatched to attack the historic university city of Bonn. The senior intelligence officer Wing Commander Jim Rose, head of the air section at Bletchley Park, the ULTRA centre that had cracked the German operational codes, was shocked when he was first contacted by Bomber Command about the raid: 'Bomber Command rang me and asked, "What are the military targets in Bonn?" I was horrified they were going to bomb Bonn, the home town of Beethoven. "There's just a clothing factory." "It doesn't matter," came the reply, "We're going to bomb it anyway."'[6] The raid destroyed the university and a host of major public buildings, as well as killing 313 people. Wrecking the fabric of central European culture mattered no more to Harris than killing civilians. At a meeting of SHAEF, Jimmy Doolittle ruefully admitted that one of his bombers had hit Strasbourg Cathedral. 'Why Jimmy, you've done better than me,' said Harris breezily, 'I've been trying to hit Cologne Cathedral for years.'[7] Another historic city on Bomber Command's list was Freiburg on the upper Rhine near the French border. Though it was without any industry, it was hammered by 341 Lancasters on the night of 27–8 November 1944 on the basis that it had a rail junction and was full of German troops. Almost 2,000 tons fell on the city, but the railway escaped damage and the German army numbers were far lower than RAF intelligence had claimed. Just 75 Wehrmacht soldiers were killed, in comparison to almost 2,900 civilians. Much of the structural heart of the city was obliterated, including the city archives, the Holy Ghost Hospital and a medieval Franciscan convent church. Joseph Sauer, a theologian at Freiburg University, recorded in his diary the experience of walking down the main street on the morning after the raid. 'All the buildings on the right were nothing but rubble. You were taking your life in your hands to work your way through to Kaiserstrasse. We had to climb over high piles of debris and stone, beams and iron and wire mesh. All around us was a new world, a horrid desert of stone, out of which only the Minster stood out, having been left unscathed by this spook of hell. Tears came to my eyes and I saw a lot of people who were evidently in a similar state.'[8]

The pattern of prodigious attacks against targets of little strategic importance continued into 1945. On 16–17 January two successive raids by Lancasters and Mosquitoes created a firestorm in Magdeburg, northeastern Germany, which killed 4,000 people. A few weeks later, on the night of 7–8 February, 295 Lancasters bombed the town of Kleve on the Dutch border, despite its small population, just 21,000, and its lack of industry. It had been subjected to many attacks before and was largely in ruins, yet still Bomber Command thought it worthy of more attention. The famous BBC reporter Richard Dimbleby accompanied one of the Lancasters on this mission, and in his commentary he could not conceal from listeners the reality that Kleve had been 'utterly destroyed already' and was 'nothing more than a heap of rubble'. What was captivating about his account, which was recorded live, was both his eloquent description of the scene and his honesty about his nerves. 'It is the most extraordinary sight I have ever seen in the air,' he reported as the Lancaster began its bombing run towards the blazing centre of the town, heading into the flak from the ground batteries:

> Down go more target indicators, a medley of bright, indeed lovely colours, their reflections glowing on the thick white and dark grey clouds that are rolling up . . . Our bombs are going. The flak is bursting just under us. We are going over the top now. There's more fire. I don't know how we can stand this. We are shaking with the flak. But how steady the crew and skipper are as they hold to their course. Our bombs are bursting there now, flash, flash, flash. I am sorry, I tried to be steady and contained on this commentary but it is more than I can do. It is a staggering sight to see in the sky.[9]

The big raids against the Ruhr, Berlin and other major targets went on throughout this period. In Operation Hurricane in mid-October, a combined initiative with the USAAF designed to 'demonstrate to Germany the overwhelming superiority of Allied forces',[10] Duisburg and Brunswick were hit by three successive raids in the space of twenty-four hours involving 1,340 Lancasters, a figure that in itself showed the formidable riches that Harris now had at his command. In November 1944, Düsseldorf was hit by 561 Lancasters. At the beginning of January, 514 of them flew to Nuremburg, and in February 486 attacked Wiesbaden, the capital of Hesse in southwestern Germany. In March, 750 Lancasters hit Essen, and 746 attacked Dortmund on the successive nights of the 11th and 12th. Altogether Lancaster crews flew 51,685 sorties in the last six months of the war, the force having been expanded to 57 squadrons by April 1945.

But what was striking was how the smaller targets often suffered disproportionately. On the night of 23–4 February, for example, the southwestern town of Pforzheim, a place that produced mainly clocks and jewellery and had no military value, was hit by 362 Lancasters. In the space of twenty-two minutes, 1,551 tons of bombs were dropped on the town, 100 more tons than fell on Cologne in the first Millennium raid in May 1942. Because Pforzheim had not previously suffered major attacks, its narrow streets and buildings were still intact before the raid. Incendiaries therefore had a far more devastating effect than in towns where there had already been widespread destruction. A huge firestorm was created, driving a howling wind through the centre of the city, sucking oxygen out of the air and pulling people into the flames. Pforzheim resident Maria Lupus managed to escape death by running for the city's canal:

> The monstrous firestorm ripped the air right out of our mouths. Our survival instinct showed us the only way to find some oxygen was to breathe directly above the surface of the water. The child on my arm didn't budge. It was probably almost anaesthetized from the fumes that had developed. Meanwhile the lack of oxygen had also gotten worse down in the canal. The thick smoke penetrated painfully into eyes and lungs. You totally lost sense of time. Had many hours passed? Or just a few? There were some horrific scenes at the river that flowed past the canal. Injured people washed ashore who in mortal fear had jumped out of burning houses into the water. Many were already dead; others had ghastly burns. There was dead silence everywhere.[11]

In the days that followed, it was found that 17,600 people had lost their lives, around a quarter of the population. That was a higher casualty rate than at Nagasaki, where the second atomic bomb was dropped on 9 August 1945. A full 83 per cent of the core of Pforzheim had been razed to the ground. In some quarters in the old town, there were literally no inhabitants or buildings left.

Another city that largely escaped the bombing until 1945 was Würzburg, located halfway between Frankfurt and Nuremburg. As the site of an army barracks, ball-bearing plant, Gestapo office and Luftwaffe airfield, there was at least some merit in its inclusion on the list of bombing targets, but the city was also an important cultural and medical centre, dominated by medieval churches, a magnificent baroque palace, an institute for the deaf and dumb and several renowned hospitals. On the night of 16–17 March, 225 Lancasters dropped 967 tons of bombs on the city in a raid lasting seventeen minutes. In the firestorm that engulfed Würzburg, at least 5,000 people died, 66 per cent of them women and 14 per cent children. Hermann Knell, who was a nineteen-year-old at the time, recalled: 'Everywhere people were fleeing from the city, there were fires even in the outskirts and an unbelievable roar of wind. We had heard of the firestorms in Hamburg and we knew we were in for something similar.' Knell had found his way to a park to seek refuge from where he saw that 'the inner core of Würzburg had become a cauldron of fire. The roar of the conflagration was deafening and the smoke suffocating.'[12]

The most notorious RAF raid of all was the bombing of Dresden on the night of 13–14 February. The attack has been singled out as the darkest wartime deed in the record of the RAF. The very name is synonymous with indiscriminate killing and unreasoning brute force. Over the years it has come to be regarded by many as a war crime which grievously undermined the moral integrity of the Allied cause, ranking alongside other raids like Guernica, Rotterdam, Warsaw and Coventry in aerial bombardment's catalogue of infamy. The enormous death toll, the lack of any clear military objective, the fact that the war was almost over, and the architectural beauty and rich cultural heritage of the city are all ingredients that have fuelled the never-ending debate about the ethics of this raid. Even Harris himself, normally so robust in defending area bombing, seemed embarrassed about the episode and put responsibility for it on 'more important people than myself', by which he meant Churchill and the Air Staff.[13] Yet for all the outrage it has provoked, Dresden was not so different from other raids mounted by Bomber Command, either in method or outcome. Estimates of the number of deaths have varied wildly over the years, one reaching as high as 256,000, but most reliable historians agree that the maximum figure, based on burials and registrations by the local authorities, is likely to have been no higher than 25,000. In fact, a commission of 13 eminent German historians, set up in 2004 and headed by Rolf-Dieter Mueller, announced provisionally in 2008 that the total could be 18,000.[14] That puts the death toll in Dresden significantly below the overall devastation caused by the Hamburg firestorm in 1943, when around 42,000 people died. Nor was the Dresden bombing anything like as lethal, in proportion to its size, as other RAF raids in the last year of the war. Dresden was Germany's seventh largest city, with a population of around 650,000, temporarily swollen by a large influx of refugees from the eastern front. On the basis of a maximum death toll of 25,000, this means that less than 4 per cent of the city's population died during the raid, compared to 25 per cent at Pforzheim on 23–4 February or 8 per cent at Darmstadt on 11 September 1944, when 8,100 people lost their lives in another RAF firestorm. Dresden was indeed the biggest raid ever undertaken by the Lancasters, 796 of them hitting the city that night in two waves, but it was not abnormally large by the standards of the period. Fifteen other missions mounted by Bomber Command since September 1944 had involved more than 700 heavy bombers. In the two massive raids on Essen and Dortmund in mid-March 1945, over 1,000 heavy bombers had been dispatched. Nor was there anything unusual about Bomber Command's methods over Dresden that night, as the classic mix of Pathfinder markings and heavy deployment of incendiaries was adopted.

Most of the airmen who took part did not feel there was anything unique about the mission. Rex Oldland, an engineer with 455 Pathfinder squadron, said that he had 'never had any qualms' about the raid. 'I know there has been a lot of moralizing about it, but personally, it was just a target and we hit it. It was burning merrily when we left it. Callous lot, weren't we?'[15] Peter Nettleton, a gunner with 15 Squadron, regarded the sortie as only another milestone towards the completion of his tour. 'I suppose I would like to say, in retrospect, that this was a terrible thing I was doing but it had to be done. But that would not be true. At the actual time one was more concerned with one's own skin and survival. I cannot pretend that I had any qualms about what I was doing.'[16]

What made the Dresden issue extremely potent was not so much the scale of violence as the combustible mix of timing, politics, Churchillian displeasure, and inept Allied press management, which was ruthlessly exploited by Dr Goebbels. Once the row spilled onto the public stage, Dresden became the symbolic focus for the growing revulsion felt in many quarters towards the policy of area bombing. If Dresden had occurred in 1943, it would have been hailed as a triumph. But in February 1945, when Germany was broken and in retreat, there could be no such sense of pride. The roots of the controversy lay in how the decision to bomb Dresden was taken. The most vociferous critics of the raid have been in the habit of portraying the city as an isolated artistic gem, a cultural masterpiece that transcended the brutalities of European conflict. But, as Frederick Taylor pointed out in his definitive account of the bombing, this was far from the case. Unlike places such as Pforzheim or

Freiburg, Dresden was a genuine industrial centre, with at least 127 factories that were involved in military production, while its rail network was one of the most important in the eastern Reich, employing a substantial local workforce. Contrary to its gentle image, Dresden was a key base for the Nazi Party. Governed by Martin Mutschmann, one of the Reich's most hardline Gauleiters, Dresden had participated in the vicious oppression of the Jews, staging its own Kristallnacht in November 1938, when the city's synagogue was burnt down, and serving as a vital transport link in the movement of Jews to the concentration camps in the east. Slave labour was used in its munitions plants. Its main arts hall was turned into an SS barracks.[17]

Dresden had largely been spared until February 1945 not by its innocuity but by its distance from England. As early as 1941 the city had appeared on Bomber Command's list of '43 towns in Germany selected for area attack'.[18] No action was taken because of the recognized difficulties facing heavy bombers operating against tough fighter defences in eastern Germany. But in August 1944, after the success of D-Day, the Air Ministry's Bomber Operations Directorate worked up a plan known as Operation Thunderclap, in which it was proposed to launch Allied attacks of massive intensity against Berlin, with the aim of assisting the Red Army and dealing a fatal blow to German morale. Thunderclap was the Trenchard doctrine in its crudest form. Taking as its model the German bombing of Rotterdam, its explicit aim was to inflict as much terror and death as possible. 'Experience indicates that when a nation has been deprived of all hope of further resistance, a spectacular catastrophe inflicted from the air may precipitate immediate capitulation', read one passage. The paper estimated that in order to achieve 90 per cent devastation of a built-up area, approximately 2,000 tons of high explosive must be dropped per square mile. 'A pure morale air attack must achieve a far denser pattern of HE bomb strikes on the area selected than can ever be achieved in a normal night bombing operation. The risk of death or severe injury to the individual inhabitants of the area attacked is not sufficiently great in the course of area attacks to create any overwhelming effect upon morale. Air attack on morale, in order to produce decisive results, must be of such density that there is created in the mind of the individual the conviction that if he is in the area of attack, his chances of escaping death or serious injury are remote.'[19] Thunderclap remained nothing more than a theoretical proposal throughout the autumn of 1944 because SHAEF felt it had little chance of success, but the collapse of the German eastern front in January 1945 put a new impetus behind it. Group Captain Arthur

Morley, one of Bufton's colleagues at the Bomber Operations Directorate, explained in a report of 21 January urging the revival of Thunderclap: 'The launching of the Russian offensive on an enormous scale and the subsequent break-through at a number of points on a wide front presents the German High Command with an alarming military situation. Latest information indicates that the spearhead of one of the Russian drives is within 40 miles of Breslau, and is aiming for Berlin.' In pressing the case for Thunderclap, Morley was quite open about its terroristic purpose. 'That this operation is an attack on enemy morale needs no apology. The basic principle of true morale bombing is to provoke a state of terror by air attack.'[20] Sensing the chance of a possibly decisive blow against Germany in the east, Bufton showed more enthusiasm towards Thunderclap than he did towards most schemes for area bombing. 'If the operation were launched at a time when there was still no obvious slackening in the momentum of the Russian drive,' he told Bottomley on 22 January, 'it might well have the appearance of a close co-ordination in planning between the Russians and ourselves. Such a deduction on the part of the enemy would greatly increase the moral effect on both parties.'[21]

The theme of helping the Russians was swiftly taken up by the Joint Intelligence Committee (JIC), part of the planning organization of the Chiefs of Staff. With the Germans trying to bring up reinforcements for their crumbling defensive lines and a flood of refugees trekking westwards, a strategic Allied air assault 'would be bound to create great confusion, interfere with the orderly movement of troops to the front and hamper the German military and administrative machine', stated the Committee in its report of 25 January. As the idea of Thunderclap gathered momentum, Harris was asked for his views on the JIC report. He was, predictably, all for attacking Berlin again, but also stressed that the operation should include the three other major cities of eastern Germany: Chemnitz, Leipzig and Dresden, all of which had long been on his list of targets.

It was at this stage that Winston Churchill became involved. Preparing to leave for Yalta on the Black Sea for his last great summit with Roosevelt and Stalin, he wanted to be able to offer the Russian leader some concrete support. On the night of 25 January, he telephoned Sir Archibald Sinclair, asking him about plans 'for basting the Germans in their retreat from Breslau'.[22] The next morning Sinclair gave a cautious response, telling the Prime Minister that the 'target which the enemy may offer in a large scale retreat westward to Dresden and Berlin is best suited to Tactical Air Forces', since 'it would be extremely difficult for our heavy bombers to interfere with these enemy movements by direct attack on their lines of retreat'. The best use for the bombers, Sinclair added, 'is in maintaining the attack upon German oil plants', a remark that showed a degree of wishful thinking on Sinclair's part, given Harris's lack of co-operation on such a strategy. But he concluded that, if poor weather did not permit attacks on oil installations, then there might be opportunities to mount area attacks on 'Berlin and other large cities in eastern Germany such as Leipzig, Dresden and Chemnitz, which are not only the administrative centres controlling the military and civilian movements but also the main communication centres through which the bulk of the traffic moves'.[23] Churchill, who often adopted an imperious manner towards his Secretary of State for Air, was not happy with this response and wrote to Sinclair on 26 January: 'I did not ask you last night about plans for harrying the German retreat from Breslau. On the contrary, I asked whether Berlin and no doubt other large cities in East Germany should not now be considered especially attractive targets. I am glad that this is "under examination". Pray report to me tomorrow what is going to be done.'[24] Under pressure from the Prime Minister, the time for action had arrived. On 27 January, Bottomley sent Harris an official letter instructing him, subject to the oil plan and weather, to launch attacks on Berlin, Dresden, Leipzig and Chemnitz. Such a blitz, wrote Bottomley, would 'not only cause confusion in the evacuation from the east but also hamper the movement of troops from the west'.[25] On the same day, Sinclair informed Churchill that the 'Air Staff have now arranged' for bombing to be conducted against Berlin and the other three eastern cities. The chief of Bomber Command, promised Sinclair, 'has undertaken to attempt this task as soon as the present moon has waned and favourable weather conditions allow. This is unlikely to be before 4th February.'[26]

Yet there were still many details to be decided, including the involvement of the Americans, the priority to be given to each city, the size of the bomber forces and the timing of each raid. It was the Yalta conference on 4 May that led to the concentration on Dresden as a key target. There has long been a debate about what help the Russians requested on the eastern front from the Allied strategic air forces, partly because the minutes of the summit make no specific mention of a direct raid on Dresden itself but instead refer to the call by General Aleksei Antonov (Deputy Chief of the General Staff and the Russian army's spokesman at Yalta) for an air frontier running from Berlin through Dresden to Zagreb. Yet the memory of one of the British interpreters, Hugh Lunghi, is clear on this point:

I was very much involved in the talks about the bombing of Dresden, which the Russians had asked for, both at the plenary session and the opening sessions where General Antonov laid out the military position and mentioned this. Because Dresden was an important junction, they didn't want reinforcements coming over from the Western Front and from Norway, from Italy and so on; and similarly on the following day, when there was a meeting of the chiefs of staff in Stalin's quarters, in the Kareis Palace, where Antonov very clearly said, 'Well, we want Dresden railway junction bombed because we are afraid the Germans are putting up a resistance, a last stand as it were.' And we agreed to this. We agreed to pretty well everything.[27]

In the light of the discussions at Yalta, Portal sent a message to Bottomley on 6 February with the agreed Allied priorities, urging that a new directive be issued to meet them. The following day, the Air Targets Committee met at the Air Ministry. It was decided that no new directive was needed but a new list of objectives was issued. The first city on the list was Berlin, which was already being hit heavily by the USAAF, the second Dresden, the third Chemnitz. The Air Targets Committee list was sent to Bomber Command and to SHAEF, the Americans agreeing to launch a daylight bombing assault on Dresden before the main RAF attack at night. Dresden's fate had been sealed. The attack was only a matter of days away.

According to some historians, it was at this very moment, when the die had been cast, that Sir Arthur Harris began to develop severe doubts about Operation Thunderclap. The revisionist agenda holds that the bomber chief was unfairly made a scapegoat for a policy he opposed, while the politicians evaded responsibility for a raid they had demanded. The chief protagonist of this theory has been David Irving, whose deep archival scholarship has not prevented him espousing some extreme causes, including holocaust denial. In his book on Dresden, Irving claimed that Harris was so angered by the Air Targets Committee list that he actually drove to London to challenge the order. Furthermore, in the papers of Sir Norman Bottomley at Cambridge University, there is a fascinating letter from Irving, written in December 1961, just as he was finishing his book. In it, Irving told Bottomley that he had held lengthy discussions with Harris and Saundby for the purposes of his research:

Air Marshal Saundby's recollections are very clear. He describes how the original order from the Air Ministry was queried by Bomber Command and how Harris even refused to carry it out until there were clearer details given of what the objective of the raid was going to be. Until he was apprised of the purpose of the raid, he said, he could not allocate the most suitable aiming points. When the order for the big raid finally came, Harris again refused (according to Saundby) on the grounds that such a raid would detract from the oil offensive. The Air Minister who had undertaken to represent his views replied that the order to bomb Dresden came from the Prime Minister's office. In the presence of Saundby, Harris then telephoned Churchill to try to have the order taken back, but without success. 'With a heavy heart', writes Saundby to me, 'I was forced to lay this raid on.'[28]

No credibility can be attached to this letter. The idea that Harris saw Dresden as an unwelcome distraction from the oil plan is almost laughable in its absurdity, given his stance over previous months, and it was Harris who first suggested that Dresden be incorporated within Operation Thunderclap. There was no reason for him to object to a raid on Dresden. It was, after all, the ultimate display of area bombing.

The emptiness of this desperate attempt to rewrite history was exposed by the testimony of Jim Rose, the Air Intelligence Officer at Bletchley Park, who had been shaken the previous autumn by the order to attack Bonn. Rose later recalled his feelings when he heard that Dresden had been made a priority target:

> It seemed to me tragic that this beautiful city should be destroyed. We were getting near the end of the war. My authority stemmed from the ULTRA channel of intelligence. I rang up General Spaatz, head of the American Air Force in Europe, at his base in Normandy. I said, 'Is it true you are going to bomb Dresden?' He said, 'Yes, in agreement with the British.' When I asked why, he said, 'Because I'm told that one of the Panzer divisions from the Ardennes offensive is being moved through Dresden for the defence of the Hungarian oil fields.' I said, 'Through ULTRA we have the division's movement order. It is going nowhere near Dresden. It's being routed west of Prague.' Spaatz replied, 'I have no wish to bomb Dresden. If the British agree not to, I'm willing not to.'

Rose then rang Bomber Command and was put through to Saundby, whom he told about his conversation with Spaatz. He then reiterated that the city had no military importance. 'Saundby said, "I don't care what you say. We are going to bomb Dresden." And that was that.'[29] Rose, who died in 1999, may have been trying to paint himself in a flattering light, as so many others tried to do after the war, but his account is more believable than Irving's.

Everything was now in place for the raid, which was fixed for the night of Tuesday 13–14 February. After all the debate about the USAAF's involvement, it turned out that poor weather prevented the Americans flying to Dresden during the day as planned. The RAF were, however, able to take off in the evening. As always, there was a high degree of tension at the start of the briefing before a big raid, since the crews did not know the target. Leslie Hay of 49 Squadron recalled his reaction: 'The squadron commander draws back the curtain and he said, "It's going to be Dresden." Right at the back of Germany. And my heart sank and I thought, Crumbs, that's a long way.'[30] Inured by the exhausting cycle of night bombing, most airmen felt it was just another job. 'If Harris had told us to bomb Timbuktu I suppose we would have done. It meant nothing to me,' said John Aldridge, another member of 49 Squadron.[31] Frank Musgrove, who was making his thirtieth and last operational trip, said that there was a general mood of acceptance: 'No one was shocked when the target was at last revealed. The briefing officer made crystal clear that this attack was one the Russians had particularly wanted. We understood that Dresden was an important communication centre and assembly point for German troops destined for a crucial sector of the eastern front. No one walked out or refused to go. I am quite sure that it never occurred to anyone among these hundred well educated men to do so.'[32]

But there were a few Lancaster airmen who had deep reservations. One of them was Donald Feesey, a navigator with 166 Squadron, whose memoirs include this account of the briefing: 'After we had settled in our seats, the Commanding Officer stood and regarded us in silence for a few seconds. Then came his opening remarks, "I hope you all slept well last night, for tonight you are going on a long one."' Then the CO disclosed the target:

> We were clearly going to be airborne for some nine or ten hours. However, it was not the hazards of the distance which appalled me but the fact that I was to be part of a tremendous bomber force setting out to demolish completely what was regarded as the architectural jewel of Germany and all its history. It was an operation on which I was reluctant to go and several others felt the same and made our feelings known. We were told that it was something which had to be done as the city was of significant military importance.[33]

Bomb aimer Miles Tripp wrote that he initially felt cheerful when he learnt the target, because he felt that Dresden would have nothing like the defences of the Ruhr or Berlin. But then his mind wandered to thoughts of the refugees who were fleeing into the city. 'I remembered newsreels taken early in the war and in my mind's eye saw a long stream of French refugees, their possessions piled in handcarts and prams, scattering in panic from the Stuka dive-bombers. The memory was instant and vivid and left me feeling disturbed.'[34] After the briefing, the men went to change into their flying gear. They each had two special pieces of equipment to carry: a small Union Jack and a small notice in Russian which read 'I am a British aviator', to reveal themselves as Allies if they came down behind Russian lines.

Accompanied by nine Pathfinder Mosquitoes, whose Master Bomber was Wing Commander Maurice Smith, the Lancasters left on 13 February for the 700-mile, five-hour journey to Dresden in two waves. The first, comprising 244 aircraft, began to take off from six o'clock. Due to the weakness of the Luftwaffe at this stage of the war, little fighter resistance was encountered along the route. At the appointed hour of 10 p.m. local time, the Pathfinder Lancasters dropped their white magnesium parachute flares to light up the target area. Soon afterwards the Mosquitoes flew down to lay their red target indicators on the aiming point, which was a stadium of the leading football club in the heart of the city centre. Within minutes, it was glowing with blood-red lights. Amidst mounting panic, the air-raid sirens started and people began to make for the shelters, but there was precious little anti-aircraft fire, the guns having been moved to other, more important, sites. In clear visibility and the absence of opposition, the marking had been almost perfect. Master Bomber Maurice Smith now called in the main force of the first wave. The Lancasters poured over the city, dropping 880 tons of explosives and incendiaries in the space of just fifteen minutes. Buildings were blasted apart by 172 cookies. Flames quickly engulfed the narrow streets, lit by 700,000 incendiaries. 'Everywhere we turned, the buildings were on fire. The spark-filled air was suffocating, and stung our unprotected eyes,' said Otto Grebiel, a distinguished painter, who was drinking in a pub when the bombs from the first wave fell. 'Entire chunks of red-hot matter were flying at us. The more we moved into the network of streets, the stronger the storm became, hurling burning scraps and objects through the air.'[35] As Bomber Command had intended, the city's emergency services were quickly overwhelmed. Even the rubble on the ground seemed to be on fire as the conflagration swept all before it. People suffocated in shelters and cellars, or were incinerated in the open air. The Reich's chief of fire-fighting, Major-General Hans Rumpf, wrote in his subsequent report of the experience of his crews: 'The sights with which they were presented filled these men, hardened on the inside and out by experience of a hundred nights of fire, with horror and dismay. The buildings along the streets, shattered under the hail of bombs and seared by fires from the incendiaries, had collapsed and blocked the exit routes, consigning thousands to death in the inferno.'[36]

By the time the fires were raging, the second wave of Lancasters was on its way to Dresden. Even larger than the first, it was made up of 552 planes. They started taking off at 9 p.m., ready to bomb from 1 a.m. local time. The blaze was so colossal that target indicators were almost redundant. In fact the designated aiming point in the historic marketplace between Alstadt and the Schloss (castle) was already burning fiercely, so the Pathfinders dropped their green markers on fringe areas. Long before they even reached Dresden, they could see the enormous fire burning in the distance. Pilot Robert Wannop recorded in his journal:

> As we approached the glow could be seen, fifty miles away. The target area was almost like day. Down below, 19,000 feet, the town was simply a mass of flames, a pool of fire. It was awe-inspiring, breathtaking. I had never before, nor ever will again, see such a sight. Searchlights flickered aimlessly around, even their usual brilliance lost by the blazing inferno. Around us we could see other Lancasters. It was light enough to format had we wished. Even vapour trails were plainly visible, an unusual phenomenon at night. The opposition was negligible – like taking candy from a baby. We saw one night fighter as we left the area but he wasn't interested in us, which was a good thing.[37]

Michael Bradford, a gunner with 50 Squadron, was not so lucky when a fighter encountered his Lancaster just as it was about to begin the bombing run:

> As we came in, it was like a curtain of steel met us. The wings were hit and I know there was a hole torn in the fuselage and one of the tailplanes. Anyhow, we went in, dropped our bombs, the aircraft gave a lurch and we knew the weight had gone. The skipper put the throttles full forward and we dived away out of the sky, narrowly missing a few aircraft on the way. The light from the target itself, which was burning fiercely, lit up the sky to such an extent that we were able to spot aircraft about. This of course made the fighters' job easier but they did not have much luck because once the bombers had got rid of the bombs we were weaving, diving, climbing out of the way and getting on our way home. That was a night to remember, especially from the fires on the ground. They were terrible. It was the worst inferno I had ever seen. It seemed to be spread over miles and miles of territory. It was just fire, fire, fire.[38]

Between 1.21 and 1.55 a.m., the Lancasters dropped almost 2,000 tons of bombs, including over 350 cookies.

One of those who claimed to have deliberately not dropped his bombs on the target was Miles Tripp, who recorded how he gave the pilot erroneous instructions so the Lancaster's load would fall away from the fires. Flying over Dresden, 'It was as though one was looking down at the fiery outlines of a crossword puzzle. Blazing streets stretched from east to west, from north to south, in a gigantic saturation of flame. I was completely awed by the spectacle.' Tripp thought it was pointless to contribute more to the horror on the ground. 'I told Dig to turn to starboard, to the south of the city. He swung the aircraft away from the heart of the inferno and when we were just beyond the fringe of the fires, I pressed the bomb release. I hoped the load would fall in open country. I couldn't forget what we had been told at briefing or the old newsreels of German dive-bombing atrocities.'[39] But the credibility of such high moral conduct is disputed by Frank Musgrove. An account of this sort, he wrote, 'is a gloss on events by a man carrying the burden of sixty years of guilt, for a situation not of his making. I have been tempted over the years to take part in this sort of evasion myself. I hope that I have not too often succumbed.'[40]

Bomb aimer Frank Tolley of 625 Squadron told how, on leaving the target, 'I remember thinking, seeing the fire, "Bloody hell, I wouldn't like to be down there." '[41] The scenes within the bombed area were truly like something from a gruesome fantasy. As in Hamburg, the merging of the fires had created a tornado which demolished buildings and pulled trees from their roots. As temperatures soared, the streets turned to a molten quagmire. Huge crowds made for the city's central reservoir and dived into the water. But the sheer numbers, combined with the roaring heat that sucked oxygen out of the air, made the place unbearable. People tried to clamber out but the smooth cement edges made it impossible to do so. Far from being a refuge, the reservoir turned into a watery graveyard. The next morning, when the raid was over and much of the water had evaporated, a thick ring of charred corpses could be seen along the walls. Other parts of Dresden had become a vast crematorium. One survivor said the city centre was like 'a boiling cauldron', another that 'charred corpses' were everywhere.[42] Nora Lang was in a basement cellar when the second wave started bombing. 'There was no beginning and no end to the bombing, it seemed, just these endless explosions everywhere.[43] Even when the Americans arrived the next day to carry out their raid which had been postponed from 13 February, the fires were still burning. The US bombing, aimed at the marshalling yards, had only a fraction of the RAF's destructive power but it still worsened the cataclysm that enveloped the ruined city.

In the immediate aftermath of Dresden, the British press and public reaction was generally favourable. 'Smashing blows against Dresden,' proclaimed *The Times*. 'As the centre of a railway network and a great industrial town, it has become of the greatest value in controlling the German defence.'[44] The *Daily Express* rejoiced that 'The Dresden artery is severed' and even coined a new verb 'to Dresden'.[45] Some of the crews were pleased, not just that another raid was over but that they had provided a further demonstration of the awesome power of Bomber Command. Prevented by illness from flying to Dresden, Frank Broome, a rear gunner with 626 Squadron, recalled that 'when our lads returned, they joked about breaking all the Dresden china'.[46] But behind this bravado was a creeping awareness that the raid was a form of overkill. Pride began to be replaced by shock. Squadron Leader Arthur Carter, who had been switched from operational duties to a desk job at the Air Ministry, called on his old comrades the day after Dresden. 'There was a feeling in the mess that it was a horrible mistake. The firestorm had been horrendous and nobody knew why it had been done. They had been briefed that it was at the Russian request but nobody wanted to help them anyway. Both we and the Americans hated their guts.'[47] Bill Utting, an Australian with 460 Squadron, said he 'felt disgust when I learnt of the numbers that had been killed. I was very, very sorry but it was too late then.'[48]

Concern about the raid soon became a matter of fierce public debate, thanks to blunders by the RAF Press Office where, just two days after the raid, the liaison officer Air Commodore Colin Grierson gave an in-judiciously frank briefing, in which he said that Dresden had been hit because it was a centre 'to which evacuees are being moved', before adding that the RAF wanted to destroy 'what was left of German morale'.[49] This was far from the usual bland assurance that strategic bomb-ing was aimed at military and industrial targets, the line that the Air Staff had pursued since 1941. With his natural journalistic instincts, Howard Cowan of the Associated Press wanted to give full coverage to this change of tone. 'Allied air bosses have made a long awaited decision to adopt deliberate terror bombing of great German population centres as a ruth-less expedient to hasten Hitler's doom,' he wrote in his draft report. Amazingly, the government's official wartime censor compounded the Press Office's folly by approving this article.

The admission of terror bombing, while literally true in the case of Thunderclap, was a tremendous propaganda gift for Goebbels and, even in the dying days of the war, he was keen to exploit the situation. Through leaflets, broadcasts, agency output and articles, he spoke of the 'Allies' massacre of the refugees', 'annihilation' and 'mass murder', all the time increasing the estimate of the death toll. His characterization of the bomber crews as 'terror-flyers' now appeared to have become a reality.

All this undoubtedly had an effect on public opinion in Britain and the USA. Questions were asked in Parliament about 'terror bombing', while the air strategy was earnestly debated in the press. Even Churchill, one of the driving forces behind the raid, succumbed to the growing mood of incrimination. In one of the less creditable episodes of his wartime leadership, he wrote to Portal on 28 March, suggesting that 'the moment has come when the question of bombing German cities simply for the sake of increasing the terror, though under other pretexts, should be reviewed, otherwise we shall come into control of an utterly ruined land'.[50] Portal was indignant at Churchill's charge, and, through Bottomley, sent a copy of the Prime Minister's letter to Harris. On 29 March the Bomber Chief produced one of his most waspish replies, describing Churchill's reference to terror attacks as 'an insult both to the bombing policy of the Air Ministry and to the manner in which that policy has been executed by Bomber Command'. Harris then claimed that 'We have never gone in for terror bombing and the attacks which we have made in accordance with my Directive have in fact produced the strategic consequences for which they were designed and from which the armies now profit.' In another passage, he dismissed the controversy over Dresden as nothing more than sentimentality: 'The feeling, such as there is, over Dresden could easily be explained by a psychiatrist. It is connected with German bands and Dresden shepherdesses. Actually Dresden was a mass of munitions works, an intact government centre, and a key transportation point to the East. It is now none of those things.' Then in a notorious passage that in the years to come would be widely quoted against him, he gave his own sterling defence of area bombing:

> Attacks on cities like any other act of war are intolerable unless they are strategically justified. But they are strategically justified in so far as they tend to shorten the war and so preserve the lives of Allied soldiers. To my mind we have absolutely no right to give them up unless it is certain that they will not have this effect. I do not personally regard the whole of the remaining cities of Germany as worth the bones of one British Grenadier.[51]

This had always been Harris's sincerely held view, and in his support he could cite how the bombing of industrial centres drew the German economy to a grinding halt in the spring of 1945, with the Reich's rail system, gas, water and electricity all paralysed.

On Dresden itself, it is possible to argue that the raid was the blow that finally cracked German morale, making even the tyranny of the Nazis an irrelevance in the final weeks of war. Götz Bergander, who was a teenager during the time of the Dresden raid and later became a leading journalist and author, said: 'It is true that most Germans no longer believed in victory, but nevertheless they could not imagine unconditional surrender. The shock of Dresden contributed in a fundamental way to a change of heart. This expressed itself at that time in words: Better an end to terror than terror without end.'[52] As well as destroying the last vestiges of the German people's spirit, Dresden also provided hope to the Jews facing extermination, as this testimony from Jewish prisoner Ben Halfgott reveals: 'We saw the bombing of Dresden from the satellite camp at Schlieben where we worked with German women making *Panzerfausts*, anti-tank rockets. The fires in the sky, a huge red glow – it was like heaven for us. We went out to watch and it was glorious, for we knew that the end of the war must be near and our salvation was at hand. I was fifteen years old when the Russians arrived and I weighed 50 kilos. You could see all my bones.'[53] Interrogated by the Americans just after the war, Göring himself made this intriguing admission: 'He considered the Allied raids on Dresden this February, when one blow followed the other in quick succession, as the most deadly, the most demoralising and therefore the most effective raids of the war. "Nothing is more terrible than an attack which is made on the same target three times in a row. That really undermines the resistance of the people."'[54]

Through all this bitter controversy, two of the outstanding qualities of Bomber Command, the excellence of the Lancaster and the courage of its aircrews, continued to endure. In all the epochal episodes of the last year of the war, from D-Day to Dresden, the Lancaster's power, resilience and strength were never more in evidence. It was in the last two months of the war that the Lancaster gave a unique demonstration of its phenomenal lifting power, which exceeded any other bomber of the Second World War, even the celebrated Boeing B-29 Superfortress. March 1945 saw the introduction into service of the awesome 'Grand Slam' bomb, weighing 22,000 pounds, or almost ten tons. The 'most destructive missile in history until the invention of the atom bomb' to use the words of Harris,[55] it was designed by Barnes Wallis and was essentially a much larger version of the Tallboy. A ten-ton bomb had long been a cherished project of Wallis's, and by 1944 he had made good progress on its development. But in September 1944, work on the Grand Slam was halted on the instructions of the Air Ministry because there was a widespread belief that the war could be finished by Christmas. A month later, with characteristic vision, Sir Wilfrid Freeman, the Chief Executive of MAP, reversed this short-sighted decision and production recommenced. By 13 March the first Grand Slam bomb, filled with Torpex, was ready. Tested at Ashley Walk experimental range in the New Forest, it produced a crater 30 feet deep and 124 feet in diameter. Because of its colossal size, 26 feet 6 inches in length and 3 feet 10 inches in diameter, it could only be accommodated in a specially modified Lancaster known as the B1, which featured a strengthened undercarriage and beams along the bomb bay. In addition the doors were removed from the bay and fairings fitted in the front and rear. Harris, an enthusiast of this monster, had to borrow a special Ransome and Rapier Super Mobile Crane from A&AEE at Boscombe Down to enable the Grand Slam to be loaded into the Lancaster.

The heavyweight bomb was first used in action on 14 March in a raid against the Bielefeld Viaduct on the vital railway line between Hamm and Hanover, when the B1 Lancaster, flown by Squadron Leader C. C. Calder, accompanied 14 other Tallboy-carrying Lancasters of 617 Squadron. The viaduct had been under attack several times, even sustaining some damage, but the Germans had always managed to repair it. On this occasion it was different. Descending to the ground with a terminal velocity of 4,600 feet per second, having been dropped from 12,000 feet, Calder's Grand Slam penetrated the soft earth by the side of the bridge, then exploded underground with such devastating effect that the subsequent earthquake demolished seven arches of the bridge. With the war drawing to a close, only 41 Grand Slams were produced. Apart from the Bielefeld Viaduct, they were used in four other raids, two against U-boats and two against railway viaducts, where their astonishing penetrative power meant they could destroy a concrete roof 23 feet thick.

The last months of the war were not as dangerous for Allied bombers as early 1944, with the loss rate falling to less than 1 per cent. Yet the risks of being shot down were not negligible, as the German fighters and flak operators fought with a near-irrational ferocity. A total of 19 Lancasters, out of a force of 520, were downed on a raid to Dessau in east Germany in early March, and a week later 24 were lost on another of those grim raids to Nuremburg, this latter mission reaching a loss rate of almost 9 per cent as a result of what the official history called 'a temporary resurgence of the German night fighter force'.[56] Joe Williams, a rear gunner with 625 Squadron, was one of those who experienced the continuing tenacity of the German fighter force when he flew to Chemnitz on 5–6 March, a night when 13 Lancasters were shot down out of a force of 417. Williams's Lancaster had already run into trouble before it even reached Germany, as the starboard outer engine started to stream smoke and had to be feathered. Bravely, the crew decided to carry on, even though the starboard outer drove both the generator for the Gee set and the hydraulic pump which operated the mid-upper turret:

> Here we were committed and we were really dead ducks from that moment on. On three engines, we were on maximum climbing power for three hours – whereas a maximum of one and a quarter hours was permitted. Everything got terribly hot, red hot. We lost our position in the stream, and we never got our height. We were meant to get to 18,000 feet but we only got to 15,000 feet, then levelled off as we plodded on. It was the wrong decision. We must have thought we were fireproof. We approached the target, which was burning and glowing. All the other planes had gone home. We made our bombing run and dropped the bombs. We exited the target. And there in the glow of the target I saw a Ju 88 night fighter.

Williams told the pilot to do some flat turns to check whether the Ju 88, armed with upward-firing cannon, had seen the Lancaster. The fighter followed the bomber's every move:

> I opened fire, fully depressing my guns, but he got in underneath us. I ordered a corkscrew to starboard. We went into the corkscrew, hoping to get him in my sights. But this fellow could do the corkscrew manoeuvre as well as we could. He was right underneath us. The bomb aimer could see him through the nose panel, which shows how close he was. He gave us the works. We could hear the shells banging into the fuselage. Nothing was working in the rear turret. Hydraulic pipes were burning like candles. My intercom had gone. No hydraulic power. Upfront, the order was given to bail out. The engineer later said that, looking back at the rear, he could see the tailplane falling off in lumps. So we were burning very well. I realized I had to get out.

But Williams struggled to open the turret doors, which had been damaged by cannon shell. 'I sat back in the turret and I shouted, "For God's sake, get me out of this." I think He above must have heard me, because next time I had a go at the door, it opened.' To his anguish, he found that his parachute, stowed near the rear door, was burning. But by a stroke of good fortune, he remembered that one crew member, on a previous trip, had left a spare parachute in the cockpit. 'I realized my only hope was that spare chute. I went up through the fuselage. I lost the skin off my face and a lot of the clothing was burnt off me, although I was moving as quickly as I could towards the cockpit.' The pilot was just about to leave the cockpit to bail out when Williams arrived. He selflessly returned to steady the plane while Williams looked for the spare parachute. 'He was having difficulty controlling the aircraft because of the lack of tail surfaces. The plane kept wanting to go up and stall. That would have been the end of us.' Williams found the parachute, clipped it on and he and the pilot went out through the front escape hatch. After his parachute had safely opened, he came down in some bushes, and struggled to a nearby farm, where there was a light shining from the outside toilet. 'There was a gentleman in there doing his business. So I have the rare distinction of having surrendered to a man on a toilet.' He spent two months as a POW in Bavaria before escaping in April 1945 and reaching American lines.[57]

The selfless and indomitable spirit highlighted in Williams's story was typical of Bomber Command right up to May 1945. Three of the ten Victoria Crosses won by Lancaster airmen were for deeds in the last five months of the war. In each of this trio of cases, the medal was awarded posthumously. On 23 December 1944, Acting Squadron Leader Robert Palmer led a formation of Lancasters on a daylight attack against a marshalling yard in Cologne. Carrying G-H equipment, his bombing run was crucial to guide the rest of the formation onto the target. Under ferocious fighter fire but oblivious to his own safety, he kept his exact course for the bombing run even as shells tore through his aircraft. 'With his engines developing unequal power, an immense effort was needed to keep the damaged aircraft on a straight course. Nevertheless, he made a perfect approach and his bombs hit the target.'[58] But moments later his plane burst into flames and he fell to earth. His VC was awarded soon afterwards for 'heroic endeavour beyond praise'.[59]

The penultimate Lancaster VC was awarded to wireless operator George Thompson for the selfless gallantry he showed on a daylight raid against the Dortmund-Ems canal on 1 January 1945. Just after releasing its load, his Lancaster was badly hit by flak. Flames and smoke swept through the aircraft, but Thompson fought his way down the fuselage to rescue the badly injured mid-upper gunner from his turret. With his bare hands, Thompson put out the fire on the gunner's clothing, sustaining serious burns in the process. In great pain, he then worked his way to the rear of the Lancaster to drag the rear gunner from his blazing turret. Again, he used his hands to extinguish the flames on his comrade's flying gear. Having pulled the two gunners to safety, he then went to report to the captain. So severe were his burns that at first the skipper did not even recognize him. After the Lancaster crash-landed, Thompson was taken to hospital, where he died three weeks later. 'His signal courage and self-sacrifice will ever be an inspiration to the service', read his citation.[60]

The last Lancaster VC of the war was gained by Edwin Swales in his role as Master Bomber in the Pforzheim raid of 23 Febuary, overseeing the attack even though his plane was severely damaged by enemy fighter fire. On the way back to England, his crippled Lancaster kept losing height until he had to tell the rest of the crew to bail out. Fighting desperately with the controls, he kept the plane steady enough so the other six men could escape. Hardly had the last airman jumped out when the aircraft fell to earth. Captain Swales was found dead at the controls, having given 'his life that his comrades might live'.[61]

As always, it would be wrong to pretend that this was the entire picture, with bravery a universal quality. For a very few airmen, the approach of the war's end elevated the instinct for survival above obedience to orders. Gunner Peter Nettleton had this insight:

> When the war was at its fiercest and the outcome was in doubt, morale was uniformly high. But in the last weeks of the war, when fighter and flak opposition was comparatively light because the Germans were crumbling, there were definitely instances where crews would drop their loads in the North Sea or use fairly minor technical excuses, such as the non-functioning of a heated flying suit, to abort the exercise. This, in retrospect, is very understandable but at the time I felt slightly offended and shocked.[62]

The loosening of discipline was mirrored in the Lancaster workforce, where the imminence of victory sparked a mood of rebellion against the Avro management. From February until the end of the war, the factories in Manchester were plagued by unrest, some of the strikes even bigger than those that occurred in 1943. One February strike, which took place at Chadderton, had a whiff of almost demobbed irresponsibility about it, for, according to MAP, 'the cause is said to be due to the failure of one employee to pay his arrears on union dues. The strikers are agitating for this employee's dismissal and the management refuse to dismiss the man.'[63] The strikers went back to work when the employee made a token payment of his arrears. But that was only a rehearsal for the massive dispute that engulfed Chadderton in April 1945, when the whole plant was brought to a standstill in a row over the abolition of piece rates. Union efforts secured an end to the strike, but the air of rebellion continued inside the factory. 'A very small number of conscientious employees are carrying on with their work, but their efforts are hampered by the lack of complementary work on the part of other employees who are still on the premises but not actually working,' complained MAP.[64] With VE Day barely a month away, the whole episode had an air almost of irresponsibility and irrelevance.

April 1945 saw the last raids of the Lancaster. The final big area attack took place on the night of 14–15 April when 500 Lancasters flew to Potsdam, near Berlin. It was a mission that infuriated Churchill, who thought that the RAF had been instructed to cease area bombing on 6 April, following the row over Dresden. 'What's the point of going and blowing down Potsdam?' he asked Portal.[65] The Chief of the Air Staff replied: 'In accordance with your decision on the recommendation of the Chiefs of Staff, we have already issued instructions to Bomber Command that area bombing designed solely with the object of destroying industrial areas is to be discontinued. The attack on Potsdam, however, was calculated to hasten the disintegration of enemy resistance.'[66] On 18 April more than 900 aircraft, including 617 Lancasters, attacked the North Sea island fortress of Heligoland, which included an airfield and naval base. Henry Hooper of 115 Squadron recalled: 'It was a demonstration of the power of Bomber Command. When I got there, it had been turned into a piece of earth. There was nothing but a pall of dust and smoke and we bombed through that.'[67] The next day, 36 more Lancasters arrived, six of them carrying Grand Slams, just to ensure that the place was completely destroyed.

The very last major raid by the Lancasters occurred on 25 April, when 361 of them flew to bomb Hitler's remote mountain retreat at Berchtesgaden. Right up to the end of the war, Eisenhower was convinced that Hitler was funnelling troops and materiel into his Alpine redoubt to stage a violent last stand against the Allies, a fear that was apparently confirmed when Bletchley Park intercepted an ULTRA message from the Führer to one of his generals ordering 'a last bulwark of fanatical resistance'.[68] Peter Marshall recalled the mood amongst his 619 Squadron when the target was revealed:

> Excitement spread through the briefing room as crews burst into noisy chatter. Everyone knew the war in Europe was drawing to a close but to be going after Adolf Hitler, with him and his henchmen as the target, made this operation different. Targets don't usually have identifiable faces attached to them, but this time we knew names and what they looked like. This time it was personal. But we knew it was going to be heavily defended and we would have to be on our toes if we weren't going to get the chop.[69]

There were three targets at Berchtesgaden: the Berghof itself, the SS barracks and the Eagle's Nest, Hitler's personal retreat high in the mountain where in 1938 he had negotiated the dismemberment of Czechoslovakia with Neville Chamberlain.

Accompanied by a substantial escort of American Mustangs and Thunderbolts, the Lancasters left in the early hours and flew southwards over the breathtaking scenery of the Alps towards the target. But the German threat had still not evaporated, as Jeffrey Goodwin of 150 Squadron found. 'It was the first time I have ever seen the Alps and it was glorious. It was dawn, fantastic. Between us and the Alps, I suddenly saw a German jet fighter, the Me 262. I realized he was parallel to us and then he was getting further away. I think he was returning to base, running short of fuel. I had a slight gulp.'[70] The first Lancasters at the head of the stream glimpsed the target high in the Bavarian mountains. Just before 9 a.m. they started to throw Window strips out to confuse the German radar defences. Then the Pathfinders moved in to drop their markers. David Ware of 635 Pathfinder Squadron recalled the sense of ease compared to previous raids: 'We were bristling with Allied fighters all over us. This was complete air superiority. There was no fear of anything. We found Berchtesgaden and we were the first to drop flares because we were the primary visual crew. Not that you really needed flares because you could see the target. Berchtesgaden was on a mountain and you could see it very clearly. We had a great run in and we did some great marking, very accurate. Then we turned for home.'[71] Navigator Ian Dunlop, also of 635 Pathfinder Squadron, had this memory: 'It was brilliant daylight. The scenery was glorious. We were at 18,000 feet but the mountains were at 12,000 so in fact we were only 6000 feet above the border. I put in my log book, "Wizard prang". We really used slang like that in those days.'[72]

But this confidence from the Pathfinders was not reflected within the main force, where there was mounting confusion over the radio communications. Some could not hear the instructions from the Master Bombers; others heard only the US fighter escorts. The circling of so many aircraft over the small target increased the risk of collisions, while the anti-aircraft guns had now gone fully into action. 'We were right in the mountains, just clearing the tops and the sides and there was fierce gunfire coming at us from the fortified positions on both sides and the valley below,' said bomb aimer Dickie Parfitt. 'It was hot. There would be only one chance for one bombing run. We wouldn't want to go round again. The Master Bomber was on the air giving me instructions. Our bomb doors were open and suddenly we were there and not far off track. I called for a few corrections and then it was "Bombs gone". We climbed away and headed for home.'[73] The closeness of the other bombers in the tight environment was what shook Bob Woolf, flying with 9 Squadron. He was in the astrodome of his Lancaster during the bombing run, when suddenly he saw a 617 Squadron Lancaster directly above with its bomb doors open. 'I watched in utter horror as the bomb was released and began its curving flight. It was heading absolutely straight for us. I had no alternative, even though we were on our run. "Starboard, skip, a touch starboard," I shouted. The bomb missed our port wing tip by nothing at all. I could read the word Torpex on it as it went past, the name of the explosive inside. Well, the run-up was spoiled and we couldn't make another, so we brought our Tallboy home for the last time.'[74]

In this messy situation, it was hardly a surprise that the raid only had limited success. The SS barracks and the Berghof were hit, but the Eagle's Nest remained untouched. Worse still, two Lancasters were shot down, a tragic outcome on what was almost the last trip of the war. Some of the crews felt bitter about the poor planning of the mission which, to them, seemed little more than a public relations exercise. But on the way home and back at base there was a mood of celebration. On the return flight to England, recalled David Ware:

> we only had to worry for about half an hour because we were soon back over Allied territory. This was wonderful. This was the end of the war, no more living with that gnawing fear, "Am I going to survive?" When we got back, I think about 11 o'clock, the ground crew had got a big table out, with lots of glasses and champagne. They had been our ground crew throughout the campaign and we were pretty close. But we could not get too pissed because we had to go to debriefing. That night, we were a bit over the top.[75]

Dickie Parfitt felt a surge of elation as he saw the White Cliffs of Dover. 'I thought, I've made it. I'm through this. I'm safe. That evening we all went into Lincoln and had a few beers. It felt a bit of an anti-climax after having been over Adolf Hitler's house that very morning!'[76] Contrary to Eisenhower's fears, the Führer had not been there. Hitler killed himself in his Berlin bunker five days later.

The last wartime raids by the Lancasters were carried out on 25–6 April in two separate attacks. A force of 107 Lancasters hit the Tonsberg oil refinery in southern Norway, causing severe damage to the target. One plane, piloted by Flying Officer A. Cox, was shot down over Sweden, the last of more than 3,300 Lancaster losses during the war, but fortunately all the crew survived. After a brief spell in a Swedish POW camp, the airmen were released on VE Day. The second, much smaller raid, was by 14 Lancasters carrying out mine-laying in the Oslo fjord against the non-existent German naval menace. All the Lancasters returned safely. But before VE Day, Bomber Command had two huge missions to undertake that were both very different to the destructive tasks for which they were usually employed. Essentially humanitarian in nature, these two operations involved ferrying large quantities of food to the Dutch people and bringing back British POWs from Germany. It is an irony that only a few weeks after Dresden, the Lancasters should be called on to act as a saviour of humanity. Operation Manna, the transport of food supplies to the Netherlands, began on 26 April, the day after the Berchtesgaden raid. The mission was vital because the infrastructure of the country had all but collapsed and the people of western Holland were on the verge of starvation. According to British intelligence, there had not been a live baby born in this part of Holland for nine months owing to the malnutrition of mothers. Since late February, with the end of the war imminent, the RAF had been practising for this exercise, developing the right dropping technique for the cargo. The method adopted was for the Lancaster to be loaded with eight specially built panniers. Within each pannier, there were 70 sacks weighing 25 pounds, containing essential foodstuffs like tea, sugar, dried eggs, tinned meat, flour and chocolate. The panniers were then either suspended within the aircraft on hooks attached to special cables, which would be released like bombs by pressing the tit, or, more simply, they just rested on the bomb doors and fell out when the doors were opened. Before Manna could begin, one other step was necessary: securing the acquiescence of the occupying Germans. Though the Reich had not yet surrendered, negotiations between British agents, led by Air Commodore Arthur Geddes, and Nazi officials led to a written agreement whereby the Germans pledged, first, not to open fire on the Lancasters, and second, to allow a series of designated drop points to be established across Holland.

The first planes to embark on Operation Manna were from 115 Squadron and over the next nine days up to VE Day, the Lancasters flew 2,835 sorties and dropped 6,684 tons of food on Holland. For the men carrying out this mission, it was a relief to be greeted with cheers rather than antiaircraft fire. David Ware, the pilot of 635 Squadron, remembered the experience of flying over Rotterdam harbour at 200 feet. 'On the ships and the quayside, you could see everybody waving. Holland had been so isolated by the Germans. It was a wonderful experience, flying so low, as low as you could make it because Holland is so flat. We flew down a canal and reached a town, where there were hundreds of people waving at us. We each got our rations, sent them down to the gunner and I did a run down the high street and he threw the sweets out. It was great.'[77] Robert Wannop left this moving account in his journal:

> We crossed the Dutch coast at 2000 feet and commenced losing height down to 500. Much of the land was under water. We then went onto the Hague. Children ran out of school waving excitedly – one old man stopped at a cross-roads and shook his umbrella. The roads were dotted with hundreds of people, waving, a white blob showing for their upturned faces, faces that we knew were wreathed in smiles of happiness. A hell of a lump came to my throat. Nobody spoke in the aircraft. It wasn't the time for words. My vision grew a little misty. Perhaps it was rain on the Perspex, perhaps it wasn't. We had a great reception in The Hague, where Union Jacks were spread out on the tops of building. One building was painted with huge white letters, 'Thank you RAF' – they were thanking us. Those brave people who had so often risked their lives to save an RAF aircrew and return him safely to England. Who had spied for us and done countless other deeds that may never be revealed. They were thanking us for delivering a little food. I felt very humble.[78]

The process of dropping the panniers was described by Henry Hooper of 115 Squadron:

> We took off and flew individually. We flew as low as was safely possible, between 100 and 200 feet. The Germans knew we could not bomb from that height so they felt safe. We got to the dropping zone which was marked with a very large white cross. We dropped the food and a lot of it burst and broke but most got through. What stands out in my mind was seeing all the Dutch people in the streets and on their rooftops, waving and cheering as we flew by. Messages were set out in sheets on the ground, 'Thank you'. I felt it was marvellous. One minute I had been dropping bombs to kill people, now I was dropping food to save people.[79]

The intelligence officer Bill Jones, who had been involved in the development of the dropping technique, travelled with one of the Manna Lancasters and was also deeply affected by what he saw: 'It brought a lump to my throat and I think we all had tears in our eyes to see those people waving at us and cheering us on our way.'[80] But not all the crews were happy with the experience. Some were shaken by low-level flying. 'If pilots can hop over the tops of windmills and electric pylons, they're having a lovely time but it is not so good for the other people in the aeroplane. I did not like that one little bit,' recalled navigator Ian Dunlop.[81] Others, like wireless operator Ian Wolstenholme, worried about the Germans keeping their word. 'Manna operations were more nerve-racking than general operations because as you flew over, you could see the

Germans on the 88mm guns, following us over. I used to think to myself, "If one of them has got an itchy finger, they cannot miss us."' But the Germans never opened fire and the food got through to the Dutch. One seventeen-year-old, Arie de Jong, recorded in her diary the thrill of seeing the Lancaster stream, a beacon of hope at last:

> There are no words to describe the emotions experienced on that Sunday afternoon. More than 300 four-engined Lancasters, flying exceptionally low, suddenly filled the western horizon. One could see the gunners waving in their turrets. A marvellous sight. One Lancaster roared over the town at 70 feet. I saw the aircraft tacking between church steeples and drop its bags in the south. Everywhere we looked, bombers could be seen. No one remained inside and everybody dared to wave cloths and flags. What a feast! Everyone is excited with joy. The war must be over soon now.[82]

Just as stirring, in its own way, was that other liberation exercise: the return of the British prisoners of war from the former occupied territories. Code-named Operation Exodus, this began on 4 May when the first Lancasters flew to Juvincourt in northern France and to Brussels, picking up the POWs who had been taken to these holding centres before the journey back to England. The Lancaster was not ideal as a transport plane, given its cramped interior and big spars for the mainplane and tail, but, as so often before, it adapted superbly to its temporary new role. As far back as November 1944, Bomber Command had been considering the Lancaster for just this task and Don Bennett, the head of the Pathfinder Force, conducted experiments to see how many passengers the aircraft could carry. 'I took a crew of five and 24 passengers very comfortably. From the centre of gravity point of view, it is of course necessary to put some of them in the nose,' he reported to Harris.[83] Once Exodus was underway, the maximum number of ex-POWs was limited to 24 per aircraft for safety reasons, and figures going from 1 to 24 were painted on the floor of the Lancaster so the men would know where to sit. Some pilots, however, were known to exceed the total on occasions, as pilot Robert Wannop admitted when recalling his trips from Juvincourt:

> I was torn off a strip for carrying too many passengers, as we were only supposed to carry 24 and each skipper had a list of names. However when my Lanc was loading two very dejected Tommies came up and asked if I could find room for them. They looked so miserable and disappointed that I had not the heart to refuse. It was OK until we reached Blighty and then questions were asked – but it was too late then and anyhow, did those boys look happy. The most touching moment on each trip was when the White Cliffs of Dover came into sight. Then as many chaps as possible

would crowd into the navigator's and engineer's compartments and peer out with eager eyes. I used to wonder what their thoughts were. I couldn't ask them. That damned lump again in my throat.[84]

David Ware, the Pathfinder pilot, was equally moved, especially by the time he had a squadron leader sitting beside him with tears rolling down his cheeks as the Lancaster crossed the English coast.

Ware was also deeply impressed by the efficiency of the operation, under which the Lancasters landed from northern Europe at RAF bases in southern England, where the ex-POWs had all the arrangements made for their readjustment to life in Britain. 'It was fantastic. We went to Lübeck on 10th May to bring back POWs and when we landed, there must have been all of 200 planes, British and American nose-to-nose. The POWs were coming by van or foot. Each time we came back to RAF Wynne. It was an amazing set-up there. A terrific operation.'[85] Flight engineer Danny Boon felt that Exodus was 'one of the best organized things I ever saw in all my time in the air force. They were taken to a hangar, stripped off, deloused, seen by doctors, given their pay and documents. Before we took off again, some of the ones we had brought back had already passed through the system.'[86] Many of the ex-POWs needed sympathetic handling, since some of them had been incarcerated for almost the whole war. Thomas Tredwell described the scene on the base where he operated:

> Some of the prisoners were in danger of collapse. When they went into hangars, they were sprayed with the newfangled DDT – and this was a little undignified. Many of them, having been in German hands less than 24 hours earlier, were in a state of complete confusion. They had to be led in certain directions. Some of them had been in a POW camp for four years, and they had their little pile of belongings, like a small bar of soap, which they had to put down while they were deloused. To begin with, their eyes would never leave these little piles on the floor. After a while, they began to relax, and they would just walk straight past their possessions which they had jealously guarded and now had completely forgotten. It was rather pathetic.[87]

But at the other end of the emotional scale, a lot of the prisoners were only too elated at returning to England, and could not hide their jubilation. 'They were an incredibly cheerful collection, members of all services and all ranks, mixed up in one laughing, talking and smoking conglomeration,' said the engine fitter Stephen Rew, who helped with the processing of the ex-POWs at Coningsby.

Those were the feelings that shone through the account left by Doug Fry, a former Stirling air gunner who had been a POW since July 1943 and was flown from Lübeck on 10 May:

There were 23 of us. I pointed out to the skipper that his crew had no Mae Wests or parachute harnesses. He replied, 'Yes, we left them behind. We knew you wouldn't have this equipment so we thought we would fly without it as well.' Again, I thought that was a wonderful gesture. The flight back was wonderful. There was no mid-upper gunner so I asked the skipper if I could go in the mid-upper turret and he agreed. We got back to an airfield in the Midlands and when we got off the aircraft, there were two WAAFs to meet each of us. They took us into a hangar, where there were tea, cakes and sandwiches laid out and a dance band playing. We were there for half an hour. We were then taken by trucks through the countryside to Cosford. There had obviously been some spring rain because it smelt beautiful and fresh, wonderful English countryside. Then we were put up in billets at Cosford with clean sheets. Fish and chips that night in the canteen and then a good soak in the bath. X-rays and medicals the next day, kitted out in new RAF uniform. Briefly interrogated, and then given our rail passes, plus a bit of pay. All the houses along the railway had their bunting up and big signs saying 'Welcome Home Lads'.[88]

Safety was of paramount importance, because there was nothing more tragic than a Lancaster crew and a score of prisoners perishing just as they reached the end of their arduous journey. It was not just a question of numbers, as 50 Squadron gunner Michael Bradford remembered: 'We had to be very careful. These chaps were great for bringing back bits and pieces that they had picked up. It was found out that some of them were bringing back German grenades and explosives as souvenirs. So we had to do a body search on everybody. If we did not know what they were carrying, the object was thrown out. As a gunner, I had to act as a steward, make sure these fellas behaved themselves.'[89] At the start of Exodus, Sir Archibald Sinclair was so concerned that on 3 May he urged Harris to give strict instructions that 'if there is any doubt about any particular sortie, on the grounds of weather or the experience of the crew, then that sortie will be abandoned, even if it involves delay, inconvenience or disappointment to the passengers'.[90]

In fact, on 9 May there was an accident when a Lancaster of 514 Squadron, having taken off from Juvincourt, ran into technical difficulties and had to attempt a forced landing. Unfortunately, the plane stalled, crashed and everyone on board was killed. The following day Harris replied to Sinclair, telling him that, although everything possible was being done to protect the ex-POWs, tragedies were inevitable. 'We must face the fact that flying especially in wartime is a dangerous trade.' He concluded by asking Sinclair whether the risks in transporting the ex-POWs were really worth it. 'I cannot understand why there should be any trouble in providing one or two ships for a shuttle service from Antwerp, of a size which would take far more prisoners than we could ever take.'[91] Sinclair told him that evacuation by sea had been considered but 'the case against it is the disorganisation of land communications with the ports, aggravated by the shortage of motor transport. Moreover, while I agree with you that risk is inseparable from flying, especially in wartime, the risk of travel by sea before the mines are swept up is at least comparable and the loss of even one ship would probably entail a great loss of life.'[92]

The anxieties of Harris and Sinclair turned out to be unfounded. The accident of 9 May was Exodus's only loss. Altogether 3,000 round trips were flown over the 24 days of the operation, bringing home 74,000 troops. At the end of Exodus, Eisenhower wrote to thank Harris in generous terms for the way he organized the operation. It was, said the American commander, 'an achievement of great magnitude, comparable to the remarkable results of the offensive war waged by Bomber Command. The assistance rendered by your Command not only greatly accelerated the return of many British repatriates to their home but it also relieved the over-worked transport aircrews.'[93] Harris expressed gratitude for Eisenhower's praise. 'It was a task which caused us considerable apprehension, the aircraft not being particularly suitable for the work and the aerodromes available being very hard on the tyres. A burst tyre in a Lancaster taking off is a serious matter. Consequently I was relieved when the work was concluded with only one accident, unfortunate as that was.'[94]

The war in Europe had come to an end. Relief, gratitude and sadness were joined together as the bloodiest conflict in mankind's history drew to its close. Amidst all these emotions was imprinted in both the RAF and the British people a heartfelt spirit of admiration for the plane that, in its tenacity and resolution, had become one of the symbols of the triumphant struggle against tyranny. The engine fitter Stephen Rew put it well at the close of his richly evocative account of life on a bomber base:

> Personally, I find it impossible to recall the sights and sounds of Ops without a deep sense of nostalgia, mingled with great pride, that I was involved in such stirring events, albeit in a very insignificant role: the sound of four

sweet-running Merlins on full power, the squat, dark shape becoming somehow slimmer and more deadly-looking as she becomes airborne; the smell of burnt 100 octane petrol, acrid yet sweet; the summer twilight; the air heavy with the thunder of engines; the sky speckled with lean black shapes, with here and there a glint of gold as the last rays of the dying sun touch the gleaming Perspex of a cockpit canopy or turret; the gradual return of silence and the beauty of the night; the drone of the returning engines; the harsh ring of the telephone shattering the tension in the hut; the twinkle of the navigation lights; the changing engine notes as the propellers and throttles are altered for landing; the final tired sigh and the 'pop-pop-pop' as the engines are throttled right back as she comes over the fence and the sharp screech of tyres kissing the concrete; the flurry of guiding her into dispersal and, when safely parked, the quick little prayer of thanks that she hasn't run into anything on the way; the cheerful chatter of the aircrew and their cheery 'goodnight' from the crew bus; the indescribable, though not unpleasant smell of the aircraft after flight; checking that everything is switched off, and drinking the remaining coffee; the queer little noises from the cooling engines and the quiet hum of the dying gyros; the silence and the stars; and perhaps, above all, the knowledge that the minor part that one has played has not let the aircrew down.[95]

At an Avro dinner in December 1945, Sir Arthur Harris paid this tribute to the company, his words encapsulating the feelings of a nation: 'As the user of the Lancaster during the last three and a half years of bitter and unrelenting warfare, I would say this to those who placed that shining sword in our hands – without your genius and your efforts we could not have prevailed. The Lancaster was the single greatest factor in winning the war.'[96]

18

'A deadly silence'

Squadron Leader Peter Russell was standing by one of the hangars at RAF Scampton in the week that victory in Europe was declared. Gazing out across the airfield, he reflected on his survival through the dark nights of conflict: 'It was over. A new way of life was beginning, a life without the zest that living so close to danger and oblivion gives.' On this early summer's day the sun climbed high in the skies over Lincolnshire. 'Though everyone was in battledress, the sunshine glinted in the polished brass buttons of men's caps. There was no sound of aircraft engines. Across the green field Lancasters, which would no longer drop death on the good and on the bad in German targets or be a blazing sarcophagus for stricken men within them, rested in their dispersal pans. Their awesome duty was done.'[1]

On VE Day itself impromptu celebrations were held throughout Bomber Command. There were long drinking sessions in the mess or the pubs of local towns, often followed by frivolous antics. On some stations all the magnetos were removed from the Lancasters as a precaution against any drunken pilot who might decide to give a celebratory aerobatic display or something even more adventurous. Sticking firmly to the ground, Flight Lieutenant Dennis Steiner and his comrades ferried a group of WAAFs in a builder's wheelbarrow through the town of Gainsborough, then climbed up lamp posts to pull down the bunting that decorated the streets. 'Returning to base in an Austin Ruby car, our Bombing Leader drove it between the undercarriage and the fuselage of the line-up Lancasters. There was not a lot of room to spare! The next day the mess was decorated with our purloined bunting until the Mayor arrived in high dudgeon to reclaim it. He was well and truly entertained and had to be driven home, having lost all interest in his bunting.'[2]

Yet to some of the Bomber Command personnel, there was an unnatural, forced element to the festivities. The scars of war ran too deep, the memories of the fallen were too vivid. At her station, the radio telephony operator Pip Beck thought that the drinks in the mess were 'curiously muted'. It was 'as if everyone was putting on an act. Perhaps we were. Perhaps too much had happened. So many people had died – so many known personally.'[3] In the days after 8 May, Peter Nettleton of 15 Squadron based at Mildenhall was gripped by a sense of 'anti-climax', a feeling reinforced by the decision of his station commanders to keep up a heavy schedule of flying Lancasters on cross-country trips. Such a move, he said, led to an unprecedented revolt from some of the airmen. 'It was a waste of time and petrol. The Aussies at Mildenhall dug their heels in and said, "No, balls to that, we're not going to be buggered around." My sympathy was very much with the crews, though technically it was a mutiny. Flying just for the sake of flying in these vast Lancasters was quite pointless.' Nettleton was also exasperated by the return to peace-time discipline and ceremony, hardly what war-weary airmen wanted.

This mood of anticlimax was exacerbated by the perception that Churchill's government was reluctant to give the bomber aircrews the recognition they deserved, something that rankled deeply with Harris. On 10 May he issued his own moving 'Special Order of the Day' to the person-nel of Bomber Command, honouring their achievements and expressing his heartfelt thanks for their contribution in the defeat of Germany:

> To those who survive I would say this. Content yourself and take credit with those who perished, that now the 'Cease Fire' has sounded count-less homes within our Empire will welcome back a father, husband or son whose life, but for your endeavours and sacrifices, would assuredly have been expended during long further years of agony to achieve a victory already ours. No Allied Nation is clear of this debt to you.

He concluded on this note: 'Your task in the German war is completed. Famously have you fought. Well have you deserved of your country and her Allies.'[4] But to Harris's anger, such sentiments were not echoed by Winston Churchill in his victory broadcast to the nation on 13 May. Addressing the nation in his inimitable whisky-soaked growl, Churchill provided a sweeping narrative of the war's progress, from the dark but heroic days of 1940 to the final land operations through western Europe. At almost every milestone along the route to victory, he was full of praise for the different branches of the armed forces, whether it be the RAF in the Battle of Britain or the Royal Navy or the 8th Army in North Africa. Even Northern Ireland was deemed worthy of inclusion in this cavalcade of honour. Harris at High Wycombe and the bomber crews at their bases kept listening expectantly, hoping that Churchill was saving the best for last. But the Prime Minister reached the final triumph without a single mention of Bomber Command. This omission was a severe disappointment to Harris, especially from a politician who had played such a key role in the development of the strategic air offensive. It was, he wrote to Sinclair a fortnight later, 'an insult not to be forgotten, if it is forgiven'.[5]

The failure to give any public acknowledgement of Bomber Command's efforts may have been an oversight on Churchill's part, though that is unlikely given not only his mastery of the English language but also the diligence he always showed in the preparation of his speeches. It is more conceivable that, with an eye on his place in history, he was distancing himself from the most controversial aspect of Britain's war, just as he had done in his letter to Portal condemning the bombing of Dresden. Privately, Churchill was more generous to Harris, sending him a message in which he referred to the 'deep sense of gratitude which is felt by all the Nation for the part which has been played by Bomber Command in forging the victory'. He continued: 'All your operations were planned with the greatest care and skill. They were executed in the face of desperate opposition and appalling hazards. They made a decisive contribution to Germany's final defeat. The conduct of these operations demonstrated the fiery gallant spirit which animated your aircrews and the high sense of duty of all ranks under your command.'[6] Harris only regretted that such words could not have been uttered in public.

But there was another grievance that outweighed even his annoyance at omissions in the Churchillian rhetoric. This was the failure of the government to provide a special medal for all the men and women who served in Bomber Command. Again, the refusal to award such a medal seemed to him all too indicative of a shameful eagerness by the politicians to dissociate themselves from a campaign that, for all its success in defeating Germany, had been tainted by growing controversy since Dresden. What particularly enraged him was the failure to honour the role of the ground crews with anything more than the 1939–45 War Medal, awarded to all who served full-time in the armed forces, and the standard 1939–45 Defence Medal, which was given to non-operational personnel serving at home. As Harris never tired of pointing out, many civilians, including firefighters, the Home Guard, the Royal Observer Corps, police, lighthouse keepers and even local authority mortuary attendants, were eligible for the Defence Medal, a wide criterion that he thought devalued the unique work of the ground crews in ensuring the bombers could carry out their operations. 'Few people appreciate the terrible miseries and discomforts and the tremendous hours of work under which the ground personnel of Bomber Command on the airfields have laboured for nearly six years and through six winters, two of which have been notoriously bitter,' he told Sinclair on 1 June 1945.[7] He did not feel quite so much injustice about the position of the aircrews, for they could qualify for the 1939–45 Star, awarded for missions overseas, or the prestigious Aircrew Europe Star, given to personnel who flew over Europe between 1939 and June 1944, or the France and Germany Star, a decoration introduced to mark service in northern Europe after D-Day. But still, Harris felt these awards were insufficient recognition for men who had risked their lives on a far greater scale than any other members of the armed forces. One classic anomaly he highlighted was that RAF crews who served with the Tactical Air Forces in the Mediterranean between 1943 and 1945 qualified for the Italy Star, yet heavy-bomber crews who had attacked northern Italian cities in 1943 were ineligible.

Harris poured out his indignation in a series of long letters to Portal, Sinclair and Trenchard, arguing that the treatment of his personnel was typical of the official indifference towards his Command. He complained to Sinclair that the idea of a 'defence' medal was a contravention of the very purpose of Bomber Command. 'The only task which we have not been asked to perform, other than negatively, is that of "defence". Everything else we have done has been not only of an offensive nature but a continued offensive over five-and-a-half years, for many of those years the only offensive aimed at the German enemy in his own land.'[8] Given the scale of the bomber force's contribution to the Allied victory, he argued, it was 'incredible and intolerable' that the 'men and women of this Command are denied the Campaign medal'. It was, he wrote, 'a slight which emphasises and underlines the omission of any reference to the strategic offensive in the Prime Minister's speech'. In conclusion, he warned that if Bomber Command were not offered its own medal:

> then I too will have the Defence medal and no other – *nothing else whatever*, neither decoration, award, rank, preferment or appointment, if any such is contemplated or intended. I will be proud indeed to wear the Defence medal and that alone – and as bitter as the rest of my personnel. I will not stand by and see my people let down in so grossly unjust a manner without resorting to every necessary and justifiable protest which is open to me.[9]

Portal and Sinclair were sympathetic but they could not force a change from the Honours and Decorations Committee. Harris's protests were ignored. The government refused to strike a Bomber Command medal. The issue has remained one of political controversy ever since, and over the recent decades there have been a number of campaigns, motions in the House of Commons and petitions demanding that the government retrospectively award such a medal. All have failed, which has often been interpreted as another indication of the political establishment's cynical unwillingness to honour its debt to the bomber personnel because of unease about strategic bombing. Yet, going right back to May 1945, the argument about a separate Bomber Command medal has never been as clear-cut as its supporters claim. Second World War medals were awarded on the basis of campaigns and operational service, not on attachment to certain organizations within the armed forces. If a medal had been struck solely for Bomber Command, the cry would invariably have gone up for special medals for Fighter Command, Coastal Command, Training Command and the Fleet Air Arm. Moreover, a whole new set of invidious anomalies would have arisen with such a move. If, for instance, those who flew in bomber streams over northern Europe in 1944–5 merited a special medal, then why not the pilots from Fighter Command who sometimes escorted them? If Bomber Command ground crews had received an additional medal, then those in the ATA or the WAAF would have had a case to feel aggrieved at being excluded. But Harris was never one to embrace the wider picture. With his ferocious integrity, he stuck to his resolution not to accept any personal honours if Bomber Command did not receive its medal. This explains why, unlike nearly all other senior commanders, he was not made a member of the House of Lords at the end of the war.

It has often been claimed that the absence of a peerage was due to a prejudice against him from within Clement Attlee's Labour Government, because of its revulsion at area bombing. But this is entirely untrue. A major in the First World War, wounded in both Mesopotamia and France, Clement Attlee had a deep personal admiration for military heroism and, in Churchill's absences, had frequently defended the aerial offensive against Germany. Indeed, he had been in charge of the War Cabinet at the time of Dresden when Churchill was at Yalta. With this record, he was unlikely to have snubbed the Bomber Chief. The reality is that Harris was offered a peerage by the Labour Government, but turned it down. He did so for two reasons, firstly because he had decided to retire to South Africa to embark on a business career and felt 'a handle' would be no advantage in the Dominion, and secondly because he was determined to stick by his word to Sinclair and Portal.

While the debate about medals, decorations and speeches raged through the early summer of 1945, a large number of Lancaster airmen were preparing for more conflict. The war in Europe might have been finished, but the one in the Far East was not, as Japan continued to fight with a tenacity which matched that of the Reich armed forces until the fall of Berlin. The RAF had been heavily involved in the fight against the Japanese forces in this theatre with a wide range of aircraft, from 'tropicalized' Spitfires modified for missions in the Far East to the American B-24 Liberator. But Lancasters had never served outside Europe. In fact, apart from the attempt to bomb the *Tirpitz* in 1944 and a few 'shuttle runs' to Italy and North Africa in 1943, no Lancaster had ever operated from anywhere but a British airfield. Typically, Harris was dismissive in 1944 of the idea that the Lancaster might be able to operate from airfields in France or Russia, thereby increasing the plane's petrol endurance over Germany. Neither country, said Harris, had the facilities on the ground that were required by the Lancasters. But victory in Europe meant an end to the argument that Lancasters could not be diverted from their central objective of maintaining the strategic offensive. As a result, aircrews throughout Bomber Command had to begin training for an entirely new war thousands of miles away.

Intriguingly, as early as mid-1943, the Lancaster had briefly been considered by the Americans for a highly specialized role in the Pacific Theatre because of its unique loading capacity. When the atomic bomb was under development and the massive B-29 Superfortress had yet to go into operational service, US researchers needed to identify a combat aircraft capable of carrying the 17-foot long weapon. Norman F. Ramsey, a young physicist from Columbia University, conducted the survey and concluded that, apart from the B-29, only the Lancaster would be suitable. But even the B-29, 'would require considerable modification so that the bomb could extend into both front and rear bomb bays,' he wrote. 'Except for the British Lancaster, all other aircraft would require such a bomb to be carried externally.'[10] Though the B-29 programme was beset with early difficulties, the USAAF was still reluctant to allow America's historic new weapon to be carried by an RAF aircraft. When, in late 1943, plans were being drawn up for the first full-drop tests of a dummy atomic bomb in early 1944, Ramsey again suggested that the Lancaster should be used because production on the B-29 had only just started. But again he was overruled, partly because General 'Hap' Arnold, the head of the USAAF, had invested so much energy in the B-29 programme. On 29 November 1943, the first modifications began on the Superfortress to adapt it for the new bomb. The question of using the Lancaster never arose again.

In the more conventional role of strategic bombing in 1945, the Lancasters were to be regarded as a support arm for the USAAF's area attacks of Japanese towns and cities. The concerns that had, at least in theory, prevented the Americans from launching all-out saturation bombing of Germany did not apply in Japan, which was subjected to the sort of repeated bombardment that Dresden, Würzburg and Pforzheim endured in the last months of the war. The RAF's determination to use the Lancaster alongside the Americans in Japan partly reflected a political desire to prove that Britain was still a global power capable of decisive action in any theatre. As Portal put it to Harris in late March 1944: 'We have no intention of tacitly accepting in any phase of the Pacific War a situation in which we should leave full prosecution of the air offensive to the Americans.'[11] This was a point reiterated confidently by Sinclair the following month, when he stressed to Harris that 'British bombers will be represented in the war against Japan by the Lancaster IV and for the rest we shall have to use in that theatre American types, as, indeed, we are doing now'.[12]

The biggest problem about the bombing of Japan was the sheer distance from Allied bases on Pacific islands to the enemy mainland, far beyond anything that had been demanded of Bomber Command in Europe. In such circumstances, the amount of fuel required would be so large as to make the bomb load almost worthless. To increase the range of the Lancasters, the RAF embarked on plans for a series of experiments in mid-air refuelling, using the techniques pioneered by the aviator Sir Alan Cobham, who in 1934 had set up Flight Refuelling Limited. One of the early ideas was to use half the Lancasters in the Far East force as fuel tankers, filling up the other half during their sorties. Because of other heavy commitments, especially D-Day, little progress was made on this plan. But in August 1944 the Air Staff sent Harris a 'top secret' minute with further details of the scheme. By means of mid-air refuelling, stated the minute, 'it is estimated that the radius of action of the standard Lancaster can be increased by about 45 per cent. This would allow operations from bases in Formosa or in the China Coastal Area, opposite to or northward of that island. The intention is that after the defeat of Germany a force of up to 40 Lancaster squadrons from the United Kingdom should be moved to the Far Eastern theatre. Twenty of these squadrons would be equipped as bombers and the other twenty as tankers.' The report promised that the technique of refuelling 'is not expected to raise special difficulties from the point of view of handling in the air' but in order to test the logistics properly six Lancasters were to be allotted to the Bomber Development Unit, three of them as tankers.

Preparing for the inevitable outburst from Harris at this diversion, the Air Staff assured him, 'beyond the provision of these six aircraft and five others, there will be no other interference in the flow of aircraft to your command'.[13] But by the autumn, it was clear that this scheme would not be effective, since it would drastically limit the bombing capability of a Lancaster squadron. Nor was the technique fully reliable. At this stage Group Captain Leonard Cheshire, now working on policy, warned how difficult it would be for the Lancasters to mount any sort of offensive against Japan. 'I should estimate that it takes at least three aircraft to do the work of one in Europe,' he wrote in a report of October 1944. 'Apart from the substantial decrease in disposable bomb load occasioned by extreme range and reduced aircraft performance; inferior airfields, inadequate maintenance facilities, poor communications and climate, all contribute towards decreased serviceability.'[14]

But the Air Ministry persisted. As an alternative to flight refuelling, the RAF also worked on the installation of a massive 1,200-gallon saddle tank on top of the Lancaster's fuselage just behind the cockpit. Roy Chadwick's engineering skills on the plumbing and pumps ensured that the huge amount of additional petrol did not slosh about dangerously, while he also developed a system for air purging to stop the build-up of explosive gases as the tank was emptied. Carrying 3,650 gallons of fuel and a bomb load of 8,000 pounds, the modified Lancaster had a potential range of 4,340 miles. But in practice, the saddle tank proved impracticable. The first version was damaged in an accident, which required the undercarriage to be strengthened. The next was sent for trials under tropical conditions in India but the results were mixed, raising severe doubts as to whether this type was a feasible proposition for the Japanese war. A more successful but less ambitious change was simply to develop a 'tropicalized' Lancaster by removing the mid-upper turret and installing a 400-gallon extra fuel tank in the fuselage, which increased the Lancaster's range to 3,180 miles. The ever-reliable Avro was given a contract for this programme.

An additional potential difficulty for Lancasters operating in the Pacific was navigation over long stretches of sea, so the RAF began another experiment. A special Lancaster, serial number PD328, was equipped with the latest navigational aids, including Loran, a US development of Gee that had a range of over 1,200 miles, and Rebecca, an advanced radio transmitter. In October 1944 this plane, code-named Aries, was loaned to the Empire Central Navigation School and began a record-breaking, long-distance flight all the way across the globe to New Zealand and back to Britain via Cairo, in the process testing the serviceability of the Lancaster and its equipment. Few problems were encountered on the journey, proving that navigation would not be a problem for the Lancaster in the Pacific. While the Air Staff worked on their plans, Avro was turning out the first 'tropicalized' Lancasters ready for service in the war against Japan. Designated the Mark I FE (Far East) and Mark VII FE, these special Lancasters were equipped not only with their special fuel tanks but also with Gee, Loran and Rebecca, and had FN 82 turrets with their 0.5-inch Browning guns. In addition, they had a different colour scheme to the wartime European Lancasters. They kept the black underside, but in place of the usual green and brown camouflage they were painted bright white on the upper half. Also coming into service were the first Lincolns, originally the Mark IV Lancaster, some of which could be prepared for operations in the Far East.

By 1945 the problem with operating the Far East Lancasters and Lincolns was more political than technical. The fact was that the mighty USAAF, with its unrivalled resources, did not absolutely need the RAF in the final thrust of the war against Japan. The determination to send the Avro heavy bombers to the Pacific was really an exercise in geopolitical power play, with Churchill and Portal desperate to prove that Britain still mattered in every quarter of the world. On a more elevated level, the creation of what was known as 'Tiger Force' was also a way of repaying the solidarity that the 8th Air Force had demonstrated in the bombing of Germany. But the Americans were not especially enthusiastic. The commander of Tiger Force, Air Marshal Sir Hugh Lloyd, who had fought with distinction at Malta and North Africa, visited America in the spring of 1945 and reported despondently that 'we can expect no help for British redeployment and a lot of opposition. We will have to pay our way. Our seats in the stalls will be expensive.'[15] Lloyd pointed out that because the B-29s would be using existing runways on the Pacific islands day and night, the RAF would have to build its own airstrips. 'We will want a port detachment, lighters, dredges perhaps, landing quays and certainly a pipe line out to sea for petrol and oil.'[16] The government agreed in February 1945 that, despite the costs and the huge logistical difficulties, the Tiger Force of 400 Lancasters and Lincolns should be sent to the Pacific. It would be the biggest self-supporting operation in the history of the RAF, involving potentially 15,000 operational RAF personnel and 7,500 for construction purposes.

While Lloyd was in Washington in March trying to negotiate a suitable base for Tiger Force, Churchill attempted to put pressure on the USAAF to be more amenable. 'With all your wealth of aerodromes, you would not deny me the mere pittance of a few for my heavy bombers,' he wrote to Hap Arnold.[17] Lloyd believed that one of the causes of America's lack of co-operation was the failure to recognize the superiority of the Lancaster over most US bomber types, and its greater practicability than the B-29. He wrote later in his dispatch:

> The B29s needed specially constructed runways of 8500 feet for take-off. The B17, B24 and the Lancaster, on the other hand, could operate from a runway of 6000 feet without considerable climbing restrictions, but neither the B17 nor the B24 could carry the bomb load of the Lancaster for any given range or carry, even under the most favourable conditions, a load of 18,000 pounds of bombs from a runway of 6000 feet. The Americans did not appreciate what the Lancaster could do, neither did they appreciate it could drop a greater weight of incendiary bombs over Japan than even the B29. The B29, for example, has 40 hooks and on each can be carried a cluster of 38 bombs, each bomb weighing 6 pounds, total bombs 1520; total weight 9210. The Lancaster has eighteen hooks with the adaptor and on each can be carried a cluster of 28 bombs each weighing 20 pounds, a total of 504 bombs, total weight 10,080 pounds.[18]

Eventually, in June 1945, the Americans agreed that the Tiger Force could share the base on the island of Okinawa. 'This is a very handsome gesture on your part and in full accordance with all the kindness we have received from the US Chiefs of Staff,' wrote Churchill to General Marshall, the US Chief of Staff.[19] The size of the operation, however, had to be scaled back to 10 squadrons, totalling 220 aircraft. The first Lancasters due to arrive were those of 617 and 9 Squadron, carrying their Tallboys, a weapon that had particularly impressed the Americans. On 7 July the first convoy of air crews and support staff left Britain for the Pacific, bringing 15,000 tons of airfield construction equipment, 522 vehicles, together with trailers and motorcycles. But Sir Hugh Lloyd, who inspected the men, was concerned at their morale. 'I observed that although there would be no doubt of their efficiency once in the theatre, there was a lack of enthusiasm for visiting new places or gaining new experiences. All war interest had been lost with the end of the German war. The Japanese war was too remote for them.'[20] It was not surprising that most of the men felt apprehensive, given some of the warnings they received about the risks of disease and operational flying in unique conditions.

In his private memoir, navigator Jack West recalled his time in training for Tiger Force during the early summer of 1945, when he was billeted in a hotel in Morecambe. At one stage, he was told that he would need 17 different inoculations for tropical diseases. On another occasion, he and his comrades received a talk, with a shocking twist, from Wing Commander C. A. Morris, leader of the initial Tiger Force, who told them that 'if we had to ditch in the South China Sea there was little chance of being picked up due to lack of rescue aircraft or ships. Consequently, a cyanide tablet would be available and would be given out before each op.'[21] It was disturbing for West to learn that the RAF was willing to offer cyanide in an emergency to avoid the agony of a lingering death in the Pacific. This is a revelation that has not appeared before in any history, but it was confirmed in a subsequent letter to the RAF Museum of July 2004, in which Jack West wrote: 'Now regarding the cyanide tablets, they were not issued to us. We were simply told they would be available to us before each flight to bomb Japan.' West added that he was informed the 'anticipated loss rate' could be as high as 80–85 per cent.[22] Fortunately, neither these mathematical forecasts nor the administration of cyanide were ever tested. On 6 August the USAAF dropped the first atomic bomb on Hiroshima, followed by the second over Nagasaki on 9 August. On 15 August 1945 Japan surrendered.

For the Lancaster airmen not involved in Tiger Force, there were many other tasks to be undertaken in the summer of 1945. Norman Ashton, the engineer of 103 Squadron, had the pleasant duty of flying on a goodwill mission to South America with two other Lancasters. Not renowned for his diplomatic skills, Sir Arthur Harris was at the head of the mission but on this occasion, with the burden of war removed and the sun of Rio beckoning, he was in genial form. After the grey austerity of war-torn Britain, Ashton was amazed at the abundance, glamour and excitement of South America.[23] Everywhere the three Lancasters flew, resplendent in their post-war white, they received an enthusiastic reception. A more demanding overseas mission carried out by the Lancasters was Operation Dodge, where the planes made a series of fourteen- to fifteen-hour trips to Italy to pick up British army veterans, some of whom had been away from home for five years. For Richard Gration of 44 Squadron, the Dodge sorties were a welcome relief after the offensive against Germany. 'On each occasion we returned with twenty soldier passengers on board who were delighted to be going home in a few hours instead of a few weeks by sea, regardless of the discomfort, noise of the four Merlins and sometimes airsickness. So the aircraft specially built to carry bombs and destroy cities were at the last used for a more humanitarian reason and the aircrew who flew them were given a pleasant job to carry out and at the same time have a mini holiday. It was very rewarding experience and a memory to cherish.'[24]

After VE Day, Lancasters also flew back to Germany, although in very different circumstances to their visits over the previous three and a half years. As a reward to the ground crews and the WAAFs, Bomber Command offered each of them a trip in a Lancaster to Germany so they could see the destruction in the Ruhr valley and have an experience of the plane they helped to keep in the air. These unarmed, sightseeing trips were known in the RAF as 'Cook's Tours'. A few pilots became carried away with the exhilaration of flying at low level over Germany and thereby put the lives of their crews at risk. One such foolish incident occurred on a 'Cook's Tour' near Hanover when Bill Adams, a pilot with 617 Squadron, was showing off by roaring over fields and sending local Germans scattering in fear. But suddenly he allowed the starboard wing to dip too far. It hit the ground with a grinding thud, smashing both propellers and setting fire to the two starboard engines. Adams managed to keep the stricken Lancaster in the air for a few more yards, but then it came crashing down in a neighbouring field. As the broken plane shuddered to a halt through ploughed earth, the crew were terrified that the plane might burst into flames. The navigator Tom Collin later recalled: 'Death by incineration on a Cook's Tour would have been a shocking waste of a life. I jumped through an escape hatch on the port side. We all got out safely, then found that both fires had been put out by the earth that had sprayed over the aircraft.' Adams himself, looking at the wreckage, failed to raise a laugh with his quip: 'Goddammit! I've always liked chopping the tops off German corn with the props, but how was I to know the bloody crop was backward this year.'[25]

To all who witnessed it in the months immediately after VE Day, the devastation of Germany was an awesome sight. The Biblical metaphor of the whirlwind was truly appropriate, with cities and towns reduced to wastelands of rubble, dust and ashes. A vivid picture of the scenes was painted for readers of the *Sunday Chronicle* by the paper's editor J. W. Drawbell, who visited Germany on a 'Cook's Tour' in July 1945:

> You know nothing until, just an ordinary civilian with a civilian's outlook, you go down over what is left of these decimated cities and fly over town after town of havoc and ruin. It is as though a giant bulldozer had run amok, or an immense flail tank, a hundred times its normal size, had threshed its way from end to end in a town. Here are chaos and death and ruin, utter and complete. The heart of industrial Germany has been gouged out. The homes of millions of workers have gone beyond hope of rebuilding. Whole towns stand derelict.

Drawbell found it hard to believe that life could go on, but there were people trying to piece the threads of their lives together, struggling for food, emerging from cellars, looking haunted. He was sitting in the Lancaster alongside a navigator who had taken part in raids on Dortmund. 'It must have given him satisfaction to see how completely raids had destroyed the area. What a wilderness. The whole target area is circled like a gigantic crater. It is as though a piece of the earth had been scorched and blasted. Nothing grows.' Essen, where the Krupps works had stood, was 'an unbelievable spectacle. There is no sign of life in all this vast factory of war covering more than 2000 acres. With millions of others, I was all through the London blitz and that was terrifying and destructive enough. But it was nothing – I mean nothing – to what the Germans had.'[26] Lancaster navigator Frank Musgrove was another who saw the apocalyptic wilderness for the first time in daylight, having spent so many nights attacking the Reich: 'We flew at low level over Essen and Cologne and other industrial cities beyond. We observed the blackened ruins, the rubble and the complete desolation extending mile after mile. We could see little sign of life, no movement in this vast, shattered landscape. We were looking at destruction on a scale without precedent.'[27]

It seemed impossible to believe that this epic ruination could not have played a central role in bringing Nazi Germany to its knees. The war machine, early observers concluded, must have ceased to function under the sheer weight of bombing. As Air Commodore Claude Pelly of the British Bombing Survey Unit, set up to analyse the effects of the strategic offensive, wrote after a visit to the Ruhr in late April: 'There is a deadly silence in the Ruhr areas which creates a deep impression on the visitor's mind. At the vast Krupps works at Essen, a tangle of steel beams and twisted machinery is super-imposed on the stratum of rubble which one soon comes to regard as normal in this part of Germany. The RAF's great achievement in rendering the biggest armament works in the world incapable of producing a hairpin is brought home very forcibly, even during a cursory inspection.'[28] Yet as the British Bombing Survey conducted its investigations, it gradually came to the conclusion that the area bombing had not been nearly as efficient as the appearance of devastation implied, certainly not before the autumn of 1944 when Germany's fate had almost been sealed. The survey found, for instance, that it was not until March 1945 that production in Essen had finally collapsed, despite the deaths of 7,000 people and the destruction of 88 per cent of its housing. Peter Johnson, who had taken part in the air offensive during the war before joining the Unit, recorded that he left Essen in a state of despair: 'It seemed that all that had been done in the long and often terrible summer of 1943 had been in vain. All the agonies and casualties, the numbers of the dead and missing aircrew . . . the civilian men, women and children we had killed in Germany by our rain of bombs, all this had been for nothing.'[29] The Unit's final verdict was that area bombing had not achieved the goals set for it by Bomber Command, and had failed to break the morale of the German people. In contrast, argued the Unit's report, the precision attacks on transport and communications had been highly efficient.

These findings concurred with those of the Americans' own survey, headed by the economist J. K. Galbraith, which also argued that assaults on transport and oil were far more effective than those on cities, and pointed out that German production actually increased between 1943 and 1944. In fact, Galbraith's study concluded that, in some industries, area bombing had actually helped to streamline the production process. Albert Speer, the Nazis' organizational mastermind, agreed. 'Area bombing alone would never have been a serious threat,' he wrote.[30] Despite the efforts of Harris, who produced his own memoirs in 1947, it gradually became the conventional orthodoxy that area bombing had failed, especially after the publication in 1961 of the highly readable four-volume official history of the strategic air offensive by Sir Charles Webster and Noble Frankland, who was himself a Lancaster navigator. Webster and Frankland's view was that Bomber Command's 'contribution to victory was indeed, a great one, though in direct terms at least, it was long delayed'.[31]

In recent years, this judgement has been subjected to serious challenge by historians such as Richard Overy, who have highlighted the way strategic bombing forced the Germans to divert huge resources in man-power, equipment and raw materials away from the front. The strategic offensive, wrote Overy, set 'a strict ceiling' on Germany's production. 'The harvest of destruction and disruption reaped by bomb attack, random and poorly planned as it often was, was sufficient to blunt German economic ambitions.'[32] The historian Thomas Childers has been even more un-equivocal: 'Strategic bombing did make a major contribution to the Allied victory over the Third Reich. It depleted Germany's economic might, depressed the morale of its subjects, weakened the Wehrmacht on all fronts, shortened the war and saved Allied — particularly British and American — lives. In the brutal moral calculus of total war, that is exactly what it was intended to do.'[33] Apart from questions of production and resources, it has also been argued that the onslaught brought home to the German people the suffering that Nazism had inflicted on other nations. Furthermore, the widespread devastation meant that no Germans could ever be in any doubt about the scale of their defeat, ensuring that the country which had gone to war against its neighbours three times in the previous seventy years, would never do so again. In this context, area bombing was a way of purging Germany's soul of militarism.

But even recognizing the strength of some of these points, it is difficult to deny that after mid-1944, concentrated attacks on oil and transport would have achieved so much more, given the enormous capabilities of the Lancaster force. Even the most fervent defenders of area bombing cannot dispute the tragic reality that at Dresden, neither the railways nor the local industries were properly hit, unlike the historic streets. At the height of the row over oil installations in January 1945, Harris perversely complained that Portal was just looking for a 'quick, clever, easy and cheap way out' of the war.[34] It would not have been 'cheap' or 'easy', but it would have been quicker.

After VE Day the Lancaster was never to be involved in any offensive campaign again, unlike that other legendary British plane of the Second World War, the Spitfire, which fought in Israel, Korea and Malaya, before its final flight in Commonwealth service in 1955. The Lancaster actually kept going marginally longer in RAF service, but only in maritime, reconnaissance and experimental duties in its later years. From the moment the war was finished, the Lancaster force was rapidly reduced, down from 57 squadrons to 22 before the end of 1945. Gradually, the longer-range, heavier Avro Lincoln started to replace the Lancaster in the Bomber Command squadrons. The last Lancaster to be built came off the production line at Armstrong Whitworth of Coventry, delivered to the RAF on 2 February 1946. Exactly 7,377 planes had been built since 1941. It might seem odd that Lancasters were still being produced after the surrender of Germany. In fact, 500 Lancasters were built after May 1945, but this was because the factories could not suddenly halt production, given that raw materials had been ordered, workers employed, parts made and contracts signed. Switchovers, as the history of the Lancaster demonstrated, were never straightforward in the aircraft factories. The year 1946 also saw a continuing rapid rundown of the Lancaster force as 13 more squadrons disappeared. The last Lancaster unit in Bomber Command was 49 Squadron based at Upwood in Cambridgeshire. Having first changed from Manchesters in June 1942, the squadron finally said farewell to the Lancaster in March 1950. It was the end of a momentous era in the history of Bomber Command.

But it was not the end of the Lancaster as a viable plane. Since the end of the war, it had been employed in a variety of other fields apart from bombing. One was civil aviation, where a version of the aircraft, known as the Lancastrian, was created for passenger and mail transport. The Lancastrian had its roots in Canada during the first part of the war, when the chronic shortage of suitable transports led the Canadian Government to ask London whether a Lancaster might be supplied that could serve as a prototype for such an aeroplane. The British Government were initially reluctant, but once there was a steady supply of the Mark IIIs, it was agreed in October 1942 that a Mark I, which had not yet gone into operational use, could be flown across the Atlantic to be modified by Victory Aircraft of Ontario. Stripped of its guns and bomb gear but fitted with extra fuel tanks, the Mark I Lancaster was taken to Canada, where it had all three turrets removed and faired over. Then it was flown back to Britain for further modifications, including improved electrical systems, ten passenger seats, a new nose fairing and a bigger fuel tank, which increased the range to 4,000 miles. From then on, it proved a reliable workhorse operating on the North Atlantic route between Britain and Canada, mainly carrying forces mail. Trans Canada Airlines were so impressed that seven Mark X Lancasters were converted into Lancastrians.

Roy Chadwick was also impressed by the simplicity and reliability of the Canadian adaption. From 1943 he was working on his own major long-term project to build a new four-engined advanced airliner, known as the Avro Tudor, a plane that would cast a black shadow over the company. But because there was a short-term gap in the market for a civil transport, Chadwick tried to persuade the government to author-ize the production of its own Lancastrian, Type 691, a more sophisticated version of the Canadian model. In late 1944 the government agreed and the first prototype flew in February 1945 before undertaking its maiden commercial flight in April 1945 with the newly formed British Overseas Airways Corporation (BOAC). With its huge petrol tanks, the Lancastrian had an unprecedented range for a British civilian plane and so was initially used on BOAC's 'Kangaroo Service' between Sydney and Britain via New Zealand. But carrying just nine passengers, it was hopelessly un-economic and, for all the prestige of its long-distance endurance, it lost significant amounts of money for BOAC. Even less successful were the six Mark III Lancastrians, with 13 passengers, ordered for British South American Airways, four of which crashed between August 1946 and

November 1947. Before this series of disasters, the RAF had ordered 51 of the type, most of which were used for ferrying VIPs or for work at navigation and flying schools. In all, 82 Lancastrians were built, but they added little lustre to the name of the original and were largely phased out by 1950.

Another important role carried out by the post-war Lancaster was as an experimental aircraft for testing new equipment, guns, engines and electronics. Throughout the war, when pressure on Lancaster numbers was intense, Harris was always reluctant to permit his heavy bombers to be used for such purposes, but he could not completely halt such trials. In fact many of them, especially on navigational aids, were extremely beneficial to Bomber Command. After May 1945 the Lancaster had a valuable career in evaluation work for both industry and the RAF. Tests were continued, for instance, on refining techniques for mid-air refuelling long after the Tiger Force had been disbanded. In a historic flight in July 1947, an Avro Lancastrian flew non-stop from London to Bermuda, having been refuelled en route by a Lancaster tanker based in the Azores. The aim of the journey was to prove to the Air Registration Board that such long refuelled flights were both safe and reliable, which the plane demonstrated triumphantly. A journalist from *Flight* magazine, E. W. Young, was on board the Lancastrian, and he described the moment when the supply was connected:

> As the time of interception by the tanker Lancaster drew near, we all began to take a renewed interest in events, and necks and eyes were strained to find our consort. In actual fact, the tanker found us, almost magically to the uninitiated but very scientifically with the aid of Eureka/Rebecca. The tanker, having appeared quite suddenly through a 10/10th layer of stratus below us, formated nearly to our starboard side, slightly below and astern of our aircraft. Before it arrived our refuelling engineer, who had taken up his station in the tail, had trailed out our hauling line and grapnel. About 260 feet of it now curved in a graceful arc. From the harpoon-like gun of the tanker, the projectile, with its contact line attached, shot out underneath and at about 90 degrees to our hauling line. It immediately made contact with the pawl and grapnel. Electrical potential is neutralised at the moment of contact on the bare portion of both lines and the two aircraft are then bonded throughout the operation. It was only a matter of minutes before the pipeline had been wound to our aircraft and secured in the coupling of the tail.

In less than twenty-five minutes, 1,750 gallons had been fed into the Lancastrian's No. 1 and bomb-bay tanks.[35]

In a move signalling the changing nature of aviation, the last series of refuelling trials performed by the Lancaster was on the Gloster Meteor, the RAF's first jet fighter, which had an exceptionally high rate of fuel consumption. These jets were refuelled simply by flying the Meteor's nose probe into a cone attached to a supply line trailing behind the Lancaster. Later Meteors had larger fuel tanks fitted which obviated the need for mid-air refuelling. The last of the tanker Lancasters were scrapped in 1951. But the Avro machine had its own part to play in the arrival of the age of jet propulsion, serving as a test bed for some of the early engines, since its endurance and reliability made it ideal for this work. It was used for airborne trials on the Armstrong Siddeley Sapphire and the AS Mamma turboprop, as well as a Swedish turbojet called the Stal Dovern, which was fitted in a large ventral pod beneath the Lancaster's bomb bay for its trials in 1951. By far the most successful engine that the Lancaster helped to develop was the supreme Rolls-Royce Dart turboprop. The Dart's trials with the Lancaster began in 1953 and the engine was subsequently used to power the Vickers Viscount, the best-selling British airliner of all time.

In other programmes at A&AEE at Boscombe Down, the Royal Aircraft Establishment at Farnborough and various centres during the 1940s and 1950s, Lancasters were also involved in research on aerofoils and rudders, high-pressure tyres, power-assisted elevator controls, wind sensors and the effect of deep winter on aircraft equipment. The most famous of these research Lancasters was the PA474, which had a varied career in flight refuelling and photo-reconnaissance in Africa before it was sent to the College of Aeronautics at Cranfield, where it undertook aerofoil experiments. When it was withdrawn in 1964, it was on the verge of being scrapped, like almost all other Lancasters, but thanks to the foresight of the Air Historical Branch and the College, it was saved for the nation and now forms part of the Battle of Britain Memorial Flight, one of only two airworthy Lancasters in the world, the other being the FM213 at the Canadian Warplane Heritage Museum in Ontario.

Given Harris's contempt for the navy, there was something incongruous about the fact that six Lancasters were transferred from the Air Ministry to the Admiralty in 1945, becoming part of the 780 Advanced Training Squadron based at HMS *Godwit* in Shropshire. There they joined a variety of other aircraft, including Oxfords, Tiger Moths and Fireflies, all designed to give recruits a breadth of experience. The sheer size of the Lancaster, compared to the other planes, left Petty Officer Air Fitter (Engines) Ron Swinn 'speechless' when he first had to work on the aircraft so it would be airworthy after a long spell in storage. 'My first priority was the power plants, Merlin 55s,' he recalled. 'How proud I was as I started them up, one after the other firing with no difficulty whatsoever. It was a feeling of sheer delight to have these four monsters working away at my command, the aircraft bucking, bouncing and straining at the brakes and chocks.'[36] But the Royal Navy Lancasters were not in use for long. Most were either scrapped or returned to the RAF by 1947.

The French naval aviation force, Aeronavale, also operated Lancasters through an agreement of March 1948 negotiated by the Labour Government's Foreign Secretary Ernie Bevin. Under this deal for military co-operation between the western European powers, Britain agreed to provide 54 ex-RAF Lancasters to the Aeronavale, having modified them for maritime reconnaissance work through the provision of advanced navigation aids, extra fuel tanks and an airborne lifeboat. The French Lancasters operated mainly off the African coast during the 1950s, but one of them remained in service at New Caledonia in the Pacific up to 1964. Other foreign air forces to operate Lancasters were those of Argentina, which received 15 of them in 1948, and Egypt, which acquired 9. The largest foreign contingent, however, belonged to Canada, which flew around 260 of them after the war, most of which were built by Victory Aircraft and had served with the RCAF squadrons of No. 6 Group. As with the French, the Canadians used the post-war Lancasters on maritime duties, including reconnaissance and search-and-rescue, though some were also used for photographic surveys and even as water bombers in fire-fighting. Again, as in France, the last Canadian Lancaster was not withdrawn until 1964.

The only two overseas actions undertaken by British Lancasters or Lancastrians in the post-war period were both highly charged politically. One took place in the Berlin Airlift, the other during the Arab-Israeli conflict. The airlift began in June 1948 in response to the attempt by the Soviet Union to gain control of the western Allied sector of the city through the imposition of a food and fuel blockade. It was a remarkable logistical effort by the Allied aircraft, which succeeded in delivering 5,000 tons of supplies a day and thereby broke the Russian siege by May 1949. The role played by the Lancastrians was small but vital. Exploiting the skills learnt in the refuelling trials, 13 of them belonging to two commercial firms, Flight Refuelling Limited and Skyways, were deployed to bring fuel supplies to the German capital. Between them they flew 5,600 sorties, delivering 14 million gallons of fuel. They operated from Wunstorf, a former Luftwaffe bomber base near Hanover in northern Germany, and flew into the Berlin airfield of Gatow. Each daily operation had to keep to a strict schedule and within a specific air corridor because there were so many aircraft flying into the city, with one plane landing in Berlin every ninety seconds, twenty-four hours a day.

The crew in each Lancastrian comprised the pilot, a navigator, an engineer and a radio officer. 'The aircraft was basically a Lancaster bomber converted into a petrol tanker by the simple expedient of fitting petrol tanks into the bomb bays,' said Bob Allen, a radio operator with Flight Refuelling. 'The aeroplane itself had four petrol tanks, two in each wing, but in this operation the outer two wings were used for carrying ordinary petrol, as used by the service transport, and the inner two were filled with high octane fuel for use by the aeroplane. The total cargo capacity was seven to eight tons.'[37] Flying at 3,500 feet and at a speed of 180 knots, the Lancastrians spent three and a half hours in the air on the return trip between Wunstorf and Gatow, but much of the crews' time was taken up waiting for planes to be loaded and unloaded. Though guided throughout the journey by instructions given over the radio, the pilots had to land at Gatow visually. If they could not land at the first attempt, there was no possibility of turning around for a second try, since there were aeroplanes coming onto the landing circuit every three minutes. It was tiring and often dangerous work.

Bob Allen, who personally flew on 270 flights into Berlin, recalled some of the anxious moments. 'The Russians flew fighters at the transports, pulling up at the last minute. That was known as buzzing. There was also occasional flak. Once flying into Gatow at approximately 2.30 a.m., flak was put up in front of the aeroplane. Although not directed at it, I can assure you that it was an uncomfortable moment, especially sitting on eight tons of petrol.' Severe weather could also be a problem: 'Once, when we returned to base after a hailstorm, we were surprised to see that the aluminium nose cone had been punched back some three feet.'[38]

On the first trips, the ventilation systems of the Skyways Lancastrians had not been properly fixed. 'By the time we got to Gatow we were a bit under the weather with the petrol fumes. So we had to fly with the top escape hatch off for ventilation. It took them a while to sort out where the fumes would go to,' said Cyril Hagues of Skyways.[39] But despite such hazards, the airlift was a resounding success, perhaps changing the course of European history. 'I was very elated at having been given the opportunity to take part in such a tremendous operation,' said Bob Allen.[40] The Lancaster, which had spent so much of the war trying to destroy Berlin, had played its role in the city's post-war salvation.

A different sort of history was experienced by pilot Henry Hooper of 115 Squadron, who served in the Middle East after the war. The majority of the FE 'tropicalized' Lancasters, originally destined for the Tiger Force, were dispatched to North Africa and Palestine to replace the B-24 Liberators which had gone back to America. At first, said Hooper, the Lancasters had little to do except cross-country runs, training and fighter affiliation. But then the planes were partially converted to carry passengers, mail and freight by the installation of panniers and 16 tubular seats, 8 on each side of the fuselage. Operating between Cairo and Algiers, Hooper had to keep his Lancaster below 10,000 feet because there were no oxygen facilities on board. 'We flew at night because during the day it was very bumpy. We operated like a poor quality airline.'[41] It was an enjoyable life but that began to change with the growing conflict between the Arabs and the Israelis. Hooper caught a glimpse of the impending trouble when he was asked to ferry some captured members of the Israeli terror group, the Stern gang, to Tel-Aviv. Having landed and been told by flying control to await further instructions, he got out of the plane and went to speak to a wing commander. While he was walking across the airfield, some shots suddenly rang out. When he ran back, he found one of the gang members lying on the ground dead, and another seriously injured just outside the Lancaster. What had happened was that the terror suspects, manacled together, had been allowed out of the aircraft to relieve themselves against the tail wheel, but a jittery rear gunner had accidently let off his Brownings at them. 'That caused a bit of a kerfuffle,' said Hooper laconically.

In March 1947 he was transferred to 38 Squadron based in Palestine, with the duty of flying Lancasters on reconnaissance and maritime patrols. His main task was to search the eastern Mediterranean for illegal immigrant ships which were busy ferrying Jewish immigrants from Europe, mainly down the Adriatic. 'The British were trying to see fair play and ensure that UN-quotas on the numbers of Jews going into Palestine were not exceeded. But to get round this, the Jews in their desperation used any old ship and sailed them furtively at night down the Adriatic and then across to Palestine, where their passengers were met by the Jewish underground army.' The flights lasted 10 to 11 hours:

> If we found a suspicious ship, we flew down very low alongside and then we flew across the stern to get the name of the ship and if possible the port of registry. This information would be radioed to Jerusalem, where it would be decided whether it was a suspect ship or not. But you could tell a suspect one. On a normal ship, everyone would come on deck to wave at the Lanc. On the immigrant ships, no one appeared to be on

board. They looked like ghost ships. So they just gave themselves away. Plus they had open air latrines built on the rails at the back, with the resultant distinguishing marks. But they were long tedious trips and we often did not find anything.[42]

In practice, these Lancaster patrols did little to stem the tide of migrants heading for the fledgling Israeli state.

Less exotic maritime duties were also carried out by other Lancasters throughout this period. The return of the B-24 Liberators to America meant that Coastal Command needed a new heavyweight aircraft. The growing surplus of Lancasters as a result of the contraction in Bomber Command meant that the Avro plane was the obvious replacement. From July 1945, Lancasters were therefore adapted to maritime reconnaissance and air/sea rescue roles, the changes carried out by the firm of Cunliffe-Owen Limited of Southampton. Over the next two years, 130 Mark III Lancasters and one Mark I were converted in this way and given the new designation of ASR (Air Sea Rescue) Mark III. The main features of these maritime Lancasters were: the removal of the mid-upper turret and the guns from the rear turret, which was to be used purely as an observation post; the provision of small windows on each side of the fuselage near the rear; and the enlargement of the astrodome. The latest aids and scanners were also installed, including Rebecca and ASV radar, while a 30-foot 6-inch lifeboat was installed in the bomb bay. In July 1946 three home-based squadrons of Coastal Command operated the maritime Lancasters: 179 and 210 Squadrons at St Eval in Cornwall, and 120 Squadron at Leuchars in Scotland. Other Coastal Command Lancasters served abroad in Malta and other parts of the Mediterranean. Gradually the ASR Mark III was superseded by the more advanced GR (General Reconnaissance) Mark III, which had better radar and more powerful Packard Merlin 224 engines.

Squadron Leader Roy Dye was one of those who flew the maritime Lancasters from St Eval. 'I was very, very impressed with the plane, having previously been flying on Wellingtons. Everything seemed so smooth, there was never any problem,' he said. 'It was very reliable. Even when one engine failed, it just drifted slightly until the engine was feathered, then it was fine. We generally flew over the sea at about 2,000 feet. If you're out across the ocean, 600 miles from land, reliability is quite comforting. It was a superb aircraft. The one thing about the Lanc was that it was awkward to get around because of the main spar. And the noise was so loud you could barely hear. Our reconnaissance trips would generally last seven or eight hours, but sometimes we would do up to eleven. That is why we had three wireless/radar operators on board, because after looking at a screen for thirty minutes, you lose your concentration.' Squadron Leader Dye also had praise for the lifeboat carried by the Lancaster. 'It was a very, very good design, taking up the size of the bomb bay. It was released at about 700 feet into the wind and had a parachute so it would drop down on a marker. As it touched the water, rockets would shoot out.'[43]

But the Lancaster's days were numbered in reconnaissance. A new plane had arrived on the scene, the Avro Shackleton, which was directly descended from the Lincoln and therefore the Lancaster. First arriving in service in 1951, the Shackleton was, for many, an advance on the Lancaster, which of course had never been designed as a long-range reconnaissance aircraft. Astonishingly, the Shackleton, even though it was sometimes derided as nothing more than a thousand rivets flying in loose formation, was to remain in RAF service until 1991, another tribute to the inherent greatness of Chadwick's design. As the Shackleton came in, the Lancaster went out. The last overseas Coastal Command Lancasters were withdrawn from the Mediterranean in 1954. Then on 10 October 1956, just months after the Shackleton had first gone into wartime action during the Suez crisis, a press release from the RAF announced that the very last of the Lancasters in operational service, which was then serving with the School of Maritime Reconnaissance, would be making its final flight in five days' time. On 15 October 1956, at St Mawgan in Cornwall, an RAF Lancaster came in to land for the final time. A special ceremony was held on the runway to mark the event, with a band and speech by the wing commander. Then the plane was retired and flown away to be scrapped.

The Avro Lancaster now belonged to history, not the RAF. But so many of the plane's ties with the epochal days of the war had already been broken. Guy Gibson had been killed in his Mosquito over the Netherlands in August 1944, living up to his bleak prediction that he would not outlive the war. Arthur Harris had returned from South Africa in 1953 and was living in retirement in Goring-on-Thames. He had still refused a new offer of a peerage but had accepted a baronetcy from Churchill, largely because he believed his immediate post-war stance on the campaign medal for Bomber Command was no longer relevant. Leonard Cheshire, following a nervous breakdown at the end of the war, had devoted his life to the care of the disabled and distressed, a role that would ultimately win him as much honour as his exploits in Bomber Command. Don Bennett, after several unsuccessful ventures in the aviation business, had become involved in Liberal party politics. Sir Archibald Sinclair had lost both his seat in the House of Commons and his leadership of the Liberal Party, and now sat quietly in the House of Lords as the Earl of Thurso. Charles Portal had resigned as Chief of the Air Staff in 1951 and entered the commercial world. Winston Churchill, at the age of 80, had left the Premiership. Wilfrid Freeman had died in 1953. The only two of the great public figures of the Lancaster's wartime history who were still at their desks, still trying to develop new planes and new ideas, were Barnes Wallis and Sir Roy Dobson of Avro.

But Dobson no longer had alongside him the colleague and genius who had made the entire saga possible. Throughout much of 1947, Roy Chadwick had been working on designs for a revamped version of his new airliner, the Avro Tudor. The first one, Mark I, had been unsuccessful, but Chadwick, with his usual determination, thought that he had cracked the problem with the Tudor Mark II. In brilliant sunshine on Saturday, 23 August 1947, the Tudor II took off from Woodford. Avro's chief test pilot Sidney Thorn was at the controls, Roy Chadwick beside him. Suddenly the aircraft faltered, skimmed over a farm and struck the ground. It ploughed across two fields, had both its wings ripped off and then plunged nose first into a pond. As the plane disintegrated, the fuselage split behind the centre section. Thrown more than 60 yards, Chadwick smashed into a tree, fractured his skull and died instantly. His end was as savage as that suffered by many of his Lancaster pilots. On investigation it was discovered that the aileron controls had been disconnected the night before, then wrongly reattached on the morning of the flight, which meant that any movement by the pilot would bank the plane in the opposite direction to the one intended. When the phone call was received at the Chadwick household and the family was informed that Roy was dead, 'all our world seemed to have crumbled in ruins,' said his daughter Margaret.[44] In an emotional public tribute Sir Roy Dobson said:

> His whole life was devoted to the cause of aviation. From the personal point of view, I have lost an old and trusted friend and colleague who stuck with me through thick and thin. I know that, had he been spared another few years, his name would have been blazoned forth as a man who had again jumped ahead of modern thought in his line. The country, as well as the company, has lost someone quite irreplaceable: Mr Roy Chadwick, designer of the Lancaster bomber.[45]

Writing to Chadwick's daughter Margaret, Sir Arthur Harris reflected on the historic contribution of her late father:

> Your father never received a tithe of the recognition and honours due from the nation for his services. The Lancaster took the major part in

winning the war with its attacks on Germany. On land, it forced the Germans to retrieve from their armies half their sorely needed anti-tank guns for use as anti-aircraft guns by over a million soldiers who would otherwise have been serving in the field. The Lancaster won the naval war by destroying over one-third of the German submarines in their ports, together with hundreds of small naval craft and six of their largest warships. Above all, the Lancaster won the air war by taking the major part in forcing Germany to concentrate on building and using fighters to defend the Fatherland, thereby depriving their armies of essential air and particularly bomber support. But the Lancaster was Roy Chadwick, and it was he who did all that for his country.[46]

In the journal he kept during the war, recording his missions over Germany, the young wireless operator John Byrne often contemplated his own mortality. At the start of 1945, he wrote out these words as a dedication 'to those aircrew who have proudly flown their last flight'.

They will no longer see the patches of cloud that dappled the countryside with shadow. Or scan the lie of the country, the compass bearings of the railways, the shape of the largest fields. They will no longer feel the damp coldness of a cloud. Or sight the horizon tilting and rolling and spinning about them, the irritability of their aircraft when banking and climbing. They will no longer smell burnt oil, the wind clutching the flat surfaces of their goggles, the sunlight flashing back in streamers from the bracing wires of their aerofoil and dancing in a spinning circle on the airscrew. They will no longer hear the motor dying into shrillness in a take-off, the instant response to the throttle, the very familiarity of these things will no longer suddenly please them. No longer as they glide back to their aerodrome will the wind cry softly in their ears. Nor will they sing aloud, their words swept away by the slipstream and lost.[47]

Byrne was killed in a collision with another Lancaster over Dresden on the night of 13–14 February 1945.

Notes

INTRODUCTION: 'GODDAM, IT'S A FLYING BOMB BAY'

1. Adolf Galland, *The First and the Last*.
2. David C. Isby (ed.), *Fighting the Bombers*.
3. James Taylor and Martin Davidson, *Bomber Crew*.
4. John Sweetman, *Bomber Crew*.
5. Interview with Michael Maltin, IWM (Imperial War Museum) sound archive tape 27315.
6. James Taylor and Martin Davidson, *Bomber Crew*.
7. Jack Currie, *Lancaster Target*.
8. Garrod to Harris, 27 May 1942, Harris papers H90.
9. Sir Arthur Harris, *Bomber Offensive*.
10. James Taylor and Martin Davidson, *Bomber Crew*.
11. Gordon Thorburn, *Bombers First and Last*.
12. Leo Amery, *The Empire at Bay*, diary entry for 12 May 1942.
13. Harris to Lord Halifax, British ambassador to the USA, 23 July 1942, Harris papers H34.
14. Harris to his Group Commanders, 4 May 1942, Harris papers H49.
15. Interview with Michael Maltin, IWM sound archive tape 27315.
16. Interview with Henry Hooper, IWM sound archive tape 27807.
17. Interview with David Ware, IWM sound archive tape 24932.
18. Interview with Larry Curtis, IWM sound archive tape 9211.
19. Diary of Wireless Operator John R. Byrne, IWM 04/24/1.
20. Paper from Directorate of Bombing Operations, Air Ministry, 6 September 1942, Bufton papers Buft 3/15.
21. Morley to Assistant Chief of the Air Staff, 21 January 1945, Bufton papers Buft 3/43.
22. Harris to Sinclair, 30 December 1942, Harris papers H78.
23. Interview with J. W. Henderson, IWM sound archive tape 16374.
24. Interview with John Sanders, IWM sound archive tape 14803.
25. Jack West DFM (Distinguished Flying Medal), private memoir *My Life in the RAF*, RAF Museum X001–6422.
26. Jack Currie, *Lancaster Target*.
27. Interview with Frank Waddington, IWM sound archive tape 17365.
28. David Scholes, *Air War Diary*.

29. Interview with Bob Knights, IWM sound archive tape 9208.
30. Noble Frankland, *History at War*.
31. Memoir of Stephen Rew, IWM 96/58/1.
32. Campbell Muirhead, *Diary of a Bomb Aimer*.
33. Harry Yates, *Luck and a Lancaster*.
34. Memoir of Stephen Rew, IWM 96/58/1.
35. Noble Frankland, *Bomber Offensive: The Devastation of Europe*.
36. Leo McKinstry, *Spitfire: Portrait of a Legend*.

CHAPTER 1: 'MAKE IT SIMPLE'

1. *The Times*, 10 November 1932.
2. Tami Davis Biddle, *The Rhetoric and Reality of Air Warfare*.
3. Mark Connelly, *Reaching for the Stars*.
4. Chaz Bowyer, *Bomber Barons*.
5. Robin Neillands, *The Bomber War*.
6. Max Hastings, *Bomber Command*.
7. Richard Overy, *Why the Allies Won*.
8. Dudley Saward, *'Bomber' Harris*.
9. Mark Connelly, *Reaching for the Stars*.
10. Leo McKinstry, *Spitfire*.
11. Louis Manzo, 'Morality in War: Fighting and Strategic Bombing in World War II'.
12. Peter Smith, *Avro Lancaster*.
13. Gordon Thorburn, *Bombers First and Last*.
14. Frederick Taylor, *Dresden*.
15. Churchill to Portal, 30 December 1940, Portal papers, folder 1.
16. Portal to Churchill, 7 January 1941, Portal Papers, folder 1.
17. Colin Sinnott, *The Royal Air Force and Aircraft Design 1923–1939*.
18. Ibid.
19. Ibid.
20. Harris to Sir Douglas Evill, 15 July 1944, Harris papers H15.
21. Mel Rolfe, *Bomber Boys*.
22. Draft specification P13/36, 11 June 1936, Air Ministry papers AIR 16/194.
23. Ibid.
24. O. T. Boyd to Air Defence of Great Britain HQ, 17 June 1936, Air Ministry papers AIR 16/194.
25. Minutes of meeting of Operational Requirements Committee, 22 June 1936, Air Ministry papers AIR 16/169.
26. Ibid.
27. Oxland to group commanders and ADGB HQ, 11 June 1936, Air Ministry papers AIR 16/194.
28. Minutes of meeting of Operational Requirements Committee, 22 June 1936, Air Ministry papers AIR 16/169.
29. Francis K. Mason, *The Avro Lancaster*.

30. Harry Holmes, *Avro: The History of an Aircraft Company*.
31. Unpublished interview with Roy Chadwick, 6 January 1944, Air Ministry file AVIA 46/115.
32. Arnold Hall, entry on Dobson in the *Oxford Dictionary of National Biography*.
33. Harald Penrose, *Architect of Wings*.
34. Recollection of his sister May, recorded in Penrose, *Architect of Wings*.
35. Harald Penrose, *Architect of Wings*.
36. Sir Roy Dobson, entry on Chadwick in the *Oxford Dictionary of National Biography*.
37. Harald Penrose, *Architect of Wings*.
38. Ibid.
39. Interview with Geoff Bentley.
40. Harald Penrose, *Architect of Wings*.
41. Interview with Dick Marsh.
42. Historic note of Design Conference on P13/36, March 1936, Air Ministry file AVIA 46/115.
43. Historic note on the Manchester, Air Ministry file AVIA 46/115.
44. Unpublished interview with Roy Chadwick, 6 January 1944, Air Ministry file AVIA 46/115.
45. Harald Penrose, *Architect of Wings*.
46. Len Deighton, *Blood, Tears and Folly*.
47. Unpublished interview with Roy Chadwick, 6 January 1944, Air Ministry file AVIA 46/115.
48. Peter V. Clegg, *Avro Test Pilots since 1907*.
49. History of the Manchester Trial at Boscombe Down, Air Ministry file AVIA 18/699.
50. Letter from J. L. Serby, Ministry of Aircraft Production, to Avro, 20 June 1940, Air Ministry file AVIA 15/2323.
51. Portal to Robert Saundby, 12 September 1940, National Archives AIR 2/2149.
52. Francis K. Mason, *The Avro Lancaster*.
53. Note by Secretary of State, 2 April 1940, Air Ministry file AIR 6/60.
54. Harald Penrose, *Architect of Wings*.
55. This is the date given in D. C. Wood, *The Design and Development of the Avro Lancaster*.
56. Arthur Tedder, *With Prejudice*.
57. Unpublished interview with Roy Chadwick, 6 January 1944, Air Ministry file AVIA 46/115.
58. N. E. Rowe to Roy Dobson, 19 July 1940, Air Ministry file AVIA 15/590.
59. Leo McKinstry, *Spitfire*.
60. Freeman to Harold Balfour, Under-Secretary for Air, undated, Air Ministry file AIR 20/2828.
61. Unpublished interview with Roy Chadwick, 6 January 1944, Air Ministry file AVIA 46/115.
62. N. E Row to RAE Farnborough, 7 August 1940, Air Ministry file AVIA 15/590.
63. Minute by Captain Liptrot, 22 August 1940, Air Ministry file AVIA 15/590.

64. Minute by N. E. Rowe, 25 August 1940, Air Ministry file AVIA 15/590.
65. Unpublished interview with Roy Chadwick, 6 January 1944, Air Ministry file AVIA 46/115.
66. National Archives, AVIA 46/115.

CHAPTER 2: 'OH BOY, OH BOY, WHAT AN AEROPLANE!'

1. Anthony Furse, *Wilfrid Freeman*.
2. Unpublished interview with Roy Chadwick, 6 January 1944, Air Ministry file AVIA 46/115.
3. Chadwick to Freeman, 16 August 1941, National Archives AIR 20/2966.
4. Chadwick to RAE, 6 September 1940, National Archives AVIA 46/115.
5. Mike Garbett and Brian Goulding, *Lancaster at War: Volume II*.
6. Francis K. Mason, *The Avro Lancaster*.
7. Preliminary consideration of Lancaster prototype, National Archives AVIA 46/115.
8. Note on Lancaster history, National Archives AVIA 46/115.
9. Mike Garbett and Brian Goulding, *Lancaster at War: Volume II*.
10. Unpublished interview with Roy Chadwick, 6 January 1944, Air Ministry file AVIA 46/115.
11. Farren to Hennessy, 19 November 1940, National Archives AVIA 46/115.
12. Chief Superintendent of RAE to Hennessy, 27 November 1940, National Archives AVIA 46/115.
13. Norbert Rowe to Hennessy, 20 November 1940, National Archives AVIA 46/115.
14. Harald Penrose, *Architect of Wings*.
15. Ibid.
16. Mike Garbett and Brian Goulding, *Lancaster at War: Volume I*.
17. 3 March 1941, Lancaster Handling and Performance Trials, National Archives AIR 18/715.
18. 10 March 1941, Ibid.
19. Bottomley to Pierse, 1 February 1941, quoted in Sir Charles Webster and Noble Frankland, *The Strategic Air Offensive Against Germany 1939–45: Volume I*.
20. Interview with Wing Commander Thomas Murray, IWM sound archive tape 12805.
21. Minutes of the Air Council, 24 January and 24 March 1941, National Archives AIR 6/60.
22. Sinclair to Beaverbrook, 10 February 1941, Beaverbrook papers BBK/D/33.
23. Beaverbrook to Sinclair, 22 February 1941, Beaverbrook papers BBK/D/33.
24. Sinclair to Beaverbrook, 26 February 1941, Beaverbrook papers BBK/D/33.
25. Mike Garbett and Brian Goulding, *Lancaster at War: Volume II*.
26. Dobson to Westbrook, MAP, 24 April 1941, National Archives AVIA 15/233.
27. Westbrook to Dobson, 25 April 1941, National Archives AVIA 15/233.
28. Mike Garbett and Brian Goulding, *Lancaster at War: Volume II*.
29. Harald Penrose, *Architect of Wings*.

30. Mike Garbett and Brian Goulding, *Lancaster at War: Volume II*.
31. Unpublished interview with Roy Chadwick, 6 January 1944, National Archives AVIA 46/115.
32. Minutes of Lancaster Group meeting, 9 September 1941, National Archives AVIA 15/1465.
33. Dobson to J. S. Buchanan, 29 August 1941, National Archives AVIA 15/1465.
34. Folder presented to Sir Charles Craven, 1941, RAF Museum AC 94/26.
35. Mike Garbett and Brian Goulding, *Lancaster at War: Volume III*.
36. Chan Chandler, *Tail Gunner*.
37. Portal to Beaverbrook, 29 April 1941, National Archives, AIR 8/339.
38. Mark Connelly, *Reaching for the Stars*.
39. Henry Probert, *High Commanders of the Royal Air Force*.
40. Diary entry for 28 November 1940, in Robert Rhodes James (ed.), *The Diaries of Sir Henry Channon*.
41. Sinclair to Churchill, 2 April 1941, Beaverbrook papers BBK/D/52.
42. Ibid, 1 May 1941, Beaverbrook papers BBK/D/52.
43. Churchill to Sir Edward Bridges, Cabinet Secretary, 5 May 1941, Beaverbrook papers BBK/D/52.
44. Sinclair to Portal, 16 June 1941, quoted in Sir Charles Webster and Noble Frankland, *The Strategic Air Offensive Against Germany 1939–45: Volume I*.
45. Sinclair to Churchill, 25 June 1941, Beaverbrook papers BBK/D/52.
46. Dudley Saward, *'Bomber' Harris*.
47. Don Bennett, *Pathfinder*.
48. James Taylor and Martin Davidson, *Bomber Crew*.
49. Tami Davis Biddle, 'Bombing by the Square Yard'.
50. Ibid.
51. Mark Connelly, *Reaching for the Stars*.
52. Sir Charles Webster and Noble Frankland, *The Strategic Air Offensive Against Germany 1939–45: Volume I*.
53. *Daily Mirror* editorial, 12 September 1940, quoted in Mark Connelly, *Reaching for the Stars*.
54. Mark Connelly, *Reaching for the Stars*.
55. John Wheeler-Bennett and Anthony Nicholls, *A Semblance of Peace*.
56. Note by Portal, 18 August 1941, Portal papers, Folder 1.
57. Denis Richards, *Portal of Hungerford*.
58. Paper on Night Bombing Policy, 25 August 1941, Bufton papers Buft 3/9.
59. Churchill to the War Cabinet, 7 September 1941, National Archives AVIA 10/377.
60. Freeman to Craven, 15 September 1941, quoted in Anthony Furse, *Wilfrid Freeman*.
61. Anthony Furse, *Wilfrid Freeman*.
62. Sir Charles Webster and Noble Frankland, *The Strategic Air Offensive Against Germany 1939–45: Volume I*.
63. Portal to Churchill, 25 September 1941, Portal papers, folder 2.
64. Churchill to Portal, 27 September 1941, Portal papers, folder 2.
65. Interview with Professor John Ellis, IWM sound archive tape 18538.
66. Jon Lake, *Lancaster Squadrons 1942–45*, Vol. II.

67. Portal to Churchill, 2 October 1941, Portal papers, folder 2.
68. Churchill to Portal, 7 October 1941, Portal papers, folder 2.
69. Sir Charles Webster and Noble Frankland, *The Strategic Air Offensive Against Germany 1939–45: Volume I.*
70. Pierse to Sinclair, 12 August 1941, National Archives AIR 4/41.
71. Ibid, 4 November 1941, National Archives AIR 4/41.
72. Hopkins to Freeman, 30 September 1941, National Archives AIR 20/2966.
73. Handwritten exchange on Hopkins letter, National Archives AIR 20/2966.
74. H. B. Howard of the British Air Commission to MAP, 17 September 1941, National Archives AIR 38/725.
75. Mark Connelly, *Reaching for the Stars.*

CHAPTER 3: 'THE IMPORTANCE OF KILLING AND TERRIFYING THE BOCHE'

1. Sir Arthur Harris, *Bomber Offensive.*
2. The quotation is from the Hosea, chapter 8, verse 7. According to Harris's memoir, he told Portal: 'Well, they are sowing the wind,' to which 'Portal made some comment to the same effect as mine, that the enemy would get the same and more of it.'
3. Mark Connelly, *Reaching for the Stars.*
4. Sir Wilfrid Freeman, MAP to Sir Richard Pierse, Bomber Command, 2 July 1941, National Archives AIR 20/2966.
5. Pip Beck, *Keeping Watch.*
6. Note to Avro on 'skin wrinkling', 21 December 1941, National Archives AIR 15/1565.
7. Mike Garbett and Brian Goulding, *Lancaster at War: Volume I.*
8. Harald Penrose, *Architect of Wings.*
9. Churchill to Roosevelt, 29 March 1942, Churchill Archives CHAR 20/72.
10. Ralph Sorley to Freeman, 29 March 1942, National Archives AIR 20/2914.
11. 'Notes on Accident to Lancaster 1', R559 at A&AEE, 18 April 1941, National Archives AIR 15/1565.
12. Note by J. E. Serby, 21 April 1942, National Archives AIR 15/1565.
13. Minutes of meeting on Lancaster riveting, 24 April 1942, National Archives AIR 15/1565.
14. Air Ministry historical note, National Archives AIR 16/590.
15. Ben Pimlott (ed.), *The Second World War Diary of Hugh Dalton.*
16. James Taylor and Martin Davidson, *Bomber Crew.*
17. Interview with Alec Flett, IWM sound archive tape 16068.
18. Operations Training Requirements for Heavy Bombers, 8 February 1942, National Archives AIR 2/7684.
19. Ibid.
20. Minute by Air Ministry Technical Directorate, 17 February 1942, National Archives AIR 2/7684.
21. Harris to the Air Ministry, 27 February 1942, National Archives AIR 2/7684.
22. Ibid.

23. Henry Probert, *Bomber Harris*.
24. Interview with Thomas Murray, IWM sound archive tape 12805.
25. Jack Currie, *Lancaster Target*.
26. Max Hastings, *Bomber Command*.
27. Interview with Rex Oldland, IWM sound archive tape 20918.
28. Solly Zuckerman, *From Apes to Warlords*.
29. Henry Probert, *Bomber Harris*.
30. Ibid.
31. Dudley Saward, '*Bomber' Harris*.
32. Charles Carrington, *Soldier at Bomber Command*.
33. Sinclair to Portal, 14 February 1942, quoted in Sir Charles Webster and Noble Frankland, *The Strategic Air Offensive Against Germany, 1939–45: Volume I*.
34. Air Staff Directive, 14 February 1942, quoted in ibid.
35. Portal to Bottomley, 15 February 1942, quoted in ibid.
36. Cherwell's paper to the Prime Minister, 30 March 1942, Portal papers, folder 3.
37. Paper by Bottomley, 23 September 1941, Bufton papers Buft 3/26.
38. A thorough, if somewhat jaundiced analysis of the RAF's range of incendiaries appears in Jorg Friedrich, *The Fire*.
39. Joseph Goebbels, *Diaries*.
40. Freeman to Harris, 27 April 1942, RAF Museum, Harris papers H16.
41. Harris to Freeman, 29 April 1942, RAF Museum, Harris papers H16.
42. Bufton to Freeman, 10 May 1942, RAF Museum, Harris papers H16.
43. Squadron Leader D. A. C. Dewdney, Air Intelligence, Bombing Operations, to Freeman, 1 and 7 May 1942, RAF Museum, Harris papers H16.
44. Roger Beaumont, 'The Bomber Offensive as a Second Front'.
45. Amery to Churchill, 27 July 1942, Leo Amery, *The Empire at Bay*.
46. Entry for 12 May 1942, Leo Amery, ibid.
47. Richard Overy, *Bomber Command 1939–45*.
48. John Nettleton, interview recorded with the BBC, 19 April 1942, IWM sound archive tape 2148/G/B.
49. Richard Overy, *Bomber Command 1939–45*.
50. Ibid.
51. Pip Beck, *Keeping Watch*.
52. Selborne to Churchill, 27 April 1942, National Archives AIR 20/2795.
53. Churchill to Selborne, 27 April 1942, National Archives AIR 20/2795.
54. Harris to Churchill, 28 April 1942, Harris papers H65.
55. Churchill to Harris, 18 April 1942, Harris papers H65.
56. John Nettleton, interview recorded with the BBC, 19 April 1942, IWM sound archive tape 2148/G/B.
57. Alfred Price, *Battle over the Reich: Volume I, 1939–1943*.
58. Chan Chandler, *Tail Gunner*.
59. Interview with Hugh Parrott, IWM sound archive tape 16279.
60. Dudley Saward, '*Bomber' Harris*.
61. Jorg Friedrich, *The Fire*.
62. Mark Connelly, *Reaching for the Stars*.
63. *Daily Mail*, 1 June 1942.

64. Dudley Saward, *'Bomber' Harris*.
65. Sir Arthur Harris, *Bomber Offensive*.
66. Noella Lang (ed.), *The Rest of my Life in 50 Squadron*.

CHAPTER 4: 'A PIDDLING MISSION FOR THE MIGHTY LANC'

1. Interview with FO Dim Wooldridge, IWM sound archive tape 2149/G/C.
2. *Flight* magazine, 9 July 1942.
3. *Flight* magazine, 13 August 1942.
4. Harald Penrose, *Architect of Wings*. This may sound a little too close to that dreary corporate joke which has been in circulation since the late 1950s: 'You don't have to be mad to work here but it helps.' On the other hand, Penrose's book is a model of restraint and diligent research, and the author did work at Avro alongside Chadwick.
5. Franklin D. Roosevelt, 'Fireside Chat' broadcast, 30 December 1940.
6. Statistics on output from Harry Holmes, *Avro Lancaster: The Definitive Record*.
7. Ken Delve, *Avro Lancaster*.
8. Don Charlwood, *No Moon Tonight*.
9. Mike Garbett and Brian Goulding, *Lancaster at War: Volume II*.
10. Harris to Churchill, 6 July 1942, quoted in Henry Probert, *Bomber Harris*.
11. Harris to Freeman, 25 August 1942, RAF Museum, Harris papers H16.
12. Llewellin to Freeman, 11 September 1942, National Archives AIR 20/2914.
13. Freeman to Sinclair, 12 September 1942, National Archives AIR 20/2914.
14. Ibid., 25 September 1942, National Archives AIR 20/2914.
15. Sinclair to Freeman, 19 September 1942, National Archives AIR 20/2914.
16. Harris to Freeman, 8 October 1942, RAF Museum, Harris papers H16.
17. Minutes of the Cabinet, 11 December 1942, National Archives AIR 8/714.
18. Note by Cherwell to the War Cabinet, 8 December 1942, National Archives AIR 8/714.
19. Minutes of War Cabinet sub-committee on Aircraft Production, 13 October 1942, National Archives AIR 8/714.
20. Paper on the B3/42 by Ralph Sorley, ACAS Technical, 10 October 1942, National Archives AIR 8/714.
21. Sorley to Sinclair, 13 December 1942, National Archives AIR 8/714.
22. Harris to Air Marshall John Linnell, 16 October 1942, RAF Museum, Harris papers H91.
23. Linnell to Harris, 30 October 1942, RAF Museum, Harris papers H91.
24. Harris to Linnell, 4 November 1942, RAF Museum, Harris papers H91.
25. Harris to Portal, 12 November 1942, National Archives AIR 8/714.
26. Harris to Sinclair, 30 December 1942, RAF Museum, Harris papers H78.
27. Harris to Portal, 29 October 1942, RAF Museum, Harris papers H81.
28. 'Summary of Bomber Commands Achievements in 1942, report by Harris, January 1943, RAF Museum, Harris papers H28.
29. Ibid.
30. Max Lambert, *Night after Night*.

31. Harris to Portal, 7 July 1942, RAF Museum, Harris papers H81.
32. Henry Probert, *Bomber Harris*.
33. Jon Lake, *Lancaster Squadrons 1942–45*, Vol. I.
34. Guy Gibson, *Enemy Coast Ahead*.
35. Ibid.
36. Minute on the Role of Bomber Command, August 1942, RAF Museum, Harris papers H14.
37. Jack Currie, *Lancaster Target*.
38. Robin Neillands, *The Bomber War*.
39. Harry Yates, *Luck and a Lancaster*.
40. J. Norman Ashton, *Only Birds and Fools*.
41. Kevin Wilson, *Bomber Boys*.
42. Guy Gibson, *Enemy Coast Ahead*.
43. Gordon Thorburn, *Bombers First and Last*.
44. Robert Raymond, *A Yank in Bomber Command*.
45. Harris to Portal, 25 October 1942, RAF Museum, Harris papers H81.
46. Portal to Harris, 11 December 1942, RAF Museum, Harris papers H81.
47. Noella Lang (ed.), *The Rest of my Life in 50 Squadron*.
48. John Terraine, *The Right of the Line*.
49. Minutes of Air Staff Conference, 12 July 1941, National Archives AVIA 14/2176.
50. Note to No. 5 Bomber Group, 17 May 1942, National Archives AVIA 14/2176.
51. Freeman to Harris, 26 May 1942, quoted in Sir Charles Webster and Noble Frankland, *The Strategic Air Offensive Against Germany 1939–45: Volume I*.
52. Harris to Freeman, 1 June 1942, RAF Museum, Harris papers H16.
53. Freeman to Harris, 3 June 1942, RAF Museum, Harris papers H16.
54. Anthony Furse, *Wilfrid Freeman*.
55. Harris to Freeman, 6 June 1942, RAF Museum, Harris papers H16.
56. Handwritten note by Freeman, 5 October 1942, National Archives AVIA 20/2966.
57. Harris to Churchill, 17 June 1942, RAF Museum, Harris papers H65.
58. Harris paper for the War Cabinet, August 1942, RAF Museum, Harris papers H16.
59. Harris to Portal, 6 August 1942, quoted in Dudley Saward, *'Bomber' Harris*.
60. Harris to his Group Commanders, 4 May 1942, RAF Museum, Harris papers H49.
61. Harris to Bottomley, DCAS, 16 April 1942, RAF Museum, Harris papers H47.
62. Harris to Group Commanders, 21 September 1942, RAF Museum, Harris papers H49.
63. Field Marshal Lord Alanbrooke, *War Diaries*.
64. Minute by Winston Churchill, 22 October 1942, Portal papers, folder 1.
65. Sinclair to Churchill, 23 October 1942, Churchill to Sinclair, 26 October 1942, Portal papers, folder 1. Sir Charles Webster and Noble Frankland, *The Strategic Air Offensive Against Germany 1939–45: Volume II*.
66. Cunningham to Wing Commander Arthur Morley, Bombing Operations Directorate, 14 November 1942, Bufton papers Buft 3/12.

67. Sir John Slessor, *The Central Blue.*
68. Cherwell to Portal, 27 February 1942, Portal to Cherwell, 28 February 1942, RAF Museum, Harris papers H81.
69. Max Hastings, *Bomber Command.*
70. Bufton to Harris, 17 March 1942, RAF Museum, Harris papers H53.
71. Harris to Bufton, 17 April 1942, RAF Museum, Harris papers H53.
72. Bufton to Harris, 8 May 1942, RAF Museum, Harris papers H53.
73. Reports sent to Bufton, April 1942, Bufton papers Buft 3/12.
74. John Sweetman, *Bomber Crew.*
75. Anthony Furse, *Wilfrid Freeman.*
76. Sir Charles Webster and Noble Frankland, *The Strategic Air Offensive Against Germany 1939–45: Volume I.*
77. Paper by Bufton, 6 September 1942, Bufton papers Buft 3/15.
78. Freeman Dyson, *Disturbing the Universe.*
79. Andrew Maitland, *Through the Bombsight.*
80. Interview with Group Captain Jack Goodman, IWM sound archive tape 16075.
81. Don Bennett, *Pathfinder.*
82. Paper by Bufton, 2 August 1942, Bufton papers Buft 3/12.

CHAPTER 5: 'THE TARGET FOR TONIGHT'

1. Dudley Saward, *'Bomber' Harris.*
2. Henry Probert, *Bomber Harris.*
3. Charles Carrington, *Soldier at Bomber Command.*
4. Edward Smithies, *Aces, Erks and Backroom Boys.*
5. Patrick Bishop, *Bomber Boys.*
6. Frank Broome, *Dead Before Dawn.*
7. Mike Garbett and Brian Goulding, *Lancaster at War: Volume II.*
8. Max Lambert, *Night after Night.*
9. Gerald Myers, *Mother Worked at Avro.*
10. BBC broadcast by Churchill, 9 February 1941.
11. Mike Garbett and Brian Goulding, *Lancaster at War: Volume II.*
12. Memoir of Stephen Rew, IWM archive 96/58/1.
13. Ibid.
14. Norman Ashton, *Only Birds and Fools.*
15. Mike Garbett and Brian Goulding, *Lancaster at War: Volume II.*
16. Memoir of Stephen Rew, IWM archive 96/58/1.
17. Les Bartlett, *Bomb Aimer over Berlin.*
18. Gordon Thorburn, *Bombers First and Last.*
19. Interview with Jim McGilveray, IWM sound archive tape 27798.
20. Slessor to Harris, 21 February 1942, and Harris to Slessor, 24 February 1942, RAF Museum, Harris papers H59.
21. Gordon Thorburn, *Bombers First and Last.*
22. Harry Holmes, *Avro Lancaster.*
23. Mike Garbett and Brian Goulding, *Lancaster at War: Volume II.*
24. Memoir of Stephen Rew, IWM archive 96/58/1.

25. Mike Garbett and Brian Goulding, *Lancaster at War: Volume II*.
26. John Sweetman, *Bomber Crew*.
27. Gordon Thorburn, *Bombers First and Last*.
28. Interview with George Bilton, IWM sound archive tape 13444.
29. Chan Chandler, *Tail Gunner*.
30. Bill Jones, *Bomber Intelligence*.
31. Patrick Bishop, *Bomber Boys*.
32. Ron Smith, *Rear Gunner Pathfinders*.
33. Clayton Moore, *Lancaster Valour*.
34. Unpublished memoir of Flight Lieutenant R. E. Wannop, IWM archive 80/30/1.
35. Martin Davidson and James Taylor, *Bomber Crew*.
36. Jack Currie, *Lancaster Target*.
37. John Nichol and Tony Rennell, *Tail-End Charlies*.
38. Les Bartlett, *Bomb Aimer over Berlin*.
39. Guy Gibson, *Enemy Coast Ahead*.
40. Donald Feesey, *The Fly By Nights*.
41. Les Bartlett, *Bomb Aimer over Berlin*.
42. Interview with Thomas Murray, IWM sound archive tape 12805.
43. Campbell Muirhead, *Diary of a Bomb Aimer*.
44. Interview with Joe Williams, IWM sound archive tape 15471.
45. Unpublished memoir of Flight Lieutenant R. E. Wannop, IWM archive 80/30/1.
46. Norman Ashton, *Only Birds and Fools*.
47. Gordon Thorburn, *Bombers First and Last*.
48. Interview with Ronald Olsen, IWM sound archive tape 15743.
49. Harry Yates, *Luck and a Lancaster*.
50. Memoir of Stephen Rew, IWM archive 96/58/1.
51. John Colville, *The Fringes of Power*.
52. Unpublished memoir of Flight Lieutenant R. E. Wannop, IWM archive 80/30/1.
53. Interview with Hugh Parrott, IWM sound archive tape 16279.
54. Campbell Muirhead, *Diary of a Bomb Aimer.*
55. Interview with Ian Anderson, IWM sound archive tape 10759.
56. Interview with John Sanders, IWM sound archive tape 14803.
57. Chan Chandler, *Tail Gunner*.
58. John Nichol and Tony Rennell, *Tail-End Charlies*.
59. Interview with John Duffield, IWM sound archive tape 9590.
60. An excellent description of the layout of a Lancaster is contained in Michael V. Nelmes and Ian Jenkins, *G for George*.
61. Mike Garbett and Brian Goulding, *Lancaster at War: Volume II*.
62. Bruce Barrymore Halfpenny, *Bomber Aircrew in World War II*.
63. Unpublished memoir of Flight Lieutenant R. E. Wannop, IWM archive 80/30/1.
64. Frank Broome, *Dead Before Dawn*.
65. James Taylor and Martin Davidson, *Bomber Crew*.
66. Memoir of Stephen Rew, IWM archive 96/58/1.

67. Jack Currie, *Lancaster Target*.
68. Harry Yates, *Luck and the Lancaster*.
69. Frank Broome, *Dead Before Dawn*.
70. Jack Currie, *Lancaster Target*.
71. Interview with Doug Tritton, IWM sound archive tape 17132.
72. Interview with Joe Williams, IWM sound archive tape 15471.
73. Unpublished memoir by J. W. Walsh, IWM archive 03/32/1.
74. Memoir of Stephen Rew, IWM archive 96/58/1.
75. Bill Jones, *Bomber Intelligence*.
76. James Taylor and Martin Davidson, *Bomber Crew*.
77. Frank Broome, *Dead Before Dawn*.

CHAPTER 6: 'THE LIGHT IS SO BRIGHT THAT IT HURTS'

1. Jack Currie, *Lancaster Target*.
2. She was describing how he was awed by a visit to St Peter's basilica in Rome. Harald Penrose, *Architect of Wings*.
3. Interview with Peter Huggins, IWM sound archive tape 13245.
4. Squadron Leader Peter Russell, *Flying in Defiance of the Reich*.
5. Interview with John Toombes, IWM sound archive tape 28633.
6. Interview with David Day, IWM sound archive tape 15479.
7. Andrew Boyle, *No Passing Glory*.
8. Martin Davidson and James Taylor, *Bomber Crew*.
9. Donald Feesey, *The Fly By Nights*.
10. Peter Russell, *Flying in Defiance of the Reich*.
11. Interview with Arnold Easton, IWM sound archive tape 12652.
12. Ron Smith, *Rear Gunner Pathfinders*.
13. Interview with Rex Oldland, IWM sound archive tape 20918.
14. Memo by the Directorate of Technical Development, 29 January 1942, National Archives AVIA 15/1617.
15. Report of Conference at Avro, 30 April 1942, National Archives AVIA 15/1617.
16. Note by Directorate of Operational Requirements, 8 November 1942, National Archives AVIA 15/1617.
17. Interview with Doug Tritton, IWM sound archive tape 17132.
18. John Sweetman, *Bomber Crew*.
19. Norman Franks, *Ton-Up Lancs*.
20. Norman Ashton, *Birds and Fools*.
21. Interview with Eddie Dawson, IWM sound archive tape 13284.
22. Michael Nelmes and Ian Jenkins, *G for George*.
23. Jack Currie, *Lancaster Target*.
24. Gordon Thorburn, *Bombers First and Last*.
25. Harris to Guy Garrod, Air Member for Training, RAF Museum, Harris papers H90.
26. Harris to Drummond, 10 December 1943, RAF Museum, Harris papers H90.

27. Patrick Bishop, *Bomber Boys*.
28. Interview with Kenneth Grantham, IWM sound archive 10225.
29. Ibid.
30. Patrick Bishop, *Bomber Boys*.
31. Frank Musgrove, *Dresden and the Heavy Bombers*.
32. Richard Knott, *Black Night for Bomber Command*.
33. Miles Tripp, *The Eighth Passenger*.
34. Frank Musgrove, *Dresden and the Heavy Bombers*.
35. Max Hastings, *Bomber Command*.
36. Freeman Dyson, *Disturbing the Universe*.
37. Harris to Slessor, 24 February 1942, RAF Museum, Harris papers H59.
38. Ron Smith, *Rear Gunner Pathfinders*.
39. Interview with Bob Knights, IWM sound archive tape 9208.
40. Max Lambert, *Night after Night*.
41. Martin Davidson and James Taylor, *Bomber Crew*.
42. Ibid.
43. Privately printed memoir by Jack West DFM, RAF Museum X001-6422.
44. Interview with David Day, IWM sound archive tape 15479.
45. Miles Tripp, *The Eighth Passenger*.
46. Interview with Ronald Olsen, IWM sound archive tape 15743.
47. Gordon Thorburn, *Bombers First and Last*.
48. Statistics from Jorg Friedrich, *The Fire*.
49. Wynford Vaughan-Thomas, commentary from inside 207 Squadron Lancaster during raid on Berlin, 3 September 1943 (BBC Radio).
50. Report for Air Ministry by Pilot Officer Oliver Matheson, 1942, RAF Museum P358.
51. David Isby, *Fighting the Bombers*.
52. Kevin Wilson, *Bomber Boys*.
53. Wilhelm Johnen, *Duel Under the Stars*.
54. Interview with Bob Knights, IWM sound archive tape 9208.
55. Harris to Freeman, 14 June 1943, RAF Museum, Harris papers H85.
56. Harris to Portal, 13 October 1944, RAF Museum, Harris papers H83.
57. Interview with Arnold Easton, IWM sound archive tape 12652.
58. Wilhelm Johnen, *Duel Under the Stars*.
59. Sir Charles Webster and Noble Frankland, *The Strategic Air Offensive Against Germany 1939–45: Volume II*.
60. David Isby, *Fighting the Bombers*.
61. Interview with David Day, IWM sound archive tape 15479.
62. Peter Russell, *Flying in Defiance of the Reich*.
63. Kevin Wilson, *Men of Air*.
64. Bill Jones, *Bomber Intelligence*.
65. Harry Yates, *Luck and a Lancaster*.
66. Gordon Thorburn, *Bombers First and Last*.
67. John Nichol and Tony Rennell, *Tail-End Charlies*.
68. Interview with Arnold Easton, IWM sound archive tape 12652.
69. Richard Overy, *Bomber Command 1939–45*.
70. Gordon Thorburn, *Bombers First and Last*.

71. David Isby, *Fighting the Bombers*.
72. Interview with Donald Falgate, IWM sound archive tape 11587.
73. Interview with Rex Oldland, IWM sound archive tape 20918.
74. Interview with Peter Huggins, IWM sound archive tape 13245.
75. Mel Rolfe, *Bomber Boys*.
76. Peter Russell, *Flying in Defiance of the Reich*.
77. Clayton Moore, *Lancaster Valour*.
78. Interview with Thomas Murray, IWM sound archive tape 12805.
79. Harry Yates, *Luck and a Lancaster*.

CHAPTER 7: 'LIKE ENTERING THE JAWS OF HELL'

1. Noël Coward, 'Lie in the Dark and Listen' in Sheridan Morley, *A Talent to Amuse: A Biography of Noël Coward* (1985), quoted by kind permission of Alan Brodie Representation.
2. Interview with Joe Williams, IWM sound archive tape 15471.
3. Gordon Thorburn, *Bombers First and Last*.
4. Interview with Joe Williams, IWM sound archive tape 15471.
5. Interview with Doug Tritton, IWM sound archive tape 17132.
6. Peter Russell, *Flying in Defiance of the Reich*.
7. Ron Smith, *Rear Gunner Pathfinders*.
8. David Isby, *Fighting the Bombers*.
9. Les Bartlett, *Bomb Aimer over Berlin*.
10. Pip Beck, *Keeping Watch*.
11. Max Hastings, *Bomber Command*.
12. Clayton Moore, *Lancaster Valour*.
13. Frank Musgrove, *Dresden and the Heavy Bombers*.
14. Martin Davidson and James Taylor, *Bomber Crew*.
15. Interview with Rex Oldland, IWM sound archive tape 20918.
16. Interview with Larry Curtis, IWM sound archive tape 9211.
17. Andrew Maitland, *Through the Bombsight*.
18. Noble Frankland, *History at War*.
19. Norman Franks, *Ton-Up Lancs*.
20. Robin Neillands, *The Bomber War*.
21. Harris to Portal, 12 June 1942, RAF Museum, Harris papers H81.
22. Interview with Thomas Tredwell, IWM sound archive tape 10743.
23. Harris to Freeman, 9 July 1943, RAF Museum, Harris papers H85.
24. Unpublished memoir of J. W. Walsh, IWM archive 03/31/1.
25. Peter Russell, *Flying in Defiance of the Reich*.
26. BBC commentary by Wynford Vaughan-Thomas, 3 September 1943, IWM sound archive tape 2178/1.
27. Ibid.
28. Campbell Muirhead, *Diary of a Bomb Aimer*.
29. Interview with Leonard Miller, IWM sound archive tape 28556.
30. Robert Raymond, *A Yank in Bomber Command*.
31. Interview with Rex Oldland, IWM sound archive tape 20918.

32. Private memoir of Jack West, RAF Museum X001–6422.
33. Interview with Peter Huggins, IWM sound archive tape 13245.
34. Clayton Moore, *Lancaster Valour*.
35. Interview with Donald Falgate, IWM sound archive tape 11587.
36. Norman Franks, *Ton-Up Lancs*.
37. Jack Currie, *Lancaster Target*.
38. Campbell Muirhead, *Diary of a Bomb Aimer*.
39. Interview with Alfred Watson, IWM sound archive tape 23198.
40. Sean Feast, *Master Bombers*.
41. Frank Musgrove, *Dresden and the Heavy Bombers*.
42. Interview with John Duffield, IWM sound archive tape 9590.
43. Ron Smith, *Rear Gunner Pathfinders*.
44. Don Charlwood, *No Moon Tonight*.
45. Interview with Joe Williams, IWM sound archive tape 15471.
46. Interview with Ken Parfitt, IWM sound archive tape 18539.
47. Log book of J. S. A. Marshall, IWM archive 94/37/1.
48. BBC commentary by Wynford Vaughan-Thomas, 3 September 1943, IWM sound archive tape 2178/1.
49. Interview with Jack Goodman, IWM sound archive 16075.
50. Jack Currie, *Lancaster Target*.
51. Ron Smith, *Rear Gunner Pathfinders*.
52. Unpublished memoir of Stephen Rew, IWM archive 96/58/1.
53. Interview with Hugh Parrott, IWM sound archive tape 16279.
54. Norman Ashton, *Only Birds and Fools*.
55. John Sweetman, *Bomber Crews*.
56. There is an excellent description of the system in Jenny Gray's book about the landing disaster at RAF Bourn in December 1943, *Fire by Night*.
57. Richard Knott, *Black Night for Bomber Command*.
58. Churchill to Lloyd, 26 September 1942, RAF Museum, Harris papers H88.
59. Don Bennett, *Pathfinder*.
60. Peter Russell, *Flying in Defiance of the Reich*.
61. Jenny Gray, *Fire by Night*.
62. Interview with Freddie Watts, IWM sound archive tape 21029.
63. Richard Knott, *Black Night for Bomber Command*.
64. Sean Feast, *Master Bombers*.
65. Interview with Kenneth Grantham, IWM sound archive tape 10225.
66. Clayton Moore, *Lancaster Valour*.
67. Jenny Gray, *Fire by Night*.
68. Interview with Geoff King, IWM sound archive tape 28657.
69. John Nichol and Tony Rennell, *Tail-End Charlies*.
70. Chan Chandler, *Tail Gunner*.
71. Bill Jones, *Bomber Intelligence*.
72. Interview with Bob Knights, IWM sound archive tape 9208.
73. Interview with Sid Pope, IWM sound archive tape 9667.
74. Gordon Thorburn, *Bombers First and Last*.
75. Frank Broome, *Dead Before Dawn*.
76. Norman Ashton, *Only Birds and Fools*.

CHAPTER 8: 'LIVING UNDER A SENTENCE OF DEATH'

1. Interview with David Day, IWM sound archive tape 15479.
2. John Nichol and Tony Rennell, *Tail-End Charlies*.
3. Ibid.
4. Frank Musgrove, *Dresden and the Heavy Bombers*.
5. James Taylor and Martin Davidson, *Bomber Crew*.
6. Interview with Eddie Dawson, IWM sound archive tape 13284.
7. Interview with George Atkinson, IWM sound archive tape 6176.
8. Interview with Stephen Masters, IWM sound archive tape 10597.
9. Interview with George Bilton, IWM sound archive tape 13444.
10. Unpublished memoir of Peter Antwis, IWM archive 01/35/1.
11. Frank Musgrove, *Dresden and the Heavy Bombers*.
12. Noble Frankland, *History at War*.
13. Ibid.
14. Interview with Donald Falgate, IWM sound archive tape 11587.
15. Donald Feesey, *The Fly By Nights*.
16. Miles Tripp, *The Eighth Passenger*.
17. Frank Musgrove, *Dresden and the Heavy Bombers*.
18. Max Lambert, *Night after Night*.
19. Interview with Terry Kearns, IWM sound archive tape 9302.
20. Harris to Portal, 30 October 1942, RAF Museum, Harris papers H81.
21. Portal to Harris, 1 November 1942, RAF Museum, Harris papers H81.
22. Cochrane to Harris, 4 August 1943, RAF Museum, Harris papers H59.
23. Harris to Cochrane, 11 August 1943, RAF Museum, Harris papers H59.
24. Cochrane to Saundby, 24 October 1943, National Archives AIR 14/1564.
25. Report by Harris to the Air Staff, 30 October 1943, National Archives AIR 14/1564.
26. Harris to Peter Drummond, Air Member for Training, 17 November 1943, RAF Museum, Harris papers H90.
27. Report of Air Ministry TG2 staff, *Note on Lancaster Accidents*, November 1943, RAF Museum, Harris papers H90.
28. Interview with David Day, IWM sound archive tape 15479.
29. Interview with Danny Boon, IWM sound archive tape 17113.
30. Kevin Wilson, *Men of Air*.
31. Clayton Moore, *Lancaster Valour*.
32. Patrick Bishop, *Bomber Boys*.
33. Les Bartlett, *Bomb Aimer over Berlin*.
34. Bruce Barrymore Halfpenny, *Bomber Aircrew in World War II*.
35. Memoir of R. E. Wannop, IWM archive 80/30/1.
36. Miles Tripp, *The Eighth Passenger*.
37. Ibid.
38. John Nichol and Tony Rennell, *Tail-End Charlies*.
39. Mel Rolfe, *Bomber Boys*.
40. Memoir by J. W. Walsh, IWM archive 03/32/1.

41. Interview with Joseph Williams, IWM sound archive tape 15471.
42. Interview with Harold Davis, IWM sound archive tape 9194.
43. Interview with Joseph Williams, IWM sound archive tape 15471.
44. Mel Rolfe, *Bomber Boys*.
45. Interview with Doug Tritton, IWM sound archive tape 17132.
46. Dr Vanessa Chambers, research paper: 'Gremlins, World War Two and the Supernatural'.
47. Interview with Harold Davis, IWM sound archive tape 9194.
48. Interview with Larry Curtis, IWM sound archive tape 9211.
49. Max Lambert, *Night after Night*.
50. Mark Connelly, *Reaching for the Stars*.
51. Tom Docherty, *No.7 Bomber Squadron in World War II*.
52. Max Arthur, *Dambusters*.
53. Gordon Thorburn, *Bombers First and Last*.
54. Kevin Wilson, *Men of Air*.
55. Pip Beck, *Keeping Watch*.
56. Memoir by J. W. Walsh, IWM archive 03/32/1.
57. Peter Russell, *Flying in Defiance of the Reich*.
58. Miles Tripp, *The Eighth Passenger*.
59. Mel Rolfe, *Hell on Earth*.
60. Interview with John Duffield, IWM sound archive tape 9590.
61. Interview with Thomas Tredwell, IWM sound archive tape 10743.
62. Cochrane to Harris, 11 May 1943, RAF Museum, Harris papers H59.
63. Interview with Ronald Olsen, IWM sound archive tape 15743.
64. Interview with Doug Tritton, IWM sound archive tape 17132.
65. John Terraine, *The Right of the Line*.
66. Interview with Thomas Murray, IWM sound archive tape 12805.
67. Mel Rolfe, *Bomber Boys*.
68. Interview with Arthur Cole, IWM sound archive tape 15558.
69. Interview with J. W. Henderson, IWM sound archive tape 16374.
70. Private memoir of Jack West, RAF museum X001-6422.
71. Andrew Boyle, *No Passing Glory*.
72. Entry for 8 June 1944, Campbell Muirhead, *Diary of a Bomb Aimer*.
73. Harry Yates, *Luck and a Lancaster*.
74. Robin Neillands, *The Bomber War*.
75. Martin Davidson and James Taylor, *Bomber Crew*.

CHAPTER 9: 'IT WAS A REAL BEAUT TO FLY'

1. Sir Arthur Harris, *Bomber Offensive*.
2. Harris to Portal, 24 September 1942, RAF Museum, Harris papers H81.
3. Portal to Harris, 26 September 1942, RAF Museum, Harris papers H81.
4. Harris to Portal, 9 July 1943, Portal papers, folder 10.
5. Harris to Freeman, 4 September 1942, RAF Museum, Harris papers H66.
6. Harris to Freeman, 5 September 1942, RAF Museum, Harris papers H66.
7. Harald Penrose, *Architect of Wings*.

8. Portal to Churchill, 14 September 1942, Portal papers, folder 3.
9. Churchill to Portal, 17 September 1942, Portal papers, folder 3.
10. Portal to Churchill, 18 September 1942, Portal papers, folder 3.
11. Sir Wilfrid Freeman to Ralph Bell, Director General of Aircraft Production, Ottawa, 24 July 1943, National Archives AIR 20/2914.
12. Portal to Churchill, 13 July 1943, Portal papers, folder 3.
13. Portal to Churchill, 16 June 1943, Portal papers, folder 3.
14. Air Staff paper, 'Approaching Obsolescence of the Halifax', 14 November 1942, National Archives AIR 2/7781.
15. Harris to Freeman, 8 January 1943, National Archives Air 2/7781.
16. Sorley to Harris, 16 March 1943, National Archives AIR 20/1769.
17. Harris to Sorley, 18 March 1943, National Archives AIR 20/1769.
18. Note by Sorley to Portal, 23 March 1943, National Archives AIR 20/1769.
19. Note by Portal to Sorley, 24 March 1943, National Archives AIR 20/1769.
20. Sorley to Harris, 24 March 1943, National Archives AIR 20/1769.
21. Paper by Ralph Sorley, 23 March 1943, National Archives AIR 8/714.
22. Churchill to Cripps, 27 October 1943, National Archives AIR 20/1769.
23. Cripps to Churchill, 11 November 1943, National Archives AIR 20/1769.
24. Harris to Sorley, 30 April 1943, National Archives AIR 2/7781.
25. Breakey to Harris, 18 July 1943, National Archives AIR 2/7781.
26. Harris to Portal, 7 September 1943.
27. Harris to Freeman, 8 September 1943, RAF Museum, Harris papers H85.
28. Freeman to Harris, 10 September 1943, RAF Museum, Harris papers H85.
29. Portal to Harris, 14 September 1943, RAF Museum, Harris papers H85.
30. Minutes of Air Staff meeting, 21 December 1943, National Archives AIR 2/7781.
31. Note by G. S. Whitlock, Air Ministry, 18 December 1943, National Archives AIR 2/7781.
32. Paper by MAP, 24 December 1943, National Archives AIR 2/7781.
33. Harris to Portal, 14 April 1944, RAF Museum, Harris papers H83.
34. Paper by Bufton, 'Appreciation of the operational effectiveness of the Halifax compared with the Lancaster', December 1944.
35. Interview with Charles Calder, IWM sound archive tape 17748.
36. James Taylor and Martin Davidson, *Bomber Crew*.
37. Interview with Thomas Tredwell, IWM sound archive tape 10743.
38. Freeman Dyson, *Disturbing the Universe*.
39. Harris to Sorley, 21 April 1942, RAF Museum, Harris papers H17.
40. Harris to Harold Macmillan, Secretary of State for Air, 9 June 1945, RAF Museum, Harris papers H80.
41. Interview with Jim Porter, IWM sound archive tape 18505.
42. Interview with John Sanders, IWM sound archive tape 14803.
43. Interview with Harold Davis, IWM sound archive tape 9194.
44. Unpublished memoir by Stephen Rew, IWM archive 96/58/1.
45. Paper by MAP, 24 December 1943, National Archives AIR 2/7781.
46. Minutes of Air Staff meeting, 21 December 1943, National Archives AIR 2/7781.
47. Henry Probert, *Bomber Harris*.

48. Richard Overy, *Why the Allies Won*.
49. Dudley Saward, *'Bomber' Harris*.
50. Donald Miller, *Eighth Air Force*.
51. Quote from a lecture given by Sir Norman Bottomley, Deputy Chief of the Air Staff, 1947, RAF Museum, Bottomley papers AC71/2/78.
52. *Aeroplane Spotter*, 28 January 1943.
53. Donald Miller, *Eighth Air Force*.
54. Ibid.
55. Max Hastings, *Bomber Command*.
56. Sir Charles Webster and Noble Frankland, *The Strategic Air Offensive Against Germany 1939–45: Volume II*.
57. Simon Read, *The Killing Skies*.
58. Sir Charles Webster and Noble Frankland, *The Strategic Air Offensive Against Germany 1939–45: Volume II*.
59. Max Hastings, *Bomber Command*.
60. Dudley Saward, *'Bomber' Harris*.
61. Sinclair to Harris, 17 January 1943, RAF Museum, Harris papers H79.
62. Interview with J. W. Henderson, IWM sound archive tape 16374.
63. Don Bennett, *Pathfinder*. Bennett wrote that he would 'hate to confirm or deny' this story. Another version is that the two TRE researchers dreamt up the name.
64. Harris to Churchill, 17 April 1943, RAF Museum, Harris papers H65.
65. Harald Penrose, *Architect of Wings*.
66. Interview with Bob Knights, IWM sound archive tape 9208.
67. Interview with Thomas Tredwell, IWM sound archive tape 10743.
68. Harris to Tizard, 6 July 1942, RAF Museum, Harris papers H26.
69. Harris to Freeman, 14 June 1943, RAF Museum, Harris papers H85.
70. Harris to Coryton, 23 February 1943, RAF Museum, Harris papers H59.
71. Bennett to Harris, 18 April 1943, RAF Museum, Harris papers H57.
72. Article in February 1943 edition of *Tee Em*.
73. Bennett to Harris, 4 February 1943, RAF Museum, Harris papers H90.
74. Harris to Garrod, 5 February 1943, RAF Museum, Harris papers H90.
75. Article by Don Bennett in March 1943 edition of *Tee Em*.
76. Figures from Francis K. Mason, *The Avro Lancaster*.
77. Harris to Group Commanders, 6 April 1943, RAF Museum, Harris papers H59.
78. Joseph Goebbels, *Diaries*, entry for 6 March 1940.
79. Ibid., entry for 7 March 1940.
80. Norman Ashton, *Only Birds and Fools*.
81. James Taylor and Martin Davidson, *Bomber Crew*.
82. Kevin Wilson, *Bomber Boys*.
83. Ibid.
84. Stalin to Harris, 23 April 1943, RAF Museum, Harris papers H49.

CHAPTER 10: 'WHAT THE HELL DO YOU DAMNED INVENTORS WANT?'

1. Harris to Slessor, 22 March 1942, RAF Museum, Harris papers H59.
2. Susan Ottaway, *Dambuster: The Life of Guy Gibson*.
3. Richard Morris, *Guy Gibson*.
4. Memoir of the Dambusters Raid by Wing Commander D. J. Shannon, IWM archive 008177/03/1.
5. Max Arthur, *Dambusters*.
6. Richard Morris, *Guy Gibson*.
7. Interview with Larry Curtis, IWM sound archive tape 9211.
8. Max Arthur, *Dambusters*.
9. Richard Morris, *Guy Gibson*.
10. Max Arthur, *Dambusters*.
11. Interview with Norman Boorer, IWM sound archive tape 13076.
12. Richard Morris (ed.), *Breaching the German Dams*.
13. Interview with Norman Boorer, IWM sound archive tape 13076.
14. Richard Morris (ed.), *Breaching the German Dams*.
15. John Sweetman, *The Dambusters Raid*.
16. Ibid.
17. Quoted in Peter Pugh, *Barnes Wallis*.
18. John Sweetman, *The Dambusters Raid*.
19. Harris to Portal, 18 February 1943, RAF Museum, Harris papers H82.
20. Portal to Harris, 19 February 1943, in ibid.
21. John Sweetman, *The Dambusters Raid*.
22. Ibid.
23. Harald Penrose, *Architect of Wings*.
24. Ibid.
25. Peter Pugh, *Barnes Wallis*.
26. Max Arthur, *Dambusters*.
27. Interview with Norman Boorer, IWM sound archive tape 13076.
28. Ibid.
29. Guy Gibson, *Enemy Coast Ahead*.
30. Ibid.
31. Ibid.
32. John Sweetman, *The Dambusters Raid*.
33. Guy Gibson, *Enemy Coast Ahead*.
34. Interview with Edward Johnson, IWM sound archive tape 8204.
35. Paul Brickhill, *The Dambusters*.
36. Chaz Bowyer, *Bomber Barons*.
37. Interview with Larry Curtis, IWM sound archive tape 9211.
38. Interview with John Elliott, IWM sound archive tape 13904.
39. John Sweetman, *Bomber Crew*.
40. Interview with Edward Johnson, IWM sound archive tape 8204.
41. Guy Gibson, *Enemy Coast Ahead*.
42. Ibid.

43. Max Arthur, *Dambusters.*
44. Ibid.
45. John Sweetman, *The Dambusters Raid.*
46. Speech about the Dambusters given by David Shannon to the Royal Aeronautical Society, 10 November 1986, IWM sound archive tape 16256.
47. Interview with Edward Johnson, IWM sound archive tape 8204.
48. Max Arthur, *Dambusters.*
49. Peter G. Masefield, entry on Lockspeiser in the *Oxford Dictionary of National Biography.*
50. Interview with Dave Shannon, IWM sound archive tape 8177.
51. Interview with Edward Johnson, IWM sound archive tape 8204.
52. Speech about the Dambusters given by David Shannon to the Royal Aeronautical Society, 10 November 1986, IWM sound archive tape 16256.
53. Max Arthur, *Dambusters.*
54. Further details of the dispute are in Sir Charles Webster and Noble Frankland, *The Strategic Air Offensive Against Germany 1939–45: Volume II.*
55. Speech about the Dambusters given by David Shannon to the Royal Aeronautical Society, 10 November 1986, IWM sound archive tape 16256.
56. Interview with John Elliott, IWM sound archive tape 13904.
57. Max Arthur, *Dambusters.*
58. Guy Gibson, *Enemy Coast Ahead.*
59. Max Arthur, *Dambusters.*
60. Interview with Edward Johnson, IWM sound archive tape 8204.
61. Interview with John Elliott, IWM sound archive tape 13904.
62. Guy Gibson, *Enemy Coast Ahead.*
63. Max Arthur, *Dambusters.*
64. Kevin Wilson, *Bomber Boys.*
65. Interview with Dave Shannon, IWM sound archive tape 8177.
66. Guy Gibson, *Enemy Coast Ahead.*
67. Interview with Edward Johnson, IWM sound archive tape 8204.
68. Max Arthur, *Dambusters.*
69. Guy Gibson, *Enemy Coast Ahead.*
70. Max Arthur, *Dambusters.*
71. Interview with Edward Johnson, IWM sound archive tape 8204.
72. Ibid.
73. Max Arthur, *Dambusters.*
74. Interview with Edward Johnson, IWM sound archive tape 8204.
75. Max Arthur, *Dambusters.*
76. Memoir of the Dambusters Raid by Wing Commander D. J. Shannon, IWM archive 8177.
77. John Sweetman, *The Dambusters.*
78. Dudley Saward, *'Bomber' Harris.*
79. Interview with Dave Shannon, IWM sound archive tape 8177.
80. Richard Evans, *The Third Reich at War.*
81. Harris to Bottomley, 20 December 1943, RAF Museum, Harris papers H47.
82. Harris to Portal, 18 January 1945, RAF Museum, Harris papers H84.
83. Wallis to Chadwick, 25 May 1943, quoted in Harry Holmes, *Avro Lancaster.*

CHAPTER 11: 'A SEA OF FLAMES!'

1. Harry Holmes, *Avro Lancaster*.
2. Keith Lowe, *Inferno*.
3. Martin Middlebrook, *The Battle of Hamburg*.
4. Henry Probert, *Bomber Harris*.
5. Interview with Thomas Tredwell, IWM sound archive tape 10743.
6. David Jablonsky, *Churchill, the Great Game and Total War*.
7. Watson-Watt to Harris, 28 May 1942, RAF Museum, Harris papers H35.
8. Harris to Freeman, 31 May 1942, RAF Museum, Harris papers H35.
9. Sir Charles Webster and Noble Frankland, *The Strategic Air Offensive Against Germany 1939–45: Volume II*.
10. David Jablonsky, *Churchill, the Great Game and Total War*.
11. Ibid.
12. Frank Musgrove, *Dresden and the Heavy Bombers*.
13. Interview with Donald Falgate, IWM sound archive tape 11587.
14. Martin Davidson and James Taylor, *Bomber Crew*.
15. Martin Middlebrook, *The Battle of Hamburg*.
16. Kevin Wilson, *Bomber Boys*.
17. Interview with Thomas Tredwell, IWM sound archive tape 10743.
18. Keith Lowe, *Inferno*.
19. Ibid.
20. Ibid.
21. Richard Evans, *The Third Reich at War*.
22. Martin Middlebrook, *The Battle of Hamburg*.
23. Martin Davidson and James Taylor, *Bomber Crew*.
24. Interview with Trevor Timperley, IWM sound archive tape 27493.
25. Ibid.
26. July 1943, *The Goebbels Diaries*.
27. Keith Lowe, *Inferno*.
28. Richard Evans, *The Third Reich at War*.
29. Ibid.
30. Max Hastings, *Bomber Command*.
31. Quoted from James Barker, 'Sowing the Wind' (2005).
32. Quoted in Mark Connelly, *Reaching for the Stars*.
33. Robin Neillands, *The Bomber War*.
34. Keith Lowe, *Inferno*.
35. Martin Middlebrook, *The Battle of Hamburg*.
36. Richard Evans, *The Third Reich at War*.
37. Norman Ashton, *Only Birds and Fools*.
38. Jack Currie, *Lancaster Target*.
39. Dudley Saward, *'Bomber' Harris*.
40. Martin Middlebrook, *The Battle of Hamburg*.
41. Keith Lowe, *Inferno*.
42. Carl von Clausewitz, *On War*.
43. Martin Middlebrook, *The Peenemünde Raid*.

44. Kevin Wilson, *Bomber Boys*.
45. Interview with Bill Griffiths, IWM sound archive 25267.
46. Mel Rolfe, *Looking into Hell*.
47. Martin Middlebrook, *The Peenemünde Raid*.
48. Ibid.
49. Mel Rolfe, *Hell on Earth*.
50. Don Charlwood, *No Moon Tonight*.
51. Kevin Wilson, *Bomber Boys*.
52. Harris to Portal, 11 July 1943, RAF Museum, Harris papers H43.
53. Portal to Churchill, 13 July 1943, Portal papers, folder 2.
54. Eden to Churchill, 14 July 1943, Portal papers, folder 2.
55. Churchill to Eden, 16 July 1943, Portal papers, folder 2.

CHAPTER 12: 'AT THE MACHINES ALL THE TIME'

1. Report by W. Dunn, Deputy Director of Control, MAP, 2 August 1944, National Archives AVIA 15/1565.
2. *Aircraft Manufacturing*, January 1943.
3. *The Aeroplane*, 14 August 1942.
4. Minute by Roy Dobson, 5 October 1941, National Archives AVIA 15/1565.
5. Note by L. W. Warner, Deputy Director General of Aircraft Production, 28 February 1943, National Archives AVIA 15/1565.
6. Interview with Eva Feulou, BBC Lincolnshire, 20 July 2005, BBC WWII People's War Archive.
7. Interview with Geoff Bentley.
8. Gerald Myers, *Mother Worked at Avro*.
9. Ibid.
10. Interview with Sophie Pape.
11. Ibid.
12. Gerald Myers, *Mother Worked at Avro*.
13. Figures in report by E. W. Walton on the Avro factories, July 1943, National Archives AVIA 10/108.
14. Interview with Lillian Grundy.
15. Gerald Myers, *Mother Worked at Avro*.
16. Interview with Sophie Pape.
17. Interview with Lillian Grundy.
18. Ibid.
19. Transcript of BBC broadcast to aircraft workers, 30 December 1942, Stafford Cripps papers.
20. *The Times*, 19 November 1942.
21. Interview with Joseph Barry.
22. Gerald Myers, *Mother Worked at Avro*.
23. Interview with Lillian Grundy.
24. *The Times*, 15 March 1944.
25. Report by E. W. Walton on the Avro factories, July 1943, National Archives AVIA 10/108.

26. Story given to the author by Jack Beatty.
27. Interview with Clare Hollingworth.
28. Interview with Harry Errington, IWM sound archive tape 20961.
29. Report by MAP, 27 July 1943, National Archives AVIA 15/2548.
30. F. L. Dock, Senior Air Personnel Officer, Manchester Group, to MAP, 13 September 1943, National Archives AVIA 15/2548.
31. Interview with Dick Marsh.
32. Interview with Sophie Pape.
33. MAP report, 2 October 1943, National Archives AVIA 15/2548.
34. Interview with Harry Tulson.
35. This moving episode is recounted in Harry Holmes, *Avro: The History of an Aircraft Company*.
36. Harris to Bottomley, 7 July 1943, RAF Museum, Harris paper H47.
37. Leigh-Mallory to Harris, 2 July 1943, RAF Museum, Harris papers H47.
38. Interview with Sophie Pape.
39. Bruce Robertson, *Lancaster: The Story of a Famous Bomber*.
40. *The Aeroplane*, August 2002.
41. Mike Garbett and Brian Goulding, *Lancaster at War: Volume II*.
42. Interview with Paul Longthorp, IWM sound archive tape 10199.
43. Giles Whittell, *Spitfire Women of World War II*.
44. Interview with Margaret Gore, IWM sound archive tape 9285.
45. Interview with Frank Iredell, IWM sound archive tape 9887.
46. Harry Yates, *Luck and a Lancaster*.
47. Norman Franks, *Ton-Up Lancs*.

CHAPTER 13: 'A CALCULATED, REMORSELESS CAMPAIGN OF DESTRUCTION'

1. Figures from Sir Charles Webster and Noble Frankland, *The Strategic Air Offensive Against Germany 1939–45: Volume II*.
2. Harris to Portal, 12 August 1943, quoted in Max Hastings, *Bomber Command*.
3. John Terraine, *The Right of the Line*.
4. Harris to Air Staff, 7 December 1943, RAF Museum, Harris papers H26.
5. Response by Harris to briefing note, 25 July 1943, RAF Museum, Harris papers H47.
6. Harris to Bottomley, 20 December 1943, RAF Museum, Harris papers H47.
7. Harris to Air Commodore W. Elliott, 28 October 1943, RAF Museum, Harris papers, H35.
8. Field Marshal Lord Alanbrooke, *War Diaries*.
9. Report received by the Air Ministry, late 1943 (undated), Bufton papers 3/27.
10. Max Hastings, *Bomber Command*.
11. Churchill to Portal, 16 June 1943, and Portal to Harris, 18 June 1943, Portal papers, folder 4.
12. Mark Connelly, *Reaching for the Stars*.
13. Both newspapers quoted in Mark Connelly, *Reaching for the Stars*.

14. *The Aeroplane*, 23 October 1942.
15. Gordon Thorburn, *Bombers First and Last*.
16. Interview with Bill Reid by the Imperial War Museum, July 1978, IWM sound archive tape 4993.
17. Interview with Bill Reid for Thames Television, 1972, IWM sound archive 2892.
18. Ibid.
19. Ibid.
20. Ibid.
21. Ibid.
22. Interview with Bill Reid by the Imperial War Museum, July 1978, IWM sound archive tape 4993.
23. Francis K. Mason, *The Avro Lancaster*.
24. Quotes from Goebbels's diaries in Dudley Saward, *'Bomber' Harris*.
25. Sinclair to Harris, 24 November 1943, RAF Museum, Harris papers H79.
26. Edward Westerman, *Flak*.
27. James Taylor and Martin Davidson, *Bomber Crew*.
28. Memoir of J. W. Walsh, IWM archive 03/32/1.
29. Sir Charles Webster and Noble Frankland, *The Strategic Air Offensive Against Germany 1939–45: Volume II*.
30. Martin Middlebrook, *The Berlin Raids*.
31. Broadcast by Ed Murrow, 4 December 1943, IWM sound archive tape 2181.
32. Dudley Saward, *'Bomber' Harris*.
33. Sir Charles Webster and Noble Frankland, *The Strategic Air Offensive Against Germany 1939–45: Volume II*.
34. Freeman Dyson, 'A Failure of Intelligence' (2006).
35. Memoir of Stephen Rew, IWM archive 96/58/1.
36. Max Hastings, *Bomber Command*.
37. Ibid.
38. Ibid.
39. Mark Connelly, *Reaching for the Stars*.
40. Harris to Sinclair, 25 November 1943, RAF Museum, Harris papers H79.
41. Marquess of Salisbury to Sinclair, 26 November 1943, RAF Museum, Harris papers H79.
42. Sinclair to Salisbury 29 November 1943, RAF Museum, Harris papers H79.
43. Portal to Sinclair, Bottomley and BBC, 26 October 1943, quoted in Mark Connelly, *Reaching for the Stars*.
44. Harris to Portal and Sinclair, 25 October 1943, RAF Museum, Harris papers H67.
45. Mark Connelly, *Reaching for the Stars*.
46. Harris to Portal and Sinclair, 23 December 1943, RAF Museum, Harris papers H67.
47. A. J. Brown, *Ground Staff – A Personal Record*.
48. Interview with Trevor Timperley, IWM sound archive tape 27493.
49. Harry Yates, *Luck and a Lancaster*.
50. Interview with Arnold Easton, IWM sound archive tape 12652.

51. Interview with Bert Wolstenholme, IWM sound archive tape 27789.
52. Interview with Danny Boon, IWM sound archive tape 17113.
53. Les Bartlett, *Bomb Aimer over Berlin.*
54. Campbell Muirhead, *Diary of a Bomb Aimer.*
55. Interview with Thomas Murray, IWM sound archive tape 12805.
56. Harris to the Air Staff, 28 December 1943, RAF Museum, Harris papers H67.
57. Les Bartlett, *Bomb Aimer over Berlin.*
58. Interview with Hugh Parrott, IWM sound archive 16279.
59. Interview with Fred Gardiner, IWM sound archive tape 16366.
60. Interview with Charles Marshall, IWM sound archive tape 16356.
61. Interview with Frank Waddington, IWM sound archive tape 17365.
62. Ron Smith, *Rear Gunner Pathfinder.*
63. Kevin Wilson, *Men of Air.*
64. Interview with Arnold Easton, IWM sound archive 12652.
65. Alfred Price, *Battle over the Reich: Volume II.*
66. Miles Tripp, *The Eighth Passenger.*
67. Interview with Ferguson Smith, IWM sound archive tape 22197.
68. Ibid.
69. Interview by Sam Brookes for the BBC People's History archive, 6 November 2003.
70. Interview with Ferguson Smith, IWM sound archive tape 22197.
71. Martin Middlebrook, *The Berlin Raids.*
72. Alfred Price, *Battle over the Reich: Volume II.*
73. Martin Middlebrook, *The Nuremburg Raid.*
74. Robin Neillands, *The Bomber War.*
75. Interview with Freddie Watts, IWM sound archive tape 21029.
76. Interview with Basil Oxtaby, IWM sound archive tape 12613.
77. Kevin Wilson, *Men of Air.*
78. Henry Probert, *Bomber Harris.*
79. Dudley Saward, *'Bomber' Harris.*
80. Martin Middlebrook, *The Nuremburg Raid.*
81. Sir Charles Webster and Noble Frankland, *The Strategic Air Offensive Against Germany 1939–45: Volume II.*

CHAPTER 14: 'THE SUPREME OPERATION FOR 1944'

1. Harris to Lovett, 24 January 1944, RAF Museum, Harris papers H28.
2. Carl von Clausewitz, *On War.*
3. Richard Overy, *Why the Allies Won.*
4. John Terraine, *The Right of the Line.*
5. Harris to Portal, 28 March 1944, National Archives AIR 20/1769.
6. Statistical section report, 2 April 1944, National Archives AIR 20/1769.
7. Portal to Harris, 7 April 1944, National Archives, AIR 20/1769.
8. Harris to Portal, 7 April 1944, Portal papers, folder 10.

9. Portal to Harris, 12 April 1944, Portal papers, folder 10.
10. Harris to Portal, 15 April 1944, Portal papers, folder 10.
11. Henry Probert, *Bomber Harris*.
12. Portal to Harris, 16 April 1944, Portal papers, folder 10.
13. Harris to Portal, 18 April 1944, Portal papers, folder 10.
14. Andrew Boyle, *No Passing Glory*.
15. Ibid.
16. Christopher Foxley-Norris, in the *Oxford Dictionary of National Biography*.
17. Interview with Bob Knights, IWM sound archive tape 9208.
18. Interview with Arthur Poore, IWM sound archive tape 20261.
19. Christopher Foxley-Norris, in the *Oxford Dictionary of National Biography*.
20. Andrew Boyle, *No Passing Glory*.
21. John Sweetman, *Bomber Crew*.
22. According to the testimony of Malcolm Hamilton, IWM sound archive tape 18264.
23. Interview with Larry Curtis, IWM sound archive tape 9211.
24. Andrew Boyle, *No Passing Glory*.
25. Robin Neillands, *The Bomber War*.
26. Interview with Bob Knights, IWM sound archive tape 9208.
27. Andrew Boyle, *No Passing Glory*.
28. Report of attack on Limoges Factory, Leonard Cheshire papers, IWM archive 71/31/1.
29. Ibid.
30. Ibid.
31. Report of attack on Antheor viaduct, Leonard Cheshire papers, IWM archive 71/31/1.
32. Interview with Larry Curtis, IWM sound archive tape 9211.
33. Report of attack on Antheor viaduct, Leonard Cheshire papers, IWM archive 71/31/1.
34. Report of attack on aircraft factory at Albert, 2–3 March, Leonard Cheshire papers, IWM archive 71/31/1.
35. Report of attack on explosive works at Pouderie Nationale, Leonard Cheshire papers, IWM archive 71/31/1.
36. Report of attack on St Etienne, Leonard Cheshire papers, IWM archive 71/31/1.
37. Andrew Boyle, *No Passing Glory*.
38. Report of attack on Munich, Leonard Cheshire papers, IWM archive 71/31/1.
39. Francis K. Mason, *The Avro Lancaster*.
40. Interview with Bob Knights, IWM sound archive tape 9208.
41. Harris to Portal, 18 November 1944, RAF Museum, Harris papers H83.
42. Don Bennett, *Pathfinder*.
43. Bennett to Harris, 31 May 1944, RAF Museum, Harris papers H57.
44. Cochrane to Harris, 28 June 1944, RAF Museum, Harris papers H59.
45. Harris to Cochrane, 3 July 1944, RAF Museum, Harris papers H59.
46. Figures from Max Hastings, *Bomber Command*.
47. Interview with Donald Falgate, IWM sound archive tape 11587.
48. Interview with Geoff King, IWM sound archive tape 28657.

49. Andrew Boyle, *No Passing Glory*.
50. Kevin Wilson, *Men of Air*.
51. Ibid.
52. Gordon Thorburn, *Bombers First and Last*.
53. Unpublished memoir of Stephen Rew, IWM archive 96/58/1.
54. Paper by Harris entitled 'The Employment of the Night Bomber Force in Connection with the Invasion of the Continent from the UK', 13 January 1944, Portal papers, folder 10.
55. Response by Air Staff and AEAF, 30 January 1944, Portal papers, folder 10.
56. Arthur Tedder, *With Prejudice*.
57. Ibid.
58. Ibid.
59. Ibid.
60. Ibid.
61. Harris to Lovett, 3 April 1944, RAF Museum, Harris papers H28.
62. Arthur Tedder, *With Prejudice*.
63. Harris to Portal, 24 March 1944, Portal papers, folder 10.
64. Arthur Tedder, *With Prejudice*.
65. Henry Probert, *Bomber Harris*.
66. Paper on Overlord from the Bombing Operations Directorate, 5 April 1944, Bufton papers Buft 3/51.
67. Max Hastings, *Bomber Command*.
68. Sir Charles Webster and Noble Frankland, *The Strategic Air Offensive Against Germany 1939–45: Volume III*.
69. Harris to Lovett, 3 April 1944, RAF Museum, Harris papers H28.
70. Portal to Churchill, 13 April 1944, Portal papers.
71. Diary entry for 19 April 1942, Field Marshal Lord Alanbrooke, *War Diaries*.
72. Sir Charles Webster and Noble Frankland, *The Strategic Air Offensive Against Germany 1939–45: Volume III*.
73. Henry Probert, *Bomber Harris*.
74. Arthur Tedder, *With Prejudice*.
75. Bill Jones, *Bomber Intelligence*.
76. Interview with Denis Burns, IWM sound archive tape 17179.
77. Campbell Muirhead, *Diary of a Bomb Aimer*.
78. Harris to Bottomley, 8 March 1944, RAF Museum, Harris papers H68.
79. Kevin Wilson, *Men of Air*.
80. Ibid.
81. Charles Carrington, *Soldier at Bomber Command*.
82. John Keegan, *The Second World War*.
83. Arthur Tedder, *With Prejudice*.
84. Transcript of interview with Hermann Göring, 1 June 1945, Bufton papers Buft 3/60.
85. Interview with Danny Boon, IWM sound archive tape 17113.
86. Interview with Rex Oldland, IWM sound archive tape 20918.
87. Interview with John Sanders, IWM sound archive tape 14803.
88. Interview with Malcolm Hamilton, IWM sound archive tape 18264.
89. Charles Carrington, *Soldier at Bomber Command*.

CHAPTER 15: 'GET ON AND KNOCK GERMANY FINALLY FLAT'

1. Peter Pugh, *Barnes Wallis: Dambuster.*
2. Sir Arthur Harris, *Bomber Offensive.*
3. Kevin Wilson, *Men of Air.*
4. Ibid.
5. Interview with Malcolm Hamilton, IWM sound archive tape 18264.
6. Interview with John Gedney, IWM sound archive tape 13943.
7. Dave Birrell, *Baz: The Biography of Squadron Leader Ian Bazalgette.*
8. *London Gazette*, 17 August 1945.
9. Interview with Malcolm Hamilton, IWM sound archive tape 18264.
10. Francis K. Mason, *The Avro Lancaster.*
11. Stephen Darlow, *D-Day Bombers.*
12. *London Gazette*, 11 October 1946.
13. Interview with Bob Knights, IWM sound archive tape 9208.
14. Diary entry for 3 August, Campbell Muirhead, *Diary of a Bomb Aimer.*
15. Ibid.
16. David Scholes, *Air War Diary.*
17. Memoir by Peter Antwis, IWM Archive 01/35/1.
18. Ibid.
19. Max Lambert, *Night after Night.*
20. Ibid.
21. Stephen Darlow, *D-Day Bombers.*
22. Arthur Tedder, *With Prejudice.*
23. Montgomery to Harris, 9 July 1944, RAF Museum, Harris papers H49.
24. Charles Carrington, *Soldier at Bomber Command.*
25. Ian Gooderson, *Air Power at the Battlefront.*
26. Arthur Tedder, *With Prejudice.*
27. Charles Carrington, *Soldier at Bomber Command.*
28. Interview with Donald Falgate, IWM sound archive tape 11587.
29. Dudley Saward, *'Bomber' Harris.*
30. Ian Gooderson, *Air Power at the Battlefront.*
31. Private Memoir by Jack West, RAF Museum X001-6422.
32. Report by Harris on Operation Tractable, 25 August 1944, RAF Museum, Harris papers H49.
33. Ian Gooderson, *Air Power at the Battlefront.*
34. David Scholes, *Air War Diary.*
35. Harry Yates, *Luck and a Lancaster.*
36. Henry Probert, *Bomber Harris.*
37. Sir Arthur Harris, *Bomber Offensive.*
38. Max Hastings, *Bomber Command.*
39. Harris to Evill, 27 June and 3 July 1944, Evill to Harris, 1 July 1944, RAF Museum, Harris papers H15.
40. *London Gazette*, 26 October 1945.

41. Entry for 13 June 1944, Campbell Muirhead, *Diary of a Bomb Aimer*.
42. Tom Docherty, *No 7 Squadron in World War II*.
43. Courtney to Harris, 30 March 1942, RAF Museum, Harris papers H88.
44. Figures from Terry Hancock, *Bomber County*.
45. Sir Arthur Harris, *Bomber Offensive*.
46. Ibid.
47. Ibid.
48. Michael Wieck, *A Childhood under Hitler and Stalin*.
49. Ils Mar Garthaus, *The Way We Lived in Germany during World War II*.
50. Alfred Price, *Battle over the Reich*.
51. Sir Charles Webster and Noble Frankland, *The Strategic Air Offensive Against Germany 1939–45: Volume III*.
52. Dudley Saward, *'Bomber' Harris*.
53. Sir Charles Webster and Noble Frankland, *The Strategic Air Offensive Against Germany 1939–45: Volume III*.
54. Henry Probert, *Bomber Harris*.
55. Figures from Max Hastings, *Bomber Command*.
56. Interview with Ian Dunlop, IWM sound archive tape 17831.
57. Frank Broome, *Dead Before Dawn*.
58. Journal of John Byrne, IWM archive 04/24/1.
59. Harry Yates, *Luck and a Lancaster*.
60. Sean Feast, *Master Bombers*.
61. Robin Neillands, *The Bomber War*.
62. Interview with Ian Dunlop, IWM sound archive tape 17831.
63. Tom Docherty, *No 7 Squadron in World War II*.
64. Norman Ashton, *Only Birds and Fools*.
65. Harris to Portal, 1 November 1944, RAF Museum, Harris papers H83.
66. Portal to Harris, 5 November 1944, in ibid.
67. Harris to Portal, 6 November 1944, in ibid.
68. Portal to Harris, 12 November 1944, in ibid.

CHAPTER 16: 'THE *TIRPITZ* WAS DOOMED'

1. Harris to Portal, 27 June 1944, RAF Museum, Harris papers H83.
2. Note by J. D. Breakey, Director of Operational Requirements, 3 December 1944, National Archives AIR 2/7838.
3. Minutes of Air Ministry Conference, 12 January 1943, National Archives AIR 2/7939.
4. Harris to Freeman, 14 June 1943, RAF Museum, Harris papers H85.
5. Sir Arthur Harris, *Bomber Offensive*.
6. Ibid.
7. Minutes of Air Ministry Conference, 24 June 1943, National Archives AIR 2/7839.
8. Ibid.
9. Sorley to Evill, 21 July 1943, National Archives AIR 2/7839.
10. Ken Delve, *Avro Lancaster*.

11. Ibid.
12. Harris to Evill, 20 October 1943, National Archives AIR 2/7839.
13. Note by Air Commodore A. R. Wardle, 19 December 1943, National Archives AIR 2/7839.
14. Harris to Evill, 11 July 1944, RAF Museum, Harris papers H15.
15. Harris to Portal, 19 April 1944, RAF Museum, Harris papers H83.
16. Harris to Evill, 28 August 1944, RAF Museum, Harris papers H15.
17. Sorley to Portal, 24 July 1944, National Archives AIR 2/7839.
18. Harris to Portal, 11 July 1944, RAF Museum, Harris papers H83.
19. Harris to Sorley, 7 October 1944, National Archives AIR 2/7838.
20. Harris to Portal, 13 October 1944, RAF Museum, Harris papers H83.
21. Sir Arthur Harris, *Bomber Offensive*.
22. Minutes of conference on heavy bomber armament, 22 November 1944, National Archives AIR 2/7838.
23. Ken Delve, *Avro Lancaster*.
24. Minutes of conference on heavy bomber armament, 22 November 1944, National Archives AIR 2/7838.
25. Evill to Portal 18 October 1944, National Archives AIR 20/3393.
26. John Nichol and Tony Rennell, *Tail-End Charlies*.
27. Bennett to Harris, 12 February 1945, RAF Museum, Harris papers H58.
28. Harris to Bennett, 19 February 1945, RAF Museum, Harris papers H58.
29. Sinclair to Harris, 8 September 1944, RAF Museum, Harris papers H79.
30. Harris to Evill, 9 September 1944, RAF Museum, Harris papers H68.
31. Miles Tripp, *The Eighth Passenger*.
32. Message from Churchill to RAF, 25 March 1942, RAF Museum, Harris papers H81.
33. Sir Arthur Harris, *Bomber Offensive*.
34. Ibid.
35. Harris to Trenchard, 22 September 1943, RAF Museum, Harris papers H50.
36. Interview with Bob Knights, IWM sound archive tape 9208.
37. Gordon Thorburn, *Bombers First and Last*.
38. Interview with Malcolm Hamilton, IWM sound archive tape 18264.
39. Interview with Thomas Andrew, IWM sound archive tape 14834.
40. Tape of a lecture delivered by Tony Iveson to the Royal Aeronautical Society, 1986, IWM sound archive 16255.
41. Interview with Larry Curtis, IWM sound archive tape 9211.
42. Interview with Freddie Watts, IWM sound archive tape 21029.
43. Tape of a lecture delivered by Tony Iveson to the Royal Aeronautical Society, 1986, IWM sound archive 16255.
44. Ibid.
45. Interview with Thomas Andrew, IWM sound archive tape 14834.
46. BBC Interview with Wing Commander James Bazin, recorded 5 October 1944, IWM sound archive 2510.
47. Interview with Larry Curtis, IWM sound archive tape 9211.
48. Interview with John Sanders, IWM sound archive tape 14803.
49. Interview with Larry Curtis, IWM sound archive tape 9211.
50. Interview with John Sanders, IWM sound archive tape 14803.

51. Tape of a lecture delivered by Tony Iveson to the Royal Aeronautical Society, 1986, IWM sound archive 16255.
52. Interview with John Sanders, IWM sound archive tape 14803.
53. Tape of a lecture delivered by Tony Iveson to the Royal Aeronautical Society, 1986, IWM sound archive 16255.
54. Interview with Thomas Andrew, IWM sound archive tape 14834.
55. Interview with Bob Knights, IWM sound archive tape 9208.
56. Tape of a lecture delivered by Tony Iveson to the Royal Aeronautical Society, 1986, IWM sound archive 16255.
57. Gordon Thorburn, *Bombers First and Last*.
58. Ibid.
59. Report by Fl. Lt. Cussons, 12 November 1944, National Archives AVIA 40/2015.
60. Gordon Thorburn, *Bombers First and Last*.
61. Harris to Lovatt, 24 November 1944, RAF Museum, Harris papers H28.
62. Tami Davis Biddle, 'Bombing by the Square Yard'.
63. Max Hastings, *Bomber Command*.
64. Ibid.
65. Interview with Ian Anderson, IWM sound archive tape 10759.
66. Bufton to Portal, 21 December 1944, Bufton papers Buft 3/51.
67. Sir Charles Webster and Noble Frankland, *The Strategic Air Offensive Against Germany 1939–45: Volume III*.
68. Harris to Portal, 28 December 1944, RAF Museum, Harris papers H70.
69. Bufton to Portal, 3 January 1945, Bufton papers Buft 3/51.
70. Transcript of interrogation of Herman Göring, 1 June 1945, Bufton papers Buft 3/51.
71. Portal to Harris, 8 January 1945, RAF Museum, Harris papers H84.
72. Harris to Portal, 18 January 1945, RAF Museum, Harris papers H84.
73. Portal to Harris, 20 January 1945, RAF Museum, Harris papers H84.
74. Henry Probert, *Bomber Harris*.
75. Churchill to Portal, 28 January 1945, Portal papers, folder 6.
76. Harris to Christopher Courtney, 23 March 1942, RAF Museum, Harris papers H88.
77. Denis Richards, *Portal of Hungerford*.
78. Exchange of correspondence in ibid.
79. Richard Overy, *Why the Allies Won*.
80. David C. Isby, *Fighting the Bombers*.
81. Thomas Childers, '*Facilis descensus averni est*'.
82. Richard Evans, *The Third Reich at War*.
83. Thomas Childers, '*Facilis descensus averni est*'.
84. Transcript of talk by Bottomley, 1944, RAF Museum, Bottomley papers AC71/2/53.
85. Frank Musgrove, *Dresden and the Heavy Bombers*.

CHAPTER 17: 'A PURE MORALE AIR ATTACK'

1. Andrew Roberts, *'The Holy Fox'*.
2. Paper by SHAEF, 1944, Bufton papers Buft 3/51.
3. Dr Richard Davis, 'Bombing Strategy Shifts, 1944–45'.
4. Ian Gooderson, *Air Power at the Battlefront*.
5. Quoted in Robin Neillands, *The Bomber War*.
6. David Spark, 'The Man Who Tried to Stop the Dresden Raids'.
7. Charles Carrington, *Soldier at Bomber Command*.
8. Jorg Friedrich, *The Fire*.
9. Transcript of broadcast by Richard Dimbleby, 8 February 1945, IWM sound archive tape 1969/G/E.
10. Sir Charles Webster and Noble Frankland, *The Strategic Air Offensive Against Germany 1939–45: Volume III*.
11. Jorg Friedrich, *The Fire*.
12. Hermann Knell, *To Destroy a City*.
13. Henry Probert, *Bomber Harris*.
14. *Daily Telegraph*, 3 October 2008.
15. Interview with Rex Oldland, IWM sound archive tape 20918.
16. Interview with Peter Nettleton, IWM sound archive tape 9348.
17. Frederick Taylor, *Dresden*.
18. Report for Air Ministry, National Archives Air 8/714.
19. Paper on Thunderclap by the Bombing Operations Directorate, August 1944, Bufton papers Buft 3/43.
20. Morley to Bufton, 21 January 1944, Bufton papers Buft 3/43.
21. Sir Charles Webster and Noble Frankland, *The Strategic Air Offensive Against Germany 1939–45: Volume III*.
22. Frederick Taylor, *Dresden*.
23. Sir Charles Webster and Noble Frankland, *The Strategic Air Offensive Against Germany 1939–45: Volume III*.
24. Ibid.
25. Ibid.
26. Frederick Taylor, *Dresden*.
27. Ibid.
28. David Irving to Sir Norman Bottomley, 11 December 1961, RAF Museum, Bottomley papers AC71/1/113.
29. David Spark, 'The Man Who Tried to Stop the Dresden Raids'.
30. Frederick Taylor, *Dresden*.
31. Interview with John Aldridge, IWM sound archive tape 18499.
32. Frank Musgrove, *Dresden and the Heavy Bombers*.
33. Donald Feesey, *The Fly By Nights*.
34. Miles Tripp, *The Eighth Passenger*.
35. Frederick Taylor, *Dresden*.
36. Ibid.
37. Journal of R. E. Wannop, IWM archive 80/30/1.
38. Interview with Michael Bradford, IWM sound archive tape 17328.

39. Miles Tripp, *The Eighth Passenger*.
40. Frank Musgrove, *Dresden and the Heavy Bombers*.
41. Interview with Frank Tolley, IWM sound archive tape 29049.
42. Frederick Taylor, *Dresden*.
43. Ibid.
44. *The Times*, 15 February 1945.
45. *Daily Express*, 15 February 1945.
46. Frank Broome, *Dead Before Dawn*.
47. John Nichol and Tony Rennell, *Tail-End Charlies*.
48. Interview with Bill Utting, IWM sound archive tape 30079.
49. Frederick Taylor, *Dresden*.
50. Sir Charles Webster and Noble Frankland, *The Strategic Air Offensive Against Germany 1939–45: Volume III*.
51. Harris to Bottomley, 29 March 1945, RAF Museum, Harris papers H9.
52. Frederick Taylor, *Dresden*.
53. Robin Neillands, *The Bomber War*.
54. Transcript of interrogation of Göring, 1 June 1945, Bufton papers Buft 3/60.
55. Sir Arthur Harris, *Bomber Offensive*.
56. Sir Charles Webster and Noble Frankland, *The Strategic Air Offensive against Germany 1939–45: Volume III*.
57. Interview with Joseph Williams, IWM sound archive tape 15471.
58. *The London Gazette*, 23 March 1945.
59. Ibid.
60. *The London Gazette*, 20 February 1945.
61. *The London Gazette*, 24 April 1945.
62. Interview with Peter Nettleton, IWM sound archive tape 9348.
63. Report by MAP, 20 February 1945, National Archives AVIA 15/2548.
64. Report by MAP, 11 April 1945, National Archives AVIA 15/2548.
65. Churchill to Portal, 19 April 1945, Portal papers, folder 6.
66. Portal to Churchill, 19 April 1945, Portal papers, folder 6.
67. Interview with Henry Hooper, IWM sound archive tape 27807.
68. John Nichol and Tony Rennell, *Tail-End Charlies*.
69. Ibid.
70. Interview with Jeffrey Goodwin, IWM sound archive tape 27793.
71. Interview with David Ware, IWM sound archive tape 24932.
72. Interview with Ian Dunlop, IWM sound archive tape 17831.
73. John Nichol and Tony Rennell, *Tail-End Charlies*.
74. Gordon Thorburn, *Bombers First and Last*.
75. Interview with David Ware, IWM sound archive tape 24932.
76. John Nichol and Tony Rennell, *Tail-End Charlies*.
77. Interview with David Ware, IWM sound archive tape 24932.
78. Journal of R. E. Wannop, IWM archive 80/30/1.
79. Interview with Henry Hooper, IWM sound archive tape 27807.
80. Bill Jones, *Bomber Intelligence*.
81. Interview with Ian Dunlop, IWM sound archive tape 17831.
82. Article on Operation Manna, Nanton Lancaster Society Air Museum.
83. Bennett to Harris, 9 November 1944, RAF Museum, Harris papers H57.

84. Journal of R. E. Wannop, IWM archive 80/30/1.
85. Interview with David Ware, IWM sound archive tape 24932.
86. Interview with Danny Boon, IWM sound archive tape 17113.
87. Interview with Thomas Tredwell, IWM sound archive tape 10743.
88. Interview with Doug Fry, IWM sound archive tape 27255.
89. Interview with Michael Bradford, IWM sound archive tape 17328.
90. Sinclair to Harris, 3 May 1945, RAF Museum, Harris papers H80.
91. Harris to Sinclair, 10 May 1945, RAF Museum, Harris papers H80.
92. Sinclair to Harris, 12 May 1945, RAF Museum, Harris papers H80.
93. Eisenhower to Harris, 15 June 1945, RAF Museum, Harris papers H55.
94. Harris to Eisenhower, 19 June 945, RAF Museum, Harris papers H55.
95. Unpublished memoir of Stephen Rew, IWM archive 96/58/1.
96. Toasts at Avro dinner, 6 December 1945, RAF Museum, Bottomley papers AC71/2/66.

CHAPTER 18: 'A DEADLY SILENCE'

1. Peter Russell, *Flying in Defiance of the Reich*.
2. John Nichol and Tony Rennell, *Tail-End Charlies*.
3. Pip Beck, *Keeping Watch*.
4. Henry Probert, *Bomber Harris*.
5. Harris to Sinclair, 1 June 1945, RAF Museum, Harris paper H70.
6. Dudley Saward, *'Bomber' Harris*.
7. Harris to Sinclair, 1 June 1945, RAF Museum, Harris papers H70.
8. Ibid.
9. Ibid.
10. Richard Rhodes, *The Making of the Atomic Bomb*.
11. Portal to Harris, 28 March 1944, National Archives AIR 20/1769.
12. Sinclair to Harris, 8 April 1944, National Archives AIR 20/1769.
13. Air Staff note to Harris, 21 August 1944, National Archives AIR 14/689.
14. Report by Cheshire, 11 October 1944, National Archives AIR 20/4694.
15. Report by AM Lloyd, March 1945, RAF Museum B1729.
16. Ibid.
17. Andrew Roberts, *Masters and Commanders*.
18. Dispatch by Lloyd, August 1945, RAF Museum B1729.
19. Ibid.
20. Ibid.
21. Private memoir of Jack West, RAF Museum X001-6422.
22. Jack West to Stuart Haddaway, RAF Museum, 16 July 2004, RAF Museum X001-6422. I am grateful to Stuart Haddaway for showing me this correspondence.
23. Norman Ashton, *Only Birds and Fools*.
24. Interview with Richard Gration, BBC World War II People's War archive.
25. Mel Rolfe, *Looking Into Hell*.
26. James Drawbell, *Sunday Chronicle*, July 1945, R. E. Wannop papers, IWM archive 80/30/1.

27. Frank Musgrove, *Dresden and the Heavy Bombers*.
28. Denis Richards, *Portal of Hungerford*.
29. Patrick Bishop, *Bomber Boys*.
30. Ibid.
31. Sir Charles Webster and Noble Frankland, *The Strategic Air Offensive Against Germany 1939–45: Volume III*.
32. Richard Overy, *Why the Allies Won*.
33. Thomas Childers, '*Facilis descensus averni est*'.
34. Harris to Portal, 8 January 1945, RAF Museum, Harris papers H84.
35. *Flight* magazine, July 1947.
36. 'The Avro Lancaster in Navy Service', The Royal Navy Research Archive (website).
37. Interview with Bob Allen, IWM sound archive tape 18670.
38. Ibid.
39. Interview with Cyril Hagues, IWM sound archive tape 18766.
40. Interview with Bob Allen, IWM sound archive tape 18670.
41. Interview with Henry Hooper, IWM sound archive tape 27807.
42. Ibid.
43. Interview with R. M. Dye.
44. Harald Penrose, *Architect of Wings*.
45. *The Times*, 25 August 1947.
46. Harald Penrose, *Architect of Wings*.
47. Journal of John Byrne, IWM archive 04/21/1.

Bibliography

Unpublished Sources

Air Ministry Papers (National Archives, Kew)
Antwis, Peter (Imperial War Museum)
Attlee, 1st Earl (Bodleian Library, Oxford University)
Balfour, Harold (House of Lords Records Office)
Bance, A. M. (Imperial War Museum) – logbooks
Barratt, R. C. (Imperial War Museum) – logbooks
Bashford, T. G. (Imperial War Museum) – logbooks
Beaverbrook, 1st Baron (House of Lords Records Office)
Boorman, J. (Imperial War Museum) – logbooks and diaries
Bottomley, Sir Norman (RAF Museum, Hendon)
Bufton, Sydney (Churchill Archives, Cambridge)
Byrne, Pilot Officer John (Imperial War Museum) – journal
Chambers, Dr Vanessa (Exeter University) – research paper on RAF superstitions
Cheshire, Group Captain Leonard (Imperial War Museum)
Churchill, Sir Winston (Churchill Archives, Cambridge)
Cordner, Flying Officer J. (Imperial War Museum)
Cripps, Sir Stafford (Bodleian Library, Oxford University)
Davies, Wing Commander H. J. (Imperial War Museum) – logbooks
Doran, B. J. (Imperial War Museum) – logbooks
Easton, Flight Lieutenant Arnold (Imperial War Museum)
Ebsworth, Sergeant W. N. (Imperial War Museum)
Fenwick, C. (Imperial War Museum) – memoir
Fox, Flight Engineer T. W. (Imperial War Museum) – memoir
Freeman, Sir Wilfrid (National Archives, Kew)
Gayler, C. (Imperial War Museum) – memoir
Harris, Sir Arthur (RAF Museum, Hendon)
Hayes, David (RAF Museum, Hendon) – report on aircraft inspections 1944–5
Hazeldean, Squadron Leader Hedley George (Imperial War Museum) – logbooks
Johnstone, H. (Imperial War Museum) – logbooks
Lupton, Pilot Officer H. (Imperial War Museum) – notes on training courses
Marshall, Flight Lieutenant J. S. A. (Imperial War Museum) – logbooks
Matheson, Flight Lieutenant O. R. (Imperial War Museum)
Meggeson, Flight Lieutenant O. J. (Imperial War Museum) – logbooks
North, Pilot Officer W. (RAF Museum), Hendon – journal
Patterson, Flying Officer J. (Imperial War Museum)

Pierse, Sir Richard (RAF Museum, Hendon)
Portal, 1st Viscount (Christ Church College, Oxford)
Rew, Stephen (Imperial War Museum) – memoir
Saundby, Sir Robert (RAF Museum, Hendon)
Searle, Kenneth A. (RAF Museum, Hendon) – diary
Sunderland, G. R. (RAF Museum Hendon) – history of A.V. Roe factory at Yeadon
Swann, Wing Commander P. H. (Imperial War Museum)
Tedder, 1st Baron (RAF Musem)
Tiger Force (RAF Museum, Hendon)
Walsh, J. W. (Imperial War Museum) – memoir
Wannop, Flight Lieutenant Robert (Imperial War Museum) – memoir
Watts, Sylvia (Imperial War Museum)
West, Jack (RAF Museum, Hendon) – privately printed memoir

Transcripts of Audio Interviews and Speeches

Acquier, John (Imperial War Museum tape 6091)
Aldridge, John (IWM, tape 18499)
Allen, Bob (IWM tape 18760)
Anderson, Ian (IWM tape 10759)
Andrew, Thomas (IWM tape 14834)
Atkinson, George (IWM tape 6176)
Baker, Eileen (IWM tape 27234)
Baker, William (IWM tape 28123)
Batchelor, Group Captain Kenneth (IWM tape 10429)
Bazin, Wing Commander James (IWM tape 2510)
Berry, Jimmy (IWM tape 20926)
Bilton, George (IWM tape 13444)
Blair, John (IWM tape 18413)
Blanchard, Eric (IWM tape 21580)
Boon, Danny (IWM tape 17113)
Boorer, Norman (IWM tape 13076)
Booth, John (IWM tape 18770)
Bracegirdle, Albert (IWM tape 30003)
Bradford, Michael (IWM tape 17328)
Brown, Peter (IWM tape 10036)
Burns, Denis (IWM tape 17179)
Burroughes, Hugh (IWM tape 7255)
Buswell, Ernie (IWM tape 7276)
Calder, Wing Commander Charles (IWM tape 17748)
Coe, George (IWM tape 26803)
Cole, Arthur (IWM tape 15558)
Cooksey, Thomas (IWM tape 15346)
Cordon, Alec (IWM tape 6135)
Cornish, Geoffrey (IWM, tape 23327)
Crisford, Ray (IWM tape 28661)
Curtis, Lawrence (IWM tape 9211)
Davis, Harold (IWM tape 9194)

Davy, Herbert (IWM tape 29898)
Dawson, Eddie (IWM tape 13284)
Day, David Alan Royston (IWM tape 15479)
Dimbleby, Richard, Commentary on Lancaster raid on Kleve, 2 February 1945 (BBC Radio)
Dove, Margaret, 'Roy Chadwick Remembered' (February 2003, Air League)
Duffield, John (IWM tape 9590)
Dunlop, Ian (IWM, tape 17831)
Easton, Arnold (IWM tape 12652)
Edmondson, Roy (IWM tape 27515)
Elliott, John Charles (IWM tape 13904)
Ellis, Ken (IWM tape 20525)
Ellis, Professor John (IWM tape 18538)
Errington, Harry (IWM tape 20961)
Falgate, Donald (IWM tape 11587)
Flett, Alec (IWM tape 16068)
Frankland, Noble, and Robert Saundby, 'Reflections on the Strategic Air Offensive', lecture given 13 December 1961 (Royal United Services Institute)
Fry, Doug (IWM tape 27255)
Gardiner, Fred (IWM tape 16366)
Gedney, John (IWM tape 13943)
Gibson, Ken (IWM tape 18501)
Goodman, Group Captain Jack (IWM tape 16075)
Goodwin, Fred (IWM tape 27793)
Gore, Margaret (IWM tape 9285)
Grant-Dalton, Hugh (IWM tape 26589)
Grantham, Kenneth (IWM tape 10225)
Griffiths, Bill (IWM tape 25267)
Hagues, Cyril (IWM tape 1876)
Hamilton, Squadron Leader Malcolm (IWM tape 18264)
Harris, Sir Arthur (IWM tape 8904)
Henderson, J. W. (IWM tape 16374)
Hill, James (IWM tape 9541)
Holdham, Alfred (IWM tape 12311)
Hooper, Henry (IWM tape 27807)
Howarth, Flight Lieutenant, Report on Flying Training, recorded 28 February 1944 (BBC Radio)
Hudson, Douglas (IWM tape 27042)
Huggins, Squadron Leader Peter (IWM tape 13245)
Iredell, Frank (IWM tape 9887)
Irons, Harry (IWM tape 27796)
Irving, George (IWM tape 12283)
Iveson, Tony, Lecture about Tirpitz Raids given on 10 November 1986 (Royal Aeronautical Society)
Johnson, Edward (IWM tape 8204)
Kearns, Terry (IWM tape 9302)
King, Geoff (IWM tape 28657)

Knights, Robert (IWM tape 9208)
Lee, Edgar (IWM tape 28769)
Longthorp, Paul (IWM tape 10199)
Lummis, Ernie (IWM tape 27800)
McDonnell, Douglas (IWM tape 9259)
McGilveray, Jim (IWM tape 27798)
Maltin, Michael (IWM tape 27315)
Marsh, Philip (IWM tape 18752)
Marshall, Charles (IWM tape 16356)
Masters, Stephen (IWM tape 10597)
Melville, Alan, Commentary on attack on Caumont, 30 July 1944 (BBC Radio)
Miller, Leonard (IWM tape 28556)
Murray, Wing Commander Thomas Charles (IWM tape 12805)
Murrow, Ed, Commentary of raid on Berlin, 2–3 December 1943 (BBC Radio)
Nettleton, John, Report on raid on Augsburg, recorded 17 April 1942 (BBC Radio)
Nettleton, Peter (IWM tape 9348)
Oldland, Rex (IWM tape 20918)
Olsen, Ronald (IWM tape 15743)
Oxtaby, Basil (IWM tape 12613)
Parfitt, Ken (IWM tape 18539)
Parrott, Hugh (IWM tape 16279)
Perkins, Harry, 'The Longest Lancaster Operation' (BBC People's Archive of World War II)
Poore, Arthur (IWM tape 20261)
Pope, Sid (IWM tape 9667)
Porter, Jim (IWM tape 18505)
Powell, Egbert (IWM tape 18410)
Read, John Joseph (IWM tape 9945)
'Reaping the Whirlwind: Symposium on the Strategic Bomber Offensive 1939–45', 26 March 1993 (Royal Air Force Historical Society)
Reid, Bill, Account of his raid on Dusseldorf, 3 November 1943 (Recorded in 1972 by Thames Television)
—— (IWM tape 4993)
Sanders, John (IWM tape 14803)
Sanderson, Eric (IWM tape 15207)
Shannon, Wing Commander David (IWM tape 8177)
—— Lecture about the Dambusters, given on 10 November 1986 (Royal Aeronautical Society)
Sheppard, Robert (IWM tape 3198)
Simpson, Elizabeth (IWM tape 18201)
Smith, Ferguson (IWM tape 22197)
Taylor, John (IWM tape 30416)
Timperley, Trevor (IWM tape 27493)
Tindall, Arthur (IWM tape 29991)
Tolley, Frank (IWM tape 29049)
Toombes, Jack (IWM tape 28633)

Tredwell, Thomas (IWM tape 10743)
Tritton, Doug (IWM tape 17132)
Utting, Bill (IWM tape 30079)
Vaughan-Thomas, Wynford, Commentary from inside 207 Squadron Lancaster during raid on Berlin, 3 September 1943 (BBC Radio)
Waddington, Frank (IWM tape 17365)
Wall, John (IWM tape 27806)
Ware, David (IWM tape 24932)
Watson, Alfred (IWM tape 23198)
Watts, Freddie (IWM tape 21029)
Wilson, Ian, Commentary on return of Lancaster *N-Nan* to base, 14 August 1944 (BBC Radio)
Williams, Joseph (IWM tape 15471)
Wolstenholme, Bert (IWM tape 27789)
Wooldridge, Flying Officer Dim, Account of raid on Rostock, 23–4 April 1942 (BBC Radio)

Published Sources

Addison, Paul, and Crang, Jeremy, *Firestorm: The Bombing of Dresden* (2006)
Alanbrooke, Field Marshal Lord, *War Diaries 1939–1945* (2001) ed. Alex Danchev and Dan Todman
Amery, Leo, *The Empire at Bay: Diaries 1929–1945* (1988) ed. John Barnes and David Nicholson
Arthur, Max, *Lost Voices of the Royal Air Force* (1993)
—— *Forgotten Voices of the Second World War* (2004)
—— *Dambusters: A Landmark Oral History* (2008)
Ashton, J. Norman, *Only Birds and Fools* (2000)
Barker, James, 'Sowing the Wind', *History Today* (March 2005)
Barker, Ralph, *Strike Hard, Strike Sure* (1963)
—— *Men of the Bombers* (2005)
Barnes, C. H., *Handley Page Aircraft Since 1907* (1976)
Bartlett, Les, *Bomb Aimer over Berlin* (2007)
Beaumont, Roger, 'The Bomber Offensive as a Second Front', *Journal of Contemporary History* (1987)
Beck, Pip, *Keeping Watch: A WAAF in Bomber Command* (1989)
Beevor, Antony, *Berlin: The Downfall 1945* (2002)
Bekker, Cajus, *The Luftwaffe War Diaries* (1964)
Bennett, Don, *Pathfinder* (1958)
Best, Geoffrey, *Churchill and War* (2005)
Biddle, Tami Davis, 'Bombing by the Square Yard: Sir Arthur Harris at War 1942–45', *International History Review* (September 1999)
—— *Rhetoric and Reality in Air Warfare* (2002)
Bingham, Victor, *Merlin Power* (1998)
Birrell, Dave, *Baz: The Biography of Squadron Leader Ian Bazalgette VC* (1996)
Bishop, Patrick, *Bomber Boys: Fighting Back 1940–1945* (2007)
Bowman, Martin, *Scramble: Memories of the RAF in the Second World War* (2006)
—— *Flying into the Flames of Hell* (2007)

Bowyer, Chaz, *Bomber Barons* (1982)

Boyle, Andrew, *No Passing Glory: The Full Authentic Biography of Group Captain Leonard Cheshire* (1962)

Braithwaite, Denis, *Target for Tonight* (2005)

Brickhill, Paul, *The Dambusters* (1951)

Broome, Frank, *Dead Before Dawn* (2008)

Brown, A. J., *Ground Staff – A Personal Record* (1943)

Budiansky, Stephen, *Air Power* (2003)

Carrington, Colonel Charles, *Soldier at Bomber Command* (1985)

Chandler, Chan, *Tail Gunner: 98 Raids in World War II* (1999)

Channon, Sir Henry, *Diaries*, ed. Robert Rhodes James (1967)

Chant, Christopher, *Lancaster: The History of Britain's Most Famous World War II Bomber* (2003)

Chappell, Francis Roy, *Bomber Commander: A Biography of Wing Commander Donald Teale Saville* (2004)

Charlwood, Don, *No Moon Tonight* (1956)

Cheshire, Leonard, *Bomber Pilot* (1943)

Childers, Thomas, '*Facilis descensus averni est*: The Allied Bombing of Germany and the Issue of German Suffering', *Central European History* (April 2005)

Clarke, Peter, *The Cripps Version: The Life of Sir Stafford Cripps* (2002)

Clausewitz, Carl von, *On War* (London edition, 1908)

Clegg, Peter, *Avro Test Pilots since 1907* (1997)

Cockell, Charles, 'The Science and Scientific Legacy of Operation Chastise', *Interdisciplinary Science Reviews* (2002)

Colville, John, *The Fringes of Power: Downing Street Diaries, 1939–55* (2004)

Connelly, Mark, *Reaching for the Stars: A New History of Bomber Command* (2001)

Cooke, Colin, *The Life of Richard Stafford Cripps* (1957)

Cooper, Alan, *Beyond Dams to the Tirpitz* (1983)

—— *Born Leader: The Story of Guy Gibson* (1993)

Corrigan, Gordon, *Blood, Sweat and Arrogance: The Myths of Churchill's War* (2006)

Cotter, Jarrod, *Living Lancasters: Keeping the Legend Alive* (2005)

Currie, Jack, *Lancaster Target: The Story of the Crew who Flew from Wickenby* (1981)

Curtis, Lettice, *Her Autobiography* (2004)

Darlow, Steve, *Lancaster Down* (2000)

—— *D-Day Bombers: The Veterans' Story* (2004)

Davis, Richard, 'Bombing Strategy Shifts, 1944–45', *Air Power History* (1989)

—— 'Overlord: The Normandy Invasion', *Air Power History* (1994)

Deighton, Len, *Blood, Tears and Folly* (1993)

Delve, Ken, *Avro Lancaster* (1999)

Dick, Ron, *Lancaster: RAF Heavy Bomber* (1996)

Docherty, Tom, *Number 7 Bomber Squadron in World War II* (2007)

Dunmore, Spencer, and Carter, William, *Regs the Whirlwind* (1991)

Dyson, Freeman, *Disturbing the Universe* (1979)

—— 'A Failure of Intelligence', *Technology Review* (December 2006)

Evans, Richard J., *The Third Reich at War* (2008)

Falconer, Jonathan, *The Dambusters* (2003)

Feast, Sean, *Master Bombers* (2008)

Feesey, Donald W., *The Fly By Nights: RAF Bomber Command Sorties 1944–45* (2007)

Foster, Charles, *Breaking the Dams: The Story of Dambuster David Maltby and his Crew* (2008)

Frankland, Noble, *Bomber Offensive: The Devastation of Europe* (1969)

—— *History at War* (1998)

Franklin, Neville, and Scarborough, Gerald, *Lancaster* (1979)

Franks, Norman, *Claims to Fame: The Lancaster* (1995)

—— *Ton-Up Lancs* (2005)

Friedrich, Jorg, *The Fire: The Bombing of Germany 1940–45* (2002)

Furse, Anthony, *Wilfrid Freeman: The Genius Behind Allied Survival and Air Supremacy* (2000)

Galland, Adolf, *The First and the Last* (1954)

Garbett, Mike, and Goulding, Brian, *Lancaster at War,* three vols. (1971, 1979, 1984)

Garthaus, Ils Mar, *The Way We Lived in Germany During World War II* (1977)

Gibson, Sir Guy, *Enemy Coast Ahead* (1995)

Gilbert, Sir Martin, *Winston S. Churchill* (vols. 4–8 and companion vols., 1975–88)

Goebbels, Joseph, *Diaries*, ed. L. P. Lochner (1970)

Goff, Wilfred E., 'Avro Lancaster', series of four articles, *Aircraft Production Journal* (January to April 1943)

Gooderson, Ian, *Air Power at the Battlefront* (1998)

Gray, Jenny, *Fire by Night* (2000)

Grayling, A. C., *Among the Dead Cities* (2006)

Gregory, Pat, et al., *Heroes of the RAF* (1960)

Halfpenny, Bruce Barrymore, *Bomber Aircrew in World War II* (2004)

Hancock, Terry, *Bomber County: A History of the Royal Air Force in Lincolnshire* (2004)

Hannig, Norbert, *Luftwaffe Fighter Ace* (2004)

Harris, Sir Arthur, *Bomber Offensive* (1947)

Hastings, Max, *Bomber Command* (1979)

Havers, Richard, *Here is the News: The BBC and the Second World War* (2007)

Hecks, Karl, *Bombing 1939–45* (1990)

Henshaw, Alex, 'First off the Line', *Aeroplane Monthly* (September 1983)

—— 'Rolling a Lancaster,' *Aeroplane* (August 2002)

Holmes, Harry, *Avro: The History of an Aircraft Company* (1994)

—— *Avro Lancaster: The Definitive Record* (2001)

—— *Combat Legend: Avro Lancaster* (2002)

Holmes, Richard, *The World at War: The Landmark Oral History* (2007)

Irving, David, *The Destruction of Dresden* (1963)

Isby, David C. (ed.), *Fighting the Bombers* (2003)

Jablonsky, David, *Churchill, the Great Game and Total War* (1991)

Jackson, A. J., *Avro Aircraft since 1908* (1984)

Jackson, Robert, *The Air War at Night* (2000)

Jacobs, Peter, *Bomb Aimer over Berlin: The Wartime Memoirs of Les Bartlett DFM* (2007)

Johnen, Wilhelm, *Duel Under the Stars* (1958)

Jones, Bill, *Bomber Intelligence* (1983)

Keegan, John, *The Second World War* (1989)

Kirby, Robert, *Avro Manchester: The Legend Behind the Lancaster* (1995)

Knell, Hermann, *To Destroy a City* (2003)

Knott, Richard, *Black Night for Bomber Command* (2007)

Lacey-Johnson, L., *Point-Blank and Beyond* (1991)

Lake, Jon, *Lancaster Squadrons 1942–45*, two vols. (2002)

Lambert, Max, *Night after Night: New Zealanders in Bomber Command* (2005)

Lanchenbery, Edward, *A. V. Roe* (1956)

Lang, Noella (ed.), *The Rest of my Life with 50 Squadron: From the Diaries and Letters of FO P. W. Rowling* (1997)

Levine, Alan, *The Strategic Bombing of Germany* (1992)

Lewis, Peter, *The British Bomber since 1914* (1980)

Lloyd, Sir Ian, and Pugh, Peter, *Hives and the Merlin* (2004)

Longmate, Norman, *The Bombers* (1983)

Lowe, Keith, *Inferno: The Devastation of Hamburg 1943* (2007)

Lyall, Gavin, *The War in the Air* (1968)

McKee, Alexander, *Dresden: The Devil's Tinderbox* (1982)

McKinstry, Leo, *Spitfire: Portrait of a Legend* (2007)

Macmillan, Harold, *War Diaries 1939–45* (1984)

Maier, Charles, 'Targeting the City: Debates and Silences about the Aerial Bombing of World War II', *International Review of the Red Cross* (September 2005)

Maitland, Andrew, *Through the Bombsight* (1986)

Manzo, Louis A., 'Morality in War: Fighting and Strategic Bombing in World War II', *Air Power History* (Autumn 1992)

Mason, Francis K., *The Avro Lancaster* (1989)

Meilinger, Philip, 'Trenchard and Morale Bombing', *Journal of Military History* (May 1996)

Messenger, Charles, *Harris and the Strategic Bombing Offensive* (1984)

Middlebrook, Martin, *The Nuremburg Raid* (1974)

—— *The Battle of Hamburg* (1980)

—— *The Peenemünde Raid* (1982)

—— *The Berlin Raids* (1988)

Middlebrook, Martin, and Everitt, Chris, *The Bomber Command Diaries* (1985)

Miller, Donald, *Eighth Air Force: American Bomber Crews in Britain* (2006)

Moore, Clayton, *Lancaster Valour: The Valour and the Truth* (1995)

Morris, Richard, *Guy Gibson* (1994)

Morris, Richard (ed.), *Breaching the German Dams* (2008)

Muirhead, Campbell, *Diary of a Bomb Aimer* (1987)

Musgrove, Frank, *Dresden and the Heavy Bombers* (2005)

Musgrove, Gordon, *Pathfinder Force* (1976)

Myers, Gerald, *Mother Worked at Avro* (1995)

Neillands, Robin, *The Bomber War: Arthur Harris and the Bomber Offensive 1939–45* (2001)

Nelmes, Michael V., and Jenkins, Ian, *G for George: 460 Squadron RAAF* (2000).

Nesbit, Roy Conyers, *An Illustrated History of the RAF* (1990)

Nichol, John, and Rennell, Tony, *Tail-End Charlies: The Last Battles of the Bomber War* (2004)

Nicholson, Nigel (ed.), *Harold Nicholson: Diaries and Letters 1939–45* (1967)

Ottaway, Susan, *Dambuster: The Life of Guy Gibson VC* (1994)

Overy, Richard, *The Air War 1939–45* (1980)
—— *Why the Allies Won* (1995)
—— *Bomber Command 1939–45* (1997)
Owen, James, and Walters, Guy (ed.), *The Voice of War* (2004)
Parker, R. A. C., *The Second World War: A Short History* (1989)
Penrose, Harald, *Architect of Wings: A Biography of Roy Chadwick* (1985)
Pimlott, Ben (ed.), *The Second World War Diary of Hugh Dalton* (1985)
Pugh, Peter, *Barnes Wallis: Dambuster* (2005)
Price, Alfred, *Battle over the Reich: The Strategic Bomber Offensive over Germany*, 2 vols
    (2005)
Probert, Henry, *Bomber Harris: His Life and Times* (2001)
—— *High Commanders of the Royal Air Force* (1991)
Raymond, Robert, *A Yank in Bomber Command* (1977)
Read, Simon, *The Killing Skies: RAF Bomber Command at War* (2006)
Rew, Stephen, 'Finger Trouble', *Aeroplane Monthly* (August 1977)
Rhodes, Richard, *The Making of the Atomic Bomb* (1987)
Richards, Denis, *Portal of Hungerford* (1977)
—— *The Hardest Victory: Bomber Command in the Second World War* (1994)
Riding, Richard (ed.), *Avro Lancaster Portfolio* (1983)
Roberts, Andrew, 'The Holy Fox': A Biography of Lord Halifax* (1991)
—— *Masters and Commanders: How Roosevelt, Churchill, Marshall and Alanbrooke Won
    the War in the West* (2008)
Robertson, Bruce, *Lancaster: The Story of a Famous Bomber* (1964)
Robinson, Bill, *A Pathfinder's Story: The Life and Death of Flight Lieutenant Jack Mossop*
    (2007)
Rolfe, Mel, *Looking into Hell* (1995)
—— *Hell on Earth: Dramatic First-Hand Experiences of Bomber Command at War* (1999)
—— *Bomber Boys* (2004)
Russell, Peter, *Flying in Defiance of the Reich* (2007)
Saward, Dudley, 'Bomber' Harris: The Authorised Biography* (1984)
Schneider, Helga, *The Bonfire of Berlin* (2005)
Scholes, David, *Air War Diary: An Australian in Bomber Command* (1997)
Scott, J. D., *Vickers: A History* (1962)
Scott, Squire, *Twenty Days in the Reich* (2005)
Sinnott, Colin, *The Royal Air Force and Aircraft Design 1923–1939* (2001)
Slessor, Sir John, *The Central Blue: Recollections and Reflections* (1956)
Smith, Peter, *Avro Lancaster* (2008)
Smith, Ron, *Rear Gunner Pathfinders* (1987)
Smithies, Edward, *Aces, Erks and Backroom Boys* (1990)
Spark, David, 'The Man Who Tried to Stop the Dresden Raids', *History Today*
    (March 2005)
Spencer, Dunmore, and Carter, William, *Reap the Whirlwind: The Untold Story of 6
    Group* (1991)
Stafford, David, *Roosevelt and Churchill: Men of Secrets* (1999)
Sweetman, Bill, *Avro Lancaster* (1982)
Sweetman, John, *The Dambusters Raid* (1982)
—— *Bomber Crew: Taking on the Reich* (2004)

Taylor, Eric, *Operation Millennium* (1987)

Taylor, Frederick, *Dresden: Tuesday 13th February 1945* (2004)

Taylor, James, and Davidson, Martin, *Bomber Crew* (2004)

Tedder, Arthur, *With Prejudice* (1956)

Tempest, Victor, *Near the Sun: Impressions of a Medical Officer of Bomber Command* (1946)

Terraine, John, *The Right of the Line* (1985)

Thorburn, Gordon, *Bombers First and Last* (2006)

Thorning, Arthur, *The Dambuster Who Cracked the Dam* (2008)

Tripp, Miles, *The Eighth Passenger* (1969)

Tubbs, D. C., *Lancaster Bomber* (1971)

Verrier, Anthony, *The Bomber Offensive* (1968)

Ward, Chris, *5 Group Bomber Command: An Operational Record* (2007)

Webster, Sir Charles, and Frankland, Noble, *The Strategic Air Offensive Against Germany 1939–45,* four vols. (1961)

Westerman, Edward B., *Flak: German Anti-Aircraft Defences 1914–45* (2001)

Wheeler-Bennett, John, and Nicholls, Anthony, *A Semblance of Peace* (1972)

Whittell, Giles, *Spitfire Women of World War II* (2007)

Wieck, Michael, *A Childhood under Hitler and Stalin* (2003)

Wilson, Kevin, *Bomber Boys: The Ruhr, the Dambusters and Bloody Berlin* (2005)

—— *Men of Air: The Doomed Youth of Bomber Command* (2007)

Wood, D. C., *The Design and Development of the Avro Lancaster: 50th Anniversary* (1991)

Wragg, David, *RAF Handbook 1939–45* (2007)

Yates, Harry, *Luck and a Lancaster: Chance and Survival in World War II* (1999)

Zuckerman, Solly, *From Apes to Warlords* (1978)

Acknowledgements

I am indebted to a large number of people who helped with this book. First of all, I am grateful to the Lancaster airmen and former Avro workers who granted me personal interviews: Harold Barratt, Joesph Barry, Jack Beatty, Geoff Bentley, Norman Card, Alan Courtley, Squadron Leader R. M. Dye, Lillian Grundy, Geoff Heath, Clare Hollingworth, Frank Hillier, Sue Jones, Dick Marsh, Sophie Pape, D. Peters, Harry Tuson and Kevin Whittaker. With regard to the archive material, I received generous assistance from the staff of the National Archives at Kew, the British Newspaper Library at Colindale, the Churchill Archive Centre at Cambridge, the Bodleian Library in Oxford, the House of Lords Record Office, Christ Church College Library in Oxford, the British Library at Euston, and Cambridge University Library. I must record my particular thanks to Robert Saundby and his team at the Imperial War Museum archive, who never failed to provide wise advice and guidance. The collection of interviews with RAF crews at the Museum, built up through the dedication of staff, is a wonderfully rich resource for military researchers. Equally helpful were the staff of the RAF Museum at Hendon, headed by Peter Elliott. I wish to give my particular thanks to Stuart Hadaway and Peter Devitt, whose expert knowledge of Bomber Command was constantly enlightening during my many visits to Hendon. Both of them pointed me to material about several previously obscure episodes in the Lancaster's history, such as the creation of Tiger Force. I only hope that this book has done justice to the encouragement that they gave me.

I am grateful to Alan Brodie Representation for permission to quote from Sir Noel Coward's poem 'Lie in the Dark and Listen', and also to Dr Vanessa Chambers of Exeter University for allowing me to quote from her fascinating thesis about superstition and ritual in the RAF.

Further research was carried out with efficiency and enterprise by Alannah Barton. I was given invaluable assistance and advice on the photographs by Juliet Brightmore. On the production side, I am grateful, as always, to the excellent team at John Murray, including Roland Philipps,

Helen Hawksfield, Caro Westmore, Anna Kenny-Ginard, Polly Ho-Yen, Amanda Jones and Lucy Dixon. My copy editor, Richard Mason, did a superb job in improving the text, especially by highlighting mistakes, improving the flow of the narrative and bringing the sprawling draft into manageable size. Nick de Somogyi carried out the proofreading with superb attention to detail and historical understanding, qualities which were also displayed by the equally diligent indexer Chris Summerville. Any errors in the final version are entirely my responsibility. My agent Georgina Capel and her team, especially Rosie Apponyi, gave me their usual reassuring support.

But above all, I want to express my deepest personal thanks to my darling wife Elizabeth, who has been a tower of strength throughout this project. She never showed me anything but warmth, devotion and tenderness during the long months of research and writing, when the book completely dominated our lives. Her patience was unstinting, her wisdom invaluable. *Lancaster* would not have been possible without her and it is to her that the book is dedicated.

Leo McKinstry
March 2009

Index

Index